WORLD CITIES
SHANGHAI

WORLD CITIES
SHANGHAI

ALAN BALFOUR • ZHENG SHILING

Series editor: **Maggie Toy**

W·WILEY-ACADEMY

ACKNOWLEDGEMENTS

I thank Zheng Shiling, my guide to Shanghai for over ten years, and his colleagues at Tongji University, particularly Luo Xiao Wei and Wu Jiang, who were such generous hosts to the first workshop of the Architectural Association Asia, where the idea for this book originated.

In America my administrative assistant Barbara Stubblebine has managed all the loose ends and Tongji Professor Dia Songzuo (on a research sabbatical at Rensselaer) has been a constant source of guidance and clarification as I slowly build a history of the city. Throughout the last year the work was served by the consistent and dedicated support of my research assistant Madonna Foster, who had the complex and often frustrating task of developing the project material. I am grateful to them all for their help.

Again as in past work I reviewed the text with a small group of colleagues: Barry Russell, Kenneth Warriner, Mark Mistur and Dia Songzuo. Their comments were painfully constructive and they have helped strengthen the work, for which I thank them.

The authors coordinated their examination of the city: I dealt with the urban history, Zheng offering a detailed presentation of the architecture from the last 150 years. The architects were selected to offer a broad sense of the spectrum of architectural and urban form that is shaping the expanding city. In all but a few cases, as indicated, the text accompanying the projects has been provided by the architects. Again the authors developed a joint list but for logistical reasons the final selection was made by me. Several of the projects discussed in the Zheng essays are not present in the project section only because of the difficulties in obtaining material. In addition we recognise that many of these projects involved cooperation with architectural design institutes in Shanghai. These have been listed wherever the information was available or given. That said, the resulting range of buildings, projects and proposals gives a powerful representation of the driving ambition of this new world city, and is a powerful demonstration of the professionalism at all levels of the construction industry in Shanghai.

Both Dr Zheng and I appreciate the generous participation of so many architects from around the world. Listed alphabetically by practice are the individuals in each of the offices who have helped to build this complex picture of Shanghai architecture today: Patricia Casse, ADP (Paul Andreu); Keith Millay and Ardath Grant, Anshen + Allen; Alisa Kahn, Architectural Resources Cambridge; Dennis Wilhelm, Arquitectonica; Choupy Sauvage, ARTE Charpentier & Associates; David Fong, Fong & Chan Architects; Norman Foster and Pippa Taylor, Foster and Partners; Bruce Fowle, Fox & Fowle; Debbie Dempsey, HOK; Wendy Arrington, Jerde Partnership; Andrew Simmonds, John Portman & Associates; Samuel Fajner, KMD; Ilona Rider, KPF; Caroline Hancock, Michael Graves & Associates; Phil Castillo, Murphy/Jahn; Eli Jaeger and Janet Samples, NBBJ; Naeko Yamamoto, Nikken Sekkei International, Ltd; Henry Cobb, Ann Kirschner and James Balga, Pei Cobb Freed & Partners; Kay Bayliss, RMJM; Gretchen Bostedt and Michael McGeady, RTKL; Leung Hon Ming, Seniorman Design; Xing Tonghe, Shanghai Modern Architectural Design Institute; Angela Wang, Shanghai New Expo Center; Mingyuan Ding, ShangHai ZhongFang Design Institute; Patrick Cheung, Simon Kwan & Associates; Kim Albrecht and John Kriken, SOM; Stephen Simon and Jeffries Sydness, Sydness Architects, P.C.; Tao Ho and Peggy Lam-Woon Man, TaoHo; Josie Dee, Wong & Ouyang (HK) Ltd. In addition, I would like to thank Maggie Toy and Amie Tibble at John Wiley and Sons. Lastly, but certainly not least, my sincere thanks go to Mario Bettella, Klára Smith, Francesca Ciurlante and Francziska Wisniewska at Artmedia Press for their hard work and dedication in turning a pile of manuscripts, photographs and drawings into this beautiful book. Thank you all. *Alan Balfour, Rome.*

Illustration Credits

The cover photograph is by He Weizeng and was supplied with permission by Zheng Shiling. The photographs on pages 2, 6-7, 10, 39, 48, 106, 117, 149, 158, 310-311, 360 and all the photo essays are by Alan Balfour. The Kaifeng Scroll on pages 18-23 is from the Beijing Museum. The majority of the maps and the pictorial material in the Balfour essays were drawn from photo archives in Shanghai, and all appear in several recent Chinese publications on the city. The typographic reinterpretation (page 30) of the map from Linda Cooke Johnson's Shanghai: From Market Town to Treaty Port, 1074–1858 (Stanford, 1995), permission requested from the Michigan Center for Cartographic Research. The Introduction, page 213, the Shiling essays and the final project section on competitions have illustrations that are either photographed by Zheng Shiling or selected by him from photo archives in Shanghai. All the illustrations for the architectural projects were selected and supplied by the architects named, and they are reproduced with their permission.

For Anne, Sarah and David

Cover: Night view of the Lujiazui Financial District in Pudong from the Bund and dominated by the looming mass of the Oriental Pearl TV Tower.

Page 2: The Lujiazui Financial District viewed from the roof of the Peace Hotel at the junction of Nanjing Road and the Bund.

Pages 6-7: Morning view over Huangpu Park to the Bund. The park was formerly the preserve of the international community. Shanghainese, unless they were servants, were not allowed to enter until 1928.

First published in Great Britain in 2002 by
WILEY-ACADEMY

a division of
JOHN WILEY & SONS LTD
Baffins Lane
Chichester
West Sussex PO19 1UD

ISBN 0-471-87733-6

Design and Prepress: ARTMEDIA PRESS Ltd, London

Printed and bound in Italy

CONTENTS

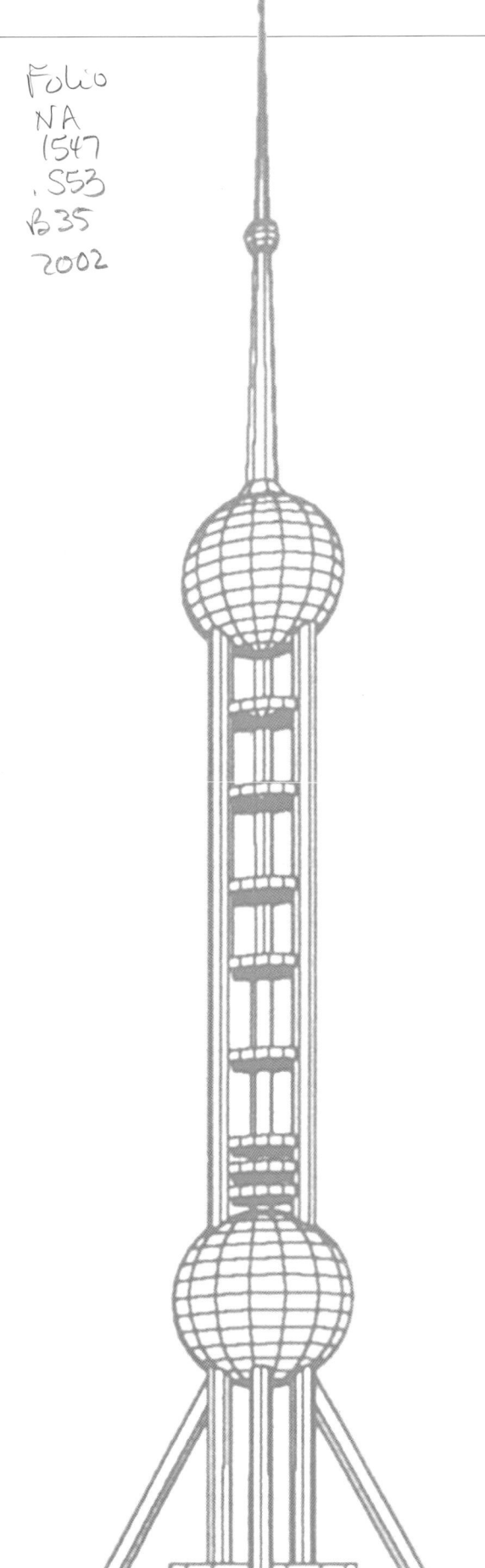

Skyline of Shanghai in the year 2000

INTRODUCTION

ALAN BALFOUR

The physical and economic transformation of Shanghai in the last decade of the twentieth century is unparalleled in urban history. The nature of this transformation is, on the surface, so crude and expedient that its character and multiple meanings must be considered carefully if we are to see behind what on the surface appears to be an excessive and vulgar display, facetiously called 'Market Leninism'. Crude though it may be, it is setting the stage for Chinese economic dominance.

In approaching this metamorphosis from the monumental relic of colonial ambition and Chinese confusion into one of the most aggressively international mercantile cities in the world, Shanghai is increasingly the centre of Asian finance. It is essential to see it emerging not as some naive representation of Western reality but out of the 3,000-year history of urban culture in China. This is a culture whose rational administrative and financial structures have in past ages effectively managed human populations in a harmony and prosperity unmatched in the West; a culture and a reality that are not only exhaustively documented but accessible and surprisingly familiar.

Chinese urbanism is perfected in the idealised capital cities that were seen as essential instruments for maintaining dynastic power. All city form and structure evolved from these. In the history of China over the last two millennia there have only been six great capital cities: Xi'an, Beijing, Luoyang, Hangzhou, Kaifeng and Nanjing. All were characterised by five dominant qualities. They were based on an idealised grid plan explicitly formed as a physical representation of Confucian hierarchy, order and harmony. Rectangular defensive walls encircled the cities which were located strategically to command either a unified nation or a region in a divided China (Xi'an in the centre, Beijing and Luoyang in the north, Hangzhou, Kaifeng and Nanjing in the south). Their objective was to establish the unique character of a new dynasty. The cities were oriented with some recognition of *feng shui* in their southern exposure and relationship to water, linked to the great water network of the nation. These qualities were revised, refined and perfected in the painful struggle for dynastic succession, and sustained by the exceptional knowledge and competence of surveyors, hydrologists, architects, engineers and builders. Over the last 2,000 years the dynastic succession has created the largest and most luxurious cities in the world – Song Kaifeng and Hangzhou – and a thousand years earlier, the great city of the golden age of the Han, Xi'an.

Europe had not known such highly ordered city planning since the fall of the Roman Empire, which was as much concerned as China with the absolute and divine power of the emperor. But then, nowhere in the evolution of the European city over the last thousand years was such total authority applied to the structuring of urban reality. Idealising earthly order was antithetical to Western religion, which thought it sinful to attempt to create a paradise on earth – until the Renaissance and the re-establishment of temporal power. This has a surprising culmination in the profound republicanism of the United States of America and the planning of its ideal cities of Philadelphia, Washington and that most rational of all plans, New York City. European society was formed in the continually shifting conflict between three forces: religion, aristocracy and trade – conflict that had the virtue of denying the concentration of power in any one of the three. In contrast, the only force limiting the absolute power of the Chinese emperor was the need to respect religious model principles, particularly Confucian teachings.

Much that follows concerns politics and the use of the city as an instrument of power. The political history of Europe is the history of numerous competitive, often warring, states controlled by cities whose defence was critical to survival. The dynastic capitals of China from Xi'an to Beijing have until the last two centuries been the absolute power centres of the nation, reinforcing the absolute divine power of the emperor. The emergence of a commercial capital able to rival Beijing in strength and influence creates a yet unresolved disturbance in the deep structure of Chinese culture. Shanghai's relationship to Beijing is not the same as that of New York's to Washington. The political project is increasingly being reformed and redefined in Shanghai with a pragmatism and expediency that have forced resistance to the dogma of Communism – a resistance lubricated by an American consumerism that has the strength to shape the political and economic project of Asia in the coming century.

This work comprises my writing on the history and formation of the city and, from my colleague Zheng Shiling, essays on its many architectural styles. I am also pleased to be able to include the vision of the Director of the Shanghai Urban Planning Administrative Bureau, Madam Xia Liqing. This is followed by an extensive review of the architecture of the last ten years, a decade of the most dramatic growth of any city in recent times. The architectural section focuses on built work and projected schemes. The latter is divided into works that are to be built and those that remain dreams by way of some uncertainty or lack of success in international competitions of the last few years. Over the last ten years, I have walked around, read about, and talked about Shanghai, and the more I have learned, the more the city has shifted and changed. So these are personal tales concerned with capturing the driving desires and ambitions – fictions of desire if you will – that have determined the physical form of the city. The underlying subject in this passage through the layers of history is the mapping of desire – social, political, metaphysical; and the pleasure of projecting possible futures from the evidence.

In the Jing'an Temple

IMPERIAL CITIES

ALAN BALFOUR

Cities are formed over long periods of time and out of such a dense fusion of necessity and cultural desire that understanding them requires both a historical perspective and some sense of the metaphysics underlying their intellectual character. This is particularly true with respect to the cities of China.

THE SUI FIGURE

I am looking at a small figure. It is only eight or so inches tall (Fig. 1). It is made from white clay with a soft green glaze apparently splashed across its top half. Such figures were probably made in quantity in moulds, and one can imagine the potter quickly splashing the brush carrying the glaze over rows and rows of unfired figures, ready to enter the kiln; little lines of the glazing still run to the base of the figure. Perhaps because it was never meant to be seen, there is something careless in its making. It was created to be one of the silent servants that would comfort the afterlife of a wealthy merchant in a small town close to the Yangtze River. It is in the form of a beautiful woman and was made during the Sui Dynasty between the years AD 581 and 618. The figure still carries the calcified residue of the soil in which it has lain for over 1,400 years.[1] She could have been one of the:

> lovely daughters of noble families, far excelling common maidens, women with hair dressed finely – in looks and bearing sweetly compliant, of a gentleness beyond compare, with melting looks but a virtuous nature and truly noble mind. Dainty features, elegant bearing, grace the marriage chamber, moth-like eyebrows and lustrous eyes that dart out gleams of brightness, delicate colouring, soft round flesh, flashing seductive glances, in your garden pavilion of long bed curtains await your royal pleasure.[2]

She is young and elegantly dressed. She wears a neatly fitted gown of great simplicity; it seems to belong more to ancient Greece than to Central China. The dress is gathered tightly beneath her breast below an elegant neckline, and the soft clinging fabric flows generously to the ground. The neck is exposed, yet the arms are fully covered and over her shoulders she wears a long wrap, which drapes over her forearms and down her sides. The hands, hidden in lengthy sleeves, as was the fashion, and clasped over a swelling stomach that suggests that she could be pregnant, appear to be contained within the fabric of the gown. The simplicity and flowing ease of a gown that would not have seemed out of place in the 19th century is matched by the strength and composure of her face beneath a great pile of hair. The eyes belong to Asia, but in every other respect the woman seems a universal presence. She has a straight, well-formed nose and an exquisite, controlling smile that conveys inner calm and supreme trust in the external world. It is the quality of worldliness, of urbanity, that is so compelling.

One can compare her with European figurative representations in the 6th century, so disturbed by the internal agonies of Christianity that individuality and naturalness are lost. Urban life in 6th-century China was experienced in the here and now, not, as in Christian Europe, in the shadow world, as Christians prepared for reality in the afterlife, in the City of God. In Byzantine Christendom there is no representation of an individual as composed as this tiny figure. Although a ritual object produced to give comfort in the afterlife, she seems free from the distortions and mental agonies caused by faith or peculiar custom. She allows the imagination to construct around her a family life, a home life. Through her we can glimpse the style of the people and the fondness man felt for woman. We know this was a consumer society with a

Figure 1: Female tomb figure from the Sui Dynasty, AD 581–618

highly developed sense of fashion and changing style. Even in this tiny fragment one feels the imagination of an advanced culture with complex technologies. It shows in the dress and in the manufacture of the figure. These were industrious mercantile societies with a fine sense of public performance and apparently a sensual delight in being. If she were to stretch out her hand and lead you back to her time, there is a feeling that you would enter a familiar world, a world in which the routines, rituals and even the dramas of urban life would hold few surprises. Contrary to the simplifications of Western prejudice, the social foundation on which Chinese culture sits was never inscrutable, rarely unreasonable, and even, as judged by the most ancient texts, always understandable. Consider this tiny figure as a sign of the confidence, self-sufficiency and refinement of Chinese culture that could only have emerged from centuries of exchange in trade and ideas, embedded in and stimulated by complex urban cultures.

These social and intellectual foundations were established between 551 and 221 BC within the dynasties of the Spring and Autumn Period (772–481 BC) and the Eastern Zhou (771–256 BC). The Chinese phrase for the many philosophies that developed during this period is 'The Hundred Schools of Thought', of which four have had a profound influence: Confucianism, Daoism, Mohism and the Legalist school of thought. Although these four seams of philosophy have intertwined and blended over the years, each dynasty giving emphasis to one or another, Confucianism has been the most influential, particularly in the last 250 years.

The School of Confucius was led by Confucius (551–479 BC),[3] but includes the works of others such as Meng Tzu (Mencius, 372–289 BC).[4] The teachings are based on the 'Five Classics of Confucianism': the *Book of Songs*, the *Book of History*, the *Book of Rites*, the *Book of Changes* (*I Ching*) and the *Spring* and *Autumn Annals* – all of which were compiled by Confucius late in his life – and on the 'Four Books of Confucianism', the *Analects*, the collection of his discourses compiled by his disciples. For 2,000 years these formed the basis of the examinations for entry into the imperial bureaucracy. The writings look back to the benevolence of the Zhou Dynasty and the ideal of a people living together in harmony. Confucius's ideal was the cultivated, superior *junzi* ('son of a prince'), noble not by birth but by developing the five virtues of benevolence, righteousness, good behaviour, wisdom and trustworthiness. The essential structure of his social order was filial piety, the respect and obedience of children toward their parents; when these relationships are in order, the rest of society will follow.

Daoism was established by Laozi in the 6th century BC and developed by others, notably Zhuangzi (369–328 BC). The Chinese have a saying that they are Confucian in public and Daoist in private. Dao translates as the 'way' or the 'path', and the major text of this philosophy is the *Daodejing* ('Way of Virtue'). This book argues that the best governments govern least. For Laozi, wisdom entails studying oneself, and the wise man 'takes no action' that will interfere with anything. Acts can thus be compared with water, which flows everywhere and seems to be weak, yet is stronger and more pervasive than anything else: 'Do nothing yet leave nothing left undone'.

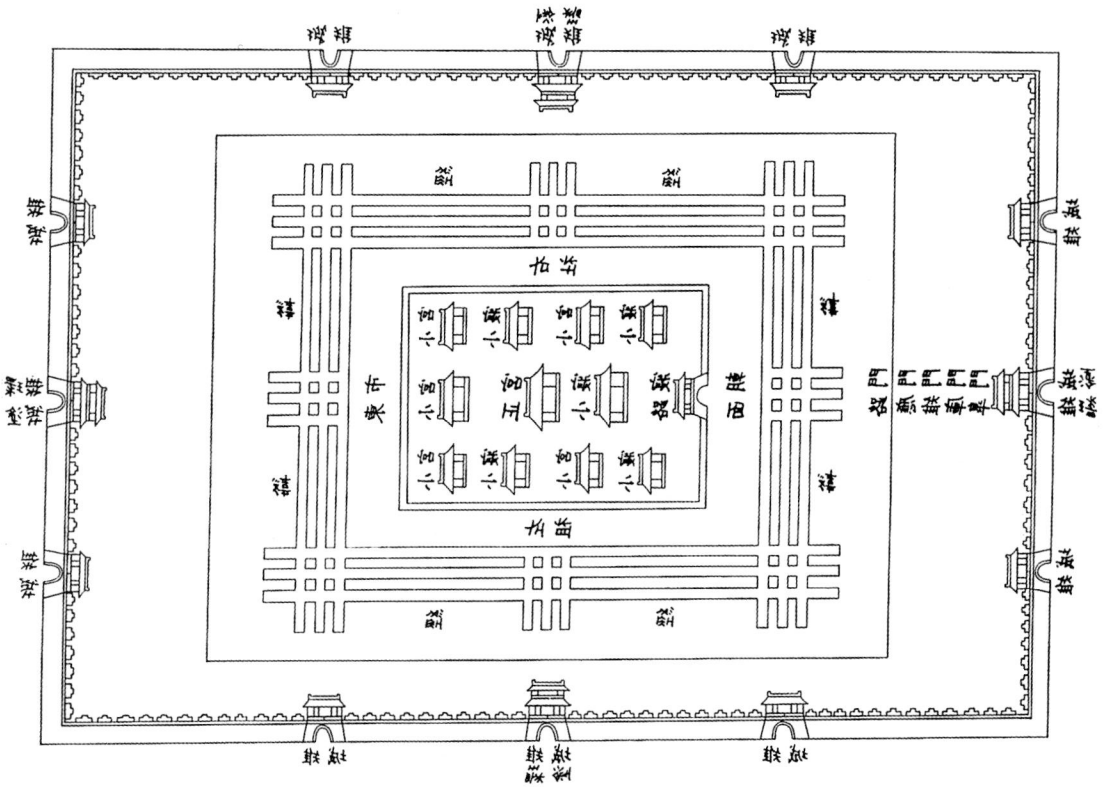

Figure 2: The ideal imperial capital derived from the *Zhou Li*

Mohism was founded by Mo Tzu (470–391 BC), whose writings are known as the *Mozi*. For Mo Tzu the Confucian emphasis on family relationships was divisive, and while the Confucians believed in the inheritance of power through birthright, the *Mozi* argued that all qualified men should be appointed to government positions regardless of class. The most distinctive aspect of *Mozi* philosophy was the teaching of universal love. The texts cite a mythological past, the 'Xia' Dynasty, where people cared for each other as one family, and treated all children as their own. It calls for all to show 'love for everyone', and claims that 'All men are equal in the sight of heaven'.

The Legalist school of thought was formed principally by Han Feizi (280–233 BC), whom the Chinese compare to the Italian Renaissance statesman Niccolò Machiavelli. Again in opposition to the Confucian view, he argues that human nature is basically selfish, and that the ruler must impose strict rules on his subjects for social order to be maintained. These rules must be obeyed without question, with harsh punishment for those who disobey; in Han Feizi's view 'the ruler alone possesses power'. This school is seen as drawing on the dark side of human nature (it offers some explanation for the more extraordinary acts of Mao Zedong).

Against the background of the rise of the imperial city, the essays that follow are concerned with the thousand-year evolution of Shanghai, not with unravelling the way in which these essential seams of thought intertwined and shaped the culture of each succeeding dynasty. Yet these ideas are embedded in all that follows.

THE HAN

Legalism shared influence with Confucianism in organising the government and society of the Han. Although recorded history reaches back much earlier, the Han Dynasty (206 BC–AD 220) is the period in which many imperial institutions were established – most significantly the imperial Civil Service – and a centralised government bureaucracy developed (a table of Chinese Dynasties is given on page 364). China was always most powerful when its entire people were formed into an empire under one sovereign.[5] The first emperor was named King of the Han in 206 BC and named emperor four years later, taking the name Gaodi. He established the capital in Chang'an (modern Xi'an), fashioning it into one of the most ordered and cultivated cities in the world. In its earliest form, it was planned before the end of the 6th century BC in a grid composed of 11 north–south streets and 15 east–west streets with market squares east and west of the central north-south axis. This led at the northern end to the palace compound enclosed behind a massive fortification more than two miles in extent. Just below the palace a denser grid of streets enclosed the imperial administration.[6] The formal origins of this idealised order predate the 6th century BC and were recorded in the official texts defining social order and behaviour, the *Zhou Li*.[7] In its perfect form the palace should lie at the centre, flanked by two sacred areas, to the west the shrine to the ancestors, and to the east that to heaven and nature (Fig. 2).

Although Gaodi was illiterate, he recognised the need for educated advisors. Guided by the teachings of Confucius he created a bureaucracy that sought to achieve order and harmony (albeit hierarchical) both in society and in the family, a new order that was reflected in the rational grids that ordered the streets of Xi'an and supported a richly diverse city life. The Han imposed the system of land tenure across the Empire, which replaced feudal servitude with a new relationship between tenant and landlord that allowed tenants to buy and sell land. This in turn led to the development of a money economy and to the rise, in cities and towns, of new social classes based on trade, manufacture and service.

The rise and fall of the late Han Dynasty is a paradigm of both the strengths and weaknesses of the dynastic process. Gaodi's son, Emperor Wendi (180–157 BC), has long been viewed as the ideal model of the virtuous ruler, whose dominant concern was for the well-being of his subjects. He continued his father's efforts to develop an effective centralised bureaucracy that would manage the affairs of the Empire with equity. Emperor Han Wudi (141–87 BC) extended the Empire into the west, and in his travels responded to the request by those in the far west for trade with China by exchanging silk for horses with such success that a permanent trade route was established, the 'Silk Road'. The Han extended the frontiers of China, pushing north, south and west almost to the extent of China's modern border. The army crossed the deserts of Central Asia as far as the Caspian Sea, creating safe trade routes not only to India, but reaching as far as Greece and Rome. The Romans are recorded to have first seen silk in 53 BC in the colourful banners of the Parthian army as it defeated the Eastern Legion. At first, silk trickled into Rome through exchanges along the eastern frontier. Then the Chinese actively developed several trade routes to take it, along with other luxury goods, to the Western Empire. By sea they went to Sri Lanka and the west coast of India and then on through the Red Sea to Rome, overland through India. The most celebrated passage, the 'Silk Route', went from Xi'an, travelling north or south across the high mountain deserts to Baghdad then on to Damascus or Constantinople and thence to Rome. This was not a continuous flow, but a sequence of exchanges, with the cost of the silk rising at each step. To satisfy the insatiable demand of the wealthy Romans, huge quantities were imported; at its peak of popularity it is recorded that they were willing to pay an ounce of gold for an ounce of silk, placing a heavy drain on the Roman economy. From AD 73 to 97, the Han army brought all of Central Asia, up to the Caspian Sea, within Chinese control. The Han were curious about the affluent Western people, whom they called Daqin (Chinese phonetic for 'Rome'), and an envoy was sent to make formal contact with Rome. At the Persian Gulf the traders, fearing that such direct contact would weaken their lucrative trade, told him that he would be in extreme danger if he continued. He turned back.

It was the weakening of the imperial household and persistent threats from rival families and neighbouring tribes that led to the collapse of the Han Empire. The court attempted to reassert itself by investing power in the eunuchs, who increasingly corrupted the court by selling first their favours and then their influence for money. Conflicts initially arose between the eunuchs and the scholars in the imperial bureaucracy in AD 166, with the eunuchs achieving complete victory in 172; this led to the massacre of many thousands of scholars and the collapse of the Civil Service. In 184 a peasant uprising, the Yellow Turban rebellion, broke out against the Eastern Han. It was led by a Daoist sect, which preached a messianic vision of the imminent arrival of a time of 'Great Well-Being', and promoted faith healing through the use of charms and magic chants. They brought more than 360,000 armed supporters into the conflict, and sapped the energy of the Empire until defeated in 196. In the aftermath, many military commanders and landowners found they had more power than the imperial court. (This most widespread peasant rebellion in Chinese history continues to make Chinese leadership deeply wary of secret cults and spiritual leaders, but history repeats itself.) Never fully crushed or dispersed, the rebellion gave the army vast control over the countryside and increased the oppressiveness of the regime. It brought to power General Cao Cao, who had emerged from the victorious coup of 189 against the eunuchs. The Han Dynasty finally collapsed when its last emperor Hsein Ti became the tool of opposing military commanders, some in league with the Yellow Turbans. General Cao Cao unified all of China north of the Yangtze under his command. His son Cao Pi forced the abdication of Hsein Ti and founded the short-lived Wei Dynasty (AD 220–300), the first in the Three Kingdoms period.

THREE KINGDOMS

Throughout the first millennium of the Common Era, China's dynastic empires enjoyed a succession of rising and falling fortunes, as imperial and aristocratic families struggled to maintain the unity of one China. Within this, and reflecting these changes in fortune, the city became the base of power, and its structure and form became increasingly complex, intensifying as it received and transformed the products of mercantile expansion.

The period between the fall of the Han in AD 220, and the establishment of the Sui in 581 was the most confused and disruptive era on record. The Han was followed by the unstable Three Kingdoms era; historians are still unable to determine where legitimate power lay. The Tsien Dynasty briefly reunited the Empire but failed to anticipate the strength of the warring nomadic peoples moving in from the north, the Hsein Pi. In AD 316, they swept south, destroying the capital Luo Yang and driving the imperial court south to Nanjing, dividing the Empire.

The subsequent division into northern and southern dynasties has been compared with the Dark Ages in Europe and the Barbarian invasions that decimated the Western Roman Empire. This, however, would seem to be an inappropriate comparison for China. A dynastic administration maintained power in the south, and the Han Chinese always outnumbered the invaders in the north. The invaders consciously sought to re-establish the culture of the Han by intermarriage, resulting in a mixed-race ruling class, and Chinese culture and language quickly overwhelmed and subsumed the culture of the invaders.

The capital of the south, Nanjing (then named Jiankang), evolved into a great and luxurious city whose form and culture had influence throughout the Yangtze Valley. However, the southern Kingdom diminished the Civil Service as a path to influence, which gave rise to a new aristocracy based on military power, and only marginally dependent on imperial favour. The result of this shift in the locus of power was the realisation that anyone of influence could become emperor, and be replaced in death by any rival within the power structure. This broke the divine element, the Mandate of Heaven, in dynastic succession, which had dominated all the ancient dynasties.

THE SUI DYNASTY

The Sui Dynasty (581–618) succeeded in reuniting the Chinese Empire. Yang Chien, the Duke of Sui, became the Sui Emperor Wendi after he usurped the throne of the northern Zhou Dynasty in 581. In 589 he captured Nanjing and quickly conquered all eight of the so-called northern and southern dynasties that had ruled China from 420. China was once again united within the harmony of a single dynasty. This was the time when Justinian was labouring to reunite the Roman world and was still trading in silk with China. For Emperor Wendi, the essential step in consolidation was to establish a new capital. He named it Chang'an (now Xi'an) and built it close to the site of the golden city of the Han. The city was both symbol and instrument. Emperor Wendi centralised and strengthened imperial administration, establishing more effective systems of taxation and imperial legislation, which formed the basis for all subsequent imperial codes of law. Millions were conscripted into the building of a system of canals that would link the lower Yangtze with Chang'an.

In 604 Emperor Wendi was murdered by his son Yang Ti, a son driven to patricide by a dream of recreating the full glory of the Han Empire. In maintaining a balance of power between the north and the south, Yang Ti re-established the northern capital of Luo Yang and built a second capital in the central Yangtze Valley at Yang Zhou. He then initiated a vast construction project, expanding the Grand Canal to link the two capitals that lay 1,000 miles apart.

The Grand Canal had evolved over 1,000 years to become the communications system that united the nation, stimulated and extended the economy, and was the principal instrument by which succeeding empires controlled wealth and expanded power. All the major cities of dynastic power were connected to the Grand Canal. Known as the Yunglianglu ('Grain Transport River'), it was first dug 2,400 years ago by the kingdom of the Wu. The Wu occupied the region south of the Yangzhi, and the first phase of the canal was built north of the river as part of a military campaign against the kingdom far to the north. (The Wu capital was in the area of present-day Suzhou, whose economy has always been based on the canal.) The first section linked the Yangzhi with the Huai River.

During the Qin Dynasty (221–206 BC) the channel had been extended by imperial decree to link the Yangzhi with the port of Guangzhou 1,200 miles to the north. Between 605 and 618 CE, Yang Ti extended the canal to link the city of Hangzhou in the fertile region south of the Yangzhi with the Sui in the capital Luo Yang, in Central China. By AD 609 the canal network, combining natural rivers and lakes linked by channels and controlled by dams or water gates, extended from Hangzhou in the south to the area of present-day Beijing far to the north. The canal was a central element in all imperial strategy, economic and military. It allowed the emperor to collect the annual tax on grain, shipping vast quantities from the fertile south to the imperial capital, where it was held in storage and used to supply the garrisons manning the Great Wall and the mountains on the western edges of the Empire. The canal evolved into the circulation system for all nationwide trade. It became, through most of its 2,000-year existence, the most penetrating and robust communication system of any nation in the world.

The Roman roads may have been strategic, but paved roads were unable to carry the mass of goods and produce supported by the canal. And while the major cities of the Roman Empire created wealth through its ports, the canal made all the major cities of China trading ports. After the collapse of the Roman Empire the Christian imagination was too preoccupied in the contemplation of the afterlife to maintain networks in anything other than the spiritual realm. From the 6th century, Christian Europe consciously avoided giving order to the real world, and in the millennia during which China was unified by thousands of miles of interrelated waterways, Europe retreated into a thousand defensive fiefdoms.

Luo Yang had been the former imperial capital of the Eastern Han and a great centre of culture and learning. It was destroyed both at the end of the Han Dynasty and at the beginning of the Sui. Given the name Dongdu by the Sui administration, the city was reconstructed on a grand scale, appropriate to the vast extension of the canal system. The rational new city lay between two wide channels structured to carry barges weighing up to 800 tons, transporting goods from the city across the length and breadth of China. Dongdu became a pivotal centre of trade and bureaucracy, attracting many foreign merchants and reaching a population of over a million in the 7th century within the European calendar. Nothing in Europe could compare. The Grand Canal had a far reaching influence on the wealth and development of the Empire, particularly south in Yangtze Delta, yet four centuries were to elapse before Shanghai would emerge.

THE TANG DYNASTY

As the Sui Dynasty gave way to the great and industrious Tang Dynasty, it appears that the major cities of the south were relatively unaffected by these imperial struggles. The Tang Dynasty (618–907) was founded by Li Yuan, a high official in the Sui government related by marriage to the royal families of both the Sui and the northern Zhou. The Sui Dynasty was brought to an end when vast expenditure on public works and obsessive engagement in wars with Korea caused rebellion in the north by a military aristocracy of mixed Chinese and Tartar descent. The Sui emperor was forced to retreat to his southern capital of Jiangdu (modern Yangzhou) in 617, only to be assassinated by a member of his own household. In the confusion Li Yuan led a coup capturing Chang'an (Sui Daxingzheng), which he made the Tang capital.

In all of these struggles, the city was the critical base of power, its institutions providing the mechanisms for running the country. All new dynasties marked their consolidation of power in either the destruction of a city or its co-option and renaming. It was a rational instrument perfected not just to support the imperial court and administration but also to provide the context in which the full cultural character of the dynasty would be nurtured.

The Tang Dynasty reasserted the role and influence of the scholar bureaucrat, the army being relegated to the task of holding the frontier. In re-establishing the capital in Chang'an (Xi'an) – the ancient seat of the Han Dynasty – it established Tang control at the heart of a united nation and far from Nanjing, the locus of Sui power in the Yangtze Valley. During these centuries Tang Xi'an became the largest and most cosmopolitan city in the world. It was linked by the Grand Canal to a network of waterways that had been extended over 30,000 miles across the nation, providing a vast and robust communications network that drove the economy and gave order to population growth and city development. As the pivotal city of the silk routes it brought traders from across the western regions: Muslims from Persia, Arabs, Uighurs and Jews, bringing Islam, Judaism, Nestorian Christianity, Manichaeism and Zoroastrianism. Strength of trade and the freedom of cultural and religious practice encouraged large communities of foreigners to settle in the city. The first mosque was established in 787, barely a century after the death of Mohammed. The dense neighbourhoods that still surround the mosque remain the centre of the Islamic community, with its streets lined with pavement cafés.

The style of the Tang survives in the *Sancai* – three-colour pottery. These camels and horses splashed with green, orange and brown glaze not only remain the most popular for tourists but in all their variety preserve the elegance and worldliness of Tang.[8] The wealth of the city, besides the economy that supplied and supported the imperial court, was based on the export of luxury goods, porcelains, and textiles – especially silks. Diplomatic ties were established from Chang'an with Byzantium and with the Sassanid Empire in Persia. And during these centuries, Japan and Korea established a stable centralised administration that was modelled on Tang policies and administration; they adopted the Chinese script, and the imperial Japanese city of Kyoto (Heian) was modelled directly on Chang'an.

Neglect of the military garrisons on the southern frontier led to an uprising and the capture first of the port city of Guangzhou, then, in a sweeping move across the country, the sacking of Chang'an (Xi'an). Subsequently, the Tang court returned to the capital as puppets of the military commanders, but finally, internal struggles among the military destroyed the dynasty, and the Empire divided. The southern court was once again established in Nanjing, and the urban culture continued its artful evolution.[9]

Except when dynastic transitions caused the ritual destruction of a city, the movement of empires did little to disturb the productivity of cities, nor the necessity for trade and agriculture. The first printed book dates from the corrupt, dying years of the Tang Dynasty. Printing became widespread, with Confucian texts enjoying the same popularity and mass diffusion as Buddhist prayer sheets. Tea drinking displaced wine, and the need to boil the water to make the tea improved the health of the people. One can still sense the sensuality of the culture in the richly embroidered fabrics and in the smooth surfaces and pure white glazes of the porcelain that enhanced all domestic activity and decoration.[10]

THE SONG DYNASTY

The Song (Sung) Dynasty (960–1279) reunited China after 50 years of turmoil in the aftermath of the Tang, turmoil that saw the nation divided into 12 military kingdoms. It began with little promise. General Chao K'uang-yin was elected to power by the palace guards, usurping the seven-year-old natural successor to the late Zhou Dynasty. He reigned under the name of Emperor Taizu. By 975, he had brought most of the warring kingdoms under control, and the southern kingdoms agreed to submit to his rule. He moved the capital some 300 miles northwest of Nanjing, placed on the dividing line between north and south. With

strong support from the urban literati, the *wenren*, he and his successors achieved major changes in the administrative and social structures of the nation. These were changes dedicated to nurturing the arts and improving the quality of life for all. They viewed perfecting city life as the most tangible measure of their achievement, and during the reign of the Northern Song, Kaifeng became both the world's largest and its most distinguished city. But more of that later.

Legislative restructuring was at its most ambitious during the reign of Emperor Shen-tsung, from 1068 to 1086. The so-called 'New Laws' were aimed at improving the condition of peasant life and increasing the revenues derived from land. The main measures were the 'Equalisation of Loss' laws, which shifted taxation from a tribute of grain supplied directly to the imperial capital to a process of storing and selling grain and other goods locally, returning only the revenue to the capital. The government also began to develop procedures for controlling and stabilising the economy by buying goods in times of over-supply and selling when supply was short.

Through the 'Young Shoots Law' the government made loans to the peasants for the purchase of seeds to be replaced after harvest, bypassing moneylenders and combating the emergence of feudal landlords, who would act as creditors and seize land for failure to repay. A remission of the services law was introduced, eliminating what had been the obligation of compulsory labour to the government, and replacing it with a money tax. Laws were passed limiting the profits from property transactions, which led to a census documenting all land-holding throughout the Empire. State shops were established to control the price of goods, easing the exploitation of the poor, which in turn led to a national banking system through which the imperial administration was able to regulate the economy.

The law that has had the most lasting effect was the 'Family Guarantee Law', which provided for the division of the total population, urban and rural, into family groups or units. These groups were mutually responsible for each other, sharing and supporting one another in times of hardship, but they were also ordered to report any seditious activity within the group to the authorities. All able-bodied men in the group received military training. Such impositions appeared to be acceptable to the communal and family-centred character of Han society. The carefully constructed laws had exact equivalents in the physical and administrative structures of the city. (This enforced interdependency survives in the street committees that still manage the local affairs in town and cities in present-day China. It is still in effect throughout Shanghai, perhaps strongest in the districts built before 1990.) The political subtlety of such laws, their concern with reducing the burden on the peasant and instilling mutually supportive behaviour, had no equivalent in the Western world in the 10th century, so completely had the spiritual overwhelmed the temporal in Europe.

Dedicating the administration to equity and social improvement was at a cost to the military and to national defence, and left the country vulnerable to attack from the north. After the death of Shen-tsung, power shifted to a much more conservative faction, and many of the reforms were abandoned, but not forgotten.

THE KAIFENG SCROLL

During the Song Dynasty, Kaifeng was known as Bianjing or Dongjing. In 1105 its population was estimated at well over a million – a concentration of inhabitants then unequalled in the world. The city was located at the junction of the Grand Canal and the Yellow River, a nexus of national trade. The strength of its institutions and its attractiveness to the ambitious had made it the locus of scientific enquiry, with new discoveries in medicine, in engineering and in chemistry – it was at this time that the first experiments with explosive powders were made. The city attracted thousands of traders from across China and from all parts of the world touched by the China trade, including the Middle East. This not only brought many Muslims to the city, but also a significant number of Jews. They had arrived first in Xi'an along the strengthened Silk Route in the 7th century, and then moved with the shifting centres of power. The first major synagogue was built in Kaifeng in 1163. (During the 14th and 15th centuries more than 1,000 Jewish traders and bankers are recorded in the city, wielding considerable influence.)

The Song Dynasty left behind extensive documentation in texts and drawings detailing city life in China in the 12th and 13th centuries. They represent the rich and varied patterns of urban society, industry, entertainment, and the institutions that maintained public order. Looking at this evidence in the present, the life of the Northern Song seems familiar, rational and tempting.

One of the most stimulating documents is an 11th-century panoramic ink drawing, 7 feet long, of the city of Kaifeng, by the Song artist Zhang Zeduan (Fig. 3). It is entitled 'Life along the River on the Eve of the Qing Ming Festival', a period when families returned to tend the graves of their ancestors.[11] It represents life on the outskirts of Kaifeng, conveying its texture and physical character: the streets, squares, canals, markets, parks and pleasure gardens – all the elements that had evolved over 1,000 years of urban development. (The scenes are also strongly reminiscent of Shanghai immediately before the Treaty of Nanjing in 1842, a character that can still be found in the restored villages in the water districts west of Shanghai, and along the still productive Grand Canal.)

The scroll takes the viewer in a continuous sequence up the river through the outer suburbs and into the city. It represents Chinese town life of 1,000 years ago with more precision and immediacy than any photograph. Nothing gives greater evidence of the profusion and complexity of shipping on the Grand Canal. The large varieties of river craft are drawn in such detail that they could act as blueprints for modern reconstruction. Wide barges, their masts lowered to pass beneath the great arched wooden bridges, teem with people busying themselves around the multiple cabins. Crowds push to the edge of a humpback bridge to watch the panicking people on the deck of a barge struggling with the current. The streets throng with people and animals: pedlars carrying their wares on shoulder poles avoid a stream of heavily laden single wheelbarrows, donkeys, camel caravans and all manner of carts and carriages. Through the city gate we see ladies peeking from behind the patterned curtains of sedan chairs, officials on horseback followed by servants on foot, and many sleepy customers gathering around the wine stores, or watching the world go by from teahouses and the terraces

of restaurants. Through this drawing one can enter so closely into the scene that it is as if one had joined the crowds on the street.

Aside from its exquisite observation of detail, the most powerful aspect of the scroll is its handling of perspective. The continuous rolling scene along the streets of the city, an actual distance of probably a quarter of a mile or so, is all viewed from a consistent height just above the rooftops. The view gives a sense of simultaneous and consistently observed action throughout the town. The people, who are drawn and behave with great naturalness, are on a continuously inclined plane with some reduction of scale into the distance, a visual structure that allows glimpses into the distance. Parallel with the picture frame are the facades of the buildings on the main street, which become three dimensional as they move up the inclined plane. The illusion is so competently handled that at no point does the imagination cease to believe in the truthfulness of the representation. It is a view of continuous action, sustained by a perceptual device only recently encountered in the West: the field of play in video games.

We can see from surviving examples that Roman wall paintings displayed a strong sense of perspective. Roman conventions also produced a highly impressionistic representation of place, in many ways similar to the structure of the scroll. However, Christianity denied a singular perspective on the world. The history of Western art can be seen to reflect continual conceptual adjustments in the imagination of the culture as it struggled to adjust to, or find release from, the God-centred view of a world. Christians did not ignore perspective, but they chose a form of representation that conveyed the idea of a world produced by an omniscient God. Byzantine mosaics, for example, in representing heavenly landscapes, rejected the single point of view, attempting to convey a vision of omnipresence free from the idea of one-point perspective. Depictions of reality were similarly constrained.

The recovery of perspective in the paintings of Giotto and Cimabue in the 13th century was achieved through a specific representational technique derived from the more disciplined paintings of ancient Rome. Giotto was the first to create visually and psychologically satisfying representations of the human form by shedding the distorted mannerisms of Byzantium. He was the first painter in the Christian world to construct a representation of three-dimensional form and space, a feat of the imagination that became feasible only when Christian spirituality softened sufficiently to acknowledge the value of life in the present. Only then was it possible to draw lessons from the arts of imperial Rome. The Chinese imagination suffered no such distortion.

Religion, then, framed all representations of reality in the Western world. Drawing and painting were merely elements in a metaphysical structure that compelled the individual imagination to surrender totally to the power of the Divine. The great fresco cycle in the Arena Chapel in Padua (painted between 1305 and 1360) contains 38 scenes from the life of Christ. It offers a revealing contrast to the Kaifeng scroll, reflecting two profoundly different cultural imaginations. Even today, the citizens who people the streets of Kaifeng in the scroll seem real and natural, their personalities defined by work, deed and social interaction. The European figures, on the other hand, seem to be suffering from a kind of

Figure 3: 'Life along the River on the Eve of the Qing Ming Festival', Zhang Zeduan, 11th century, Beijing Museum

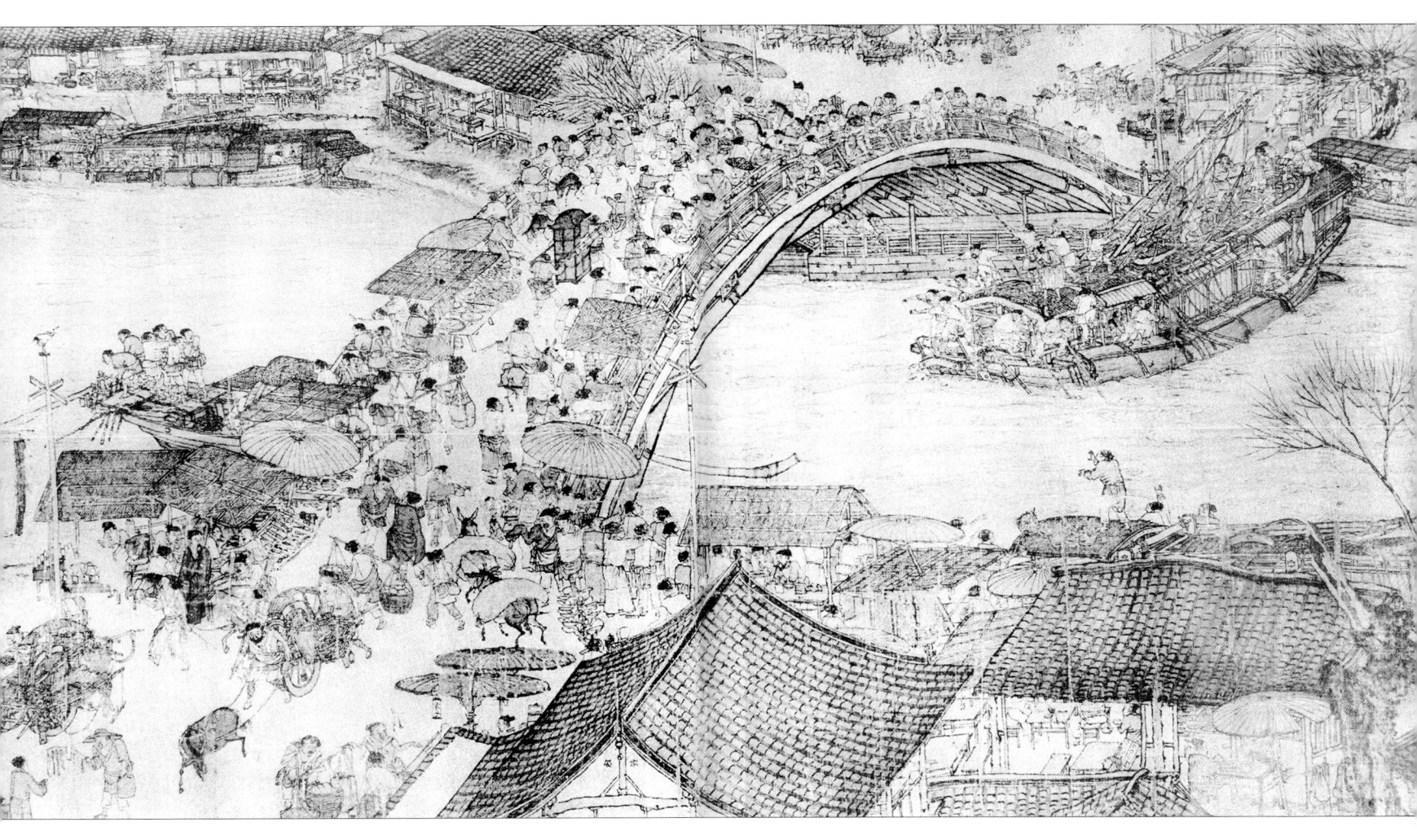

emotional distraction, as if enchanted by some strange magic. If one compares the physical settings, Kaifeng is presented as a highly integrated homogeneous place, with little sense of hierarchy either physically or socially, and with no apparent barriers or distortions in the procession of shops, taverns and homes. In the European frescos, Christ's deeds take place on a medieval stage manifestly disturbed by the struggle to reconcile the illusion of life in the present with the promise of total fulfilment in the City of God. The Christian figures seem detached from reality, ill at ease with the earthly realm, not quite touching the ground; and the only structures of significance are the churches, which appear like heavenly space ships. The Chinese figures are immediate and familiar; they could have been painted at the turn of the 20th century. This view of Kaifeng was confirmation of the success of the Song court in achieving a harmonious, balanced and industrious society. The Padua frescos are an ambiguous reminder to the Christian that one must live with the awareness that the present is merely a prelude to the reality of heaven.

An even more revealing comparison to the Kaifeng scroll can be made through another early medieval work – the great frescos of Ambrogio Lorenzetti entitled 'Allegory of Good Government' in the Palazzo Publico in Siena, 1338–40. These symbolic works dealing with the representation of place were painted two centuries after the Kaifeng scroll. They were intended to provide an ever-present lesson to the public officials of Siena on the qualities of good and evil government. Good and Evil are represented in two separate paintings, both exactly the same size, offering detached panoramic views of the city and surrounding countryside, but differing in their dramatisation of the effects of contrasting governments. Comparing the vision of the 'good city' (Fig. 4) with the Kaifeng scroll, one finds striking differences. The Lorenzetti is as politically and pictorially complex as the scroll. The artist paints Siena as a city absolutely divided from the country by its wall, which is at the centre of the painting, with the city on the left and the country on the right. (Curiously, this separating wall is much more dominant in the painting than the cathedral, which is relegated to the extreme left corner.) This implies a rigid and total division between peasant and burger. The Kaifeng work also separates town and country, with the great gate to the city shown to the left of the centre. But the division between town and country life is far softer – is shared between the two.

The highly organised, almost abstract, landscape depicted around Siena could not be more different from the untidy, sensuous glimpses the scroll gives of the Song landscape. Lorenzetti's landscape is one of the earliest in European painting and seems much more an intellectual exercise than a tangible reflection of experience. The town appears to embody the spiritual realm, whereas the country is described as an economic utility. By contrast, in the intimate multiplicity of representations in the scroll, all seems to be a harmonious combination of the social, the commercial and the agricultural, with surprisingly little concern for the metaphysical/spiritual. The Song streets are lined with businesses covered with banners and theatrical displays, promoting the various activities inside. All the buildings, regardless of their function, are similar both in scale and materials. Restaurants, shops, houses, wine sellers, and barracks are all unified in their manner of construction and accessibility; they are all also quite recognisably Chinese. The representation is of a relatively homogeneous and open culture where all activities are available to everyone, and no one building or activity stands out. In contrast, the buildings that line the streets of the Christian representation vary greatly in colour and form, but they are private, internal places with small windows and doors, and bear no relationship to street life. They seem remote, closed and hostile.

The people on the streets are in many ways similar in the two works. In both cities the citizens move freely and appear open to forms of creative expression: dancing between the porticos in Siena, listening to the storyteller in Kaifeng. However, the people in Lorenzetti's work are less well drawn, or rather more stylised; they lack a clear range of personalities and ages. Bristling with fortifications, Siena seems introverted and defensive; only the divine structures seem truly real. In contrast, the Kaifeng scroll portrays a town with a tolerant and resilient fabric, accommodating an industrious, communal people; a town of small gods without fear of conquest. Though there was a large imperial district in the city, forbidden to all but the inner circle of the court, there is not even a hint of an oppressive imperial power in this drawing. And because these village streets were close to the centre of Song culture, a city of more than a million people, the artist chooses to invest enormous time and energy to convey – in response, one presumes, to the wishes of the imperial patron – a place in which all orders and classes of society co-mingle happily.

When the Song attempted to regain the northern provinces, this provoked a war with the Manchurian Jurchen Jin Dynasty. The Song army

Figure 4: 'Allegory of Good Government', Ambrogio Lorenzetti, Palazzo Publico, Siena, 1339

was weak and the Jurchen attacked, captured and destroyed Kaifeng. Survivors of the Northern Song fled south and under the son of the emperor, re-established the dynasty as the Southern Song in the new capital of Hangzhou, which lasted from 1127 until 1279. This displaced community established Hangzhou as the centre of China's most brilliant artistic culture for the next several centuries. 'In Heaven there is paradise, on Earth there are Hangzhou and Suzhou', ran a Chinese proverb.

THE MONGOL INVASION

When Kaifeng and the Northern Song fell in the Jurchen invasion of 1127, the victorious Jurchen established the Jin Dynasty. The crushing of the Song brought an end to the middle period of the Chinese Empire.

In 1206 Genghis Khan unified the Mongol tribes of the northern steppe and in 1215 conquered part of northern China. The Mongol project was to dominate the known world from Eastern Europe in the north to the jungles of Burma in the south, Japan and Indonesia to the east and China at the centre. Through military action in 1205, 1209 and 1215 Genghis Khan destroyed the cities of the north, proclaiming the need to return the land to pasture so that he could understand it (cities were a meaningless reality to him). Though Genghis Khan died in 1227, his armies continued their battle against the Jin. In 1232 the Jin emperor, in retreat, moved the capital from Beijing to Kaifeng. The Mongols laid siege to Beijing and, on taking the city, slaughtered thousands, moving on to take Kaifeng in a battle that marked the first use of explosive grenades in warfare. The city was sacked and fell.

Genghis Khan's grandson Kublai Khan finally seized control of all China in 1280. He took the title Yuan for his dynasty and ruled as both the first Yuan emperor and Great Khan of the Mongols. The Empire at its grandest stretched from the Danube in the west to Manchuria in the east. The Yuan (1271–1368) were the first non-native Chinese to rule China; never before had it been under foreign domination, foreign systems of administration, or a foreign language. Though the Yuan retained most of the essential elements of Chinese bureaucracy, they imposed their own military form of central control. They divided the people into four classes, with the Mongols at the top, followed by their Central Asian allies, then the northern Chinese, and at the bottom the great majority of the population of the Han, which created deep resentment.

The Yuan capital was established in Beijing, which would remain the imperial city of China, save for two brief periods, until the present. In 1293, reinforcing their control of the nation, Khan's engineers closed the Grand Canal from Beijing southwards to the Yangzhi, constructing instead a water passage through mountains far from any natural waterway, and maintaining the levels by feeder dams and lock gates.

The Southern Song resisted the Mongols for 43 years longer than any other nation in their path. When Kublai Khan took the Song capital of Hangzhou, it was left, unharmed, to evolve as the major centre of Han culture.

MARCO POLO IN HANGZHOU

Kublai Khan's Civil Service was recruited from a host of miscellaneous foreign adventurers – Arab, Persian and Central Asian Muslims, some Jews, a few Jesuit priests and, most notably, Marco Polo.[12] At the beginning of the 14th century, when Polo was part of the Mongol court, Hangzhou had replaced Kaifeng as the largest and most complex administrative, industrial and mercantile city in the world. It was the very model of the ideal city of the Han imagination. To the Yuan it was Xungzaisuo, which translates as 'the temporary residence of the emperor'. Its artistic wealth was matched by its prosperous position at the centre of silk production and at the heart of the vast area of rice cultivation, products that travelled across the Empire along the Grand Canal.

The Book of Sen. Marco Polo, the Venetian, Concerning the Kingdom and Marvels of the East is a wondrous document. It is through Polo's eyes and words that we gain the most complete picture of life in the Song capital of Hangzhou in the 1300s:[13]

The position of the city is such that it has on one side a lake of fresh and exquisitely clear water[14] and on the other a very large river. The waters of the latter fill a number of canals of all sizes, which run through the different quarters of the city, carry away all impurities, and then enter the Lake; whence they issue again and flow to the Ocean, thus producing a most excellent atmosphere. By means of these channels, as well as by the streets, you can go all about the city. Both streets and canals are so wide and spacious that carts on the one and boats on the other can readily pass to and fro, conveying necessary supplies to the inhabitants.

At the opposite side the city is shut in by a channel, perhaps 40 miles in length, very wide, and full of water derived from the river aforesaid, which was made by the ancient kings of the country in order to relieve the river when flooding its banks. This serves also as a defence to the city, and the earth dug from it has been thrown inwards, forming a kind of mound enclosing the city.

In this part are the ten principal markets, though besides these are a vast number of others in the different parts of the town. The former are all squares of half a mile to the side, and along their front passes the main street, which is 40 paces in width, and runs straight from end to end of the city, crossing many bridges of easy and commodious approach. At every 4 miles of its length comes one of those great squares of 2 miles . . . in compass. So also parallel to this great street, but at the back of the market places, there runs a very large canal, on the bank of which towards the squares are built great houses of stone, in which the merchants from India and other foreign parts store their wares, to be handy for the markets. In each of the squares is held a market three days in the week, frequented by 40,000 or 50,000 persons, who bring thither for sale every possible necessary of life, so that there is always an ample supply of every kind of meat and game, as of roebuck, red-deer, fallow-deer, hares, rabbits, partridges, pheasants, francolins, quails, fowls, capons, and of ducks and geese an infinite quantity; for so many are bred on the Lake that for a Venice groat of silver you can have a couple of geese and two couple of ducks. Then there are the shambles [streets of butchers] where the larger animals are slaughtered, such as calves, beeves, kids, and lambs, the flesh of which is eaten by the rich and the great dignitaries.

Those markets make a daily display of every kind of vegetables and fruits; and among the latter there are in particular certain pears of enormous size, weighing as much as 10 pounds apiece, and the pulp of which is white and fragrant like a confection; besides peaches in their season both yellow and white, of every delicate flavour.

Neither grapes nor wine are produced there, but very good raisins are brought from abroad, and wine likewise. The natives, however, do not much care about wine, being used to that kind of their own made from rice and spices. From the Ocean Sea also come daily supplies of fish in great quantity, brought 25 miles up the river, and there is also great store of fish from the lake, which is the constant resort of fishermen, who have no other business. Their fish is of sundry kinds, changing with the season; and, owing to the impurities of the city which pass into the lake, it is remarkably fat and savoury. Any one who should see the supply of fish in the market would suppose it impossible that such a quantity could ever be sold; and yet in a few hours the whole shall be cleared away; so great is the number of inhabitants who are accustomed to delicate living. Indeed they eat fish and flesh at the same meal.

All the ten market places are encompassed by lofty houses, and below these are shops where all sorts of crafts are carried on, and all sorts of wares are on sale, including spices and jewels and pearls. Some of these shops are entirely devoted to the sale of wine made from rice and spices, which is constantly made fresh, and is sold very cheap.

Certain of the streets are occupied by the women of the town, who are in such a number that I dare not say what it is. They are found not only in the vicinity of the market places, where usually a quarter is assigned to them, but all over the city. They exhibit themselves splendidly attired and abundantly perfumed, in finely garnished houses, with trains of waiting-women. These women are extremely accomplished in all the arts of allurement, and readily adapt their conversation to all sorts of persons, insomuch that strangers who have once tasted their attractions seem to get bewitched, and are so taken with their blandishments and their fascinating ways that they never can get these out of their heads. Hence it comes to pass that when they return home they say they have been to Kinsay [Hangzhou] the City of Heaven, and their only desire is to get back thither as soon as possible.

Other streets are occupied by the Physicians, and by the Astrologers, who are also teachers of reading and writing; and an infinity of other professions have their places round about those squares. In each of the squares there are two great palaces facing one another, in which are established the officers appointed by the King to decide differences arising between merchants, or other inhabitants of the quarter. It is the daily duty of these officers to see that the guards are at their posts on the neighbouring bridges, and to punish them at their discretion if they are absent.

All along the main street that we have spoken of, as running from end to end of the city, both sides are lined with houses and great palaces and the gardens pertaining to them, whilst in the intervals are the houses of tradesmen engaged in their different crafts. The crowd of people that you meet here at all hours, passing this way and that on their different errands, is so vast that no one would believe it possible that victuals enough could be provided for their consumption, unless they should see how, on every market-day, all those squares are thronged and crammed with purchasers, and with the traders who have brought in stores of provisions by land or water; and everything they bring in is disposed of.

To give you an example of the vast consumption in this city let us take the article of pepper; and that will enable you in some measure to estimate what must be the quantity of victual, such as meat, wine, groceries, which have to be provided for the general consumption. Now Messer Marco heard it stated by one of the Great Kaan's [sic] officers of customs that the quantity of pepper introduced daily for consumption into the city of Kinsay amounted to 43 loads, each load being equal to 223 pounds.

The houses of the citizens are well built and elaborately finished; and the delight they take in decoration, in painting and in architecture, leads them to spend in this way sums of money that would astonish you.

The natives of the city are men of peaceful character, both from education and from the example of their kings, whose disposition was the same. They know nothing of handling arms, and keep none in their houses. You hear of no feuds or noisy quarrels or dissensions of any kind among them. Both in their commercial dealings and in their manufactures they are thoroughly honest and truthful, and there is such a degree of good will and neighbourly attachment among both men and women that you would take the people who live in the same street to be all one family.

And this familiar intimacy is free from all jealousy or suspicion of the conduct of their women. These they treat with the greatest respect, and a man who should presume to make loose proposals to a married woman would be regarded as an infamous rascal. They also treat the foreigners who visit them for the sake of trade with great cordiality, and entertain them in the most winning manner, affording them every help and advice on their business. But on the other hand they hate to see soldiers, and not least those of the Great Kaan's garrisons, regarding them as the cause of their having lost their native kings and lords.

On the Lake of which we have spoken there are numbers of boats and barges of all sizes for parties of pleasure. These will hold 10, 15, 20, or more persons, and are from 15 to 20 paces in length, with flat bottoms and ample breadth of beam, so that they always keep their trim. Any one who desires to go a-pleasuring with the women, or with a party of his own sex, hires one of these barges, which are always to be found completely furnished with tables and chairs and all the other apparatus for a feast. The roof forms a level deck, on which the crew stand, and pole the boat along whithersoever may be desired, for the Lake is not more than two paces in depth. The inside of this roof and the rest of the interior is covered with ornamental painting in gay colours, with windows all round that can be shut or opened, so that the party at table can enjoy all the beauty and variety of the prospects on both sides as they pass along. And truly a trip on this Lake is a much more charming recreation than can be enjoyed on land. For on the one side lies the city in its entire length, so that the spectators in the barges, from the distance at which they stand, take in the whole prospect in its full beauty and grandeur, with its numberless palaces, temples, monasteries, and gardens, full of lofty trees, sloping to the shore. And the Lake is never without a number of other such boats, laden with pleasure parties; for it is the great delight of the citizens here, after they have disposed of the day's business, to pass the afternoon in enjoyment with the ladies of their families, or perhaps with others less reputable, either in these barges or in driving about the city in carriages.

Of these latter we must also say something, for they afford one mode of recreation to the citizens in going about the town, as the boats afford another in going about the Lake. In the main street of the city you meet an infinite succession of these carriages passing to and fro. They are long covered vehicles, fitted with curtains and cushions, and affording room for six persons; and they are in constant request for ladies and gentlemen going on parties of pleasure. In these they drive to certain gardens, where they are entertained by the owners in pavilions erected on purpose, and there they divert themselves the livelong day, with their ladies, returning home in the evening in those same carriages.

Notes

1 This is a tomb figure from the Sui Dynasty (581–618) in my own collection. It was one of a group that would have represented the servants of the deceased, a centuries-old tradition that replaced what is presumed to have been human sacrifice in the earliest history of China.

2 From *The Summers of the Soul*, a prose poem written by Chu Tz'u during the Han Dynasty (206 BC–AD 220).

3 Confucius is the Latin version of the name, which in Chinese is K'ung Fu Tzu. His actual name, Kong Qui, is not used out of respect; to use it suggests inappropriate intimacy.

4 There are two systems by which Chinese characters are romanised (made readable in languages using the Roman alphabet). The first, the Wade-Giles System, has been in use for over a century and is still used outside the Chinese mainland, in Taiwan for example. The second, the 'pinyin' system, was introduced by the present government of China as, in their view, more accurately reflecting the sound and character of the language (thus 'Peking' became 'Beijing'). This is not an insignificant matter in China, since romanised versions of Chinese characters are widely used throughout the country. The great majority of the names in this text are rendered in pinyin, but some exceptions have been made with familiar historical names: Mao Zedong is pinyin, while Chiang Kai-shek is Wade-Giles, for example. It is also possible that the romanisation used by my Chinese associates has occasionally assumed a hybrid form.

5 The major source for this material and the subsequent notes on the dynastic cities is CP Fitzgerald, *The Horizon History of China*, American Heritage Publishing Co Inc (New York), 1969. There is much splendid historical scholarship on China in English. The strength of Fitzgerald, who lived and worked in China between 1920 and 1950, is his ability to convey the grandeur of Chinese history. I have drawn also on Dun J Li's *The Civilization of China: Translations and Introductions*, Charles Scribner & Son (New York), 1975, and Wolfgang Bauer's *China and the Search for Happiness*, The Seabury Press (New York), 1976, along with standard references including the *British Museum History of Chinese Art* (London), 1996, and Dorothy Perkins' *Concise Encyclopedia of China*, Roundtable Press (New York), 1999.

6 See AEJ Morris, *History of Urban Form*, John Wiley & Sons (New York), 1979. The earliest records documenting Xi'an's form presuppose a coherence and complexity that would have taken centuries to achieve, suggesting that cities in the ancient world were more unified and rational than those of later recorded history. Traces of ancient cities stretching from central China to northern India and Mesopotamia show similarities of structure and order too close to be coincidental.

7 See Paul Wheatley, *The Pivot of the Four Quarters: A Preliminary Enquiry into the Origins and Character of the Ancient Chinese City*, Aldine Publishing Company (Chicago), 1974, p411.

8 They also demonstrate the importance of these animals as the bearers of porcelains, and textiles – especially silks.

9 Nanjing, literally means 'Southern Capital', just as Beijing means 'Northern Capital'.

10 As Fitzgerald states in his *History of China*, op cit, 'Many would see the Tang and Song dynasties as China's most glorious age, an age of many-sided achievements which perhaps ran too far ahead of the norm of development in other nations to be sustained.'

11 The drawing is in the Beijing Museum. Sadly, few such artworks survive, but if compared with works such as 'The pedlar with 500 articles' by the Southern Song artist Li Sung, it clearly represents a well-developed drawing style and reflects a remarkably clear-eyed pleasure in the details of daily life.

12 Western influence in the court of Kublai Khan was the norm not the exception. It is presumed that Polo was fluent in the Mongolian language, yet he admitted to having very little knowledge of the Chinese languages.

13 There are many editions and translations of the writings of Marco Polo. This material is taken from *The Book of Sen. Marco Polo, the Venetian, Concerning the Kingdom and Marvels of the East*, translated and edited with notes by Colonel Henry Yule, third edition (revised throughout in the light of recent discoveries by Aemni Cordier), John Murray (Edinburgh), 1903, an edition with rich, eccentric footnotes and splendid illustrations.

14 This remains the most beautiful part of the city.

Tea room at the end of the Bridge of Nine Turnings, in the 19th century

SHANGHAI

ALAN BALFOUR

The Chinese were skilled cartographers and land planners, as evidenced by an exquisite map of China from the 11th century, whose accuracy is recognisable even today. Such experience was essential in administering a vast land and in gaining physical control over it through some of history's most extensive public engineering projects. The Great Wall and the Grand Canal were for centuries in a continuous process of building, rebuilding and relocating, with the guidance of surveyors, hydrologists, civil engineers, logicians – areas of knowledge either non-existent or neglected in the West.

The upper, middle and lower Yangtze regions had been the setting for town and city formation since the Spring and Autumn Era (772–481 BC). Between the 6th and 3rd centuries BC, the capital of the Wu people, Wuden, was established close to what would become the garden city of Suzhou. East of Suzhou, the Yangtze had always been too tidal and the land too marshy to provide a secure harbour or to support permanent settlement. However, during the Sui Dynasty (7th century AD) many small ports developed along the tributaries and canals flowing into the Yangtze. It was at this time that the village of the Hu or Hudu appears on the records at the confluence of the Huangpu and the Wusong (later Suzhou Creek). Three centuries later, during the Tang Dynasty, this would emerge as the river port of Shanghai. 'Shanghai' is composed of two Chinese characters: 'Shang', meaning 'on', and 'hai' meaning 'sea'.[1]

SONG SHANGHAI

Song Shanghai gained strength after river silting closed the market centre of Quinlong to its west, and although it developed in a marshy, undeveloped area at the edge of a region dominated by the great cities of Hangzhou and Suzhou, the earliest records show that it was emerging as a port of some significance. It received its official designation as a market town – *zhen* – in 1074. An office of diverse trades was established in 1119, and it was named market city – *shi* – in 1159.[2] Most of the temples and schools that gave character to the early city were formed and founded under the Southern Song Dynasty in the glorious period between 1127 and 1279 when the Empire was holding out against the might of the Moguls. Its capital Hangzhou was a brilliant centre of culture, as evidenced later by Marco Polo, and not more than three days travel from Shanghai. In the administrative reorganisation during this period, the Song divided up the former kingdom of Wu Yae to create the Jinxing prefecture, increasing the significance of the Huangpu River and consequently of Shanghai. The early population records for the county show less than 12,000 households, but this would soar to a quarter of a million in 1127, absorbing the exodus from Kaifeng during the Mongol invasion that destroyed the Northern Song. Yet, as elsewhere in China, even after the city was brought within Mogul rule under the Yuan Dynasty in 1279, it grew in modest confidence and prosperity, never suffering the abandonment or devastation of the imperial capitals.

YUAN SHANGHAI (1279–1368)

The earliest mapping of Shanghai took place during the Yuan Dynasty (1279–1368) in the 13th century (Fig. 1).[3] As with all such early maps, it restricts itself to the general positioning of the many waterways within the region. A simplified diagram, this official record is a factual display of the complex of arteries that sustain this small city, linking it to the Huangpu River, then to the Yangtze, and then across all of China via the Grand Canal. The abstract mapping is reminiscent of the London Tube

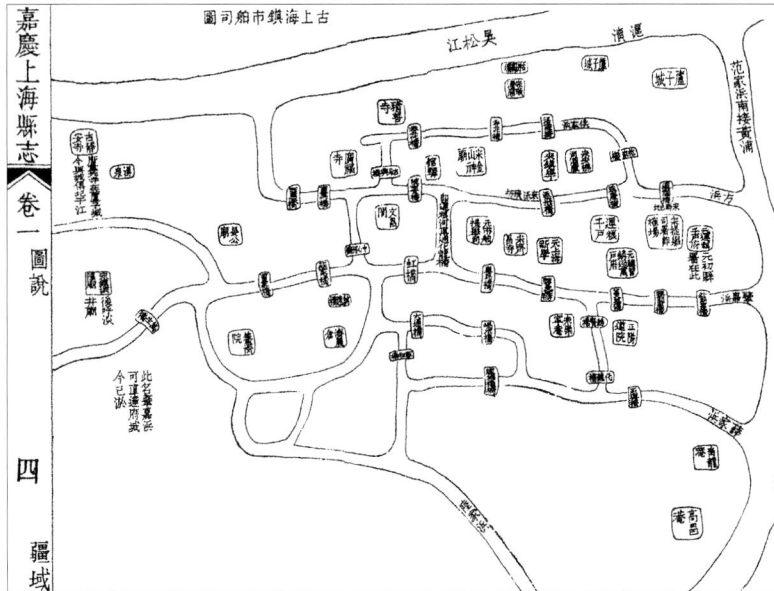

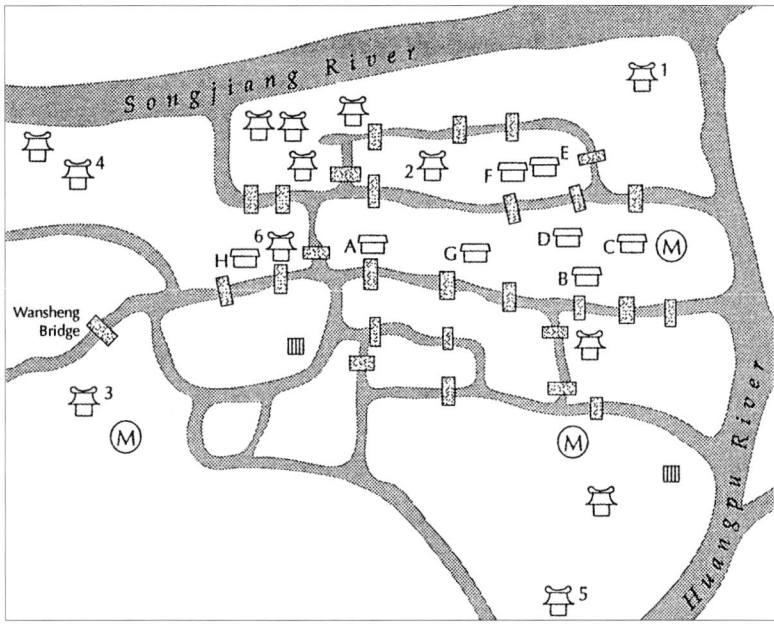

Centre for Cartographic Research & Spatial Analysis, Michigan State University

(M) **Marketplaces**

▱ **Offices**
    A. Office for Overseas Trade
    B. Yuan Military Circuit Office
    C. Yuan Dynasty Office for Grain Transport
    D. Commercial Meeting Hall
    E. Wine Distribution Warehouse
    F. Old Song Dynasty Market-Town School
    G. Yuan Dynasty "New" School
    H. Yuan Dynasty *Xian* College

▥ **Private *Shuyuan* Academies**

⛩ **Temples**
    1. Shunji Temple (Tian Hou Temple)
    2. Jinshan Temple
    3. Song Danjing (City God) Temple
    4. Song Jingan Shrine
    5. Longhua Buddhist Temple
    6. Wengchang Temple

Figure 1: Shanghai in the Early Yuan Period, late 13th century

map: it represents essential relationships and shows no concern for specific geographical or topological features. Most of those who made their living on the waterways would have been illiterate, and this is a diagram by and for the local administration. The Huangpu River flows upwards to the right edge, with the Suzhou Creek running across the top. Only the major canals are named. Emphasis is given to the names of the bridges over the canal, which are shown in lozenge-shaped frames. Throughout the town centre, between the main canals, several character blocks in frames show the location and title of the various offices of the imperial administration. The short stretch of canal at the very centre of the town runs alongside the central food market. Despite its simplicity, the map also attempts to present the changing order of the city and the shifting locations of major functions – food, temples, administration – recording not only their present location but where they stood in previous dynasties. This unadorned document provides us with a simple description of the commercial waterways with Shanghai at the centre.

From this earliest plan there is a suggestion that the old city of Shanghai was based on the grid-like network of canals flowing from the Huangpu River. But as the city grew, changed and intensified, the grids were softened and the canals filled in by the dense buildings growing in every available space.

Yuan Shanghai became the county seat of the Songjiang region in 1292, with a population of 64,000 households. Given the relatively large size of an average family, this was a considerable number. The Yuan town continued to form around the three major canals flowing east into the Huangpu, which had been opened during the Song era. This town between the waterways was a mass of houses, workshops, stores, linked across the canals by 27 bridges and 'packed together like the scales of a fish' according to one contemporary record. The Yuan were tolerant of all religion, and the major temples were restored and extended. Extensive land reclamation projects developed south of the town, with the damming and poldering of marshland funded by taxes and special grants.[4] The Yuan administration established a new school, which, following Song practice, was endowed with the proceeds from extensive agricultural holdings. Underscoring the commercial significance of the town they established Yuan Xi'an Prefecture College to train the county administrators, the Yuan Military Circuit Office, the Yuan office for grain transport, the Yuan Wine Distribution Warehouse and the Office of Overseas Trade; a second office for overseas trade and taxation was soon established.

The Yuan oversaw improvements in agricultural tools and water control, and the introduction of a new strain of early ripening rice greatly increased yields.[5] But it was the development of a new cash crop, cotton, that transformed the economy of the entire delta. The cotton revolution propelled the Songjiang region and Shanghai from a marshy periphery, at best a land of rice and fish, into national prominence as one of the most prosperous and progressive districts of the Empire. The cotton bush and its cultivation came to China from India in the 13th century and quickly became central in the brackish lands to the west of Shanghai. Cotton not only became the cornerstone of

Shanghai's market economy, but also improved the dress of the masses. Until cotton arrived, silk was a fabric exclusive to the court and the wealthy, while the poor who produced it had to make do with rough cloth of hemp or ramie. Production was continually improved by innovations in technology. The Chinese cotton gin, mechanically similar to Eli Whitney's invention of some 400 years later, was in use by the 13th century, and equally inventive devices were developed for pummelling and fluffing the ginned material. Two crops dependent on water – rice relying on flooded fields, and cotton on waterways for its transport – forced the development around Shanghai of elaborate and precise water management, but it was cotton that transformed and strengthened the structure of the region's economy. Linda Cooke Johnson quotes from the contemporary Chinese historian Zhang Zhongmin's 1987 book on the city[6]: 'the lands in front of the Huangpu were planted with cotton from the river to sea. The land was white like the sky with the cotton flowers; men planted, women spun and wove.'[7]

MING SHANGHAI (1368–1644)

A Ming map of 1533 maintains the pragmatism of the earliest records of Shanghai, showing the network of waterways and villages across the country (Fig. 2).[8] It is a practical document in which the Huangpu River forms a diagonal across the sheet, joined recognisably by the Suzhou Creek east of centre. Just below the junction the boxed text establishes the location of the imperial administration.

Unlike the map makers of Europe, who felt the need to embellish their descriptions of cities with the evocation of Divine forces and exaggerated effects, the Chinese map maker was a strict recorder of facts. This, again, is a document for administrators by administrators. It makes no attempt to represent any other aspect of the town. There is no indication of the many paths that must have linked the sequence of bridges, nor of the homes and workshops that would have been crowded onto the land between the canals. No attempt is made to represent the actual physical qualities of the city. This is not a document

Figure 2: Ming Shanghai and surroundings, early 16th century

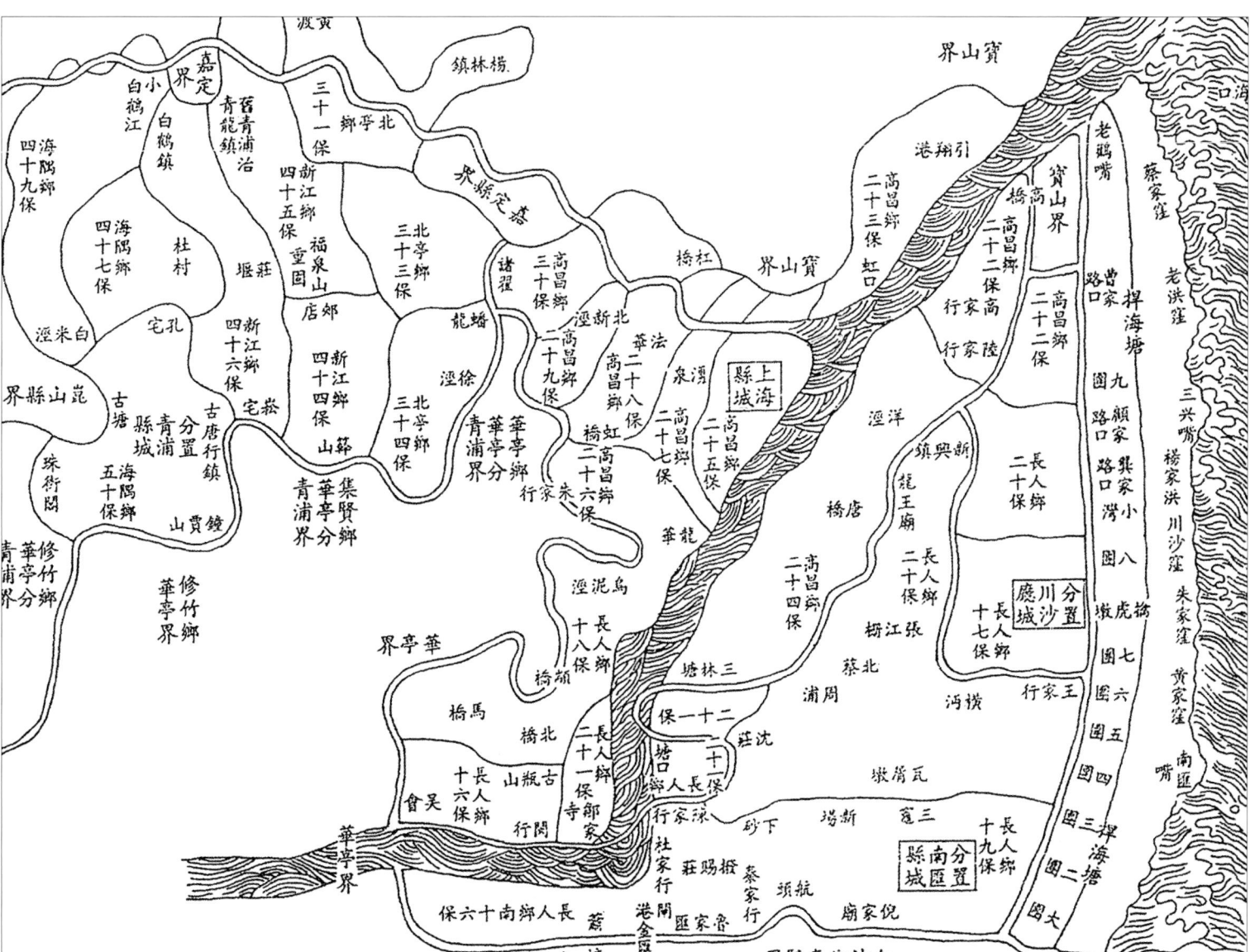

about what might be, but wholly about what is. The map had only one function – to register those elements of the city that were the specific concern of the town administrators and tax collectors: the volume of shipping and the movement of goods on the canals. All elements presented can be considered as aspects of public works. So on the one hand this map is a pragmatic diagram of the key transportation networks within the town, and, on the other, it documents the imperial sphere of influence. Underlying the gently wandering paths of the three lateral canals is an indication that when first laid out, these were formed in a regular set of parallel channels intersected by a partial grid of transverse connections. So flat is the delta, and so wayward the path of the rivers and streams, that this 16th-century description accurately reflects the result of several centuries' struggle between the man-made order and nature.

During the Ming period, Shanghai differed only in scale and population from the many small market towns throughout the region – towns whose planning and structure were the product of reason and circumstance rather than imperial ideal. On coming to power, the greatest of Ming emperor, Yongle (1360–1420), moved the capital from Nanjing to Beijing and immediately began the restoration of the Grand Canal. The canal linking Beijing with the Yangtze was reopened in 1415, becoming once again the major artery of the nation and carrying the great part of the emperor's annual grain tax. Of the total tax, 10 per cent came from Suzhou and Shanghai alone, giving some indication of the productivity of the region and the volume of shipping passing through it. To effect this transportation and to strengthen the river connection between Shanghai and the Yangtze, the decision was made to dredge the Wusong and the Huangpu. Though linked to imperial strategy the decision was taken locally and work was funded by commercial tariffs and local agricultural taxes. Shanghai had developed just south of the confluence of the Wusong and Huangpu, and east to the Yangtze estuary, which made them subject to the build-up of both silt and sand as the river mixed with the tidal sea currents.[9] Ming officials resolved the problem by dredging a channel to allow both rivers to flow north to the Yangtze. This combined force reduced the effect of the tidal currents and greatly lessened the problems of silting. Just as significantly, it allowed shipping entering the estuary of the Yangtze the choice of sailing in many directions, where previously all shipping into the China Sea had been forced by winds and currents to sail south. The new channel would link Shanghai permanently to the Yangtze and to all the important internal and external shipping routes.

THE WALL

The most significant construction in the city between its emergence as a market town in the 12th century and the arrival of the British in the 19th century was the building in 1554 of the city wall.[10] The commercial strength of Shanghai during the 15th and 16th centuries attracted continual and destructive raids from the sea by pirates – the Wukou (Wu – 'short' or 'ugly', and Kou – 'invader', referring presumably to the Japanese). These eventually threatened the very survival of the city. During the reign of Yongle (1403–24), there had been extensive international trade with Japan, the states of the Southern Seas, Indonesia and the Philippines. In the succession of short-lived empires that followed the death of Yongle, however, a far-reaching and destructive imperial decree prohibited all maritime trade, and made outlaws of all those attempting to maintain commercial links with the islands to the east. It also led to the withdrawal of imperial naval defence, leaving the coastal cities open to attack. The source of the piracy is presumed to have been Chinese sailors in co-operation with the Japanese. Politically, Japan was experiencing a period of extreme instability with no effective authority controlling either land or sea.

The problem assumed crisis proportions during the reign of Jiajing (1522–67) with continual raids along the coast. The response from the imperial court was to increase the prohibition of sea traffic and close down all port activity. In some areas, people living near the coast abandoned their homes and moved inland to escape the threat of attack. Imperial forces sent to defend the coast were so neglected by the administration that they were forced to steal from the very people whom they were meant to protect. In 1553, despite the presence of the Ming army, a pirate force of several thousands sacked Shanghai. The population fled, leaving the town to be plundered, the barges on the canals and river burned or sunk.

On reoccupying the town the citizens appealed to the city administration:

> In earlier times though the city has not had a wall marauders have not dared to come in because the population, on the whole, was of valiant, sturdy sailors, able to protect themselves and their families against all threats . . . now the population of the county has increased many times over, now there are many rich men in the city who have cash and property . . . wealth from commerce has accumulated. Less than one *li* outside the city is the Huangpu river offering access to evildoers. In the reign of the present emperor [1522–67] alone, no fewer than 100 gentry and merchant families have lost their lives, money and property. [Now] all the population (the old hundred names) of the county have come together to request official permission to build a city wall.[11]

The wall was begun in 1554. It was not designed to enclose the entire town but was formed as an oval ring around the old heart of the city, some distance back from the river, cutting through the dense buildings of the city and diverting the canals to form a moat. Strictly rectangular enclosures were reserved for imperial orders. The effect was to create two cities: the old administrative one within the wall and an extensive residential, ship-building and warehousing area outside the wall to the south and east. The canny Chinese engineers kept all dimensions to an effective minimum: the wall had a circumference of 3 $\frac{1}{2}$ miles and was 12 feet in height, while the moat was 7 feet deep; there were six land and three water gates. The wall helped, but the piracy was finally brought to an end by more effective imperial intervention and by the emergence of a unified and stable Japan. The city quickly returned to business as the threat of attack diminished. By the end of the 16th century, international trade resumed, as illustrated by the arrival of four galleons from Manila taking on board silks and porcelain bound for the

Mexican port of Acapulco. The lasting effect of the wall was to form a subtle psychological barrier between the discipline of the official city and the polyglot profusion of the industrial port.

The public policy of the Ming administration was encapsulated in the phrase *Tian Xia Wei Gong* ('All under heaven is for the benefit of the people'). The plan of the Ming city shows the degree to which the emperor's officials controlled its affairs. At the centre was the *Yamen*, the buildings of the county magistrate and the official (Xi'an) school. It is recorded that the compound of the imperial administration was viewed by the population as a place of harsh authority and was entered only under duress or necessity. To the northeast were the city temple and the Yu Yuan Gardens. Waterways were the major transportation routes and, in many senses, the major focus of public life. The city streets, many marked by commemorative arches, were narrow, lined with workshops and stalls, markets and a great number of wine shops. The majority in the town lived above their businesses in small rooms, but many of the houses had little courtyards where friends would meet.

Large formal gardens were laid out for the pleasure of elite officials and merchants to stimulate the intellect and the senses. Shanghai's most significant garden, the Yu Yuan 'garden of preparedness' or 'pleasure garden', was established in 1559 by Pan Yunduan as a tribute to his father's leadership in building the city wall. (It is the only surviving Ming garden in the city and now virtually the only place in the city that provides an enveloping sense of the past.) It was designed by Zhang Nanyung, a landscape artist from Suzhou, and during the Qing Dynasty it was incorporated into the grounds of the city temple. Other gardens, the Spring Dew Garden and the Crane Crossing Pavilion, later called the Pearl Bud Garden, are memorable only for their seductive names.[12]

One of the great sights of the town, then as now, was the Longhua Buddhist temple far to the southwest. It has a history far more ancient than the town itself, dating back before the second century. The end of the 16th century, the most active period of temple building in the Ming Dynasty, saw 100 new temples built and four restored.[13] Shanghai has had temples dedicated to the Dragon King, the Three Dragons King, the Yellow Emperor, the Three Officials, and Buddhist Bodhisattvas have become part of the celebration of popular heroes and spirits. However, the city temple was and remains the most important. City temples traditionally house the City God, a real person, who in life offered exemplary service to the city. Shanghai chose, shortly after his death, the Yuan scholar and bureaucrat Oum Yubo (born in 1295), who was deemed uniquely virtuous because he had continuously refused the invitation to join the imperial court. The temple was rebuilt and rededicated in 1602 and still stands beside the Yu Yuan Gardens, most recently rebuilt and re-dedicated in the mid 1990s. Chinese gods are much more friendly and accessible than their counterparts in the West. Temple rituals and symbols have none of the cold mystery and uneasiness of Christian rites. The performances around the city temple remain at the public heart of Shanghai.

Set among the winding lanes that lace through the dense fabric of the town, the temple precinct was the most significant place of gathering, ritual and performance. Meetings with family and friends, sermons, sacred festivals, theatrical and operatic performances both secular and sacred, all took place within the temple precinct. The ritual surrounding ceremonies, processions, sacred days, festivals and popular events determined the sequence of daily life and marked the intervals of the year. This is not so dissimilar to the towns of Renaissance Italy, where parishes defined neighbourhoods and the grand spaces in front of the cathedral were as much secular as sacred. But the mythic gods at the heart of these two communities could not have been more different. In Europe was a people spiritually under the control of an omniscient and dreadful God who demanded the suppression of life in the present in preparation for the afterlife. In China many small gods offered spiritual guidance, and even lesser deities, who existed exclusively to offer comfort, gave advice, eased the chores of daily life and celebrated the pleasures of the seasons. In entering the numerous temples to the three alternative spiritual paths – the City Gods, Buddha and the Dao – one never experiences a feeling of intrusion, of being unwelcome. Nature and the world are self-created in Chinese thought: the forms in life and nature are immanent, not imposed externally by divine decree. And the delicate metaphysics of the temples is far more rational and appropriate to this belief than the tragic scenes central to the imagery of Christianity. China's tragedies are man-made.

In two maps from the 17th and 19th centuries, the old city sits within the distorted circle of the wall, an order that frames it to this day. These are maps from the official records of the city, the only context in which the city would be so described. Judging from the use of signs and symbols, both appear to have evolved out of the earlier maps of the city, which is consistent with the continuity within the Chinese Civil Service, but each adds some surprising new visual effects. The basic pattern of the early city – transverse canals flowing into the Huangpu River – continues to dominate the order. The canals trace a slightly more wayward course than a century earlier, however, and several channels have been closed, and new ones opened. The bridges are again named in lozenge-shaped boxes over the canals, and significant buildings are named in framed boxes. Now, in addition to the text, they are illustrated by small pictorial representations – the buildings are symbolised by a wall and a roof, some larger than others, suggesting relative importance. The first map (Fig. 3) begins to record the organisation of the city, dotted lines showing the main paths through neighbourhoods, suggesting a dense and complex fabric. The later map (Fig. 4)[14] depicts many more lanes, some dotted more heavily than others, suggesting major and minor routes. The later map also gives slightly more detail to the building symbols, adding roof tiles and a window and door. It is significant that, although they have very different functions, temples, administration buildings and schools are each represented by the same symbol, while the fortifications dominate these new maps, forming an imperfect circle, or squashed oval, around the city. (It is interesting to compare the informal order of these walls with the geometrically perfect 16th-century defences of many cities in southern Europe.) A moat encircling the city outside the walls is linked to the canals. The three major canals pass through arches in the walls as they flow east to the Huangpu. In both maps, the walls are given architectural detail and shown in simple three-dimensional projection as seen from the air. There is more elaboration

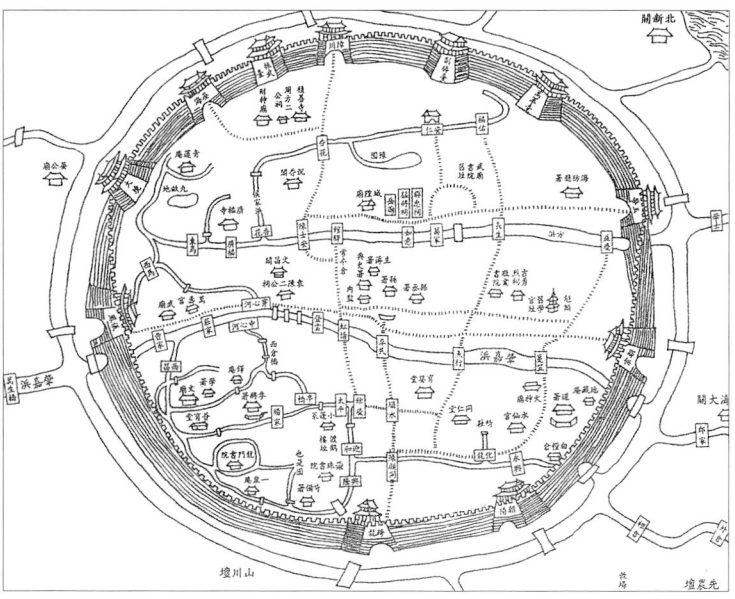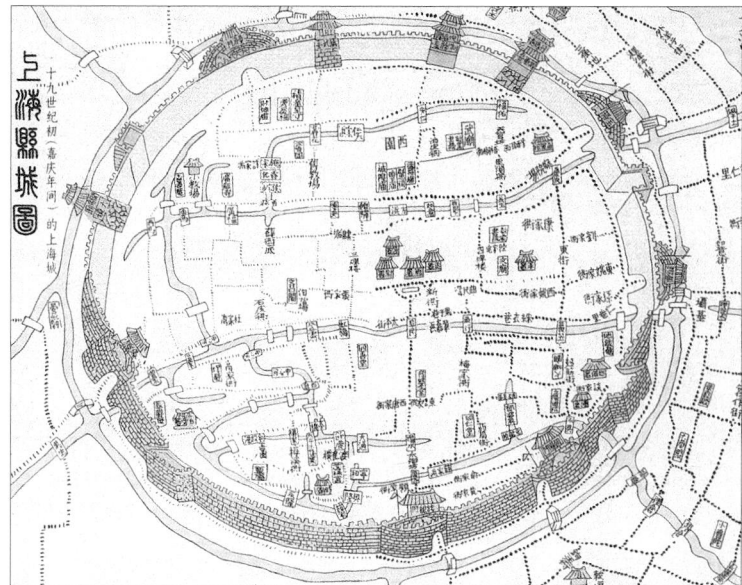

Left: Figure 3: Ming Shanghai, early 17th century
Right: Figure 4: Jianqung map of Ming Shanghai early 19th century

and accuracy in the later drawing, but both pay a great deal of attention to the representation of the thickness and texture of the wall, its crenellations and the architecture of the gatehouses sitting above the arched entries. There are single gates into the walled city on the north, south and west, and several on the east side, the wall arching over the main canals that flow into the old city.

This shift from the purely diagrammatic to a system of symbolic representation suggests changes both in the way the map was viewed and in its intended audience; the map was no longer merely an instrument of bureaucratic control, but a representation of place. These are still official documents, representing official property or issues of concern to officialdom. Yet this is not a major city; it is not marked in any way by the grandeur of the imperial order. It is a circumstantial place, dominated by commerce. The flow of the canals and the pressure of landowners compromise any attempt to establish a regular order in the streets, canals and walls. It suggests that Shanghai, both its structure and its people, has always been an informal, imperfect place, a place ordered by circumstances and reason, free from unnecessary regulation.

To the people of this town, change is slow, almost imperceptible. Place is constant, and only the seasons change. Imperial order was controlled and supported by an unyielding nationwide system of laws and taxes. These were administered by a strictly disciplined Civil Service dedicated to serving the emperor and maintaining Confucian harmony and balance in the order of all things. The only Confucian element evident in these plans of Shanghai is the location of the various offices of the imperial administration at the centre of the city. The many temples that offer comfort via the three religious paths are placed in neighbourhoods around the city at some distance from the centre.

The wall is presented in this way not as a picturesque flourish, but as a document of the technologies of defence and warfare, whose forms, even in the drawings, would have been fully understood in Europe. The crenellations protected the archers, and the semi-circular extensions of masonry that flank all the major gates may reflect Chinese superiority in firearms, the wall, high and curved to deflect the impact of cannon fire. The wall acts to cut the city off from the river. In the later map, the

stretch of land along the river's edge is crisscrossed with paths, suggesting the emergence of new activities and industries able to develop more freely outside the constraints of the city.

This place of small, helpful gods was the antithesis of the Divinely distorted cities of Europe in the 16th century. The paths through the neighbourhoods offer the only evidence of the life of the townspeople. These are somewhat informal and meander circuitously through the islands formed by the canals. The paths on the east of the city are much more direct than those on the west and seem more concerned with defining property boundaries than with efficient movement through the town. We can assume from the evidence that these were people with the freedom of self-determination, able to use their wealth to rise within the community, to develop property. More than 60 arches each carry a plaque stating the name of the place and noting its distinction from various districts of the city. There are no signs of imperial luxury here, no marks of an idealised order. The city temple is only presented as a sign, not rendered symbolic, and no attempt is made to suggest the presence of the Yu Yuan Gardens – the public heart of the city.

One can think of the city as a natural system, a crude physical organism. And like natural systems, its essential moving parts are dedicated to the transportation and exchange of materials. The city dwellers are its life's blood. The parts of the system are given attractive exteriors – its architecture – which help explain their function and smooth their operation and experience. This is a place without any illusion – no false promises or exaggerated differences. It is much less interesting, less distinguished than the major cities in the region. The cities visited by Marco Polo were formed, above all, to entertain the imperial tastes and desires of Kaifeng, Nanjing and Suzhou. However, the very ordinariness of Shanghai marks its subsequent evolution and its particular interest in terms of this examination. This was never a city distorted by illusions, yet in its difference from more favoured places it can be said to have become a city of suppressed desire, whose ordinariness would later make it able to absorb European confidence and order.

Even today, in the small trading towns on the rivers to the west such as Tongli and Zhou Zhuang, it is possible to experience the quality of life in late Ming Shanghai. It seems only a short distance from the fields to the edge of the canal. The paths lead straight onto the bridge, so one is unaware of the grandeur of the span until one looks back: a spectacular and effortless leap of stone leads onto a narrow curving street running toward the heart of the town. This passes between two- and three-storey buildings, stores, shop houses and the occasional merchant house, marked by circular moon gates in the walls that screen elegant courtyards. The street ends in the Temple Square, a generous, regular space with a pair of symmetric braziers at its centre, burning incense in front of two slightly neglected bronze lions flanking the path to the temple portal. Inside is a gloomy, sweet-smelling space. On a recent trip I was met by a small man in modest religious dress: a dark grey, long-sleeved gown, belted and reaching to the ground. His bright eyes and wispy beard made him seem like some character from central casting, but he was real. He smiled gently and handed me a well-worn board with a type-written sheet pasted to it. 'This will help you', he said in English. 'You will find we have most kinds of gods here; some may seem familiar.'

Nearby, in the neatly restored City Temple in Zhu Jia Jiao, a carving on a very large abacus – at least 8 feet in length – hung over the entrance gateway. 'Life is a continual calculation', said the woman at the gate as she busied herself preparing lunch for the gatekeeper, 'and one should continually keep an account of good fortune.' The inner temple court was a space of elegant order and tranquillity, perfectly formed to support all the performances, sacred and secular, demanded by the community. The sacred shrine faced a simple, high, covered terrace, essentially a stage for all forms of public performance. Such stages were always built high up, I was told, because performance must always be seen as detached from the ordinary.

In the 17th century, into the last years of the Ming Dynasty, the high official and devout Christian Xu Guong built, in the characteristic Jesuit style, a Catholic mission just outside the north gate to the old city.[15] He had been converted by Jesuit missionaries in southern China in his youth and was renamed Paul; he is still known in the West as Paul Xu. It was he who, working with the Italian missionary Matteo Ricci, translated mathematical texts and wrote scientific treatises based on an oral translation of European works. It was also he who persuaded the Ming court to buy a European cannon in the fight against the Wukou pirates. The site of the mission of Paul Xu was confiscated during the anti-Christian repression in the Kangxi period (1662–1723). (Though this was Catholic not French property, when the French arrived in Shanghai in 1845, they claimed it, and the city authorities returned the land to them.)

Some sense of the fabric of religious life in the late Ming period can still be found in the more conservative parts of Japan. Japan's religious traditions and rituals were influenced by, and parallel, those of China. Buddhism and Shintoism were both equally egalitarian, and there are shops in the most conservative towns in Japan that sell a wide range of household altars and shrines. The Shinto shrines have an elemental simplicity; they offer solace with nothing more than the simple wooden figure of steps leading to the door of the house. The Buddhist shrines are made in a wide range of sizes, the largest being close to the scale of a

wardrobe. Beyond the doors of the cabinet are layers of gilded arches surrounding the Buddha. Though suppressed during the socialist years, such household gods are omnipresent in Hong Kong and Macao (the Shanghainese claim, however, that in Hong Kong the shrines are used only to ask for money).

A poetic evocation of the mood of the city toward the end of the Ming Dynasty can be found in the *Kangxi Gazetteer* under the title 'View from a High Chamber'. A sensitive eye looks at the city from the upper terrace of one of the administration buildings on a summer's afternoon and sees that the city has all the qualities of a painting:

> Mist and clouds wind and coil together with the smoke from cooking fires above the streams and flat lands, swallowing up [the view] and spitting [it] out again; rising and setting like the sun and moon, fleeting and disappearing before our eyes; whether in winter's snows or autumn's gusts [the view of Shanghai] is ever more beautiful.[16]

This description is reinforced by a marvellous drawing from the early Ming period, more immediate even than the Kaifeng scroll, and so fresh that it could be a contemporary scene. This careful, elegant drawing is of the northeast quadrant of the city, the Fang Bang ('square by a small river') (Fig. 5). It shows the crowded streets of the town centre in the foreground, the wall rising through a haze in the middle distance, and beyond the port city, spiked with the masts of numerous ships to the far bank of the Huangpu River, the tower of the Customs House in the distance. On the right of the drawing is the great gate of the city wall, through which flows the central canal. Just visible at the centre, barges are being polled between the houses, heading toward the town centre. They pass under the first of the bridges, which is named 'More and more celebration' in the *I Ching*, and then under the second bridge and the sign for 'long life'. Just left of centre is the great drum, or town clock, housed in a bell tower, whose booming sound set the rhythm and pace of daily life. Close by is the temple to the city god, Guandi.

The drawing shows great charm and variety in its depiction of the homes, businesses and public buildings. Its high vantage point also allows us to peek into the gardens and squares, showing a town with many tree-lined streets and much less congestion than records suggest. We look down on the backs of the houses and across the canals into the speciality stores, the snack shops and even the terrace of a restaurant. The drawing presents a picture of town life that can still be found in the small, highly picturesque water towns to the west of the city between Shanghai and Suzhou, whose main streets are the canals and rivers, and the embankments on either side. High arched bridges dominate the scene, and the many simple structures that together form the town have the rich variety in the detail, yet much of the uniformity of structure, conveyed in the Kaifeng drawing. A small number of materials and building forms is able to encompass all the needs of the community. The drawing conveys an impression of satisfying balance and equity. This is a place without mystery, formed from the familiar, almost universal, patterns produced by community and trade. The simplicity and elegance of the architecture are unified by the limited palette of materials: whitewashed walls, wood framing, either oiled or painted Chinese red, and the roof tiles, which are mostly grey but occasionally, on significant

Figure 5: 17th-century Ming Shanghai

buildings, are brightly coloured in reds and greens. The official buildings of the town shown just to the right of centre – and given no special prominence – would have been especially well made. These, and the exceptionally well-engineered stone bridges and embankments were built to last.

The composite effect is of a pragmatic, intelligent society that had formed coherent principles of constructing and organising reality over many centuries. In almost every respect, this drawing shows a Shanghai that differs little in its town life from Kaifeng 500 years earlier, as represented in the scroll. It represents the refinements of an urban life that had at least 2,000 years of previous history. The simple conclusion one draws from such continuity is that this was a culture that had long since become fully realised, and had developed all the necessary instruments to ensure its survival.

QING SHANGHAI (1644–1911)

The Qing Dynasty was founded by the Manchu in 1644. In 1643 a Han Chinese, Li Zicheng, led an army of rebellion against the Ming, capturing Xi'an and proclaiming himself emperor. He then marched on the Ming capital of Beijing. The Ming army had positioned itself along the Great Wall as security against Manchurian incursion. As the rebel army approached, the Ming general made the fatal error of inviting the Manchurian forces to help oppose the rebellion. The resulting confusion allowed part of the rebel army to take Beijing. The emperor and empress hanged themselves. In June of 1644 the Manchu army entered Beijing unopposed, and proclaimed the Qing Dynasty with a seven-year-old as its first emperor.

The first three Qing emperors had long reigns, which, when taken together, historians consider to be the greatest period of premodern Chinese history. The Manchus retained the imperial Civil Service and continued to staff it with Confucian-trained Han Chinese literati. Each Chinese province was governed by both a Manchu governor general and a Chinese governor. By imperial decree, marriages were forbidden between the Manchu and the Han Chinese, and men were forced to wear their hair in the Manchu style, gathered into a long pigtail or 'queue'. However, by the 18th century the Manchu had been Sinicised, wholeheartedly embracing Chinese culture while maintaining racial separation. Shanghai, far from Beijing, had a minimal Manchu presence and nothing interfered with the development of its trade and commerce.

Under the Ming and Qing Dynasties, cotton cultivation and handcraft manufacturing, water control measures, and the market towns, were all linked in the emerging commercial economy of the Shanghai Songjiang region. As Linda Cooke Johnson writes, 'a near industrial level of handcraft manufacturing developed using specialised weaving looms and techniques, and employing dying and finishing processes that called for large scale equipment and heavy labour – well beyond the capacity of peasant households or industrial shops to provide.'[17] Imported commodities included rice, sugar and tobacco from Zhejiang, Hunan, Szechwan and the southern coastal ports. Together they helped create such prosperity that by the High Qing period (in the 18th century) the Songjiang prefecture and the Shanghai district in particular were among the richest regions of China.[18] Trade routes for the long-distance transportation of commodities were expanded, and an astonishing variety of products was exported, judging from the list of the Shanghai *Daguan Zeli*, the customs handbook for 1785. Included were all sorts of apparel, from sable furs to straw hats and shoes; food stuffs including tea (for local consumption or to be exported on northern shipping routes), wine, beans, rice, sugar, beef, vegetables; tobacco; many varieties of cotton from unprocessed raw cotton and cotton balls, thread and yarn to the finished fabrics in a wide range of grades and weights; silk in all stages of production from silkworm eggs to the finest finished damasks; paper of many varieties manufactured in Suzhou; candles, cooking and lighting oils; leather goods; lumber and bamboo in bulk; gold, jade and fine jewellery; items made of bone, horn, feathers and fur; medicines of many kinds; charcoal; and stinking mud shipped north as ballast and sold as fertiliser. Imported goods such as paper from Japan, Japanese knives, foreign yarns and luxury items such as birds' nests for gourmet soups were taxed at a much higher tariff than locally produced imports. It was at this time that the British began to plan their development of trade with China and to take a special interest in Shanghai.

The most powerful government official in the city after 1736 was the Yamen of the Circuit Intendant. Through a fusion of offices, the Intendant was in charge of military defence for the whole region, as well as administering the city Customs House, the Daguan. Standing on the banks of the Huangpu, and painted bright red, this was the most visible building south of the city beyond the walls. Nearby, just inside the wall, was the office of the Intendant, far from the old Confucian centre of administration, but close to the heart of the trading city. The city walls limited growth within the city, but a counter city developed south and east between the walls and the Huangpu. Inside the walls, the city retained its Ming formality.[19] Outside, along the river, development continually intensified in the dense mat of shop houses that were

served by hundreds of narrow lanes leading to shipyards and docks, warehouses and processing sheds and, at the heart, the new, tall Customs House. Compared to the ordered, sombre texture and Confucian regulation of the official city, the counter city outside the walls was a place of expediency, driven by commerce and industry.

These oppositions, to quote Cooke Johnson again, 'reflected a deeper dichotomy in Chinese society. From the earliest times, theories of urban organisation in China always emphasised centrality.'[20] The Confucian emphasis on the centre extended from the imperial capitals to lowly county seats. City organisation had from the earliest times created a division between government and trade; the government agencies were in the centre, surrounded by districts, each with their own religious establishment and academic institutions, and though the many streets to and from the town were lined with shops, all the major market activity was pushed to the edge. But with the coming of the Qing Dynasty, markets were deregulated and left to find their own levels of operation and location within the town; a market economy evolved, independent of state control, leading to a double nuclei of urban growth – one centre based on the pattern of Confucian administration, the other on the locus of markets and mercantile activity.[21] This striving for Confucian harmony also shaped the buildings. While European architecture strove for confrontation and exaggerated difference between the varying types of building that formed the fabric of the city, Chinese architecture sought harmony and unity in all contexts: palaces, temples, schools, houses, are all composed of the same elements and all made from the same material,

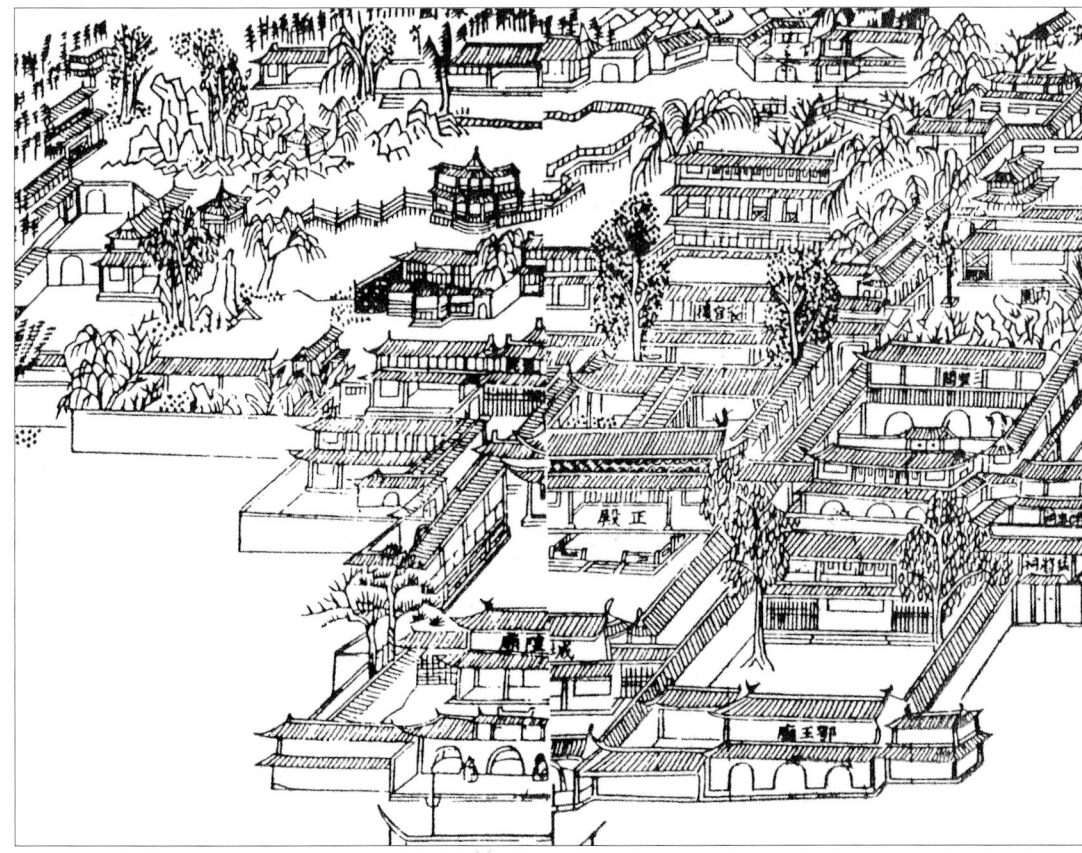

Figure 6: The City Temple and the Yu Yuan Gardens in the Qing Dynasty, early 19th century. Top centre is the splendid tea room which still stands at the end of the Bridge of Nine Turnings.

in the same way. (This is strikingly evident, as we have seen, in the Kaifeng scroll, and even today the surviving towns on the waterways west of the city have an essential pragmatism that demands that the form and structure of the town should be, above all, a useful armature and stage for the unified performance of town life.)

The Qing also saw the rise of benevolent societies, which greatly increased the influence of the merchants and corporations, allowing the private sector to play an increasingly dominant role in public service. All Chinese social groupings were based on three key affiliations: family or clan, ties to native place, and guild membership, the latter forming the basis for the benevolent societies. These were run by independent boards and supported by contributions from members involved in trading activities large and small. They undertook to house the homeless, finance water-control projects, support public jury service, invest in public schools and orphanages, and provide funerals for the poor. Their activities were administered from highly visible structures, such as the Tongrentang, whose great facade was brightly painted and gilded, symbolising the generous and comforting sharing of wealth with the needy. The Christian missionaries, who offered similar services as a means of gaining influence and converts, saw the benevolent societies as a threat. (The Confucian spirit of seeking harmony and balance was far removed from the objectives of the missionaries, who were making investments towards their place in heaven by saving as many souls as possible.) The strength of the economy and the prosperity of the merchants produced a marked lessening of class division in the city, laying the basis for far-reaching political change in the 20th century.

Prosperity allowed the Qing city to develop strong institutions. Schools were important to all levels of Chinese society.[22] There were three major types, the private school, the Confucian academies, and the official schools. Xi'an College, the key institution in preparing for the Civil Service exams, appropriately positioned close to the offices of the city magistrate, the major portion adjoining the Confucian temple, was its guiding spirit. That process of seeking meritocracy by examination had shaped the official administration of China for six centuries. (During the Qing Dynasty, Shanghai had achieved the political status to award 20 degrees annually, 12 on the civil list and nine to the military.) There were also private academies whose structure and presence in the city resembled the private homes of the wealthy, with pavilions, courts and terraces, and explicitly formed gardens of contemplation. An early 19th-century gazetteer contains woodcuts illustrating several schools. The Duisha Academy resembled one of the great houses of Suzhou; the Jungye Shajuan School, in contrast, seemed to be a much more practical environment. The Lunhuen Academy, founded in 1865, resembled the home of a wealthy merchant and offered an advanced curriculum blending Confucian classics with Western studies in mathematics and sciences.

Prosperity also allowed the transport merchants of the city to build the Yu Yuan Gardens in 1760 and donate them to the City Temple, transforming a formerly private, elite world into a public pleasure garden – by far the largest public area in the old city[23] (Figs. 6 and 7). Though the City Temple was never a forbidding or sacrosanct place, the addition of the gardens increased the secular mood of the public performances.

The pavilion and many halls that formed the complex were rebuilt and furnished by the numerous mercantile groups and common trade guilds that had taken up residence in the surrounding streets. This ceremonial heart of Shanghai became an engaging blend of business, pleasure and religion, a blend that was emblematic of the emerging style and character of the 19th-century city. Surrounding the City Temple, business halls, shops and teahouses flourished, none more grandly than the Huxuting tea house, reached across the Bridge of the Nine Turnings (see page 28). Such was its overriding secular character that this would become one of the few areas of the city that Europeans could visit with ease. (It remains popular and, along with the gardens, is the only significant survivor of the old city.) Each of the five wards within the walled city had its own temples. Buddhist shrines became family shrines and popular cult temples. They are still present in the northwest quadrant of the city, but elsewhere many temples have disappeared. Temples came and went based on the utility and appeal of the spirits. There were strong alignments between the merchant guilds and some of the more popular cult temples, such as the relationship between traders from the southeast of China and the Temple to Guandi, who in his earliest form was the God of War, but was subsequently redefined as the God of Loyalty in War and Trade.

Despite the thoroughness of the records kept by the imperial bureaucracy, attempts to determine the population of Shanghai in the years before the arrival of the British in 1841 have produced no definitive results. Johnson draws the conclusion that the population of the city itself was 250,000,[25] including children and the elderly, in a county of half a million. This is substantial but not unusual in the highly urbanised province, with its continual process of town formation along the many waterways in the region for which Shanghai was the administrative centre. Housing varied as widely as the distance between rich and poor.[26] The norm for the poor worker was the shop house, in which the business was accommodated in a single room at street level and the family lived above. The more affluent lived in family compounds around a courtyard. As had always been the case, most structures were built of wood (there was no local stone), the wall surfaces plastered and painted white, with the dressed-wood frames of windows, balconies and doors painted red or black. The streets of shop houses are marked to this day by their dull red paint and a continuous line of windows on the upper storey. Most roof tiles were grey; only the major public buildings, the temples and public halls, were permitted to use bright glazed tiles in reds and greens. Each distinct neighbourhood had its own character, and the entrances to many of the lanes were marked by handsome gates named after the dominant families. The city's main streets had hardly changed in 600 years; they remained 6 to 12 feet in width, flagged and paved with stone, brick or edge-laid broken roof tiles, and still teeming with street traders, pedlars, food stalls, tea stands and fortune tellers, just as shown on the Kaifeng scroll.[27]

The city was dominated by the activities of the port and by trade and manufacture. At the beginning of the 19th century, the port of Shanghai was described by one of the missionaries on the *Huron* expedition of 1835 as 'a forest of innumerable masts'.[28] The *Huron* was one

Figure 7: In the Yu Yuan Gardens

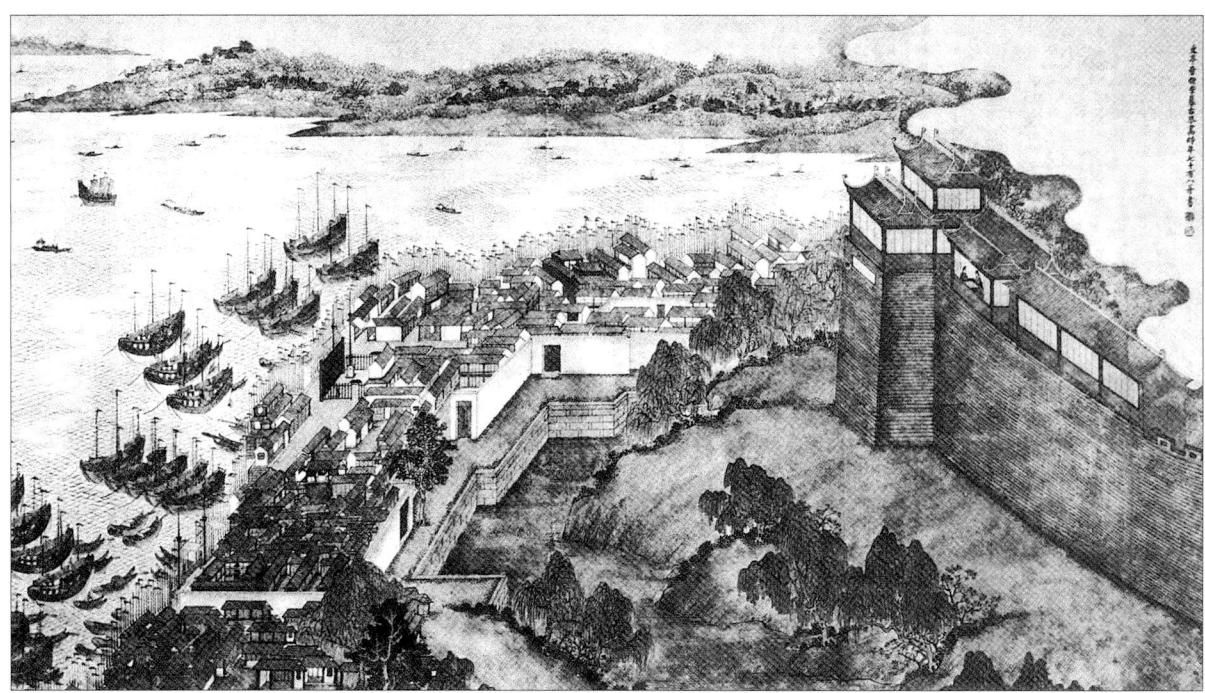

Figure 8: Early 19th-century Shanghai, between the walls and the river from the pavilion of the Red Phoenix

of several British vessels that had begun to chart the waters in the 1830s. Records from this period show that the volume of Chinese shipping through the port was twice that of Canton, despite an imperial decree that blocked all international transactions in Shanghai between the years 1760 and 1843, and limited international trade to the port of Canton. There were three main levels of merchant activity: the most powerful handled the long-distance shipping of cotton, silk and fertiliser; the middle level dealt in services, banking, the supply of fresh meats and clothing; and lastly the merchant brokerages constructed warehouses and ran brokerage yards for cotton, silk, tea and beans. They were all served by a multitude of local craftsmen, artisans, pawnbrokers, shopkeepers, oil-pressing yards, bamboo workshops and cotton/silk weaving, finishing and dying operations.

The city both inside and outside the walls buzzed with activity: weaving and cotton traders gathered around the great West Gate, bookstores clustered round the Xi'an College, and by the North Gate (that would eventually lead to the European city), among the restaurants and brothels, were jade carvers, goldsmiths, jewellers, makers of eyeglasses and shops selling paintings and calligraphy. Throughout the commercial area the street names reflected the nature of the businesses they contained: Salt Wharf, Pickled Melon Street, Bamboo and Wood Workers Street, Oil-pressing Lane.[29] The name of the riverbank changed from Outside Street to Horse Road as it widened by the city to accommodate heavy transport. The riverbanks carried all the equipment for long-distance commerce, supporting the wharves and docks, dry docks, shipyards and the 'go-downs' – great storage warehouses. Behind were the dense lanes of shop houses and cheap lodgings for the boat hands. Just outside the walls were the extensive Huiguan – the compounds of the Native Place associations (tribal groups settling in the city from other parts of China), which included temples, performance stages, halls, offices, dormitories and rental housing, all in a cluster of courtyards and gardens. The obligation was to house anyone coming to Shanghai from the native region, particularly those preparing to take the Civil Service exams. The complex also included mortuaries, and at some distance

from the city were the extensive cemeteries. Along the southern edge of the river were the Hongs (the Fujian tea merchants), the guildhalls of the shipping merchants, and the Huiguan of the sand-junk merchants, with its shipyards, docks and warehouses. In the midst of all this were manufacturers processing soya-bean oil using animal-powered machines. Crowning the view was the red tower of the Customs House, and close by, the Long Life Hall, the major provider of charity for the poor.

By 1858 all the major common trade activities, from copper to bean oil, were clustered in the lanes and squares surrounding the Yu Yuan Gardens, while the compounds of most of the Native Place associations formed an arc around the eastern districts of the city, outside the walls.[30] These supported a rich mix of social services, from rental housing to the comforts of the cult temple. By the 19th century the buildings of the Native Place and Common Trade associations had more influence on the population than government or religion. Together they moulded the character of the city in the 19th century, and their strength and broad base of support led directly to the political independence of Shanghai in the 20th century. By the end of the 19th century this combination of popular trading groups and immigrant associations allowed the working majority to begin to define the civic identity of Shanghai, displacing the centuries of imperial dictate guided by the Confucian principle.

An early 19th-century drawing, made in the years shortly before the British arrived, gives a view from a high vantage point looking south across the narrow band of the city, between the walls and the river (Fig. 8). It is one of the eight famous scenes of the city and shows a view south beyond the walls from the pavilion of the Red Phoenix, the most elaborate of the city gatehouses. A series of ordered streets runs down to the river, framing rows of white-washed walls beneath tiled roofs. The water's edge is dense with the sails of sampans, beyond which heavy cargo ships are lined up in groups of three or four. The most curious aspect of the drawing is at the centre. On the landward side, the buildings end in a highly formal screen wall that encloses not just the moat that surrounds the city, but an elegant landscaped park beneath the city walls. The steeply sloping banks beneath the walls have been planted with picturesque clusters of willows, and across the moat is a splendid formal promenade. This defies the Western perception of the city at the time of the Treaty of Nanjing (1842) as that of a squalid village. Contrary to the simple, pragmatic maps of the same period, the impression here is of an active commercial harbour combined with civic pleasure gardens. On the right of the drawing two figures contemplate the scene below from pavilions on the walls that are almost lost in the swirling clouds, heightening the lyrical mood.

However, when the Europeans were assessing the possibilities for colonisation of the Chinese coastal cities in the 1830s, Shanghai had become a less gracious city, with fewer gardens and more popular cult temples. In many ways, the strength of its popular and commercial culture had begun to undermine respect for the imperial administration.[31] The increasing strength of the benevolent societies developed by the merchant groups, and the growing confidence and prosperity of the merchant community, produced a continual weakening of the social

and political elite. As a result of this, much of the city was poorly managed. The wall was badly maintained and had collapsed in several areas. The canals, according to Western reports, were rarely dredged, silting up with mud and refuse, all but drying up at low tide. This was partly also due to a collapse in the cotton trade, caused by Western manipulation, and created a weakness that made Shanghai more pliable to Western ambition.

It is still possible to experience the quality of life recorded in these drawings in the many little market towns that survive on the rivers and small lakes west of the city. This network of towns, such as Zhu Jia Jiao west of Quingpu, remain small but active commercial ports, connected to the Grand Canal, continuing the ancient water-borne trade across central and southern China. They still offer the experience of narrow lanes, food vendors, the sweet, rich smells of banana-leaf-wrapped meats and fruit concoctions, the formality of the specialist stores, the elegant merchant houses and the welcoming and often witty decorations in the local temple.

Notes

1 Sometimes the reverse term, 'Haishang' is used in referring to Shanghai. The author Zhang Ailing, for example, named one of his books *Hai Shang Hua Lie Zhuan* ('Legend of flowers [or women] in Shanghai').

2 See Linda Cooke Johnson, *Shanghai From Market Town to Treaty Port 1074–1858*, Stanford University Press (Stanford, California), 1995, p 67. (Four main sources inform my text, the two primary ones being maps and my own experience in and around the city. The third is the writings of travellers to the city, and the fourth is the exceptional work of the small number of Western scholars who have studied the city. Principal among them is Dr Cooke Johnson in the work cited above, and in collections such as *Cities of the Jiangnan in Late Imperial China*, State University of New York Press (New York), 1993. The quality of Dr Cooke Johnson's substantial scholarship, which has made her work such an asset to these essays, is her ability to convey the evolving physical character of the city as well as its multiple social levels. There is a certain amount of Chinese scholarship available in English, but, largely due to problems of language, none offers the rich overview presented by Dr Cooke Johnson. My major Chinese source was translations from *The Evolution of Shanghai Architecture in Modern Times*, Shanghai Educational Publishers (Shanghai), 1999, which offers an insightful overview of the city's evolution and reproduces the major historical maps of the city.

3 Cooke Johnson, op cit, Reproduced in *Hucheng beikao* (Official Gazetteer, 18th century), translated and redrawn by the Centre for Cartographic Research and Spatial Analysis, Michigan State University. (Such city gazetteers were continually updated records of taxes, trade and the specifics of the imperial bureaucracy.)

4 Cooke Johnson, op cit, p67.

5 Ibid, pp44–6.

6 Zhang Zhongmin, 'New discoveries in the evolution of Shanghai's port in the early Qing period', Zhongguo Jingji Shi Yanjui, cited in Cooke Johnson, *Shanghai*, op cit.

7 Cooke Johnson, *Shanghai*, op cit, p52. 'The population rose faster than the rice production, and as even western lands switched from labour-intensive paddy-grown rice to dry-field cotton, more labour was released for employment ancillary manufacturing and small commercial establishments. By 1588, over 60 different kinds of cotton, cotton thread and cloth were listed in the *Wanli* (Shanghai) gazetteer'.

8 Ibid, reproduced in the Shanghai *Xian Zhi* (Official Gazetteer, 1872).

9 Cooke Johnson, op cit, p72.

10 Ibid, pp78–82.

11 Ibid, p80.

12 Ibid, p90.

13 Ibid, p89.

14 Jiajing Shanghai *Xian Zhi* (Official Gazetteer, 1814).

15 Cook Johnson, op cit, p93.

16 Ibid, p82.

17 Ibid, p59.

18 Ibid, p63.

19 Ibid, p96.

20 Ibid, p97.

21 One can see in this similarities between Willhelmine Berlin in the 18th century and industrial Berlin in the 19th.

22 Cooke Johnson, op cit, p103.

23 Ibid, p99.

24 Tongzhi Shanghai *Xian Zhi* (Official Gazetteer, 1872).

25 Cooke, Johnson op cit, p118.

26 Ibid, p118.

27 Ibid, p62.

28 Ibid, p164.

29 Ibid, pp113–16.

30 Ibid, p131.

31 Ibid, p117.

The pavilions and the many different landscapes within the Yu Yuan Gardens.

Between Shanghai and Suzhou the many small towns such as Tongli and Zhou Zhuang in the network of waterways still linked to the Grand Canal, retain the form and character of Shanghai in the Ming and early Qing periods.

Perspectives of the few remaining commercial streets and residential lanes in the old city.

Incense and icon sellers cluster round the city temple (top right).

BRITISH SHANGHAI

ALAN BALFOUR

The British were the major foreign traders along the China coast in the late 18th century. Tea was the principal commodity. While trading between China and its neighbours involved simple tariffs paid to customs officials, foreign trade was managed by the so-called Canton system – the channelling of all Western trade through Canton by imperial decree, and the payment of obligatory tax as a tribute to the emperor. This greatly angered foreign traders, particularly the British. Even before transactions were possible, a mission had to travel to Beijing, and the representatives of the nation seeking a trading relationship had to prostrate themselves before the emperor, the 'Son of Heaven'. Taxes were collected through Chinese merchants in Guangzhou called the Hong (or Cohong for combined merchant companies), who had the power to set the price for imports and exports, and collected duties and tariffs for the Qing administration.

British trade was under the control of the British East India Company, whose business interests stretched across Asia and who supported its expansion with a large, well-trained military force. The British used the profits from opium grown in India, which it illegally traded with the Cohong, to offset the tribute they were paying to the imperial administration on tea and cotton. This process cultivated a huge appetite for the drug, and pushed China's balance of payments from a strong surplus in 1826 to a deficit of 40 million *yuan* in 1838. During this period, Western manipulation of the cotton trade caused the core of the Shanghai economy, the international market in the indigo-dyed cotton, nankeen, to collapse.[1] The major problem for China was Western resistance to handling Chinese currency, and increasing competition in the price and quality of cotton from British and US mills. The collapse of the nankeen trade created an overall depression, which

led to disruption of the southern trade routes caused by trade disputes. In a short space of time, China was forced to exchange its previous status as the major exporter of finished cotton for a role as the major importer of goods and cloth from the UK and US. The British took advantage of the much-weakened Shanghai. The collapse of the nankeen trade and the subsequent economic depression greatly aided their prosecution of the Opium War.

THE OPIUM WAR (1839–42)

The Chinese government's efforts to end opium smuggling and the British merchants' resentment of the Canton system were the major ingredients for the war. On 19 June 1841, a double column of British ships towing men-of-war, steamed up the Huangpu to anchor alongside Shanghai. At the same time, an artillery regiment came ashore on the estuary of the Yangtze and moved on the city over land. Such was the force of the advance that the Chinese guns, on the ramparts to the north of the city, were never even fired. There was such fear of the approaching foreigners that the whole population, including the imperial officials and the military, fled the city, leaving the British to enter without resistance. They made their headquarters in the Yu Yuan Gardens, and although a British letter written during the occupation described the gardens as 'extensive and built in good style . . . [with] many summer and grotto houses . . . affording quarters for the soldiers',[2] in only five days of occupation the British army demolished the exquisitely carved garden pavilions for use as firewood. The city had not been so violated since the raids of the Wukou pirates. In those five days there was much looting and plundering, a reported rape, and several people killed.

Opposite: The Bund.

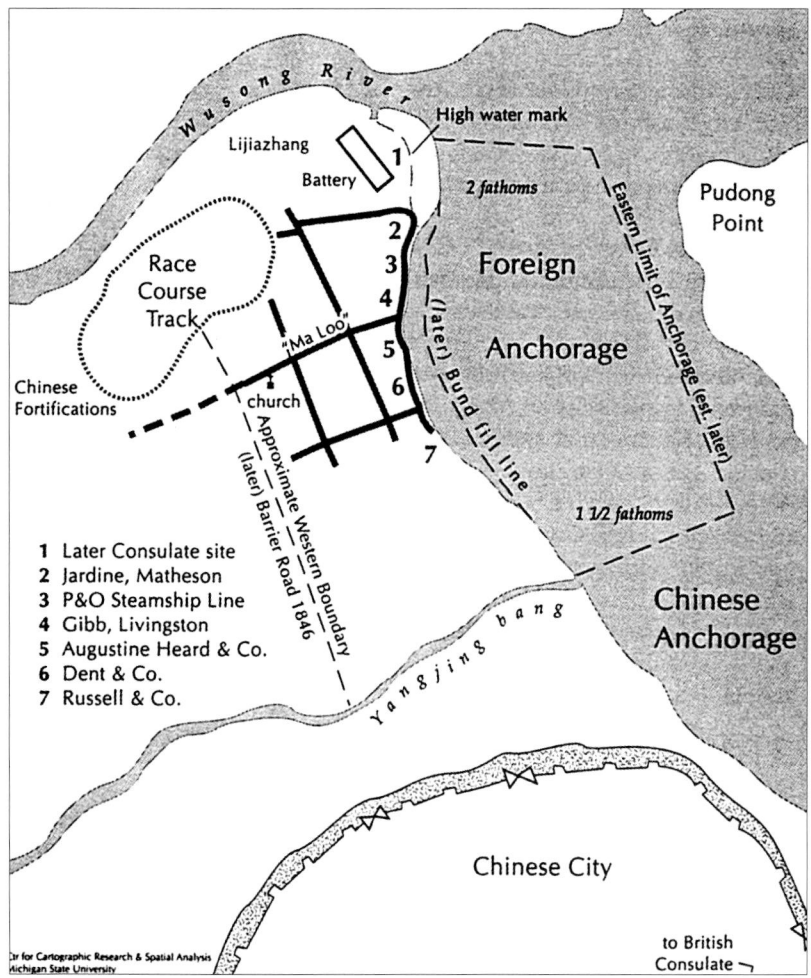

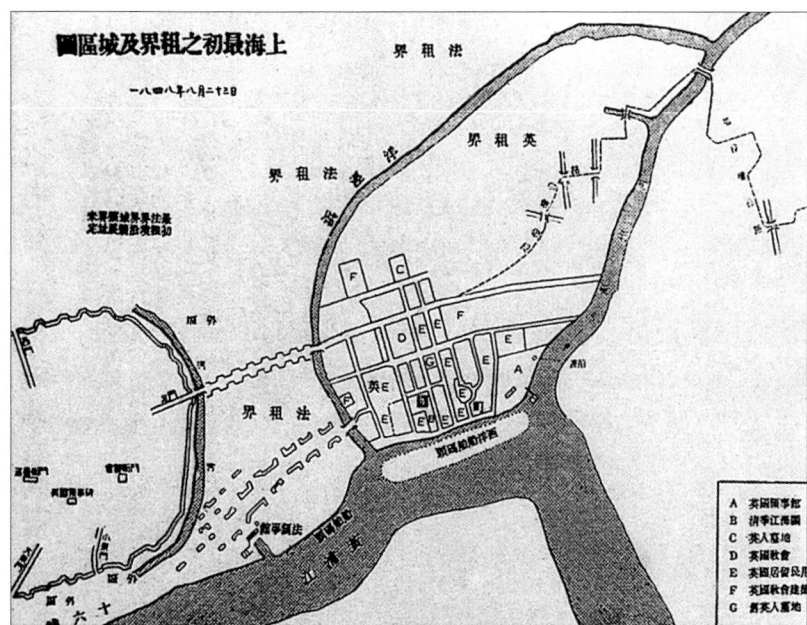

Above: Figure 1: The British settlement and anchorage at Shanghai, 1846

Below: Figure 2: Chinese mapping of the relationship between the new settlement and the old city, 1848

British naval power overwhelmed Qing forces. They took control of the major ports north to Guangzhou, and when the British moved on Nanjing, the emperor sued for peace. The result was the Treaty of Nanjing. The treaty, signed in 1842, established most of the trading freedoms that had been sought in the first British mission to China in 1793. It led to the opening of the four 'Treaty' ports of international trade in addition to Canton, and established British Shanghai. The articles of agreement were as follows:

1. An indemnity to be paid to Britain by China of 21 million Mexican silver dollars as compensation for war expenses, opium confiscated by the Chinese government, and debts owed by the Cohong merchants in Guangzhou to British merchants. (Britain had already received six million dollars as ransom for the opium that had been confiscated by Lin Zexu, the Qing commissioner.)

2. The opening of the five so-called Treaty Ports of Guangzhou, Xiamen, Fuzhou, Ningbo and Shanghai for foreign residence and trade.

3. The abolition of the Cohong and the establishment of a moderate fixed tariff on imports and exports, which China could not alter without British consent.

4. The granting to Britain of most-favoured-nation treatment by China, meaning that Britain would automatically be given any privilege that China might later extend to any other nation.

5. The appointment of foreign consuls at Treaty Ports, who would be able to communicate directly with officials of equal rank in the Qing government. This included the principle of extraterritoriality in civil and criminal cases. British consuls would have jurisdiction over British subjects accused of crimes or involved in disputes with Chinese citizens. British citizens would be tried by the Consul under British law, while Chinese citizens would be tried under the laws of China. This principle, exempting the British from Chinese laws, violated China's judicial powers.

7. The cession of Hong Kong, a barren island near Guangzhou, to Britain in perpetuity. Under the Convention of Beijing, in 1860 China also ceded Kowloon, on the mainland across from Hong Kong, to Britain. In 1898 Britain acquired a 99-year lease over the New Territories adjoining Kowloon. Hong Kong, Kowloon and the New Territories reverted to China in 1997.

The British Parliament revoked the East India Company monopoly on trade in 1843. Thus the British government became directly responsible for trade and for the development of a power-base in China. When the first British delegation arrived in the city, it was led by the newly appointed Consul, Captain George Balfour, as the representative of the British plenipotentiary in Hong Kong. Out of respect for the significance of the occasion, Consul Balfour was met by Senior Administrative Gong Mujiu, Intendant of the Susongpang Circuit, and tariff collector for the entire region. Shanghai was declared open as a Treaty Port on 18 November 1843.

Why did the British choose Shanghai? Hugh Hamilton Lindsay was the first to explore the city's trading potential for the East India Company.[3] He arrived in 1832 with an interpreter and called it the principal emporium of Eastern Asia. In 1843 the Hong Kong Legislature described it as 'containing at least 300,000 souls'. He reported that in addition to Chinese shipping, vessels came to Shanghai from Singapore, Malacca, Penang, Java, Sumatra, Borneo and cities surrounding the Persian and Indian seas, and from as far as the isles of Polynesia. At a parliamentary enquiry in 1847 investigating the potential for trade with China, Consul George Balfour argued the case for the city. First, he cited its proximity to Suzhou and the Chinese interior. It was, he argued, 'destined to become the great Emporium for the China trade'.[4] His reasoning was primarily based on a belief that Shanghai's strategic location, close to the mouth of the Yangtze, would let British trade penetrate the interior of China, gaining access for British goods to a population in the hundred millions (a familiar tale).

The difference between an imperial capital such as Beijing – utterly conservative and ordered to maintain an absolute and unchanging authority – and the informal structure of trading cities such as Shanghai, was sufficiently extreme to lead to the emergence of quite distinct urban cultures. Those within imperial control lived with numerous constraints on freedom and expression not enforced in Shanghai. At a fundamental level, those living under imperial domination formed highly conformist and conservative societies, both insular and xenophobic. Those living in the competitive, diverse trading cities on the coast were opposite in almost all respects. It would have been inconceivable for a great European city to emerge on the edge of Beijing. It was only in the resilient informality and expediency of Shanghai that such a disturbing growth could have been tolerated. (Beijing itself had been occupied by European forces after the sacking of 1806, and by the end of the 19th century the commercial district south of Tiananmen Square had acquired a distinctly European character. Even today, a self-conscious Victorian clock disturbs the view south from the tomb of Mao Zedong.)

Article 2 of the treaty stated that cities and towns should be opened to British subjects, where they might reside for the purposes of carrying out mercantile pursuits without molestation or constraint. This was read by the British to mean the right to live within the city – an interpretation never accepted by the Chinese. At first the Shanghai administration treated the British as just another foreign trading group, viewing their needs and demands as equivalent to requests from the Native Place societies. China was a land of many peoples with distinct languages and ethnic traditions, and Ningbo, Shaoxing and several others all had their own Huiguan north and east outside the walls of the old city. The Chinese imagined that all the British needed was the equivalent of a Native Place Huiguan – a compound within which to conduct their business and house their people.

Although British records describe the difficulties of finding temporary accommodation within the city, in these first months Consul Balfour insisted on, and was successful in establishing, a consular office inside the walls of Shanghai, close to the great red tower of the Duguan Customs House that dominated the river's edge. According to Chinese documents, the first request made by Consul Balfour was for land on which to build their Huiguan. Senior Administrative Gong Mujiu gave the British 'a piece of wasteland' to the north of the city.[5] This 'wasteland' contained a mixture of small farms, craft workshops, silk weavers,

cotton furnishers and dyers, wood carvers and candle makers and most significantly the Huiguan of the Fujian and Ningbo merchants, which had been established in 1796, and had evolved into a complex of meeting halls, temples and mortuaries, all of which the British and subsequent foreign incomers would have to remove.

THE BALFOUR PLAN

It was Consul Balfour who administered the laying out of the settlement's master plan, a plan that would establish streets, quays and river frontage within the agreed boundaries – the west bank of the Yangtze to the Yangtze Creek at the southern end and close to the Wusong River (Suzhou Creek) at the northern end. In the first years of settlement the major trading merchants had strips of land along the river's edge, and later the Consulate moved from within the walled city to the strategic and prominent stretch of land to the north, at the confluence of the two rivers, which had been the site of the major Chinese fortification in the defence of Shanghai from attack from the Yangtze.

Balfour's plan for the city was very simple, and even today the informal alignments of the major streets show that it was not a work of military surveying, although Balfour had been a captain in the Indian army. The plan he achieved was an imperfect grid (Fig. 1),[6] neither straight nor parallel, with each of the major sections varying in width.[7] This was not the result of artistic licence, but derived from the continual struggle to reconcile the new plan to the previous uses and paths in the area, and to come to agreement with a patchwork of Chinese owners, all with differing demands and all resentful of the foreign presence. However, it is of interest that this informality had typified the form and character of Shanghai since the earliest times.[8] From the old paths that ran along the river's edge, three roughly parallel major streets were laid out, running westward, and cut by two transverse streets that formed six, roughly similar rectangles of developable land. All major streets led to the waterfront, along which the great trading houses gradually established their operations and eventually built their palaces. The plan also included sites set aside for the European cemetery, the church, and that essential element in all colonial cities, the racetrack.

The scale of the resulting plan is very European and, from the beginning, the overall texture was utterly different from the dense circumstantial order of the Chinese city. The same six rectangles still form the heart of the foreign city. The plan, however, was not implemented without many years of struggle. Many different owners, tenant farmers, craftsmen and small-scale manufacturers, occupied much of the so-called wasteland. Most sensitive of all was the fact that there were numerous family tombs in the area, involving careful negotiation to remove the graves in releasing the land for development. The British, it was felt, did not respect the significance of these grave sites, whose positions had been carefully established by geomancy – an issue complicated by the British wish to own, not lease, the land. This led to highly inflated prices and claims against the British, and in the end the Shanghai authorities had to establish a set price for all acquisitions. Both issues were symptomatic of the tensions and divisiveness that were embedded in the foundation of Shanghai's foreign concessions.

Along with planning the town, Balfour's most formal achievement was the Land Regulations of 1845: 'This code, which has been subjected to numerous revisions . . . defines the boundaries of the settlement, provides for the acquisition and lease of lands (originally in perpetuity from the Chinese), defines the qualifications of electors, who must be landowners or taxpayers, and otherwise provides a structure for administrative government.'[9] Balfour also reached agreement on the rules for foreign anchorage, which from the beginning defined the way in which the British city would grow. It established 'The place of anchorage for loading and unloading as close over as possible to the left bank, at the bend of the (Huangpu) river adjacent to Wusong [Creek], which is at a distance of three quarters of a mile below the walls of Shanghai.'[10] The site within which the foreigners could trade and evolve was immediately adjacent to the foreign anchorage.

The Chinese administration mapped the newly established foreign area in 1846 (Fig. 2). The document shows nothing of the old city save the walls and moat enclosing the northern half, the interior a blank save for the Customs House and Yu Yuan Gardens, the only places that could have any significance for the foreigners. The new settlement is well to the north of the old walls and separated by the creek that flows from the Suzhou to the Huangpu. A path runs straight from the North Gate to the European settlement. On the plan, it appears to be enclosed by a fortified fence. An older road runs from the Chinese port, bridging into the settlement close to the river. In contrast to the absence of any attempt to indicate paths and roads in the Chinese areas, the road pattern of the settlement is carefully and fully set out, each road marked by parallel lines. The only major road through the Chinese area is defined by the outline of buildings that line its route. The plan indicates that there is only one route available to foreigners visiting the old city, a route that leads directly to the Customs House.

A European map from 1855 illustrates that this was a fairly ambitious town, given that it was just over ten years old. Yet it was a town without any apparent connection to the Chinese city, on the left of the map (Figs. 3). The names of the European streets betray neither pride nor personality, called after neither administrators, politicians nor businessmen as one might have expected. But this is a practical town given to practical names; the major routes back from the river are called Mission Road, Customs House Road and Ropewalk Road. The only hint of romance comes in the name Park Lane, a central street that ends in a little park that survives to this day. This would later be renamed Nanjing Road, in celebration of the treaty. At the northern end, Consulate Road runs by the Consulate. Transverse roads are equally practical – Church Street, Bridge Street, Barrier Road – naming use very much in the Chinese manner.

The strangest map of the period, from around 1853, shows the 'Shanghai Walled City', and the 'English Ground', with a tiny patch of 'French Ground' squeezed between, and, well to the right, the 'American Ground'. It appears to reflect accurately on the major element of the new settlement but shows a city filled with Christian missions and chapels. These make the settlement palatable to a prospective visitor from the West, and were presumably to show the extent of missionary work among the heathens.

Figure 3: British Shanghai in 1855

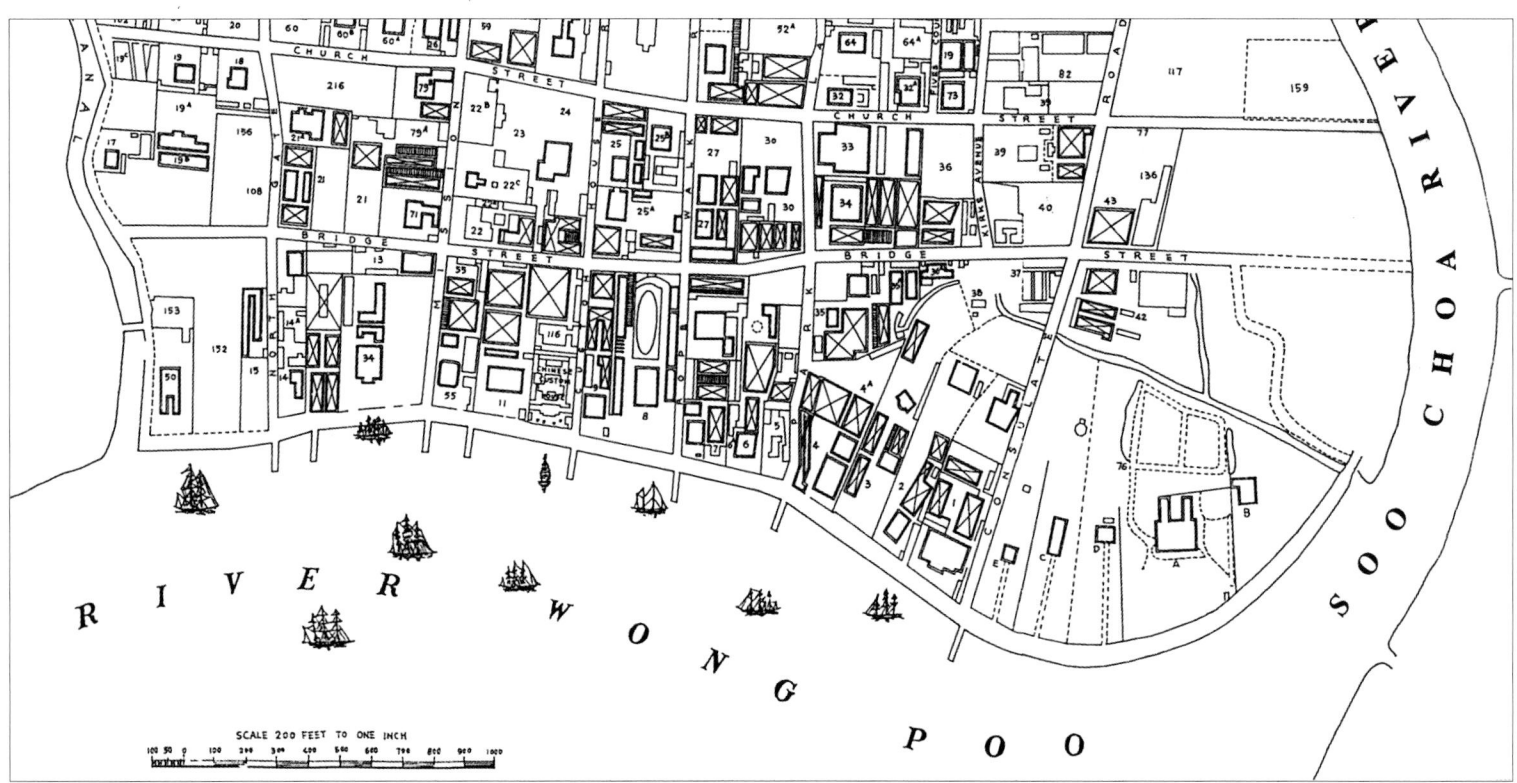

The United States acquired the right to trade in the Treaty Ports on 3 July 1844, followed closely by the French on 24 October. The French had established a political base in Canton in 1776, and in 1843 their envoys signed a convention establishing a trade relationship with China. On its ratification, France's new Consul, Theodore Layreine, arrived in China in the company of Roman Catholic prelates, proudly waving from the prow of a gunboat. Though this was a relationship based on commerce, the French never lost sight of the larger project – to pursue with China an agreement that would equal the commercial and diplomatic advantages enjoyed by Britain. In these negotiations, a significant clause (Article 22) protected French churches and missions.[11] This was aligned with imperial decrees from 1844 and 1846, which allowed the Chinese to practise Christianity. It also allowed, the French argued, for the restoration of property confiscated during an imperial crackdown on foreign religions in the 18th century.

Across China, French interests were closely allied to those of the Roman Catholic Church, and Article 22 led the French to claim several parcels of land around the city – sites of Catholic buildings constructed in the Ming Dynasty. These included a small lot just inside the walls of the old city and a large tract of land in the southern suburbs that had been the site of the first Catholic mission. Work quickly began on this southern site on the construction of a cathedral for a Chinese congregation, and the new Consul found accommodation within this French property in the old city; for him, it was a little piece of France.

With the expansion of the settlements, the Chinese believed that the British Consul should manage all Westerners, but the French would have none of it. After persistent negotiation over a period of years, and a threat from gunboats, France was granted exclusive tenure to the French settlement in Shanghai.

By 1846, 24 merchant firms, three of which were American, were in operation in the international concession. There were by this time five retail stores, 25 private residences, a church, a hotel, a dispensary, a clubhouse at the racetrack, and the first burials in the cemetery. In this same year, the committee on roads and jetties was set up to oversee the construction of the Bund (they used the Hindu name meaning embankment or dyke). It is of interest that during these early years, citizens formed these private voluntary organisations to initiate and carry out public works, which in England would have been the responsibility of the municipality – exactly the same shift from public to private altruism that had so changed Shanghai in the first decades of the 19th century. In both cases, merchant culture underpinned a system whereby major institutions in the city were supported by a self-governing, self-taxing financial structure combined with a belief in public service. However, compared to the tens of thousands of merchants in Chinese Shanghai, the foreign population was in the low hundreds.

THE TAIPING REBELLION AND THE SMALL SWORD SOCIETY

No more than ten years after its foundation, the character of this fragile foreign settlement would be shaped by events that were affecting all of China. The Taiping Rebellion was the largest and most damaging uprising anywhere in China during the Qing Dynasty. It had a deep impact upon the structure and stability of the nation, and a direct effect on the growth and evolution of Shanghai. The leader, Hong Xuiguan, was a Hakka, and part of a subgroup of the Han, with a distinct language and customs. Though born poor, his ability allowed him to receive a public education, although he failed in the Civil Service exams. As a young man in Guangzhou he was given pamphlets on Christianity, written by the first Chinese convert to Protestant Christianity, and these were the source of the revelation that came to him several years later – that he was the younger brother of Jesus Christ and had been commanded by God to destroy all pagan idols and bring the Chinese people to the true God. After a brief period of Christian study in Guangzhou with an American missionary, he drew attention to his claims by destroying ancestral tablets in neighbourhood Confucian temples. Moving north to Jiangsu Province, he began to attract converts to his movement, the Worship of God Society. It was particularly attractive to minorities, such as his own Hakka people. Within three years it is estimated that he had more than 30,000 followers. By July 1850, the Society had become sufficiently strong to confront the regional forces of the Qing army. As word of his increasing power spread, impoverished peasants and unemployed labourers joined the ranks. In 1851, Hong Xuiguan proclaimed himself leader of a new imperial dynasty, Taiping Tiangu ('Heavenly Kingdom of Great Peace'). Hong would share power over his kingdom with five other kings, one of whom he named general of all his forces.

The Christian ideals on which Hong's vision was based led to policies of vast revolutionary change. Peasants would own the land they farmed, and money, food and clothing would be shared equally. All the cultural and social practices that had caused such pain to the majority of Chinese – slavery, concubinage, arranged marriages, foot binding, legalised torture, prostitution – would be eliminated. In his kingdom, men and women were strictly separated, yet given equal roles in all aspects of society, from war to bureaucracy.

By 1852, the kingdom had amassed an army of sufficient force to march through Hunan Province to the Yangzi. In the spring of 1853 Taiping forces captured Nanking, former capital of the Ming and southern capital of China. They renamed it Tianjing ('Heavenly Capital'). By 1855, its forces had control over 600 walled towns and cities. Though they established a strong power base, the Taiping were never able to take the Qing capital in Beijing and gradually, in the last years of the decade, imperial forces began to push back.

The Christianity of the Taiping was seen by many both within and outside China as an adoption of Western values. As the rebellion spread, many Westerners gave implicit support to the movement and were openly hostile to the Qing administration. The leading English-language newspaper in Shanghai the North China Herald called the Taiping the 'Nanking Patriots'.[12] Beijing was particularly concerned by the visits foreigners were making to the Taiping capital, Nanking, including those by the US envoy and British Consul in Shanghai. Although there was no evidence of it in public documents, the imperial administration suspected that the foreigners were negotiating with the revolutionary government against the Empire.

Over several years the Taiping did establish an effective government and their eventual failure came from the collapse of leadership rather than defeat by the inept Qing army. Its founder, Hong, became increasingly reclusive. Yang, one of his chosen kings, plotted his overthrow, but was assassinated, causing in the process the murder of thousands of Hong's followers. This so disgusted the military commander that he abandoned the movement, leaving a demoralised and divided army and a leaderless revolution, yet this peasant-ruled dynasty survived several more years, such was the appeal to the masses of its ideals.

In 1860, to renew the struggle, the Qing emperor appointed a new commander of the anti-Taiping forces and commissioner for Taiping-held territories. That winter the Taiping army, marching on Shanghai, was halted by an unprecedented snowstorm that left more than three feet of snow across the region, an act of nature that spared the city the massive destruction that the war had caused to Nanjing and the nearby Suzhou. In the last years of the rebellion, the Western powers actively supported the Qing armies. Imperial troops assisted by Western forces formed 'The Ever Victorious Army', led by the American, Frederick Ward Townsend. The struggle was a complex one, and Townsend was killed in battle in 1862, his place taken by the Englishman Charles George Gordon. The sympathy that the West had at first shown faded as the movement became increasingly capricious and uncontrollable. In the end, commitment to help end the revolution was based on the greater benefits to the West in maintaining a malleable and decrepit Qing Empire than in sustaining an unstable revolution. Imperial and Western forces defended both Chinese and Western Shanghai. The British were again quartered in the Yu Yuan Gardens around the City Temple and in native compounds in the old city.

The fight for control of the Shanghai region continued intermittently from 1860 until the revolution collapsed four years later. Shanghai was never taken, but was transformed by the political destabilisation in the region and the vast movement of refugees that flocked into the two cities. Imperial and Western forces laid siege to Nanjing in May of 1862; a siege that lasted for two years and ended in 1864 after 15 days of continuous attack, bringing to an end the Taiping revolution. The surviving Taiping king committed suicide the month before the fall of Nanking. The leadership refused to surrender and fled the city, only to be hunted down and executed in the months that followed. During the 14 years of rebellion, over 30 million people had been killed.

The movement, however, would be a great inspiration to Mao Zedong and a powerful influence on the evolution of revolutionary politics in China into the 20th century. The palace home of Hong in Suzhou remains a major revolutionary tourist site. But recent scholarship portrays the Taiping revolutionaries as typically bourgeois with strong feudalist tendencies, who, had they succeeded, would have reinstated the dynastic structure. Perhaps this is just one more stage in the continual reassessment of the Mao Zedong legacy. The experience of the Heavenly Kingdom of Great Peace and the force that religion can exert in stimulating the masses to revolution have had a fundamental influence on Chinese political thought up to the present day.

Early in the rebellion, from 1853 to 1855, Shanghai was facing a related revolution of its own. the Small Sword Society, a branch of the Triads, rebelled against the Qing administration within the Shanghai region.[13] The Small Sword Society was founded in 1850 and drew its membership from artisans and unemployed sailors, many of whom were disaffected by the economic impact of increasing foreign trade within the city. Its leader, Lui Lichuan, spoke some English, was effective in dealing with foreigners, and also professed an interest in Christianity. As the Taiping rebellion grew in strength, the Small Swords infiltrated the city militias formed to defend Shanghai from the Taiping. In September 1853 the Small Swords captured the city and during the following months occupied other cities in the region. Once their position was consolidated, they aligned both their military strategy and their political cause with the Taiping Revolutionary Government, which by then had established its capital in Nanjing. For both political and military reasons, the Small Swords carefully respected the independence of the foreign settlements and limited their occupation of Shanghai to the Chinese city.

The Western community, though publicly neutral, gave significant private aid to the Society; at the height of its influence, over 40 Westerners were employed in the Shanghai administration. The Qing were particularly concerned that foreign merchants from Shanghai had established trade contacts with the revolutionary government in Nanjing. The struggle to draw the foreign concession – particularly the British – out of their neutrality lasted many months. The Chinese requested that the administration of the international settlement build a trench around the city to interfere with the supply of food and ammunition to the revolutionary government. The French were willing but lacked resources; the Americans were passive; and the British would not commit themselves. The imperial authorities believed that the British were actively supporting the revolution in Shanghai and indirectly showing favour to the Taiping government in Nanjing. The French, however, both by political inclination and because their settlement was on the front line of the conflict, gave full support to the imperial forces against the rebels in the city.[14]

The British never did commit themselves to opposing the Small Sword Society, and stood by while the French made an all-out attack in January 1855, with a mixed force of French sailors and Chinese imperial troops. This was repelled by the militia of the Small Sword Society with the help of many British and American sailors; all of whom, it was later claimed, were deserters. The foreigners were able to use small arms with much more effect than the Chinese forces on either side. However, the idea of Westerners fighting Westerners across the wall of the old city embarrassed the British into changing their position slightly; they helped blockade the flow of supplies into the old city and arrested British naval deserters, though there was never clear British support for the Qing forces. The rebellion ended in 1855 on the eve of the Chinese New Year, when imperial troops invaded the city from the West. The many diverse members of the Society quickly dispersed and faded back into the narrow lanes of the city.

In the first decades of the international settlement, Chinese who were not the servants or employees of the foreigners could not live within the concession. (The majority of the Chinese employees came not from Shanghai but from Canton, and believed themselves superior and different from the Shanghainese.) In the ten months during which the Small Swords controlled the city, large numbers of refugees poured out of the old city into the foreign concessions, a movement that began to break down the strict division between white and native towns that characterises so many colonial cities.

The Small Sword rebellion was over by the beginning of 1856; the Taiping revolution would last eight more years. In the spring of 1859, the second wave of refugees began to impact on both Chinese and Western Shanghai. Thousands of people fleeing Taiping invaded all parts of the city, willing to pay any price to feel safe. From 1859 until 1864, Shanghai was under constant threat. The militias were digging in, fortifying positions throughout the city. Refugees were flowing uncontrolled into the already overcrowded neighbourhoods and into the settlements. To those living in the city, both Chinese and Western, they were like waves of locusts devouring their way into the tissue of both cities and consuming everything in sight. Although this caused many problems, it created an economic boom in Shanghai and forced the convergence of Chinese and Western interests. The law of 1845, forbidding the Chinese from renting property in the international settlement was wholly undermined by this flood of refugees. During the 1850s, the foreign authorities revised the law without even consulting the beleaguered Chinese administration, making it legal for Chinese to live in the settlements and allowing foreigners to be actively involved in the development of real estate, even though they never had ownership of the land.[15] Shanghai records of 1853 show 500 Chinese in British Shanghai. By the spring of 1864, 20,000 people had settled in temporary huts and in houseboats along the Huangpu River within the settlement.

Fortunes were made in land speculation in the construction of dense, cheap accommodation, sold at inflated prices, the profits for foreign investors exceeding all other major trade, including opium. These were basic wooden houses in crowded rows, warrens of tiny rooms, each housing several families – reportedly with 16 people to a room that was no more than 50 metres square. (The resulting squalor and the continual danger of fire led the authorities to ban wooden constructions in 1870.) This invasion caused much disquiet among the foreign population, who accused the Chinese of petty crime and rudeness, and led to the establishment of a police force, which the British staffed with loyal Sikhs from India. It also led the British to attempt to remove the Chinese brothels and opium dens, a move strenuously opposed by the French, not on moral grounds, but because the money from taxing such activity was the financial basis of the economy of the French settlement. The boom was over almost as quickly as it began. Within months of the defeat of the Taiping armies in 1864, an estimated two-thirds of the hastily built rental properties in the international settlement, and probably more in the Chinese city, stood empty.

However, there were three effects of the refugee crisis that would have a lasting impact on the city and on China: the evolution of the *li long*, the creation of the Foreign Inspectorate of Customs, and the

establishment of the Self Strengthening Movement; and there was a fourth: despite differences in language and appearance, it made the international settlement a predominantly Chinese city.

THE LI LONG

The most influential marriage of Western and Chinese culture was in the expansive development of slum housing, hastily erected in the Western city during the refugee crisis created by the Taiping revolution. This was known as the *li long* ('neighbourhood lane'; Shanghainese also uses the variation *longtang,* which has essentially the same meaning). The settlement law of 1870 forced these squalid firetraps to be rebuilt substantially in freestanding wood frames, backed by brick walls. As the *li long* evolved, they were refined to suit Chinese taste and social styles. Chinese records comment that such construction could not be compared to the ideal family home, which had sheltered southern societies for centuries, where several households all from a single family would co-exist around a courtyard, hidden from the street by a wall. Yet at their best, the homes in the *li long* had many pleasant small saloons, parlours and bedrooms with, most importantly, planted terraces.

Though designed and developed by Western enterprise, this community housing was as much a Chinese as a Western solution. In scale and character the houses were similar to the shop houses that dominated the old city. Formed from two-storey structures, they were laid out in narrow lanes like fish bones, on either side of a wider lane, which formed the spine of the neighbourhood. The most significant and explicitly Chinese element of the *li long* was that each neighbourhood and each lane was made exclusive through being closed off by substantial gates (Fig. 4). Behind the gates, each lane of houses became a tightly knit community, providing respite from the hectic activity on the public streets, and recapturing memories of the courtyards that once formed the centre of Chinese family life. Though dressed up in a hybrid of Western and Chinese styles, often proclaiming the name of the lane in large elegant characters, these gates were not merely for decoration. Built of stone, with heavy wooden doors, they were stronger and more secure than the front door of the houses themselves.

Created out of instability and speculation, developed in the midst of social unrest, this unique housing form was not only formative in the culture of both Chinese and Western Shanghai, but was much loved by the Shanghainese. It cultivated dense, mutually supportive social structures, safe behind the gates and lanes, unpoliceable and invisible to any authority.

THE FOREIGN INSPECTORATE OF CUSTOMS

The most distinguished refugees fleeing the Small Swords were of the city's imperial administration. To find the servants of the emperor seeking the protection of British law within a community less than ten years old was a dramatic illustration of the weakness of the Qing Dynasty. Deeply concerned at the loss of tax revenues from the port, these refugee administrators, the *Daotai,* agreed that the foreign consuls should immediately appoint customs inspectors to collect the port

Left: Figure 4: The lanes in the *li long*
Right: Figure 5: Opium hulks on the Huangpu, 1880s

duties. Thus in 1854 the Chinese Mercantile Customs Office was established, wholly staffed by foreigners yet answerable to the Chinese government. Subsequently renamed the Foreign Inspectorate of Customs, it was viewed by the *Shanghai Mercury* as 'the most telling Western [institution] ever introduced into the official administration of the empire ... of inestimable benefit to the Chinese government [in] foreign trade, fiscal ... financial, and even diplomatic achievements'.[16] The paper added that its effect was 'nothing short of a revolution' compared to the past 'corruption of the native regime'. The Foreign Inspectorate was, in essence, responsible for collecting taxes and regulating the conduct of all foreigners in the settlement. Though the Inspector General was always a foreign subject (no Chinese ever held the position), the Inspectorate was part of the Qing administration, and changed the status of Western Shanghai from a native trading enclave to an imperially recognised administration. The Superintendent of the Inspectorate had the responsibility of supervising and administering the collection of duties in all ports, as well as preventing smuggling and maintaining the port boundaries. (The Inspectorate was eventually renamed the imperial Maritime Customs Service and provided a standard of incorruptible public service well into the 20th century. This allowed a British agency to demonstrate to the Chinese the highest traditions of Confucian government.)

THE SELF-STRENGTHENING MOVEMENT

Yet another legacy to Shanghai of the Taiping crisis was that it brought to the city some of the most significant artists, writers and intellectuals from the cultural centres of Suzhou and Nanjing. With them came a level of cultural sophistication unusual for Shanghai. They also brought with them the capital, vision and desire to build new institutions that would strengthen China after the crisis passed. This resulted in the formation of the Self-Strengthening Movement, driven by a burning conviction that the youth of China must be prepared to understand and apply the best of Western and Chinese knowledge, particularly in science, industry and warfare. The Movement was active in the 1860s and 1870s. Its name was taken from one of the graphic characters in the *I Ching* (Book of Changes), which translates as 'Superior men strengthen themselves'. Choosing the name of the Movement from this figure in classical literature helped deflect the concern that engaging Western thought could undermine Chinese cultural traditions.

The Movement led to the creation of the Official Foreign Office in 1861 and its language school in 1862. It initiated major military and industrial projects across the nation, constructing arsenals in Juanguan and Nanjing, dockyards in Fuzhou, and factories in Tianjin and Shanghai. One achievement that would affect Shanghai was the creation of the Chinese Merchants' Steam Navigation Company, formed to compete with the foreign shipping companies that by 1900 dominated China's trade.

Throughout the latter half of the 19th century, inspired by the spirit of the Self-Strengthening Movement, a few of the most gifted young Chinese scholars studied Western thought in science, technology and government, with the most able travelling abroad to universities in America, France and Germany. The most talented, it was said, were sent to England. However, unlike in Japan, Chinese culture had been unable, despite the best efforts of scholars and administrators, to establish a basis for scientific and technological culture. While the last two decades of the Chinese Empire were marked by isolationism and destructive eccentricity, Japan was committed, by imperial decree, to industrialisation based on European models. Many more of the elite of that nation were sent to Europe to study science and technology; the emperor's children attended British and German schools. And this new knowledge was used to build not only industry, but a formidable navy and land army, thus creating an imbalance of power with China, and feeding an imperial ambition that was brought to an end only by the atomic bombing of Hiroshima and Nagasaki by America in 1945.

All the well-meaning efforts of the Self-Strengthening Movement were brought to nothing by the persistent refusal of the imperial court to tolerate or acknowledge the need for change. While it created a generation of scholars and scientists who effectively applied Western methods and knowledge to medicine, military affairs and industry, it failed to penetrate deeply into the traditional institutions of the nation. Crucially, it failed to change the imperial bureaucracy. The weakness of the Empire debilitated every element of Chinese culture and made it increasingly vulnerable. It was a vulnerability that an inadequate imperial army could not protect.

By the 1860s, an essential order for the two cities was established that would remain unchanged until the Maoist revolution of 1949.

THE RISE OF THE FOREIGN CITY

Though the conflicts seriously damaged international trade and the movement of goods for several years, after the rebellion, two Shanghais had clearly formed. To the south, behind the walls and into the dense industrial suburbs, lay the Chinese city; immediately to the north were the gridded streets of the Western settlement, recognisably European with its mercantile palaces freestanding on regular plots of neatly attended land.[17]

Despite the tiny population – in the hundreds in the first decade – the British settlement was the dominant influence on the culture and form of the foreign city. Its pragmatic and rational plan quickly concentrated development between the commercial centre along the Bund and the residential streets leading up to it, with industry limited to the north. The English maps of Shanghai from the 1850s (Figs. 1 and 2) show in great detail the ordered streets, the Bund, the church cemeteries, the British and US Consulates, the Chinese Customs House, and the most important commercial structures. All the buildings in the European city – the homes of the merchants, the churches, clinics and dispensary – sat on discrete pieces of land. Though the maps show the line of the wall that once enclosed old Shanghai, they leave the Chinese city as blank as the interest the Westerners had in the culture they had invaded. The suburbs of the Chinese city are either omitted or defined only by the roads that would be needed by the traders.

Although Balfour negotiated the land for the British settlement and laid out the streets, it was his successor, Rutherford Alcock, who consolidated the terms and boundaries of the concession. He removed the Consulate from within the walls of old Shanghai, first to temporary quarters within the south settlement, and established the permanent Consulate compound on a key location at the junction of Suzhou Creek and the Huangpu. In 1846 the North Customs House was built on the river, physically inside the British settlement, and dedicated exclusively to the administration of foreign tariffs. From then on, Western merchants no longer had to leave the familiarity of their settlements to conduct their business. At this point, these two communities – Chinese and foreign – became increasingly separate. Trade was based wholly on the exploitation of the weak by the powerful.

The great British merchant houses, such as Jardine Matheson and John G Russell & Co, were founded on the opium trade. The magnificent commercial palaces springing up along the Bund were also built from the proceeds of opium. The drug never appeared in Chinese correspondence, nor is it mentioned in British trade records, yet all the editorials in the North China Herald contained weekly records on the prices and qualities of the opium coming to the port.[18] The laws of one nation saw opium as a social evil and banned its importation, while the Western traders made it the financial basis of all trade. Opium produced trading practices of spectacular duplicity. Maintaining this activity was seen as significant to two world economies – India depended on it and great merchant fortunes rested on it. The Chinese and British authorities struck an unspoken bargain: opium was kept separate from legitimate trade and not brought into open treaty ports. Instead, opium hulks (Fig. 7) were permanently anchored on the river near Wusong, and the British traders discharged their illegitimate cargo in the estuary before proceeding to Shanghai.

There was no discussion of opium in the records of Consul Balfour. His successor, however, deplored the trade. In a letter to Sir George Bonham in 1848, Alcock wrote that the Chinese view of the opium trade was a major obstacle to Britain's interest in China, since the Chinese (with justification) regarded opium as a poison and saw the British as its producers, carriers and sellers for their own profit, to the undoubted impoverishment and ruin of the Chinese. 'They believed that the British had made war and dictated a humiliating peace in order to maintain the traffic in opium', he wrote.[19]

Not only illegal and deeply destructive, opium, in the central decades of the 19th century, underwrote all the legitimate British trade. Again, to quote Consul Alcock, writing in 1849 in a report to the British Plenipotentiary in Hong Kong, Sir John Bowring:

The import of opium, illegal by Imperial Decree, and therefore officially ignored by the authorities of both countries, more than equals in money value the whole of our exports from China to Great Britain, amounting to some five million pounds Sterling annually, tea having the volume of some 3.5 million, and silk 1.5 million … The opium trade, illegal as it is, forms an essential element, inextricably mixed up with every trading operation between these three countries [Great Britain, India, China].[20]

Opium trade affected not only the health of the Chinese, but also the economy of the region. The fact that foreign traders distrusted the Chinese currency meant that trading was conducted principally in silver, resulting in the vast silver drain out of China and ruinous tax rates on the farmers and peasants in districts around Shanghai – of which there is no record of British knowledge or concern.[21] With cash and silver in short supply, as often happened in Shanghai, actual bulk opium, or drafts on opium holdings, were drawn on local banks as a substitute for silver.

THE PHYSICAL CITY

After restoring the extensive damage done during the Small Swords rebellion, the Chinese Shanghai returned, at least on the surface, to its traditional form and activity. The rebellion caused several adjustments in trading practices and the north gate was realigned to meet the roads to the foreign settlement.

In the settlement the mercantile palaces and homes had a highly consistent form.[22] They were square, two or three storeys tall, with great hip roofs, and verandas and loggias on the lower floors (Fig. 8). The ground floor would often be used for storage, with the offices and residences of the principal officers on the upper floors. There was no fired brick in the Shanghai area, so construction was of wood and sun-dried brick. In the beginning, the style was an elegant and simple Classicism, and as the settlement developed, the architecture began to assume the styles and fashions of Victorian England. The architectural history of the British in Shanghai mirrors the manners of London at its most urbane. Shanghai attracted Western architects, and the British in Shanghai demanded the most fashionable realities from home, as, subsequently, did the French, Americans and, later, the Japanese.

From its first development along the river's edge, the Bund, became the centre of trade. The river bank was raised, the edge consolidated, and a broad path laid down. The width of the river, and the presence of ocean-going ships docking across from the powerful banking and merchant companies, was reminiscent in scale and character of the Thames in central London, both comforting to the British, and perhaps guiding development. Equally significant was British achievement in convincing the Shanghai authorities to mark the difficult channel upriver with buoys, and to allow a lightship to be stationed at the dangerous entrance to the river.

Since the building of the wall, on the other hand, the Chinese city had become increasingly distanced from the river, although a few connecting canals survived, which remained the basis of the city's significance and wealth. The British settlement had created a modern port for seagoing vessels; the Chinese port, some way upstream and shallower, served coastal shipping – sand junks and the many shallower draft river and canal junks that travelled across China on the vast internal waterways.

The only irrational element in the plan, something present in every major colonial British city since the 18th century, was the racetrack. This was established within months of the signing of the Treaty of Nanjing and was the first coherent element in the new settlement. Its presence had to do with temptation and desire; an obvious symbol of the fantasy that drove British ambition.

The first racetrack was set out on the most convenient available land to the north, a site that later became the setting for the centre of British rule, the Consular compound. The second location of the track was turned into cheap refugee housing in the 1860s. The final location, far distant to the west of the Bund, was laid out and ready for the fall meet of 1861. It evolved into the social heart of the British city in China and was subsequently reformed at the end of the 20th century to become the People's Square of this great Communist city. As it grew, it changed from a field of exercise and competition for young males to the social centre of the expatriate community, gambling being the ruin of many of them. The imported horses, often collapsing from the heat, were ridden with great expertise by slender young Chinese jockeys.

The ostensible reason for having a racetrack was to provide exercise for the young men staffing the government and mercantile offices of the settlement. But this is hardly an adequate explanation for such an elaborate and costly business. The maintenance of one's horses was an exclusively aristocratic activity in Britain. Ownership of horses for pleasure was, and still is, limited to the wealthy. (The breeding of horses for racing and hunting is still a defining mark of English royalty. It appears to be the only creative engagement of the present royal family, from the Queen's pleasure in the race to Charles' participation in polo.) Most of the new arrivals to this illusory culture from England, a century and a half ago, would have come from the middle classes emerging from the new industries and cities created by the Industrial Revolution. They were being afforded the sensation of entering into aristocratic orders and values, as they served the British Empire's distant outposts. The racetrack can be viewed as an idealised landscape that would tempt the youthful and ambitious to risk all in leaving home to be part of this imperial project. Like the promise of unlimited land that drew millions from Europe to the Americas, the promise of an aristocratic lifestyle, with servants and luxury goods, children sent to private schools in England, and the most indulgent pastime, horseracing, would be deeply attractive to the newly educated urban proletariat. Though different in form and not so destructive, it was like opium, a stimulator of dreams and fantasies. But the habités of the racetrack were only a handful of individuals, around 10,000 at the end of the century, compared with the tens of thousands of Chinese living in the extensive *li long* housing west and south of the racetrack.

Many clear-eyed writers have attempted to convey the character of these two cities. At the turn of century, a 68-year-old English woman, Isabella Bird, wrote a book entitled *The Yangtze Valley and Beyond*, published in 1899, which begins with her visit to Shanghai. It is of interest that at the time of her visit, just 50 years after the foundation of the Western city, the name, Shanghai, had been co-opted by the West for their part of the city, referring to the Chinese city as the 'native city'. Reflecting on this, Bird writes that 'there was a Shanghai before Shanghai'. Particularly surprising is her note that despite all efforts to the contrary, Western Shanghai was a very Chinese place:

THE ENGLISH TRAVELLER IN SHANGHAI, 1893[23]

Within four miles of Shanghai the vivacity of the Huangpu and its banks becomes overpowering, and the West asserts its ascendancy over the slow-moving East. There are ranges of great godowns, wharves, building yards, graving docks, 'works' of all descriptions, filatures, cotton mills, and all the symptoms in smoky chimneys and a ceaseless clang of all presence of capital and energy. After the war with Japan there was a rapid increase in the number of factories.

The life and movement on the river become wonderful. The channel for large vessels, though narrow, shifting, and intricate, and the subject of years of doleful prophecies as to 'silting up' and leaving Shanghai stranded, admits of the passage of our largest merchantmen, and successful dredging enables them to lie alongside the fine wharves at Hongkew. American three and four-masted and other sailing vessels are at anchor in mid-stream, or are proceeding up or down in charge of tugs. Monster liners under their own steam at times nearly fill up the channel, their officers yelling frantically at the small craft, which recklessly cross their bows; great white, two-storeyed paddle arks from Ningpo and Hankow, local steamers, steam launches owned by the great firms, junks of all builds and sizes, manageable by their huge rudders, sampans, hooded boats, and native boats of all descriptions, lighters, and a shoal of nondescript craft make navigation tedious, if not perilous, while sirens and steam whistles sound continually. 'The plot thickens.' Foreign hongs, warehouses, shipping offices, and hotels are passed in Hongkew, the American settlement, and gliding round Pu-tung Point, the steamer anchors abreast of the Bund in a wholesomely rapid flow of water 2,000 feet wide.

I arrived in Shanghai the first time on a clear, bright autumn day. The sky was very blue, and the masses of exotic trees, the green, shaven lawns, the belated roses, and the clumps of chrysanthemums in the fine public gardens gave a great charm to the first view of the settlement. Two big, lofty, white hulks for bonded Indian opium are moored permanently in front of the gardens. Gunboats and larger war-vessels of all nations, all painted white, and the fine steamers of the Messageries Maritimes have their moorings a little higher up. Boats, with crews in familiar uniforms, and covered native boats gaily painted, the latter darting about like dragon-flies, were plying ceaselessly, and as it was the turn of the tide, hundreds of junks were passing seawards under their big brown sails.

The broad carriage-road and fine flagged side-walk are truly cosmopolitan. Well-dressed men and women of all civilised nations, and of some which are not civilised, promenade gaily on the walk and in the garden. Single and two-horse carriages and buggies, open and closed, with coachmen and grooms in gay and often fantastic cotton liveries, dash along the drive. Hackney

Figure 6: The Bund and the palaces built by opium in the 1870s

victories abound, and there are jinrickshas (from which foreigners drop the first syllable) in hundreds, with Chinese runners, and Shanghai wheelbarrows innumerable, some loaded with goods or luggage, while the coolies of others are trundling along from two to four Chinese men or women of the lower classes, seated on matted platforms on either side of the wheel, facing forwards.

I was not prepared for the Chinese element being so much in evidence in the foreign settlement. It is not only that clerks and compradors dressed in rich silks on which the characters for happiness and longevity and the symbols of luck are brocaded are in numbers on the Bund, and that all the servile classes, as may be expected, are Chinese, but that Chinese shops of high standing, such as Laou Kai Fooks, are taking their places in fine streets which run back from the Bund, that some of the handsomest carriages on the Bund and the Bubbling Well Road, the fashionable afternoon drive of Shanghai, are owned and filled with Chinese ladies and children richly dressed drive in the same fashion, and that of late, specially, wealthy Chinese have become keen competitors for British houses, and have even outbid foreigners for them. Is Shanghai menaced by the 'Yellow Peril' as Malacca, Singapore, and Penang have been?

A great trading Chinese city, with an estimated population of 200,000, has grown up within the foreign boundary, subject to foreign municipal laws and sanitary regulations, but so absolutely Chinese, that were it not for the wide streets and the absence of refuse-heaps and bad smells, one might think oneself in one of the great cities of the interior. The Chinese are quite capable of appreciating the comfort and equity of foreign rule, and the various advantages which they enjoy under it. They pay municipal taxes according to their rating, and 'feu duty' for their land, which it is usual for them to hold in the name of a foreigner. They are under the jurisdiction of the Chinese Government, but civil cases in which foreigners are concerned and breaches of the peace are tried in what is known as the 'Mixed Court', an apparently satisfactory and workable arrangement, and serious criminal cases belong to the Chinese Shanghai magistrate.

Shanghai has two telegraph lines embracing London; daily papers well conducted, the *North China Daily News* specially maintaining a deservedly high reputation; several magazines, and communication with Europe always once a week, and usually oftener, by well-appointed mail steamers of four lines. Telegraphic news from all parts of the world appears simultaneously in London and Shanghai; it is thoroughly in touch with Europe and America, and European politics and events in general are discussed with as much zest as at home. Excellent libraries, and the large book-store of Messrs. Kelly & Walsh, cater for the intellectual needs of the population, but it is likely that the depressing climate in spring and summer, and the whirl of society and amusements in winter, indispose most of the residents for anything like stiff reading.

The French Bund is a continuation of the British; but the French settlement is small, markedly inferior, and gives one an impression of arrested development, the only noteworthy buildings being the Consulate, the Town Hall, and the large but plain Roman cathedral.

The English settlement makes a proud display of the wealth of the insular kingdom in the number of its stately buildings, the Consulate, the cathedral, the municipal buildings, the four-storeyed and elaborately designed clubhouse, the banks and shipping offices, and the massive mansions of historic firms, standing in their secluded grounds; though of the magnates of eastern commerce in the days of the rapid making of great fortunes almost none remain. British, too, in design, architecture, and arrangement, in all indeed but cost, is the magnificent pile of buildings in which the Imperial Maritime Customs and the new Post Office, under the same management, are housed.

But there was a Shanghai before Shanghai, a Shanghai which still exists, increases, and flourishes a busy and unsavoury trading city, which leads its own life according to Chinese methods as independently as though no foreign settlement existed; and long before Mr Pigou, of the HEIC, in 1756, drew up his memorandum, suggesting Shanghai as a desirable place for trade, Chinese intelligence had hit upon the same idea, and the port was a great resort of Chinese shipping, cargoes being discharged there and dispersed over the interior by the Yangtze and the Grand Canal. Yet it never rose higher than the rank of a third-rate city.

It has a high wall three miles and a half in circuit, pierced by several narrow gateways and surrounded by a ditch 20 feet wide, and suburbs lying between it and the river with its tiers of native shipping as crowded as the city proper. This shipping, consisting of junks, lorchas, and native craft of extraordinary rig, lies, as Lu Huew said, 'like the teeth of a comb'.

Shanghai is a mean-looking and busy city; its crowds of toiling, trotting, bargaining, dragging, burden-bearing, shouting, and yelling men are its one imposing feature. Few women, and those of the poorer class, are to be seen. The streets, with houses built of slate-coloured, soft-looking brick, are only about 8 feet wide, are paved with stone slabs, and are narrowed by innumerable stands, on which are displayed, cooked and raw and being cooked, the multifarious viands in which the omnivorous Chinese delight, an odour of garlic predominating. Even a wheelbarrow, the only conveyance possible, can hardly make its way in many places. True, a mandarin sweeps by in his gilded chair, carried at a run, with his imposing retinue, but his lectors clear the way by means not available to the general public.

All the articles usually exposed for sale in Chinese cities are met with in Shanghai and old porcelain, bronzes, brocades and embroideries are displayed to attract strangers. Restaurants and tea houses of all grades abound, and noteworthy among the latter is the picturesque building on the Zig-Zag Bridge … The buildings and fantastic well-kept pleasure grounds of the Ching-hwang Miao, which may be called the Municipal Temple, the Guild Hall of the resident natives of Chekiang, and the temple of the God of War, with its vigorous images begrimed with the smoke of the incense sticks of ages of worshippers, its throngs, its smoke, its ceaseless movement, and its din are the most salient features of this native hive.

Yamens, of course, exist for yamen runners, for Shanghai has the distinction of being the residence of a Taotai, or Intendant of Circuit, and a magistrate in whose hands the administration of justice is placed, involving responsibility for the interests of over 560,000 Chinese, the estimated native population of the city and the settlements, the total population being estimated at 586,000.

This was compared to a foreign population in the order of 8,000, who behaved as if the city was all theirs. Bird goes on to offer some very pointed advice:

Of the men I write tremblingly! Chinese tailors seem as successful as Chinese dressmakers, and the laundrymen equal both, no small matter when white linen suits are in question. May it be permitted to a traveller to remark that if men were to give to the learning of Chinese and of Chinese requirements and methods of business a little of the time which is lavished on sport and other amusements, there might possibly be less occasion for the complaint that large fortunes are no longer to be made in Chinese business.

For indeed, from ignorance of the language and reliance on that limited and abominable vocabulary known as 'Pidgun', the British merchant must be more absolutely dependent on his Chinese compradore than he would care to be at home on his confidential clerk. Even in such lordly institutions as the British Banks on the Bund it seems impossible to transact even such a simple affair as cashing a cheque without calling in the aid of a sleek, supercilious-looking, richly-dressed Chinese, a shroff or compradore, who looks as if he knew the business of the bank and were capable of running it. It is different at the Yokohama Specie Bank, which has found a footing in Shanghai, in which the alert Japanese clerks manage their own affairs and speak Chinese. May I be forgiven?

Notes

1 Cooke Johnson, *Shanghai*, op cit, pp173–4.

2 Ibid, p179 (from the dispatches of Lieutenant General Sir Hugh Gough).

3 Ibid, pp182–5.

4 Ibid, p183 (from UK parliamentary papers).

5 Ibid, p189.

6 Ibid, Centre for Cartographic Research and Spatial Analysis, University of Michigan.

7 Balfour may not have been familiar with John Randel's plan for New York City from 1811, the ruthless grid controlling the development of Manhattan, which had become one of the fastest growing cities in the world in the years during which Balfour was laying out Shanghai. The Manhattan plan can be seen as representing an ideal of rational, uniform order that characterised the most progressive Western imaginations in the first half of the 19th century.

8 Even today, the extensive development in Pudong, across from the Bund, developed by the omnipotent Communist administration, has still resulted in a wavering, informal grid of streets.

9 HJ Lethbridge, *All About Shanghai*, The University Press (Shanghai), 1934–5 (reprinted by Oxford University Press, Hong Kong, 1983), p14. This is a curious document, whose credentials are unclear, but whose authentic feel has allowed it to stay in print.

10 Cooke Johnson, op cit, p188.

11 Ibid, p245.

12 Ibid, pp276–7.

13 Ibid, pp279–82.

14 Ibid, p298.

15 Ibid, pp326–9.

16 Ibid, p315 (from CA Montalto de Jesus, 'Historic Shanghai', *Shanghai Mercury*, 1909).

17 The evolution of these two cities into such distinct entities paralleled the development of most major colonial settlements in Asia, from Cairo to Saigon.

18 Cooke Johnson, op cit, p228.

19 Ibid, p230.

20 Ibid, pp230–1 (from Foreign Office documents, Alcock to Bowring).

21 Ibid, p230.

22 *The Evolution of Shanghai Architecture in Modern Times,* Shanghai Educational Publishers (Shanghai), 1999.

23 Isabella Bird, *The Yangtze Valley and Beyond*, John Murray (Edinburgh), 1899.

本世紀30年代上海市區一角

From the 1930s, *Li long* fill the foreground below the racetrack

TWIN CITIES

ALAN BALFOUR

Imagine two maps: the first is an English map from the mid-19th century, the other a Chinese one from the end of the century. In the first, all the conventions of English map engraving convey with great precision this settlement with its government and commercial buildings, cemetery and churches. It is precise in defining the new Western reality, yet barely acknowledges the existence of an extensive, complex, ancient city to its south. For the map-maker, Chinese Shanghai simply did not exist. A faint line shows the wall that surrounded the old city and some small group of structures that might have been of importance to anyone forced to visit this other world, but there is no sense of the city whose population was in the hundreds of thousands, whose port boasted a volume and variety of shipping craft the equal of London. Nothing is offered of the reality of the dense, clustering, ancient city and nothing in all this complexity is seen to have any significance for the few thousand foreigners who were creating the illusion of European life in China.

The West, however, was not alone in representing a partial reality; in the second map, executed by the Chinese authority at the end of the century, Chinese Shanghai was recorded using similar graphic conventions. All the lanes, streets and canals of the city are essentially identical to those mapped in the 17th century (see page 36). The three transverse canals still flow through the city and out to the Huangpu, and most of the subsidiary channels survive. Bridges, which were such a dominant element in the earlier mapping, have lost their singular importance, but not their location, though they are now linked to a network of paths and streets and reflect a broader interest on the part of the administration in the land activities in the city. These paths have no larger order, running informally throughout the city. They are more a record of property boundary than of passage. The characters listing the administrative

offices are still framed just right of centre and now only the Yu Yuan Gardens merit a drawing, along with a few symbolic trees. The imperial Customs House is shown on the river, but there is nothing to indicate the great European city that surrounds it.

More devious and curious than either is a French map from the same period. At a time when the population of the French concession was little more than 300, the map showed extensive streets and roads that existed only on the map and in the ambition of the French administration, while ignoring the many lanes and significant Chinese institutions that actually occupied the land, standing in the way of French desire. These included two major compounds: the Native Place associations of the Ningbo and the Tan Hou Miau. The French concession lay between the sewage ditches and open coffins in the Chinese graveyards that sat outside the northern gate to the old city, and the muddy creek that marked the lower edge of the British settlement. From the outset, the French administration acted independently and, in some ways, in opposition to the other foreign governments, with particular animosity reserved for the British. Perhaps memories of the Napoleonic Wars still lingered, though the USA had also been at war with Britain not 50 years earlier. The French used the demoralisation and political confusion following the Taiping revolution to expand their territory, and in so doing wilfully destroyed temples and trading compounds, but were met with aggressive opposition when they attempted to dig up the burial grounds of the Ningbo, one of the most influential of the Native Place Associations. With such a small population, only nationalism and politics can explain their actions. It led to years of animosity.

But other maps illustrate a much more complex fusion and assimilation of cultures. An exquisite British survey map from the 1890s treats

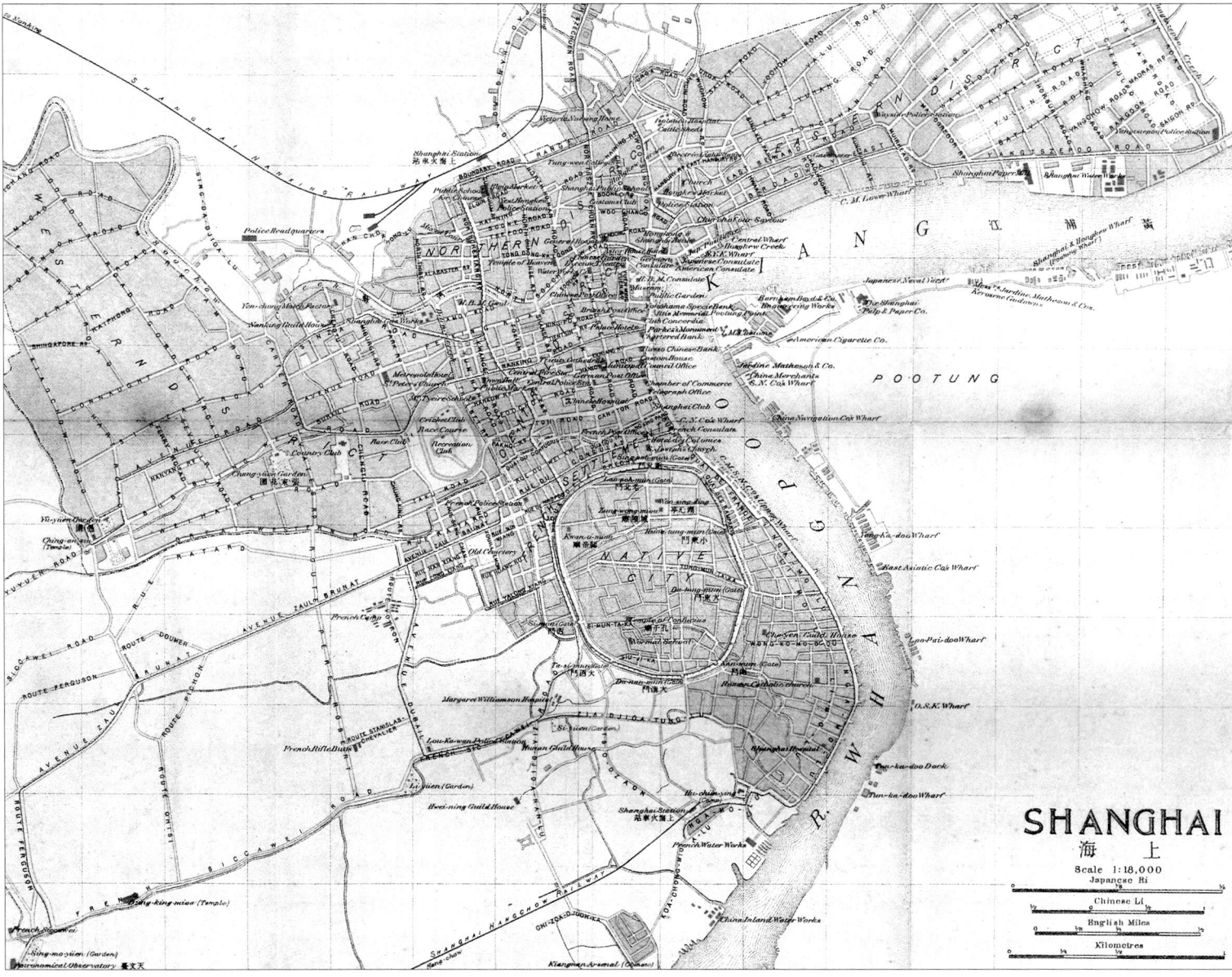

both the Chinese and the international settlement equally, not simply in the conventions of representation but in the identification and labelling of societies, guild houses, temples, churches and banks, all significant institutions in the new fusion of cultures (Fig. 1). More surprising is a Chinese map from 1902, made in the fading years of the imperial administration. Though the streets and even the bridges are still more important than the institutions, here, inscribed in mapping conventions that have evolved over a thousand years, the international settlement and the Chinese city are represented as one. This oneness unites the uneven canal order of the walled city with the wavering, near-rational grid of the basically English city. In a peculiar parallelism, the confines of the walled city have a strange affinity with the addictive confines of the racetrack. And in the unpredictability of history, the racetrack, born of forces remote from the old walled city, would eventually become the heart of revolutionary Shanghai (Fig. 2).

Consider the effect of the invasion of new realities, knowledge and politics on this hard-working port town, a town never given to reflection, a town in which nothing was ever idealised, and nothing was ever shaped by imperial dreams. Such idealising, as we have seen, was irrelevant to the practical imagination of Shanghai. Its many forms were always the result of a rational, pragmatic, sensible friction. However, the arrival of the Europeans created a new Shanghai out of forces as

complex as imperial ambition, but much more understandable to the Shanghainese traders. This was a new Shanghai shaped by modern technologies in transportation, power supply, financial management, and by the desire for European reality. It was this, above all, that disturbed and caused envy.

Though Shanghai saw little growth in its economy, it had achieved fairly consistent patterns of trading by the end of the century. Business activity in the foreign city was based wholly on the import and export of goods, none of the foreign powers having any interest in investing in manufacturing. It was as if the foreign city had drained all the energy and confidence out of the Chinese city. However, one legacy of the Self-Strengthening Movement was in the development of young leaders familiar with Western methods of business and industry, who were determined to apply these lessons for the benefit of China.

Nothing in the previous 800 years of Shanghai's existence had necessitated any significant change in the life and structure of the city. Population pressures rarely became unmanageable; all the patterns, the fabric of family life, of society, its class divisions, rituals, hardships and pleasures remained constant, fluctuating only with the cycle of the seasons. Changes that are apparent from the long view can be seen in the tiny shifts in style and decoration that mark the art of each succeeding dynasty, all proceeding within an elegant yet narrow frame of desires and beliefs. Suddenly, all such habits were overturned and over-whelmed by the technology and force of the new industrial world. The results of such a confrontation could have been catastrophic; however, the resilient and entrepreneurial character of the Shanghainese was much more concerned with gaining access to such power than with the demise of a previous way of life. Political leaders arose, seeking to create a new political order the equal, yet the opposite, of past dynasties.

Chinese Shanghai at the turn of the century, then, was a walled city whose every element – social, cultural, political and physical – had remained essentially unchanged for five centuries; a walled medieval city living in the shadow of the great modern metropolis, each belonging to profoundly different nations and cultures. The old city was much weakened by the dying imperial regime and the opium-fuelled predations of Western mercantilism, forcibly twinned with an aggressive modern city created with all the confidence of the British Empire. The structures, physical and social, the tools, trades, mood and smells that were played out in the lanes of old Shanghai had changed little in over 700 years. It is easy, then, to imagine the effect of burgeoning European technology on the Shanghainese imagination. The population felt deep bitterness about the way they were treated by the Europeans, but they quickly saw the need to understand and control foreign tools. Shanghai was more able than any city in China to absorb the lessons from the implantation next to its heart of a powerful advanced culture. By the turn of the century, the Western city gloried in the speed and power of its technology. All the elements of modern urban infrastructure were passed on to Shanghai as soon as they were established in Europe. Gas production and distribution, water purification and distribution, sewage treatment and electricity were all installed throughout the city as soon as these technologies were understood. Unlike the cities of Europe, foreign Shanghai was young and able to adapt without restraint to every new system. This was a city living wholly in the promise of its future, without roots, without history. The Europeans established the Wusong Shanghai Railway Company in 1875. By the end of the 19th century, the European rail network linked all the major cities of China. Foreign Shanghai imported all the newest technologies from Europe and America: telephones, trolley cars and, early in the new century, the automobile. In these same years the barges on the canals and the coolies remained, as they had been for centuries, the beasts of burden. Even the rickshaw, the *jinrikisha*, was a European import from India, a simple machine that gave the coolies employment throughout the new city. Few of the lanes through the old city were wide enough even for rickshaws. There, the wheelbarrow remained the means of transport, even into the second decade of the 20th century, and for the wealthy and powerful the sedan chair, with each displaying insignia appropriate to the status of the occupant. This could not continue.

It was as if a European or American city, say Liverpool, Hamburg or even Boston, had been pressured into allowing Japan, for example, to develop a wholly independent port and trading centre immediately next to it. The comparison is awkward at first because the West had such overwhelming technological advantage in the settlement of the Treaty Ports. Even so, the sophistication and complexity of Chinese culture

Opposite: Figure 1: Map of Shanghai, 1920s, positioning with great precision the international institutions of both the Chinese and international cities

Above: Figure 2: Official Chinese map of Shanghai, 1901

would have been able to assert an equal and opposite influence on the invaders, had not the state of the Empire been in such decline.

The threat came not only from the West: the Japanese concession in Shanghai was increasingly aggressive in business and politics. Japanese colonies in Korea and Taiwan, lands formally held by China, brutally imposed Japanese order and culture on its colonised subjects.

By the end of the 19th century the Western settlement had expanded to cover an area four times bigger than the Chinese city within the walls. The British cultivation of their empire was not a casual affair, but heavily informed by the study of past empires, particularly Rome. The merchant class was as imperial in ambition and desire as the military and the aristocracy, which were frequently one and the same. From the lessons of history the British sought the most prominent and advantageous order for the maintenance of power and for the conduct of trade. And decade by decade towards the end of the 19th century, they constructed along the river a wall of bristling imperial structures, as permanent and as autocratic as their vision of empire. Even now, at the beginning of the 21st century, the Bund retains a strong resemblance to the Thames Embankment in London, from Whitehall to the Waterloo Bridge. Along with the monumental street, European measures of time and order were established, both actually and symbolically, with the rebuilding of the Customs House. This, the earliest structure built on the river in the British settlement, in elegant Chinese administrative style, was demolished in 1907 and replaced by a much larger complex in English Collegiate Gothic, dominated by a tower carrying a large clock on every face, demolished again in 1927 and rebuilt as a great temple to the mercantile empire.

Because of the restrictive terms of the Treaty of Nanjing, there was never a basis for contact between the populous and complex Chinese city to the south and the British settlement. Many European guides and histories of Shanghai refer to the Chinese city as the village, and imply that it was a place of no significance before the Westerners arrived. Over time, the British bypassed Shanghai and imported Chinese managers, or compradors, from their settlements in Canton and Hong Kong, who compounded the problem by building a Cantonese support structure for British trade. The evolution of this duality was shaped more by convention than by prejudice on either side. Shanghai had evolved over 1,000 years as a palimpsest of ancient laws and habits at every level of a stratified society. All immigrant groups in the city, be they Asian or European, were accommodated in their own Huiguan, and left alone to worship, socialise and administer justice according to their own laws and customs. However, Shanghai had an ancient and pragmatic business culture with all the equivalent institutions and procedures of Western trade, arguably the most highly developed of any of the Treaty Ports and more independently powerful than any other base of Western imperial trade. One would not expect, therefore, the commercial success of the foreign settlement to be ignored by the Chinese.

The Western city, not yet 50 years old but rapidly building on cleared land for a small and at first homogeneous population, could afford to create an order representing the best of Europe, an order unfettered by either history or poverty. The Westerners never owned any of the land on which they lived, but nothing in the laws prevented rapacious speculation in the development of property for all takers.[1] The migrant population of the town – merchant adventurers and their wives – were upwardly mobile, nouveau riche; they would have no interest in the Chinese except as inferiors and servants. Certainly they could take pleasure in living in a society in which they were richer than those whose land they invaded. They had come to this new place to fulfil the dream of making a fortune and it was a bonus that they could live in a modern society, free from the constraints and conflicts of the world from which they had come and to which they would return, often maladjusted. China, except as the context for business, was of no interest. Yet slowly, year by year, the population of the city became more and more dominated by the Chinese, a population that was acquiring with great enthusiasm experience of Western technology and Western business practice.

TWO CITIES
Houses

In the first decade of the 20th century the affluent Chinese official or merchant lived behind high walls, with rooms opening onto internal courtyards. The very fortunate had an adjoining garden shaped as a model of perfect harmony, but none of this would be visible from the street. Until the end of the century, the great majority of the Western homes were in every way the antithesis of their Chinese counterparts. The affluent lived in tall, freestanding homes surrounded by simple lawns, with some trees, a herbaceous border, and three sides of the house fully exposed to the street. It would not be clear to the Chinese whether this arrangement, which made such a public display both of affluence and social status, was to do with arrogance, or was the result of a society without a private realm.

And then, unexpectedly, expanding in all directions came the *li long*. The first *li long* districts quickly filled out large areas of land to the west of the French settlement and the racetrack. So successful and appropriate was this form of housing that by the end of the century new neighbourhoods were being built in the Western suburbs of the old city on Chinese property. (See page 62. The *li long* are the numerous parallel structures that dominate all but the central business district of the international settlement.) The earliest types of development, formed around a dense network of rationally gridded lanes, made no distinction between major and minor lanes, but slowly the central spines widened sufficiently to carry vehicles. Aerial views of central Shanghai show that orientation was not a major issue in laying out the *li long*; *feng shui* had little place in the metaphysics of the Western developers.

By the second decade of the last century the *li long* had begun to change and expand. While each family unit remained relatively compact, the outside became much more decorative and Western in appearance. These homes became Western in habit, as well as in form, with flushing toilets becoming a much-desired amenity. In the 1920s more than 300 real-estate developers are recorded as being involved with the management and the development of the *li long/longtang*, refining the form until the best resembled the garden apartments of Europe and America.

External decoration evolved from the gloomy medievalism still prevalent at the end of the 19th century to all the fashions and fantasies of Europe in the 1930s – from Spanish vernacular to Art Deco.

It is worth noting that it would be within the security of the Shanghai *li long* that a group of young revolutionaries founded the Chinese Communist Party and developed the strategies and the ambition that would result in the 1949 Chinese Communist Revolution. Throughout Shanghai, the *li long* are now being torn down to make way for a much less subtle vision of Modernism. Yet, in several districts, the houses have been carefully restored – reminders of the context in which Mao Zedong, Zhou Enlai, Deng Xiaoping and their colleagues planned a revolution.

Streets

Moving away from the imperious business palaces along the river, the main streets of the settlement were broad, drained and lit by gas, fashionable shops slowly giving way to garden apartments and town houses. The streets became more and more affluent towards the west, where leafy suburbs with luxuriant gardens surrounding large detached houses apparently transposed in every detail the suburbs of some great Western city. All was held within an informal grid, in contrast to the labyrinthine lanes of the Chinese. As we have seen, when the city was young, it had been a place of bustling, tree-lined canals and many charming homes, of squares of temples, in a simple range of rich colours and materials. All the buildings were composed of whitewashed walls, painted woods and grey or red tiles. They sat on carefully cut stone embankments facing great arched bridges (qualities delicately present in the Ming drawing), but in all the confusion of 1,000 years, particularly the troubles in the mid-19th century, much of this was lost. Not only the daily refuse from homes and markets, but all the rubble from the wars of rebellion was dumped in the canals. The fluctuations of the great river frequently failed to provide enough scouring action to clear this away, and the canals filled up. The final demise of the canals came when trade was no longer in goods that needed to be transported in barges. The winding narrow lanes that wove their way through the old city were described by one Western observer as 'narrow, filthy and close to a degree that cannot be conceived from any description'.

The Spiritual

The Western city was slow to develop the more complex institutions – schools, hospitals and charitable associations – that were embedded in the fabric of the Chinese city. Schools only emerged in the settlements as the population of school-age children became significant. However, the preferred education for the few families with children was a boarding school in Europe or America. The incentive for Western Christian communities to develop social programmes was much more the result of the aggressive proselytisation of the Christian sects: the desire to encourage the Chinese to convert to Christianity.

Both cities had places for religious worship. There were many popular temples throughout the old city and its suburbs, and Chinese Shanghai housed several ancient Buddhist temples and respected Confucian shrines. There was a scattering of Christian mission schools and small churches throughout the city, and the large cathedral built by the French to the south. As Linda Cooke Johnson has observed, the Chinese attitude to religion was inclusive, whereas Western religious practice could be exclusive, and this created demonstrably different religious structures in the two cities. Chinese places of worship are kindly and relaxed, with no deep mystery but a sense of sharing and caring. This is a personal religion filled with recognisably human gods, gods that are always in attendance at the temple to give confidence and ease the pain of life, and are helped along in this task by daily offerings of small sums of money and the burning of incense. None of the Chinese religions centres on a god-creator; none demands obedience to a moral code. These are lively places, brightly painted in reds and oranges and covered in graphic exultations. Such hyper-reality would seem to be an expression of the wish to provide immediate sensual engagement with the gods in a reality far removed from the commonplace. In contrast to the sectarian and class-conscious fantasies that inform the housing of God in the West, the mood of these temples, large and small, is egalitarian in the broadest sense.

In Shanghai the Western mode of ecclesiastical architecture is at its most spectacular in the Anglican Cathedral, a red-brick Gothic pile attributed to England's most celebrated architect at the time, Giles Gilbert Scott, although he never visited the city (Fig. 3). Behind the vivid exterior the cathedral contains stained glass that has some of the same raw colour and otherworldliness of the local temples, but illustrates strange tales of torture and suffering, without any equivalent in the Chinese imagination. This sombre and dominating structure, still filling the square near the Bund, and restricted to Anglican Christians of the highest social level, now appears as a sad and useless legacy of colonial practice. That which was built for extreme permanence, in terms of faith, ideology and structure, now seems the product of 19th-century arrogance and illusion. Unlike the essential, permanent simplicity of the Chinese temple, it seems lost in time. The complex, abstract metaphysics of the West demanded the continual extension of the imagination to recover and rediscover both the idea and the presence of God, compelling the faithful in Shanghai with fantastic reconstructions of medieval monasticism and Renaissance Classicism. Such structures, set out in this distant land, reveal the degree to which Christianity depends on fantasy and illusion to sustain the faithful.

For the Catholics, Anglicans, Methodists and all the subsets of Christianity, the House of God was, of necessity, not just removed from reality, but offered an illusion of the spiritual realm within which the religious experience could be intensified. Chinese gods, on the other hand, happily share the streets and market places with the people. The lawns that surrounded the Anglican Cathedral were intended only to enhance its symbolic power; while those around the City Temple, along with the Yu Yuan Gardens, offered the only place of public recreation in the old city. The temple and gardens were the centre of commercial life in the city, a throbbing integration of leisure, recreation, business and worship, all the activities that the Europeans segregated and separated not according to activity but by class. Strolling along the Bund was the major social, recreational activity in the settlement and brought all the peoples of old and new Shanghai together. However, leisurely afternoons in the public park located at the northerly end of the Bund were limited to foreigners. Myth reports a sign at the entrance stating that neither dogs nor Chinese were permitted to enter – mythical, but not wholly false. The park was limited to English families and their Chinese servants and amahs (maids); the sign giving this instruction also included a restriction on dogs.

Seeking God's presence was a private affair for the Europeans. More similarly than perhaps is at first obvious, the affluent Chinese sought spiritual comfort and peace in the private beauty of their constructed gardens. These were formed as works of art, employing the most celebrated landscape architects of the period, many from Suzhou, to allow the contemplation of beauty in nature, the harmony that was possible in all things; the experience of all things being in a state of continual change. This was a private world at first hidden to Western eyes, but as the gardens were gradually opened and experienced, they presented an idea of beauty, not only acceptable to the West, but with a level of refinement and delicacy all their own.

Law

Although in both the Western and Chinese cities the law courts were administered by government officials, both administrations remained completely separate. The Chinese consciously employed people who were not from Shanghai, as they were believed to be more impartial, less likely to be corrupted by the city (a pattern that still exists within the city today). In the Chinese city, public works and major improvements were the initiative of the city's benevolent associations. At the end of the 19th century, the Tongreng Tang was the most active group in municipal affairs. It dredged waterways and collected taxes from shopkeepers and vehicle owners to pay for the cleaning and lighting of streets and the upkeep of the small police force. Additionally, it oversaw the construction of bridges and roads, the repair of temples and the management of the militia. Though such associations were wholly private, they were given high public status, and were much respected by the citizenry. The effectiveness of the Tongreng Tang and the influence of Western administrative practice led Chinese Shanghai to create a self-government office in 1905.

In a similar manner, the Shanghai Municipal Council, selected from the local community, managed the affairs of the Western city. Formed very early on in the city's life, in 1854, it was dominated by business people, since government employees were not considered appropriate. It was through the success of the Municipal Council that, within two or three decades after the turn of the century, Shanghai had a municipal infrastructure the equal of any in Europe. Well-surfaced and drained roads were gas-lit along raised sidewalks, and the municipal water supply not only brought drinkable water into every home, but also promoted the unusually widespread acceptance of water closets, public and private.

However, the central legal distinction of Shanghai, and one that stimulated a continual flow of refugees, was extraterritoriality, in

Figure 3: The Anglican Cathedral, Sir Giles Gilbert Scott, 1866

legalese: 'a treaty arrangement whereby a nation acquires exclusive jurisdiction, in both civil and criminal matters, over its recognised citizens residing in a foreign country.'[2] Thus, for example, if a Chinese or an American sued a British citizen, the trial would be in a British court under British law. There were 14 'favoured nations' who had extraterritorial rights and privileges in Shanghai: Belgium, Brazil, Denmark, France, Great Britain, Italy, Japan, The Netherlands, Norway, Portugal, Spain, Sweden, Switzerland and the United States. The two major courts were His Britannic Majesty's Supreme Court, and the United States Court for China. Surprisingly, Russia had no such rights and the concessions to Germany, Austria and Hungary were cancelled after the First World War. All these were subject to the jurisdiction of the Chinese court. As Shanghai developed, the French actively asserted their separateness, but the British concession willingly became part of the international settlement. French legal activity was consistent with the other favoured nations, but they maintained their own police force.

Ominously, the Japanese, by right of the treaty of 1896, in the settlement of the war with China over Korea, maintained their extraterritoriality in China while denying China similar powers in Japan.

Two issues are central to any appreciation of the complexity of the foreign city, as it emerged in the 20th century. First is that its form and culture were produced by a very small percentage of the population – 11,000 foreigners in 1910.[3] Despite appearances, Shanghai, in terms of population and character, was a predominantly Chinese city (Fig. 4). Second is that as the fabric of this foreign culture became evident, its technology, lifestyle and habits began to transform all aspects of Chinese life. This profound cultural infection was directly related to the end of the Qing.

THE END OF THE QING

The collapse of imperial China came in a series of catastrophic events caused by the nation's inability to respond to scientific and technical change, particularly in failure to modernise its military and naval forces. In the Sino-French War of 1884–5 a small nation from the other side of the world was able to defeat Chinese forces and gain control of Vietnam. In the process, a French naval expedition destroyed the Chinese fleet, the docks at Fuzhou and the Chinese defences in Taiwan. In the Sino-Japanese War of 1894–5 for the control of the Korean peninsula, Japan became the first Asian nation to defeat China in battle. Chinese land forces were no match for the modern Japanese army, and once again the Chinese fleet was destroyed. A harsh settlement followed defeat, in which Japan gained control of Korea and Taiwan, and was granted permission to establish industries in four of the Treaty Ports, one of which was Shanghai. The crippling weakness in all aspects of imperial administration laid the basis for Japanese conquest of China. Though Korea would become a Japanese colony in 1910, fearing Japanese ambition Western powers blocked its base in eastern Manchuria. However, Manchuria was crucial to long-range Japanese military strategy and the Russian attempt to build a railroad through Manchuria led to the Russian-Japanese War of 1904–5.

Defeat by Japan and Korea led to the formation of a faction within the imperial government who established the Reform Movement in 1898. In the same year they presented a petition to the young Emperor Guangxi. The wide range of reforms it called for were accepted by the emperor and became the basis for the 40 Reform Decrees. These sought to reform the imperial bureaucracy, to revise the educational and legal systems, to industrialise the economy and modernise the police and military. Immediately, senior members of the imperial administration, seeing their power and influence threatened, hatched a plot to depose the emperor. His adoptive mother, Dowager Empress Cixi, the 63-year-old former imperial concubine (and a schemer of deep malevolence), was informed that her emperor son planned to have her imprisoned. She quickly drew the most conservative faction of the court administration into a *coup d'état,* executed leaders of the Reform Movement, placed the emperor under house-arrest, and proclaimed herself his regent. The unfortunate 23-year-old emperor, whose reign is recorded as running from 1875 until 1908, since he was named emperor when only four years old, was never released.

In the following year, the conservative faction within the Qing court gave strong support to the Society of Righteousness and Harmony, a bitterly anti-foreign secret society linked to the Boxer Uprising of 1900[4] This rebellion against the foreign presence laid siege to the foreign legations in Beijing and Tianjin. In reaction, the combined forces of the eight foreign powers within China quashed the revolt, forcing the imperial court to flee to Xi'an. Paradoxically, after the Western powers allowed the Regent Empress to return to Beijing in 1902, she quickly enacted many of the proposals made by the Reform Movement. Throughout the Empire there was growing support for the need for massive revolution to remove the imperial system and modernise China. In 1905 Sun Yat-sen organised the Revolutionary Alliance, explicitly aimed at overthrowing the Qing, and making China a republic. Five uprisings were provoked between 1905 and 1908, each of which failed, but with each failure support for the cause spread.

Dowager Empress Cixi died in November 1908; the imprisoned Emperor Guangxi died the following day – it is believed he was poisoned on the orders of the Empress. Just days before her death, Cixi had chosen her three-year-old great nephew Xuantong to be the new emperor (he was later known as Henry Pu-yi – the Last Emperor).

As part of the modernisation programme, the Qing administration nationalised the railroads in 1911. This threatened the autonomy of the regions. The Revolutionary Alliance had infiltrated the Qing military and responding to regional protests staged a successful uprising in Wuchang on 10 October 1911. (The Wuchang uprising is still celebrated by Nationalists in Taiwan as the beginning of the Chinese Revolution.) This success spread revolt across China and by the end of November 1911, 14 of the 15 Chinese provinces had declared independence from Beijing. Sun Yat-sen, fundraising in the USA at the time of the uprising, returned to China, and in Nanjing was named first President of the Provisional Government of the Chinese Republic.

With the fall of the Empire, the merchants of old Shanghai requested that the city wall be pulled down so that they could have access and

Figure 4: The heart of the British trading city in the 1920s

exposure to the trade, technology and style of the settlements. By 1912, with the wall down, the old city presented a dilapidated collection of buildings and abandoned canals to the southern edge of the brisk modern French settlement, and the Chinese merchants directed their energies to doing business with the foreign population.

There followed years of struggle to form a stable government. In January 1912, Dr Sun Yat-sen became President of the newly proclaimed Republic of China, whose capital was Nanjing. In the political manoeuvring surrounding the establishment of the Revolutionary Government, Sun Yat-sen resigned in favour of a northern warlord, Yuan Shikai, who had achieved the essential task of persuading Henry Pu-yi to abandon the Chrysanthemum Throne. Though he formally abdicated on 12 February 1912, the emperor was allowed to remain in the palace. He was briefly reinstated as emperor in 1917, for twelve days by a monarchist general. Finally, he was driven out of the city in 1924 by a Chinese Christian warlord, and later became puppet emperor of Manchuria under the Japanese. Yuan moved the capital to Beijing and, with Sun Yat-sen, established the Kuomintang Party (the KMT), a National People's Party aimed at establishing a modern Chinese Republic. In elections held in 1913, the Kuomintang (KMT) became the major force in the new Chinese assembly. President Yuan Shikai increasingly opposed the KMT and mounted a military campaign to gain control of their major strongholds, including Nanjing.[5] Chiang Kai-shek and Sun Yat-sen fled to Japan. The death of Yuan in 1916, shortly after an unsuccessful attempt to establish a dynasty in his name, led to the emergence of many competing warlords, carving up China into regions under their individual control. The era of 1916 to 1928 is known as the 'the warlord period'.

The struggles to find a stable government for China lurched on. After failing to establish a nationalist government in Guangzhou, the KMT, headed by Sun Yat-sen and Chiang Kai-shek, regrouped in Shanghai. The Wuchang uprising had brought many young revolutionaries to Shanghai and it was here that the ambitious dreams for revolution were formed by the group of youthful leaders who would later shape China. It was in Shanghai that the Chinese Communist Party (CCP) was born.

The CCP was founded in July 1921 during a meeting in a girls' school at the edge of a prosperous *li long* in the French concession. (This is now a national shrine and, ironically, the focus of a redevelopment including the most expensive restaurants and shops in the city.) The labouring classes of all ages, particularly the very young, were exploited across China, and never more so than in the export-driven industries encouraged by the foreign traders. Ten to 14-hour workdays, seven days a week in backbreaking and health destroying industries were the norm. These were the conditions for the vast majority in the city, alienated, unrepresented and unrecognised until the rise of Communism. The workers in the European silk mills, Japanese match factories, and tens of thousands of coolies and rickshaw pullers that were ever-present on the streets of the city, were the most receptive audience to politicisation by the youthful and passionate CCP.

The English authors WH Auden and Christopher Isherwood, writing a decade later, gave a vivid sense of the plight of the workers:

Most of the factories are very small – two or three rooms crammed with machinery and operatives. The majority of the operatives are young boys who have been bought from their parents outright for 20 dollars: they work from 12 to 14 hours a day. Their only wages are their food and a sleeping place in a loft above the workroom. There are no precautions whatever against accident or injury to health. In the accumulator factories, half the children have already the blue line in their gums which is a symptom of lead poisoning. Few of them will survive longer than a year or eighteen months. In scissors factories you can see arms and legs developing chromium-holes. There are silk-winding mills so full of steam that the fingers of the mill-girls are white with fungus. If the children slacken in their work the overseers often plunge their elbows into the boiling water as a punishment. There is a cotton mill where the dust in the air makes TB almost a certainty. In this city the gulf between society's two halves is too grossly wide for any bridge. There can be no compromise here.[6]

In May of 1925, in the midst of a strike, the Japanese manager of a silk mill killed a Chinese worker and Communist organiser. This led, two weeks later, on 30 May, to a protest march on Nanjing Road. Without warning the marchers, numbering several thousand, were fired on by the settlement police, killing eleven and wounding many more. The Communists called for a general strike on 1 June, and within a few days a CCP organisation had created 117 separate unions in the city, which were joined to form a General Labour Union. On 16 June, Chinese workers had walked out of every British and Japanese-owned business. Suddenly the majority Chinese within the European city had lost all sense of inferiority and fear of their colonisers. For some among the foreign community, it was clearly the beginning of the end.

The victims of the march became known as the 'May 30th Martyrs', and as news spread it gave rise to riots and protests in Shanghai and in 28 other cities. In Guangzhou, British and French soldiers fired on protesters, killing 52 people. In response, the Communists organised a strike in Hong Kong, which crippled the city's business and industries for almost 16 months.

In Shanghai on 6 July, the Municipal Council shut off all electrical power to Chinese factories in the city. This quickly changed the attitudes of the Chinese industrialists, who had remained neutral in the face of labour action. They moved rapidly to break the unions by withdrawing their financial support. The May 30th Movement not only revealed the depth of anti-Western feeling, it also increased the despair regarding the total inadequacy of the rule of the Beijing warlords, who were seen as selfish, aimless and corrupt.

In March 1925, Sun Yat-sen died suddenly in Beijing. Just before his death, he had agreed that the KMT should join forces with the CCP to mount a military expedition to drive the warlords from Beijing and establish a responsive government. For a nation that had never in its 3,000 years of recorded history known anything other than divinely ordained imperial rule, and a culture of deeply ingrained class and tribal divisions, establishing a new political order was profoundly difficult. There appeared to be only two choices: the simplistic right-wing nationalism of the KMT, which would attempt to reconcile the past with the future, and the CCP, concerned only with the future and the need to break with the order and values of the past. From the first, the KMT feared that the CCP, backed by Russia, would seek to gain control by the infiltration of CCP operatives into its ranks; it was a fear that was completely justified.

During the period of co-operation between the CCP and the KMT, political agents had worked extensively throughout the country, particularly among the peasants, to cultivate broad support for their shared agenda, socialist and nationalist revolution, and the need to drive out the northern warlords. This intense, grass-roots organisation radicalised the urban proletariat and organised labour across the country, particularly in Shanghai, creating widespread political action that was directly opposed to Chiang Kai-shek's independent nationalist programme.

In May 1926, Chiang Kai-shek won the approval of the cultural committee of the Revolutionary Government in Guangzhou to end co-operation with the Communists. In June he was named Commander in Chief of the National Revolutionary Army. In July 1926 he launched the Northern Expedition – Sun Yat-sen's long-awaited attack on the northern warlords. The expedition was a sweeping success, due more to the advance action of CCP operatives under the direction of Chou En-lai, than to the strength of military strategy.[7] They were easily able to politicise peasants and industrial workers into strike action and attacks on police stations and militia posts across the region. By 1927 Chiang's forces had regained territory as far north as Shanghai and Nanjing. Chiang established a new national capital in Nanjing. However, his actions split the KMT. Those supporting a continued alliance with the Communists established a base in Wuhan, in the Hubei Province. Chiang moved his Central Military Academy to Nanjing, dedicated to the task of producing officers who were pledged to his cause.

The Communists were gaining ascendancy within the KMT. This split the party still further. The KMT leftists moved the Nationalist capital from Wuhan to Hangzhou where, with surprising speed, they succeeded in gaining widespread support from industrial labour. In January 1927 a mob fuelled by left-wing inspired, anti-Western fervour, rushed the British concession in Hangzhou, overpowering the British troops and forcing Britain to return Hangzhou to China. Similar politically inspired mob action also forced the British to cede first Kaifeng in February, and then Nanjing in March, back to China. Shanghai, the centre of foreign power, was to be next. The city panicked. Women and children were sent away and more than 40,000 foreign troops were rushed into the foreign city to defend and fortify it; 40,000 troops guarding a privileged foreign population of less than 30,000, within a city whose overall Chinese population was well in excess of one million, a measure that dramatises the arrogance and absurdity of the situation. Most of that one million lived in poverty and were exploited and oppressed by the foreign industries, a vast majority for whom Communism offered salvation.

The American writer Vincent Sheen, who visited the city during the unrest, wrote that the international settlement was a place where foreigners 'considered that they had built Shanghai out of nothing' and 'frankly asserted themselves as a superior race designed by nature to make money out of the Chinese'.[8] However, there were foreigners who understood the need for effective national political order, and the necessity to end the 'Unequal Treaties'. Of these, the most vocal were the Americans associated with the China Weekly Review.[9] During this period the review itself was split between those who favoured the Nationalists and those who sided with the CCP.

In October 1926 CCP-led organised labour began an attempt to end the rule of the gangster-controlled warlords running Shanghai. Though more than 350,000 workers had been mobilised, the CCP, hoping to co-ordinate the uprising with the entry of Nationalist troops from Hangzhou, held back. This gave the warlords an excuse to unleash a reign of terror, with arrests and very public executions of anyone with leftist leanings, creating massive panic throughout the Chinese city. Shanghai had to fall to the control of either the KMT or the CCP. The chief strategist of the CCP, and former deputy of the Wampu Military Academy under Chiang Kai-shek, was Chou En-lai. On 20 March 1927, after KMT forces had routed the warlord armies in the region, Chou once again initiated a worker revolt in the city, calling a general strike on 21 March. Eight hundred thousand workers responded, shutting down all business. At the same time CCP militia fanned out across Shanghai, attacking police stations and the barracks of the local militia. Within days, Shanghai, outside the foreign concession, had come within the control of the workers and the CCP. Chou claimed that 'the working class is the most revolutionary and that it can take leadership of the expedition against the [Beijing] warlords'.[10] He called for a 'new revolutionary democratic power' to be established. This brief Revolutionary victory forced the foreign business community to begin to make concessions to the Chinese; it also led both foreign and Chinese business leaders to begin, covertly, to cultivate the KMT.

Among the stream of foreign businessmen, consular officials and Chinese taipans visiting the KMT at their headquarters in Kiukiang, was the boss of the Green Secret Society, Pockmarked Huang, a friend of Chiang Kai-shek from the previous decade, when he had supplied gangsters to support the revolutionary activities of Chiang's mentor Chen Chi-mei.[11] He offered to help Chiang take Shanghai back from the CCP in exchange for protection of his gang's opium monopoly.

In March 1927, as the Nationalist Army made a triumphant entry into Shanghai, Chiang Kai-shek launched a massive covert counterattack against the Communists and their worker supporters. A wholly contrived labour union, the Society for Common Progress, had been created to diminish the dominance of the CCP General Labour Union, made up of gangsters from the Green Secret Society. Loyal KMT officials carefully screened all senior officers in the Nationalist Army, and removed all those having affiliations with the left wing of the party. The foreign concessions were complicit. The French supplied rifles and ammunition to the gangsters. The Municipal Council, with the agreement of its American chairman, allowed the gangster army to pass through the concession, an unprecedented involvement in Chinese affairs. The all-important motive was to secure a political order in the city that would support foreign business interests and the survival of the concessions.

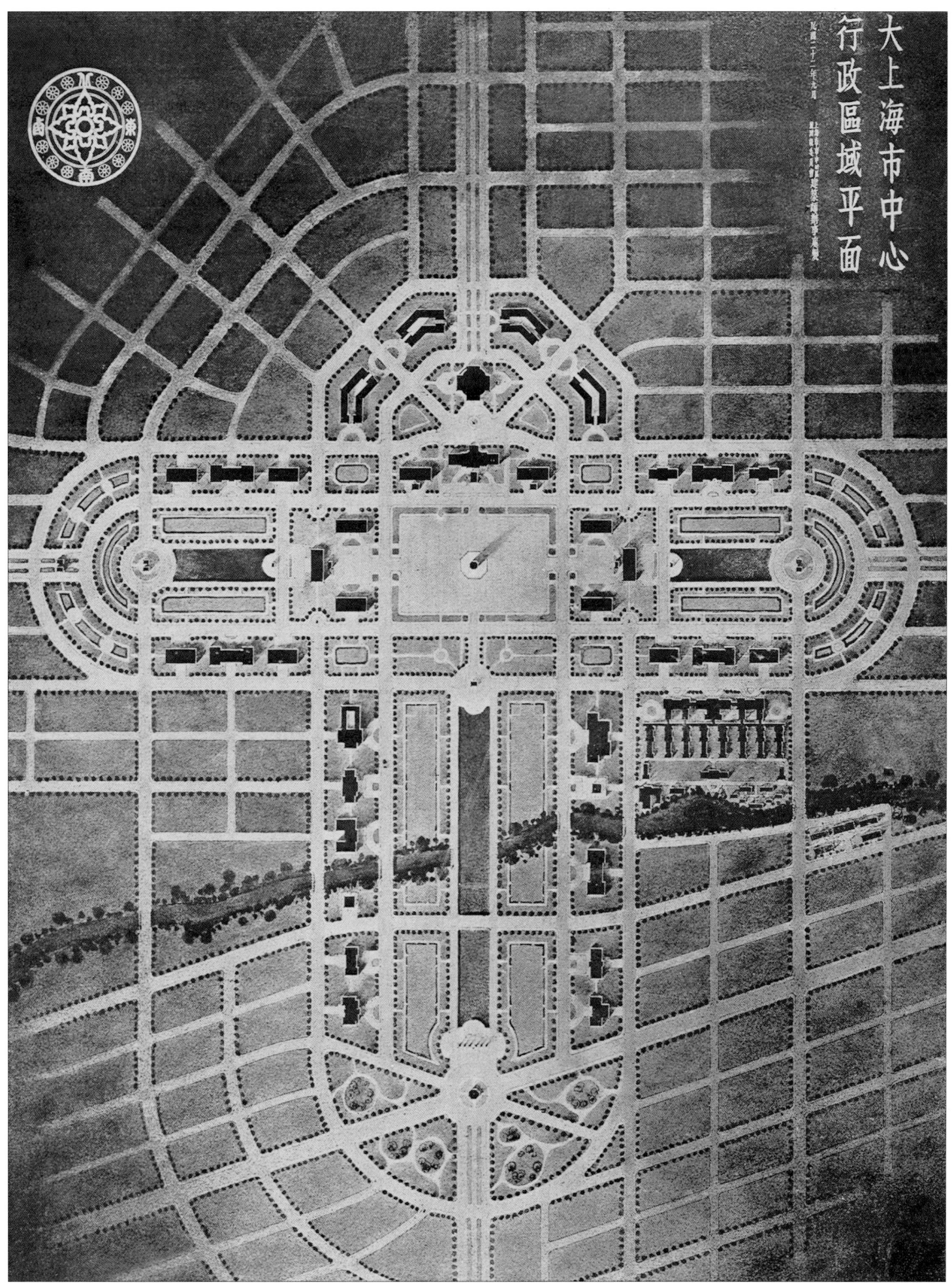

大上海市中心
行政區域平面

Figure 5: Shanghai City-Centre Zoning Plan, 1929

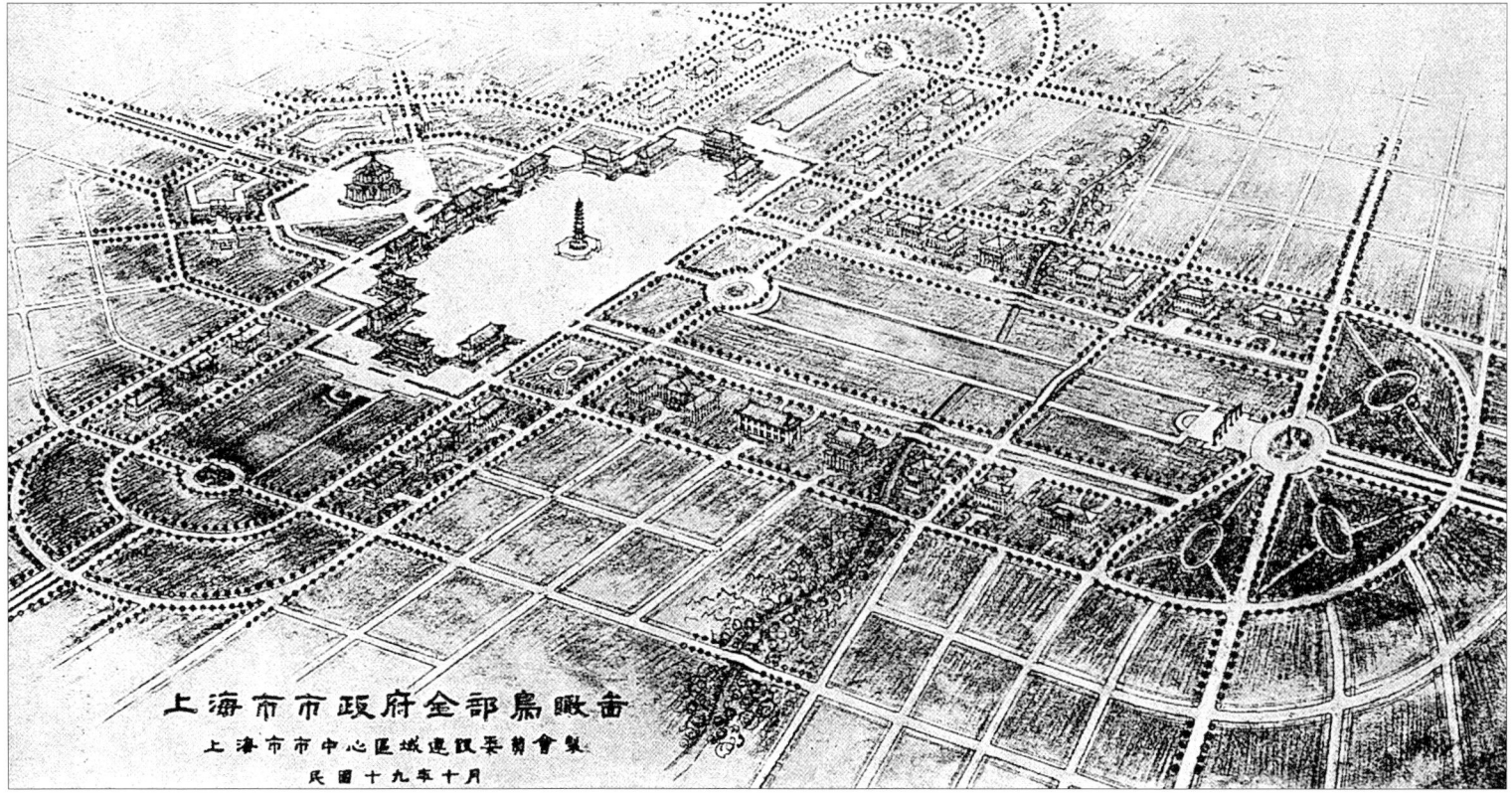

上海市市政府全部鳥瞰圖
上海市市中心區域建設委員會繪
民國十九年十月

Figure 6: Shanghai City-Centre Zoning Plan, 1929

This bloody play was directed, not by Pockmarked Huang, but by the most vicious force in the Shanghai underworld, Tu Yueh-sen, a monstrous product of the dislocated society. From the countryside near Shanghai, he had come to the city when he was 20. The employee of a fruit seller on the waterfront in the French concession, he was soon recruited to the Ch'ing Pang, the Green Gang. In 1927 he became the leader, and the most powerful among the triumvirate of secret societies (to use too polite a term), in the support of Chiang Kai-shek's passionate plan to destroy the Communists.

Early in the morning of 12 April 1927, hundreds of members of the Green Gang, all in uniform, with the character for 'labour' cynically sported on their armbands, raided the strongholds of the trade unions and their militia. Taken totally by surprise, they quickly surrendered. All who were not killed in the clash or executed on the spot were marched to the Nationalist base in the grounds of the ancient temple at Longwha, to be executed *en masse*. (The most ancient Buddhist temple in the city, 1,700 years old, is now the site of a memorial to the 'martyrs'.)

The next morning, barely aware of what had happened, 100,000 citizens gathered in the pouring rain to petition the commander of the local Nationalist forces. Partly in defence and partly as a symbol, women and children led the procession along the Poashan Road. Without warning, the KMT and their gangster allies opened fire, killing 36 people and wounding many more. The marchers panicked and soldiers loyal to the KMT began a house-by-house search to eliminate every known Communist and Communist sympathiser in the city. Five to ten thousand Shanghainese were estimated to have been killed during the three weeks of the purge. The wide disparity of these totals reflects the mass confusion caused by the attack and the insignificance of the poor in the city.

Many more thousands fled the city, including Chou En-lai. And even as the desperate struggled to find refuge in the settlements, the international community viewed the atrocities, not as a warning about the

future, but as a boon for real-estate speculation. Chiang had taken these actions unilaterally, without any authorisation from the central committee of the KMT. For this he was censured, and removed as Commander in Chief of the Army. He reacted by attempting to create an independent government in Nanjing, but the KMT forced his resignation and he fled once again to Japan. Chiang had succeeded in saving Shanghai from Communism. The business leaders in the foreign enclave were very satisfied, but the 'Shanghai massacre' laid the basis for the hatred that fuelled the continuing war with the Communists and led to the defeat of the KMT by the Communists some 20 years later.

It was in the midst of this chaos that the decision was made to create a strategic master plan for Shanghai, as if a clear, stable vision for this most progressive of Chinese cities could help bring order to the political project.

THE CHIANG KAI-SHEK CITY
Between 1927 and 1929, the Nationalist Government in Nanjing initiated the production of this master plan for Shanghai, the first in recorded history;[12] the result of this process would shape the evolution of the city through most of the 20th century. The intention of the plan was to lay the basis for a new modern Chinese Shanghai. It was conceived and evolved during a period of great instability in China. As China fell apart, the foreigners, through a combination of indifference and arrogance, increased their investment in making Shanghai the European capital of Asia. While British business interests maintained the controlling influence on Shanghai, British imperial ambition reached its climax in the construction of the vast new capital of British India in New Delhi. The symbolic heart of the new city presented an imperial power and majesty on a scale unequalled in British history. Some were led to wonder whether, as Rome had moved to Constantinople, the centre of the British Empire would move from London to Delhi.

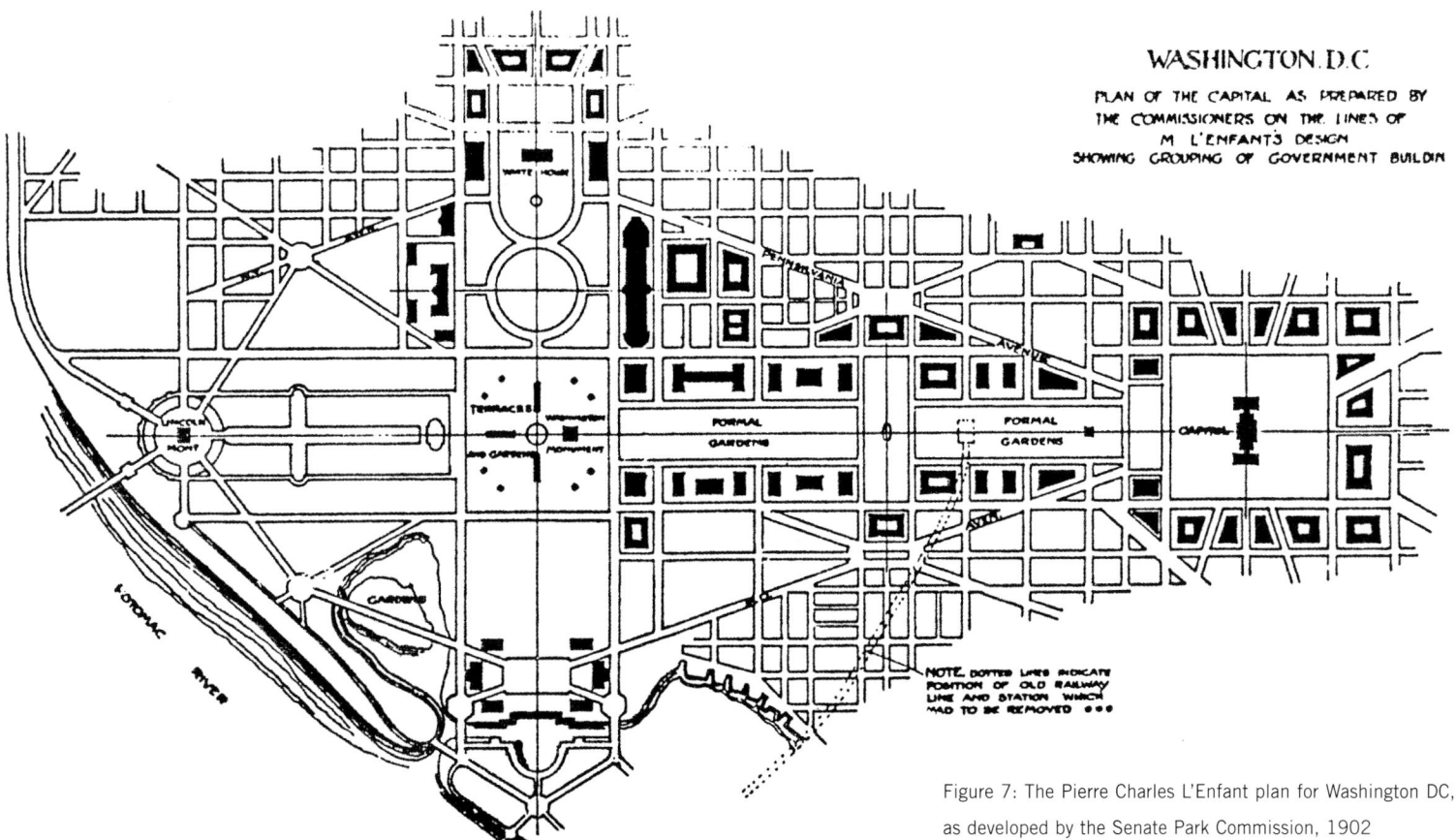

WASHINGTON.D.C

PLAN OF THE CAPITAL AS PREPARED BY
THE COMMISSIONERS ON THE LINES OF
M L'ENFANT'S DESIGN
SHOWING GROUPING OF GOVERNMENT BUILDIN

Figure 7: The Pierre Charles L'Enfant plan for Washington DC, as developed by the Senate Park Commission, 1902

The Shanghai City Centre Zoning Plan of 1929–31[13] was based on extensive surveys of all aspects of city life. While this was being done, the left wing of the KMT made public their belief that the Chinese Communist Party was wholly under the control of the Soviet Communist Party and had agreed to the covert agenda of destroying the KMT. This brought the left and right wings of the party together, and led both to the creation of yet another National Government of China and the outlawing of the Communist Party. Chiang returned to head the Nationalist Army and immediately renewed the campaign against the northern warlords, taking Beijing in 1928. This action revealed the extent of Japanese complicity with the warlords. In October, Chiang became Chairman of the reformed National Government and moved the capital to Nanjing. It was a government that refused to allow the emergence of any other political party; a government whose obsession with the destruction of Communism dominated all actions and policy. The Nationalists, under Chiang Kai-shek, held power until 1949, when they fell to the Communists.

The Nationalist Government made the decision to create a master plan for Shanghai soon after it established its base in Nanjing in 1927. The central intention was to lay the basis for the creation of a modern industrial Shanghai, independent of, and in time able to diminish the power and the presence of, the foreign enclaves. The settlement had been allowed to sprawl west and north, the final major extension being granted in 1915. By the end of the 1930s, the area was covered, and its internal organisation was effectively blocking the development of Chinese Shanghai to the north. In response to this, the Nationalists' plan had two major elements. First was the creation of an extensive road and rail network, moving around the settlements east and west with one major north–south road running along the edge of the settlement to the west. Second was the proposed creation of an extensive new city, well north and east of the foreign settlements,

which would not only have the freedom to be formed as a modern automobile-based organisation, but would also allow the development of an extensive port facility close to the Yangtze, upriver from the foreign port.

The plan, as it developed, assumed a revealing form – a form that was as much the product of desire as of reason (Figs. 5, 6). Interestingly, it is an explicit amalgam of Pierre Charles L'Enfant's plan for Washington DC (Fig. 7) and Edwin Lutyens' plan for New Delhi (Fig. 8).[14] This was the work of Chao Chein, a 1922 graduate of the University of Pennsylvania. The central element is an extensive mall, formed in the intersection between axes running north–south and east–west. This creates the figure of a cross, the north–south being the longer, dominant axis. The scale is vast, yet the drawing contains a suggestion of the structures that would have dramatised the composition still further. At the southern end, it shows a series of arches forming a monumental screen, a Chinese tower, having the same relation to the centre as did Lutyens' tribute to the dead, the All-India War Memorial in New Delhi. At the intersecting axes, the equivalent point where the Washington Monument links the White House and Congress, there is a many-storeyed pagoda. A mall on the north side ends in a great public square, which the report describes as a military parade ground, enclosed by a succession of elaborate public buildings in the Chinese manner. Each would house an agency of the city. The City Hall at the centre is flanked by the Office of Finance, and departments of construction, police, health, infrastructure, education, land use and social issues. These screen what appears to be the power centre: an extensive symmetrical hall, like a small mountain, forming a vast memorial to Sun Yat-sen. This, along with a fragment of the river that appears to run across the southern section, satisfies the laws of *feng shui*. At the extreme east and west of the plan sit the library and museum. Flanking all sides of the composition would be a series of institutional buildings in the mall, which would have been laid out in a succession of gardens and lakes.

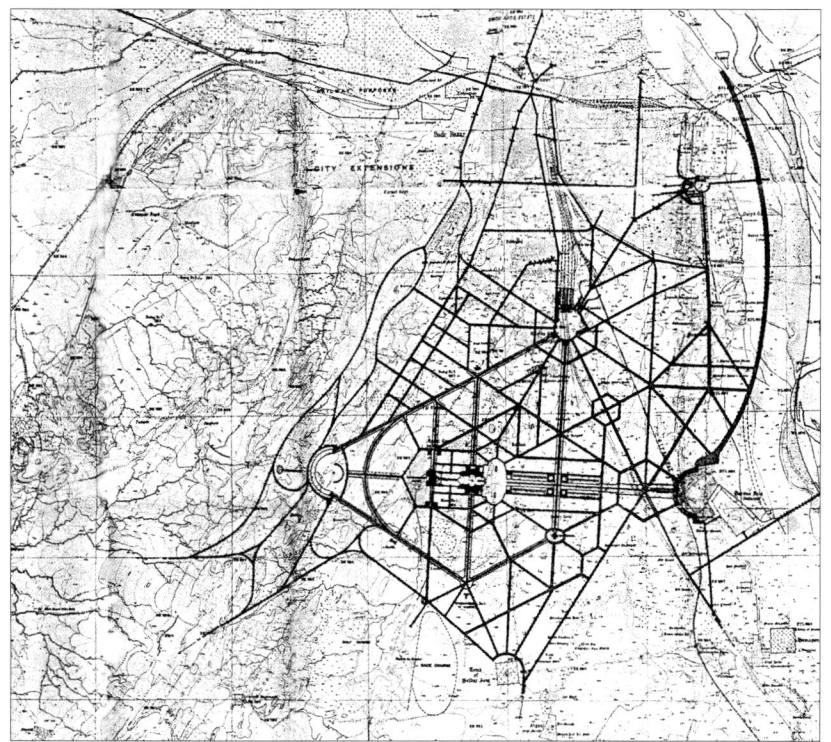

Figure 8: Plan from 'Final Report' of the Delhi Town-Planning Committee on the planning of the new imperial capital

Figure 9: The administrative centre of the new Shanghai in the Nationalist style that sought to renew traditional architectural forms

Beyond the centre, the overall order of the plan is based directly on Lutyens' New Delhi, which was begun in 1912, though its scale and ambition would become evident only during the 1920s. The size and geometry of the radial road systems, set out west and south of the formal centre, replicate, even in small details, elements of the New Delhi plan. Where Lutyens separated the centre of political (royal) power from the business heart of the city, however, the Shanghai planners appear to fuse business and political power in one. Yet the Shanghai planners placed at the heart of this new city the symbolic apparatus of the British Empire, including a Chinese version of the All-India Memorial at the southern end (anticipating the sacrifice that would have to be made to build a new modern China). The administrative buildings around the public square would be the exact equivalent to the buildings designed by Sir Herbert Baker in New Delhi, and the memorial to Sun Yat-sen, representing the seat of power, would be the exact equivalent to Lutyens' Palace of the Viceroy. It must be asked how it was possible for the symbolic equipment of the British Empire – essentially concerned with framing the omnipotence of the race through its monarch – to have any relevance to a commercial city in a new republic, unless it unwittingly offered evidence of the ambitions of those who would lead this new republic. Even more curious is why such apparatus would have been applied to a city that was not the centre of power, since the capital was in Nanjing, unless it was the Nationalist intention to make this new modern Shanghai the capital.

Lutyens was much influenced by the plan for Washington DC, but imperial power in colonial India was absolute and had no need for a central stage to create a balance of forces. The British Empire of India and British Asia had none of the constitutional limits to power that constrained the monarch in Britain. Attempting to impute a political significance to the intersecting axes in this plan for Shanghai equivalent to the interrelationship of presidential power with Congress on the Washington Mall may be fanciful, given the wholly autocratic and

oppressive nature of the Nationalist Government, but it is through such fancies that illusions are created. As Charles Baudelaire said of Baron Georges-Eugène Haussmann's rebuilding of Paris, 'Art veils mightily the terrors of the pit'. It is worth considering the idea that this plan, for a brief moment in the late 1920s, is evidence of the youthful optimism of the planners, believing that the creation of a new Shanghai could be a symbol for a free, democratic China.

When the Nationalist Government was established in 1928, Shanghai was the financial and commercial capital of China. The antithesis of autocratic and conservative Beijing, Shanghai could offer China a powerful financial base, if and when the foreigners left. The rational, strategic and far-seeing decision to build a modern Chinese nucleus in Shanghai to the north of both the concessions and old Shanghai laid the basis for the evolution of a greater Shanghai within which the foreign settlements would have been subsumed. The aesthetic decision to form this plan from the combined influence of Lutyens' New Delhi and L'Enfant's plan for Washington DC is both irrational and revealing of much about the way in which power is manifested in the physical form of the city. It reflects a desire for an end to the Western presence and a naive sense that some of the omnipotence of the British Empire would rub off on Shanghai if it assumed the guise of a great Western capital. As much as they distrusted the West, the Chinese Nationalists had a compelling desire to acquire its knowledge and equal its achievements.

Several objectives had to be met in giving form to a new Shanghai: it had to accommodate all the new technologies of transport and land management; it had to present and dramatise Chinese power and authority; and it had to offer to the imagination of the world the idea of the emergence of a great Chinese city – a city the equal of any power centre in the world, rivalling the dreams of the British Empire. In the late 1920s, nothing rivalled New Delhi in revealing the scale and ambition of British imperialism. Many were asking by then why the British were investing so much in India. To some, it was the climactic gesture of the dying Empire. For others, it was seen as a means by which the Empire was tightening its grip on the world, shifting the centre of British power from London to Delhi to be near the heart of all its domains, just as the Roman Empire had shifted from Rome to Constantinople to allow it more effectively to manage its borders and expand its sphere of influence. What effect did the collapse of the Chinese Empire have on the small group of men who shaped the project of British Empire? Were there moments in which they considered absorbing China within the Empire, absorbing a nation in chaos – a nation of critical importance to British mercantilism? And if the British planners dreamt of administering China from New Delhi, so too, in a peculiar reflection of this desire, the planners of Shanghai sought to create a base of power that would be Delhi's rival. By the 1920s, the British were in competition with several emerging empires. In Europe, Benito Mussolini sought to create a new Roman Empire, moving into North Africa, and the Japanese ambition must have become an obvious threat to British Asia.

Thus, the Nationalist master plan for Shanghai can be seen not only as the adoption of a rational order appropriate to a powerful city, but also as a reflection of the desire to reform Shanghai as the equal and opposite of British plans for Delhi. The plan would also, in those first months of Nationalist Government, represent the assertion of Chinese order and the Chinese future of Shanghai. Its extensive and theatrical public centre matched the drama of Lutyens' New Delhi monument for monument. The grand axis has a scale its equal, much more suited to a nation's capital than to the administrative centre of a commercial city. However, with the benefit of hindsight, an imperial Shanghai would have been well suited to the character of Chiang Kai-shek. We can see in this unfulfilled dream evidence of how the Nationalists viewed power as well as an unavoidable tendency towards an imperial style of leadership, despite the collapse of the Qing Dynasty.

This is perhaps only to be expected. After all, China had known no other model in its 3,000-year history, no other way of demonstrating authority, or of organising a nation. The failure of Chiang Kai-shek to respond effectively to the Japanese invasion was in part an acknowledgement that the Nationalist army was no match for the Japanese, but it also reflected his conviction that the Marxist socialist revolution was a far greater threat to the future of China and, perhaps more importantly, to his imperial ambitions. In all complex human plans there is a confusion of intentions. However, a document such as this master plan provides a way of freezing and consolidating complex patterns of desire at a certain point in time. Thus, the Nationalist plan for Shanghai suggests a global ambition for the city and a leaning towards imperial power that are far less clear in other documents. Of course, these plans are the translation by a small group of people of the desires of those in power; they must also reflect their own dreams and hopes for the nation. Despite the subsequent collapse of the Nationalist Government, this plan influenced the growth and development of Shanghai throughout the remainder of the 20th century.

The Nationalist Government never managed to regain control of all China. By 1930, Japanese armed forces had begun the move into Manchuria and those loyal to the Communist cause were helping to build a base of operations in the west of the country. The strategic importance of Chinese Shanghai, both politically and economically, justified the plan and the need to build a modern city in a modern China that would one day end foreign occupation/dominance. And for the Chinese planners, there were no models for a powerful modern city as compelling as the plan for New Delhi. This was the vision of the most powerful empire. This was the vision of the nation that had led the formation of foreign Shanghai. The question that must be asked is whether the grandeur and symbolism of the plan reflected the Nationalists' intention of making Shanghai the new capital. Nothing else can explain the vast public stage management and the wish to be compared with New Delhi and Washington. Nothing else could justify the vast expense that such a construction would incur. (A decade later, Lutyens' plan for Delhi was a forceful stimulus to the imaginations of Adolf Hitler and his architect Albert Speer, as they began planning the reconstruction of Berlin to become the new eternal Rome.)

The symbolism aside, this was a strategically effective plan. It created a new nucleus for the city on relatively underdeveloped land. As old Shanghai grew to join the new city to the north it would eventually subsume and neutralise the foreign city. The planners were most effective in creating extensive new port facilities and laying the basis for a modern industrial sector to the north. The harbour would be formed by excavating back from the west bank of the river close to the estuary. The intention of the plan was to force Chinese Shanghai to move at Western speed using Western technologies.

As ambitions grew, the Shanghai City-Centre Zoning Plan was extended in 1930 into the 'Big Shanghai Plan',[15] which incorporated all the research conducted over the previous three years. This included documentation on the city's history, its geography and climate, population, farming, manufacturing, the trade status of the roads and railways, and irrigation and sewage. Power supply and generation were given less attention. The report set out for the first time comprehensive regulations on zoning, transportation, the creation of public parks, hospitals and schools, and was fairly specific about the architectural qualities to be present in public buildings. The plan remains the most comprehensive assessment of the city to this day and still forms the basis of all subsequent public planning. Many elements from the Shanghai City-Centre Zoning Plan were implemented between the years 1930 and 1937, before Japan declared war on China. Its effects can be seen in a series of avenues radiating out from Wujia Chiang, in the northeast of the city. Remnants of the great symbolic centre remain in the layout of what was built as the new administrative centre.[16] It is now much neglected, but there remains a cluster of public buildings in the Nationalist-ordained style, at its centre a handsome town hall in the style of the buildings of the imperial administration, looking south across Chiang Lu and flanked on either side by administrative buildings, schools and the city library. What was once intended as a place of public gathering is now sealed off, the library abandoned, and the great town hall now houses some official activity that discourages visitors (Fig. 9).

THE LAST FANTASIES

Despite the image of Shanghai as a great European city in China, the foreign population remained an insignificant percentage of the total: 23,000 in 1920 and 36,000 in 1930,[17] less than 2 per cent of a total population estimated at more than three million (at the time the sixth largest city in the world).[18] Yet the imagination and desire of this modest community were able to dominate and transform Shanghai's Chinese culture. Even as China was falling apart, they continued to construct their fantasies. In these final decades the foreign city, with a confidence that belied the political and military crises facing China at the time – Japan's invasion of Manchuria and the desperate struggles between the Nationalist and Communist factions – produced a spectacular display of future desire in the construction of numerous hotels, apartment build-

ings and movie houses, all in the most exuberant European *moderne* style. The movie houses, concentrated on the road to the east of the racetrack, were given a drama equal to their role as temples of desire. These were temples in which to worship at the altar of the new world, in which to experience the emotions, humour and personalities that were shaping the future in the form of movie stars. It was a world that by the 1920s was no longer concerned with the mercantile imperialism of the British, but whose design was increasingly inspired by the United States. Traces of these fantasies survive, and are among the most poignant constructions in the city, particularly the cinemas to the east of People's Square, with their tragically inappropriate gay façades. Any view north of the Bund is dominated by the once-named Broadway Apartment Building, a confident little skyscraper. Rumour had it that the top 12

Figure 10: A day at the racecourse in the 1920s

floors were occupied by the American intelligence services as the Japanese prepared to invade China and initiate a process that would bring about the collapse of Western dreams for Shanghai.

The Racetrack

Horse racing, like chariot racing, was as much a reflection of a fatalistic view of life as it was about speculation, winning and losing. The true metaphor for the English Shanghighlander (as they called themselves) cannot be found in the bombastic architecture, nor in their obsession with whores and opium, nor in the portentous medievalism of the Anglican Cathedral, but in the weekly performances at the racetrack, in the cultivation of winners and losers, and in the dreary socialising, lubricated with quantities of gin.[19] This preoccupation was at first quite incomprehensible to the Chinese, who could not understand such waste of time and resources on a useless activity.[20] In many ways, however, the racetrack in its heyday resembled in its socialising, deal-making and flirting, the activities surrounding the Yu Yuan Gardens (Fig. 10). As the racetrack evolved, it became a setting that combined the instability of the international population with the corruption of gangsters and warlords, a metaphor for a vacuous, synthetic culture. It is ironic that the site for such escapist entertainment would later become the symbolic heart of the Communist city: the People's Square.

The Brothels

The better-class brothels in the lanes of Fuzhou Road retained the traditions of Chinese prostitution: a formal procedure in elegant interiors carried out by very young women. The little picture cards advertising their services show them wearing thickly padded silk coats and dresses, with only their faces and hands bare; but the image always displays the brilliant colours of the embroidered slippers covering the prime objects of sexual desire: bound feet. In the 1920s and 1930s opium was much more debilitating to the Chinese than to the Europeans, but sex was everyone's obsession. During these first decades of the 20th century, Shanghai became the refuge for people fleeing disturbance across the world. Even in the face of Japanese expansion in the 1930s, anyone who could get there was free to enter foreign Shanghai. For some there was truly nowhere else to go.

The Russian Revolution brought thousands of once-affluent white Russians, now dislocated and impoverished. As HJ Lethbridge has described it, they included:

White Russian women, refugees from Asiatic Russia, driven off their homeland by the triumphant Bolsheviks. They settled, together with their male companions, mostly in the French Concession, which was more residential than the International Settlement, the latter was cluttered with businesses and offices and the rents were high. In 'Frenchtown' (as locals called the Concession), they established themselves as *entraineuses*, hostesses, cabaret artists, 'taxi dancers' (metred for the time spent on the floor), and as courtesans. In plain language, a large number were whores. In racially conscious foreign Shanghai, they offended by consorting equally with Occidentals and Orientals.[21]

In 1935, 18 years after the Bolshevik Revolution, there were an estimated 25,000 displaced Russians on the streets of Shanghai. (Evidence of this is surely present in the current gene pool of the city.) Selling sex became a much more explicit and public process, elaborated and expanded by the Russians. Countless women, united only by their slit-sided *qi pao* (the silk sheaths worn by Chinese women), and whose stories could have colourfully filled a thousand novels, took their beauty onto the streets and into the fashionable restaurants and dancehalls. They filled the cafés and cheap hotels in the 1920s, until they grew old or had made enough money to become someone else. These were the lives that gave shape to the fictional persona of Jelena Trubova, one of the nine characters who become intertwined in Vicki Baum's novel *Shanghai '37*.[22]

The favourite English guide to the city in 1934, *All About Shanghai*, is positively giddy with sexual promise:

Dancing and Music. Shanghai flames with millions of flashing jewels at midnight. The centre of nightlife is a vast crucible of electric flame.

The throb of the jungle tom-tom; the symphony of lust; the music of a hundred orchestras; the shuffling of feet; the swaying of bodies; the rhythm of abandon; the hot smoke of desire under the floodlights; it's all fun; it's life.

Joy, gin, and jazz. There's nothing puritanical about Shanghai.

The 'dancing hostesses', they amiably entertain at a dime to a dollar a dance; Russians, Chinese, Japanese, Koreans, Eurasians occasionally others.

They can dance and drink.

'Vun small bottle of vine?' It's the battle cry of the far flung bottle front.

'S'funny how a little girl can hold so much champagne!'

It's not wine; it's cider or ginger ale, but not on the chit (bill).

Shura or Vera or Valia gets a commission. It all helps. Give this little girl a great big bottle.

'S'getting late.' Rose tints the sky beyond the Whangpoo. 'Let's go for ham'n eggs and one last round.'

One swaying, sinuous embrace and a moist kiss with the last strains of the dance. 'Hey, kid; why don't you marry the girl?' The modish matron cuffs the gigolo. The dancing girl nods surrender but grabs her stack of dance tickets and flees into the night.

'Boy! Call a car!'

Whoopee!

One night in Shanghai is ended.[23]

The Great World

Nowhere in European Shanghai was the strangeness of the city before the Japanese invasion more palpable than in the Great World. Recently tidied up but essentially the same as it always has been, the Great World is five floors of entertainment around an open-air stage, with sideshows, cinemas, acrobats, Chinese opera, children's rides, sleazy bars, all housed in a cold, hard concrete fantasy at what was the busiest intersection in the city. In its heyday it was visible from the racetrack, its wedding-cake steeple almost lost behind huge advertisements for movies and automobiles. A surviving photograph from the early 1920s shows that, with the exception of the words 'Chrysler' and 'Goodrich', all were in Chinese characters and aimed at Chinese Shanghai. This was a mysterious and complicated place for a Westerner, with too many signs, too many unexplained activities, too many people watching and waiting (Fig. 11).

The German film director Joseph von Sternberg wrote a much reproduced paragraph about it in his book *Fun in a Chinese Laundry*, when it was controlled by criminal gangs linked to Chiang Kai-shek. He described it as:

> seething with life and all the commotion and noise that go with it, studded with every variety of entertainment Chinese ingenuity had contrived. When I had entered the hot stream of humanity, there was no turning back had I wanted to. On the first floor were gambling tables, singsong girls, magicians, pickpockets, slot machines, fireworks, birdcages, fans, stick incense, acrobats and ginger. One flight up were restaurants, a dozen different groups of actors, crickets in cages, pimps, midwives, barbers and earwax extractors. The third floor had jugglers, herb medicines, ice-cream parlours, photographers, a new bevy of girls, their high-collared gowns slit to reveal their hips, in case one had passed up the more modest ones below who merely flashed their thighs; and under the heading of novelty, several rows of exposed toilets, their impresarios instructing the amused patrons not to squat but to assume a position more in keeping with the imported plumbing. The fourth floor was covered with shooting galleries, fan-tan tables, revolving wheels, massage benches, acupuncture and moxa cabinets, hot-towel counters, dried fish and intestines, and dance platforms serviced by a horde of music makers competing with each other to see who could drown out the others. The fifth floor featured girls whose dresses were split to the armpits, a stuffed whale, story tellers, balloons, peep shows, masks, a mirror maze, two love-letter booths with scribes who guaranteed results, 'rubber goods' and a temple filled with ferocious gods and joss sticks. On the top floor and roof of that house of multiple joys a jumble of tightrope walkers slithered back and forth, and there were seesaws, Chinese checkers, mah-jong, strings of firecrackers going off, lottery tickets, and marriage brokers. And as I tried to find my way down again, an open space was pointed out to me where hundreds of Chinese, so I was told, after spending their coppers, had speeded the return to the street below by jumping from the roof.

This vivid collaging of images established a form for writing about Shanghai in the 1930s that many followed. However, as recorded in *Anecdotes of Old Shanghai* (1985),[24] the fantasies of the Great World became much more menacing after the Japanese seized the city in 1937:

> When the Japanese aggressors occupied Shanghai, the 'Rong's Great World' became a 'special amusement' centre where people were brain-washed with ideas of enslavement to benumb their will to fight for the nation. After the victory of the Anti-Japanese War, the US imperialists and the Kuomintang reactionaries used it as a propaganda instrument to whip up an anti-Communist and anti-popular campaign. American movies made in Hollywood on pornography and violence dominated the screen and obscene and superstitious operas flooded the stage. Pick-pockets, swindlers, prostitutes and rascals mixed with the audience with an axe to grind. Traitors and enemy agents of every hue were found spying for information or plotting against people's lives among the artists, staff and audience of the Great World. The Great World was, in fact, a paradise for monsters and demons and a den for enemy agents and traitors camouflaged by beautiful music and graceful dancing. After Liberation the Great World returned to the embrace of the people. The People's government took it over in 1954.

It returned to satisfy in multiple performances all the desires and fantasies of the real Shanghainese.

I went there last one rainy evening in March a few years ago. There was no one about downstairs except for two old women almost hidden behind the food stalls. The building has an unfinished feeling despite its age and the hard, cold concrete and tile. The activity is still on five levels partly surrounding a great courtyard that has the largest stage. That night four young performers were working very hard outside in the courtyard in the light rain, and I felt embarrassed being the only spectator. I climbed the open stair to the terrace. On the stage two young acrobats were rotating huge ceramic barrels with their feet. I could see that the rain had made the surface of the barrels wet and slippery, and I felt such guilt that all this dangerous effort was just for me. I knew they could see me so I edged my way inside, relieved to be free of this peculiar relationship. Immediately inside I was faced with a broad curtain pulled back across the entrance to a small theatre for Chinese opera. Many middle-aged women, sitting in pairs, were watching with sad smiles and nodding confirmation at each step of the tortuous romance: they knew every nuance. Down the hall more old women attended to a steaming food counter. At the end, double doors opened into a bar that reeked of cigarettes and had a soft orange glow with a cinematic mood of menace. On the next floor a large audience of older men was transfixed in the yellow light of a grainy movie. All entertainment is open to everyone so I sat and watched, and it took several minutes to realise that it promised to become slightly pornographic. It is a place of astonishing ghosts and memories around which has swirled 80 years of brutality, violence and madness.

Figure 11: The Great World, drawn in the 1930s

Notes

1 The physical permanence of the structures they built was not just the result of a wish to create the illusion of stability and establishment, but also reflected the need to satisfy the demands of a novel American invention: insurance.

2 Lethbridge, *All About Shanghai*, op cit, p21.

3 Tess Johnson, *Welcome to Shanghai*, Old China Hand Press (Hong Kong), 1997, p118, Chinese Heritage Centre, Singapore. Population figures are never totally reliable. The significance of the numbers quoted here and subsequently is in the extraordinary influence that a very small group was able to wield over a vast urban population. Tess Johnson, an American writer and photographer living in Shanghai, has produced a series of remarkable books on colonial architecture in China

4 A rebellion in Northern China against most things Western, in which the protagonists used weaponless martial arts that Westerners called 'shadow boxing'.

5 Stella Dong, *Shanghai 1842–1942: The Rise and Fall of a Decadent City*, William Murrow, HarperCollins (New York), 2000, p89.

6 WH Auden/Christopher Isherwood, *Journey to a War*, Random House (New York), 1939, p246. They concluded with a peculiarly English detachment: 'And we ourselves, though we wear out our shoes walking the slums, though we take notes, though we are genuinely shocked and indignant, belong, inescapably to the other world. We return, always, to Number One House (the British Ambassador's private residence) for lunch.'

7 Dong, *Shanghai*, op cit, p173.

8 Ibid, p176 (from Personal Histories, 1969).

9 Ibid, pp176–8.

10 Ibid, p180.

11 Ibid, p182.

12 *The Evolution of Shanghai Architecture in Modern Times*, Shanghai Educational Publishers (Shanghai), 1999, p52

13 Ibid, p54.

14 Robert Grant Irving, *Indian Summer: Lutyens, Baker and Imperial Delhi*, Yale University Press (New Haven), 1981, p77.

15 *The Evolution of Shanghai Architecture*, op cit, p56.

16 Ibid, p241.

17 Chinese Heritage Centre, Singapore.

18 Lethbridge, *All About Shanghai*, op cit, p33.

19 See Harriet Sergeant, *Shanghai: Collision Point of Cultures 1918–1939*, John Murray (Edinburgh), 1999. No English writing on Shanghai since 1949 has so completely, through colourful and extensive interviews, evoked the expatriot life.

20 The Chinese have now not only accepted horseracing but in some postcolonial cities such as Hong Kong they have become obsessed with it.

21 Lethbridge, *All About Shanghai*, op cit, p xi.

22 Vicki Baum, *Shanghai '37*, Oxford University Press (Hong Kong), 1986 (first published in 1939 as *Hotel Shanghai* in the US and *Nanjing Road* in the UK).

23 Lethbridge, *All About Shanghai*, op cit, p76.

24 From *Anecdotes of Old Shanghai* reproduced in Tess Johnson's *Welcome to Shanghai*, Old China Hand Press (Hong Kong), 1997.

Surviving pockets of European realities; north and west along Nanjing Road, the Anglican Cathedral is just visible upper left.

Among the affluent *Li Long*, south of the Huaihai Road, the former girls' school that was the setting for the First National Congress of the Chinese Communist Party (CCP) is now a place of pilgrimage.

毛泽东遗物展
2001年6月18日-7月15日

文明单位
Model Unit
上海市人民政府颁发
Issued by
Shanghai Municipality

Life on the Bund, day and night, its embracing power essentially unchanged in a hundred years.

Top: The new walls and entry pavilions to the temple complex, which contain an entrance to the Shanghai Subway

Centre and below: The rituals within the old pavilions.

Above: Religious observance within the old pavilions.
Below: Demolition.

ARCHITECTURE BEFORE 1949

ZHENG SHILING

Shanghai, literally meaning 'on the sea', is a startling and remarkable city that has been given many imaginative names, such as 'the largest city in the Far East', 'the Paris of the East', 'the Whore of the Orient', 'the Queen of the Pacific', 'New York in the East', etc. In the course of its development, the city, which links the north and south domestically and the east and west internationally, has enjoyed certain advantages in its geographical location, economic conditions, culture and inhabitants that have led to its specific character. With its ability to compromise and to blend different cultures, it has become not only totally different from all other cities in China, but unique in the world.

In its prime during the 1930s and 1940s, Shanghai was China's most urbane conurbation, a metropolis that exhibited all the different hues of humanity. At that time, no other Asian city, not even Tokyo or Hong Kong, could match Shanghai's sophisticated cosmopolitanism. By 1936, it was the seventh largest city in the world, with a population of 3.81 million. The centre for new Chinese culture and modern architecture, it established itself as an important economic and cultural metropolis that has never been displaced by any other Chinese city.

Over the past 160 years, the history of Shanghai has closely echoed that of China itself. Shanghai has therefore been regarded as the key to understanding the modern history of China. It has certainly played a special role in that history.

Cities and the buildings in them are the crystallisation of the country's culture and history, and historical buildings are the most potent symbols of the city's spirit and expression of human civilisation. To some extent, historical buildings simultaneously represent the past, present and future of a city. There are few cities in the world with so many well-preserved and diverse historical buildings as Shanghai. The city's existing

architectural relics date back as early as AD 859, the year in which the Dhanari Column was built. The next oldest is the Mao Pagoda, created in 887–9 during the Tang Dynasty, followed by the Song Dynasty Xing-Sheng-Jiao Temple Pagoda (the Pagoda of the Rising Sacred Buddhist Temple, also known as the Square Pagoda, 1068–94) (Fig.1); the Yuan Dynasty Mosque (1341–68); and the Yu Yuan Gardens, built in 1559–77 by Pan Yunduan, a provincial governor of Sichuan and the son of a native of Shanghai, Pan En. In the late 18th century the gardens were annexed to the Temple of the City God and renamed Xi Yuan, the West Gardens. In the first half of the 19th century, they were used by certain guilds as a market place. A large artificial hill of yellow rock that ornaments

Figure 1: Xing-Sheng-Jiao Temple Pagoda, 1068–94

Opposite: Sincere Co. - one of the surviving monuments of prewar European commerce

the gardens is considered the masterpiece of Zhang Nanyang, a Ming Dynasty master of Chinese garden stonework and design.

Today, one can still find the old 19th-century 'go-down' warehouses within the territory of the former International Settlement (Fig. 2). At the turn of the century, Atkinson & Dallas, Ltd, Civil Engineers and Architects designed many such masonry structures in the Queen Anne style until they shifted to the Neoclassical style in the 1910s. All these historic buildings from throughout the centuries coexist with a wide range of 20th-century styles.

As early as the late Ming Dynasty, Western culture came to Shanghai as the result of religious dissemination (Fig. 3).

Before Shanghai was opened as one of the five Treaty Ports in November 1843, however, Shanghainese architecture was mostly a continuation of traditional architecture. Since then, over 150 years of change, the city has witnessed the incorporation, transformation and evolution of many different cultures, from Europe, America and Japan, which have coexisted with both its own culture and with various regional Chinese cultures; these now conflict with, accept and draw lessons from each other.

For Shanghai, the compulsory introduction of Western culture greatly shook thousands of years of feudal reign and ethics, bringing about a political, economic and cultural crisis. This longstanding and controversial mix of tradition and modernity, old and new, foreign and Chinese, good and bad, high and popular, has constituted the specific characteristics of Shanghai and is reflected not only in every aspect of life but also in the city and its architecture.

Most of the facilities of modern urban life were introduced to the concessions soon after the mid-19th century: banks (first introduced in 1848), Western-style roads (1856), gaslight (1865), electricity (1882), telephones (1881), running water (1884), automobiles (1901) and trams (1908). Thus by the beginning of the 20th century, the foreign concessions already boasted the infrastructure of a modern city, even by Western standards. By the 1930s, Shanghai was on a par with the major cities of the world.

Since the beginning of the 20th century, Shanghai has been a stage for international architects. Chinese architects educated in the West and their foreign counterparts co-operated and competed with each other in the construction of the city. The result was the introduction of a European architectural culture to China that broke with traditional architectural style and space, producing in the second half of the 19th century and the beginning of the 20th a large number of buildings that were both highly artistic and functional. Some of these reached an international standard, but were also original in the way in which they took into account the characteristics of Shanghai. This internationalisation is a reflection of the city's open sense of values and lifestyles.

At the prime of its development in the 1920s and 1930s, Shanghai's culture experienced severe political and social unrest. It seems never to have been free from civil wars and jostlings between different political forces, and has to a certain extent been shaped by war and cultural movement. The modern architecture of Shanghai was closely related to the development of the society and the city. The turbulent situation in

Above: Figure 2: Gibb Livingston & Co, 1908, Atkinson & Dallas, Ltd, Civil Engineers and Architects

Below: Figure 3: Paul Hsu Kuang-ch'i and Matteo Ricci

翁文宝公興味愚寶糖草圖

From above, left to right:

Figure 4: Residence of Sheng Xuanhuai, 1900, architect unknown

Figure 5: The Residence, 1905, architect unknown

Figure 6: The Banque de L'Indochine, 1910–11, Atkinson & Dallas, Civil Engineers and Architects, now Everbright Bank

Figure 7: China Mutual Life Insurance Company, 1910, Atkinson & Dallas, Civil Engineers and Architects

Figure 8: Shanghai Municipal Council Building, 1913–22, Palmer & Turner, now Shanghai Municipal Bureau

Figure 9: The China & South Sea Bank, 1917–21, Moorhead & Halse

Figure 10: Shanghai Post Office Building, 1924, Stewardson & Spence

Figure 11: Kincheng Bank, 1925–6, T Chuang, now Bank of Communication

Figure 12: Nanking Theatre, 1929–30, Robert Fan, now Shanghai Concert Hall

Left: Figure 13: St Ignatius Cathedral, 1910,
Dowdall & Co

Right: Figure 14: Hong De Tang Church, 1928,
architect unknown

China in the 1920s drew talented people from all parts of the country to the concessions in Shanghai, where life was relatively safe. As a result, Shanghai became the birthplace of contemporary Chinese literature, movies, music, fine arts and urban planning. The city was not only the place in which modern Chinese culture originated, however; it also saw the birth of modern industry, commerce and architecture, and was the cradle of the Chinese Communist Party in 1921.

In the modern period, architects tried to shape Shanghai into a classical city according to the Western pattern, aiming to replace traditional Chinese values with European and American ones. As a result, the buildings of modern Shanghai were dominated either by Western architectural culture and methodology or its imitation, utilising Western Neoclassicism, Gothic Revival and Modernism. In the late 1920s and 1930s, Shanghai was greatly influenced by the internationally popular Art Deco style, becoming one of its major centres. The American writer Tess Johnston noted that: 'Shanghai has the largest array of Art Deco edifices of any city in the world.'[1]

Therefore, Shanghai became a quasi replica of Western civilisation. However, different political, economic and cultural factors contributed to its multiple, complicated, colourful urban and architectural forms, thus cultivating a unique Shanghai culture that is simultaneously harmonious and dissonant, demonstrating both historical sediment and contemporary faults. Due to the lack of historical background, Western architectural culture has been greatly deformed in Shanghai. Even the buildings designed by Western architects were mostly an eclectic transplantation and variation of Western architecture. This eclecticism was the inevitable outcome of a semi-colonial, semi-feudal society in which property owners and designers varied in their ability to appreciate and design, and wide differences existed in social lifestyles as well as technological and economic conditions. Having undergone a process that ranged from imitation to producing varieties, Shanghai's buildings have become a harmonious and contradictory part of the urban

environment. Some of these buildings are outstanding, whether Chinese or foreign.[2] Others are more mediocre. In the 1930s, the city became like a vast international exhibition of architecture.

The representative buildings of the European Neoclassical style are: Residence of Sheng Xuanhuai, 1900 (Fig. 4), Residence of the Director of la Compagnie Française des Tramways et d'Eclairage Electriques de Shanghai, 1905 (Fig. 5), the Banque de L'Indochine, 1910–11 (Fig. 6), China Mutual Life Insurance Company, 1910 (Fig. 7), Shanghai Municipal Council Building, 1913–22 (Fig. 8), The China & South Sea Bank, 1917–21 (Fig. 9), Shanghai Post Office Building, 1924 (Fig. 10), Kincheng Bank, 1925–6 (Fig. 11), Nanking Theatre, 1929–30 (Fig. 12).

Typical Gothic Revival buildings are: The Commercial Bank of China (1893), and St Ignatius Cathedral (Fig. 13).

Examples of traditional Chinese architectural form are: Hong De Tang Church, 1928 (Fig. 14), the Shanghai Special Municipal Government Building, 1931–3, the YMCA Building, 1929–31 and some commercial buildings with traditional Chinese decoration.

Representative buildings of eclectic style are the Mercantile Bank of India, London & China, 1913–16 (Fig. 15), the Residence of Wang Boqun, 1934 (Fig. 16), and Moller House, 1936 (Fig. 17).

Art Deco buildings, to name just a few, include Sassoon House, 1926–9 (Fig. 18), Cathay Mansions, 1925–9 (Fig. 19), Shanghai Power Company, 1929–31 (Fig. 20), Astrid Apartments, 1933, Grosvenor House, 1934–5 (Fig. 21). Some Art Deco buildings incorporated a Spanish style, for example the Haig Court, 1925–34, Cosmopolitan Apartments, 1934 (Fig. 22), and many apartment buildings in the Western part of Shanghai.

Typical buildings in the Modern Style are: Park Hotel, 1931–4, Broadway Mansions, 1934 (Fig. 23), the Grand Theatre, 1938 (Fig. 24), Picardie Apartments, 1934–5 (Fig. 25), the Residence of DV Wood, 1935–7 (Fig. 26) and many other garden residences. The Czechoslovakian architect Ladislaus Hudec played an important role in modern

From above, left to right:

Figure 15: The Mercantile Bank of India, London & China, 1913–16, Palmer & Turner

Figure 16: Residence of Wang Boqun, 1934, Liu Shiying, now the Children's Palace of Changning District

Figure 17: Moller House, 1936, architect unknown, now the headquarters of Henshan Groups

Figure 18: Sassoon House, 1926–9, Palmer & Turner, Architects and Surveyors, now Peace Hotel

Figure 19: Cathay Mansions, 1925–9, Algar & Co, Architects

Figure 20: Shanghai Power Company, 1929–31, Elliott Hazzard

Figure 21: Grosvenor House, 1934–5, now Jingjiang Hotel, Palmer & Turner, Architects and Surveyors

Figure 22: Cosmopolitan Apartments, 1934, Poy Gum Lee

Figure 23: Broadway Mansions, 1934, Freizer and Palmer & Turner, Architects and Surveyors, now Shanghai Mansions

From above left to right:

Figure 24: The Grand Theatre, 1931-33, Ladislaus Hudec

Figure 25: Picardie Apartments, 1934–5, Ledreux, Minutti & Co, now Hengshan Hotel

Figure 26: Residence of DV Wood, 1935–7, Ladislaus Hudec, now the Shanghai Urban Planning & Design Institute

Figure 27: The Sassoon House under construction, 1932, Palmer & Turner

Figure 28: The prosperous commercial centre of Shanghai

Figure 29: Terraced houses

Figures 30-31: Garden residences

Figure 32: Sassoon Villa, 1932, Palmer & Turner

Shanghainese architecture. There are more than 60 buildings designed by him in the city, and most of them could be classified as masterpieces. His architectural style covered a vast area including Neoclassicism, country style, the Modern Style and Art Deco.

In 1927, the Shanghai Architects Institute was founded, becoming the Architects Institute of China the following year. The first issue of the periodical *Chinese Architecture* was published in November 1931, followed by the monthly *Architecture* in November 1932. In April 1936, the first Chinese Architecture Exhibition was held in Shanghai. Since then, leading architects in Shanghai have made great efforts to promote a revival of traditional Chinese architecture and initiated Chinese Neoclassicism, which aimed to revive traditional Chinese architecture.

By the end of the 19th century, Shanghai had become the centre of construction technology in the Far East. Composite, reinforced concrete, and steel structures were brought into use, leading to the appearance of high-rise buildings. By 1949, there were 38 buildings of more than ten floors in Shanghai, more than any other city in Asia. Many buildings demonstrated an advanced construction technology, and the appearance of new building types and the application of new building materials and technology had a great impact on the architecture of Shanghai (Fig. 27).

Shanghai's modern buildings embraced nearly every conceivable building type, including residences, apartments, villas, department stores, office buildings, banks, schools, hospitals, recreation grounds, cinemas, railway stations, post offices, hostels, libraries, museums, clubs, stadiums, churches, factories, public utilities and gardens. These buildings have always been related to significant historical events and figures. Some have illustrated social and economic history; some display the progress of technology; some have important historical value in terms of urban planning; some are unique in typological meaning; some represent the Shanghainese culture; some are prototypes in the history of architecture; some are designed by famous architects both from home and abroad; some are landmarks of modern Shanghai: all are graded and preserved according to their historical and artistic value.

In 1986, Shanghai was designated the National Historical City by the State Council, and the preservation of its buildings was laid down in 'The Preservation Plan for the Historic City of Shanghai'. The buildings were classified according to their historical, artistic and scientific value. This includes 13 cultural relics for preservation at state level, five of which are related to modern architecture, namely the former residence of Sun Yatsen on Xiangshan Road; the former site of the Central Committee of Chinese Socialist Youth League; the site of the First NPC of the Chinese Communist Party; the group of buildings on the Bund; and Shanghai Post Office. At city level, 113 cultural relics were cited for preservation, 37 of which are modern buildings. Also listed for preservation are 398 Modern Style buildings. Besides these, there are 82 cultural relics for preservation at district or county-level; 15 sites of ancient cultural relics for preservation; and 21 memorial sites. The Preservation Plan for the Historic City of Shanghai covers 234 complete blocks of 22 historical areas and 440 building groups. The whole land area is about 13.85 square kilometres, with buildings occupying 10 million square metres.

The range of the preservation of historic buildings is constantly widening. Eleven categories for the preservation of historical styles and features have been set up: Excellent Buildings of Modern Times at the Bund; Revolutionary Historical Sites on Si Nan Road (the former Rue Massenet); the Old City of Shanghai; Excellent Buildings of Modern Times around the People's Square; Excellent Buildings of Modern Times on Mao Ming Road (the former Route Mercier); the Metropolitan Planning Area of the 1930s in Jiangwan; Modern Commercial Culture of Shanghai; Garden Residence of Shanghai; Longhua Cemetery of Martyrs; Longhua Temple; Modern Residence Buildings in Hongkou District; and Country Villas on Hongqiao Road. Work is also being done to preserve the terraced and *li long* houses in Shanghai.

The modern commercial culture of Shanghai is mainly represented by the story of the East Nanjing Road. Modernisation of commercial buildings started in Shanghai following the completion of the Sincere Company in 1917. The East Nanjing Road had already become the most prosperous of Shanghai's commercial areas (Fig. 28). The Sun Company Department Store (1934–6) is the highlight of modern commercial activities.

The Revolutionary Historical Sites on Si Nan Road, the Garden Residences of Shanghai, the Modern Residence Buildings in Hongkou District, and the Country Villas on Hongqiao Road are characteristic of lane residences, garden-lane residences, detached residences and country villas, which are the mainstay of Shanghai's modern architecture. These were designed by architects such as Atkinson & Dallas, Civil Engineers and Architects, Ledreux, Minutti & Co, Algar & Co, architects Ladislaus Hudec, T Chuang, Robert Fan, Dayu Doon and others. The colourful regional styles of Shanghai's modern architecture are also reflected in these residential buildings. The residence of Chen Guichun (1925) is a typical traditional courtyard house of south China.

The *li long* and terraced houses, covering an area of 23 million square metres, demonstrate the unique building styles that came into being during the urbanisation and commercialisation of Shanghai. They resulted from the blending of Chinese and Western architectural forms and lifestyles. Concrete, brick and stone were used decoratively

Figure 33: The Hong Kong and Shanghai Bank Corporation Building, 1921–1923, renovated in 1999 by Palmer & Turner, Architects and Surveyors

to imitate the Western neoclassical pattern. *Li long* houses that imitated the European town house turned up in the 1870s. The structure and building materials of the early *li long* houses were essentially traditional. Subsequently, they underwent a series of shifts to the new-style *li long* house and finally to the terraced house, which gradually became increasingly Westernised and modern (Fig. 29-31). In southwest Shanghai, there are also many villas (Fig. 32).

The current functional replacement of the buildings on the Bund has opened a new chapter: the renewal of historic buildings. The renovation of the former Hong Kong and Shanghai Bank Corporation Building (1921–1923) in 1999 is a good example, allowing for the recognition of the value of Shanghai's architectural heritage (Fig. 33). The former Yokohama Specie Bank of Shanghai (1923–4) was also renovated in 2000 (Figs. 34-35). The Shanghai Art Gallery (Spence, Robinson & Partners), is a renewal of the former Shanghai Hippodrome Building of 1933.

In order to develop the historical cultural line, Shanghai has laid plans to preserve and make use of the historical buildings and districts with special styles and features. However, these have been neglected in the past, when the city's development and construction focused instead on novelty and change. The government could not provide any overall control or guaranteed system to carry out research on historical buildings. Developers tended to seek quick success and instant benefits. Many buildings with first-class design and construction were pulled down. Fashionable but mediocre buildings were built to replace those of great historical and cultural value that had given the city its identity. Some buildings were badly damaged through misuse or change of function. Billboards, air-conditioners, shop signs and some random constructions destroyed the appearance of the buildings and the landscape of the neighbouring areas. Some new buildings constructed in the historical area are not co-ordinated with the old buildings. With the destruction and disappearance of some of these historic buildings, people have become aware of the seriousness of the situation and set about taking measures to prevent this.

Many cities in the world are currently trying to cultivate their city's culture, and have paid special attention to the development of multiculturalism. As a historic cultural city, which has created over the centuries its own unique and glorious culture, Shanghai needs to make full use of its historical and humanistic advantages to optimise the urban environment. Its excellent historical buildings need to be protected while the large-scale development is being carried out. Efforts will also be made to improve awareness of preservation. In the course of urban development, these buildings need to be taken into consideration in urban planning, in order to maintain the identity of the city and preserve its historic buildings.

History and time have created the city of Shanghai. Its construction has involved the painstaking efforts of people for generations. Its historic buildings are the treasures of Shanghai and the Shanghai people, as well as the main artery of the city. The task of Shanghai for the future is not only to build a new Shanghai, but also to preserve the historic one. As a city boasting both the sedimentary accretion of history and the glory of the present, there is great potential for a splendid future.

Notes

1 Tess Johnston, *A Last Look*, p70.

2 Among the modern Chinese architects were T Chuang, Guan Songsheng, Robert Fan, Liu Shiying, Huang Jiahua, Liu Dunzhen, Chao Shen, Dayu Doon, Yang Xiqiu, Chuin Tung, Poy Gum Lee, Yang Tingbao, Chih Chen, Xi Fuquan , Tan Yuan, HS Luke, Wu Jingxiang, Wang Dingzeng. Foreign practitioners included the English architects Gabriel J Morrison, Henry Lester, John Smedley, Brenan Atkinson, Albert E Algar, Robert B Moorhead, RE Stewardson, Gilbert Davies, Palmer & Turner, the German architect Heinrich Becker, the American architect Elliot Hazzard, the Czech architects Ladislaus Hudec and CH Gonda, the French architects Alaxandre Leonard and Paul Veysseyre, and the Japanese architects Hirano and Fukui.

Opposite and below:

Figures 34-35: Yokohama Specie Bank of Shanghai, 1923–4, Palmer & Turner, Architects and Surveyors, renovated in 2000

JAPANESE OCCUPATION

ALAN BALFOUR

An English view of Shanghai immediately after the Japanese invasion provides yet another collage of Shanghai sensations:

Seen from the river, towering above their couchant guardian warships, the semi-skyscrapers of the Bund present, impressively, the facade of a great city. But it is only a facade. The spirit that dumped them upon this unhealthy mud-bank, thousands of miles from their kind, has been too purely and brutally competitive. The biggest animals have pushed their way down to the brink of the water; behind them is a sordid and shabby mob of smaller buildings. Nowhere a fine avenue, a spacious park, an imposing central square. Nowhere anything civic at all.

Nevertheless the tired or lustful businessman will find here everything to gratify his desires. You can buy an electric razor, or a French dinner, or a well-cut suit. You can dance at the Tower Restaurant on the roof of the Cathay Hotel, and gossip with Teddy Kaufman, its charming manager, about the European aristocracy or pre-Hitler Berlin. You can attend race-meetings, baseball games, football matches. You can see the latest American films. If you want girls, or boys, you can have them, at all prices, in the bathhouses and the brothels. If you want opium you can smoke it in the best company, served on a tray, like afternoon tea. Good wine is difficult to obtain in this climate but there is enough whisky and gin to float a fleet of battleships. The jeweller and the antique dealer await your orders, and their charges will make you imagine yourself back on Fifth Avenue or in Bond Street. Finally, if you ever repent, there are churches and chapels of all denominations.[1]

The two young but celebrated writers, the poet WH Auden and novelist Christopher Isherwood, had gone to China explicitly, and with considerable publicity in England, to experience the war with Japan. In 1928, increasing Japanese military intrusion into Manchuria led the Chinese warlords to side with the Nationalist Government. The Nationalists faced threats on three fronts: Japanese military activity in Manchuria, large areas in the west and north still under the control of warlords, and an undeclared state of war with the Communists in the south. Though the Japanese clearly posed the most serious military threat, Chiang Kai-shek still saw Communism as a major enemy and launched a campaign against their headquarters in south Central China. This he renewed every year in the following five years, with no resolution and little effect.

Japan invaded Manchuria in 1931. Recognising that his forces were no match for the Japanese army, Chiang withdrew from any attempt to confront the invasion. In 1932, Manchuria became a puppet state of Japan. The deposed Henry Pu-yi was renamed emperor, and the Japanese immediately began preparations for the invasion of China.

In Shanghai, the Japanese were agitating for more influence on the Municipal Council. The people reacted to the invasion of Manchuria by boycotting all Japanese goods and trade. Japanese foods and products were removed from the stores, Japanese businesses avoided, dockers refused to unload cargo from Japan, and even passenger ships were prevented from disembarking. Violence erupted in June, when a crowd attacked a group of five Japanese monks, members of a militant sect.[2] The monks had been deliberately sent into the working-class district of Chapei to provoke an incident. In the fighting, one of the monks died and two were injured. Under threat of military action, the Japanese authorities demanded the arrest of those responsible and the break-up of all anti-Japanese organisations. The city administrator accepted all these terms, but it soon became clear that it was a pretext to justify military action in the city. Again, Chiang Kai-shek sought to avoid confrontation with the Japanese. However, the 19th Route Army, an intensely patriotic faction of the Nationalist Army based outside Shanghai's north station at the edge of Chapei, refused to accept Japanese aggression and confronted the Japanese army. In response, the Japanese subjected the district to five weeks of intense and continual bombardment, levelling all the buildings and industrial infrastructure. This Japanese action in Shanghai in 1932 marked the first time a civilian population had been subject to large-scale and indiscriminate bombing. Some 10,000 civilians died in the conflict, far more than the total military casualties, and hundreds of thousands sought protection in the foreign settlements. Only intense pressure from the international community forced an end to the conflict, with the Japanese agreeing to remove all troops from the city except those in its garrison units, and the Nationalists agreeing to keep their forces outside a 30-mile limit around the city.

This unprecedented demonstration of high-tech aerial bombing on an undefended urban area was watched by the largest concentration of the world's press east of Suez. Yet moves to enact sanctions against Japan had little effect. Within months, Chapei was being rebuilt and the residents in the foreign settlement plunged happily into enlarging and enriching their fantasy city. Hotels, apartment buildings, department stores and spectacular cinemas all formed in a giddy exuberant Art Deco, as if nothing could harm their way of life. Between 1933 and 1937 the streets around the racetrack matched the *moderne* veneer with a round of entertainments and diversions. This fantasy island of foreign culture, floating in the middle of a deeply troubled nation, was always secure in the power of the parent nations. Certainly the great British Empire would protect its inhabitants.

The state of war that existed between the Nationalists and the Communists was driven by an intense hatred that blinded both sides to the threats of Japanese invasion. In 1934, in the final and most violent campaign, the Nationalists made an all-out attack on the Communist forces. This resulted in the legendary Long March, the year-long journey that took the CCP leadership and their closest supporters into the mountains of Ya'an in Shanxi Province. The march was led by the young Mao Zedong and Zhou Enlai, and the military commander, Zhu De, who was later to lead the forces that defeated the Nationalists in 1949.

In 1936, in a bizarre display of instability, Chiang Kai-shek was kidnapped in Xi'an by a former Manchurian warlord, whom he had gone to rebuke for failing to punish the Communists.[3] His release was secured only after he had agreed to form a united front with the Communists to confront Japanese aggression. Six months later, using the pretext of the kidnapping of a Japanese soldier, the Japanese invaded China, seizing Beijing and Tianjin by the end of the year.

In Shanghai, the Japanese doubled the size of the landing parties, evacuated the civilians and declared authority over all parts of the foreign settlement. In response, Chiang sent the 87th and the 88th Divisions of the Nationalist Army into the Shanghai area. The Japanese replied by sending a fleet of 26 warships down the Huangpu, and anchored the cruiser *Idzumo* at the foot of Nanjing Road, immediately across from the Cathay Hotel.

Sporadic gunfire on the morning of 14 August created immediate and widespread panic. Fearing a repeat of the aerial bombing of 1932, tens of thousands of people from across the city moved to seek refuge in the settlements. Entry was sought into the foreign city by the only open crossing, the Garden Bridge across Suzhou Creek, north of the Bund. By midday, a frightened mass of people in a line 10 miles long, was slowly flowing in across the bridge onto the Bund. Many slipped and fell, to be crushed by the crowd. Panic on the ground was matched by a dreadful error in the air. In the morning, Chinese aircraft had tried to sink the Japanese cruiser, but failed. In the late afternoon they returned to try again. One pilot, it was later claimed, while manoeuvring out of the reach of the cruiser's guns, released his bombs prematurely. Two fell, one in front of the Cathay Hotel, the other through the roof of the adjoining Palace Hotel, onto the mass of refugees streaming down from the Garden Bridge, refugees who believed they would be safe in the settlement. Within seconds, 729 people died and 861 were wounded. And on this most unlucky of days another inexperienced Chinese pilot panicked and dropped two more bombs on the French settlement close to the New World, killing 1,011 Chinese and foreigners and injuring 570. Two pilots' mistakes and four bombs produced the worst civilian carnage in modern warfare up to that time.

In 1937 Japanese forces moving across a wide front quickly captured the North China Plain. The Japanese deployed a combined military force of more than 200,000 to win the battle for Shanghai. Three and a half Japanese divisions made an amphibious landing east of the city on Hangzhou Bay on 5 November 1937 and the Japanese Air Force began an indiscriminate bombardment of the city. A report ran as follows:

TWO HUNDRED REFUGEES KILLED IN RAID ON SOUTH STATION
Japanese Bombers Litter Nantao Streets
With Death and Destruction
Chinese Deny any Soldiers in Area

Shanghai's civilian casualties mounted considerably yesterday when Japanese bombers raided densely populated Nantao, littering the South Railway Station area with death and destruction. According to a conservative estimate, well over 200 persons, most of whom were refugees, were killed or wounded. The list is by no means complete, as the over-worked hospital authorities in the Chinese city, French Concession and the Settlement were checking the number of cases last night.

The death-dealing mission was composed of 12 Japanese planes at about 1:45 p.m. Leisurely circling over the South Station sector, the raiders dropped no less than eight bombs, most of which exploded.

Crowded with over 1,000 refugees, most of whom were women and children, the station was worst hit. Other places where missiles exploded were Kuo Ho Road (Native Goods Road), two blocks to the north of the station; San Kuan Tang Street, and Loh Ka Pang area.

Altogether four bombs landed around the station. As the airplanes finally left the scene, dense smoke shot up high into the sky, while on the platforms and tracks were scattered charred and badly mutilated bodies.

The first bomb exploded a short distance from the station, wrecking a water tower close to the tracks. Many fell, killed by shrapnel outright or pinned down by debris. As wounded persons ran for shelter, a second one descended, tearing down an overhead bridge and damaging a section of tracks. Blood and wreckage strewed the immediate vicinity. At the same time, terror reigned in streets close by as additional missiles exploded one after another.

The South Railway Station has been the gathering place for refugees seeking transportation to the interior ever since the outbreak of hostilities two weeks ago. Many of those killed yesterday were known to have been patiently waiting accommodation in Hang-chow-bound trains during the past two or three days.

The bombardment of Nantao evoked the bitterest denunciation from the Chinese military spokesman at the daily press conference yesterday afternoon.

Japanese allegation that the station was bombed 'because it was used for the transportation of Chinese units from the south' was most emphatically refuted. The spokesman stated that not a single soldier could be found anywhere in Nantao yesterday or recently.

Nantao is a densely populated city and entirely devoid of Chinese troops or military positions, he said. It was pointless for the Japanese to justify their attack by alleged intentions to 'harass Chinese military positions'.

The spokesman was at a loss to understand the wanton destruction of Chinese civilian lives. He said it was perhaps aimed at terrorising the Chinese populace, or else as a retaliation for the loss of Japanese lives in Hongkew during the hostilities. He emphasised that no warning of the raid had been given by the Japanese.[4]

In this month, November 1937, the Japanese military committed acts of animal ferocity, abusing, maiming and killing thousands of the civilian population in the rape of Nanjing. The only explanation for these unforgivable acts is that the Japanese, careful students of history, applied the lessons from the Manchurian massacres at the foundation of the Qing Dynasty, believing that a brutal demonstration of force would break the spirit of the Chinese.

In Shanghai, to protect their rear, the retreating Nationalist Army set fire to Chapei, which greatly added to the sense of despair across the city. Both armies, however, avoided the international settlement. Immediately the Japanese had control of the city they began stripping all its assets, material and industrial. Every piece of metal that could be removed was taken; rails were ripped up, buildings dismantled, and every usable scrap of material was shipped back to Japan to feed the war machine:

As early as October 1937 one could observe at Shanghai uniformed Japanese soldiers and Chinese labourers, most of them impressed workers, removing in a wholesale manner property consisting mainly of metals. In almost every case the property was loaded onto Japanese Army trucks and taken to Japanese controlled wharves along the Whangpoo River, where it was subsequently shipped to Japan on military transports. What property escaped damage from military operations was completely looted after the battle lines had left Shanghai.[5]

At this time, the Japanese assumed administrative control of the Chinese city and dominated the Shanghai Municipal Council. On 8 December the Council gave permission for a Japanese victory parade to be held on Nanjing Road. A grenade, thrown at the marchers, killed four soldiers, an act that the Japanese would not forget. By the end of 1939, Japan controlled more than half of the population and the landmass of China, and their Government of Occupation stretched from Manchuria to the Chinese border with Vietnam.

In Shanghai, refugees continued to pour into the settlements and were leaving just as quickly, whenever and however possible, travelling back to towns and villages in safer parts of China. In the months following the Japanese invasion, 350,000 people were reported as leaving on steamers travelling inland. Many of the foreign residents decided it was also time for them to leave.

Isherwood and Auden were in and around the city in the spring of 1938, approaching as close to the action as possible without getting hurt. This strange note conveys the atmosphere of suspended reality in the foreign concession after such massive destruction and loss of life:

It is the Ambassador's turn to give an official garden-party. The preparations are elaborate. They require the co-operation of the ladies of the British colony, the Seaforth Highlanders, the Embassy staff. Invitations are sent out. The drinks and cold buffet are organised. The portico is decorated with flags. Bowing deeply the doll-butlers usher in their national enemies, the bandy legged, hissing Japanese generals. Everyone is present including the journalists. Next morning, the local newspaper will carry photographs of the most distinguished guests. Out on the lawn, the Scottish pipers play their airs.

Everything goes off like clockwork. It is a beautifully contrived charade, the perfect image of another kind of life projected, at considerable expense, from its source on the opposite side of the earth. . .

But gaily as the charade-players laugh, and loudly as they chatter, they cannot altogether ignore those other, most undiplomatic sounds which reach us, at intervals, from beyond the garden trees. Somewhere, out in the suburbs, machine-guns are rattling. You can hear them all day long. Everyone in the settlement knows what they mean – the Chinese guerrilla units are still active here in the enemy's stronghold. If you are so tactless as to call the attention of the Japanese officers to these noises they will reply that you are mistaken – it is only their own troops at firing practice.[6]

A garden party on the lawns of a great public building in the midst, seemingly, of a powerful city; but rising above it, inexplicably, is the sense that this fragment of a city lies in a sea of destruction. Isherwood and Auden again:

The International Settlement and the French Concession form an island, an oasis in the midst of the stark, frightful wilderness which was once the Chinese city. Your car crosses the Soochow Creek: on one side are streets and houses, swarming with life; on the other is a cratered and barren moon-landscape, intersected by empty, clean-swept roads. Here and there a Japanese sentry stands on guard, or a party of soldiers hunts among the ruins for scrap-iron. Further out, the buildings are not so badly damaged, but every Chinese or foreign property has been looted and no kind of wild animal could have made half the mess.[7]

Despite being beset by such horrendous events, the foreign city returned to normal with unseemly speed. But this normality was unsettled the following year with the influx of thousands of Jewish refugees, first from Germany, then from Austria and Poland. Their arrival was the product of a dreadful realisation through trial and rejection that Shanghai was the only major commercial city in the world that did not require visas and had not been coerced into closing its borders to Jews. (The most travelled path began with the train to Genoa then passage on the Italian Lloyd Triestina Line.) Persecution followed at every step. They were limited in what they could bring out of the country, and forced to pay extortionate fares; most arrived with nothing. Yet with the support of the international community led by Jewish people of Shanghai most settled and found work within a few months, and they kept coming. In these years the foreign population of Shanghai soared, from 36,000 in 1930 to 150,000 in 1942;[8] almost all of this increase was due to refugees from Europe who had become stateless.

On 8 December 1941, at the exact time of the bombing of Pearl Harbor, US and British gun ships were attacked on the Huangpu River, their crews rounded up and imprisoned. Diplomats from the Allied countries were arrested and taken *en masse* to the Cathay Apartment Building in the French concession. Key members of the city administration were summoned to the Shanghai Municipal Building and told that the foreign city was now wholly under Japanese control. By August 1943 a Japanese puppet government formed the first administration for a unified Shanghai.

The Japanese administration was greatly helped by the support of Wang Jingwei, once the political equal of Chiang Kai-shek in the Kuomintang, who had been head of the Nationalist Government from 1932–5 while Chiang waged war against the Communists. It was Wang who had been most outspoken in calling for an alliance between the Kuomintang and the Communists. And it was Wang, after defecting to the Japanese, who was made puppet head of the Japanese-installed Nationalist Government in 1940. He remains for some a brave yet tragic figure whose defection to the Japanese can only be explained as expedient.

From the beginning of the 20th century the Japanese held equal power and influence in foreign Shanghai with the British and Americans, and dominated the Municipal Council before the invasion. Once in control of the city they began a programme of vigorous demoralisation, actively corrupting all aspects of city life. The Japanese opened clubs in the exclusive residential areas at the edges of the foreign settlement, converting the grand houses on their elegant lawns. These were districts in which the laws of the settlement applied to the roads but not to the adjoining property. Wang was rumoured to be the owner of a property on Yuyuen Road whose elegant rooms and garden pavilions were turned into brothels, opium dens and gambling halls,[9] but this may have been a smear designed to ensure that his reputation never

recovered. The Japanese consciously exploited the libertarian mood of the city, making all vices freely and widely available, destroying the surface of propriety that kept settlement life civil. They cynically manipulated the city's puppet administration to weaken the will of the Shanghainese with drugs, gambling and the illusion of entering the foreigner's way of life, corrupting the people as the British had done a century before. This time, however, the Japanese drew the foreigners themselves into the corruption. This once-exclusive district with the appearance of the most prosperous suburbs of London and New York, large villas sitting amid extensive landscaped grounds behind high walls, was slowly fractured as an increasing number of villas advertised their new role with bright neon signs at the entrance, their pavilions floodlit, their grounds turned into parking lots.

Shanghai's city plan was under reconsideration from the beginning of the Japanese administration in 1937. The city would become a central instrument of Japan's 'Asian Co-prosperity Sphere'. These plans, however, provide evidence of the difficulties of using the city as an instrument and an engine of power; difficulties that are much more metaphysical than irrational.[10] In the first reconsideration, the Nationalist plan and the plan for New Delhi were refined to accommodate a more Japanese order (Figs. 1, 2). The major axis was moved east–west and the city would be embellished with extensive parks.

With the Japanese firmly in control of the city, an ideas competition was held to prepare a master plan for Japanese Shanghai. The results were merely the ambitious speculation (both for themselves and for the Empire) of young planners, but they offer an intriguing window onto the ambitions of the time. The goals of Adolph Hitler, the Japanese emperor's ally in war, must have been on the minds of the Japanese architects (Fig. 3). Hitler was as obsessed with transforming Berlin into the new Rome as he was with winning the war; in rebuilding Berlin he believed he would restore to Germany the leadership of the Holy Roman Empire. Japanese ambition was certainly the equal of Germany's, and it is possible to see this as an imaginative exercise in developing ideas that could rival the new Berlin. Although Japan had established its presence in many of its colonies with an Asian interpretation of Roman Classicism, this was not the favoured concept for Shanghai. The project placed second in the competition was inspired by the most heroic architect of another of Germany's allies, Vichy France. The Japanese team, led by the celebrated pre-war master Maekawa Kunio, applied to Shanghai the modernist visions of the Swiss-French architect Charles-Edouard Jeanneret, also known as Le Corbusier, 'the Crow'. The Japanese had no need to diminish the foreign city since all was now under Japanese control, and it had been partly Japanese for half a century. Instead, they chose to perfect it by destroying virtually the whole of the British sector. The plan carefully leaves the French quarter intact, but removes all buildings at the centre of the former British settlement north to Nanjing Road and west well beyond the racetrack.

This vast, ordered field would be laid out with all the elements of Corbusier's utopian vision: homogeneous, rational, utterly authoritarian. Its great axis crossing the river into Pudong created two symbolic

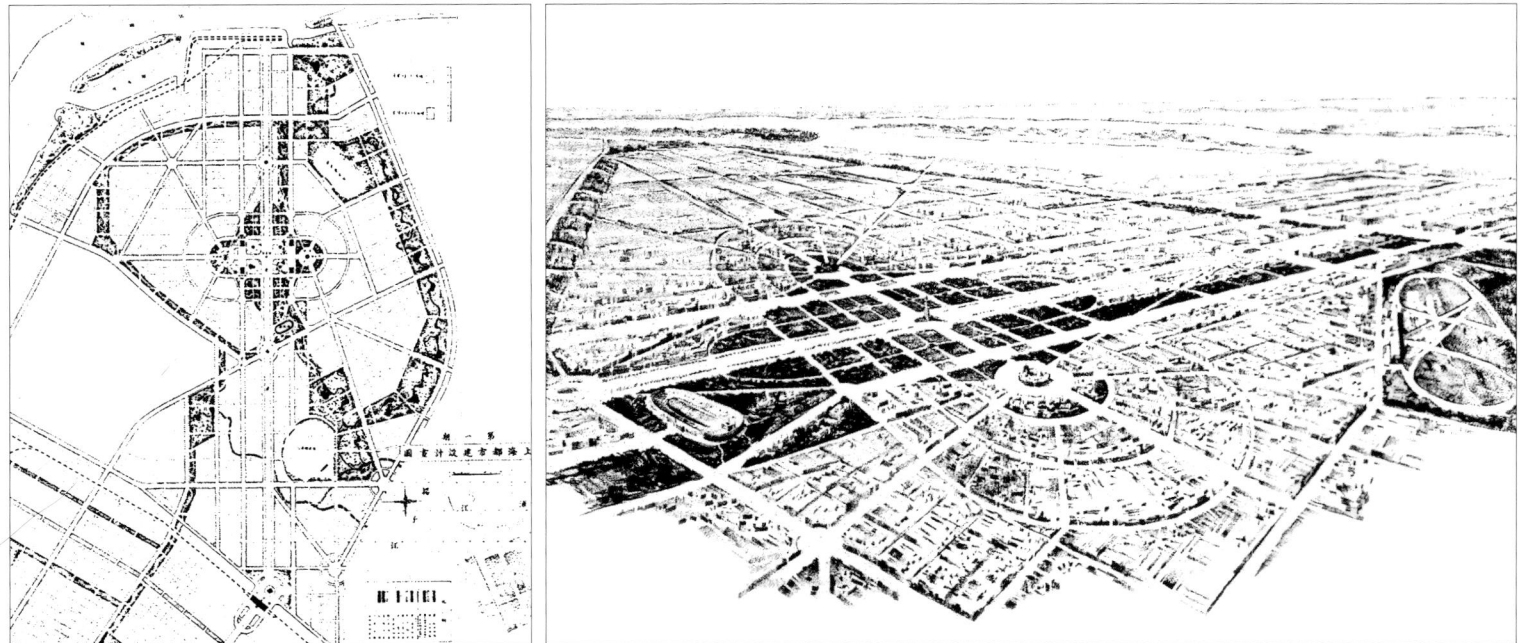

Figures 1, 2: City Planning under Japanese Administration develops the 'Big City Plan'

centres: in the west, the imperial administration; in the east across the river, a complex of buildings celebrating Japanese and Asian culture. The path to the heart of the imperial administration wends through a succession of landscaped squares enclosed by a regular wall of buildings, leading to a grand square behind which is what appears to be the seat of power. The plan is immediately reminiscent of Tiananmen Square and the Forbidden Palace in Beijing, differing only in lying on an east–west axis rather than north–south. Across the river, the long-neglected district of Pudong would be demolished. The great axis from the palace in the west continues across the river, climaxing in the vast public forum holding at its centre – and here the evidence is unclear – what appears to be an enlargement of Corbusier's proposal of 1929 for a Mundaneum – a world museum. Corbusier conceived this project for Geneva to celebrate the establishment of the League of Nations and to commemorate, in 1930, 'Ten years of efforts towards peace and collaboration among nations'[11] (Fig. 4). Extrapolating from Geneva it appears that Congress Hall, a world library and centre for international studies would surround the world museum. However, whereas Geneva would have been a place of unifying congress between all the nations of the world, those assembled in the new Shanghai would be constituents of the Japanese Pan Asian Empire. To the south would be extensive recreation areas and to the east, though not in the League of Nations plan, but certainly consistent with the Le Corbusier vision, a great airport would be laid out. Again, though none of this came from the hand of Le Corbusier, it was clearly formed in the imagination of those who had closely studied his work and who believed in the appropriateness of his vision to a highly autocratic imperial machine/regime. Given that the visions of Le Corbusier had such an influence, often destructive, on 20th-century architecture and planning, this appropriateness of his vision to an imperial dictatorship is revealing.

What does this mean in the context of this plan of Shanghai? It seems to be evidence of French complicity. As Vichy France had capitulated to Germany, the French settlement would have been viewed as an ally of Tokyo. Taking a lesson from their German comrades, the Japanese began to constrain the movement of foreign nationals from hostile countries.

By December 1943 they were forced to wear armbands whenever they appeared in public: B for British, A for American and N for Dutch. The French, however, suffered no such constraints.[12] The planners would have seen in the city evidence of the magnitude of ambition as Britain, Germany and Japan struggled to maintain or achieve world domination. (The United States was a much more shadowy presence.) Such plans as these can be viewed as reflections of desire, and to some degree, of madness. In its scale and drama this modernist vision for Shanghai was a powerful rival to Hitler's new Berlin. All that is lacking is the Great Hall. However, it should be noted that the idea of a single structure that physically contained the idea of omnipotence and omniscience had and has no place within the Asian imagination; there is no pantheon in the Asian mind. But in all other respects this is a French concept, a French view of the world that the Japanese would have willingly inhabited. The Japanese in all their imperial practice over the preceding century had shown an acute concern with the symbolism in the structure and order of buildings. In Seoul, Korea, they confirmed their grip on the city by building a vast prison-like museum across the ceremonial path to the royal palace, blocking the view and demeaning the authority of the royal family. After decades of anguish it became such a political issue in the 1980s that an election was won partly on the commitment to demolish this remnant of Japanese colonialism.

As time passes, the principal significance of such documents lies in what they reveal about ambition at a particular moment in time. So here were the French, or those who took a strong pleasure in French culture, providing a rationalist modern mask of reality for a brutal imperial machine committed to the total subjugation of Asia, a reality that at the end of the war could make the actions of the victors more palatable, worldly and progressive. And with a world divided between Japan and Germany, Shanghai would symbolise a progressive Japan against the history-burdened vision of the Germans – now rivals for the domination of the world. To the outrage of Germany, France positioned itself as the intellectual adviser to Japanese ambition; in the eventual triumph of Japan over all the world, France would maintain its rightful position of intellectual leadership.

But what of Tokyo in all this? Japan had long admired Britain's imperial effectiveness. It had controlled, among much else, both the financial capital of China and the trading capital of British Hong Kong from a small island half a world away. The Japanese would not have begun to consider transforming Shanghai in such an epic fashion were such plans not directly related to imperial ambition. Might this not suggest that Shanghai was briefly seen as the power centre of Japanese Asia? The Chrysanthemum Emperor shed the criticism of being xenophobic and racist and in one spectacular move, with French help, consolidated his power in Asia's most powerful commercial city; a city that had already seen the most effective fusion of East and West. If one looks closely at these drawings, perhaps one can find the evidence of a fleeting dream to make Shanghai the Japanese capital of the world, projected to far exceed Berlin as the locus of financial and imperial power. In victory, Japan would have invited all the defeated nations to make concrete their obedience to Japan and their respect for the divine guidance of the Chrysanthemum Throne. In this scenario the Japanese would have seen the advantage of making Chiang Kai-shek the puppet emperor of China, allowing him to occupy the Forbidden Palace in Beijing under the constant watch of the Japanese Army. But all such speculations are as fanciful and as remote as the imaginations of these planners as they struggled to give form to forces that would end in their total destruction.

From dreaming of the future the Japanese moved quickly to control the present. A secret police force, the Kenpu Tei, was established in

Bridge House, a former apartment building by the Garden Bridge. This became the most feared address in the city. The torture was continuous and vicious, concerned as much with spreading fear as with gaining information. The worst abused were released close to death. The strong pro-democracy, pro-Nationalist stance adopted by the American editor of China Press, John Powell, greatly angered the Japanese. In Bridge House he developed beriberi. His feet became swollen and turned black. Only when the flesh began to peel off his bones was a doctor called. In the ship taking him back to America both feet had to be amputated to halt the infection. He lived only a few more years, but long enough to record his ordeal in his memoirs.[13]

The Shanghighlanders, citizens of those nations at war with Japan, were subjected to a progressive process of demoralisation. Step-by-step their dignity, status and assets were removed. Finally, they were taken from the city to concentration camps in the surrounding countryside. And all the while, the French and Germans watched at an embarrassed distance; many of these people had been their friends. Germany actively lobbied the Japanese Shanghai administration to deal with the Jewish question, but this was not Berlin. Joseph Meisinger 'the Butcher of Warsaw' who had ordered the execution of 10,000 Jews in that city, was sent to Shanghai to propose a 'final solution'.[14] He made specific recommendations for the fate of the Jews, including that they should be cast adrift on ships without food or water, worked to death in salt mines, or used for medical experiments. However, the Japanese took no

Figure 3: Shanghai Competition, 1942, Maekawa Kunio and team, 2nd place

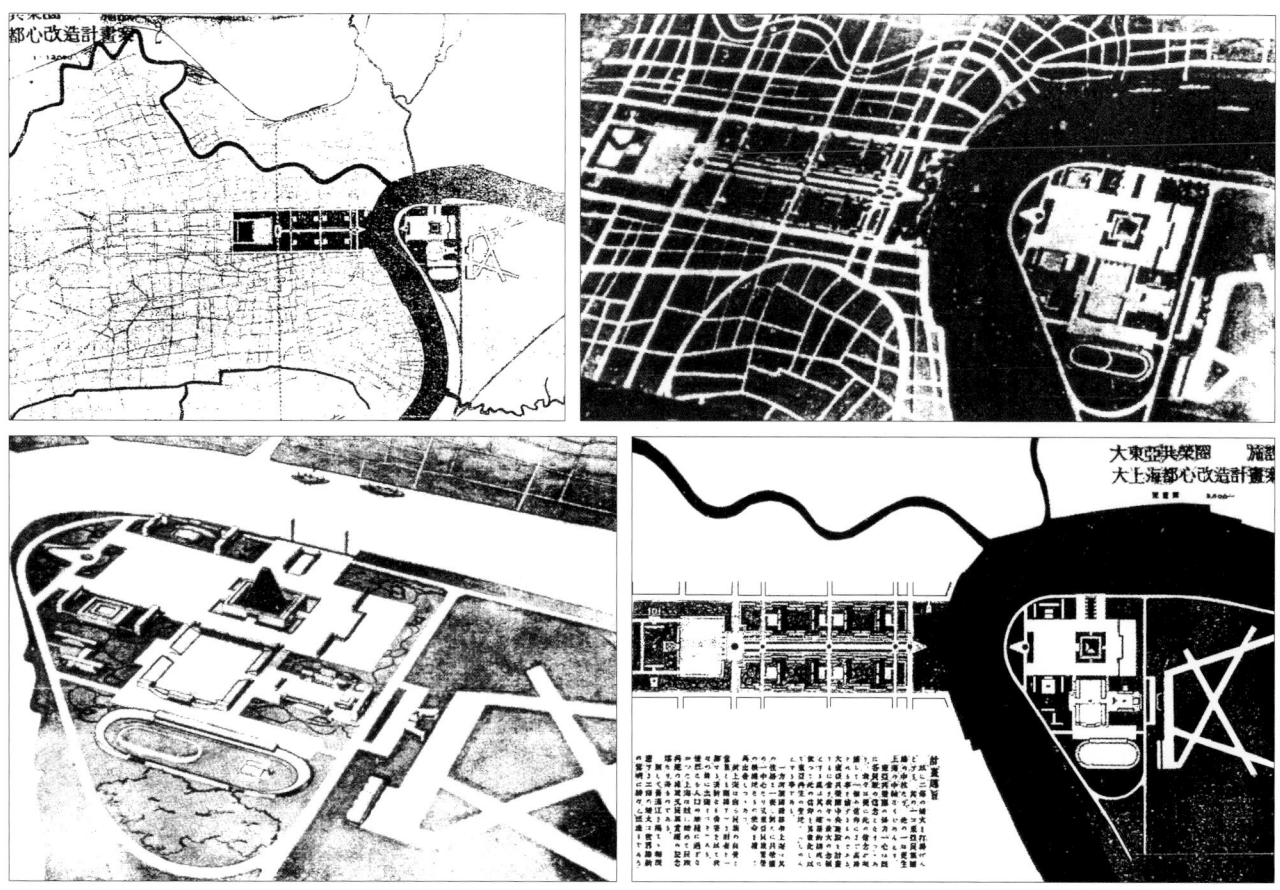

action. In the end the Jews were herded into a Shanghai ghetto one-mile square in Hongkew, where they were free to trade and allowed to continue business elsewhere in the city on day passes. They stayed there throughout the duration of the war and its aftermath. The foreign population of the city at war's end was 122,000.[15]

The British, American and Dutch Christians were subject to much more public humiliation. With the decision to move them out of the city into concentration camps, all were ordered to gather around the cathedral with as much as they were able to carry. Then began the spectacle of the procession of the former rulers, old and young, but mainly old, staggering under the weight of their most precious possessions, force-marched out of the city, many falling by the wayside. Meanwhile, a few blocks to the south, the opium dens and whorehouses in the French quarter were doing excellent business.

The first US aircraft appeared in the skies over Shanghai in July 1944. Bombing began in November, and attempted to concentrate on military targets. On 17 July a B-52 bomber missed its intended target, dropping bombs in the northwest of the city where they killed 231 people and wounded 500 more. Yet, despite this, the idea of American liberation was intoxicating.

The atomic bomb was dropped on Hiroshima on 15 August 1945. On 16 August loudspeakers around Shanghai's racetrack carried the high-pitched voice of the Japanese emperor to an incredulous audience – he offered complete and unconditional surrender. Shanghai was jubilant and vengeful.

Utter confusion followed. Japan had surrendered to a nation without effective government. The Communists, who could, and some say should, have taken Shanghai, were thwarted by an American operation airlifting Chiang Kai-shek's troops into the city, and taking it. The Nationalist leadership requested that the Japanese continue to administer the city until the US Army arrived. The Japanese used this brief respite to remove from the city everything they had stolen during the years of occupation

On return to power the Nationalists, under Chiang, began systematically to persecute all those who had remained in the city, beginning with the confiscation of property. In spite of the loss of extraterritoriality, some major foreign businesses returned and attempted to re-establish their status, but three factors prevented the formation of a supportive economic environment: corruption, retribution and, most significantly, the cost to the economy of renewing the civil war with the Communists. The war had been re-engaged in 1946 after Chiang Kai-shek refused to share power with the Communists, despite strong encouragement from the US. By 1948 the war was costing the Nationalist Government 80 per cent of the budget; the remaining 20 per cent was wholly insufficient for the nation's needs. The result was catastrophic inflation. Despite the total commitment of the economy to the war, the military campaign was ineffectual, which was in part the result of poor strategy, but mainly because the People's Liberation Army had cultivated broad peasant support across the nation.

The city planners within the Nationalist administration were far more effective. In a series of studies undertaken from 1945 until the collapse of the regime, a master plan for the city and the county was developed (Fig. 5). The most influential architects and planners had been trained in Europe and the USA since the turn of the century. The great master plan that resulted represented the best of European method (specifically CIAM, Congrès Internationaux d'Architecture Moderne) and vision from the previous quarter century. It was a 25-year plan with three major concerns: population, transportation and, surprisingly, birth control. It interrelated the activities of the city into accommodation, work, entertainment and traffic, in an organised scatter. A highly rational transport infrastructure was linked radially to a sequence of satellite towns, which were in fact garden cities in the English sense: each band of development was separated by a broad swathe of green farms and parkland. Its aim was the fusion of new Classicism, functionalism and Chinese hierarchy.

In November 1948 the Communists took Mukden and assumed control of Manchuria, humiliating Chiang Kai-shek's northeastern army. This was followed by increasing defections to the Communists, including many from within the Nationalist camp. The Nationalist forces holding Beijing surrendered peacefully on 31 January 1949. Ten days earlier, Chiang Kai-shek resigned publicly, yet privately held on to control as he organised the secret movement of troops, equipment and resources out of China to Taiwan. In Shanghai, the last weeks of Nationalist rule were as corrupt and abusive as any in the city's history. Martial law was imposed, while Nationalist soldiers were given the freedom of the city. It was a freedom to loot and abuse, with the army rounding up and executing in the streets all whom they saw as enemies.

As the Communist army approached the city, they were met by bankers and business leaders, who brokered a deal giving funds in medicine, in exchange for a peaceful occupation; an occupation that would not destroy their property. The Nationalist general, who had sworn to fight to the death, was given a large bribe by the business community and fled the city. In the retreat to Taiwan, the Nationalists took with them the most treasured objects from the Forbidden Palace. In Shanghai, in the middle of one night in February, Nationalist troops closed the Bund, and from a distance a line of coolies could be seen manhandling 1.5 million ounces of gold bullion from the Bank of China onto a ship, which left for Taiwan before first light.[16]

The peasant soldiers of the People's Liberation Army entered the city quietly, coming in from the west through the French concession. In every aspect they were strangers to all that the city had been built to represent. To the Shanghainese they were peasants, yet 'peasant' is an inadequate term to describe the hundreds of millions of people from widely different places and cultures who worked the land of China. Even now it is surprising how physically different are the young soldiers seen in the streets of the major cities. Smaller, with darker skin and pronounced features, they stand out among the smooth-skinned, complacent faces of the bourgeoisie. These peasant soldiers from all parts of China had been living and fighting for years in the most basic conditions. They slept out of doors in the constant company of their pack animals, sustained on rice, living a life without refinement of even the most basic kind. They would have had no way of comprehending the kind of people and activities that had formed this city. Their dreams had been cultivated by indoctrination and the desire to be released from feudal persecution, the ability to feed their families,

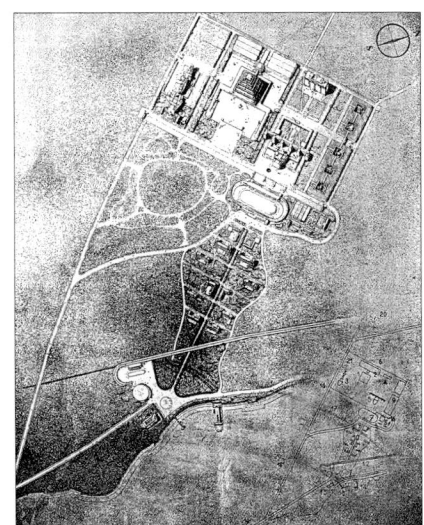

Left: Figure 4: Le Corbusier, Mundaneum, 1929
Right: Figure 5: Shanghai Master Plan, 1946

to feel secure. This host of soldiers, mainly young, carefully entering the city, refusing every offer of help, brushing aside proffered bowls of rice and cups of tea, were simply blind to the past reality of the city. They were dressed in green cotton fatigues, carrying weapons and ammunition and backpacks with essentials including emergency food in the form of crushed-locust cakes. But this was not an army of occupation, and as the nation adjusted to this most extreme revolution, the soldiers returned to their farms and villages. It was the surviving population of Shanghai that had to adjust. They were adjusting to the dislocation between the reality of the European settlement and the ideological order of Marxism/Maoism.

In one of the last 'word collages', Edgar Snow, a prolific writer on Shanghai and China who lived and worked in the city and hobnobbed with all the revolutionaries for over half a century, recalled his memories of the lost city from an austere Marxist Shanghai in 1960:

> Good-bye to all that: the well-dressed Chinese in their chauffeured cars behind bullet-proof glass; the gangsters, the shakedowns, the kidnappers; the exclusive foreign clubs, the men in white dinner jackets, their women beautifully gowned, the white-coated Chinese 'boys' obsequiously waiting to be tipped; Jimmy's Kitchen with its good American coffee, hamburgers, chili and sirloin steaks. Good-bye to all the nightlife: the gilded singing girl in her enamelled hair-do, her stage make-up, her tight-fitting gown with its slit skirt breaking at the silk-clad hip, and her polished ebony and silver-trimmed rickshaw with its crown of lights; the hundred dance halls and the thousands of taxi dolls; the opium dens and gambling halls; the flashing lights of the great restaurants, the clatter of mah-jong pieces, the yells of Chinese feasting and playing the finger game for bottoms-up drinking; the sailors in their smelly bars and friendly brothels on Szechuan Road; the myriad short-time whores and pimps busily darting in and out of the alleyways; the display signs of foreign business, the innumerable shops spilling with silks, jades, embroideries, porcelains and all the wares of the East; the generations of foreign families who called Shanghai home and lived quiet conservative lives in their tiny vacuum untouched by China; the beggars on every downtown block and the scabby infants urinating or defecating on the curb while mendicant mothers absently scratched for lice; the 'honey carts' hauling the night soil through the streets; the blocks-long funerals, the white-clad professional mourners weeping false tears, the tiers of paper palaces and paper money burned on the rich man's tomb; the jungle free-for-all struggle for gold or survival and the day's toll of unwanted infants and suicides floating in the canals; the knotted rickshaws with their owners fighting each other for customers and arguing fares; the pedlars and their plaintive cries; the armoured white ships on the Whangpoo, protecting foreign lives and property; the Japanese conquerors and their American and Kuomintang successors; gone the wickedest and most colourful city of the old Orient: good-bye to all that.[17]

For the majority of the Chinese in the city there must have been great relief in saying 'good-bye to all that'.

Notes

1 Auden/Isherwood, *Journey to a War*, op cit, p237.

2 Stella, Dong, *Shanghai 1842-1942: The Rise and Fall of a Decadent City*, op cit, p213.

3 Ibid, p250.

4 J Temperley, *Japanese Terror in China*, Modern Age Books Inc (New York), 1938.

5 Ibid.

6 Auden/Isherwood, *Journey to a War*, op cit, p239.

7 Ibid, p240.

8 Chinese Heritage Centre, Singapore.

9 Dong, *Shanghai*, op cit, p264.

10 *The Evolution of Shanghai Architecture*, op cit, pp60–3.

11 Le Corbusier/Pierre Jeanneret, *Oeuvre Complete*, 1910–29, Ginsberger

(Zurich), 1937, pp190–5.

12 Dong, *Shanghai*, op cit, p270.

13 Ibid, p274.

14 Ibid, p275.

15 Tess Johnson op cit, p118.

16 Dong, op cit, p290

17 Edgar Snow, *Red China Today*, Vintage Books (New York), 1971, p503. (In a footnote on the following page, Snow writes: 'Before the 1840s Shanghai was a fishing village on a mud flat on the Whangpoo'. It seems extraordinary that a writer who clearly found such great pleasure in the city should view its pre-Western history as that of a village: a village of 300,000 people with a range of shipping activity equal to the port of London!)

THE COMMUNIST CITY

ALAN BALFOUR

UNDER COMMUNISM

In reviewing the planning of Shanghai over the last 40 years of Communism it becomes evident that it is surprisingly free from the ideological structures that mark socialist planning in Europe. The most idealised plan in the Maoist years was that of 1953[1] (Fig. 1). This repeats certain features from the Nationalist and Japanese plans, extending the radial road system from the Big Plan of 1930 west and southwest. The need to include Pudong is carried forward from the Japanese plan. Here the interest is an area much further south and below the old city, yet proposing an equally dramatic axis running from the river's edge to a great park. The plan pays no special attention to the boundary of what had been the old walled city.

Planners from the Soviet Union developed the master plan in the early 1950s, maintaining all the major elements from the previous 25 years, and giving emphasis to bridging across the river. Housing was the main concern of the city administration in the 1950s. Large estates were developed in a pragmatic and basic form. Simple brick blocks under red-tile roofs three and four storeys high were laid out row upon row, mostly in parallel but sometimes radiating in relation to a major road. These can be seen as sensible modern equivalents of the *li long*, but with none of their oppressive density. In form they would not have been out of place within the socialist rebuilding programmes in Europe of the same decade; more basic perhaps, but in mood and character still familiar. Many of the architects from the 1950s, who were painfully disciplined in the Cultural Revolution, had looked to Scandinavia for models of an architecture appropriate to Marxist China, an architecture that was simply made, human in scale and open on all sides.

Nowhere in Shanghai was housing used to monumentalise political ideology as, for example, in Moscow. The only echo of Stalinist Classicism remains in the great House of Russian Friendship, as over-wrought and extreme as the pleasure palace of the Sassoons that it replaced.[2] The only evidence of Maoist vision is in the many tall brick chimneys of the boiler houses attached to apartment blocks built in the 1950s. These were a legacy of the subdivision of industrial effort leading to the 'Great Leap Forward' programme in 1958, which was so disastrous that Mao was removed from office from 1959 to 1965. Housing evolved into a more abstract, more modernist form in the 1960s. The demand for it was enormous and the city remains ringed by miles of concrete public housing, row upon row of six-storey flat-roof blocks tending to face north–south. The combination of time, poor construction and the pressure of occupation has transformed these once-neat white buildings into crumbling walls of washing, caged birds, flower-pots, sunscreens and miscellaneous cables and structures. What began with socialist good intentions ended in the familiar rich confusion of Shanghai life. Although shabby and careworn they are friendly places. No such benign transformations happened to the socialist housing of Moscow or Warsaw (Fig. 2).

Industrial development was the major concern of the socialist planners. The Government reconstructed large sections of the Grand Canal in 1958, benefiting Shanghai in the transporting of raw materials, coal, gravel and heavy industrial products, and it continues to provide drainage, flood control, irrigation and water supply throughout the Shanghai region. The programme of industrialisation called for the creation of self-contained industrial towns, satellites of Shanghai. Edgar Snow visited several in the 1960s:

Opposite: View of Pudong and the Lujiazui Financial District from the Garden Bridge

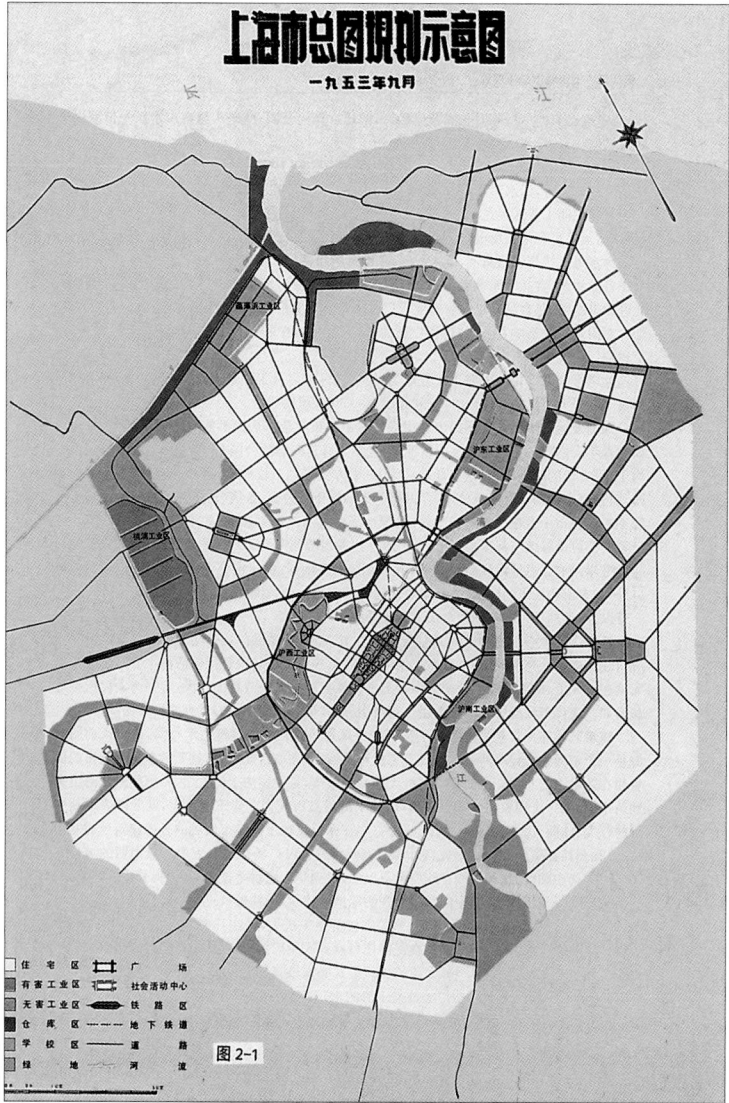

We drove for a day through the outskirts, visiting one development after another. Each of these self-contained communities was economically centred upon a sprawling new machine-building plant, a textile mill or some other factory among many dozens now built or under construction on a large scale. Some of the surrounding truck gardens, piggeries and poultry farms were owned and managed by the factories. Good highways and sidewalks led to traffic circles with shopping areas, hotels and theatres. Radiating from them were blocks of three- or four-storey apartment dwellings for the workers, some built around gardens and playgrounds for children attending the schools also newly set up for the neighbourhood. Residents were all within walking distance of their work.

Six satellites of this kind had been completed and five more were under construction. Much of the labour was spare-time effort contributed by the residents. I spent some hours in three of these new developments.

Ming Hong was typical, a community of about 70,000 workers and their families, employed by small neighbourhood factories making motors and farm machinery. More than 1,000 Ming Hong buildings of simple construction had been completed in less than two years.

We will visit Ming Hong again.

On this same day Snow investigated a former notorious 'shanty town' and was clearly convinced of the benefits of the revolution:

We got back to the city at dusk and went to see the old crazy quilt of crooked paths and lanes between 'homes' built of box wood, pieces of bamboo, matting, old oil cans and newspapers. Refugees of all kinds, people hanging on the edge of life, traditionally had camped in Pumpkin Town in squalor worse than the mud cliffs and filth where derelicts live outside Mexico City or much like the mat-shed refugee huts in Kowloon.

Some of the shelters had collapsed or been torn down but thousands survived, with improvements like roofs, glass windows and dry floors. The lanes and the alleyways were clean now, young willows were planted everywhere, water had been piped in to public fountains, and there were few flies. The grinning kids were no longer in rags and covered with sores. It was still a slum, but there were health stations in its midst, and tiny nurseries. Various workshops were busy and I saw a reading room and a bookstore.[3]

The most revealing evidence of disturbance in the project of the culture is a complete absence of any planning from the mid-1960s to the end of the 1970s. The Proletarian Cultural Revolution sought the utter destruction of bourgeois values and culture in China. People are now willing to talk about the years of the Cultural Revolution. They describe the beatings, the indoctrination, and the exile, but also the systematic destruction of all the artifacts of culture in life: porcelain, silks, scrolls and furniture; the destruction of the objects that had sustained, both by their expense and their educated refinement, class divisions in society. The most able architects and planners were victims of this cleansing process, not because of their political beliefs but because they almost always came from an affluent background. They were sent into the country to have their imagination cleaned out and reconditioned. However, this internal exile achieved nothing but fear and insecurity. (In the re-examination of this painful period this was seen as the worst demonstration of *Fajia*, or Legalism.) Those left behind had neither the ability nor the confidence to advance any vision for the city. Almost 20 years passed in which no one was allowed to imagine anything, let alone the future of the city; 20 years of being persuaded of the evil embedded in the buildings and streets of the former settlements; 20 years of having to suppress any reaction to the structures of this past life, whose luxury, indulgence and ambition now seemed inexplicable. In this state of oppression and denial all desire to invent the future of Shanghai was lost.

Hope returned slowly through the visions of Deng Xiaoping. In December 1978, two years after the death of both Mao Zedong and Zhou Enlai, Deng Xiaoping launched what he called the 'Second Revolution', commanding that the People's Republic of China build a great modern nation by the year 2000.

Planning in the 1980s was rational, scientific and mechanistic. The first order in the construction of a modern city was to renew the infrastructure, concentrating first on transport. For a decade the most visible activity across the city was the construction of an extensive, elevated highway system – a network of roads, bridges and tunnels linking both sides of the river and opening up the outlying areas. Then, in the cause of modernism, the city began to build a subway system. Confidence to dream, to shape the future only truly emerged in the 1990s. Two major projects dominated the imagination: the transformation of the settlement racetrack into the People's Square, and the creation of a business city, the Lujiazui Financial and Trade Zone across the river in Pudong. These two carefully planned set pieces brought about the widespread explosion of commercial development unequalled in any modern city.

DREAMING OF MANHATTAN

As the city came to life in response to the challenge of Deng Xiaoping in the late 1980s, the inspiration was Manhattan. On the streets between old Shanghai and the settlements, there was a flourish of public wall paintings. Painted on the gable ends of the *li long*, at the entrances to a local commercial street, even on the district police station, were many variations, some crude some fanciful, of a city of skyscrapers. These were either spontaneous expressions of desire, or carefully cultivated propaganda by the authorities, preparing the people for a spectacular transformation – cultivating a vision for the modern city promised by Deng Xiaoping. In one passageway close to the Bund there was also a large wall painting of the romantic encounter between Clark Gable and Vivian Leigh in *Gone with the Wind*. (This may have been a leftover from Steven Spielberg's movie *Empire of the Sun* of 1987, based on JG Ballard's autobiographical novel, which was filmed on the Bund. In the opening sequence the camera panned across the streets, passing a sign advertising the movie.)

No ideology inflected the infrastructure plans laid down in the 1980s. New Shanghai was being reordered to become an instrument for the dreams of Deng Xiaoping, and to become the pre-eminent modern city of China in 2000. A lattice of transportation networks coupled with numerous business zones spread across the length and breadth of the city, laying the basis for explosive change. The most spectacular production of the Second Revolution was the ungainly bulk of the Oriental Pearl TV Tower, which still dominates the view of Pudong from the Bund. Looking out recently from its observation deck on an unusually clear morning, through a haze that gave the sky a yellowish cast, I saw a vision from science fiction: multitudes of highrise buildings stretching to the horizon in every direction. By the year 2000 there were almost 3,000 such towers completed or in construction and as many again in the planning process. Shanghai was becoming not only a modern city but an emerging world power. Such forced growth in a controlled economy has been achieved, however, by the radical simplification of reality.

The 3,000 or so towers across the city are either housing or commercial, and from the outside it is often difficult to tell which is which. A striking aspect of commercial building is that although they wear wildly different styles on the outside, in general terms, they are all exactly the same. To understand this one must see the promise and significance of Shanghai through the eyes and in the dreams of business and political leaders across China, and understand the importance of real-estate development to Chinese enterprise both public and private. It is through building that power is exerted and expressed; the results have all the characteristics of towns in late medieval Italy, in which rival and often warring princely entrepreneurs built towers to mark their presence and express their power, the city of a thousand Guelphs and Ghibellines. (Even the Chinese army was heavily involved in quasi-private construction in the early 1990s, but this practice has come to an end.) Apart from establishing an effective infrastructure, the major task facing the mayor of the city and the city planning officer (Xia Liqing, Chair of the Shanghai Urban Planning Administrative Bureau and the Secretary of the CCP Planning Administration, whose essay in this publication exemplifies the unique ideological intelligence shaping the city), is to sustain a field of development broad enough to allow all those organisations, public and private, seeking power in the city a place to play. The mayor's daily task is to orchestrate the myriad claims for place and image within the city. Unlike Manhattan, the idea of which is an obsession with the Shanghainese, this is not a free market in which huge differentials in value force developments in certain directions. The prestige of the many distinct districts emerging in the city, the battery of commercial towers on the streets flanking People's Square, Huaihai Road – the Fifth Avenue of China – Pudong, have all been created through the manipulation of the central administration, always recognising the political and economic objectives of the Communist Party.

For all their seeming energy, the forces that are shaping Shanghai at this time are simplistic and crude. All activity is being forced into three distinct building types: highrise housing, lowrise housing, and mixed-use commercial development. The highrise commercial towers, though appearing to be extravagantly different, particularly in their detailing at the top, are all essentially the same.

The city remains concerned with the development of socially supportive new communities and there are several lowrise projects at the edge of the city, formed around schools, social buildings and pleasant open spaces (Fig. 3). However, these are the exceptions rather than the rule, as are the distinguished attempts to re-establish housing based on models from Chinese history. The major production of housing is being developed to suit the tastes of those whom in other places would be called nouveau riche, with all the stylistic excesses and vulgarity that marks similar housing throughout the world. This has evolved into two distinct types: single-family detached homes in a wide variety of mainly American-based styles, and highrise apartments, again styled to seem different. In the early 1990s, as the commercial potential of the Chinese market opened to the West, private housing began to be developed, specifically aimed at the foreign market, particularly the American market. The cultural complexity of Shanghai was immediately apparent to anyone flying into the old airport and driving into the city. In the midst of the construction sites and billboards were several grand houses, all from the 1900s, the gentle brick styles of Edwardian England. This had been an exclusive suburb where people would travel on weekends to visit the zoo, which is still there. And now, close by, across a hillside stripped of trees, is a development of US track housing, which would in America have been aimed at the low end of the market: mean little boxes with aluminium sidings and asphalt roofs. This activity is a reflection of one of the most complex ideological decisions affecting the future of the city – stimulating the development of housing as a commodity and not as social fabric.

Apart from the few cultural monuments – the Opera House, the Shanghai Museum of Art and the newly completed Museum of Science and Technology – educational buildings receive little attention. It took Manhattan more than a century to achieve its dramatic form; new Shanghai has emerged in little more than a decade. And as it evolves it is slowly becoming more refined, more able to control and direct its plays and players.

The People's Park and Square remains the only intentional public area in the city. Archaeologists in the far distant future, struggling to understand the form of People's Square, could well imagine that its curved edge, echoed several blocks to the east, was the residue of a sequence of walled enclosures from a very early culture, a trace of the old walled city long since gone. They might speculate that this was a place cleared for kings and gods. They would find it inconceivable that such a symbolically potent figure was merely the result of the European need to race horses.

Just as British troops had on several occasions camped out in the Yu Yuan Gardens because it was the only available space, the racetrack became a base for the People's Liberation Army after the city had been brought under control. The first action of the Communists' city government was to tear down the stands of the racetrack. The great promenade that slashes across the square is the most lasting memorial of the Maoist revolution. It appears to be a fragment of an east–west axis that was part of the first master plan produced by the revolutionary government in the

1950s. It was for decades the political and military parade ground of the city, where banners carrying the images of Chairman Mao, and later Zhou Enlai and Deng Xiaoping, would be marched past the remnants of the last crazy phase of European development, the Art Deco cinemas and hotels. As the grimness of the Maoist years drained all colour and life from the city, these gay, stylish fragments of a past reality must have seemed deeply pathetic to those who chose to look and remember. Maoist imperialism decreed that only activity in the service of the revolution could have either colour or difference. The regulation Mao jacket in blue denim that everyone had to wear was the most visible effect of the regime that repressed all expression of either character or difference, in buildings, music and literature no less than dress. It could be argued that the desire for spectacular difference in all the new buildings in the city was in reaction to decades of oppression.

The Shanghai Museum (1996, Xin Tonghe) is as awkward a work of architecture as it is a splendid collection of Chinese art and artifacts. It is, against all logic, not the product of the state or the city but results from the efforts of a few individuals. It exemplifies one of the more curious struggles faced in Shanghai in the last two decades. The Maoist years had in essence killed culture, leaving the city with no forms to build on or ideas to express. It is for this reason that the expressive forms of the new commercial buildings draw so heavily on American example. Both the education and the profession of architecture in the city have actively suppressed individualism; even in the midst of such a building boom, few individual architects have emerged with a distinct creative vision. The problem facing the architects of the Shanghai Museum was to find a form that was ahistorical, free from Western influence, yet able to symbolise the unique character and strength of Chinese culture. The resulting form is directly derived from an ancient bronze bow, a sacred thing, a thing of sacrifice. This was the first public building to occupy the People's Square, fronting the great parade ground to nowhere, and facing a wall of buildings that now constitute the public heart of the city. At the centre is the headquarters of the Shanghai Municipal Government (1995, the work of the city architectural bureau), a suitably ordered and bureaucratic mass flanked by two distinctly expressive structures. To the west is the world stage of the city, Shanghai Opera House (1994–8, Jean-Marie Charpentier). Its vast curving roof is slung between huge columns, the work of a French imagination much favoured by the city. French culture – literature, food, style and fashion – has retained its influence. Even during the grimmest of Maoist years there were French bakeries in many neighbourhoods.

To the east is a most extraordinary building, rivalling the Opera House in its structural extravagance. The Exhibition Hall for Shanghai Urban Planning (1999, the work of the city architectural bureau), is, in effect, a temple to the future of Shanghai, a place in which to worship the promise of the city, in which to cultivate desire for that future. The entrance hall is dominated by a huge sculpture, a collage of architectural forms taken from recent buildings in the city; compressed and painted gold, it has the appearance of a spaceship ready to lift off (Fig. 4). This Holy of Holies is on the piano nobile. After glimpsing the bristling city across People's Square, one enters into this

place of worship, a dark grand space filled with the 'Great Model' of the future city, carrying every building constructed in the present and planned for the near future. From the galleries above, it is a scene of claustrophobic intensity. There are side altars in the grand room and on the upper floor, in each a vignette of elements making up this extravagant project: nature preserves, regional transit systems, industrial parks with the emphasis on high-technology and, most dramatic of all, the construction of an extensive new port facility covering an island in the sea linked by bridges to the mainland, which aims to compete directly with Hong Kong. Clearly, in all this is Deng Xiaoping's desire for a modern city, without concern for history. Every sign of the old walled Shanghai has gone from the model except for the Yu Yuan Gardens and the recent faux-Chinese marketplace at its northern edge. In the last display before entering the terrace to enjoy the real city, is a completely furnished living room, a place of universal appeal: clusters of seats and a sofa around the television, bookshelves and pictures on the wall, the computer opened on the kitchen table ready for homework (Fig. 5).

Edge city in Shanghai looks like any modern commercial edge city. In no more than five years it has developed all the elements of automobile culture: strip shopping malls, Carrefour from France, and a Chinese version of Homebase dominate the entrance to the city from the west. The Chinese equivalent of highway food is served in multi-storey restaurants below a marquise flaming in neon. Along the few major roads into the city there is an almost inexplicable mixture of activities and developments. A 200-year-old village straddles the canal within sight of the highway; the decrepit sheds of abandoned industry and 1950s housing occupy the space between. Cutting into all of this is a country club, its entrance gates on the highway draped in brightly coloured paper flowers, a decoration announcing the grand opening. It not only has an English name and a very European coat-of-arms, but also boasts a golf course that somehow finds its way between the old villages and abandoned industry. Adjoining it, under construction, is a cul-de-sac of expensive villas; the picture on the promotional sign is almost, but not quite, an exact replica of an American subdivision.

Above left: Figure 3: Publicly developed housing at the edge of the city, 1998. This model project was developed to receive those pushed out from the city centre. It was designed by a faculty from Tonghi University and includes shops, schools and community buildings.

Above right: Figure 4: 'The Promise of the City'. Collage of recent Shanghai architecture in the entrance foyer of the Exhibition Hall for Shanghai Urban Planning, 2000.

Below: Figure 5: The ideal apartment.

In response to the challenge of Deng Xiaoping, it is the European, not the Chinese city that has been brought back to life. Year by year the old city behind the walls has faded from the imagination, all but disappearing in the great model of the future, save the Yu Yuan Gardens and the newly developed commercial area to the north, enjoyably designed in the grand Chinese manner. Building structures and spaces from the evolved history of Chinese building practice was briefly part of the Maoist attempt to strengthen Chinese reality. Few building traditions in the world have evolved with such care and refinement over hundreds of years. But politics and the power of international lifestyles continually subvert the wider application of Chinese tradition to the community needs of Shanghai.

It is surprising that cinema seems less popular than it once was. Television is given great attention. Nowhere in the present and future city is there the concentration of cinemas and show places that once lined the streets at the edge of the racetrack. But the Shanghainese love of food is undiminished, and the public can be seen in their thousands eating in the restaurants and strolling the Bund and the major avenues.

The streets of the European settlements continue to carry a much more complex nostalgia than the neglected lanes of old Shanghai. The cavernous lanes immediately behind the Bund feel like 1920s Chicago: great theatrical piles of stone, menacing still and always in shadow. Here and there parts of the old city remain untouched: an embassy, a club, cinemas and plenty of stylish apartment building and hotels. Many of the grand houses and gardens seem little changed – still elegant, stylish, privileged. Much of the French development of the 1920s and 1930s not only survives, but still conveys a feeling of France: tree-lined streets, Art Deco apartment buildings, bakeries and pastry shops, and little, long-abandoned shops revived again as bars or boutiques, selling clothes and antiques to tourists. Some measure of the importance of the idea of the prewar European city in the imagination of the Shanghainese is evident in the way it is reproduced in new developments, sometimes in the most extreme manner. In the summer of 2000 the favourite bar in the old residential area on the south of the French settlement was a freestanding recreation of a 19th-century German beer hall, with the beer brewed on the premises, the waitresses wearing dirndls, the young crowd dancing and singing along with a Philippino country and western band.

PUDONG AND THE LUJIANZU FINANCIAL AND TRADE ZONE
In the fall of 1993 I walked through the lanes of old Pudong. On every side, bulldozers were systematically tearing down the mud and brick walls of the densely packed old buildings. Apart from an orderly little school and the Oriental Pearl Tower looming overhead, this had been an urban peasant village with a way of life that had remained constant for hundreds of years. Now, all trace of old Pudong has gone, just as the new plan will remove almost all trace of the old walled city, and of the 19th-century *li long*. Unlike the great cities of China's past, Shanghai will not be deterred by nostalgia for a past that was exploitative and abusive, preferring to be continually reformed in the promise of the future. Regret for

such erasures of the past is felt by most architects, but China has a strong tradition of continual renewal without the distraction of nostalgia.

The seeds of the new Pudong, however, lie in plans dating from the 1930s and 1940s, and are clearly present in the first master plan from the early years of the revolution in 1953. The present plan derived from a strategy prepared in 1991. The logic is obvious: historically neglected and underdeveloped, the south and east bank of the Huangpu River provides the largest possible area for creating a new modern centre for Shanghai, immediately adjoining the former European city, and now linked to two older cities by the new highways, bridges and tunnels. Several major world architects were invited to propose an architectural master plan for the areas nearest to the Bund, including Sir Richard Rogers from England, Toyo Ito from Japan, and Dominique Perrault from France, all more able as architects than as urban planners. The task was to offer an urban design vision that would act as a guide to the stage management of the development. The overriding characteristic of the submissions was the assumption by each of the architects that they would impose their architecture and their order on the many and varied business and financial interests that would develop the area. The winning project was the least distinguished architecturally, but was the most able to tolerate a mix of architectures and developers (Fig. 6). Greater Pudong evolved in the 1990s into a grandiose plan centred on Lujiazui Dadao, the Wall Street of China, a vast boulevard running from the river several miles in a straight line southeast, ending in the Pudong Centre Park. It is flanked by an array of office buildings only distinguished from a distance, and impossible to cross as the traffic increases, yet empty of life at street level like the cities in the American Mid-west. It ends just before reaching the park in a grand civic square, with the offices of the Shanghai Municipal Administration on the east and an exuberant Museum of Science and Technology spiralling off to the west. Those arriving by subway emerge into glass pavilions that centre this new public stage, Yuanggialu. This combination of cultural and government activities contains just the echo of the Japanese plan for Pudong. The park, designed by the British landscape architects Land Use Consultants, is very young; the groves of newly planted trees are too small to convey any sense of its picturesque intention. However, the kiosk selling ice cream and the colourful boats on the lake already make it seem friendly. Looking northwest, straight down Lujiazui Dadao, presents the image of a world commercial city. Each of the many towers that form its massive effect strives to be different in shape, particularly in the sculpting of the roofs. Each forms a distinct image with almost human quality: *en masse* they have the appearance of giant warriors all wearing different armour, distinctly belligerent and obviously advanced, if one judges by the electronic gear sticking out of their heads. The Oriental Pearl seems quite lost in this new company, already a relic of past dreams and past symbols.

Standing apart and aloof, the tallest building in the year 2000 was the Jin Mao Tower. The work of the American architects Skidmore, Owing and Merrill, it is a Gothic spire of exceptional elegance. This is American corporate architecture at its most refined, blending technology and a fusion of styles with seamless ease. Here are Art Deco effects, complex formalism and high-tech manufacture. The upper part of its 88 storeys contains a Marriott Hotel that soars 32 storeys to the pinnacle of the tower. It appears with grace at the centre of the Great Model, where it is diminished by another figment of the American imagination – a vast, smooth tower with a great circle cut through its crest. This promises to be another claimant for the title of tallest building in the world. This commercial project, the work of the New York practice Kohn Pederson Fox, was at first conceived as capped by an axe-like form, the cutting edge ending the building in a flat blade pierced by an immense circle. But this disk of light seemed to the Shanghainese too close to Japan's symbol of the 'rising sun', and was amended to be less perfect. (There is tolerance but absolutely no forgiveness for Japanese brutality.) Again, the Great Model shows that this in turn will be eclipsed by what appears to be a New York Gothic extravaganza.

The view of Pudong from the Bund gives a much more confused picture, dominated in the foreground by the new Shanghai International Conference Centre (1994–9, city architectural bureau) on the river's edge, in the shadow of the Oriental Pearl. It is friendly, silly and monstrous all at the same time. A long, low building lies improbably between two unequal blue spheres. The western sphere, almost on a line with Nanjing Road as it enters the Bund, carries the outline of a map of Asia with Red China dominant. It appears as a friendly playmate to the Oriental Pearl, a funny little animal that if treated nicely will perform tricks. All the sleek smugness of American corporate weapons shy away in disgust. Chinese colleagues reject with passion the suggestion that the Convention Centre could be a more authentic representation of the

Shanghai vision than all the imported realities that surround it. They argue, with cause, that it was the product of unresponsive bureaucraticism. It was a design initiated by a powerful vice mayor, pushed through despite the objections of the public and the architectural bureaus.

THE GREAT MODEL

The Great Model allows one to play Superman and fly in one's imagination across the whole extent of the city. It becomes clear that this vast organism, capable of housing 20 million people, is in general principle similar to the old walled city now lost within its fabric. As with the old city, this as an informal, irrational organisation, whose elements – housing, culture, administration, trade and industry – are all evenly spread across the wide region. This city model is profoundly different from the equally large model of New York City that sits in the Queens Museum. There, it is evident that power is clearly concentrated on Manhattan, whereas in Shanghai there is no dominant concentration of power, political or commercial. Though there are specific industrial zones, this seemingly endless informal field is formed from a dispersal of business, trade and community into sub-centres across its whole length. The businessmen who once gathered around the Yu Yuan Gardens and the Bund now do business anywhere along the great avenues stretching in all directions. Yet, unlike its rivals in world financial power – Tokyo, New York, London – it appears to be too dispersed, lacking the potential for the dynamic intensity that marks a great city. There is no evidence in the plan of the city's military significance, though there can be no doubt of its strategic importance.

Figure 6: Pudong master plan

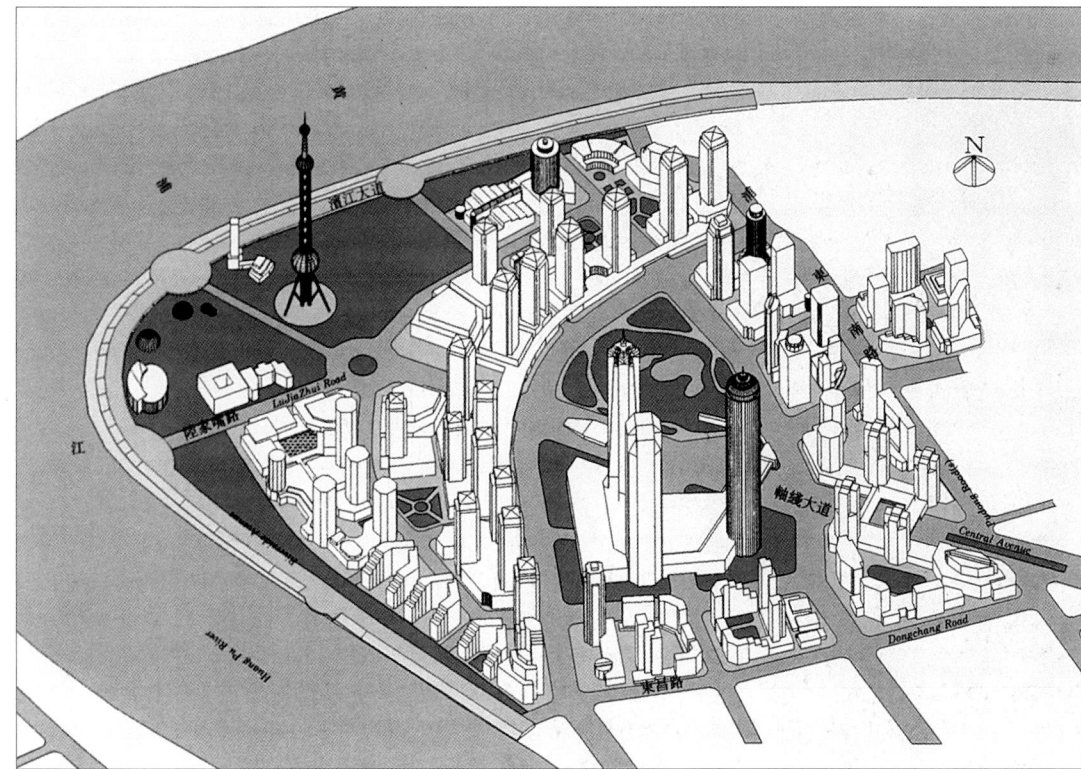

From discussion with architects and planners, it is clear that China's significant problems are twofold – population increase and population movement. Throughout China, people are continually struggling to move from the neglected rural areas into the cities. Getting access to opportunity is a continual battle for those outside the city. The farther from the big cities, the fewer are the opportunities for education and a good job. Although the process, known as *Hukou*, is being slowly relaxed, the authorities continue to control movement, and a family needs permission and a reason to move from village to town and town to city. Those who move illegally to find work are deprived of access to the slender safety-net offered by the state. Officials argue, with some justice, that these constraints are essential to maintain social stability. Politically and physically, China could not tolerate uncontrolled movement into the cities. There are an estimated 200 million people living within a day's travel from Shanghai. Uncontrolled movement could quickly collapse the social order and undermine all that has been gained from the vision of Deng Xiaoping – as has happened in India. Yet controls breed corruption: families manipulate to get their children into better schools, bribes are paid to get more prestigious jobs. The result is an increasing disparity between the wealth, health and opportunity of city dwellers and the hundreds of millions trapped within impoverished rural economies. Chinese planners have been developing what can best be described as a process of stepped urbanism, creating small, new industrial towns and industrialising existing towns and villages to provide semi-urban opportunities for rural populations. The area of Greater Shanghai has many new sub-centres that will help absorb the continual movement and growth of the population.

A decade ago, in the first confused explosion of commercialism, Shanghai seemed to be on the verge of growing out of control. Now, having witnessed an effective planning process matched by unprecedented economic growth, this great and complex city seems, at the beginning of the new millennium, to be not only dynamic and healthy but also resilient enough to accommodate the unpredictable forces of population movement and extensive industrial expansion. The city is not only comprehensible, but despite the huge volume of new construction, seems smaller than a decade ago. In part this is a product of socialist homogeneity. However, this new city is being produced through centralised control and with a very narrow set of building types. Centralised control – total public ownership of land – allows anything undesirable from the past to be removed without objection. Though old Shanghai and the *li long* are disappearing from the centre of the city, historical structures are being lovingly restored in the many small towns that still line the streams and canals around the city, which continue to conduct business along the Grand Canal. Shanghai has no shantytowns, no dangerous areas where one is advised not to walk. As the demolition of the 19th-century *li long* is completed, the authorities also intend to demolish and renew the crumbling housing projects of the 1950s and 1960s.

If we allow our imaginations to play with the vision of the Great Model, and the strategic intentions of the master plan, what can we project about their effect on the future 20 or 50 years from now? What will hold, bend, break? What, from the lessons of the last 50 years, can

be predicted? Nothing in 1950 could have anticipated the eruption that created this great commercial city in the year 2000. The potential is that this will not only be one of the world's most populous cities, but also one of its wealthiest. No city has more effectively fused the strength of China and Europe in the creation of wealth. It is a city driven by Western speculation and Chinese ambition and by a highly intelligent population, which has absorbed and been forcibly cultivated into the Western project since the late 19th century. It is a population that has shrugged off the repression of the Maoist years to rage back into life, revelling in the most crass consumption. It is easy to argue that this is far more vital than the dead hand of ideological central planning, but what seems to be missing is the unique sense of community that socialism can engender, still seen at its best in northern Europe.

Social planners have little power to influence and control the life of the people. The planners of Shanghai appear to be seeking an order that allows for a comfortable – what once would have been called bourgeois – life for the citizens. As Communism[4] evolved into Market Leninism – state-controlled capitalism – after Shengzhen, Shanghai was the first to benefit from a most unexpected product of Communism: rampant consumerism, whose giddy excess in the early days defied all reason. As Shanghai was released from the oppression of Maoism, it was drenched in a blizzard of advertising. The remnants of the prewar businesses and department stores along Nanjing Road disappeared behind cheap curtain walls of reflective glass, the occasional escalator slapped on the front dramatically demonstrating modernity. These were quickly lost in the myriad reflections of the streams of character banners and neon signs in gold, yellow and red, as the sidewalk stores vied with one another to offer the most extreme and absurd luxury goods: rare brandies, and bars of gold bullion. This must have been a product of a conscious political decision to stimulate long-suppressed consumerism. The state had to act to remove the guilt of possession. The arrival of American soft drink companies produced the same profusion of advertising that now encompasses the world. One banner greatly impressed the Shanghainese. From Mandarin it read in translation, 'Good for the mouth and good for pleasure', but the character was pronounced 'Coca-Cola'. Occasionally there was a fusion of Western advertising and political propaganda. Nanjing Road in the 1990s was lined with lamp standards along its whole length, each fitted with a circular disk to carry advertising. One summer in the early 1990s, disks running two-thirds the length of Nanjing Road extolled the virtues of Pepsi-Cola. The trademark wave of red and blue appeared behind the Pepsi slogan, which alternated between English and Chinese. Almost imperceptibly, towards the Bund the red wave changed into the red flag of China, and the characters called for all to 'Raise the flag for Deng Xiaoping'.

In the late 1990s much of Nanjing Road was transformed into a pedestrian precinct, drenched in neon like a mile-long Times Square. This has become the major gathering place for young and old – particularly in the evenings. However, in the last years of the 20th century there was increasing competition from other, more modern, commercial streets – nothing on Nanjing Road compares with the extravagance and luxury of the stores along Huaihai . Yet the reward for such speculation has been high failure rates.

The plan of the city represented by the Great Model is as dramatic and resilient as any in the city's history. Free from the distortion of imperial order or military strategy/necessity, it is for the most part a product of state-manipulated reality, and not without paradox. In two areas, housing and transportation, the influence of a wholly free market could quickly imbalance political and social stability. Allowing housing to become a commodity must in the long run produce divisions in society. Divisions defined at first by wealth and property quickly create differentials in access to opportunity. Adding to this condition the housing market is already producing widely ranging adaptations of on European and American housing models. These stylistic variations in the Western production of homes are designed to broaden the market and create prestige value explicitly related to societies where class is defined by wealth and a wide gap between rich and poor. Demand is being cultivated for variations on the American suburban home. The good life for those who make it in China is represented neither by the avant garde, nor by any interest in the exquisite homes of China's past, but by ersatz cottages, synthetic confections of a bucolic and conservative life, exactly reflecting the taste of the middle classes worldwide. The most immediate antecedents, albeit on a larger scale, are the English villas that still survive in the once-elite suburbs to the west of the foreign city, a model in their day and much favoured not just by the Europeans but by the Japanese and Chinese.

This universality of taste and image, which links the suburbs of New Delhi with Atlanta, and Jakarta with Tucson, is an unexpected effect of the multiple consumable items produced by multinational corporations. Television and print advertising create a composite of the desired good life in the combined contexts in which these global products are seen and promoted in use. All foods are taken from tall refrigerators and cooked in well-equipped eat-in kitchens, and so it goes throughout the home, from the toilet paper and shampoo in the bathroom, to the entertainment equipment in the living room. The world's favourite pet gives us a tour of the ideal home as it searches for the world's favourite pet food, and the world's favourite car sits in the driveway of the world's detached homes. Equally universal but more difficult to explain is the wish to add a touch of European Classicism to these fantasies. In Shanghai this is applied most extravagantly to the tops of private apartment buildings: 1,000 towers crowned by the illusion of a floating palace dressed in arches and columns and elaborate pediments, the most ambitious occasionally calling in the help of caryatids and recumbent lions. This horrifies the unashamedly bourgeois professors of architecture who call the style 'Neocolonialism'. Ominously, as judged by past use of such orders of architecture, this classicising is not limited to private housing. The new offices of the prosecuting attorneys and the adjoining police station, on the ring-road west of the centre, have been given full classical dress; here the drab, grey concrete colonnade that rises the full 12 storeys of the building's height, would seem to be more about authority than fantasy (Fig. 7).

A drive, taken over the last year, all the way around the edge of Shanghai would reveal a city increasingly separated by wealth; a city that allows the rich a purchased lifestyle. It is surprising how closely Shanghai resembles most of the Asian cities that have benefited from the new world industrial economy. This will only intensify with the influence of that other critical decision: support for the car. With the exception of a limited subway system, public transit in Shanghai is decrepit and underfunded; dramatically so in comparison with the enormous investment in highway infrastructure and extensive support of automobile production and consumption. In the early 1990s when market freedoms created a frenzy of expectation, the ground floor of the first (Japanese-backed) department store to open in Pudong was filled with all the world's most luxurious cars. The store has failed, however, and the fervour for extreme luxury has died down, yet the automobile is still cultivated as the most desirable object in the city, even though Shanghai, unlike Beijing, has strict controls on the ownership of private cars. The manufacture of automobiles, first by Volkswagen, then by General Motors and now by the Japanese, began with the production of simple cars for Chinese consumption. These manufacturers stimulate the development of all the subsidiary industries: glass, tyres, metal components, interior fittings and on and on. Rapidly China is developing a fully supported automobile industry that will have the ambition to compete in supplying the Asian market. All this is at the cost to Shanghai of pollution, and will undermine a street system wholly unable to take the increased volume of traffic. In ten years the city has gone from bicycles and the occasional truck and bus to total gridlock. For the economic planners, automobile production is a stimulus for industrial growth across many fields including subsequent service industries that support it. Yet the effect on the political city will be to increase division and fragmentation. Extensive though the highways of Shanghai are, they are quickly becoming inadequate as the speed and volume of traffic increase; every mile of highway will have to double in size in the next ten years simply to keep up.

Despite being a city under strict ideological control, the idealist might be disappointed to learn that in 2000, Shanghai lacked the courage to explore socialist solutions to the transport problem.[5] Imagine how different the plan and the city would have been if it had managed to develop an intricate and responsive system of public transport; if it had been less concerned with applying international solutions and more with applying its own ideological and ethical principles to the problem. Given the ingenuity of the Shanghainese, and the ubiquity of the problem for all of Asia, the city could have produced and exported to the world new solutions, new machines and new forms of transportation. Instead, too many cars are being pumped onto too few highways, while the majority of the citizens suffer in the crush and filth of the city bus system, dreaming of the day when they too will have a car. The collapse a decade from now of both the public and private transportation systems is clearly predictable from the current plan, with too many cars, inadequate highways and corrosive pollution.

The reality promised in the Great Model is an illusion, a mere pretence of a commercial city. Lacking freedom from controls and centralised objectives it attempts to hide behind a veneer of difference. The Chinese themselves would tell you that the only towers with character or personality are the product of American or French or even Japanese

Right: Figure 7: District administration building and police station 1997, north central Shanghai

Opposite: New pedestrian shopping street, just north of the affluent western reaches of Nanjing Road. It succeeds in conveying the pleasures and comfort of first world consumerism while still having a distinct Shanghai character - helped by the increasing ubiquitous commercial sentinels in the background

architects. Chinese planners and architects remain unable to produce an authentic reality (though they would say, 'Give us time'). In this city of many millions the distorted history of the last 50 years has destroyed the ability to define a meaningful reality. And even before the last 50 years, nothing in the urban or artistic history of Shanghai has ever been called upon to cultivate originality or conceptual independence. Before 1949 a privileged group of architects and planners, all from wealthy families, was able to study abroad and return to China, made confident only in a belief in the superiority of the European or American realm. These consciously imported realities were driven by imported technologies and imported ways of doing business. The Great Model offers the most graphic evidence of this reflective condition of the city and its commercial culture. All its desires and actions are borrowed from elsewhere. The excesses of the Great Leap Forward and the Cultural Revolution broke the confidence and the imagination of the urban bourgeoisie, and devastated the scholarly and professional classes, people who, given time, may have developed confidence in a Chinese vision of progress. It has had the effect of rendering the imagination of China wholly dependent on Japan and the West.[6] In calling for a modern Shanghai in the year 2000, Deng Xiaoping lacked a specifically Chinese model to which to attach his dreams.

Into the future, this city will remain a confused simulacrum unless it is able to cultivate the imagination and confidence to stage-manage its own future. The Great Model is a grotesque parody of a commercial city, utterly self-consumed and static. And when this imitation fails to create sufficiently appropriate activity to support the dream, these multiple facades will collapse. The thousands of towers will remain empty and unmaintained. Riots will break out between the poor and the homeless as they attempt to occupy long-abandoned private housing estates.

Highways will choke under the volume of traffic; roads in the city centre will be closed off in an attempt to channel the congestion. Laws will be passed and ignored that will attempt to limit and schedule all vehicular access to the city. The city will exist in the continual haze of air pollution produced by the combination of coal fumes, industrial waste and gasoline. Expanding hydroelectric generation of power, bringing online nuclear power plants, will fail to meet increasing demand and the city will continue its dependency on coal-fuelled generation.

Shanghai in the Great Model presents itself as a city overwhelmed by the desire to be a world centre of business, finance and trade. It predicts that the outcome will be a place whose order and form will be wholly derived from Western models. The cultural debate in Asia continues to be concerned with the degree to which modernism is a product of a rational scientific and technological process, culturally neutral, or has embedded within it unavoidable Western metaphysics. This future Shanghai may be derived from Western models, but from the experience of the last decade it will also be distinctly Chinese and, even more so, Shanghainese. The reality of place may not be in the surface mass and decoration of buildings, but is experienced in the intimate exchanges between individuals, in food, in conversation, in assemblies, and in the character of the workplace and the rhythms of the day.

The Great Model presents a seemingly endless field of enterprise, represented by a collage of a few object-types borrowed from the developed world. It is a simplistic and limited image of energy, competition and land speculation. It remains to be seen whether or not the state's manipulation of this field of play can match the actual reality in the future with the desires of the present. Or whether an effective reality can emerge out of the illusion. Behind this seemingly resilient inflexible field is a tough controlling bureaucracy that may be incapable, or unable, to let go.

Notes

1 *The Planning of Shanghai*, Shanghai Planning Ministry, 1994.

2 The Sassoons were highly successful Jewish traders, originally from Baghdad, whose financial empire at the turn of the 19th century extended from Shanghai to London. The house was the most grandiose in the city, matching in all its excessive detail the life of the patriarch.

3 Snow, *Red China Today*, op cit.

4 Some in Shanghai hold the view that the Maoist years should be seen more as Fascism than socialism.

5 Shanghai is viewed as one of the most politically controlled cities in the nation.

6 It could be argued that amongst the gains of the Mao years was the breaking of the influence of the rural land owners and the intellectual bourgeoisie on the mass population. In judging the vast destruction caused by Maoist policy one must set alongside it the clear egalitarian achievements in the social character of China's great cities. This does not always seem so apparent outside the cities.

The skyline of Lujiazui Central Business District in 2001

CONTEMPORARY ARCHITECTURE AND URBANISM
ZHENG SHILING

Along with the international urban construction and architecture of Shanghai, there is a concentration of Chinese history that is reflected in the old city: traditional gardens, Buddhist temples, and houses with a cultural heritage stretching back thousands of years. There was also the International Settlement and French Concession, built according to European urban and architectural patterns, as well as the new urbanised area and buildings designed by Chinese architects who followed the models of classical European cities and integrated them with traditional Chinese ideology. Shanghai had already established itself in the 19th and 20th centuries as an important economic and cultural metropolis for new Chinese culture and modern architecture, and this has never been equalled by other Chinese cities. A foundation for future development has thus been laid down.

During the 1950s, Shanghai ceased to be a centre of development as a result of the first Five Year Plan (1953–7) and the political and ideological situation. Very few construction activities took place in this former world-level metropolis, except for the Cao-Yang New Residential Area, an example of rational planning influenced by the European 'garden city'. The Wen-Yuan Building of Tongji University (1953–4), designed by Huang Yuling and Ha Xiongwen, is an example of the continuity of the Modern Movement since the 1930s in Shanghai.

In the 1950s and 1960s, based on the model of the Soviet Union, satellite cities, industrial zones and residential quarters were designed and built under the policy of national industrialisation. Some of these, especially the public buildings, adopted traditional Chinese architectural forms of monumentality and dignity. In order to bring about the industrialisation of the country, there was a boom in industrial buildings, including the Min-Hang Heavy Industry Zone (1958–62, designed by the Second Design Institute of the First Ministry of Machine Building and others) and Wu-Jing Chemical Industry Zone (1958, architect unknown). During this period, the Socialist Realist style of Russian architecture was introduced to Shanghai. The Sino-Soviet Friendship Mansions of Western Neoclassical style, designed by Russian architects Anderlev and Jislova, became a landmark and the highest tower in Shanghai until the 1970s (Fig. 1).

In an echo of the Chinese Neoclassicism of the 1930s, a trend emerged during another upsurge in construction in which China's national forms were explored. The 1959 Seminar on Architectural Art in Shanghai took place in a lenient academic atmosphere that saw such fine works as the Shanghai Lu Xun Memorial Hall (1956), in the vernacular style of this famous Chinese writer's hometown, Shao Xin (Fig. 2).

Figure 1: Sino-Soviet Friendship Mansions, Anderlev and Jislova, now the Shanghai Exhibition Centre, 1956

Above, left to right:

Figure 2: Lu Xun Memorial Hall, 1956, Chen Zhi, Wang Dingzhen, Zhang Zhimo and others

Figure 3: Cao Yang Residential Quarter, 1953, Wang Dingzhen and others

Figure 4: Fan Gua Long Residential Quarter, 1963

Below from left to right:

Figure 5: The main street of Min Hang New City, 1959, Shanghai Civil Building Design Institute

Figure 6: Shanghai Gymnasium, 1975, Wei Dunshan and others

Figure 7: Hua Ting Hotel, 1982–6, Wong & Tung International Ltd / East China Architectural Design Institute

Due to the special heritage of Shanghai's culture, Shanghainese architects differed completely from their colleagues in Beijing and other cities in their treatment of traditional urban culture. Shanghainese architects saw traditional form more as the unsophisticated vernacular of southeast China than the restoration of a monumental and palatial style.

During the 1960s and 1970s, China experienced a severe winter in the realm of architecture and of culture in general. Throughout this period, one would never dare raise the subject of art in Chinese architecture. To some extent this was for economic reasons, but it was due far more to politics and to an almighty ideology. In 1964 the so-called Cultural Revolution was launched throughout China, which profoundly affected architects' creative ability and education. The entire realm of architectural criticism became synonymous with political criticism and revolutionary slogans. Industrial buildings were thus the main field of architectural design. A few poorly designed and bad quality residential quarters were constructed to solve the housing shortage. Even though the standard of housing had been very low in the 1950s, the urban planners and architects had tried their best to create a human environment, such as the Cao Yang Residential Quarter (Fig. 3). The Fan Gua Long Residential Quarter of 1963 attempted to solve the problem of a limited site area (Fig. 4). The Min Hang New City, 100,000 square metres of buildings and housing, served the industrial area in which it was constructed (Fig. 5). As in other realms of culture, architectural design was shackled since it related to the human spirit; the medium became a tool for politics. During the 1970s, construction activities were scarce in Shanghai, and the Shanghai Gymnasium (1975) is one of the few representative works (Fig. 6).

The opening up and reform policy of China in the 1980s brought to Shanghai a prosperous new era of architectural creativity, unfolding a brand new page in the urban construction of Shanghai. A large-scale programme of urban construction and architectural activities was beginning. Shanghai, as the spearhead of China's reform initiative, has witnessed tremendous progress in the last 20 years. The magnitude of architectural and urban activities that have appeared on the desks of many young architects, planners and designers, has brought their work to rapid maturity.

During the 1980s, Shanghai again provided the opportunity for foreign architects and urban planners to display their talents. Together with Chinese architects, they designed a number of popular buildings using styles that were fashionable internationally. In 1991–6, international bidding projects amounted to about 40 per cent of the total design projects in Shanghai. In 1999, a general jury was elected to select the 50 best buildings constructed in Shanghai during the period 1949–99. Of the top 30 awards, 15 went to foreign and Hong Kong architects.

This development in which architects from abroad resumed an active role in Shanghai's architecture began in 1983 with the design of the Hua Ting Hotel (Fig. 7). A boom in hotel buildings was sparked by China's new open policy, hosting thousands of foreign businessmen and tourists. Foreign, Hong Kong and Taiwanese architects were attracted to Shanghai by these ventures. The most important hotels are the Jin An Hilton Hotel (1989), Garden Hotel (1989), and the New Jingjiang Tower (1990) (Figs. 8-10).

The use of traditional Chinese architectural expression also increased during this period. The Shanghai Centre, one of the early American

Above, left to right:

Figure 8: Jin An Hilton Hotel

Figure 9: Garden Hotel

Figure 10: New Jingjiang Tower, Wong & Tung International Ltd.

Figure 11: The Shanghai Centre, 1987, John Portman

Below, left to right:

Figure 12: The inner court of Shanghai Centre

Figure 13: Charpentier, Shanghai Opera House

Figure 14: RTKL, Scienceland.

projects, designed by John Portman, deliberately adopted traditional segments (Figs. 11-12). Some important projects were chosen through international design competitions. Architects and planners were brought in from the USA, UK, France, Germany, Italy, Canada, Japan, Australia, Singapore, Hong Kong and Taiwan.

Since the 1990s, a series of events has promoted exchange in academic study, urban planning, and architectural and urban design, between architects and planners at home and abroad: the '92 International Consultant on the Urban Design of Central Business District in Lujiazui, Pudong; the '94 International Design Contest for Shanghai Opera House (Fig. 13); the '95 International Design Competition for the Oriental Concert Hall in Pudong; the '96 International Design Contest for Shanghai Pudong International Airport; the '96 International Residential Design Contest; the '97 International Design Contest for Shanghai Scienceland (Fig. 14); the International Invited Master Plan Contest for Shanghai Huangpu Riverfront, 2000–1; the International Invited Competition for Shanghai Oriental Art Centre, 2001; the International Invited Competition for Shanghai South Railway Station, 2001 (Fig. 15) and a series of invited conceptual plans for new satellite cities and towns in Shanghai suburb in 2001.

All of these events contributed to the prosperity of architectural and urban design. Many renowned world architects and experts came to Shanghai either to give lectures or participate in projects: IM Pei, Philip Johnson, Paul Ludolf, Richard Meier, John Portman, Michael Graves, Murphy/Jahn, Kenneth Frampton, Charles Jencks, Skidmore, Owings & Merrill International Ltd, RTKL, KPF, The Jerde Partnership Ltd, JWDA Architects, Arquitectonica and others from the USA; Norman Foster,

Richard Rogers from the UK; Paolo Portoghesi, Massimiliano Fuksas, Vittorio Gregotti from Italy; Jean-Paul Viguier, Paul Andreu, Jean-Marie Chapentier, Dominique Perrault, Fredric Rolland International, Architecture Studio from France; Arthur Erickson, Eberhard Zeidler, B+H, The Webb Zerafa Menkès Housden Partnership Architects from Canada; Kenzo Tange, Arato Isozaki, Kisho Kurokawa, Fumihiko Maki, Nikken Sekkei, Nihon Sekkei, Oberyashi, Shimizu, RIA and others from Japan; Meinhard von Gerkan and Albert Speer from Germany; and Hans Hollein, Rem Koolhaas, Zaha Hadid and others.

They brought new ideas and concepts of contemporary world architecture into Shanghai and created some first-class buildings, such as IM Pei/Posco Engineering & Construction Co Ltd's Posco Building (1999) (Fig. 16) and Chinese-European International Business School (1999) (Fig. 17); Norman Foster's Kerry Centre (1999) (Fig. 18) and Jiu-Shi Tower (2001); KPF Associates PC's Shanghai World Financial Centre and KPF Associates PC/Frank CY Feng Architects & Associates (HK) Ltd/East China Architectural Design Institute's Plaza 66 (2001) (Figs. 19-20).

In return, many Shanghai architects went to study and gain experience all over the world, taking their place on the international stage. This co-operation proved fruitful, furnishing architects with new ideas.

Also due to the open policy in the 1980s and 1990s, there was a boom in urban construction that made the city into one large construction site. The Hong Qiao Economic & Technological Development Zone was the first experiment in urban design in Shanghai (1986–95). With a planned building area of 1.5 million square metres on a site of 0.65 square kilometres, the zone comprises 21 projects, including office

From above left to right:

Figure 15: The scheme of the East China Architectural Design Institute and Aménagement Recherche Poles d' Echanges

Figure 16: POSCO Building, 1999, IM Pei/Posco Engineering & Construction Co Ltd

Figure 17: Chinese-European International Business School, 1999, IM Pei/Posco Engineering & Construction Co Ltd

Figure 18: Kerry Centre, 1999, Norman Foster

Figures 19-20: Plaza 66, 2001, KPF Associates PC/Frank CY Feng Architects & Associates (HK)Ltd/East China Architectural Design Institute

Figure 21: Night view of the Hong Qiao Economic & Technological Development Zone, 1986–95

Figure 22: Shanghai International Trade Centre, 1990, Nihon Sekkei and the Shanghai Architectural Design and Research Institute

Figure 23: The New Century Plaza, 1995, H & H Architecture-Urbanism

Figure 24: Maxdo Tower, 2001

towers, hotels, shopping centres, exhibition facilities and apartment buildings (Fig. 21). The Shanghai International Trade Centre, a 33-storey office tower, is a landmark of the zone (Fig. 22). The New Century Plaza, designed by the French practice H & H Architecture–Urbanism in 1995, has a dramatic form that creates a figurative urban space (Fig. 23). The latest building in the zone is Maxdo Tower (2001), which is also the highest tower in that area (Fig. 24).

In addition, the Lujiazui Central Business District and sub-centres like Xu-Jia-Hui are being built from almost nothing to cater strategically for the needs of a large, international metropolitan information society (Figs. 25-28). Many excellent high-rise buildings are being constructed in this area, including two by Nikken Sekkei in association with the Shanghai Architectural Design and Research Institute: Shanghai International Finance Centre (2001) (Fig. 29) and the Shanghai Information Centre (1995–2001) (Fig. 30). Nikken Sekkei won an international architectural design competition for these two projects, both located at the east gate of the Lujiazui CBD and along the Century Boulevard – the central, and very visible, axis of the district. Another Japanese architects' office, Shimizu Corporation, designed the Shanghai Nextage Shopping Centre (1995), which is the landmark of the commercial area (Fig. 31).

The Canadian office Webb Zerafa Menkès Housden Partnership Architects, also in association with the Shanghai Architectural Design and Research Institute, has found success in Shanghai with its Shanghai Security Exchange Building (1997), a unique form characterised by a square opening (Fig. 32).

With the rapid development of the public traffic system, commercial centres like Xu-Jia-Hui have been booming over the last ten years (Fig. 33). The Seattle-based American architects office, Callison Architecture, in association with Frank CY Feng Architects & Associates, designed the only partly realised Grand Gateway Plaza (2000) (Figs. 34-36). The complex fills an entire block, and acts as a huge entrance gate to the Xu-Jia-Hui business district. The twin towers of the 53-storey office block are not yet constructed.

The site for the International Invited Master Plan Contest for Shanghai Huangpu Riverfront encompasses 24.7 kilometres, containing a critical mass of numerous cultural, economic and historic elements. This large-scale urban design project includes open public space, flood control, a roadway, transit and traffic system, urban renewal, and land use. Its aim is to enhance and develop the Huangpu Riverfront in order to improve the quality of life, and to revitalise the city's various urban

Below, left to right:

Figure 25: The skyline of Lujiazui Central Business District in 1992

Figure 26: The skyline of Lujiazui Central Business District in 1998

Figure 27: The skyline of Lujiazui Central Business District in 2001

Figure 28: The buildings around the central green space of Lu-Jia-Zui Central Business District

From above, left to right:

Figure 29: Shanghai International Finance Centre, 2001, Nikken Sekkei in association with the Shanghai Architectural Design and Research Institute

Figure 30: Shanghai Information Centre, 1995–2001, designed by Nikken Sekkei in association with the Shanghai Architectural Design and Research Institute

Figure 31: Shanghai Nextage Shopping Centre, 1995, Shimizu Corporation

Figure 32: Shanghai Security Exchange Building, 1997, Webb Zerafa Menkès Housden Partnership Architects in association with the Shanghai Architectural and Design and Research Institute

Figure 33: Sub-Centre Xu-Jia-Hui

Figures 34-36: Grand Gateway Plaza, 2000, Callison Architecture in association with Frank CY Feng Architects & Associates

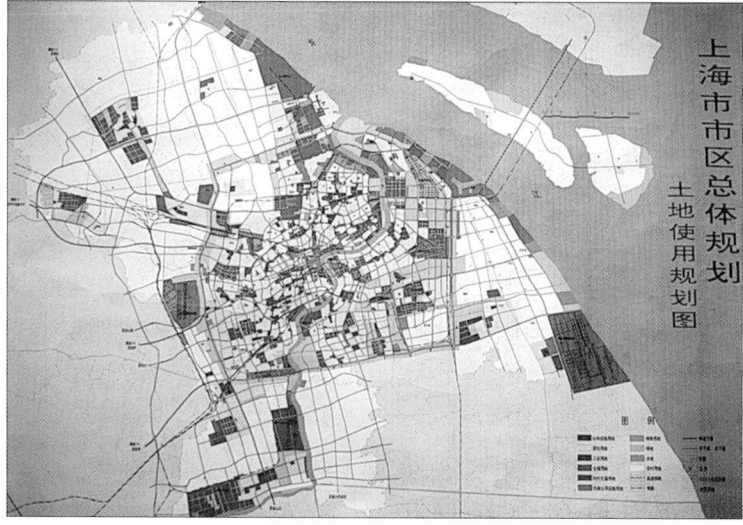

Left: Figure 37: The Land Use of the Urban Area in the New Master Plan of Shanghai, 2000

Right: Figure 38: The Square Pagoda Garden, 1978–81, Feng Jizhong

nodes. An open space system to create a city park, and public places along the river has been designed. In the next five years, several projects will be put into operation, such as an International Passenger Terminal, the development of an area adjacent to the Lujiazui CBD, and Shi-Liu-Pu Wharf.

Since the 1984 master plan for Shanghai, many changes have been executed. It is now necessary to revise the old master plan, and to put forward four objectives for a new layout in accordance with the strategic objectives of the city's economic and social development. Firstly, to establish a strategic objective for development into a world economic centre. Secondly, to foster the five great functions of a metropolis: as a collection and distribution centre, a production centre, an administrative centre, a service centre and a centre of innovation for the whole country, oriented towards the world. Thirdly, to shape a rational macroscopic urban structure and layout. Fourthly, to build a modernised urban infrastructure, both in the sense of software and hardware.

Shanghai is the biggest metropolis in China and its population amounts to 167.4 million with a territory of 6,340.5 square kilometres. Over the last ten years, its industrial structure has been undergoing a huge transformation. The tertiary industries: finance, commerce, trade, communication, real estate and other service sectors, are playing an increasingly important role in the city's economy. Shanghai is being transformed from one of the biggest industrial centres into an open, multifunctional economic centre. The open policy and reform of the 1980s and 1990s have ushered in a new era and provided much opportunity for urban construction in Shanghai. With a large-scale construction infrastructure, the urban function has been strengthened. The metropolis has witnessed an overall change and transformation of its urban structure.

According to statistics, the 1990s was a period of the most rapid development ever in the history of Shanghai. In 1990, the Gross Domestic Product was 75.65 billion *yuan*, and the per capita GDP was 5,910 *yuan*. In 1999 the GDP was 403.50 billion *yuan* and that per capita was 30,805 *yuan*. The industrial structure has also been adapted to meet the requirements of a post-industrial city. In 1990 the primary industry accounted for 4.3 per cent, the secondary industry 63.8 per

cent and the tertiary industry 31.9 per cent. But in 1999, the percentages were respectively 1.8, 48 and 50.2. All of these statistics show a rapid expansion in Shanghai's economy. Thus the city has invested much in the construction of its infrastructure. In 1990, the total investment was 22.71 billion *yuan*, while the investment in urban infrastructure was 0.75 billion. In 1999 total investment was at 185.67 billion *yuan*, and the investment in urban infrastructure was 15.65 *yuan*. Over two decades, 2,401 billion *yuan* have been invested in the urban infrastructure, 90 per cent of which was invested in the last ten years.

An ambitious plan is underway to transform Shanghai into an international economic centre at the advent of the 21st century. Shanghai is facing a significant historic opportunity to re-emerge as a world cultural, economic, financial and trade centre. Such a formidable task can only be accomplished through a solid master plan and the unremitting efforts of the citizens of the city and even of the whole nation. In revising the master plan, the city needs to put the emphasis on Shanghai's social and economic development in the coming decade, along with the readjustment of urban functions, ongoing changes to its layout, the integration of the city's past and prospective future, and the reform of its economic system.

Urban planning must be at the forefront and must play a role of macroscopic guidance in order to overcome a situation in which urban planning lags behind construction due to insufficient depth and breadth. All this urgently demands an improved scientific, forward-looking vision, the updating of concepts, exploration of new ideas, and new starting points in the reform of content and methods in urban planning and administration. On the one hand, it is important to quicken the forward-going pace, revise and optimise the master plan and simultaneously concretise the projects that will bring macroscopic guidance into play and also give scope for legislative and promotional functions. On the other hand, it is necessary to step up planning administration so that the strategic objectives of urban planning may be achieved.

Shanghai must be a truly international metropolis. The aim of urban planning is to help it reach the world's first-rate level and become an important nodal point in the global economic network. To this end, the urban structure of Shanghai must make a strategic adjustment to meet the transformation of the industrial structure. At present, the Shanghai municipal government is working on medium-term city development planning for the period 2000–25. It aims mainly to set up and develop the economic foundation required of all international cities and to foster information, finance and trade; to provide highly developed international services; to set up sound and efficient environments. In this re-adjustment of the economic and industrial structure, it is necessary to shape a modern urban structure for sustainable development.

In July 1999, after six years' hard work and many revised versions the new master plan for Shanghai was finally authorised by the State Council of China. The strategic objective for 2020 was to form a 'multi-core, multi-axis and group-oriented' urban layout consisting of the central city, sub-cities and suburban cities. In addition to the central business district and central commercial district, it planned to set up four sub-centres: in the southwest Xu-Jia-Hui area, in the northeast Jiang-Wan-Wujiao-Chang area, in the northwest Cao-Jia-Du area, and in the Hua-Mu area of Pudong. Based on such a concept, the development of Shanghai will no longer be shaped like a spilt ink mark that randomly spreads in all directions, that is to say, it will not spontaneously move in its commercial dealings step by step towards its perimeter. Instead, it should be an organic urban system and all the other sub-systems, such as land use, traffic planning, infrastructure and facilities, must serve to strengthen the city's cohesive and radiating function (Fig. 37).

In making a comparison with and analysis of the potential and advantages for the development of various metropolises in the world, it is concluded that in developing Shanghai, its natural, historical and social environments must be taken into full account and maximised. Attention should be paid to preserving and utilising not only its natural and physical features, but also to building cultural, historical and human resources. At a time when development is rapid and great in scale after a long period of excluding the outside world, people tend to aim at novelty and variety, neglecting the historical and cultural value of architecture. All too often the fine old buildings that once identified the city are demolished and substituted by fashionable commonplace buildings.

Many measures are being taken to improve the green space within the urban area. From the point of view of urban development, the water space should be made good use of. Historically, Huangpu River and Suzhou Creek have brought much vitality to the city and constituted a good part of Shanghai's identity. The future development of Shanghai should consider Huangpu River, Suzhou Creek and the whole water network in Shanghai. A transformation project for the waterfront at Suzhou Creek is now being put into operation within a 17 kilometre water channel. A new southern and northern Bund, complementing the traditional Bund, is also being planned. In the course of rapid large-scale construction and development, efforts must also be made to preserve houses, buildings and areas of historical and cultural significance.

A modernised, advanced infrastructure is a must. This includes 'hardware' such as traffic, water and electricity supply, communications, environmental engineering, housing and related facilities, as well as 'software' such as education, culture, science and technology, and urban administration. Only with a modernised infrastructure can there be both normal internal operation and close connection with other regions and the international community. In this sense, it can be said that infrastructure is a guarantee of the life of such a metropolitan city.

The updated master plan gives prominence to the construction of an 'information harbour', 'air harbour' and 'deep-water harbour'. A modernised international multimedia information centre is now under construction. The invited competition for the Pudong International Airport was won by Paul Andreu of ADP in 1996. The first phase was opened with a trial run in October 1999. The multi-purpose terminal building has a floor area of 280,000 square metres, including passenger traffic, freight transport, business, storage, information and other services related to aviation. The terminal is a rectangular building of two main levels and is 400 metres long, with a 170 metre-wide central area, and a waiting area of 1,400 metres. For the future development, the airport has a total of four terminal buildings and four runways of 4,000 metres length. After its completion, the airport will be able to handle 70 million passengers and 5 million tons of cargo and mail annually. In August 2001, nine architects and urban planners from Germany, Britain, America, Italy, Australia, Japan and the Netherlands presented their conceptual plans for a deep-water harbour city, Lu-Chao-Gang New City, with a 300,000-strong population and a land area of about 80 square kilometres, which will begin construction in 2002.

In the next five years, Shanghai plans to build 500 kilometres of highway to connect with other cities. In the city, an underground railway system will be constructed. According to the master plan, eight subway lines, four suburban railways and five light railway lines have been planned, while three subway lines of 65 kilmometres have already been put into operation.

The strategic objectives of building an international metropolis demand that Shanghai's urban-planning administration unflinchingly assume a major historical responsibility. Urban planning is based on the anticipated pattern of a city's future state and its development objectives for creating an optimised and sustainable development not only for the urban environment but also for the social and economic environment. It is by no means an idealistic blueprint for a city's 'ultimate state', but a basis for guiding its rational and orderly development. It is a macro-controlled means for the good of urban development in order to enact effective governmental intervention. Its role of legislative provision and guidance is played out at various levels: master plan, district planning, detailed planning, construction planning, and the various planning measures for the metropolitan area and its sub-divided districts and areas. Along with the development of society and the advance of science and technology, there are bound to be advances in the conception and methodology of urban planning. Thus it is important to consider how to enable urban planning to catch up with the market-oriented economy and at the same time to maintain relative steadiness; and how to improve the urban planning system, for the implementation and realisation of the strategic objectives for urban development are of vital realistic and historical significance.

With the introduction of humanistic ideas, architects are increasingly critical about issues regarding the relationship of architecture to society,

From above, from left to right:

Figure 39: The facade of He-Lou-Xuan Pavilion, 1978–81, Feng Jizhong

Figure 40: The straw roof interior of He-Lou-Xuan Pavilion

Figures 41-42: The Mu-Ru-Ju Building of Shanghai State Guest House, 1985, Wei Zhida and others

Figure 43: Tao Xingzhi Memorial Hall, 1986, Guo Xiaoling of the Shanghai Architectural Design Institute

Figure 44: Shanghai Museum, 1996, Xin Tonghe of the Shanghai Architectural Design Institute

Figure 45: Zhu Qizhan Art Museum, 1994–5, Zhen Shiling and others

Figure 46: Jin Mao Tower, 1993–9, SOM

Figure 47: The top end of Jin Mao Tower with Art Deco style

Figure 48: King Tower, 1996, Tao Ho

culture, philosophy and tradition. Influenced by world architectural development, Shanghai architecture has quickly adjusted itself. In the 1980s when Chinese society was in a period of transformation, the keynote for Chinese culture was to seek modernity, and there was unprecedented academic activity in the circle of art, culture and ideas. These drastic changes in Chinese society and its culture gave rise to a trend of seeking the root of Chinese culture. On the one hand, Western culture and ideology were introduced, and on the other, reflection was directed at history, the historical obligation of culture, and a search for the gene of Chinese cultural development. The nature of traditional culture was explored in the context of ancient Chinese philosophy. People began to understand the profound and complicated cultural significance concerning issues of social transition and reform, of whether to go forwards or backwards, to choose originality or stick to the old ways.

In this cultural atmosphere architectural circles resumed discussion of national forms after an interruption of 20 years brought about by the Cultural Revolution. In the 1980s, vernacular and regional architecture were again brought into discussion. Architectural theory laid emphasis on the cultural heritage.

At the core of traditional Chinese culture is the belief in the unity of man and nature. According to this philosophy of ancient China, everything in nature, including humans, is 'substance'. The reason why humans differ from other substances is that they are both close to nature and understand the workings of the world. Such philosophy is based on the same integration of rationality and humanity in which the grassroots of Chinese architecture resides. The Shanghai Grand Opera House (1994–8) is an expression of this ideology. The French architect's office responsible for its design, Arte Jean Marie Chapentier & Associates, won the international architectural design competition from 13 entries in 1994. Completed in 1998, the theatre skilfully demonstrates the idea of 'Life is a stage'. The upward-turned curve of the roof, holding a glass form, symbolises a traditional 'heaven'. Under the roof, the crystal transparency of another glass box containing the stage makes culture come alive to the city. The plaza below symbolises the earth, another traditional element in Chinese architecture. The theatre has a floor area of 63,000 square metres with over 1,800 seats, and it can accommodate performances ranging from concerts to opera and ballet.

Symbolism in Chinese architecture is very different from that of Western architecture, often expressed in abstract ways, and it is difficult to find a new model that combines these traditional symbols with contemporary forms. Some architects are therefore attempting to recover the symbolic meanings of Chinese culture, adopting symbols in relation to the

From above:

Figure 49: The new Lu Xun Memorial Hall, 2000, Xin Tonghe and others

Figure 50: Shanghai Yu Garden Shopping City, 1995–6, East China Architectural Design and Research Institute

Figure 51: Shanghai Library, 1997, Zhang Jiezheng, Tang Yuen and others

Figure 52: Shanghai TV Station Building, 1998, Wang Xiaoan and others

following four notions. Firstly, that Chinese architectural symbolism should be established with respect to the 'spirit' of its structure, which is understood through the 'ideal'; that the 'ideal' is expressed by means of 'form', and therefore that the ideal and the spirit are of the same importance. Secondly, a sense of space is used to represent the essence of Chinese architecture and culture. Thirdly, Chinese architecture is made plain at a philosophical level; in particular by finding the symbiotic relationship between the 'Way' (truth) and the 'Vessel' (substance): the former signifies the spirit of the architecture while the latter is its materialistic level. Only when the two supplement each other can the inner spirit of Chinese architecture be achieved. Finally, the link between modern and traditional architecture is to be formed from traditional Chinese architecture, the prototype of vernacular and regional architecture in particular.

The Square Pagoda Garden in Song Jiang, Shanghai, which was designed by Feng Jizhong in 1978–81, is a perfect example of the incorporation of form and spirit (Fig. 38). This modern Chinese public garden is composed of several historic relics and new structures designed in the vernacular spirit. At its centre is the Fang Ta (Square Pagoda), which dates back to the Song Dynasty (960–1279). Other historic elements include a wall with terracotta carvings of 1370, and a stone bridge from the Song Dynasty. A Qing Dynasty temple hall was moved from the central city of Shanghai, along with another from Songjiang Town, and placed to the north of the wall. The two new gateways and the bamboo tea-house have aroused much attention. The former consists of two pavilions with traditional Chinese roofs supported by an open steel structure, while the latter is a charming bamboo-frame structure with a saddle-formed roof (Figs. 39-40). Professor Feng Jizhong leads the field in exploring the traditional Chinese spirit in modern and vernacular architecture, and has been doing so since the 1960s. The Square Pagoda Garden is one of the most important masterpieces in contemporary Chinese architecture.

In the 1980s, the trend started by Feng Jizhong was continued in an investigation of the traditional vernacular style in architecture. The Mu-Ru-Ju Building of Shanghai State Guest House (1985), whose inner court is in the manner of traditional Chinese gardens, is a representative work (Figs. 41-42). Such an approach is also evident in the spatial arrangement of the Tao Xingzhi Memorial Hall, 1986 (Fig. 43); the Shanghai Museum, 1996 (Fig. 44); and the Zhu Qizhan Art Museum, 1994–5 (Fig. 45).

The Jin Mao Tower of 1993–9 by the Chicago practice SOM (Skidmore, Owings & Merrill LLP) exemplifies this spirit in contemporary architecture, despite the fact that it has been created by an American architect (Figs. 46-47). It is certainly one of SOM's best works of the last

From above:

Figure 53: Fuxing High School, 1996–8, Zheng Shiling and others

Figure 54: The concert hall and gymnasium of Fuxing High School

Figure 55: Night view of Shanghai Stadium, 1997, Wei Dunshan and others

Figure 56: The Hong Kou Football Field, 1999, RIA

Above, left to right:

Figure 57: Lujiazui Garden, 1999, B + H Architects International Inc

Figure 58: Ren-Heng Riverside Garden, 1999, architect unknown

Figure 59: Wanko City Garden Residential Quarter, 2000

ten years. Rising 420.6 metres above Pudong New Area, it is China's tallest building and a monument to the open policy of Shanghai. Its design recalls the ancient pagoda forms of China. The mixed-use complex consists of an 88-storey tower and six-storey podium building. With 0.278 million square metres of office space, the 555-room Hyatt Hotel, a retail gallery, service amenities and parking, the building is virtually a city in itself. In his design for the King Tower, with its 62,234 square metres of floor area, the Hong Kong architect Tao Ho has adopted a simple treatment for the facade, and conveys just an echo of the traditional Chinese roof (Fig. 48).

In the design and planning of the reconstructed Lu Xun Memorial Hall (Fig. 49) and the Shanghai Yu Garden Shopping City (Fig. 50), the architects adopted the idea of generating, duplicating and patching up, thus restoring the vernacular sense of scale and space.

In the 1990s, Shanghai paid more attention to cultural facilities, such as libraries, museums, theatres, television centres and schools. The Shanghai Library (1997) is a modern, large-scale building (a total floor area of 84,000 square metres) with 13 million books and all the necessary amenities (Fig. 51). The Shanghai TV Station Building (1998) was designed by a young architect, and harmonises with the urban centre in which it is located (Fig. 52). In the mid-1990s, 11 high schools with comprehensive education facilities were planned for construction in a suburb of the city. By the end of 2000, six new schools were opened. Amongst them, the Fuxing High School (1996–8) is the smallest and most compact, with a 26,000 square metre floor area (Figs. 53-54). In 1997, the 80,000-seat Shanghai Stadium hosted its first national game (Fig. 55), while in 1999 the first special football field in China was opened to the public. Designed by the Japanese architect office RIA, it is China's finest stadium in terms of its form and roof structure (Fig. 56).

Housing construction in Shanghai plays an important role, with about 12 to 15 million square metres built yearly. Since the beginning of the 1990s, housing has increasingly been privately owned and sold. In 2000, 97.5 percent of housing was privately bought. The quality of

housing and its environment are therefore being paid more attention by developers and architects. The Wanli Residential Area (2000), for example, has 18 million square metres of public facilities, shopping centres and offices, while the Canadian-designed Lujiazui Garden (1999), is a residential facility with a total floor area of 123,600 square metres (Fig. 57). Other representative examples are Ren-Heng Riverside Garden (Fig. 58) and Wanko City Garden (Fig. 59).

Shanghai has now become a centre of world architecture and international culture, while Shanghai architects and urban planners have adapted to the notions and trends of world architecture and urban development. However, in the future Shanghai will be exposed to new problems. The mission of Shanghai architects is to think rationally about how to provide a basis for the sustainable development of that future.

Though ideological liberation and political reform have brought about a relaxed artistic atmosphere, architects have been damaged by the many years in which they were shackled ideologically and prohibited from blazing new trails. They saw the destruction of their original value system by a succession of political movements, not least the Cultural Revolution, and a new value system is yet to be established. Now, with a market economy replacing the former planned economy, and with commercialism permeating every realm, value systems are still confused. This has resulted in a further loss for culture. Many people have abandoned their rationality and faith through eagerness for quick success and instant profit.

Such social values have resulted in a mainstream of ornamentalism and mannerism, even a ridiculous revival of European Neoclassicism, such as in the Shanghai International Conference Centre (1994–9), with its decorative capital and large concrete sphere painted like a globe (Fig. 60). Contemporary Shanghai architecture is threatening to become an imitation of a superficial Disneyland, cartoon style. The Court Building of Minhang District (2000) (Fig. 61), for example, is a ludicrous copy of Capitol Hill in Washington DC, while the Sun Wonderland Residential Quarter (1999) panders ingratiatingly to vulgar taste (Fig. 62).

From above:

Figure 60: Shanghai International Conference Centre, 1994–9, original scheme by Nihon Sekkei, developed by the Architectural Design Institute of Zhejiang Province

Figure 61: Minhang Court Building, 2000

Figure 62: Sun Wonderland Residential Quarter, 1999

CHALLENGES AND POTENTIAL

ZHENG SHILING

In his book *Invisible Cities* (1972) the Italian writer Italo Calvino identified two kinds of cities: 'those that through the years and the changes continue to give their form to desires, and those in which desires either erase the city or are erased by it'. There are few cities in the contemporary world that fall into the first category; Shanghai is one of them. Though it has experienced the vicissitudes of life, it is still youthful and dynamic. People who grew up there and now live in other parts of the world long to be back home. One might ask, what makes a city so beloved? A city full of breathtaking scenery, magnificent artworks, brilliant architecture, overlapping cultures and with creative inhabitants will inevitably attract people to live in or visit it. In Shanghai, one will always find something unique and familiar, and one can always find one's own corner or place. Old Shanghai is a concentration of international architectural history, and the developing Shanghai is a new chapter of an old book that is still being written. From the old book, one can read of a significant past and an even more brilliant future. Because of its special charm, Shanghai provides endless inspiration for artists, writers, architects, and even urban planners.

Shanghai's history can be traced back 3,000 years, with three glorious periods: the 13th century, the 1920s and 1930s, and the 1990s. Its tolerance to multiculturalism was demonstrated early on, and totally transformed the city. The 13th century established it as an administrative entity, which provided an opportunity for it to become a city of the world. Due to its great prosperity in the 1920s and 1930s, Shanghai was able to keep pace as an international metropolis (Figs. 1-3). Its open policy in the 1990s provided the chance for redevelopment as an international stage for both domestic and foreign businesses, urban planners and architects.

Shanghai has always been an open city, full of opportunity, allowing its citizens to display their talent and creativity and this competitive and commercial tradition makes the city a dynamic and progressive society. Many qualified immigrants have moved to Shanghai to put their ability to good use. The Shanghainese intelligence and skill in every field of science and technology is truly unique in China. A major factor that sets Shanghai's development apart from that of other Chinese cities is its entrepreneurial spirit and its bold drive for innovation. The importance of Shanghai is largely due to its location, midway along the China coast; it serves as an effective link not only between the port cities of north and south China, but also between cities in Japan and Korea as well as in the Asia-Pacific region. The hinterland of Shanghai is enormous and unequalled in China.

When conditions are ripe, Shanghai is uniquely equipped to develop at high speed. Since 1990, the urban landscape has undergone an unprecedented boom. The number of high-rise buildings in Shanghai has seen a particularly rapid increase. By the end of 1980, there were only 149 high-rise buildings in the city, but by 1990 the figure was 956, and by 1999, 3,185; among these, 1,350 buildings exceed 20 floors, most of them located in the city centre (Figs. 4-5). Such a rapid and large-scale urban development, however, sometimes tends to seek novelty and change for their own sake, affected by an eagerness for instant benefit to the detriment of a coherent final goal (Fig. 6).

Chinese people frequently talk about 'challenge and opportunity', both in political and ideological terms. The challenge for today's Shanghai is clearly present in its strategy of urban development: to transform the city into an international metropolis and a centre for culture, economy, finance and trade. But it is facing critical contradictions.

Opposite: Nanjing Road pedestrianised in 2000.

Above, left to right: Figure 1-3: The skyline of Shanghai in the 1930s, 1987, 2000

Below, left and centre: Figures 4-5: The skyline of the west bank of Huangpu River in the daytime and in the evening, 2000

Below right: Figure 6: The new buildings around the central green space of Lu-Jia-Zui CBD, 2001

For instance, in the course of transformation, how does one create a proper urban culture of one's own, while preserving the urban context and architectural heritage? And in transforming the social structure and economy, how does one avoid the urge for quick success and instant pay off? Given that land resources are limited, how does one maintain a balance between high density and high quality living space? To achieve all this, certain problems in the field of administration, policy and quality of personnel must be solved. If the long-term task of redeveloping Shanghai as an international metropolis is to be accomplished, it is necessary to enhance the cultural quality for both citizens and government officials, though it is almost the highest in China.

During the past ten years, no other city has achieved such improvement in the quality of the built environment as Shanghai. Since the late 1990s, a rational movement for the improvement of the urban environment has developed, following the principle that the human being should be placed at the core of every decision. In 1993, the Bund was reconstructed as a waterfront boulevard. Many other areas have also been redeveloped as public amenities, including Nanjing Pedestrian Road (Figs. 7-9); Duo-Lun Cultural Street; Century Boulevard (Fig. 10); Wujiang Road Pedestrian Area; and the public plaza of Jingan Temple Subway Station (Fig. 11). In 1865 Nanjing Road became the commercial centre of China, now visited every day by about a million people. East Nanjing Road, the cradle of China's modern commercial culture and still one of the most famous commercial streets in the world, has become the symbol of Shanghai's prosperous economy. It has been included in the preservation of commercial buildings. Established in the mid-19th century, East Nanjing Road began to take its modern shape in the 1920s and 1930s. Four great department stores, Sincere Company (1917),

Wing On Company (1918), Sun-Sun Company (1926), the new building of Wing On Company (1933) and Sun Company (1936) represented the prosperity of East Nanjing Road and of Shanghai's economy. Containing other historical buildings and heritage landmarks, Nanjing Road is also an important cultural centre.

At the same time, the amount of green space in the city has increased. In 2001, the creation of green space became Shanghai's greatest endeavour. Twelve such spaces, totalling 230,000 square metres, have appeared in the city centre, for example. Today, there are already more than 5 million square metres of public green space in Shanghai. The coverage rate of urban green areas was 12.4 per cent in 1990, with a per capita rate of 1.02 square metres. By 1999, these statistics had increased to 20.3 per cent and 3.62 square metres respectively.

Large-scale construction has taught the municipal government to pay more attention to advanced planning. The year 2001 could be that of urban planning in Shanghai. The New Master Plan of Shanghai (2000–20) has finally been approved by the State Council of China, and the 10th Five-Year Plan (2001–5) has also been conceived (Fig. 12). Today, Shanghai is becoming an international laboratory for experimental architecture and advanced urban planning concepts. The contribution of construction is truly significant. No other city in the world has planned and built so much within a period of 20 years. As early as 1992, new ideas for an Asian compact city had been worked out by the international consultation on the urban design of the central business district in Lu-Jia-Zui, Pudong, Richard Rogers from the UK, Dominique Perrault from France, Massimiliano Fuksas from Italy, and Toyo Ito from Japan.

In 2001, three satellite cities, Songjiang City, Lu-Chao-Gang New City, Jin-Shan City and six suburb towns, An-Ting Town, Pu-Jiang Town,

Feng-Cheng Town, Luo-Dian Town, Gao-Qiao Town, Zhu-Jia-Jiao Town, invited architects and urban planners from the US, UK, Germany, Italy, France, Australia, Sweden, Spain, Holland, Japan and China to present their conceptual plans. All the participants took into account a vast land area; the scale of expansion and development is truly incredible. Some plans reveal inspirational new ideas, while others have adapted to the contemporary situation historical models such as Ebenezer Howard's Garden City, Arturo Soria's *Ciudad Lineal*, and Le Corbusier's *Plan Voisin*. is also present the concept of a utopian or ideal city (Fig. 13). No one city has developed so many new urban planning concepts in such a short period, nor held so many international architectural and urban design competitions.

In 2000–1, Shanghai is systematically working on the planning of the public space for Huangpu River and Suzhou Creek. The San Francisco office of Skidmore, Owings & Merrill LLP, and Sassakki Urban Planning Office from the USA, with Philip Cox from Australia, have presented a conceptual design for the 25 kilometre-long riverfront of Huangpu River, which involves the transformation of the existing harbours, factories and warehouses into a leisure and cultural waterfront. For the World Exposition of 2010, which is under application process, a former steel plant on the Huangpu Riverfront would be an ideal site.

In the early 1990s, Shanghai had already established a strategy for the development of Pudong called 'One Dragon's Head and Three Centres', which would make it a leading area and help build up the city as an economic, financial and trade centre as quickly as possible. In this way, Shanghai set in motion its efforts to create a boom in the regional economy of the Yangtze Delta and its valley. Spurred on by speedy economic growth, urban construction has also shown great development.

However, many new problems in urban planning and administration have arisen. The slogan 'A new look for the city in one year, and astonishing changes in three years', has become the guideline of urban reconstruction and redevelopment, signalling that hasty change is overshadowing considered planning. There is now an urgent need for rational criteria for urban planning administration. For example, when planning permission was sought for Tomorrow Square (2001), the only criteria specified were for floor area and function etc, with no restriction set on height. The rocket-like office and hotel building, 282 metres high, now dominates its surroundings and somehow destroys the urban environment of the adjacent People's Square (Fig. 14). The situation is very similar with Plaza 66 (2001) (Fig. 15). Serious efforts must be made for innovation in the field of planning legislation, to impose detailed control on all construction projects, and to revise the two-tier administration policy for urban planning. Under this system, the municipal government can control only 10 per cent of new projects; and the other 90 per cent is mainly under the control of district government and even the investors.

Government officials, architects and planners, however, seem to feel they do not have time to keep a cool head. A general impulsive mood has penetrated nearly every field of social life. Slogans such as 'A well-known master of urban construction' and 'Not behind the times even over the next twenty years' have become popular. On the other hand, government officials sometimes intervene in the minor details and side

From above:

Figure 7: The Nanjing Road in 1930s

Figure 8: The Nanjing Road in 1998

Figure 9: The scheme of Arte Jean Marie Charpentier in 1998

Figure 10: A general view of the Century Boulevard, 2000

issues of architectural designs. A modern college school can be transformed into a Neoclassical building by order of a top government official without respecting the original architectural concept. The pseudo-classical Shanghai International Conference Centre even found itself on the 1999 list of the best buildings of the last 50 years, despite the fact that the experts were against it.

To meet the ever-burgeoning requirement for high living standards, about 15 million square metres of new housing are constructed every year and demand for the transformation of existing housing is also intense. The latter has constituted a major task for urban renewal since the mid-1980s. Despite a plan for the preservation of historic buildings and neighbourhoods, the old urban fabric is facing a crisis of destruction (Figs. 16-17). The urban space of Shanghai is losing its distinctiveness, and being replaced by a prevailing global internationalisation. The historic and cultural value of architecture, meanwhile, tends to be ignored. Commonplace buildings are taking the place of fine architectural works of exquisite design that were of acknowledged historical and cultural value. Having survived the vicissitudes of life for centuries, these landmarks of Shanghai have been quickly submerged in an ocean of super highrise buildings. Every client would like his building to become a new landmark. However, people are beginning to understand the consequences of this attitude and are trying to resolve such problems through the detailed and integrated Preservation Plan for the Historic City of Shanghai.

The Xin Tian Di plan offers a new approach to urban renewal: to create a compact and workable district centre, located between Shanghai's ancient walled city and its dynamic downtown. The idea of the project is to bridge the old and the new. It is a development that will ultimately accommodate 1.6 million square metres of retail, housing, offices and hotels. The main goal of its architects, SOM, is to create a sense of place and to integrate the new development sensitively into the city's existing fabric. The district's various uses are distributed around a central open space that features a 3.7-hectare manmade lake. As an approach to the renewal of the old *li long* housing it has methodological value, but cannot be an ideal model for the renewal of historical residential areas in Shanghai. Its layout arbitrarily changes the urban fabric and undermines the original context. The artificial lake was dug out from an old residential district. Only a tiny part of the historic housing is preserved and its original function has been transformed into a commercial area. The surrounding old housing will soon be replaced by highrise and luxury buildings. The Xin Tian Di Project has thus generated discussion about the rapid destruction of Shanghai's old urban fabric (Fig. 18).

In China, it is said that a six-year-old will do something first and think about it later, while a 60-year-old thinks first and acts later. The urban

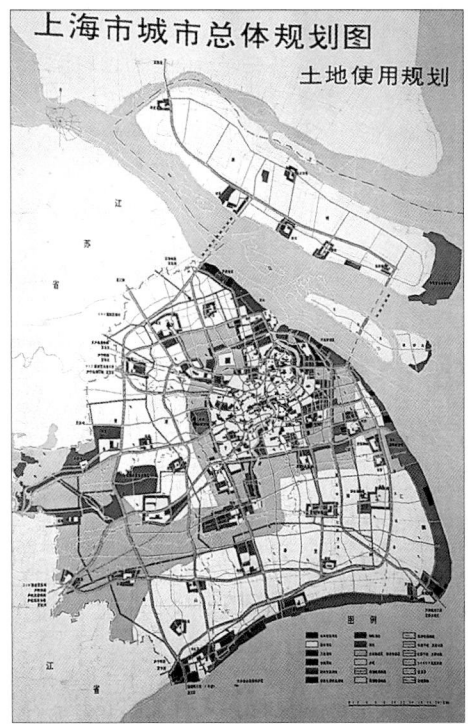

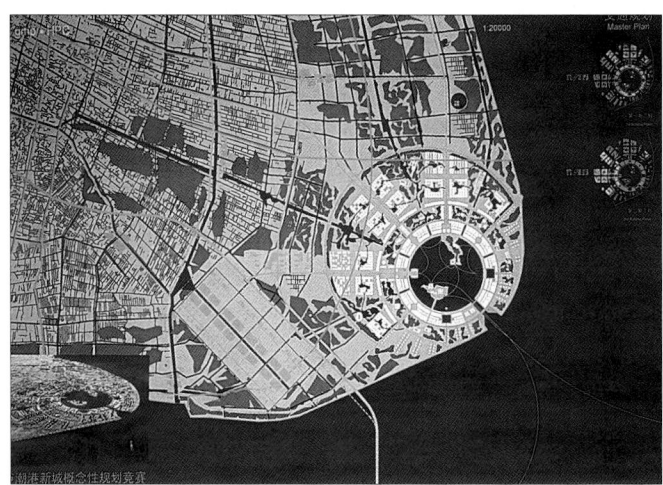

Above left: Figure 11: The public plaza of Jingan Temple Subway Station, 2000
Below left: Figure 12: The land use of the New Master Plan of Shanghai, 2000
Below right: Figure 13: Plan for Lu-Chao-Gang New City, 2001, Meinhard von Gerkan

planners of Shanghai have not yet grown up. Although there are outstanding Chinese architects and planners, who have experienced a period of the most rapid development ever in Chinese history, such vast development in other continents and countries may take 100 or even 200 years to achieve. In this sense it could be claimed that the output of Chinese architects is 25,000 times that of their American colleagues.

Some years ago, the current large-scale construction could not even have been imagined by an architect or planner with a practice in Shanghai such as myself. The young generation of architects has matured rapidly, engaging directly in real practice in a way that their teachers could never have expected. The downside is that these practitioners no longer have time for the investigation of architectural and urban theory, which has not yet been studied systematically, and most professionals have only a superficial knowledge of it. The criteria for what is excellent and what is inferior architecture are therefore unclear, even confused, in the minds of many people, who find it difficult to discriminate between good and bad. A sense of criticism and value in architectural design needs to be cultivated, both for architects and for non-professionals. In 1997, a registered architects system was established in China, but architects are still constrained by a sense of traditional hierarchy: their status, both socially and economically, is still very low. Government officials are embracing globalisation without understanding that professional knowledge is the key to the future development of a city. They believe more in foreign architects than their Shanghainese counterparts. Chinese architects are frequently discriminated against in competitions.

Shanghai City is by no means a *tabula rasa*; it is important to rearrange the urban space and to construct a clear urban identity in future developments. To realise this aim, the preservation of the historical heritage, the reconstruction of waterfront spaces and the control of random development are vital.

From above left, clockwise:

Figure 14: Tomorrow Square, 2001, John Portman in association with the Shanghai Architectural Design and Research Institute

Figure 15: Plaza 66, 2001, KPF Associates PC/Frank CY Feng Architects & Associates (HK) Ltd in association with the East China Architectural Design Institute

Figure 16: The old urban fabric before the large-scale redevelopment, 1987

Figure 17: The new urban fabric, 2000

Figure 18: The model of Xin Tian Di Project, 2001, SOM

太阳都市花园

SUN WONDERLAND

Photographs around the many layers of the Shanghai Yu Garden Shopping City, at the northern edge of the old city, east of the Yu Yuan Gardens and the City temple; all formed in a well-made exuberant Chinoiserie. An area developed in the mid 1990s dominated by stores selling traditional Chinese goods, jade and silk, and popular day and night. East China Architectural Design and Research Institute, 1995-9.

Apart from the TV tower everything in view was built in the last decade of the 20th century. Oriental Pearl TV Tower, also called the Pearl of the East, rises to a height of 468 metres: the tallest tower in Asia and the third tallest in the world. Standing by the bank of the Huangpu River in the rapidly developing Pudong district, this tower was built to symbolize the reemergence of Shanghai as a leading world trade centre.

Comprised of eleven red spheres, between 45 and 50 metres in diameter and supported by three giant columns, 9 metres in diameter, the tower dominates the skyline of the Lujiazui Financial Centre. Date of completion 1994.

Friday night on Nanjing Road, early in the 21st century, thousands of people strolling beneath the walls of neon, or hopping onto little carriages that slowly wind their way through the crowds, advertising 'Cadbury's Chocolate' and 'Sun Kist', entertained by Chinese and western music. After the football game ended on the large screen, a 'Seven Up' rap concert quickly took over center stage.

SHANGHAI: BETTER AND BETTER

XIA LIQING

Translated by Dia Songzhuo and Barbara Stubblebine

Shanghai is located at the midpoint of China's eastern coast and sits at the mouth of the Changjiang River. This location gives the city several advantages. In a 1,450,000 square-kilometre inland area and with a population of 0.4 billion, the Changjiang River, supplying broad space and strong backup, is integral to the development of Shanghai.

Shanghai's position makes it an excellent international location; it is the central point in a chain of the most important East Asian cities. A two-hour flight can easily cover the distance between Shanghai and any of these cities and this makes economic exchange and communication fast and convenient for Shanghai. The river and seacoast allow easy transportation and communication, both international and domestic, increasing Shanghai's development potential and making it a bridge that links the Chinese economy with the global economy.

The total area of Shanghai is 6,340 square kilometres, that is approximately 0.06 percent of China, and the city has a population of 14 million. It is the largest city in China, and one of the largest in the world. Presently, downtown Shanghai makes up about 670 square kilometres. Current administrative records divide Shanghai into 16 districts and four counties.

Evolving from a small fishing village, Shanghai was a simple coastal commercial town 700 years ago. Later, a county was administratively set up and the town gradually formed a concentrated place of trade and business along the Huangpu River. As merchants continued to gather, the town became known as 'The Famous Town in the Southeast'. Its residences, gardens and markets bore traditional Chinese characteristics. After the Opium War, Shanghai was forced to open as one of the harbour cities. Foreign immigrants began to build settlements, and the construction and enlargement of these areas accelerated Shanghai's urbanisation. By the 1930s, the population of Shanghai had increased to five million, making it the largest city in the Far East. The city acquired the name, 'Architectural Expo of Multi-State Style', reflecting its characteristic multiculturalism. However, the city was composed of several settlements belonging to different nations other than China. This fragmentation caused separate construction and development within the city. United urban planning for the city as a whole was absent. The urban structure was in chaos and the city function disabled.

Since the foundation of the People's Republic of China in 1949, the municipal government has paid close attention to urban planning and city construction. The built environment was thoroughly rearranged and newly planned as a whole. After 50 years' effort, especially the rapid development in the 1990s, Shanghai became what we can see today. The history of the past 50 years should be remembered. In the first 40 years, the people and the municipal government of Shanghai, through reorganisation, construction and renewal, successfully transformed Shanghai from a handicapped, developing city into a socialist city with a united structure of city layout, an advanced economy and a peaceful life. In the 1950s, suburban industrial parks were built and the small, potentially hazardous factories were moved out from the downtown area of the city. Meanwhile, workers were provided with affordable housing that became known as the 'Workers' New Village'. The racetrack was reconstructed into People's Square and People's Park. Ten more counties, one being Jiading County, were added to the Shanghai map, increasing the whole administrative area from 636 square kilometres to more than 6,000. Additionally, the municipal government planned and constructed such satellite towns as Ming Hang and Jiading. In the 1960s, Hongqiao (Rainbow) International Airport was enlarged and rebuilt. With industry and population layouts adjusted, and road and traffic in urban areas newly ordered, a united city structure was gradually evolving.

Meanwhile, plans were made to rebuild the old, slum housing areas of the city. Flood prevention facilities were enhanced and the city became more capable of handling sewage treatment. In the 1970s the south bank area of the Changjiang river mouth and the north bank area of Hangzhou bay were planned and constructed. The first cross-tunnel under Huangpu River was built during this time. In the 1980s, several housing, office and hotel building projects began. Highway systems were also under construction, as was the Joint Ventiduct Engineering sewage project. The developing districts of Hongqiao and Ming Hang were set and constructed as economic and technology districts. Research and urban renewal projects were ongoing. By the end of the 1980s the urban area of Shanghai had grown to 257 square kilometres from 82 square kilometres in the 1950s. However, even as the city worked to achieve unity and overcome legacy issues, several negative elements, such as housing shortages, traffic problems and loss of environmental quality, all stood in the way of Shanghai's progress, restraining its development.

From the viewpoint of city construction and development, the fastest and highest jump for Shanghai was in the 1990s. It was an unforgettable decade. Reform and open policy gave Shanghai much opportunity. The development of Pudong officially started. Several important infrastructure projects such as Nanpu, the Yangpu Bridge and the doubling tunnel of Yan'an Road had been built. The Waigaoqiao tax-free district, Jingqiao Industrial Park for Export Products, Rujiazui Financial and Business District, Sunqiao Modern Agriculture District, and the Zhangjiang High-tech Park were planned and constructed. A strategic blueprint that aimed at making Shanghai one of the international centres of economy, finance and business, was gradually revealed.

The construction of the city's infrastructure was emphasised more and more. The foundation of the first phase saw the construction of Pudong International Airport, Hu Ning highway (between Shanghai and Nanjing) and Hu Hang highway (between Shanghai and Hangzhou), as well as new harbours along the river and the seacoast. All these made it possible for Shanghai to enhance its function both inward and outward. In response to the urban traffic, an elevated road system with one loop and a cross was built. The foundation of the main urban road system consisted of three level avenues and three vertical streets, and with this, traffic in Shanghai reached a new peak. It broke away from the old system where all the traffic had been on a single-plan level. It was an immense improvement. Meanwhile, infrastructure construction of energy supply facilities and other services was also improved. All these efforts made a stable basis for the future development of Shanghai.

Housing projects increased both in quality and quantity. It can be said that the top priority for the municipal government was dealing with traffic problems; however, the housing shortage ran a close second. Each new government term attempted to solve it. This pushed forward a large range of urban renewal projects. The average living space per person ranged from 4.7 to 10 square metres, making the building square per person 20 square metres. In suburban districts and satellite towns, the statistics show an even higher range –13.4 square metres of living space per person, with a building square per person of 26.8 square metres. Construction of housing projects in recent decades has not only solved the severe problem of poor living conditions, but also made an improvement in the quality of life, which includes the quality of the buildings and their surrounding environment. When inspecting newly built housing areas one may find a tremendous change in the spatial layout and the amount of green space. The exteriors of residences, such as shape and colour, are now more diverse, tailored to meet the different demands of citizens with differing incomes. Apartment buildings and villas add to the richness of the city landscape.

Public buildings are continuing to develop. Supported by a group of different public centres and led by the Central Business District, a semi-core framework of urban space has been set up. Newcomers to the city are often struck by these buildings, which are vivid, attractive and diverse in style, and offer many amenities and services. Among these landmarks of the new century are the Oriental Pearl TV Tower, Shanghai Library, Shanghai Stadium and the Grand Opera House. The Rujiazui Central Financial and Trade Area and Hongqiao Economy and Technology Developing District are not only spaces for a wealth of city functions, but also form two groups of elegant skylines along the east–west axis of Shanghai's central urban area. Meanwhile, shopping streets and areas like Nanjing Road, Huaihai Road, Sichuan Road and Yu Garden Commercial City have been radically revived with projects combining the urban renewal process and adjustment of land use. Some new shopping centres have been built along those streets. With the transformation of Nanjing Road into a pedestrian street, a brand new environment of shopping and entertaining has been supplied to the public. Numerous tourists are attracted to the place. Ten years ago, inhabitants might have felt extremely curious about the mysterious world abroad, but now a modern city of their own is connecting firmly with the outer world and still progressing.

Every year the city's environmental quality is improving. In the period of high-speed economic development of the 1990s, the municipal government focused particularly on this aspect. Potentially pollution-producing industrial districts were moved out of the urban area; the inner city is mainly restricted to pollution-free tertiary urban industry. With these methods of adjustment to the production structure, the enhanced pollution control treatment and management have also provided added benefits to the city. The Suzhou River is no longer dark and odorous with sewage. With this landmark change, much has also been achieved in treating the water, atmosphere and solid waste. Tree planting is broadly encouraged. With new laws and policies in place, green projects are, one by one, becoming a reality. These include a coastal tree belt and manmade forests in suburban areas, an outer green belt along the central urban area, and a grand public green space in the central part of downtown. A good ecological environmental foundation is thus being established in Shanghai.

After more than 50 years, a modern city stands in the east. It is a great scientifically and technologically advanced metropolis composed of different towns and cities, and one whose economy is prospering. It is full of cultural diversity and sensitive to new information from elsewhere. It is planned with a rational layout, with traffic moving easily and quickly. Now, while wandering the streets of Shanghai, one can instantly feel this great progress through the city's strong, growing, living pulse.

The world has now entered the 21st century. The recent years between the old and new centuries have been the fastest developing time in human history. With world economic globalisation and a more homogeneous world economy, together with rapid economic development in the Asian-Pacific area, the revitalisation of Shanghai has been given both chances and challenges. As the capital city of the Chinese economy, Shanghai is sure to grasp all opportunities firmly, preserving its strong heritage, initiating new ones and planning and constructing a more brilliant future as a modern international metropolis. Energies will be focused on several aspects:

- Carrying out a strategy of sustainable development. Sustainable development is now common sense around the world, and it is one of the two main state strategies for national economic and social development. Urban planning and construction for Shanghai in the future will be carried out under this strategy. The

Changjiang river-mouth triangle area will be taken as a coherent urban space; productive forces, population and infrastructure layouts will be arranged to encourage the harmonious development of the economy, society, population, resources and environment. Meanwhile, human concerns will always be seen as the fundamental element. Citizens in Shanghai will enjoy a good living, working, learning and entertainment environment. A new Shanghai full of fresh strength and growth will emerge in the new century.

- Enhancing the function of the central city and creating a rational layout in order to maintain the balance between the development of the city and countryside. We will focus on the opening up and development of Pudong, as a pioneering area with increased attractions. We will make all efforts to create a market system that is fair and regulated so that Shanghai can be a prosperous commercial city that, like the sea, contains all rivers and welcomes traders from everywhere. We will enlarge the new service territories and develop business, tourism and transportation industries to make Shanghai a centre of retail, exhibitions and conferences. Urban planning will play a more important role in adjustment and control. In terms of the better configuration of resources, emphasis will be placed on different zones of mutual association and support. The city will be developed in three cycles. Inside the inner loop, we will mainly develop tertiary industry. We will build a central business district first to present an image of prosperity. Between the inner and outer loops, we will develop high-tech industry. We will accelerate the construction of substance delivery and reservation centres; and we will build up several modern-life housing parks. Outside the outer loop, we will focus on a modern industrial park and agriculture bases. We will accelerate the assemblage of suburban populations into cities and towns, industry into parks and agriculture into mass management.

- Accelerating the construction process of a key transportation port. Aimed at one of the international shipping centres, the transportation system must be improved. We will focus on developing a comprehensive container transportation system, cored with the harbour and based on a transportation net that includes both imports and exports. We will build an organised air transportation harbour with Pudong and Hongqiao international airports to actively develop passenger and product air transportation. We will set up the Shanghai international information harbour to make the state economy and society more accessible and meet the level of other advanced countries. To develop a metropolitan loop and the Changjiang River triangle zone as a whole, we will construct a highway and a high-speed rail system.

- Improving the quality of the living, working, education and entertainment environment. Shanghai is a famous city whose rich historical and cultural content is accredited by the state. The process of constructing a modern international metropolis must take into consideration all the processes of new developing districts and the conservation and renewal of old districts within an integrated

historical context. In the early years of the 21st century, there will be approximately 20 large-scale housing projects built between the inner and outer loops. With 18 square metres as the average living area per person, the quality of the outdoor residential environment will be improved. Other important aspects include architectural style, public building support and facilities, traffic, green space, community culture, urban environment renewal and the reduction of population density. Suitable housing rates and functional adjustments should preserve traditional housing as much as possible and actively preserve our excellent historical buildings and streets.

- Improving the environmental quality. With the production and industrial structure in place, there will be increased treatment of contamination, and with progress in the standard of administration – marked by the comprehensive treatment of the Suzhou River – we will achieve clear success in dealing with sewage issues. The percentage of public green space will increase inside the inner loop, making it more enjoyable for Shanghai residents. With the enhancement of the outer-loop green belt and other green areas of the city, together with the green corridors along the main streets and skeleton rivers, a green system in the downtown area composed by 'loop, point, corridor and garden' will form. Residents of Shanghai will be able to breathe fresh air freely in the central part of the city.

- Strengthening the city's infrastructure construction. A modernised city infrastructure will guarantee Shanghai's place as a modern international metropolis. With new roads and increased traffic in urban areas, a metro system will be created in the central city of Shanghai. Also, to improve the public transportation network we will open special roads for bus traffic only. With this, we can reduce inefficient traffic time. We will also further develop the water supply source, gradually making it possible to separate water according to its quality. We will finish constructing a project that ventilates east sea gas into Shanghai to allow a gas supply to the whole city. We will finish constructing a high-pressure cycle net of electricity. In addition to building new electricity factories and enlarge old ones, we will be more active in receiving outside electricity to balance supply and demand. We will reduce the number of areas inside the inner loop that have no water emission facilities. We will enhance the standard of water emission. In conclusion, we will have a better system of city infrastructure that complements Shanghai as a modern international metropolis.

The 21st century is full of promise. In the new century, we will build Shanghai into the largest economic shipping centre in China, placing it in the first rank of historical cultural cities. Furthermore, we will gradually build the city into one of the international central cities of economy, finance and trade. We firmly believe that with all the efforts that are currrently being made by the municipal government and the people of Shanghai, we will be able to carry out our plans and bring all our goals to fruition.

The Great Model in the Urban Exhibition Building

SHANGHAI BUILDS

ARTE CHARPENTIER ET ASSOCIES
CENTURY AVENUE, 2001

Century Avenue is the spine of the Pudong district, linking the main development poles of the financial and business city of Lujiazui to the scientific city at Pudong Park. This 100-metre-wide, 5-kilometre-long avenue is curved at its middle, and has nine different squares and planned crossroads.

While complying with all the requirements of a main traffic artery, the project favours the local car shopper and pedestrians through the creation of underground roads, public transport via a new subway line, and a wide footpath protected from the sun by two rows of Ginkgo biloba and camphor trees. It is hoped pedestrians will be attracted to the scattered gardens, enclosures and pergolas.

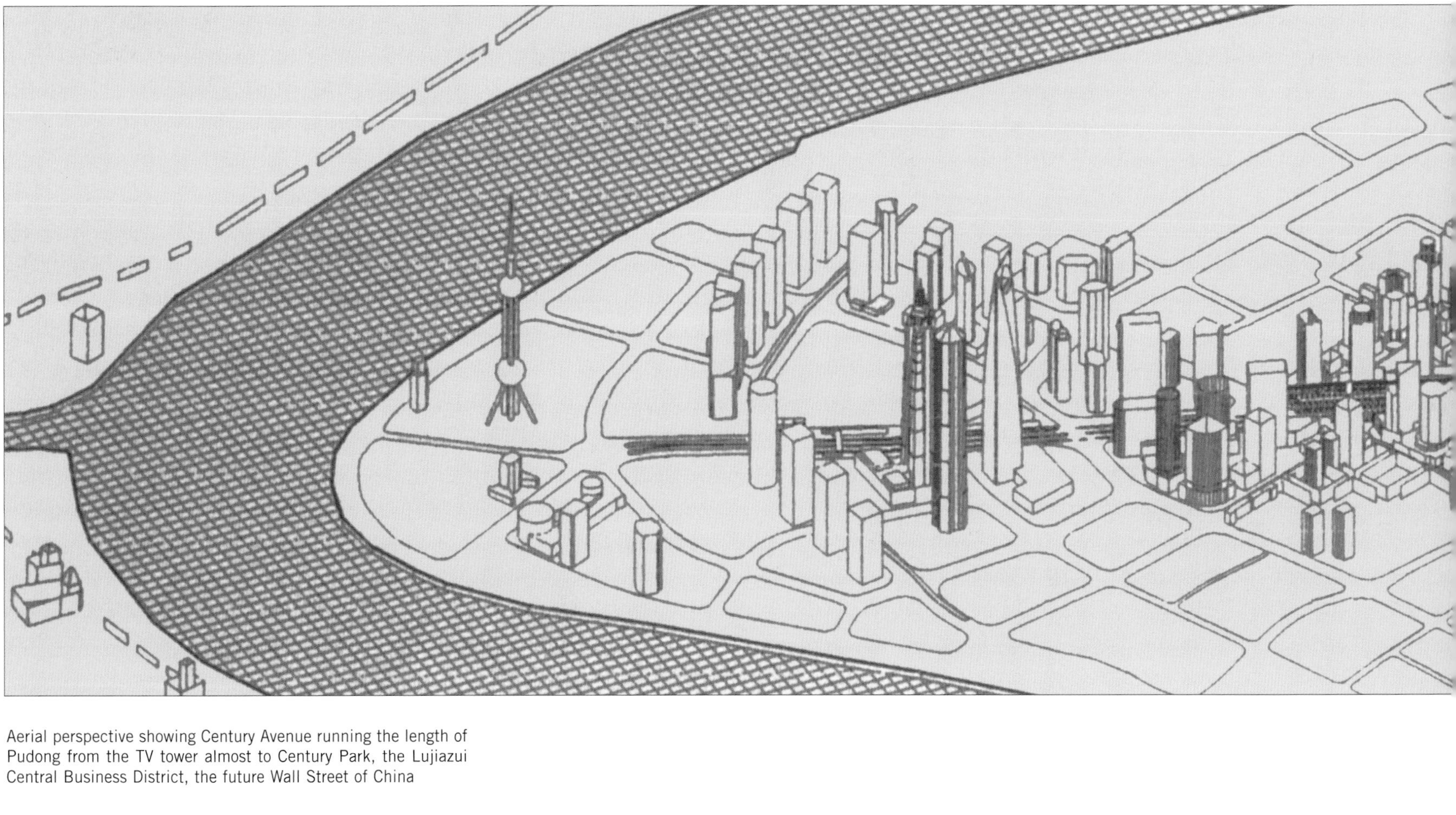

Aerial perspective showing Century Avenue running the length of
Pudong from the TV tower almost to Century Park, the Lujiazui
Central Business District, the future Wall Street of China

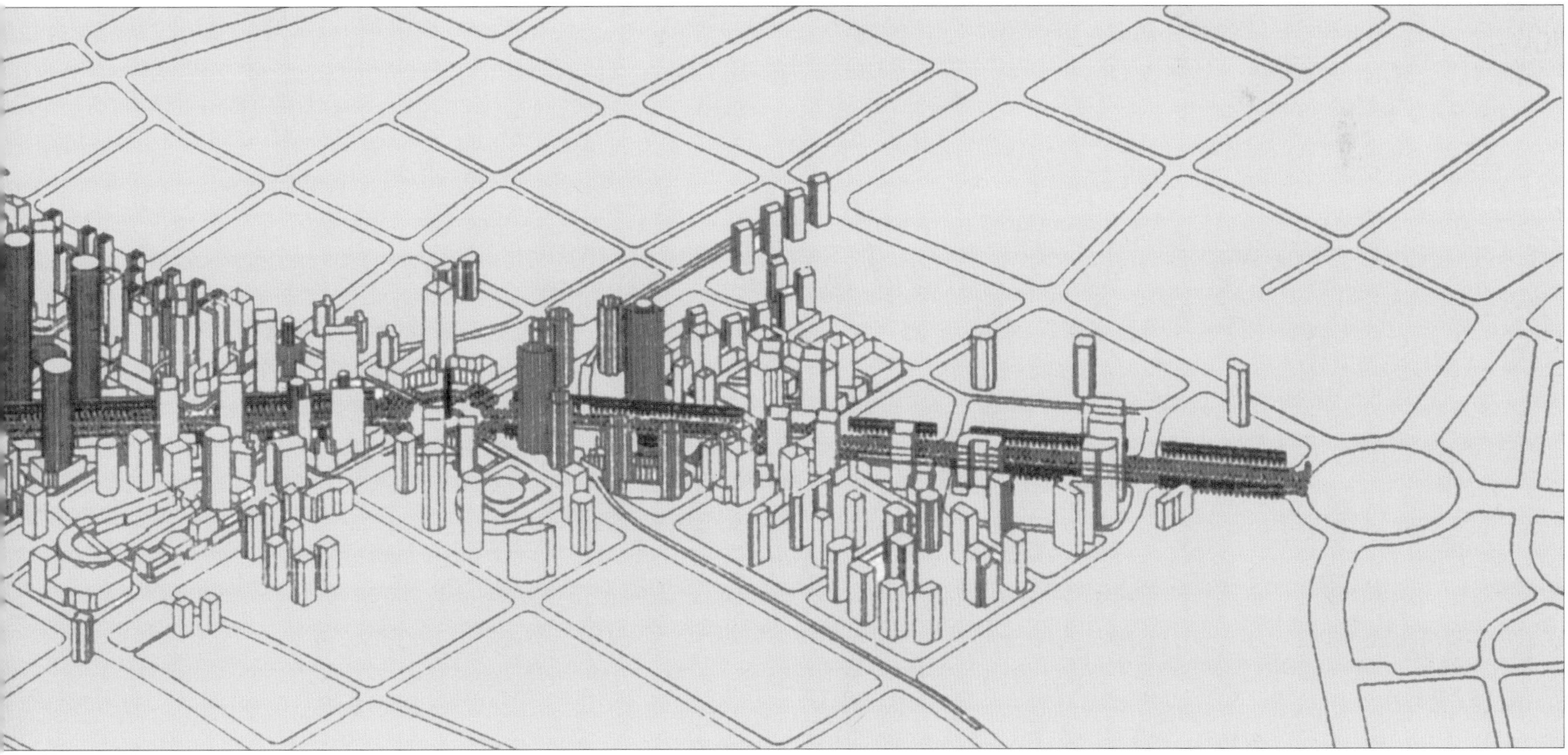

ARTE CHARPENTIER ET ASSOCIES
NANJING ROAD, 2000

The City of Shanghai commissioned a project for the development of this street, famous for its elegance since the 1920s at the time of the international concessions. Today, with the rapid extension of the town, it has become almost choked by streams of pedestrians, bicycles and cars.

The original layout of the street, which leads to the Bund by the Huangpu River, is retained. The traffic is diverted to a parallel trunk road, however, so that ithe street becomes a pedestrian space. This features street furniture such as lampposts, garden benches, telephone booths, underground exits, sculptures and planted trees at the different crossroads. The meandering layout of the centre of the street is intended to lead the pedestrian towards the windows of the prestigious buildings.

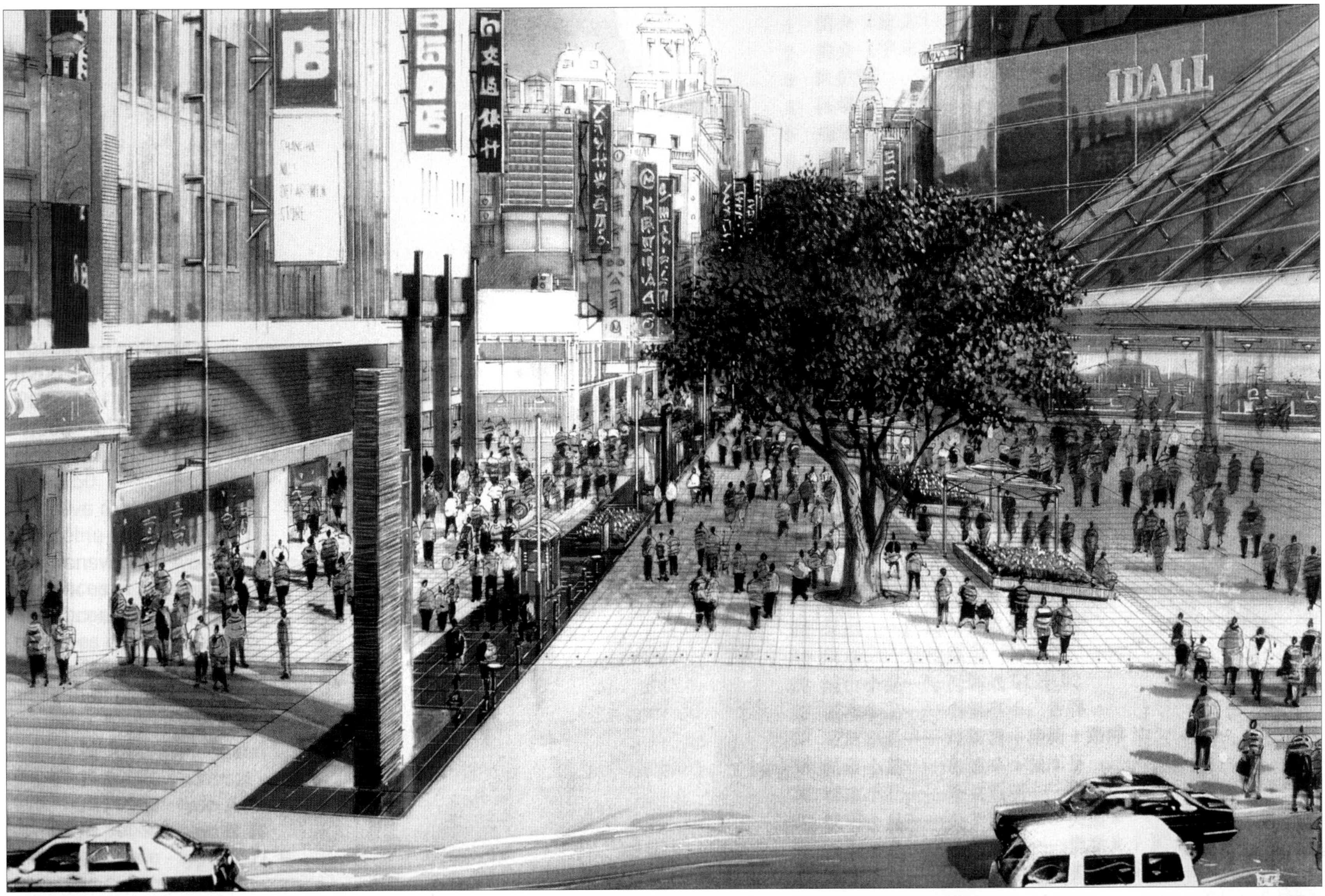
IDALL

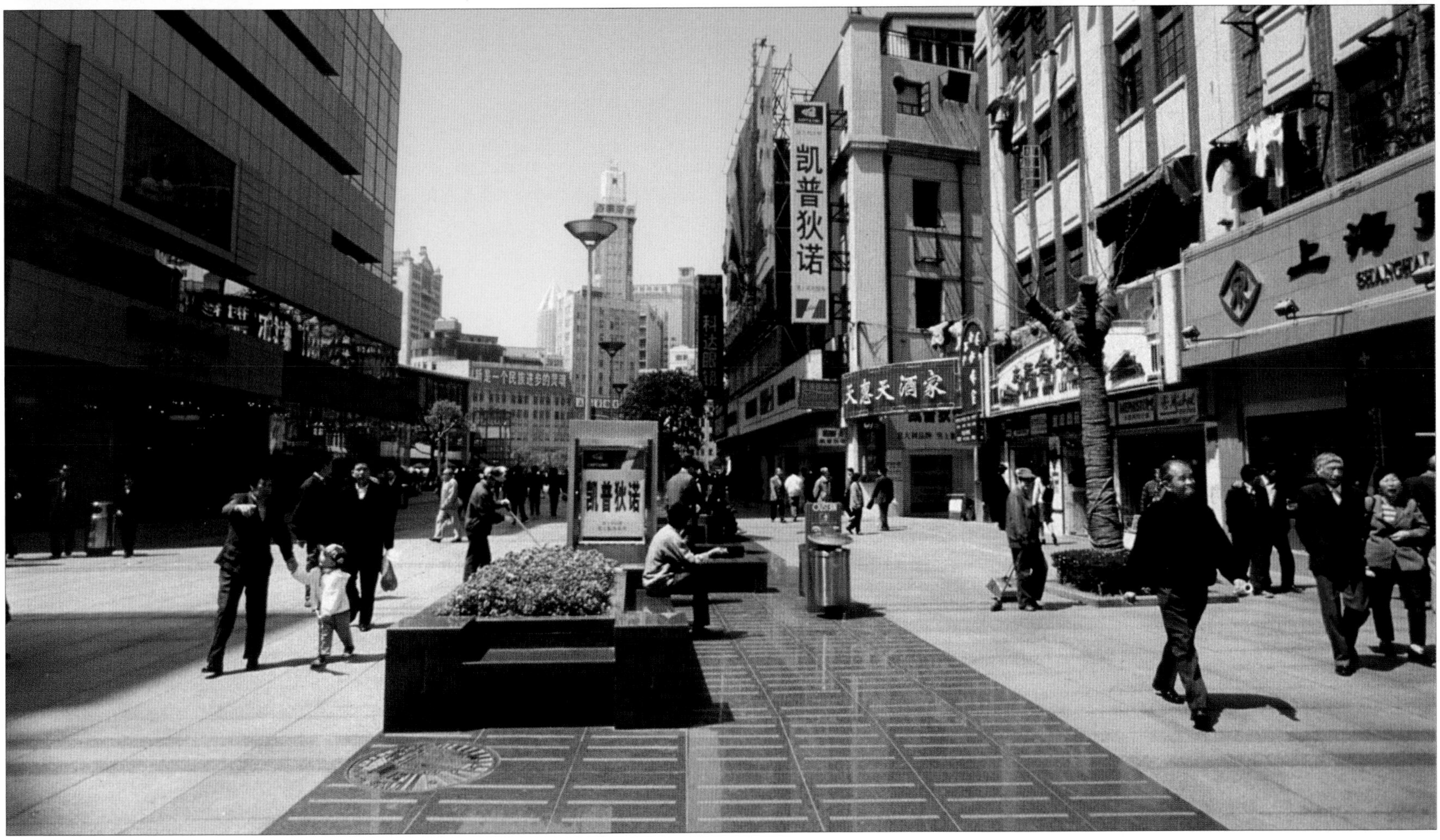
凯普狄诺
上海

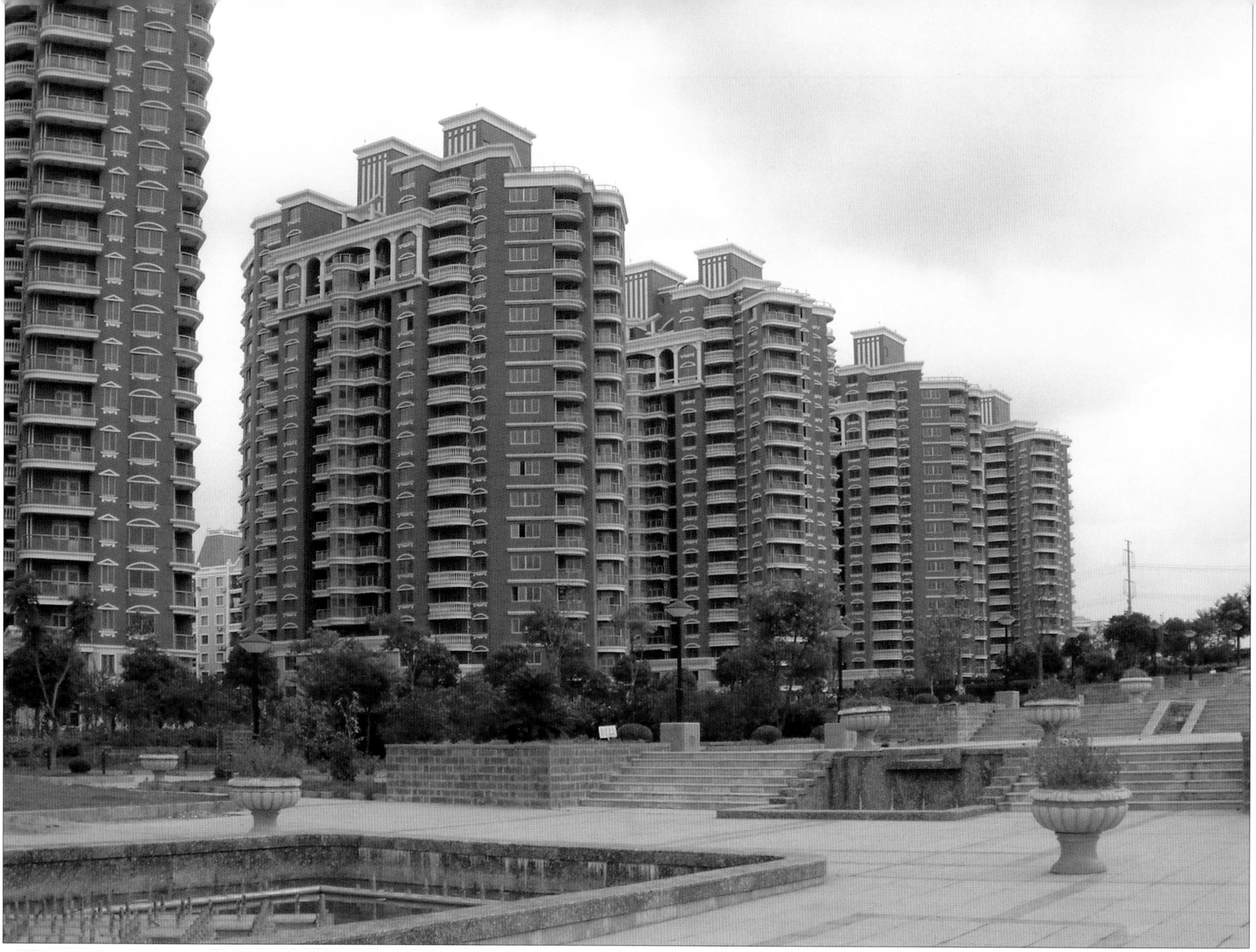

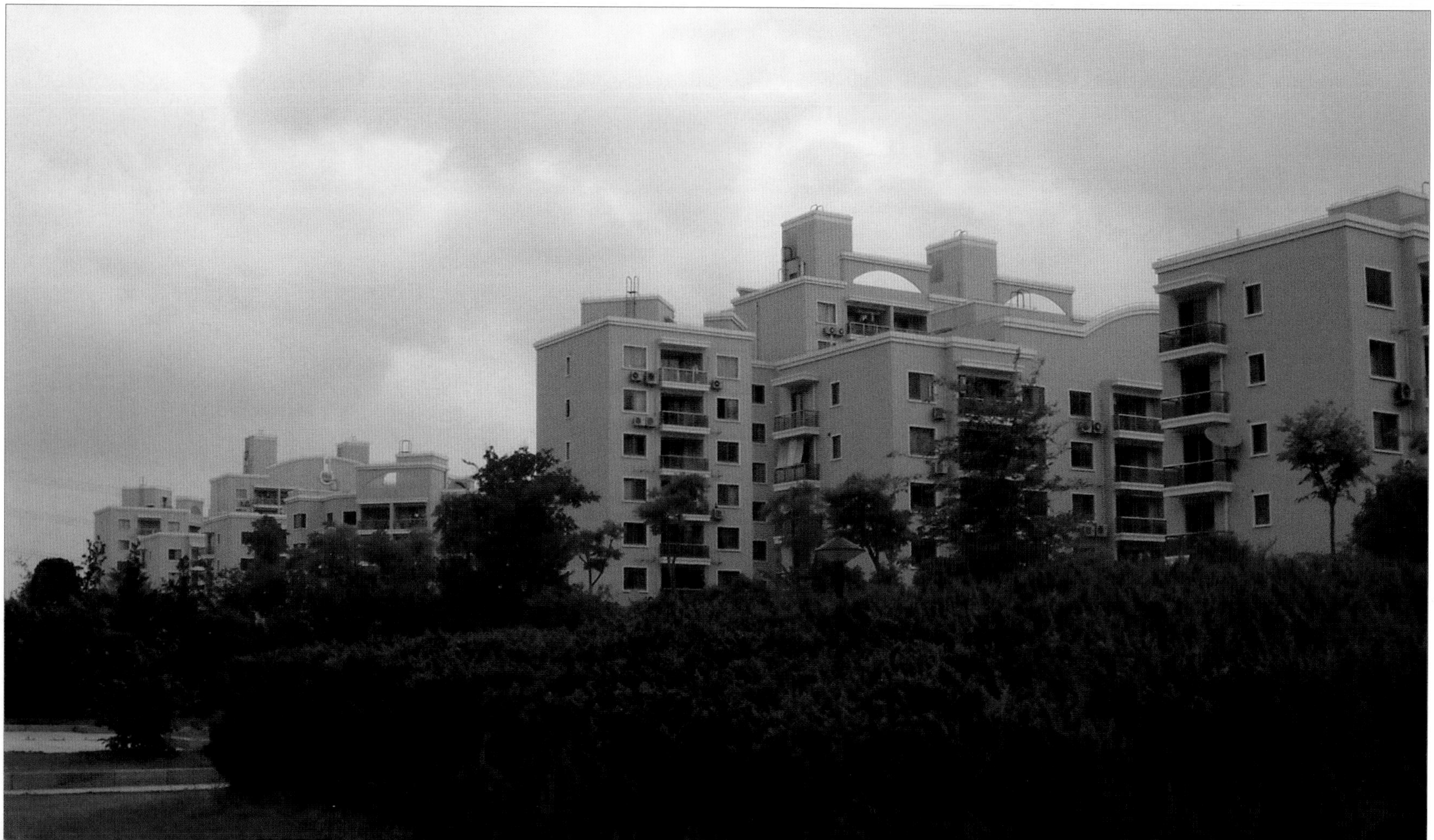

ARTE CHARPENTIER ET ASSOCIES
WANLI, 2001

This programme for a new urban district located on the north-western outskirts of Shanghai is designed to house 100,000 people in 1,800,000 square metres of lodgings, and to provide 360,000 square metres of services and public amenities. The site is in the process of completion.

Above: Plan

Opposite: Views of various housing projects that have been developed within the plan, though none designed by Arte Charpentier

HELLMUTH, OBATA + KASSABAUM

HUANGPU DISTRICT DEVELOPMENT, 1995

Huangpu district is a historical site situated in the centre of Shanghai and including the Bund. Though comprising an area of only 12 square kilometres, it occupies an extremely important position in the strategic development of the city. Since 1990 the district has been rapidly redeveloped, strengthening the growth of its tertiary activities, including finance, real estate, trade, tourism and information consultation services. To transform Huangpu district into a central downtown area with a 'prosperous economy, spiritual civili-

sation, safe social situation and a clean environment' was the objective of the urban design competition.

In response, HOK's masterplan for Huangpu establishes a clear plan and design guidelines to re-establish the area as the commercial heart of Shanghai. The plan integrates new office, commercial, retail, residential, entertainment and government facilities, dividing the district into three major focal points: (1) commerce, (2) culture and (3) government, as indicated on the plan.

Left: Conceptual master plan
Right: Design concept master plan

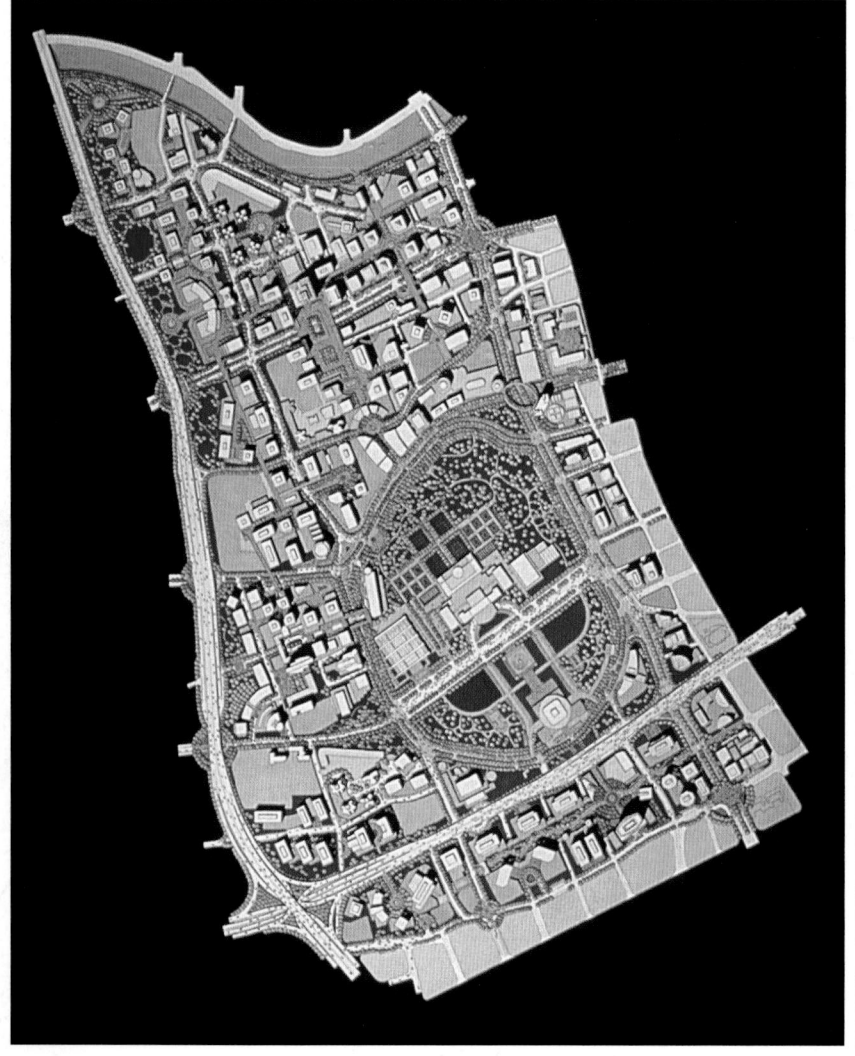
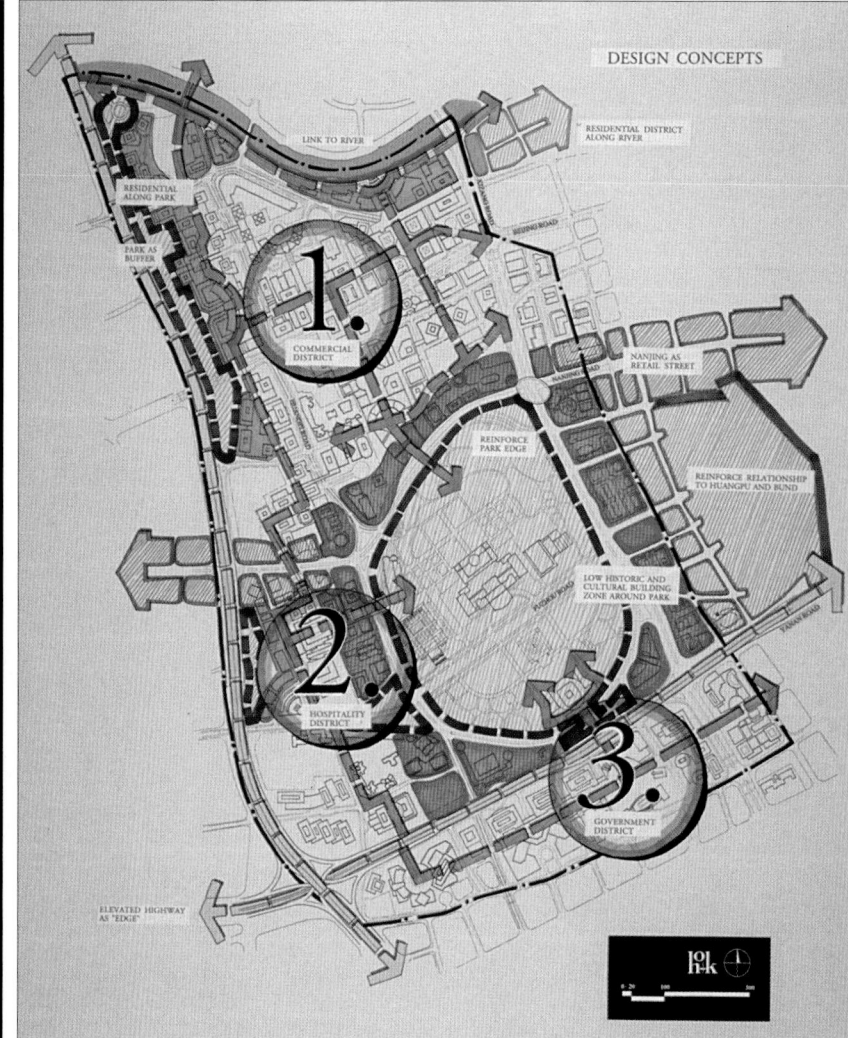

LU JIWEI, WITH GU RUZHEN, SUN GUANGLIN, ZHANG BING
JING-AN TEMPLE PLAZA, 1999

Located on West Nanjing road, Jing-An Temple Plaza is the core of the urban design of the Jing-An Temple area, also serving as a subway junction. The project is comprised of a sunken plaza, a shopping centre, a ventilation tower for the subway, and an outdoor theatre. The roof of the shopping centre is a green space, as a natural extension of Jing-An Park to the south. The unique design aims to improve the efficiency of urban public space while unifying the underground engineering with the above-ground environment.

Above: Model
Opposite above: View of the arena
Opposite below: Aerial view

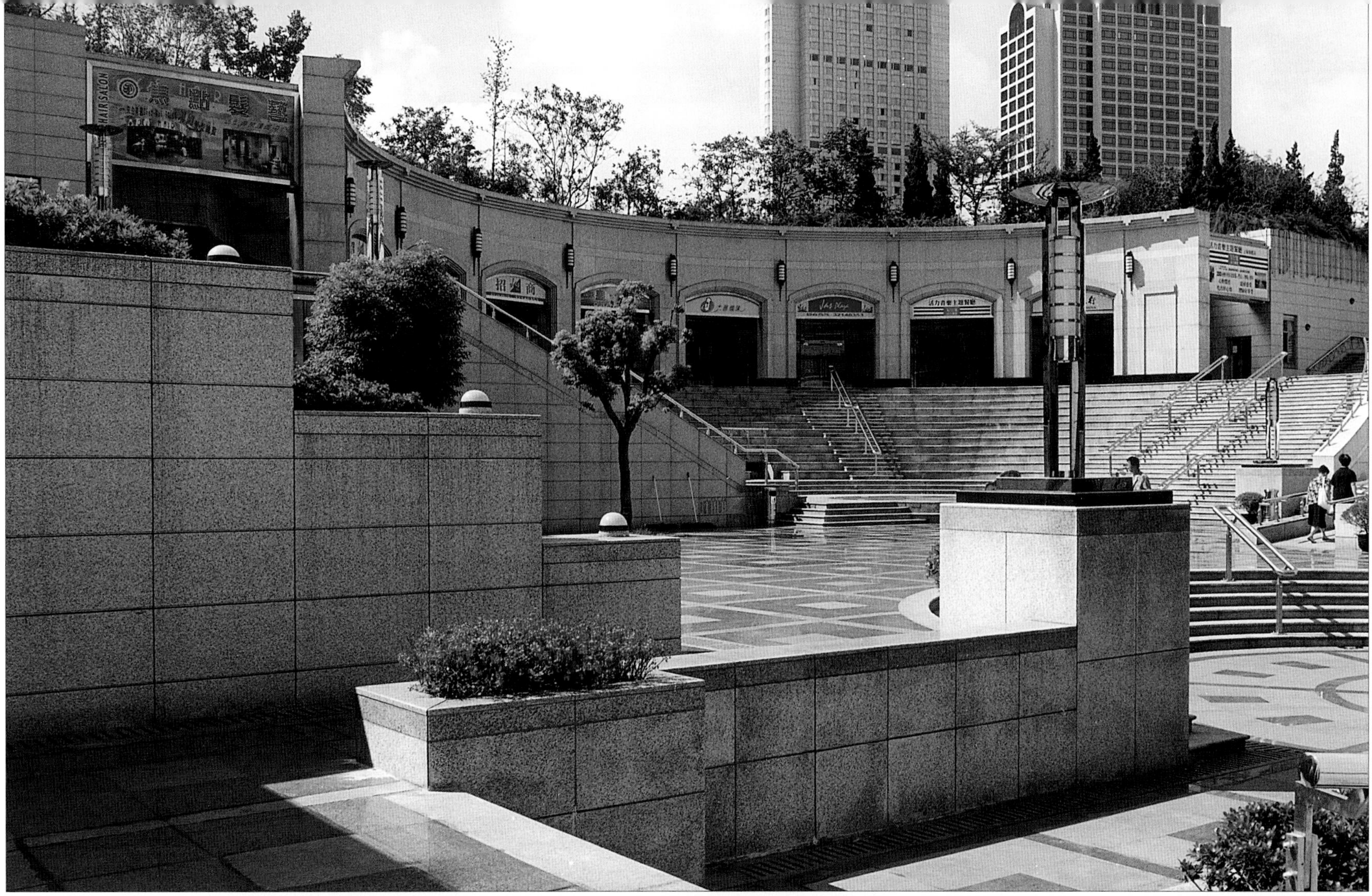
HAIR SALON
招商

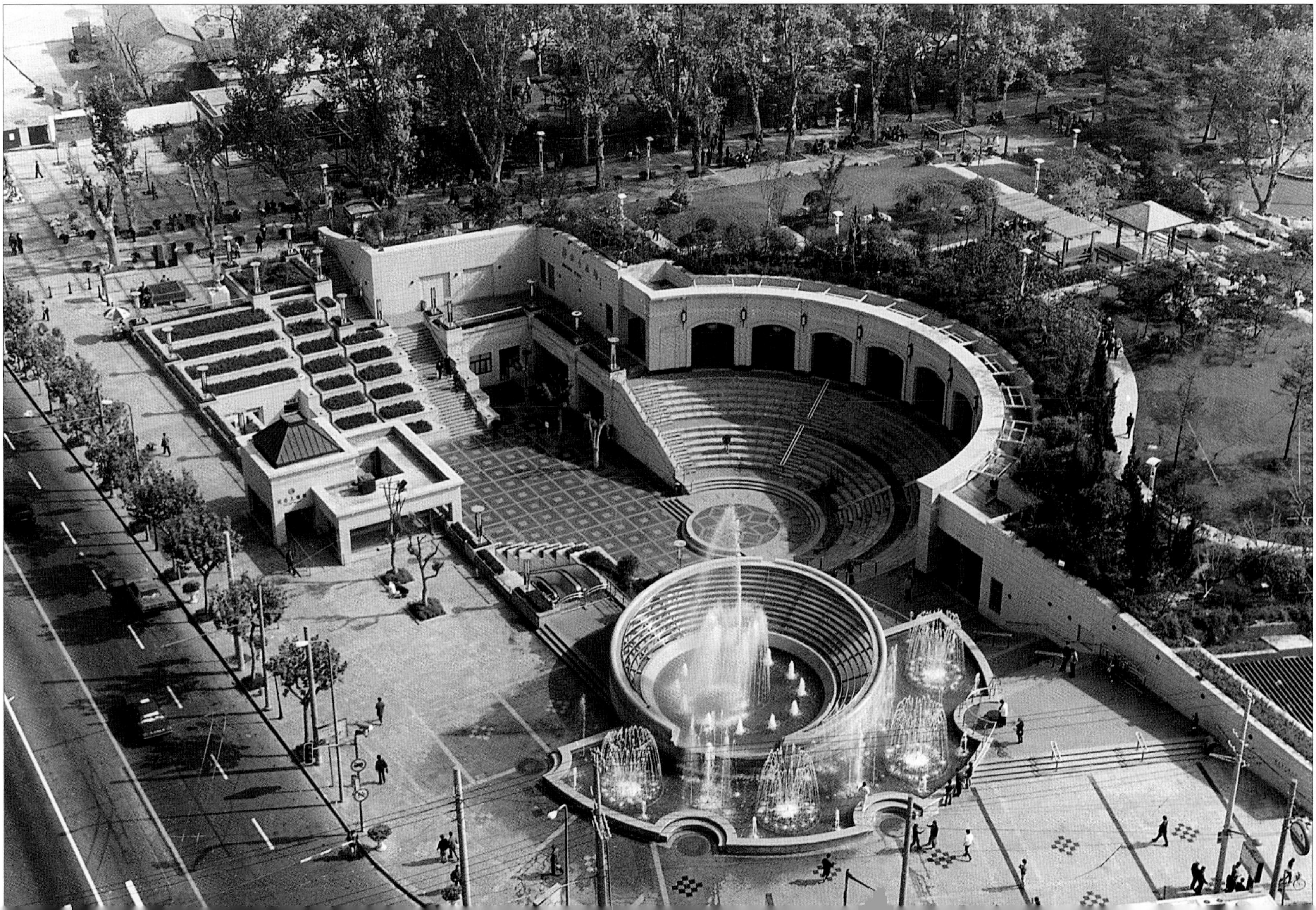

ANSHEN + ALLEN

AETNA SCHOOL OF MANAGEMENT MAIN BUILDING, SHANGHAI JIAO TONG UNIVERSITY, 2000

The Aetna School of Management's main building is designed to create a signature structure that defines a gateway entrance to the southeast corner of the Shanghai Jiao Tong University campus. The 8,000 square-metre business school, including a library, classrooms, faculty and administrative offices, conference hall, meeting rooms and computer laboratories, will serve as the primary teaching, research and conference facility for the university's graduate management programme. At the intersection of the university's main north-south axis and a secondary east-west axis, the building's gated entries will frame views to the centre of the campus, emphasising its prominence within the campus precinct. A covered, 17.5 metre-tall podium, raised slightly above a paved arrival plaza with a discreet tree pattern, will further distinguish the building from its immediate surroundings.

The planning of the Main Building anticipates the possible future development of a hotel and conference centre on the site. A separate entry for the conference centre in the two-storey portal space will allow it to operate independently, enhancing the opportunity for additional cross interaction and use by visiting School of Management faculty and lecturers while providing convenient access to the schools, lecture theatres and meeting rooms

Situated on a constrained lot, the seven-storey building is organised to encourage student and faculty interaction and accommodate the 8,838 square-metre programme of diverse functions in a vertically layered hierarchy. The most public, highest density uses, such as lecture theatres and meeting rooms, are on the lower floors, while faculty offices and meeting spaces are located above. A prominent conference room and library on the fourth floor project out, overlooking the arrival plaza. Louvred screens to shade the large expanses of operable windows in offices and meeting rooms further animate the south-facing facade.

ARTE CHARPENTIER ET ASSOCIES
SHANGHAI OPERA HOUSE, 1994–8

This was the winning project in an International Competition open to 18 architectural agencies. The brief was to design a contemporary, 1,800-seat opera house that would create a strong symbolic image of Chinese culture.

The layout has been designed as a geometric square, an ideal shape in China that symbolises the Earth. The curved roof is a segment of a circle intended to represent the sky. Both images were adopted at once by the Chinese as a symbol for the city. Shanghai residents are highly satisfied with the building's profile and the major cultural role played by the Opera House in the historical centre of Shanghai, the People's Square.

Above and opposite: Exterior views

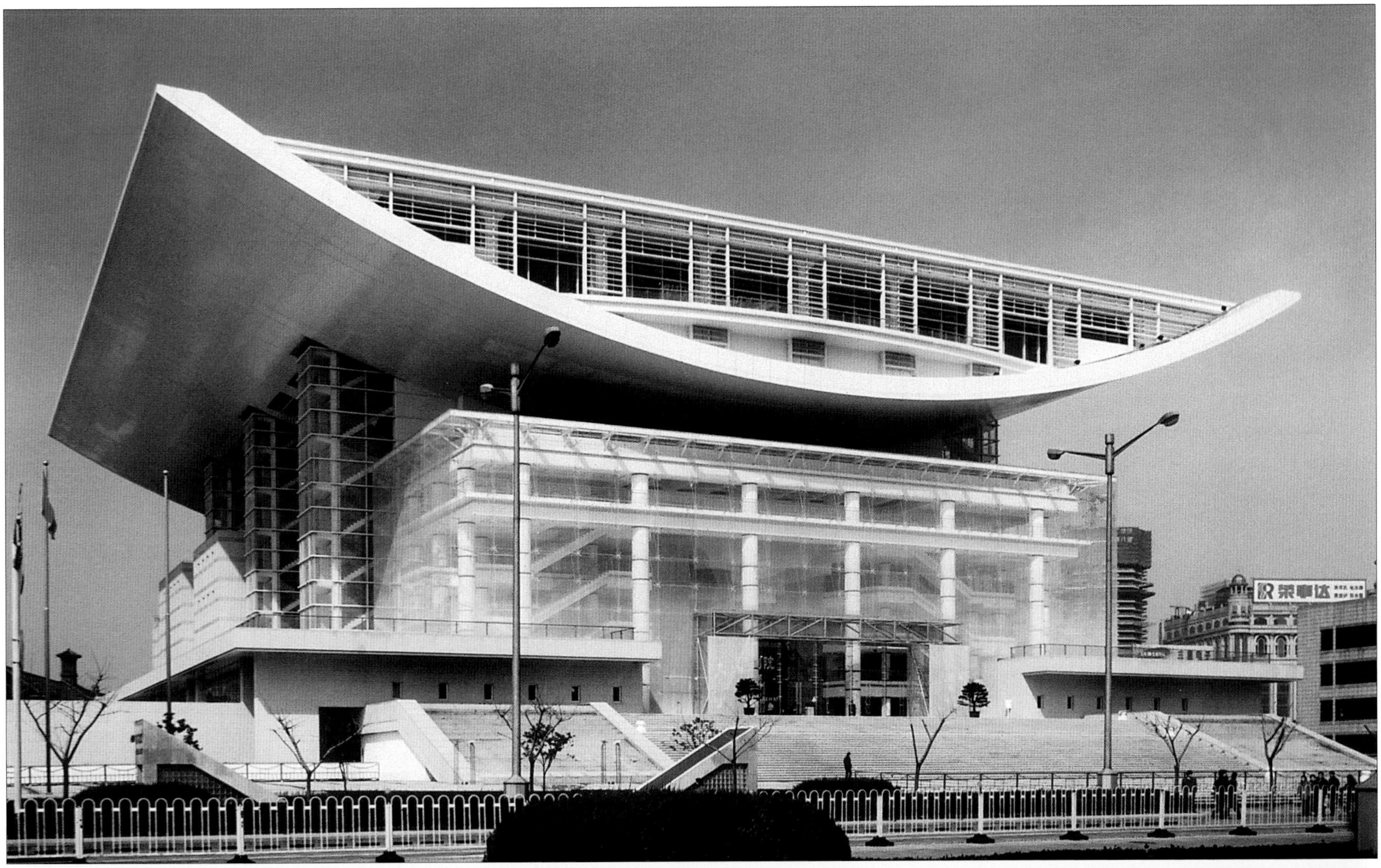

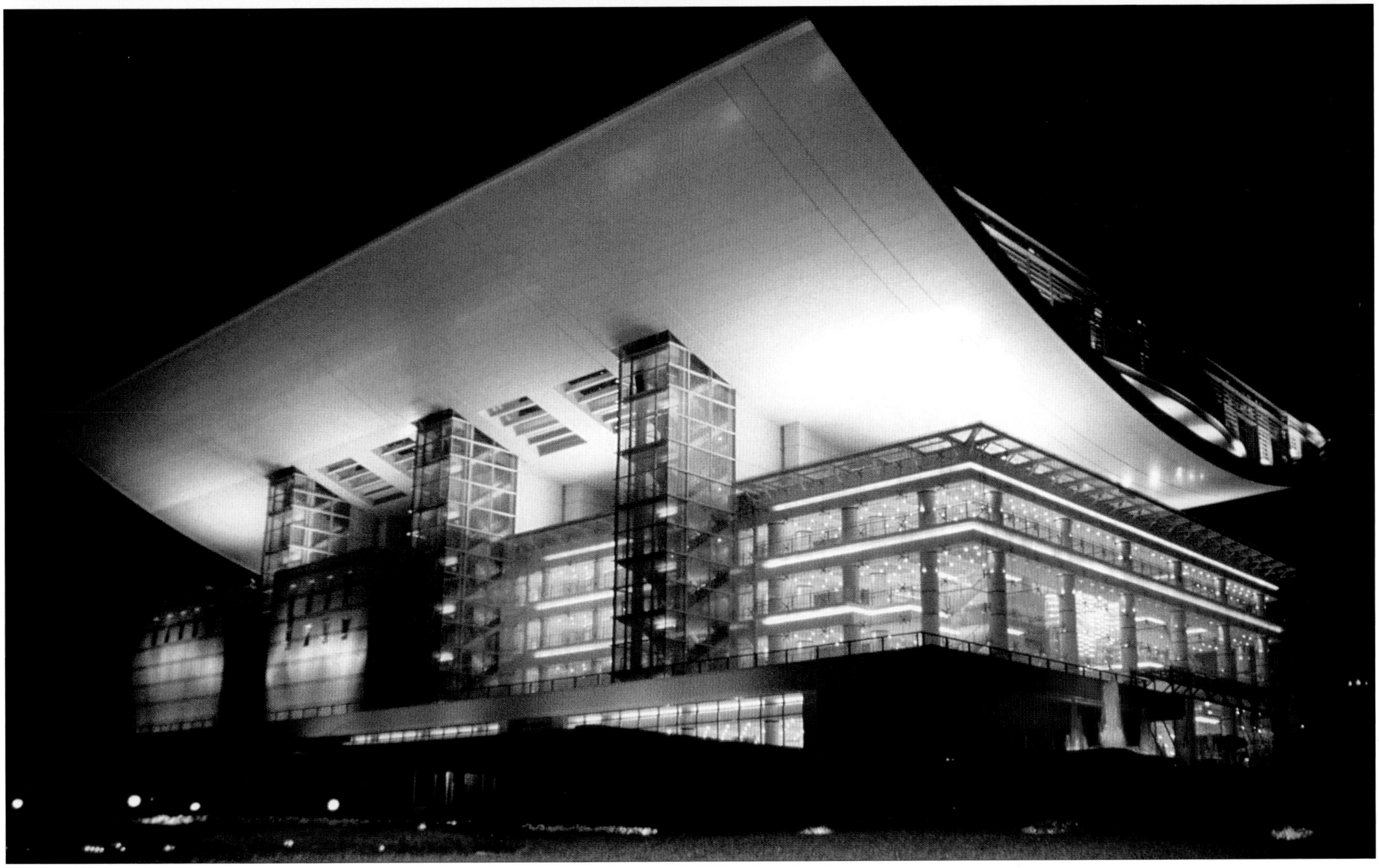

Above: Foyer
Right: View of the circle

View through a glass wall

NBBJ
ING CHANG-KI GOE SCHOOL, 1998

This 25,000-square-metre construction is comprised of two major buildings for two different tenants: the eight-storey Ing Chang-Ki Goe School, and the 18-storey Ing Chang-Ki Goe Educational Foundation. It became a reality thanks to the generosity of Goe Master, Ing-Chang Ki. He wished to carry on the tradition of the game, giving young people the opportunity to become better players. He has built many schools in China, but this is the first to focus on the game Goe. The school opened its doors to 1,800 students in 1998, so that they could study Goe while attending elementary and junior high school. It hosts both the Ing Cup international competition, and many Goe research and exchange programmes.

The architects and designers at NBBJ studied Goe in order to understand its principles and students. The result of their study was a design that incorporates various elements of the game. The four 'golden corners' and 'silver edges' of the Goe board are considered strategic places of strength. NBBJ drew inspiration from this traditional idiom, as well as from four basic principles of Goe: the grid, black and white, balance, and *qi*.

The site, located in the Huangpu district of Shanghai, has two corners. The most important is the southeast, the 'golden corner'. The six-storey entrance to the Educational Foundation stands at this corner near Nanjing Road and is a substantial presence in the city of Shanghai.

The 'silver edge' of the building lies along Tianjin Road. Here, the majority of the building is set back, creating a pleasant, raised landscaped area, the Ing Foundation Goe Plaza. The plaza provides Goe grid patterns and places for people to play Goe outdoors in the shade of the trees. The two outdoor spaces and an internal courtyard combine to give this dense, urban site, an open, humanistic feeling.

Views from surrounding streets

The Shanghai American School, founded in 1912, opened its new facilities in October 1998. These are located on 23 acres in the Pudong district, east of downtown Shanghai. To emphasise the cross-cultural nature of a Western educational institution in mainland China, the design team sought to make the design ideals of East and West work together. Instead of imposing grand gestures, as many Western firms have done in Asia, the NBBJ team built its design on a deep understanding of Chinese philosophy and design principles. The result is an effortless combination of a Western-style school with the unique qualities of a Chinese garden environment.

The Shanghai American School serves the children and families of Western diplomats and business people living in Shanghai by offering education from kindergarten through to high school, to students with English as their primary or secondary language. Phase I of the project accommodates 800 students. The completed design provides facilities for up to 2,000 students, including classrooms for specialised instruction, dormitories, a performing arts centre and outdoor sports fields. The school, fully accredited by the Western Association of Schools and Colleges, provides education from pre-kindergarten age through to grade 12.

Inner courtyard

This campus, with a gross building area of 34,203 square metres, provides international-standard teaching, research and residential facilities to serve the school's MBA, EMBA and Executive Development programmes. It occupies a 4-hectare site in the Jinquiao Export Processing Zone of the Pudong New Area of Shanghai. Acknowledging both initial funding limits and the likelihood of future growth, the campus was planned in such a way as to facilitate phased construction over time, without disruption to the ongoing life of the school.

Four key elements comprise the conceptual framework of the campus plan: a modular ordering grid laid out over the entire buildable area of the site; a large central garden shaped in the form of an L and enclosed by an arcaded walkway; a perimeter servicing zone, providing convenient vehicular access and parking on all four sides of the campus; a building zone located in the space contained between the central garden and the perimeter servicing zone, in which the various structures required to accommodate the school's programme are to be built, with each linked to its neighbours by the arcaded walkway.

The buildings are arranged around the garden so as to create functionally desirable adjacencies while at the same time fostering lively interaction between all sectors of the campus. Among these buildings, the library alone is granted the privilege of asserting a strong figural presence within the garden, thus affirming its role as the symbolic heart of this institution dedicated to the advancement of knowledge. Other buildings surrounding the garden rise to a uniform height of 15 metres, allowing three floors in the academic centre and five floors in the residence halls. Single-storey components of the campus – the convocation hall, forum, dining halls, gymnasium and bookstore – conform to the 6-metre height of the arcaded walkway enclosing the garden. These shared building heights, together with consistency in materials and details, contribute to the creation of an appropriate and memorable identity for the campus. In order to establish this identity at the outset, the garden and its enclosing arcade have been included in the first phase of construction with the library, academic centre, dining halls and two of the residence halls. Other buildings will be added as needed. The ultimate development of the campus will accommodate the present CEIBS programme plus approximately 40 per cent expansion of both academic and residential facilities. The horizontal organisation of the campus and the strategic placement of vertical circulation elements make both the garden and buildings fully accessible.

Notwithstanding the prominence given to the library, the most important principle governing this campus design is the primacy granted to open space over buildings. This principle dates back to antiquity and remains the indispensable source of civility in human environments. Thus, the extensive and varied landscape of the garden, with its enclosing arcade, is intended to affirm those values that underlie the educational mission of the China Europe International Business School: communication, teamwork, responsibility (both social and ecological) and harmony born of mutual respect in the ever more fruitful partnership between China and the West.

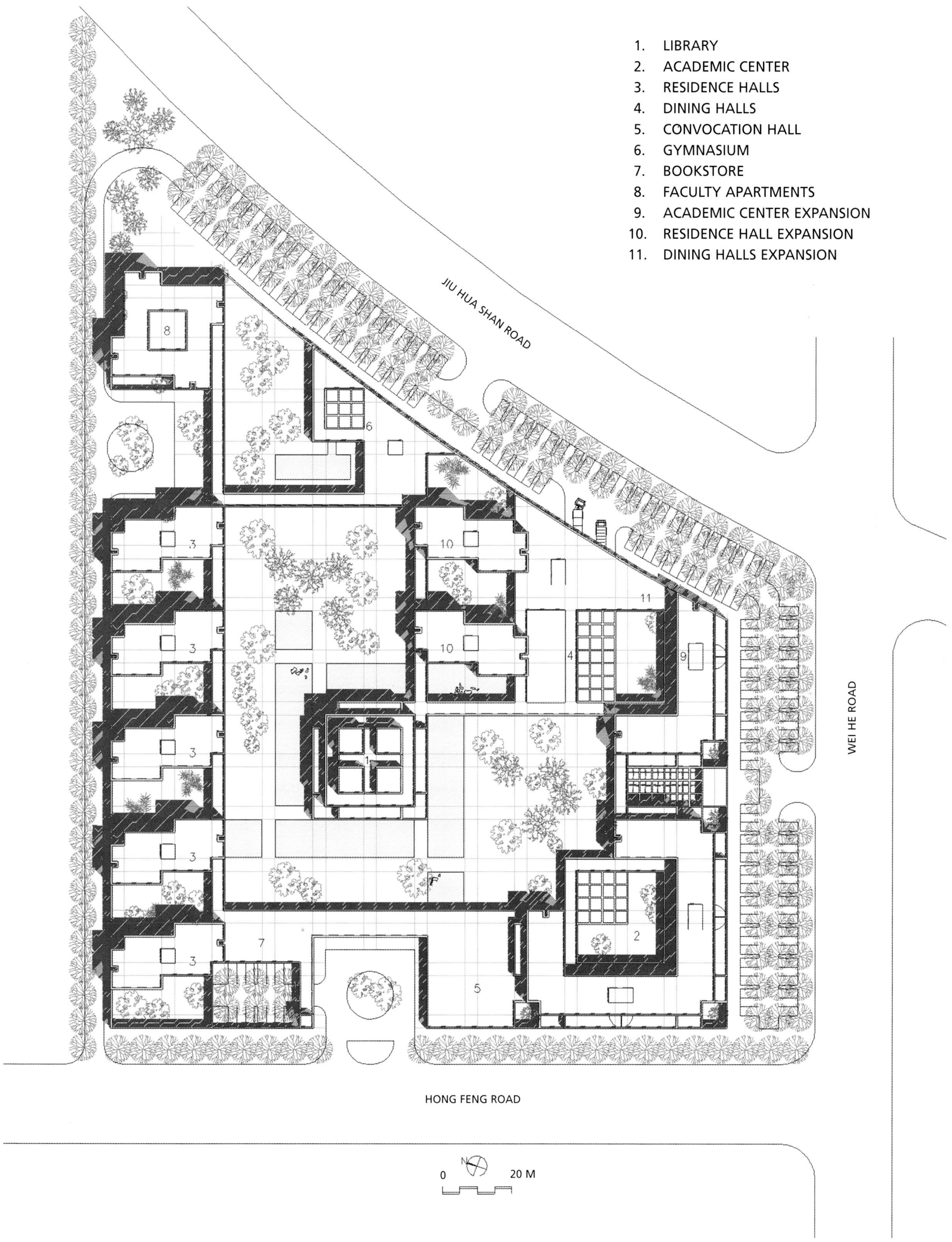

1. LIBRARY
2. ACADEMIC CENTER
3. RESIDENCE HALLS
4. DINING HALLS
5. CONVOCATION HALL
6. GYMNASIUM
7. BOOKSTORE
8. FACULTY APARTMENTS
9. ACADEMIC CENTER EXPANSION
10. RESIDENCE HALL EXPANSION
11. DINING HALLS EXPANSION

JIU HUA SHAN ROAD

WEI HE ROAD

HONG FENG ROAD

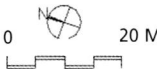

0   20 M

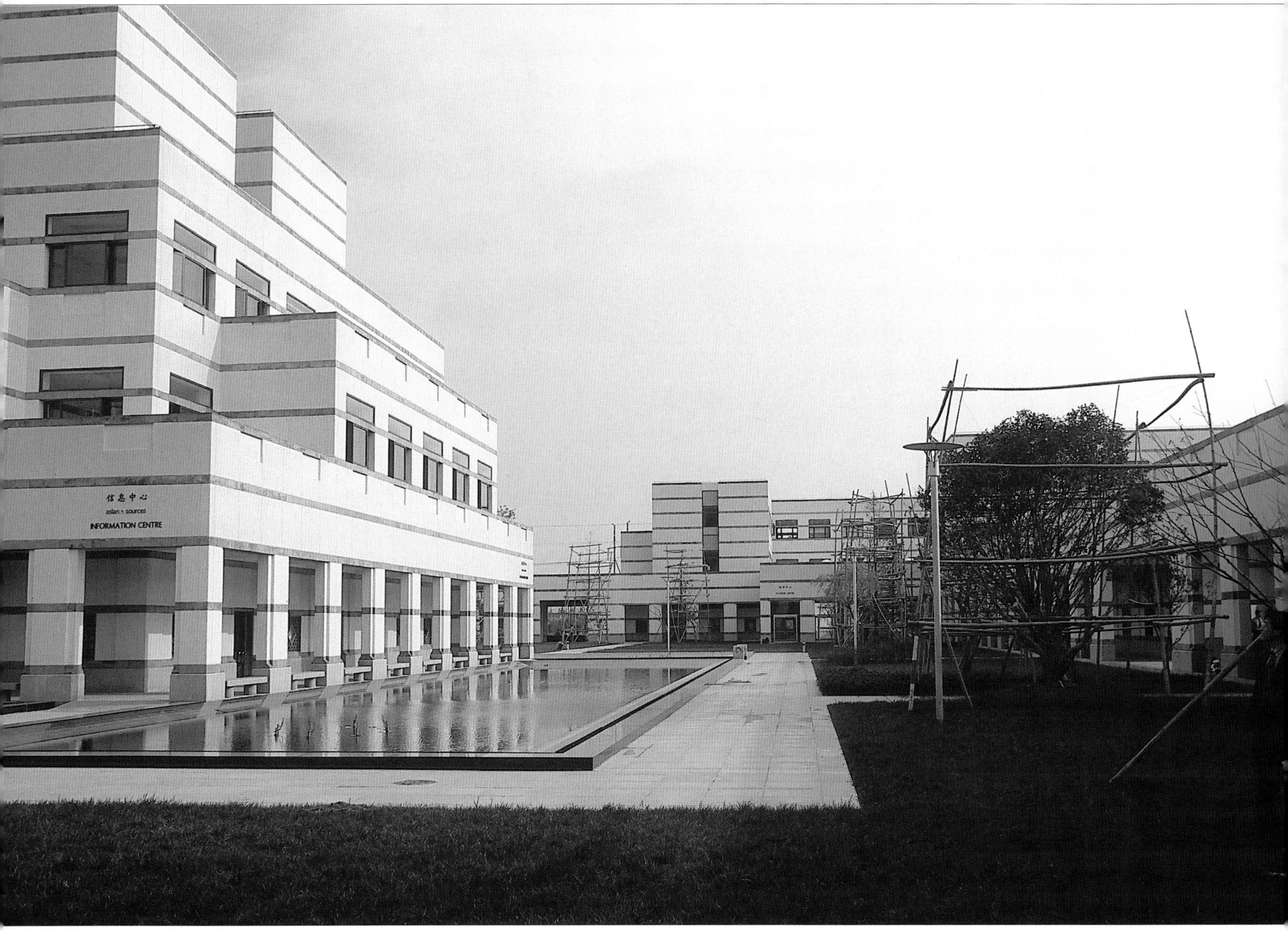
信息中心
asian sources
INFORMATION CENTRE

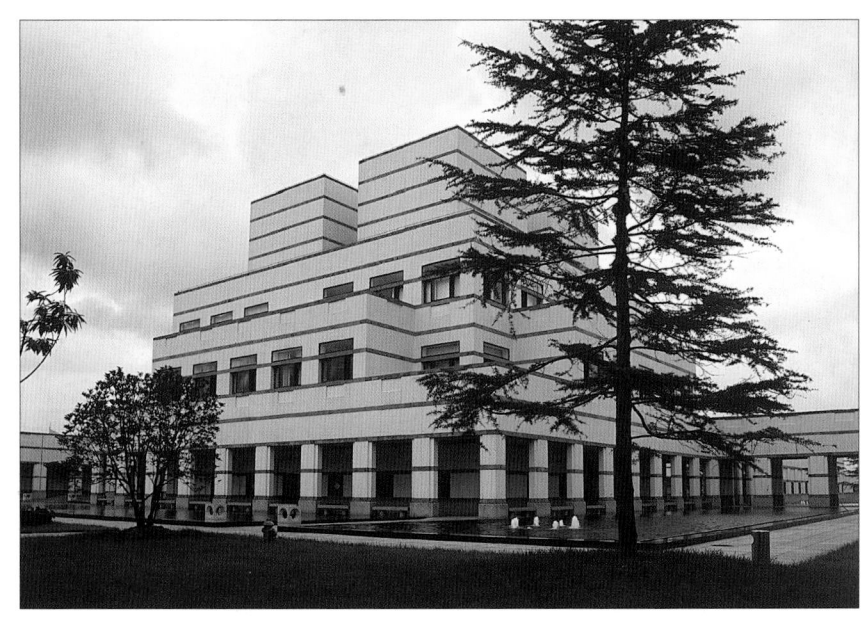

Shanghai Scienceland marks the birth of a new city as Century Boulevard links Shanghai with the new centre of Pudong. Located at the end of Lujiazui Financial Trade Zone, as a gateway to Central Park, the Civic Plaza stages an important presence in the urban design. Sited along the southern end of the plaza, Scienceland, on axis with the Shanghai Pudong New Area Government, will become an architectural and cultural landmark of Shanghai.

As an economic centre and Westernised city in China, Shanghai often presents a dual identity in its urban design. With precedents from thousands of years of Chinese history, it is also heavily influenced by periods of Western occupation. When striving for land for new development, the city faces the dilemma of how much from the past to preserve, and how to create its new portrait in the global picture. Every new building will need to respond to that challenge in its design and in every way Scienceland attempts to represent a great leap from the old to the new era.

To reflect the harmony between man, science and nature, the five essential elements of Chinese culture – metal, wood, water, fire and earth – are symbolically represented in the design of the complex and its surrounding landscape.

Restricted by a semi-circular site in a formal and symmetrical layout, the building's dynamic massing strives to break away from the ground and soar into the sky. The sweeping wing form and highly detailed glass curtain walls ascend as an icon of cutting-edge technology.

Envisioned as the world's largest science centre, the one million square feet accommodate two buildings. The four-storey main building houses galleries, restaurants, shops, a large-format theatre, a 3-D dome theatre, a multifunction hall and an interior courtyard. The annex building, linked by a bridge, houses a research library, laboratories, residences for visiting scholars and support functions.

Two memorable forms make up the building. The egg symbolises life as the origin of man and science. The wing symbolises flight as science and technology bring man and nature together, and as a symbol of rising economic and technological advancement.

Upon entering the museum, visitors will orient themselves in a central egg-shaped glass hall, which connects the museum's two gallery wings and the southern site. Within the central glass hall is a 'floating' globe-shaped space, accessible by walkways from higher floors. Symbolically, the hall and its sphere represent an egg and its yolk, an incubator for technological advancement.

Three parts make up the semi-circular museum:

The East Wing (Atrium and Galleries)

The East Wing houses galleries and a multi-function hall. Three trays of gallery floors cascading up the building are pulled back from the glass curtain wall, resulting in a linear atrium. Moving along the glass curtain wall on a series of escalators, visitors experience the ascending dynamics of the wing-shaped sloping roof. Rotated stone gallery walls display the transformation of space at the recessing edge of the platforms.

Egg and Yolk

Upon entry, visitors are greeted by the egg and the floating yolk in the central glass hall. As the origin of life the egg is also the heart of the museum. Projected shows on the yolk's surface animate the space and transform it into a colourful extravaganza in the evening. Stairs and a bridge bring people to the yolk to experience special exhibits or rides.

The West Wing

At the tail of the roof form, the West Wing emerges from the ground. It consists of a theatre complex, permanent galleries, a rainforest, and an outdoor courtyard. A grand staircase connecting the sunken plaza will bring visitors to the future rocket platform. As the world's only theatre complex with both a 3-D dome and a large-format theatre, it will continue to attract visitors even in the evening.

Opposite: Computer generated views of the preliminary designs

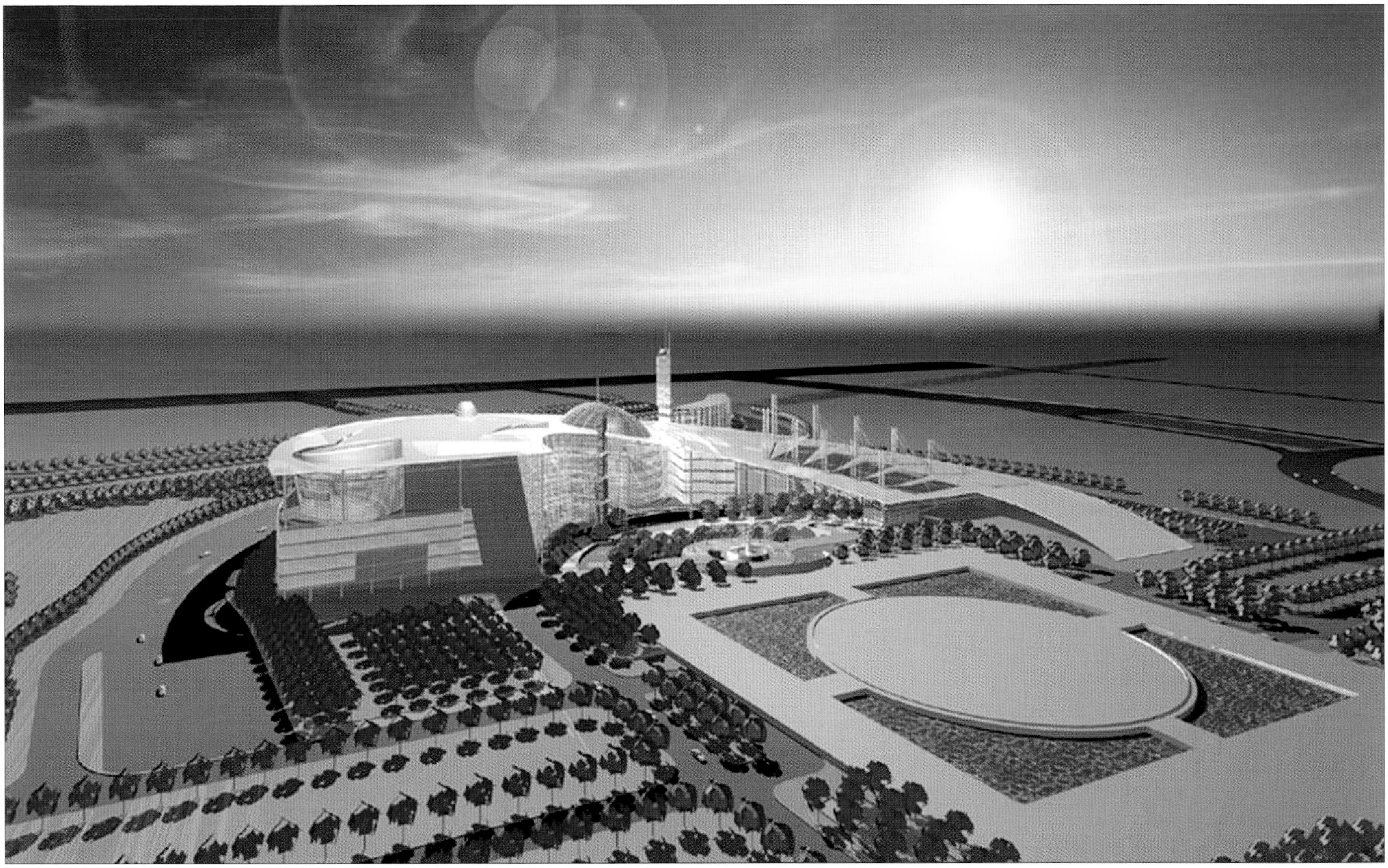

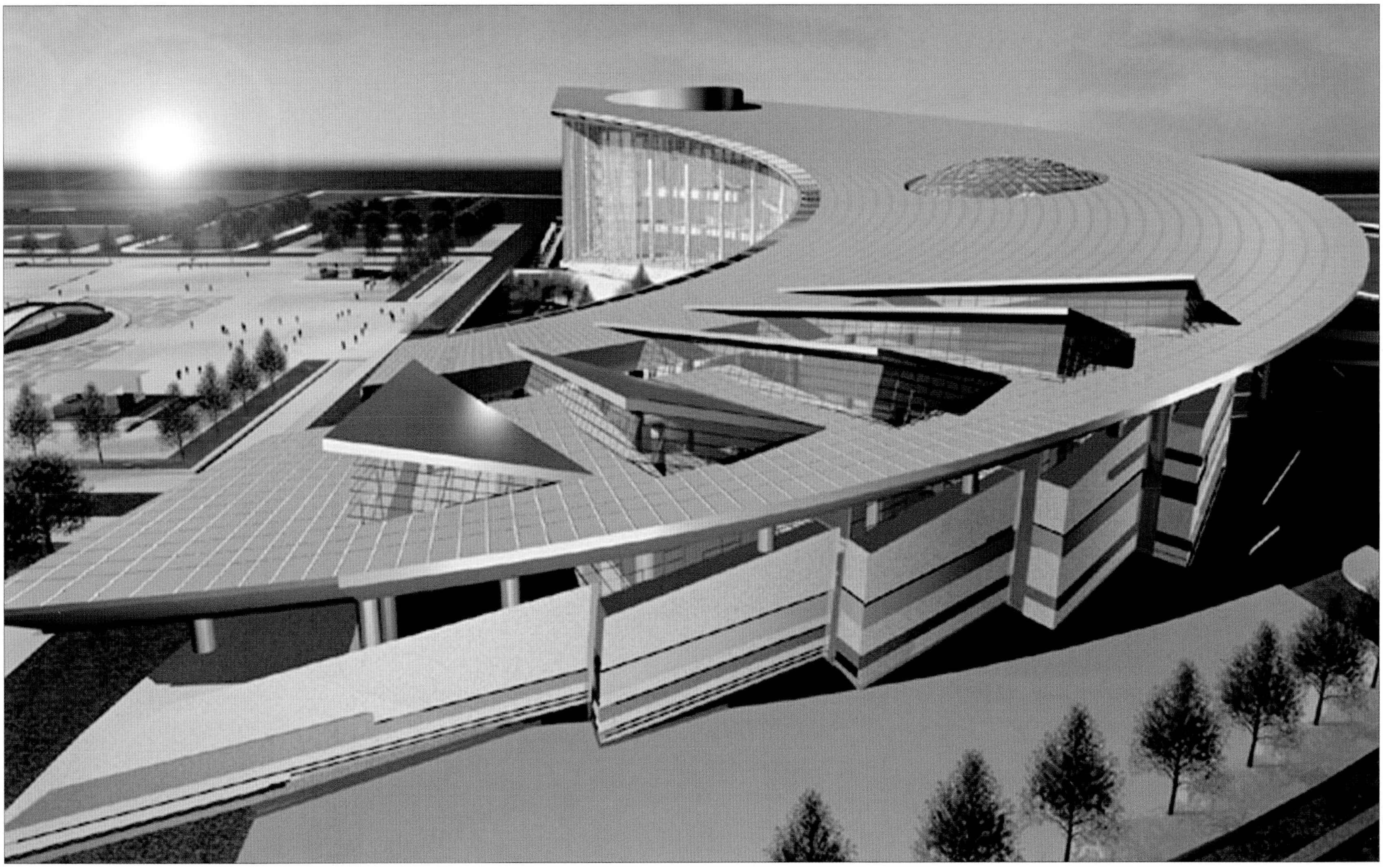

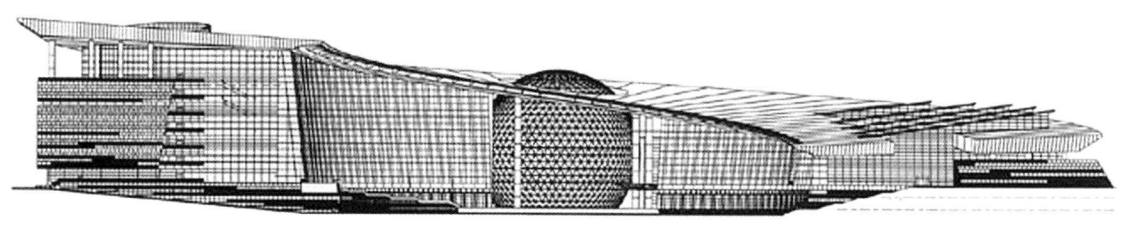

Above Right: North elevation
Right: South elevation
Below: Aerial view

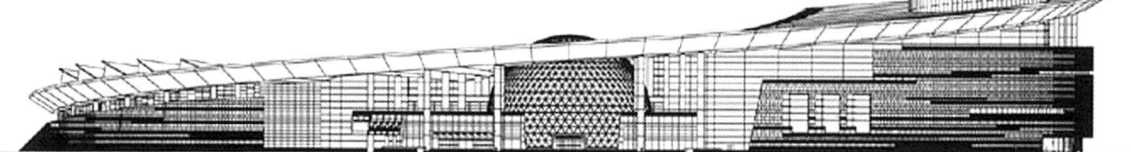

Above: Views of the completed building

Below: Cross sections through the sphere around the planetarium

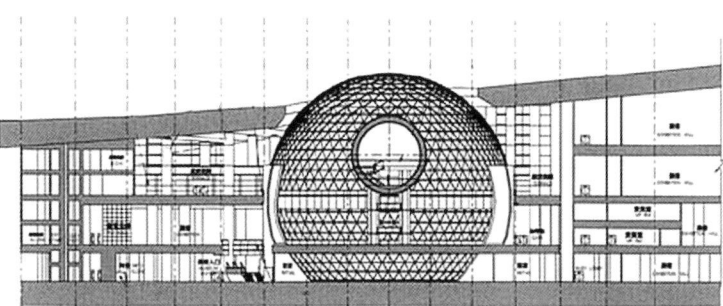
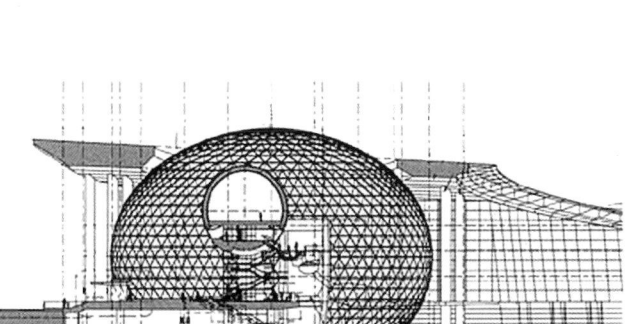

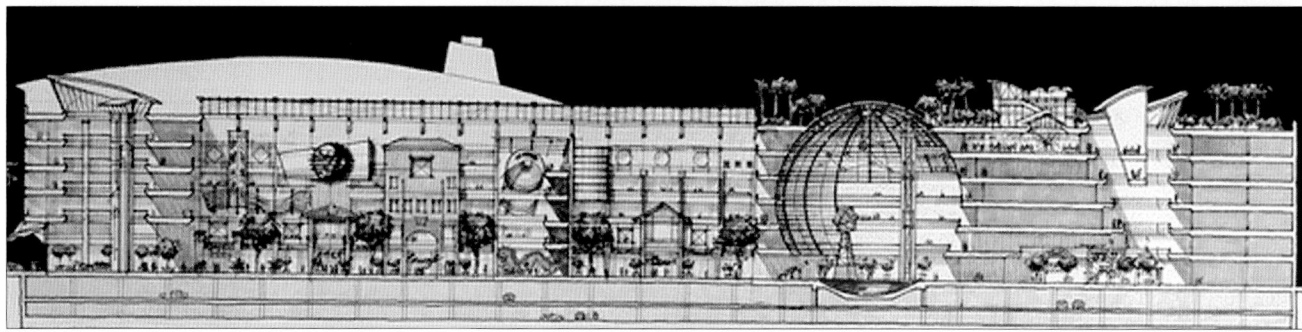

Above: Views within the glass sphere and around the planetarium
Centre: Perspective of the completed project north to the Lu-Jia-Zui central Business District
Below: Early design section showing the character of the interior

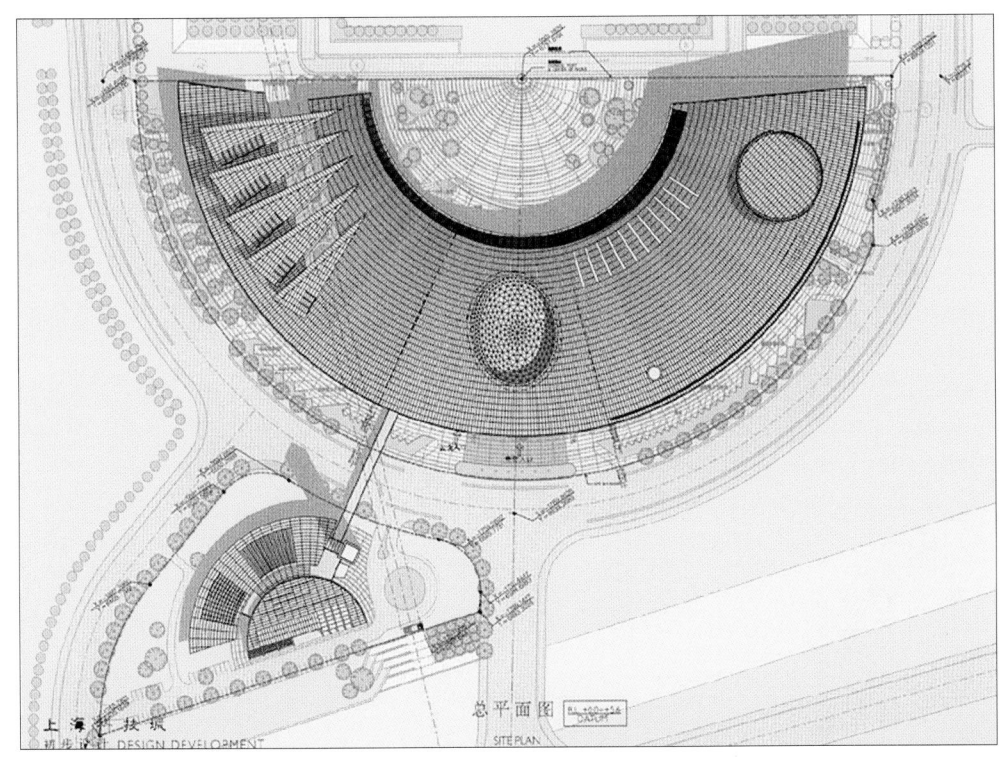

总平面图
SITE PLAN
上海科技城
机电设计 DESIGN DEVELOPMENT

Left: Site plan
Below: Interior views

The Shanghai Library was designed to be a progressive model with advanced modern facilities and functions, set in a peaceful and elegant environment. It aims to encapsulate the spirit of our times, reflecting the special cultural character of Shanghai, with its Chinese and Western cultural elements. The interior design takes the theme of the history of civilisation.

The main public entrance is on Knowledge Square, enclosed by a colonnaded corridor along Middle Huai Hai Road. The entrance lobby leads to quiet reading rooms. To the right of the lobby is an atrium, along which are distributed more than 20 reading rooms. To the left is a Jiang-Nan-style garden, enclosed by the antique books reading room. The building has a clear visual orientation, based on the column grid, which creates universal and open spaces.

The library stores 13.2 million books and has more than 3,000 reading seats. It is equipped with an advanced computer and book transportation system, and has detailed facilities for the disabled.

Opposite: General view
Above left: Vestibule
Above right: Main entrance
Left: Decorative facade

SHANGHAI MODERN ARCHITECTURAL DESIGN GROUP (LING BENLI, TANG LIN, ZHANG CHI)
SHANGHAI URBAN PLANNING EXHIBITION HALL, 1995–8

The Shanghai Urban Planning Exhibition Hall is located at the east of People's Square, corresponding symmetrically with the Shanghai Grand Opera to the west, with the Municipal Government Building located in the middle. The project is a multifunctional building, housing an exhibition of Shanghai's urban planning and city construction, together with other functions such as academic communication, consulting, research, propaganda, education and entertainment facilities. The overall building area is 18,000 square metres, while the site occupies 3,625 square metres, with five floors above ground and two floors underground.

The gallery constitutes the main part of the building, occupying the first to the fourth floors, with a square plan that is 63 metres long from east to west, and 37 metres wide from north to south. The total exhibition area is 7,000 square metres. A round multifunctional conference hall and a roof garden are situated on the fifth floor. The underground area is designed as a pedestrian street, 45 metres long, 11 metres wide and 6 metres high, which contains many shops in the 1930s building style of old Shanghai. This street is also connected with Line 1 of the People's Square subway station.

The appearance of the building emphasises a feeling of transparency. Four mushroom-shaped shells comprise a magnolia, which is the city flower of Shanghai. Colours vary with the changing light. The total height of the building is 43 metres.

XING TONGHE AND THE SHANGHAI ARCHITECTURAL DESIGN INSTITUTE
SHANGHAI MUSEUM, 1996

The Shanghai Museum is the most modern exhibition facility in China, with climate-controlled galleries applying the latest lighting and display techniques, a conservation laboratory, an auditorium, tea house, gift shops and a café. The museum is not only devoted to bringing greater recognition to one of the world's finest collections of Chinese art, a treasure trove of some 120,000 objects, but also to introducing Western art to millions of culturally isolated Chinese.

The institution gives every indication of becoming a place of openness, furthering bonds between this increasingly cosmopolitan port and the democratic world. It sits at one end of the city's principal plaza, People's Square, directly opposite City Hall. Sheathed in pink granite imported from Spain, the massive five-storey structure consists of a circular disc floating horizontally above a rectangular block. Four handle-like arches rise from the roof, creating a composition unmistakably reminiscent of an ancient Chinese bronze, an impression reinforced by the glyph that appears on the rounded wall above the main entrance.

The interior has a marble-paved central atrium surrounded by 14 carpeted galleries, most with low ceilings to accommodate modestly scaled objects. The halls are filled with rotating displays of bronzes, ceramics, paintings, calligraphies, coins, jades, statues, lacquers, seals, furniture and books, grouped by medium and arranged chronologically.

It has been observed that the new Shanghai Museum surpasses the older Taipei Palace Museum in the breadth of its displays, and in certain areas – notably bronzes, coins, Ming- and Qing-dynasty paintings – rivals even the Palace Museum in Beijing. Its collections do not, however, share those repositories' imperial lineage. Founded in 1952, the Shanghai Museum arose in the turbulent aftermath of the 1949 Communist Revolution, when many were fleeing and selling their possessions at bargain prices. The financial hub of the region, Shanghai was home to important collectors and dealers, and was the centre for the export of Chinese art to the West. It was a propitious moment and place to establish a museum, and Mayor Chen Yi decided to take advantage of it. The project was completed in less than two years, largely owing to laws that channelled private property into the hands of the government.

Several years ago, having outgrown its quarters in an Art-Deco bank building on Henan Road, the museum secured the prestigious site on People's Square. The old building was sold, and the city and central governments contributed part of the construction costs for the new museum. Another $10 million came from private donors, mainly Chinese ex-patriots in Hong Kong, many of whose fortunes had ties to pre-Communist Shanghai. A number of galleries are dedicated in their honour.

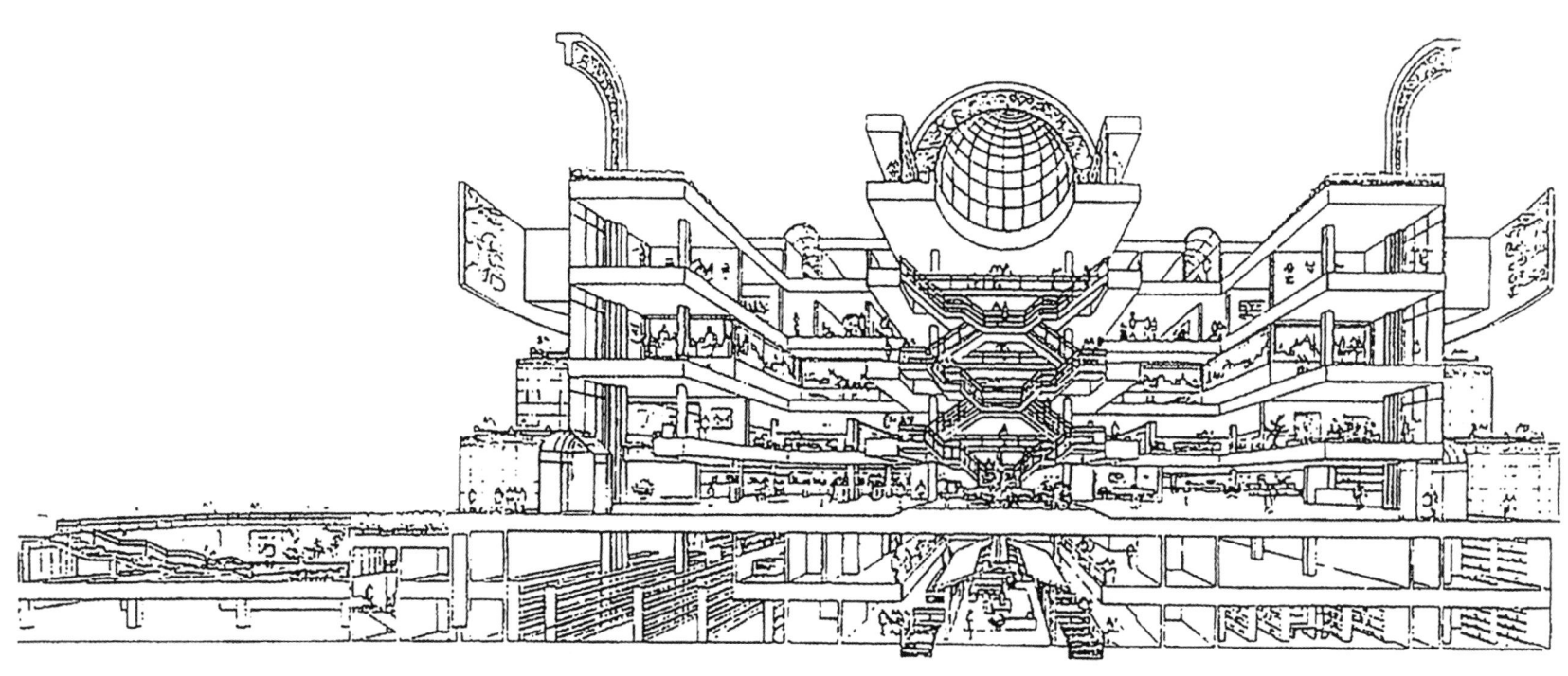

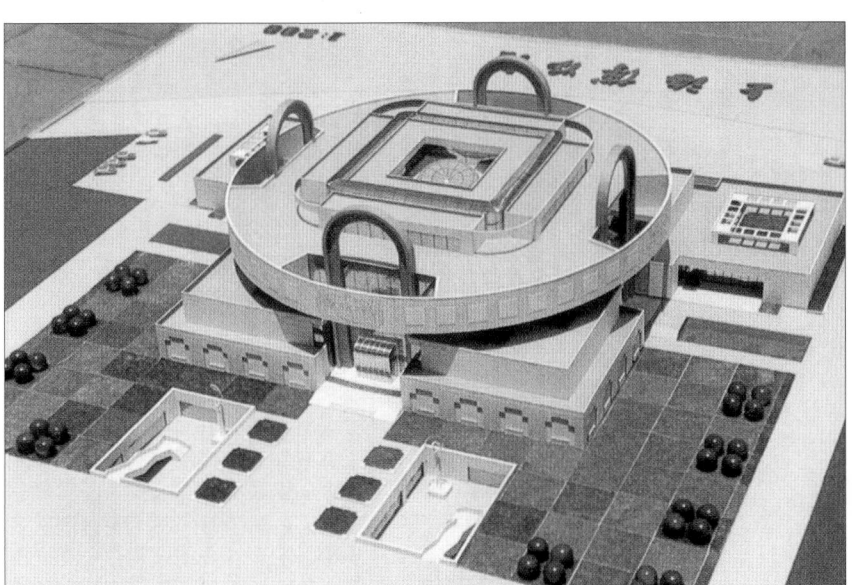

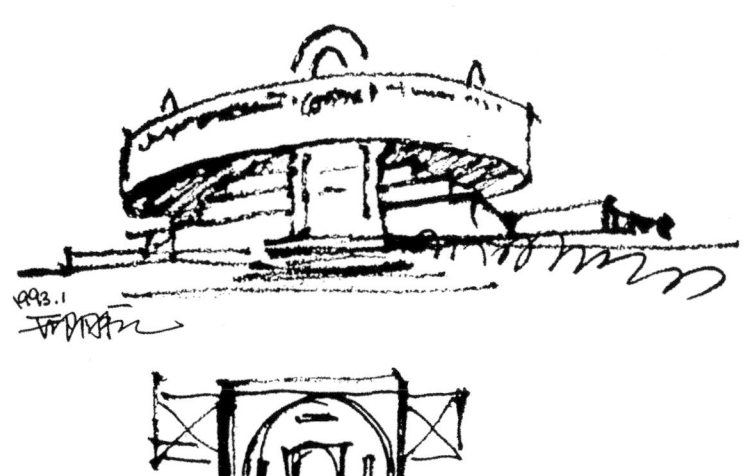

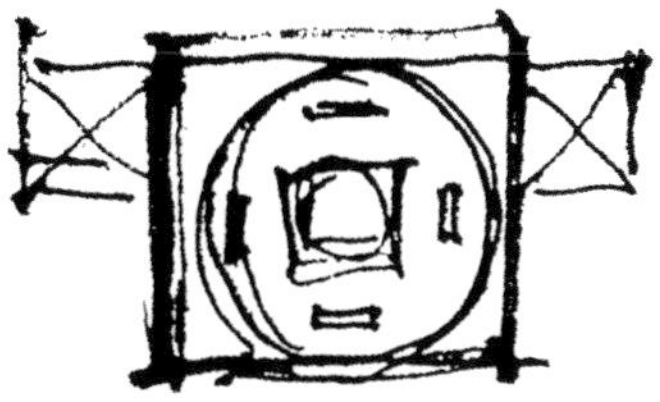

ANSHEN + ALLEN
SHANGHAI FAR-EAST INTERNATIONAL BUILDING, 1999

This 100-metre tall, mixed-use tower combines a retail base and Chinese gardens with upper floor offices to create a signature landmark on a prominent block in the emerging Lujiazui Financial District. A four-storey podium holds the edges of the triangular-shaped lot, pulling back at its apex to create an open-air entry plaza wrapped by a pergola to hold the continuity of the street edge. The lower four floors house retail arranged around a circular atrium connected by escalators. The inset mid-section of the building, articulated by two ten-storey, metal-clad wings, houses the larger floor plates of the live-work units, and serves as a transition between the tower's base and shaft. Crowned by a wide decorative cornice that encircles the top of the building, the narrower central tower, housing offices, is topped by a taller penthouse office floor and mechanical space. Curved glass-clad curtain walls project from both the narrow north facade and broader south facade, accentuating sweeping panoramic views over the city. Vertical mullions emphasise the soaring quality of these projecting bays in contrast with the regular punched openings of the more monolithic east and west elevations.

ARQUITECTONICA
SHANGHAI INFORMATION TOWER, PHASE 1 (LOWER TOWER); 1995–9

This 65,030 square-metre office development is located adjacent to the Pudong Municipal Government Building. It comprises two office towers with identical 7,000 square-metre floor plates, one of 18 storeys, the other of 33. Both are modified to create spaces and volumes only in section.

In two instances, a positive volume of the mass of the building equal to a perfect cube is displaced sideways to cantilever, preserving the clear glass corridor for access at its centre. In another instance only a cylinder containing the fire exit and a grid continuing the structure remain, revealing the essence of the building.

This project is an example of Arquitectonica's recurring interest in designing in section in addition to plan, and of their desire to dramatise the silhouette of buildings without reliance on a shaped top. Here, once again, their intentions have come to striking fruition.

Left: Detail
Right: Model
Opposite: View of projecting cube

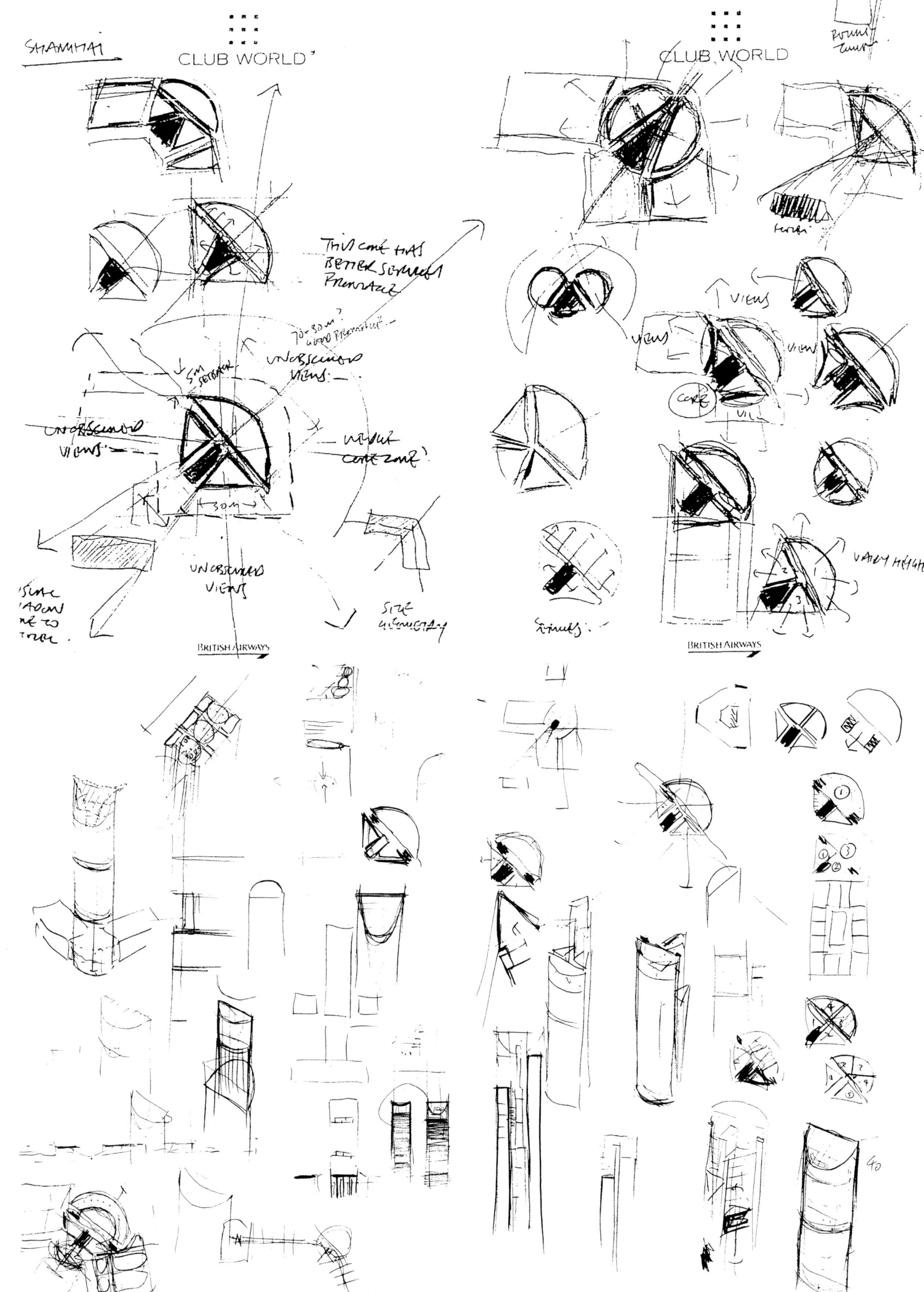

Shanghai has undergone a dramatic transformation over the last ten years. Large areas that previously contained only traditional low-rise buildings now feature thickets of office towers. This 40-storey tower is the headquarters of the Jiushi Corporation, a Chinese company that is providing the inward investment for the next wave of development in the South Bund area of the city. The competition-winning scheme is the practice's first building on the Chinese mainland.

Occupying one of the most significant sites in Shanghai, the tower looks over the Huangpu River to the historical Bund and Pudong – the new business district. These views govern the structure of the building – its concrete core is positioned away from the river to create flexible curved floor-plates on the riverside, free of internal columns. A triple-skin ventilated glazing system allows the tower to enjoy maximum daylight penetration without any attendant build-up of solar gain in the internal spaces. It is the first building in the city to employ such a system. The floor-plates step back at three points over the height of the tower to form terraces, which animate the facade and are ideally suited to conferences.

At the top is a six-storey glazed winter garden, unique in a city where most towers are capped by services installations. Adjacent to the tower a six-storey block containing shops, restaurants and bars follows the line of the street, responding to its historical context with a double-height colonnade, reminiscent of traditional Shanghai shopping arcades.

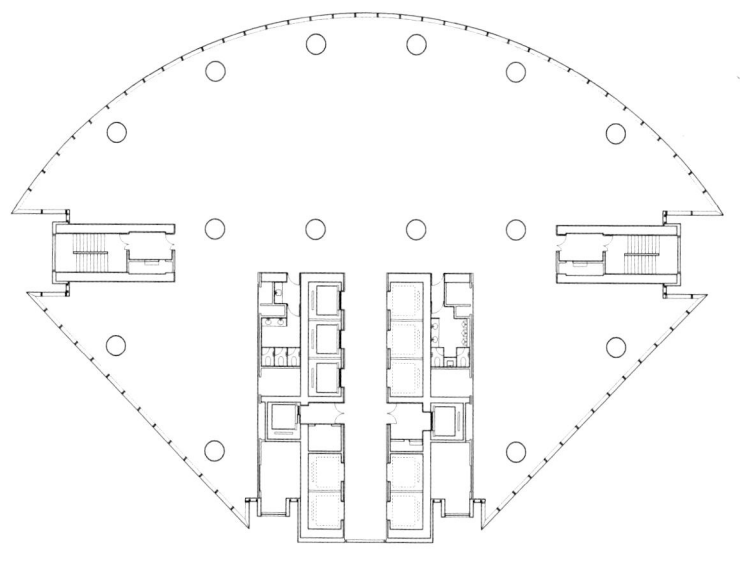

Opposite: Norman Foster's design sketches for the project
Left: View of tower with glazed winter garden
Above: Typical floor plan

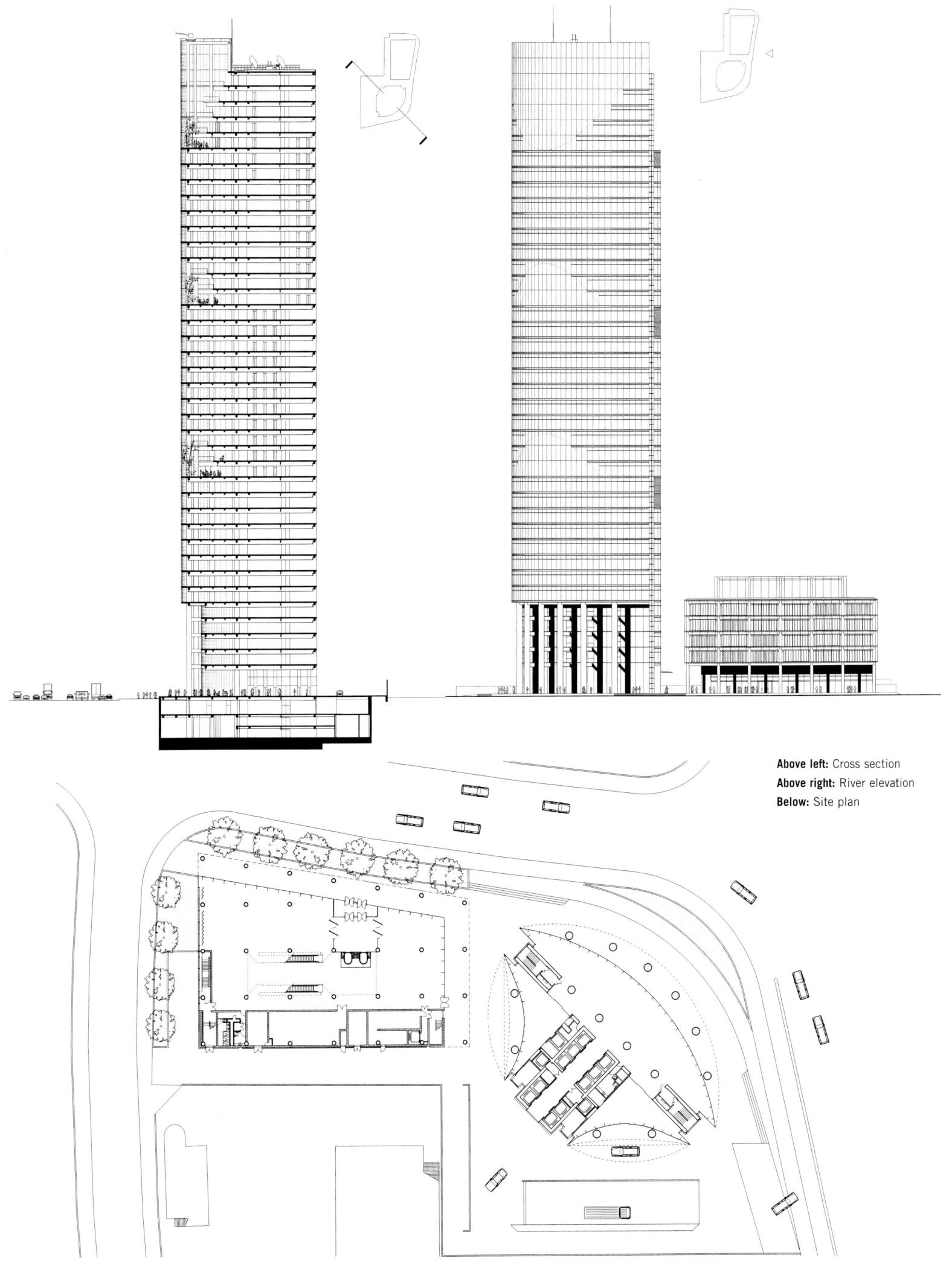

Above left: Cross section
Above right: River elevation
Below: Site plan

View from the Huangpu River

FOX & FOWLE ARCHITECTS

INDUSTRIAL AND COMMERCIAL BANK OF CHINA HEADQUARTERS, 2000

This is the first of five towers to be designed in one of the macro-blocks along Pudong Avenue in Shanghai's new economic development district. It serves as the new regional headquarters for the Industrial and Commercial Bank of China – the largest financial institution in China.

The building's main axis is parallel to the east-west traffic flow of the avenue. It was envisioned as three slab-like parallel masses. The two frontal masses form the 28-storey tower; the low mass toward the rear of the site houses retail banking functions and common spaces such as dining and meeting rooms. At the base of the tower is an elongated banking hall, the featured public space.

Shrouded in glass with brise-soleil, and capped with a semi-transparent 'parasol' at the penthouse, the frontal mass forms a transparent volume that filters light against the solid stone surface of the larger central mass. Expressed as the armature of the composition, this mass houses the fixed components of the tower. It is visually energised and accented by a communications tower that is integral to a cubic void at the top mechanical level.

The seven-storey mass toward the rear of the site is pulled away from the tower to create a skylit circulation zone.

Entrance lobbies for the tower occur at both ends. Stairs and ramps connect the tower floors to the speciality function spaces. The primary spaces, the main conference and dining halls, are expressed in a curvilinear volume that counters the curved frontal mass, creates complexity to the composition, and conveys the importance of these functions.

The large banking hall is positioned under the flared piloti of the frontal mass. It symbolises the bank's importance in the Chinese economy. The permeability of the banking hall facade, defined by horizontal stainless steel banding, provides an element of scale and enrichment to the street level experience.

The entry plaza provides an oasis in the centre of a bustling street. The trilogy of traditional Chinese bridges across a reflective pond slows the tempo of the entry experience, affords a chance to observe and enjoy the architecture, and prepares the visitor for the drama of entering the great banking hall.

At the extreme end of the hall, a large winding stair follows the circumference of the space and leads to the public banking functions on the second floor. A conical skylight marks the centre point of the space, counterbalancing the strong columnar expression and flared form at the opposite end.

Below: Ground floor plan
Right: Street view
Opposite: Interiors

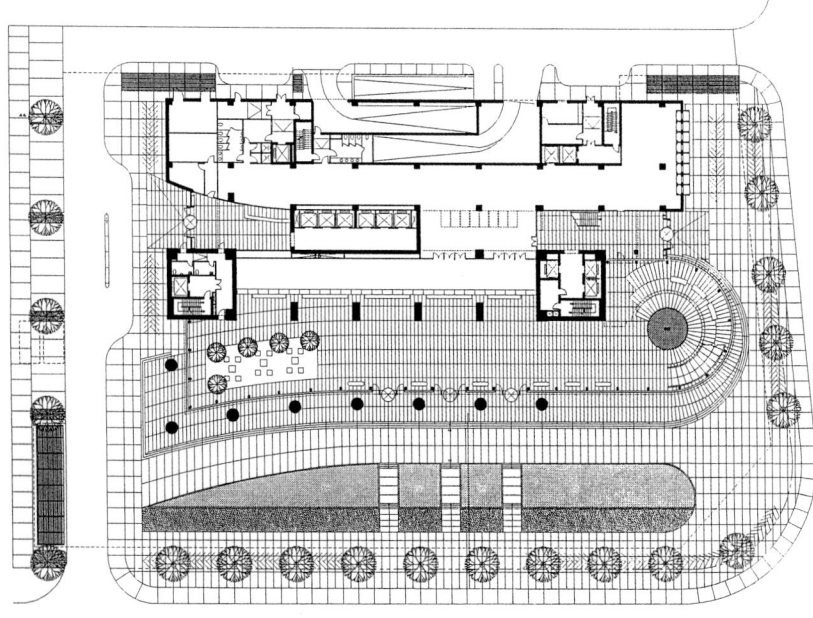

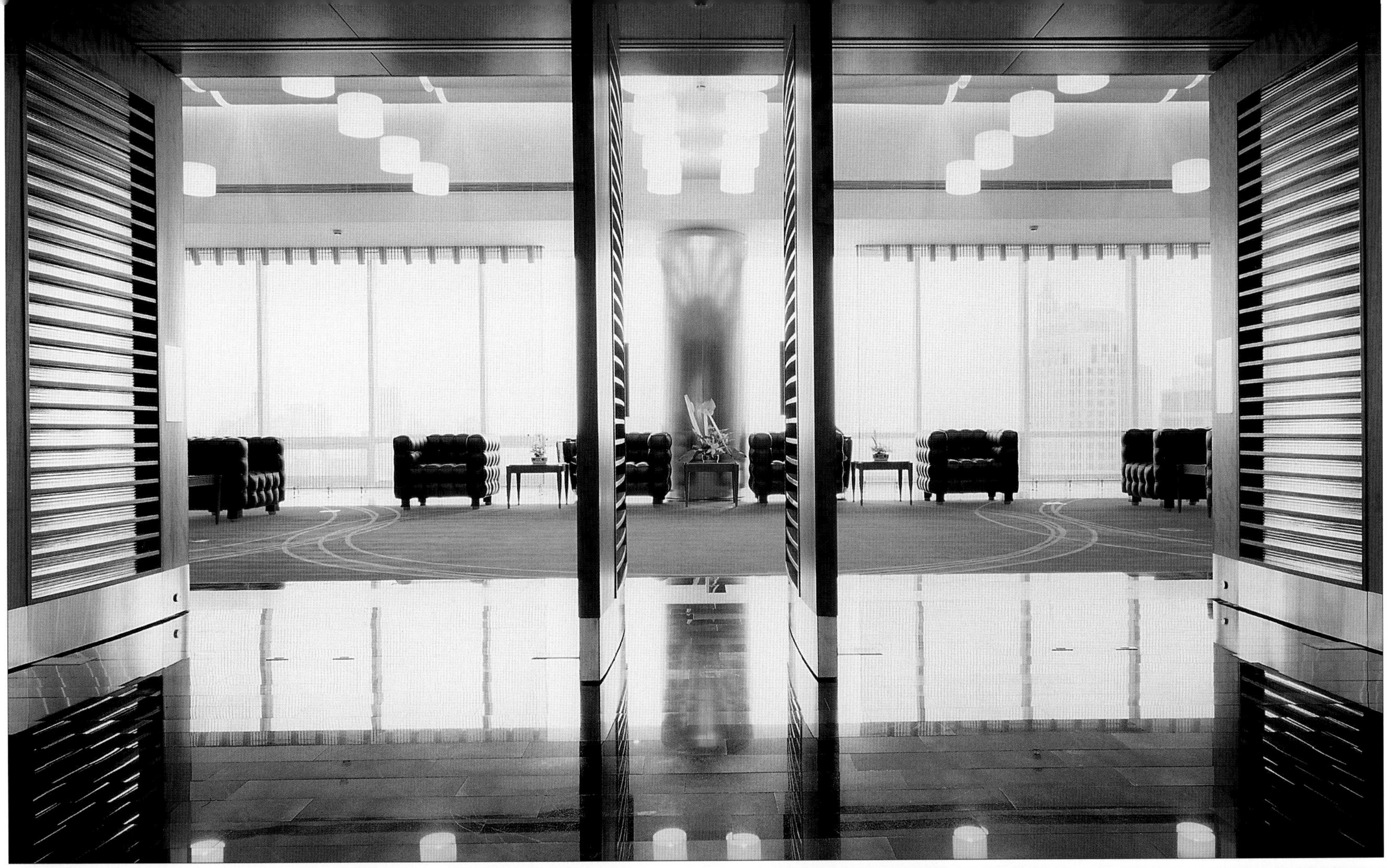

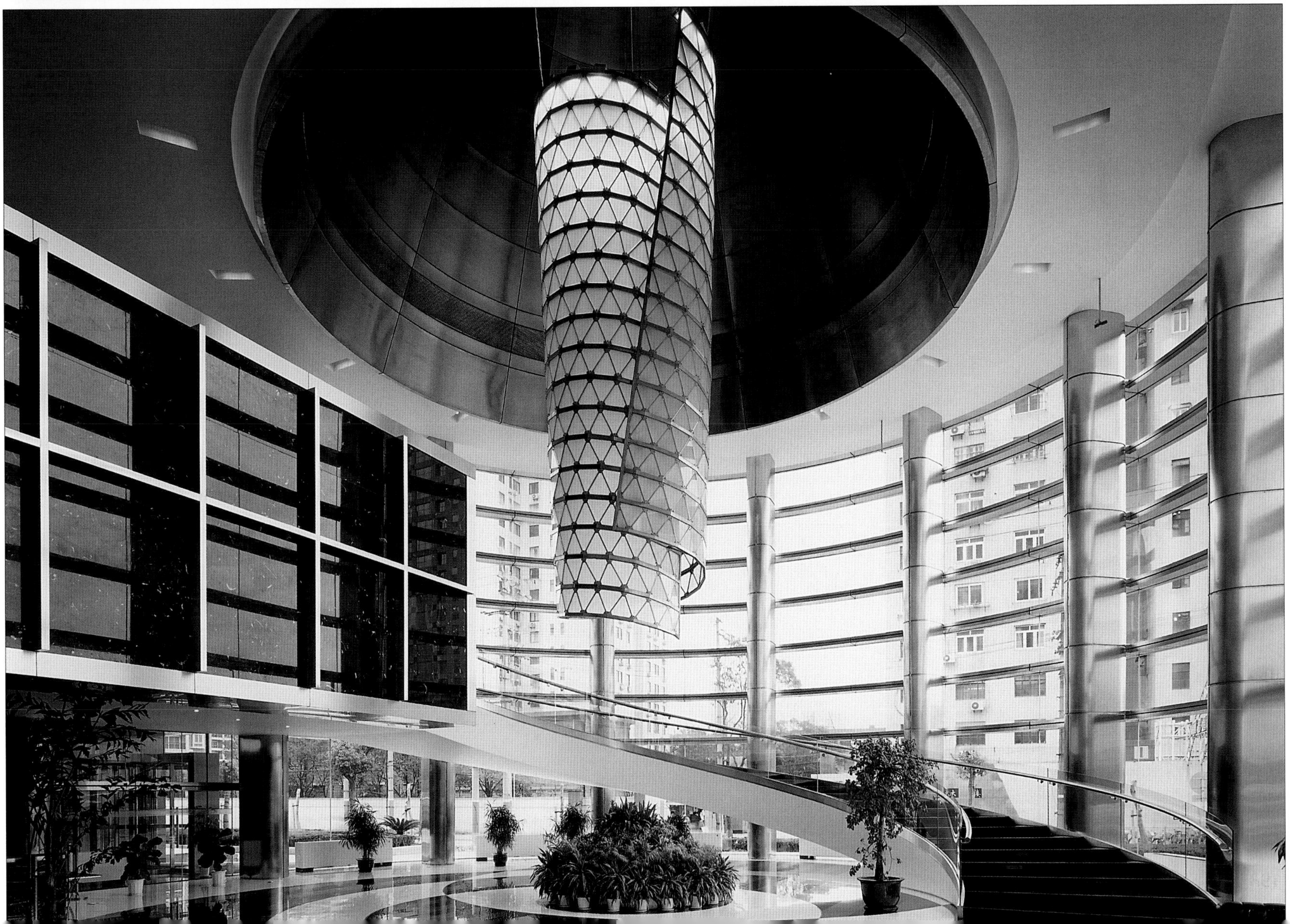

Above: Street views

Right: Fourth floor plan

Opposite: View from the building towards Jin Mao tower

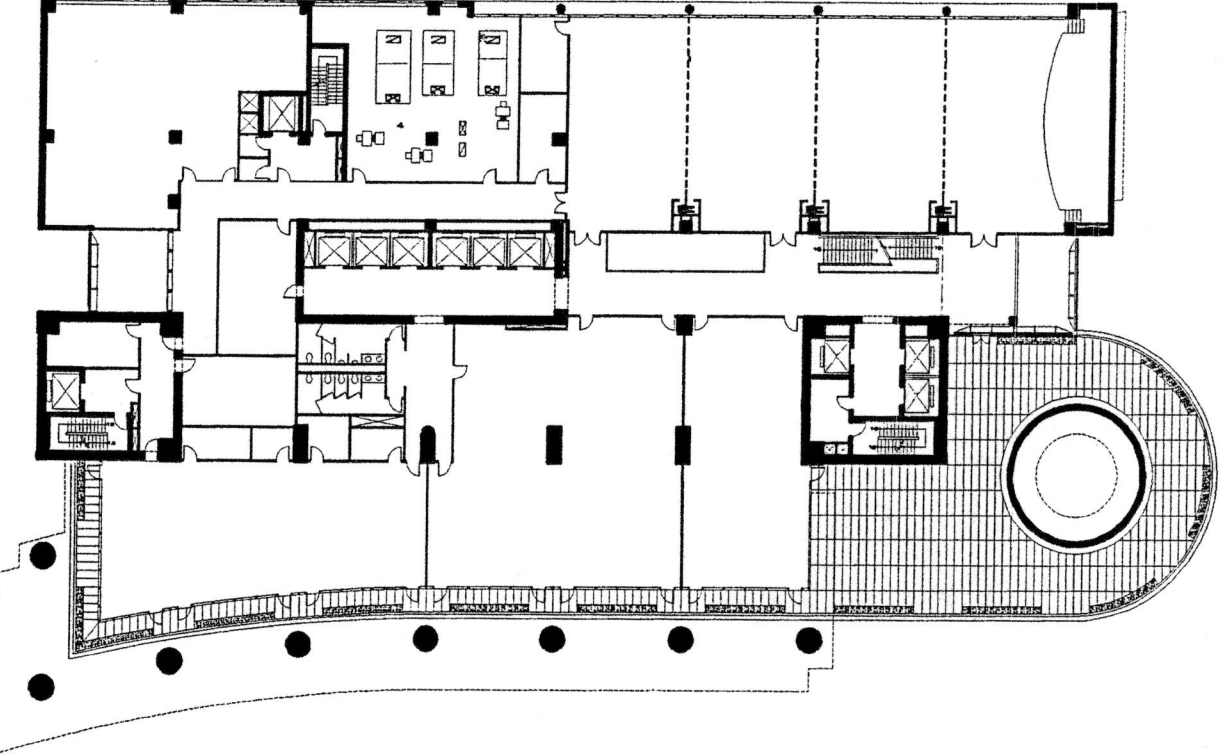

Plaza 66 seen from the
entrance of the Sino Soviet
Friendship Mansion

Kohn Pederson Fox Associates in association with Frank Cy Feng Architects and the East China Architectural Design Institute undertook the assignment of combining two high-rise office towers with a major retail mall in the heart of Shanghai's old city. This posed several major challenges. The foremost was to mediate between the scale of Nanjing Xi Lu, a celebrated pedestrian thoroughfare, and that of of such large structures.

This was resolved by arranging a series of near-primary, radially derived volumes (lozenge, cone, almond and arc) in the manner of a collage. Although bound together by a five-storey podium, each volume establishes its own entry and formal independence at ground level, where it is is distinguished by a canted sectional lean or cut. The resulting forms convey an architectural exuberance that reflects the vibrant street life of Nanjing Xi Lu.

The overall composition of the project is bound by a larger, circular geometry, as if influenced by the forces of a vortex. The resulting embrace of swirling forms gestures towards the neighbouring Stalinist exhibition building and its forecourt park. The upward spiral of building masses is terminated by the translucent lantern of the taller tower. This distinct form will be seen above the city as an icon of the commercial presence of the Hong Kong client whose headquarters will be housed within the complex.

Above: Entrance canopy

Above: The garden terrace above the mall
Opposite: Views from surrounding streets

Opposite: Main entrance
Above: Shopping centre

MURPHY / JAHN
SHANGHAI INTERNATIONAL EXPO CENTRE, 2001

The concept of the Shanghai International Expo Centre is like that of a town. The halls form a triangle with entries in between, creating a large triangular town centre, which serves as an open exhibition area. Covered arcades, connect the entries with the halls. The repetitive structure of the halls forms a soft wave, which gives the Shanghai International Expo Centre its unique image. At the northwest corner a circular tower will mark the main gate in the future. Next to the congress centre it houses offices and a 400-room hotel.

The first phase comprises four exhibition halls with an open exhibition area and one entry hall. The linear succession of drive, entry hall and arcade, tying the four halls together, gives a sense of completeness in this phase and establishes an image.

The halls measure 68 x 164 metres with core zones at both ends. Shops face the arcade at those ends and in between the halls. Restaurants are above those cores in Halls 2 and 3, served by a kitchen situated in the intervening link. The halls are column-free with a clear height of 11 metres and a high hall of 17 metres.

The halls accommodate the required technical specifications for flexibility of division, truck access, floor loading, utilities, toilets, offices, conference rooms, snack bars and restaurants, and create storage.

The primary structural system of the roof consists of simply supported steel girders with short cantilevers at both ends. Each girder has a centre span of 72 metres. Columns supporting the girders are 12 metres. Hollow steel boxes, a lower and an upper cable and V-shaped posts are the main components of each girder, which show a diamond shape in section. The girders' shapes along the span follow the bending diagram thus enabling an extremely light design. Slender, hollow box sections are under- and overslung by prestressed cables. The cables' stabilising forces are transferred through the posts to the box that takes up the compressive forces due to bending and prestressing. The top cable serves as the crescent-shaped upper ridge of the translucent fabric cladding. Along the roof's longitudinal cantilevering edge runs a hollow steel box section resembling an aeroplane's wing, forming the significantly sharp edge. This box transfers the compressive forces of the girders to the columns' axis where the cables are fixed, and provides the necessary lateral stiffness within the roof's plane. The roof rests on slender circular columns cantilevering from the ground with pin joints at the root. Lateral forces due to wind and earthquake loading are transferred through bracing between the columns.

The energy/comfort system has to take into account the relatively short occupancy time during events at which total comfort has to be achieved. During set-up and breakdown natural conditions can prevail. Particular to the use of the halls is that most loads are internally generated through people, lights and equipment. The physical properties of the envelope are thus less significant than the device of a system that responds to these special parameters.

The system developed for any individual hall is a decentralised conditioning concept composed of 28 heating and cooling units spaced at 12-metre intervals. Outside air is supplied at each unit and distributed by five outlets oriented for optimum distribution. Exhaust air is released through operable vents at the top of the longitudinal facades.

The advantage of utilising a decentralised system is that expansion is easily achieved for both the system and the building. Flexibility in heating and cooling is provided by elimination of ductwork; installation and operation are at low cost and the system is easy to maintain.

Exhibit hall elevation

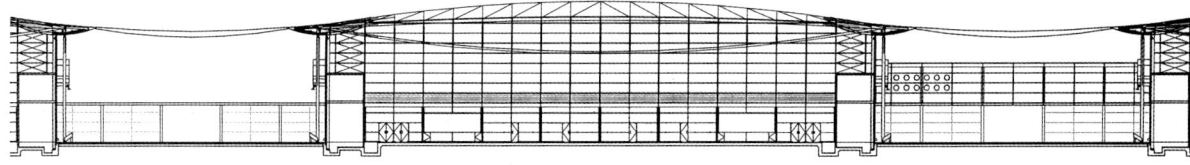

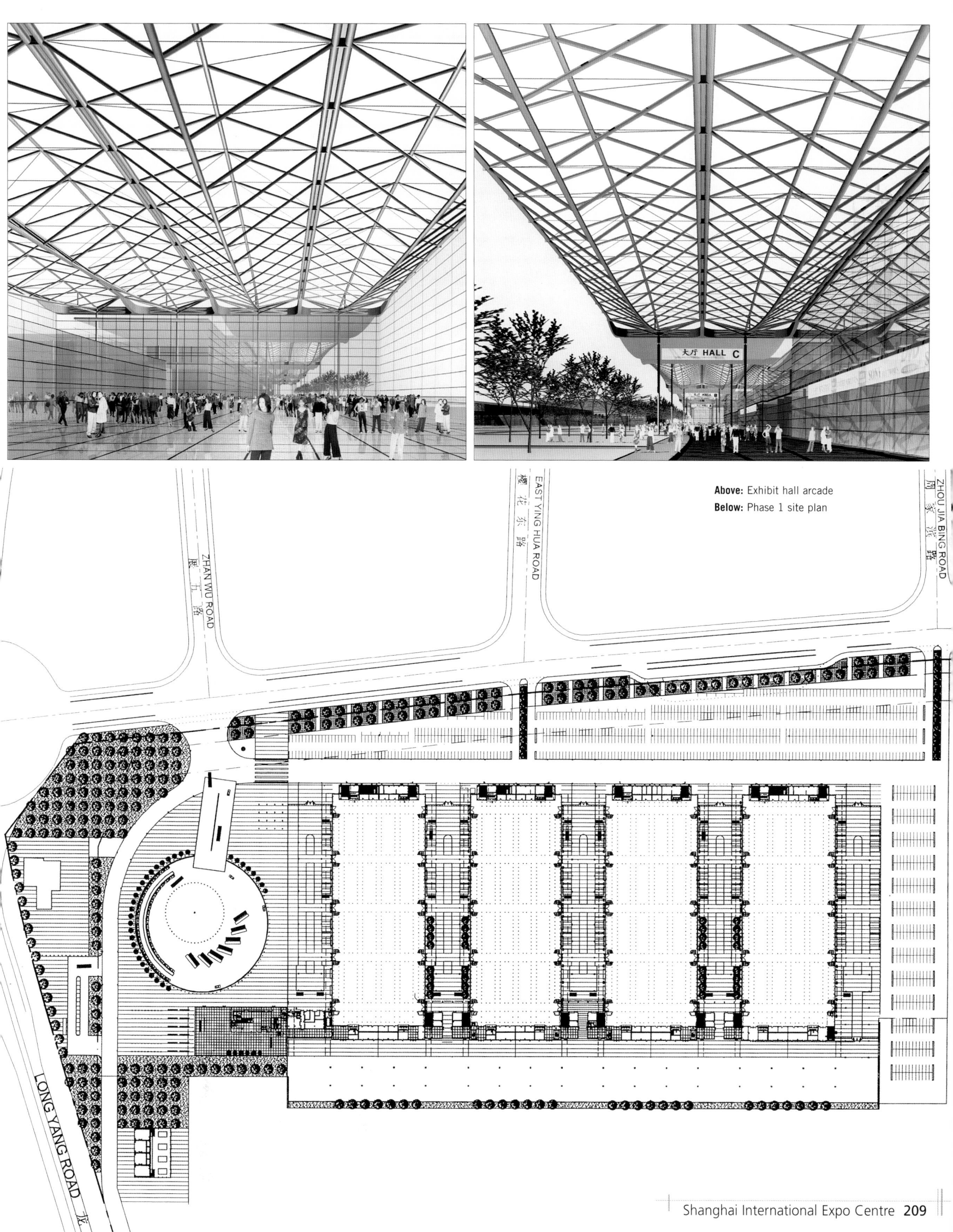

Above: Exhibit hall arcade
Below: Phase 1 site plan

ZHAN WU ROAD
展 五 路

EAST YING HUA ROAD
樱 花 东 路

ZHOU JIA BING ROAD
周 家 滨 路

LONG YANG ROAD
龙 阳 路

East elevation

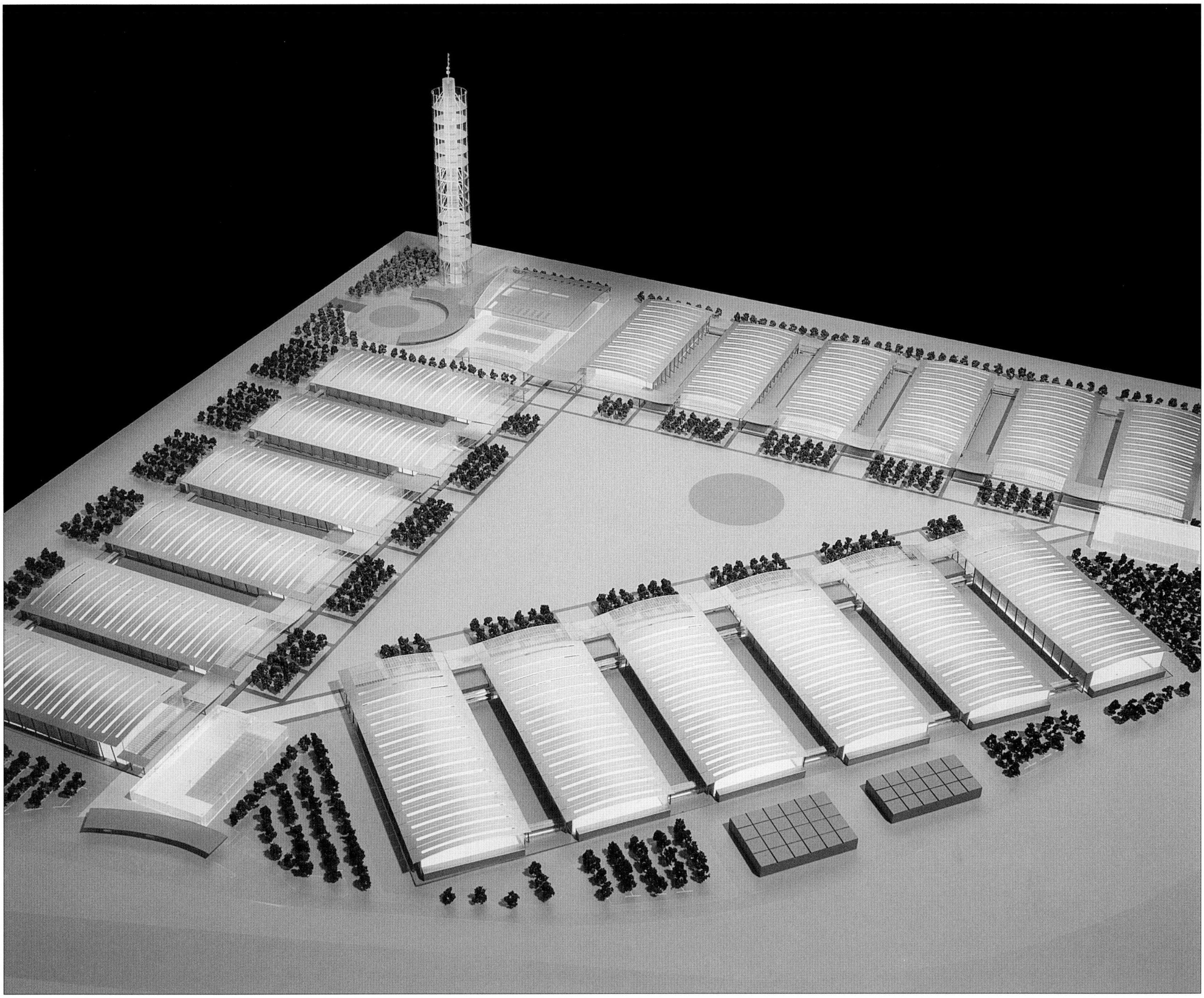

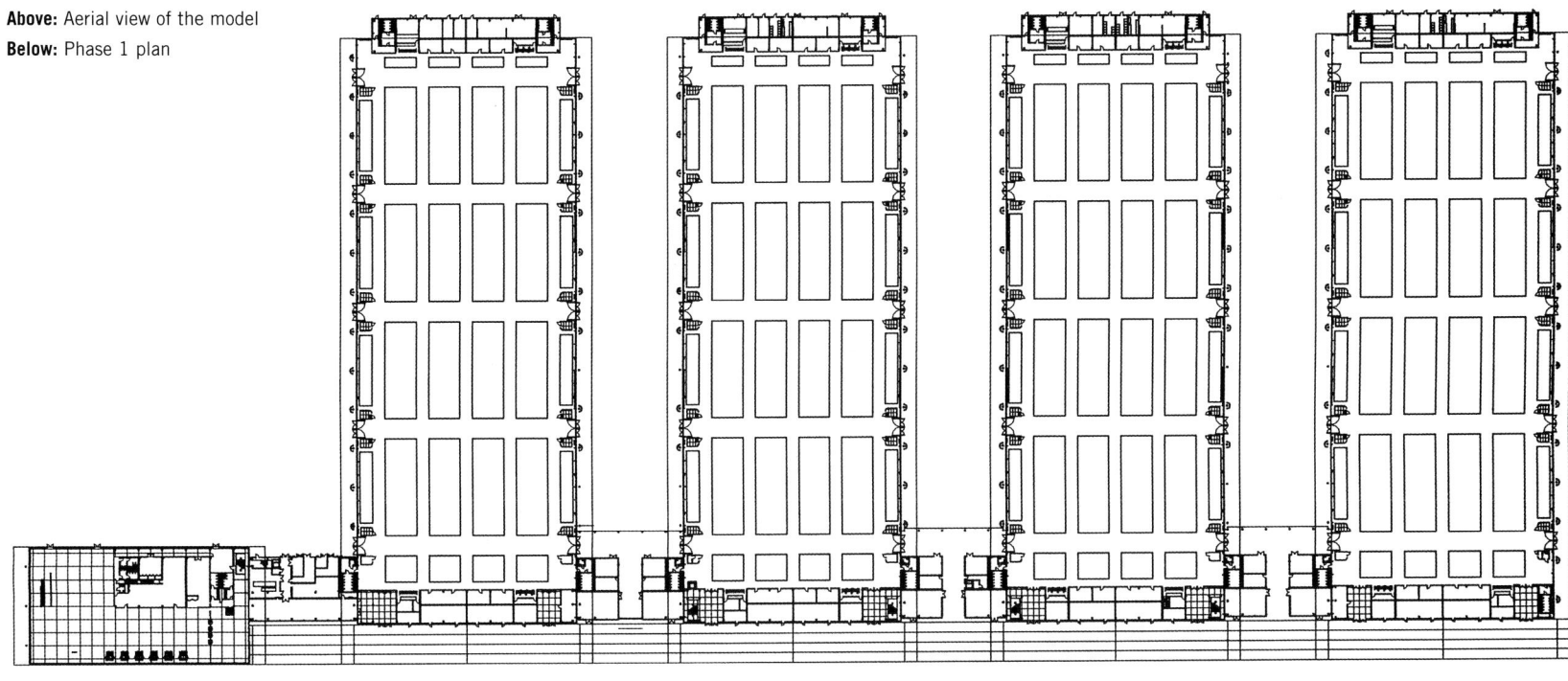

Above: Aerial view of the model
Below: Phase 1 plan

PEI COBB FREED & PARTNERS
POS PLAZA (ORIGINALLY SILVER CROWN TOWER), 1995–9

The architects, in conjunction with Poscoe Engineering and Construction, built POS Plaza, an emblematic 34-storey rectangular office tower with a concourse retail level and an accompanying circular four-storey commercial building. These are set on a 1-metre-high granite plinth, which occupies the buildable area of the site. This comprises 11,425 square metres located on Central Avenue, the major boulevard in the new Pudong development area. The flat site is bordered by streets on three sides. The two buildings frame an arrival courtyard at the same raised elevation, entered from one of the two side streets. An internal service road borders the west side of the property, separating the complex from the adjacent site. It provides access to the car park entries and exits, the bicycle parking and the truck dock; it connects to the courtyard via a slight ramp. The development has four levels of below-grade space. The first basement (concourse level) contains commercial space, service and mechanical facilities and some parking. The three other basement levels provide parking for approximately 750 cars.

The site development focuses on the large, walled, circular courtyard, which functions as a private vehicular arrival area for both buildings. The courtyard is paved with granite cobbles, forming a bold geometric pattern when viewed from the offices above. At its centre a large oculus opens to the retail concourse below, its form echoed by the fountain in this space; a display of water jets appears through the ground-level aperture. Four individually landscaped areas define the circle, framing the vehicular portals and building entries. The projecting plinth becomes a pedestrian plaza in front of the tower on Central Avenue.

The tower is clad in textured stainless steel plate, the structural bays articulated by shaped columns, suspended sunshades and broad spandrels. The aluminium-framed, lightly reflective glass window units on the typical office floors are clad in polished stainless steel. The tower is topped by a stainless steel-clad cage structure, which extends and completes the structural grid of the facade. The glass-enclosed lobby is recessed behind the plane of the tower wall on all four sides. It is of clear, monolithic float glass, framed by a stainless steel and glass mullion structural system.

The curved walls and circular columns of the drum building are clad in a rose-coloured, thermal-finish granite, matching the plinth. There is a partially covered dining terrace on the second level and a narrow terrace on the third level. A stainless steel structure framing this semi-circular terrace acts as a large-scale sunshade; at night its geometric network is defined by engaged lighting elements. At the centre of the circular building is a cylindrical atrium space ascending four floors to a skylight; this is the circulation hub linking the cafés, restaurants and shops.

JOHN PORTMAN & ASSOCIATES

BANK OF COMMUNICATIONS, 2000

The award-winning Bank of Communications is a dual-function building. The 17-storey structure, of concrete, stone and glass, provides 20,000 square metres of space for the bank's operational activities and 9,000 square metres of prime-rental office space.

In addition to the programme requirements, the design challenge was to maximise the site's location, access and scale, while blending with the surrounding historical areas. The aim was also to create a signature building with particular attention to the detail and selection of quality materials and building systems, while addressing present and future space requirements with maximum flexibility.

While distinctive, the architecture harmonises with the quality and context of neighbouring buildings in the Bund district. The plan of the granite-clad building maximises the coverage of the parallelogram-shaped site. The two functions within the building are separated at the seventh level with the bank below and the rental office space above. Each separate function has its own entrance and mechanical system.

Below: Plan
Opposite left: Front facade
Opposite right: Detail of a decorative grill

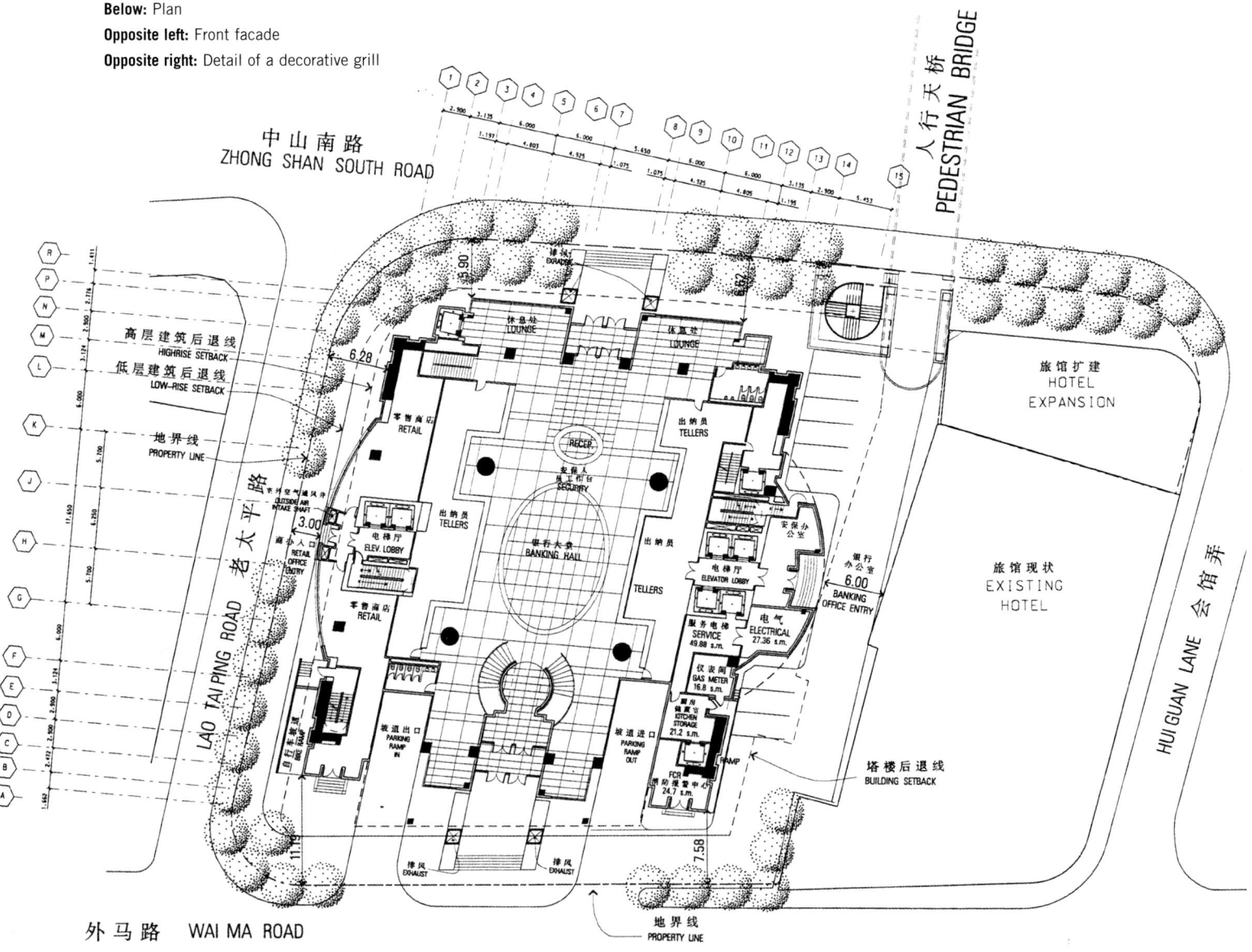

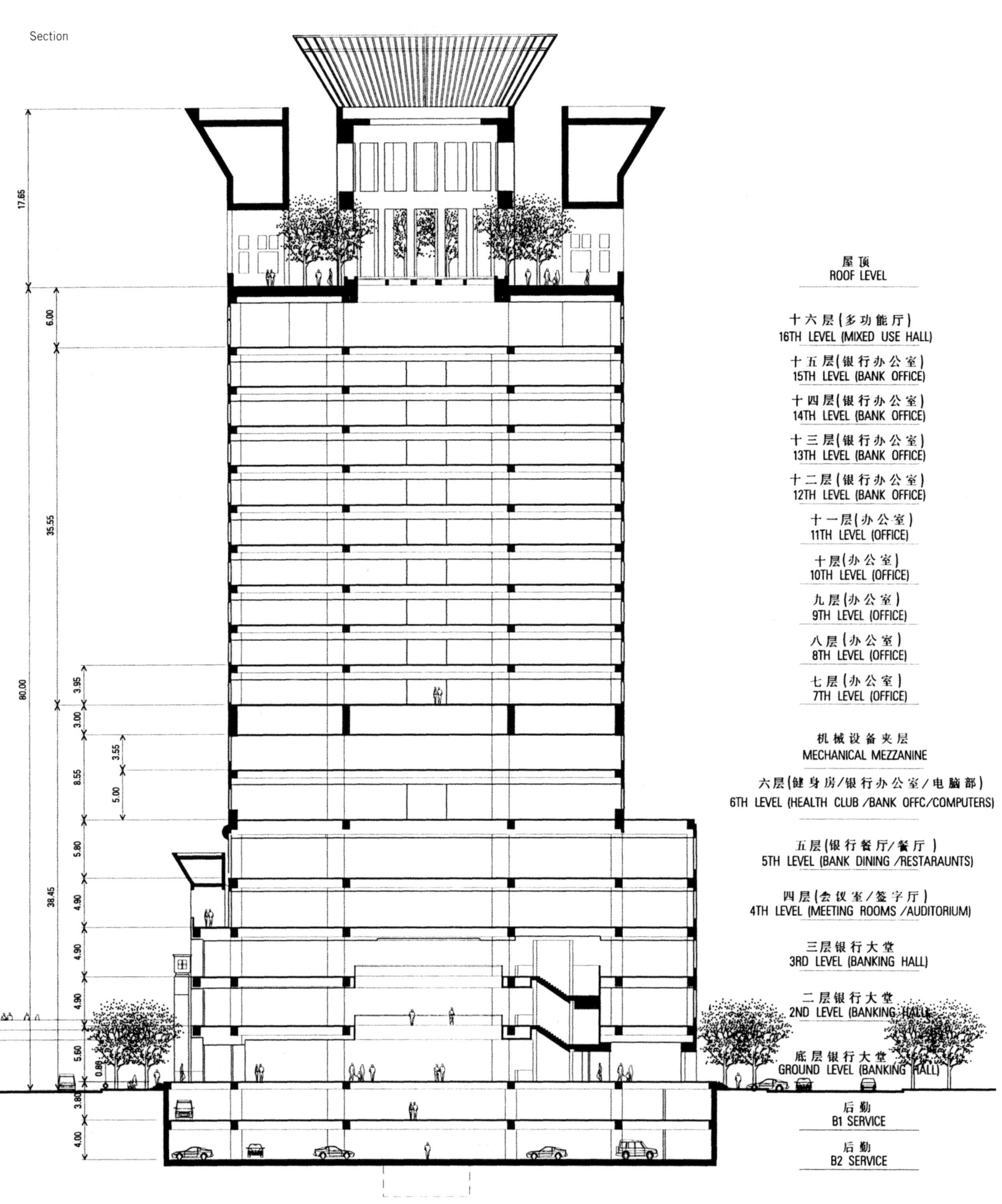

屋顶
ROOF LEVEL

十六层（多功能厅）
16TH LEVEL (MIXED USE HALL)

十五层（银行办公室）
15TH LEVEL (BANK OFFICE)

十四层（银行办公室）
14TH LEVEL (BANK OFFICE)

十三层（银行办公室）
13TH LEVEL (BANK OFFICE)

十二层（银行办公室）
12TH LEVEL (BANK OFFICE)

十一层（办公室）
11TH LEVEL (OFFICE)

十层（办公室）
10TH LEVEL (OFFICE)

九层（办公室）
9TH LEVEL (OFFICE)

八层（办公室）
8TH LEVEL (OFFICE)

七层（办公室）
7TH LEVEL (OFFICE)

机械设备夹层
MECHANICAL MEZZANINE

六层（健身房/银行办公室/电脑部）
6TH LEVEL (HEALTH CLUB /BANK OFFC/COMPUTERS)

五层（银行餐厅/餐厅）
5TH LEVEL (BANK DINING /RESTARAUNTS)

四层（会议室/签字厅）
4TH LEVEL (MEETING ROOMS /AUDITORIUM)

三层银行大堂
3RD LEVEL (BANKING HALL)

二层银行大堂
2ND LEVEL (BANKING HALL)

底层银行大堂
GROUND LEVEL (BANKING HALL)

后勤
B1 SERVICE

后勤
B2 SERVICE

The 186,000 square metre Shanghai Centre is a comprehensive living environment for the international business community comprised of three towers and a podium base. The central tower is the 48-storey, 700-room Ritz-Carlton Hotel, flanked by two 34-storey towers housing 500 apartment units. The seven-level podium is comprised of an exhibition hall, a l,000-seat theatre, office and retail space.

The owners specified that its functions and style should appeal to expatriates living in Shanghai; that it should respect the local culture; and, importantly, costs needed to be carefully controlled due to the risk associated with this uncharted early venture in China.

The contemporary architecture does not attempt to copy Chinese forms yet it reflects the essence of Chinese culture. It strives to create an environment that is respectful of its neighbouring buildings and inviting to both local and foreign visitors. The integration of space and nature are dominant factors in the design. Grand spaces are created within the entry courtyard and the atrium in the podium above; more intimate spaces are carefully woven into the architecture to evoke a variety of responses.

The inclusion of natural elements – trees, water, natural light, and plantings – permeates the complex, transforming roof tops into lush tranquil gardens. The use of concrete as the primary building material gives great flexibility in the design while at the same time being cost-effective. High-quality finishes are reserved for areas such as the lobbies and restaurants.

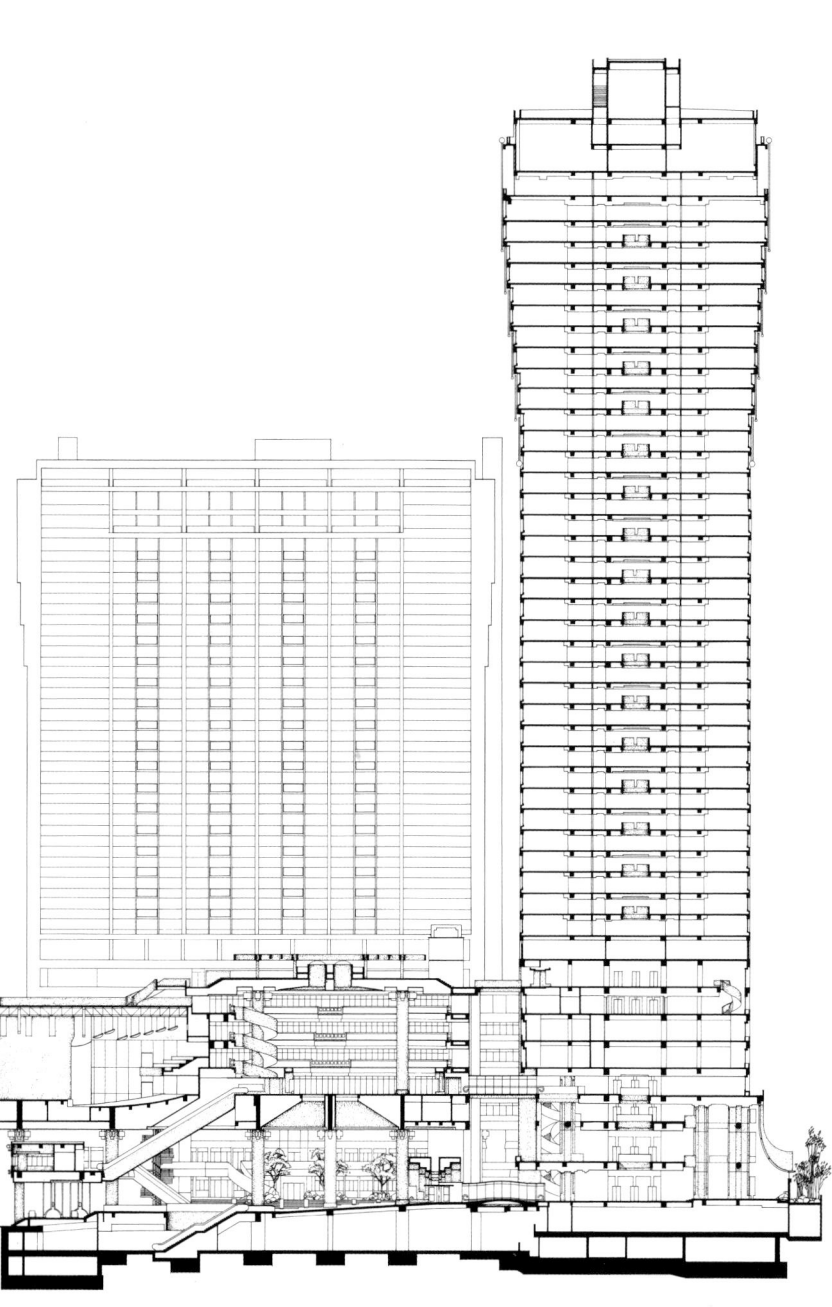

Above: Section

Right: Shanghai Centre seen across the roofs of the Sino Soviet Friendship
Mansion and affluent *li long*, from the 1920s, on the right

This was a joint project between John Portman & Associates and Shanghai Architectural Design and Research Institute. Three major elements on a landscaped plaza comprise the 93,000 square-metre Tomorrow Square. This high-rise tower with hotel and office space is connected to a low-rise podium with a retail galleria and conference centre. An atrium links the tower and podium. The client's goal was to represent the future, not the past. Incorporating the comprehensive programme of hotel, office and retail functions, Tomorrow Square creates a dramatic new landmark on Shanghai's skyline.

The 55-storey tower has facades of aluminium and glass that reach upward in a straightforward, geometric progression. By rotating the basic square plan 45 degrees at the 37th level, the building reflects the change of function within. The lower levels are offices and office apartments with the hotel located above.

The six-level podium constitutes the retail hub. The granite building extends the width of the site arcing around the tower to maximise the importance of the Nanjing Road entrance. From this main entrance, shoppers descend to a food court, bowling lanes and access to the subway system. Within the skylit atrium, escalators and elevators ascend to shops on the first three levels. Level 4 contains restaurants and entertainment venues. Level 5 houses the conference centre and health club that is linked to additional facilities on the rooftop, including the hotel swimming pool.

Left: Lower level plan
Below: Upper level plan

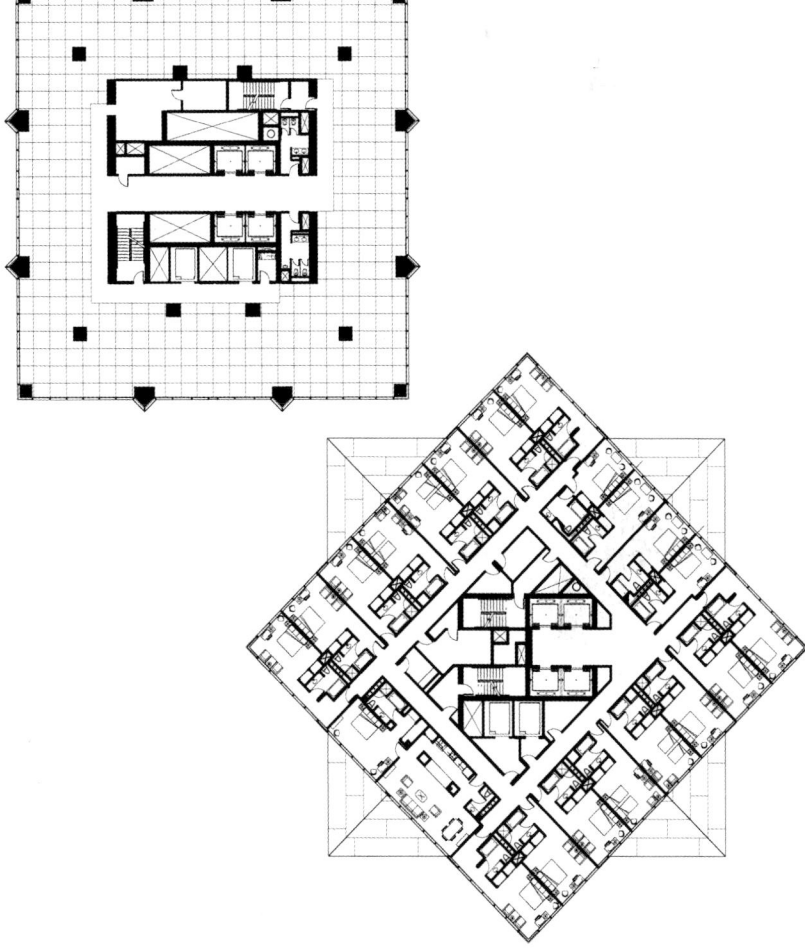

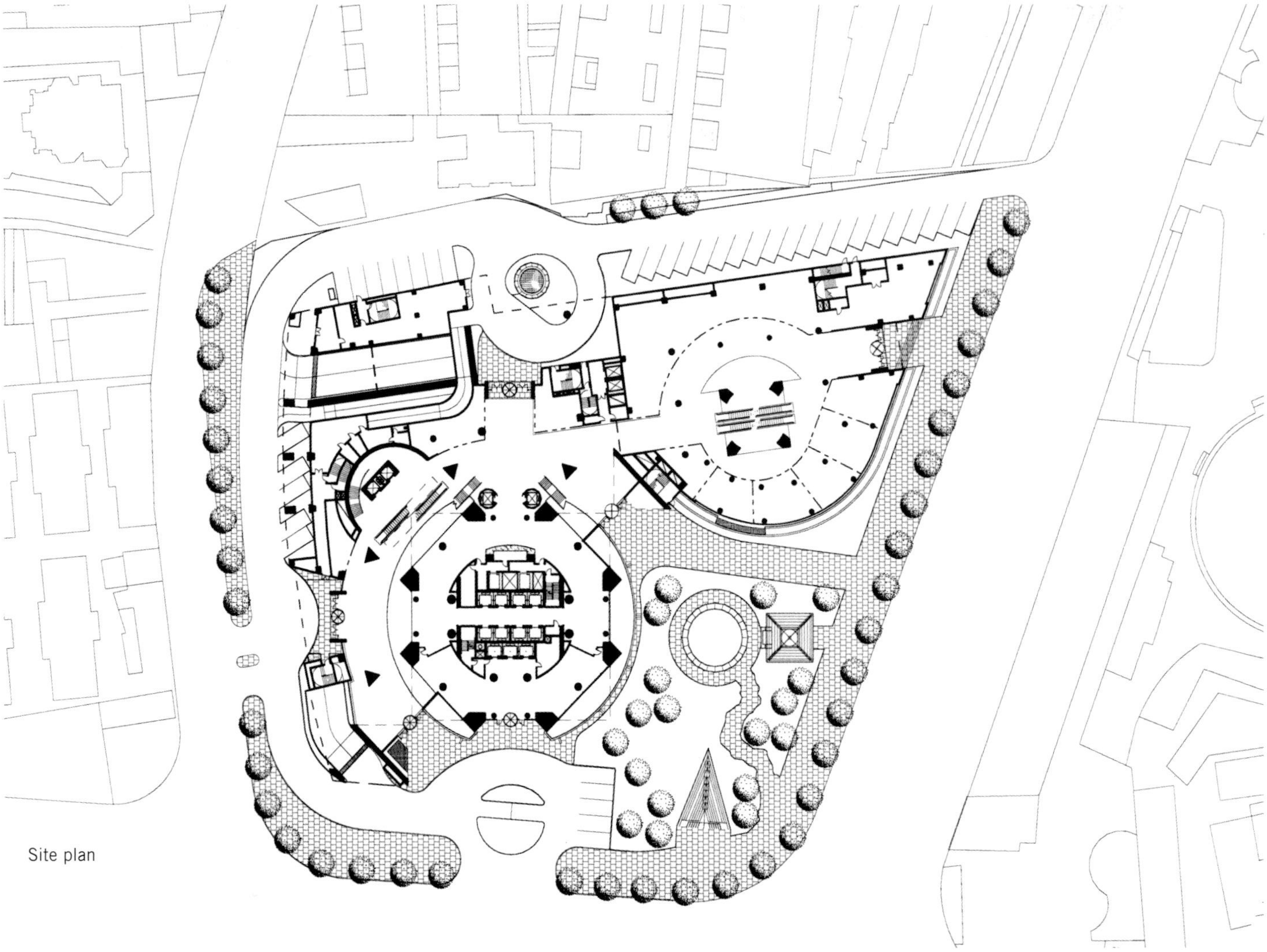

Site plan

NIKKEN SEKKEI
PUDONG INTERNATIONAL FINANCE BUILDING (ZHONGYIN BUILDING), 2000

This is a powerful element within the skyline of the Lujianzui Central finance district. The architect in collaboration with Shanghai Architectural Design and Research Institute completed this 53-storey tower in 2000, providing an additional 70,000 square metres of well-serviced office space to the heart of the new financial district. It is in a highly visible position, tucked in behind the dominating presence of the Orient Pearl TV Tower. The form of the Zhongyin Building has a simple strength that is in no way diminished by its extravagant neighbour. It is always seen from the Bund in relation to the ugly but strangely picturesque Shanghai Convention Centre, with its dubious balancing globes (one of which demonstrates the extent of the landmass of China on the map of the world). Among the myriad, essentially identical towers that cluster with ever-increasing anxiety along the Century Boulevard, there is great competition for a distinct identity on the skyline of this new Wall Street. The principal means of establishing such distinction is in the shaft of the tower and its top, like medieval warriors in armour and helmet, and there are some spectacular and quite silly variations on this theme. The Zhongyin Building, however, eschews extravagance in favour of an elegant and surprising *parti*. The lower element of the tower appears as a monolithic square column, a massive base cut diagonally, at about one third of the height, to release a highly polished slender oval tube that soars to more than 250 metres in height. At the crown this polished sleeve pulls back to form an elegant arcaded corona.

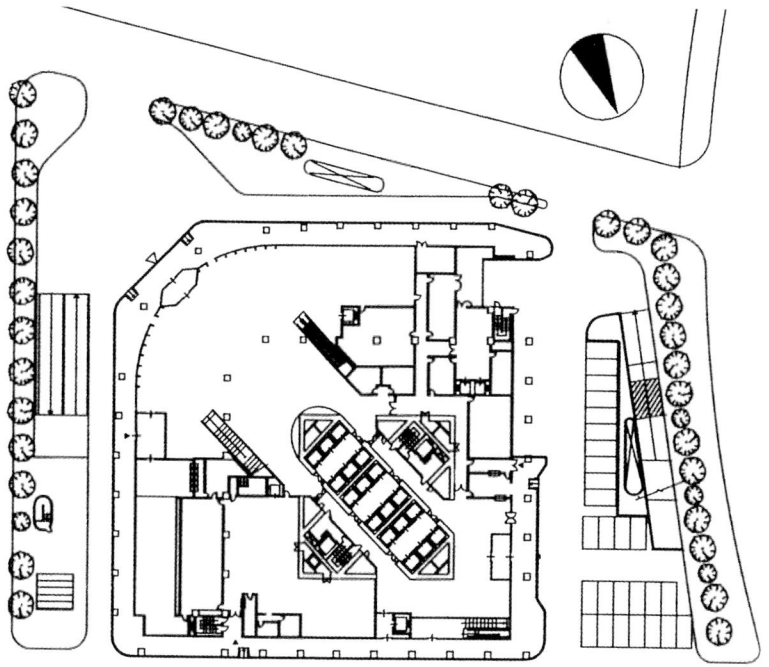

Above: View of the main entrance
Below left: Night view
Below right: Site plan and lower floor plan

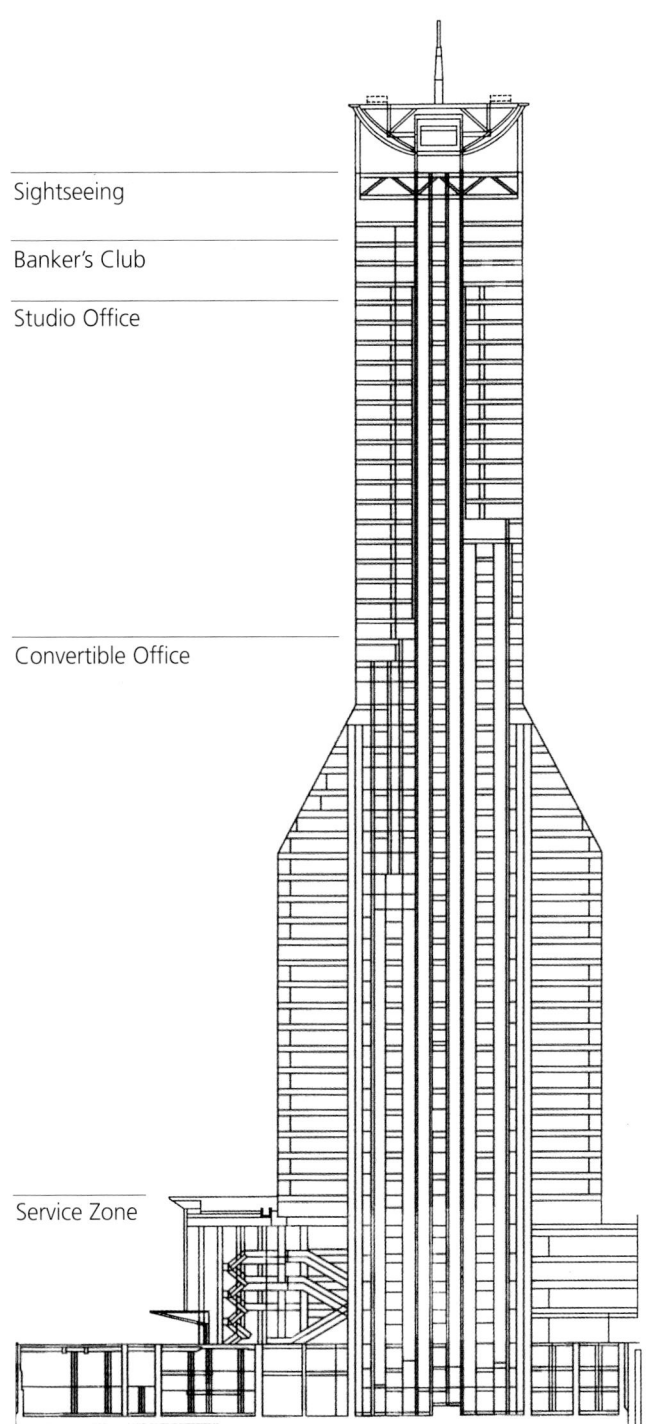

Sightseeing

Banker's Club

Studio Office

Convertible Office

Service Zone

Left: Section
Right: The main lobby on the ground floor
Opposite, above left: Looking across the Huangpu River
Opposite, above right: View from Shiji Daidao
Opposite below: Detail of the facade at night

SIMON KWAN & ASSOCIATES
CHINA MERCHANT'S TOWER, 1995

The China Merchant's Tower, a 39-storey high-rise building in Pudong, is one of Shanghai's premier office locations and major architectural landmarks. With a total floor area of 58,500 square metres, the distinctively striated tower commands prime views of the metropolitan area. The symbolically charged building form, a cylinder within a square volume, is derived from an overlay of the Chinese symbols for heaven (a circle) and earth (a square). The central core serves flexible work levels and is efficiently organised into modular zones. Contrasting materials, textures and lighting conditions carefully integrated throughout the building further enhance the accomplishment of professional tasks.

Phase 1 consists of two 35-storey office towers poised above a seven-storey commercial/entertainment podium with two levels of basement carparking. The office blocks, two gestural figments that mirror one another, feature finely articulated curtain-wall systems. The commercial podium contains a multiplex cinema and sporting facility, plus abundant retail and dining amenities. The basement carpark accommodates 460 vehicles. The total GFA is 176,528 square metres.

SKIDMORE, OWINGS & MERRILL
JIN MAO TOWER, 1998

Located in the Pudong District of the city's Lujiazui Finance and Trade Zone in Shanghai, the Jin Mao Tower is a 278,800 square-metre, 88-storey, multi-use development, incorporating offices, a hotel, retail, service amenities and parking. Situated in the top 38 storeys is the 555-room Grand Hyatt Hotel, affording impressive views of the city and the surrounding region. Office spaces, in the lower 50 storeys, are easily accessed. The six-storey podium houses hotel function areas, a conference and exhibition centre, a cinema auditorium, and a 21,000 square-metre retail galleria. The tower base is surrounded by a landscaped courtyard with a reflecting pool and seating, offering visitors a peaceful retreat from Shanghai's busy streets.

In addition to the tower and podium, Jin Mao incorporates three below-grade levels with a total area of 57,000 square metres. These levels accommodate parking for 993 cars and 1,000 bicycles; hotel service facilities; additional retail space; a food court; an observatory elevator lobby; and building systems equipment areas including electrical transformers and switchgear, a sewage treatment plant, a domestic water plant, a boiler room and a chiller plant.

The building systems design integrates intelligent features that provide safety, security and comfort; high levels of energy efficiency; ease of building maintenance, operation and control; and technologically advanced communications systems. Advanced structural engineering concepts employed in the design of the tower protect it from the typhoon winds and earthquakes typical of the area.

The tower recalls historic Chinese pagoda forms, with setbacks that create a rhythmic pattern. Its metal and glass curtain wall reflects the constantly changing skies, while at night the tower shaft and crown are illuminated. At 420.5 metres, the tower and its spire are a significant addition to the Shanghai skyline. Jin Mao's completion makes it the tallest building in China and the centrepiece of Shanghai.

View of the podium

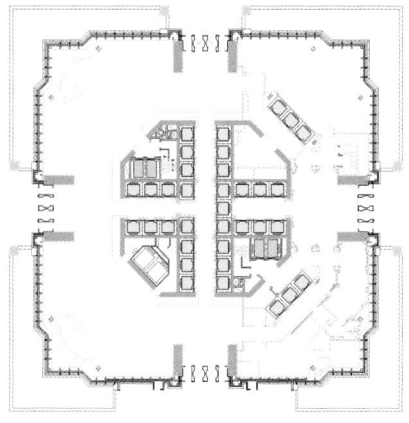

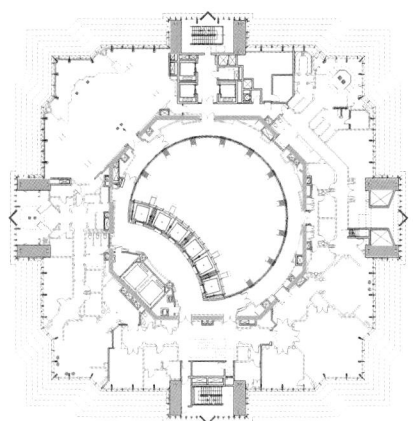

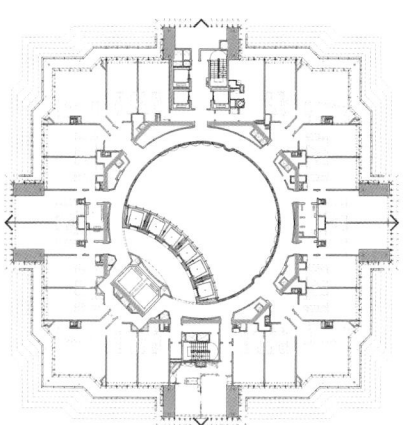

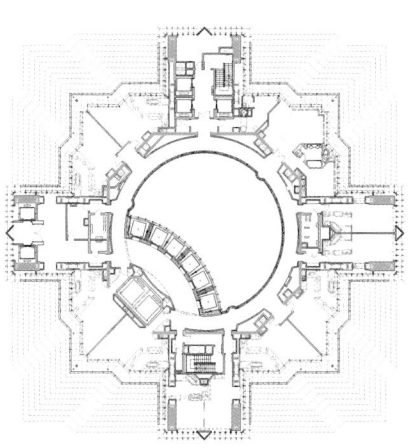

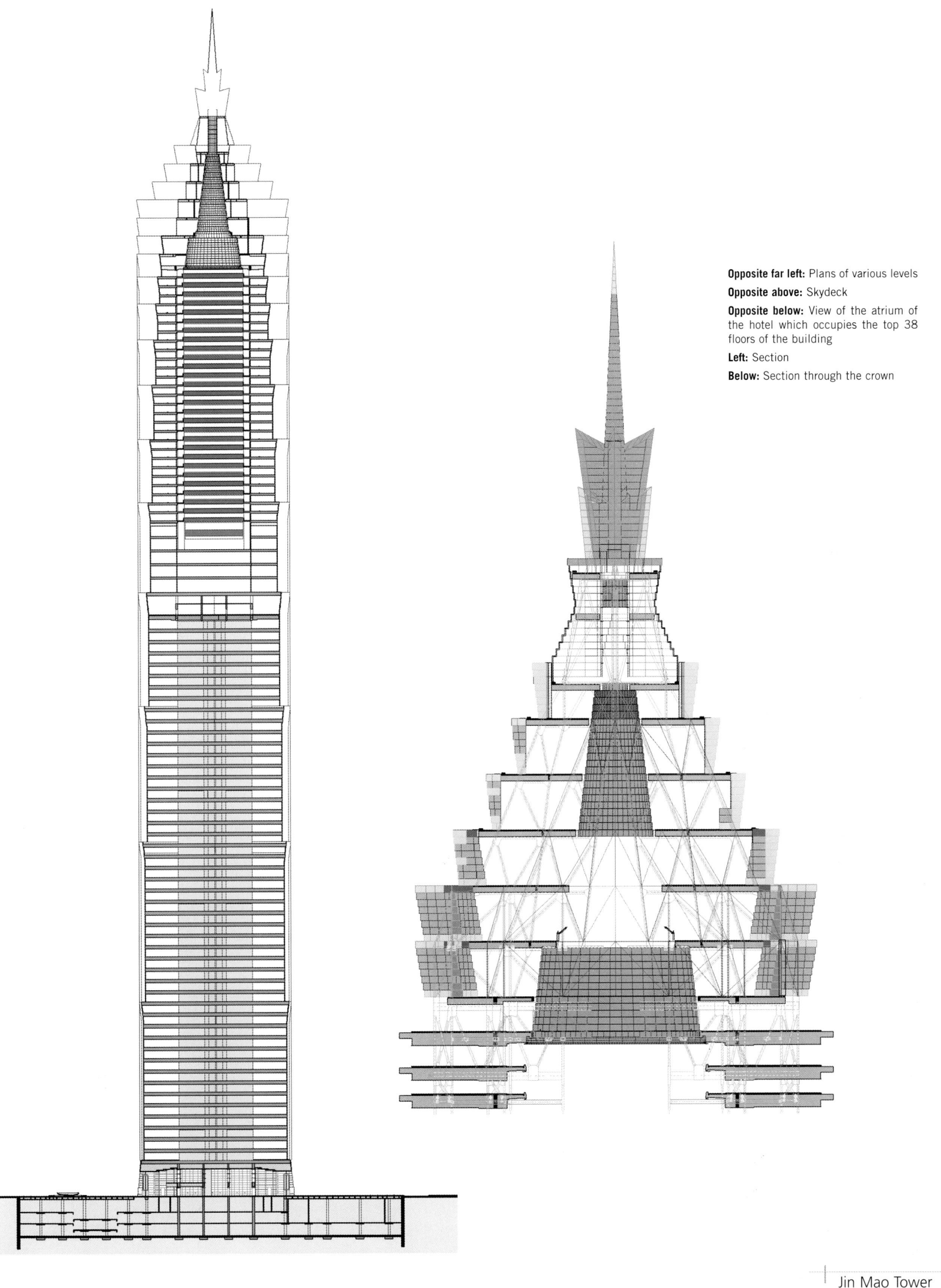

Above left: View from across the river
Above right: Detail of Jin Mao dragon
Centre: Podium plan
Below: Podium elevation
Opposite: Upward view of the atrium

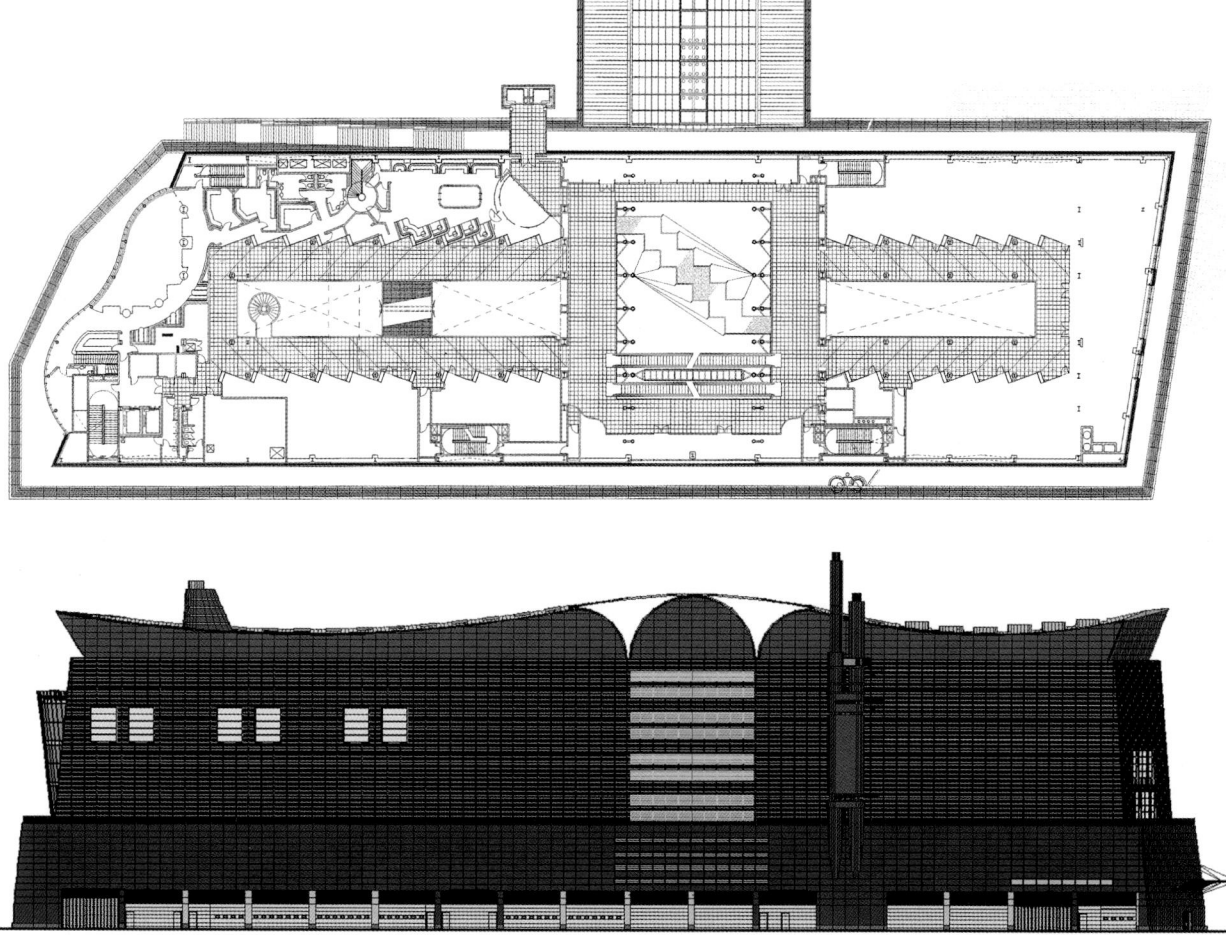

TAOHO DESIGN ARCHITECTS

KING TOWER, 1996

The King Tower is the headquarters of Jin Qiao Export Reprocessing Zone in Pudong. At 208 metres, it was the tallest modern office building in Shanghai when it was completed in 1996.

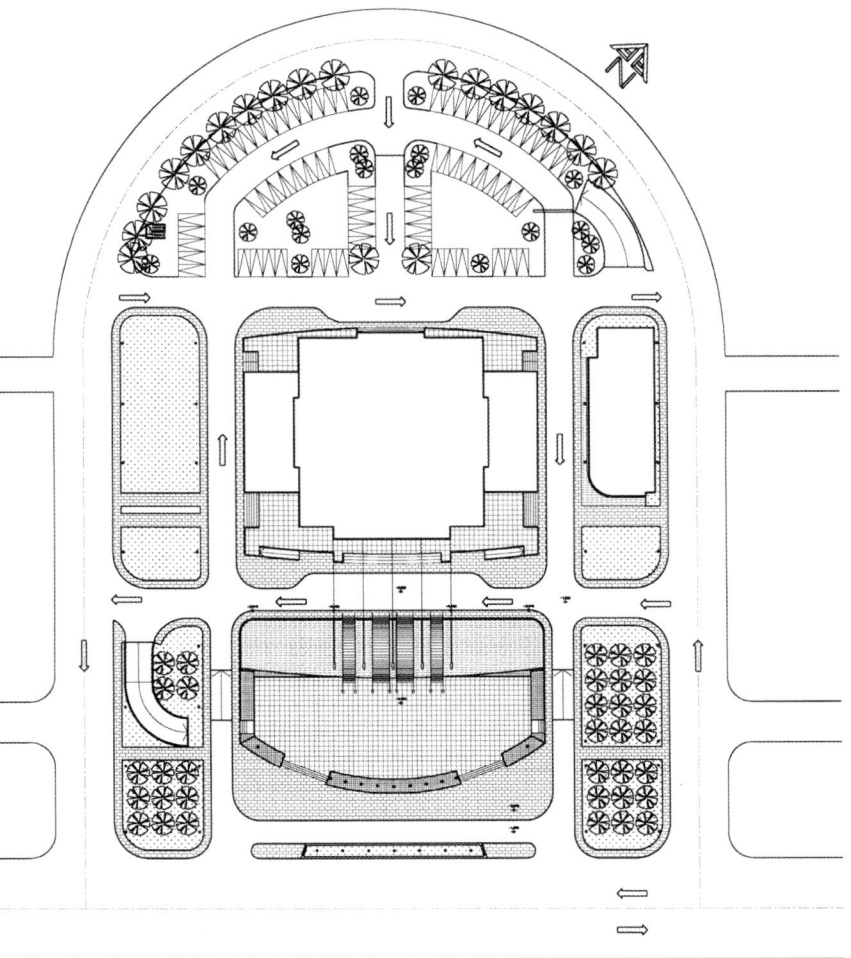

Above: Site plan
Right: View looking north
Opposite, far right: Section

WONG & OUYANG

KERRY EVERBRIGHT CITY, 1996-2003

Situated in the very heart of the city and offering a total floor area of more that 523,000 square metres, Kerry Everbright City is Shanghai's largest multifunctional development. The project is planned to include nine separate tower buildings: two office towers, three blocks of residential apartments, two commercial/residential towers, one commercial tower and one 700-room hotel over a mega mall of about 166,000 square metres. All of the buildings are linked by covered pedestrian bridges and underground tunnels, ensuring that every possible amenity is within easy reach. There is a wide range of shopping, entertainment and dining options.

Below: Interior
Right: View of the exterior

Everbright City is the only 'city within a city' complex in Shanghai. Commanding a prime position within the Shanghai Railway Station area, it is linked to two Metro (MTR) stations (Shanghai Railway Station and Hanzhong Road Station). This comprehensive development has a total construction area of over 10,7000 square metres. The project which began in 1996, is being developed in several phases.

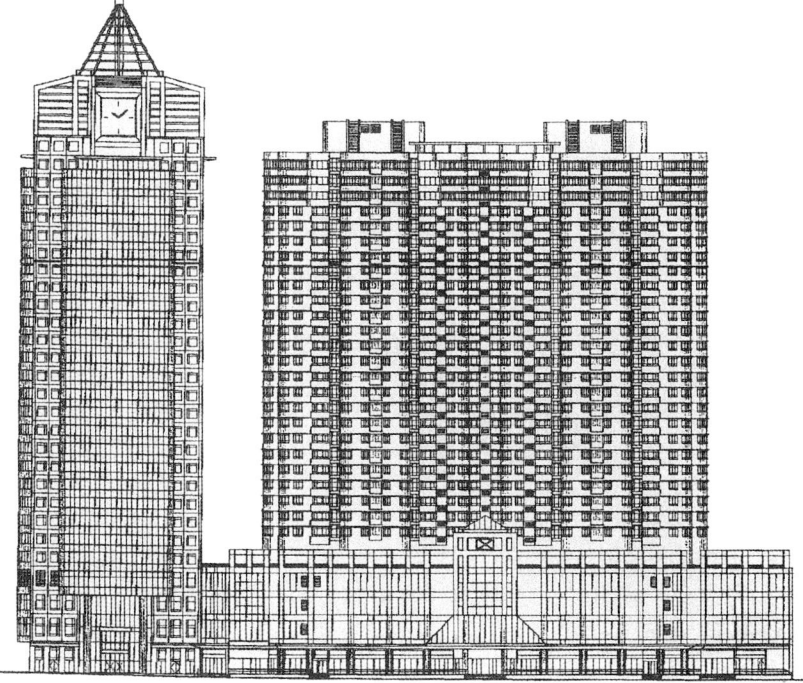

WONG & OUYANG
SAN FENG CENTRE, 1998

Located in the northern part of Shanghai's historic Bund, San Feng Centre enjoys a spectacular view of the Huangpu River. It houses the American Club 7, two podium floors of a shopping centre and 26 storeys of office space.(The building on the left is the Panorama by RSP Architects and the East China Architectural Design and Research Institute.)

Shanghai Times Square is a composite development located in the heart of Huai Hai Zhong Lu. It consists of a 30-storey office tower, a 27-storey apartment tower, which overlooks neighbouring Huai Hai Garden, a seven-storey crescent shaped commercial podium and three levels of basement.

In front of the development is a semi-circular open space, which is a popular activity area during festivals and holidays.

SHANGHAI ZHONGFANG ARCHITECTURAL DESIGN INSTITUTE
HOUSING PROJECT FOR PING-YANG VILLAGE, 1996

On a site area of 14.26 hectares, the general plan is traversed by a characteristic 45-degree, S-shaped main road. It connects with three city streets, naturally separating the site into four groups. All the housing blocks are slope-roofed. To the southwest, the blocks are four storeys high, while elsewhere they have six floors. In the middle of the main road is a central grass area, along which are situated a kindergarten and community centre for senior citizens. At the northwest corner is a refreshment centre and old people's home, while a primary school is located at the northeast. Spacing and design follow some of the traditional concepts of local *li-long* housing.

Traffic is organised in a clear plan that includes a 7-metre-wide dual carriageway connected to city streets and 4-metre-wide roads within the project. A pedestrian road paved with colourful bricks leads to all areas of the community. Outdoor parking areas are combined with the green space.

Along the main road is a 13-metre-wide green belt, with egg-stone paving. The central part of the complex is a semi-circular green plaza. East of the community is Xin-Jing-Gang green belt, which provides seats and pavilions along the city street. Landscaped courtyards provide semi-public space in front of each house, and a quiet space at the back planted with trees enhances the appearance and atmosphere.

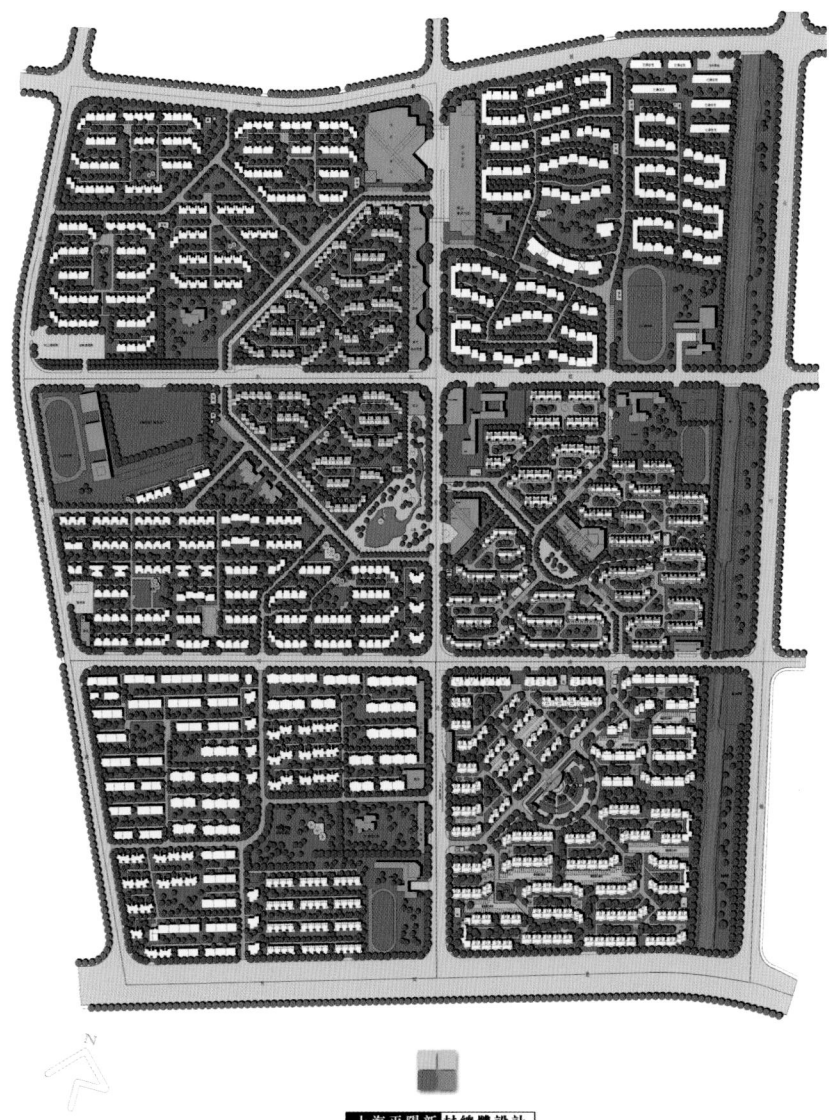

上海平陽新村總體設計

Opposite: Site plan
Above: Views within the complex

TAOHO DESIGN ARCHITECTS
COLOURFUL (WANZHAO) HOMESTEAD, 2001

The first phase of this housing scheme was to revitalise the existing, poor-quality, low-income housing facilities, which had been vacant for 3 years and to render the accommodation attractive once more, and to clean up the river. The site area is 62,419 square metres, with a total floor area of 75,580 square metres, and a unit size of 85 square metres. All sold within about a month.

The second phase was to develop the adjacent area of about 18,700 square metres, with a total floor area of 26,000 square metres.

The third phase was the Rhine Gardens development, located on the opposite side of the river to Phase 1. The site area is 25,690 square metres with a total floor area of 31,774 square metres.

Phase I

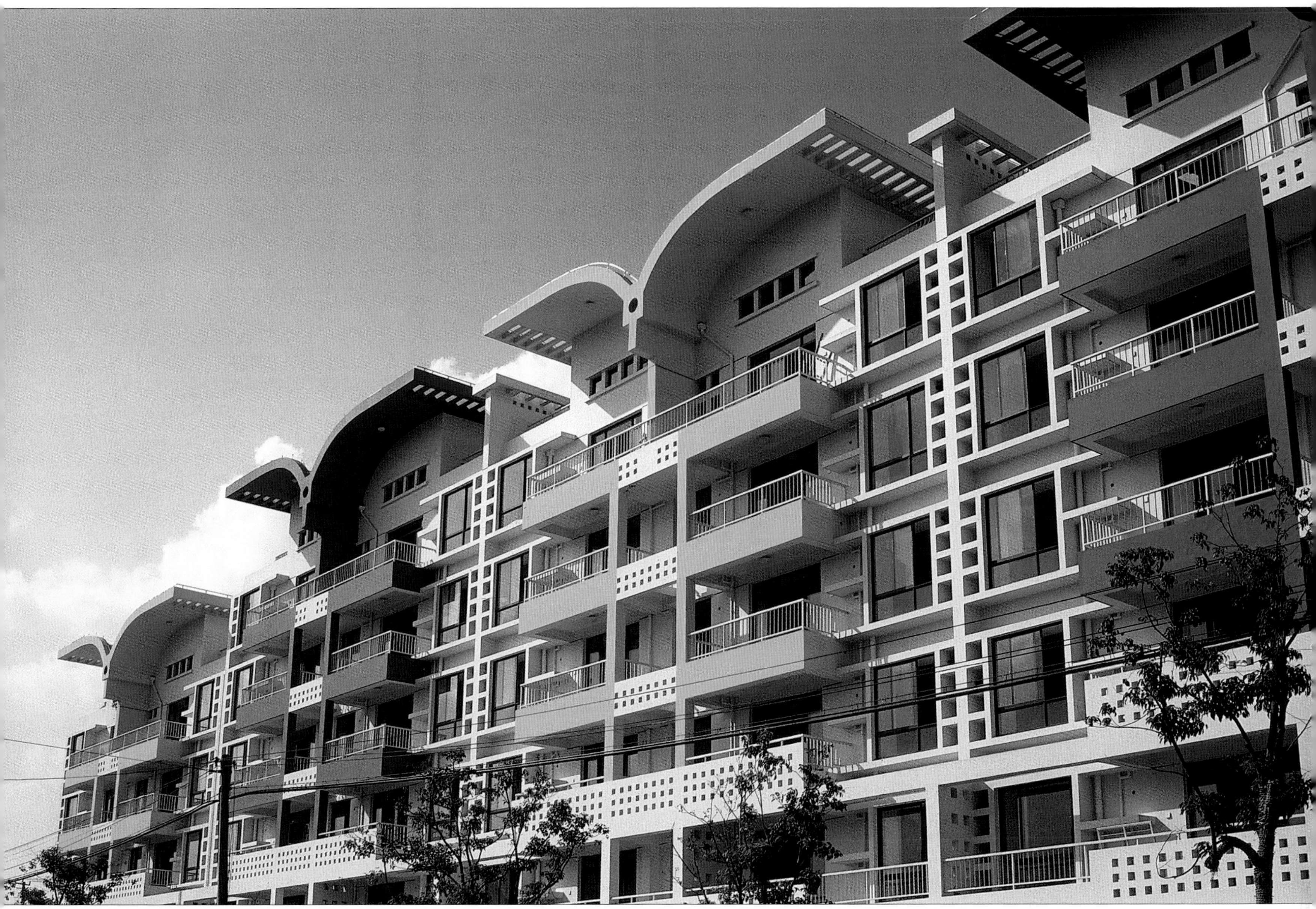

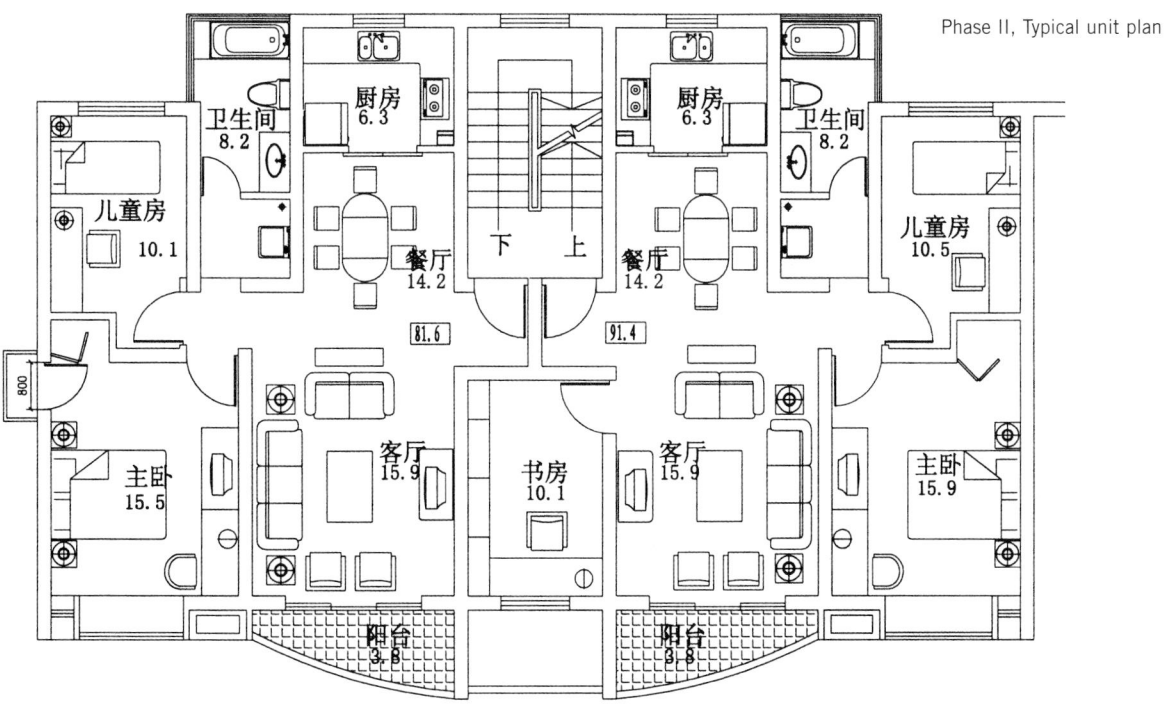

Phase II, Typical unit plan

卫生间
8.2

厨房
6.3

厨房
6.3

卫生间
8.2

儿童房
10.1

餐厅
14.2

下 上

餐厅
14.2

儿童房
10.5

81.6

91.4

主卧
15.5

客厅
15.9

书房
10.1

客厅
15.9

主卧
15.9

阳台
3.8

阳台
3.8

Above: Colourful (Wanzhao) Homestead, Rhine Gardens, Phase IIIa
Below: Colourful (Wanzhao) Homestead, Rhine Gardens, Phase IIIb

TAOHO DESIGN ARCHITECTS
VANKE WALTZ GARDENS, 2001

This project, aimed at middle-income groups, is located in the urban area of Shanghai. The total site area is 66,000 square metres, with a total gross floor area of 100,000 square metres. The ground level along the street is occupied by shops. The entire development was sold within 48 hours of the development being made public, before commencement of construction. Unit sizes range from 95 to 220 square metres.

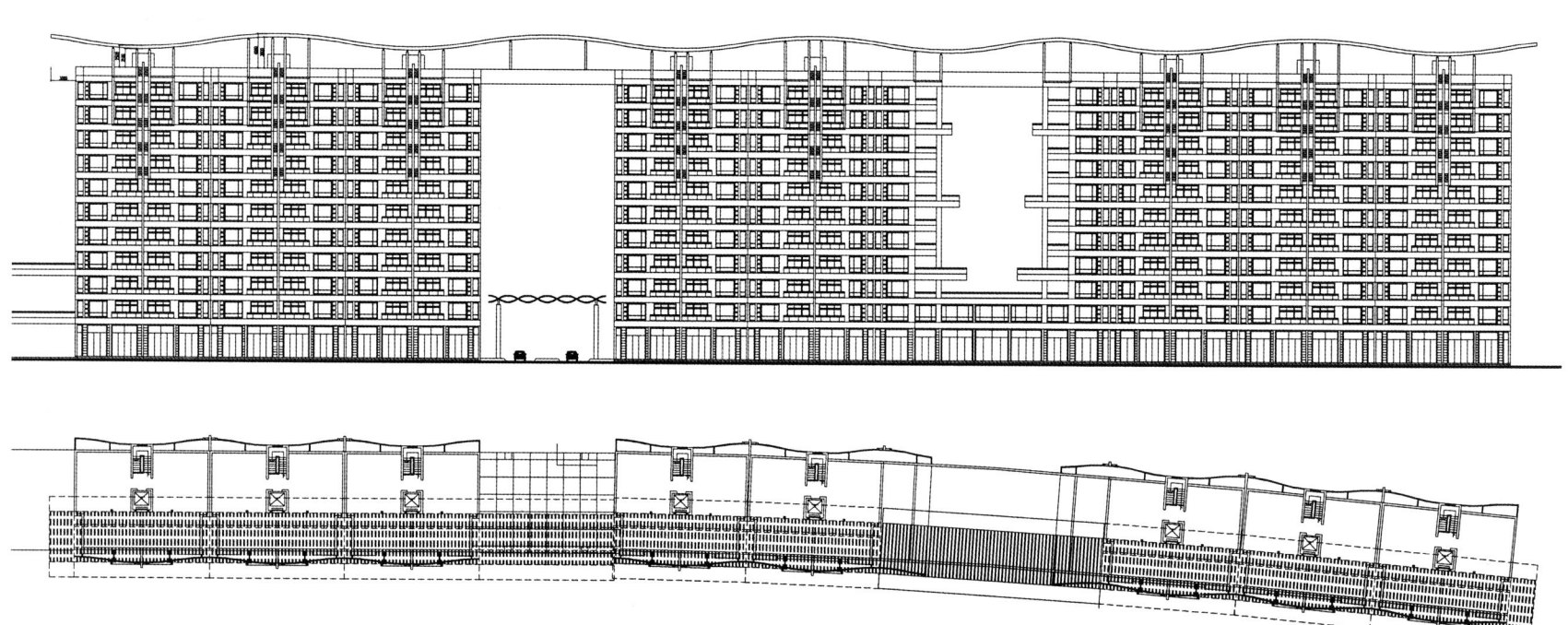

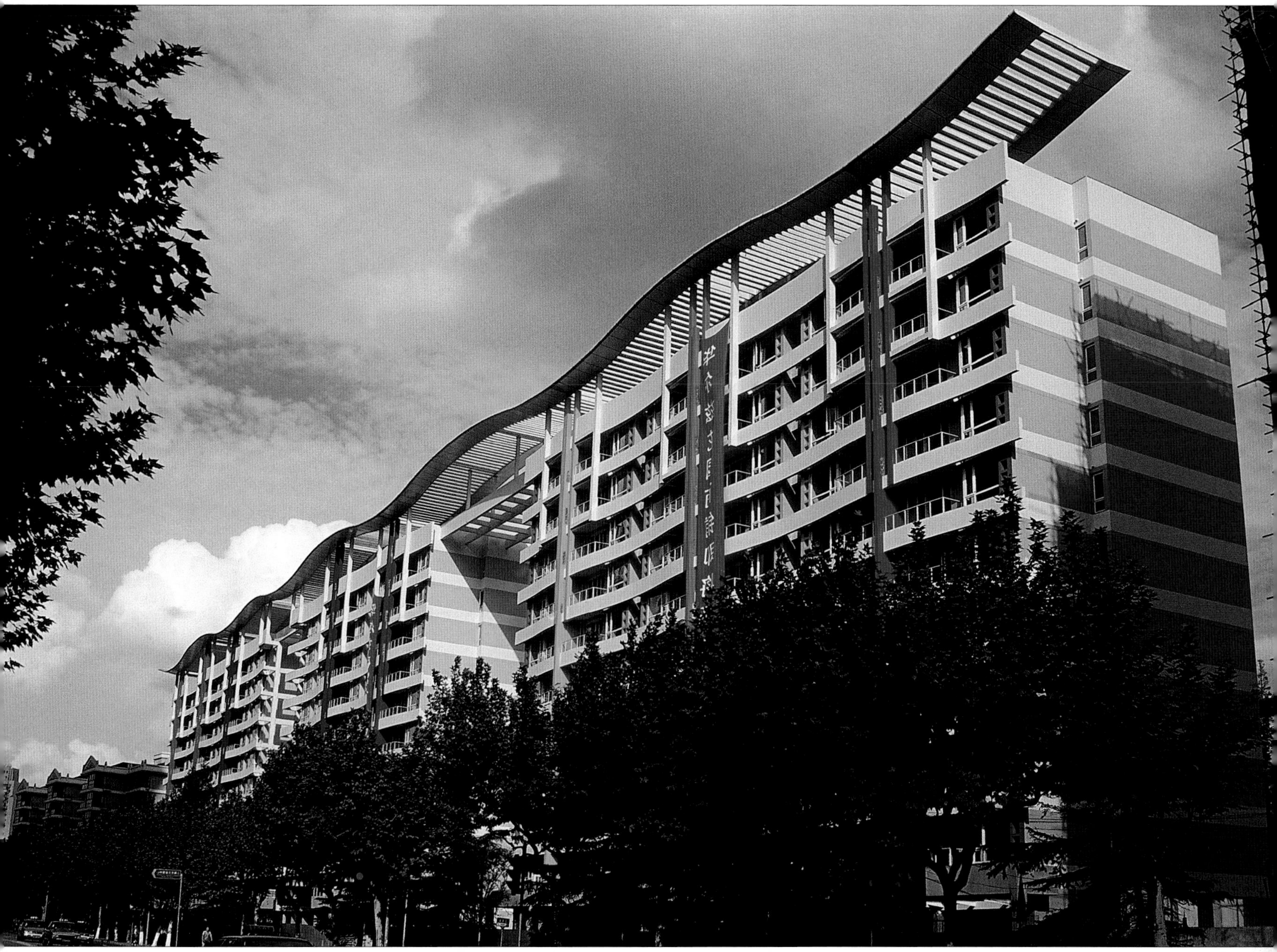

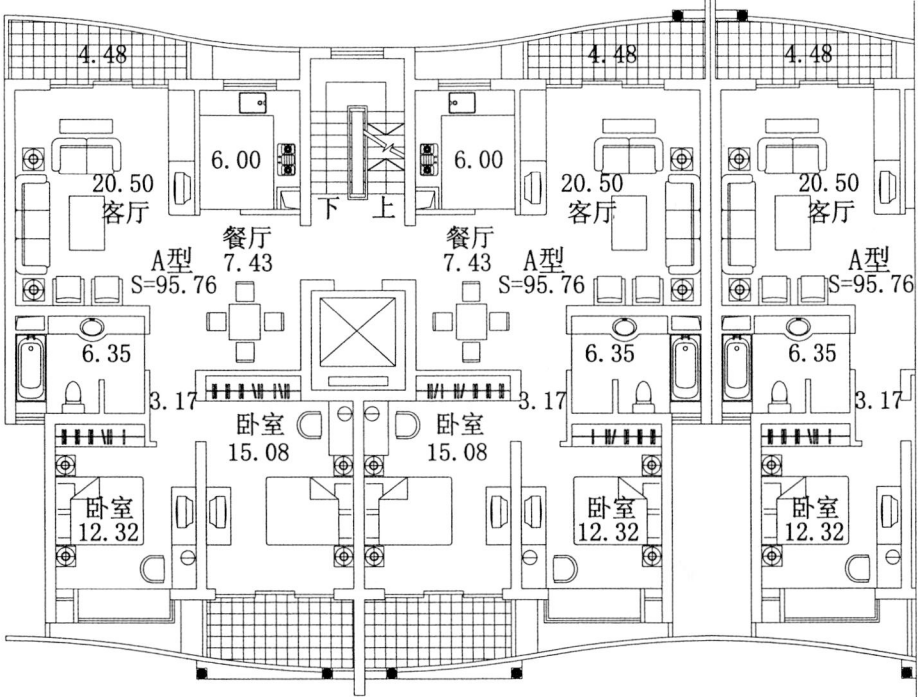

4.48
4.48
4.48
6.00
6.00
20.50
客厅
20.50
客厅
20.50
客厅
下
上
餐厅
7.43
餐厅
7.43
A型
S=95.76
A型
S=95.76
A型
S=95.76
6.35
6.35
6.35
3.17
3.17
3.17
卧室
15.08
卧室
15.08
卧室
12.32
卧室
12.32
卧室
12.32

Opposite: Street elevation of the main block

Left: Typical unit plan

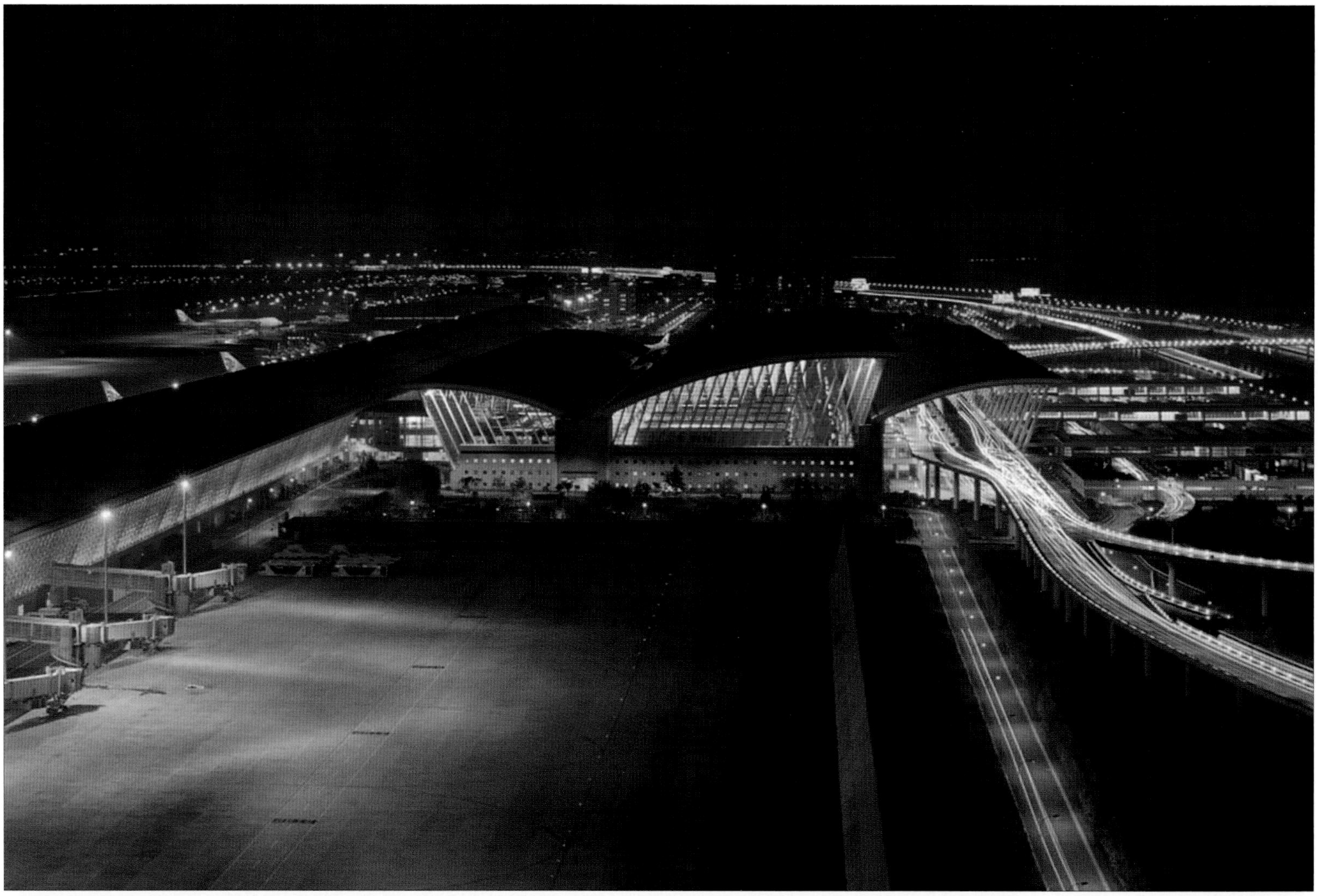

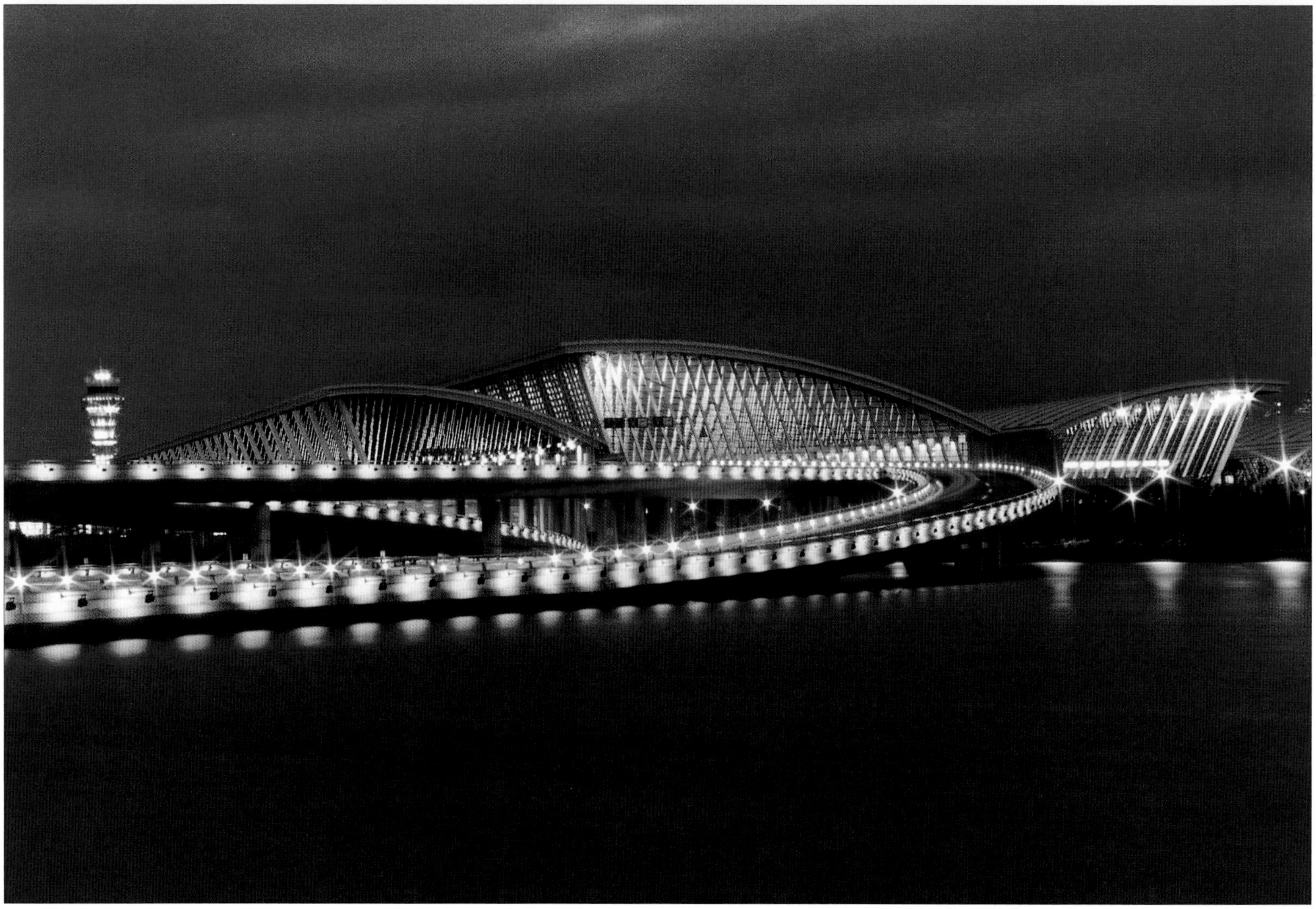

The first phase of the Shanghai Pudong International Airport (SPIA) was officially opened in October 1999. This phase includes construction of a 3,962-metre runway, a 280,000-square-metre terminal building and a 50,000-square-metre cargo complex. The total facility will be constructed in four phases with completion in 2005. When finished, SPIA will be able to accommodate 70 million passengers and 5 million tons of cargo per year. It will handle only international flights, while all domestic flights will operate out of Hongqiao. Shanghai will be the first city on mainland China to have two airports and this the only airport in Asia with four major runways. These runways will be designed to the highest international standard.

SPIA is situated on the right bank at the mouth of the Yangtze River, in the coastal area where Jiangzhen, Shiwan and Zhuqiao townships are located. It is approximately 30 kilometres from downtown Shanghai and connected to the city's highway system. The No 2 Metro line, which crosses the city, will connect SPIA with Hongqiao airport. In the future, a harbour will be built to the east of the site to provide marine links to the airport.

In order to reach a first-class international standard of advanced airport design, the overall engineering of the flying area was achieved through the collaboration of Chinese and Japanese companies. The design of the passenger terminal was by the French company Paul Andreu, chosen from a group of six competition submissions from distinguished international architectural practices. The design emphasises the theme of harmony between human beings, architecture and the environment. The terminal buildings sit within a landscaped park. Immediately adjacent to the building, the surface of a pool, rippling in the breeze, reflects its form and acts as a foil to the transparent walls of the terminal. Like a seagull preparing to rise and soar into the sky, the terminal building is a powerful symbol of Shanghai spreading its wings.

Opposite: Like a bird preparing to fly, night views of the terminal buildings
Above: Aerial view of the complex

Above and opposite above: Views of the grand concourse

Opposite below: The terminal seen across the landscapes and pools

PROJECTS

SKIDMORE, OWINGS & MERRILL
SHANGHAI WATERFRONT REDEVELOPMENT MASTER PLAN

The Shanghai Master Plan establishes a vision for the redevelopment of the Shanghai Waterfront along the Huangpu River, between the Yangpu and the Nanpu Bridges.

The most memorable image of Shanghai is the postcard view of the Bund, along the Huangpu River. The challenge of this master plan is to extend this scenic view to the entire riverfront. This plan redesigns seven places in the waterfront area: Pier 16, the Resort District, the Crescent, the Panorama, the North Bund Area, the Yangpu Bridge High Tech Centre and the Nanzhan Water Park.

Plans for the Port of Shanghai relocate existing port functions along the river and replace them with modern, containerised operations in strategic outlying areas. At the same time it is the city's goal to transform this section of the river from a busy shipping channel into a desirable area for business, tourism, housing and recreation. The coincidence of these two goals has created a rare opportunity to build a new waterfront for this world-class city.

The Huangpu River is the heart of the city, defining the centre of Old and New Shanghai. To the west lies the densely populated historic city; to the east the brand new Pudong New Development Area, poised to become the New Shanghai. Redevelopment of prime Huangpu riverfront parcels will play a pivotal role in joining Old and New Shanghai.

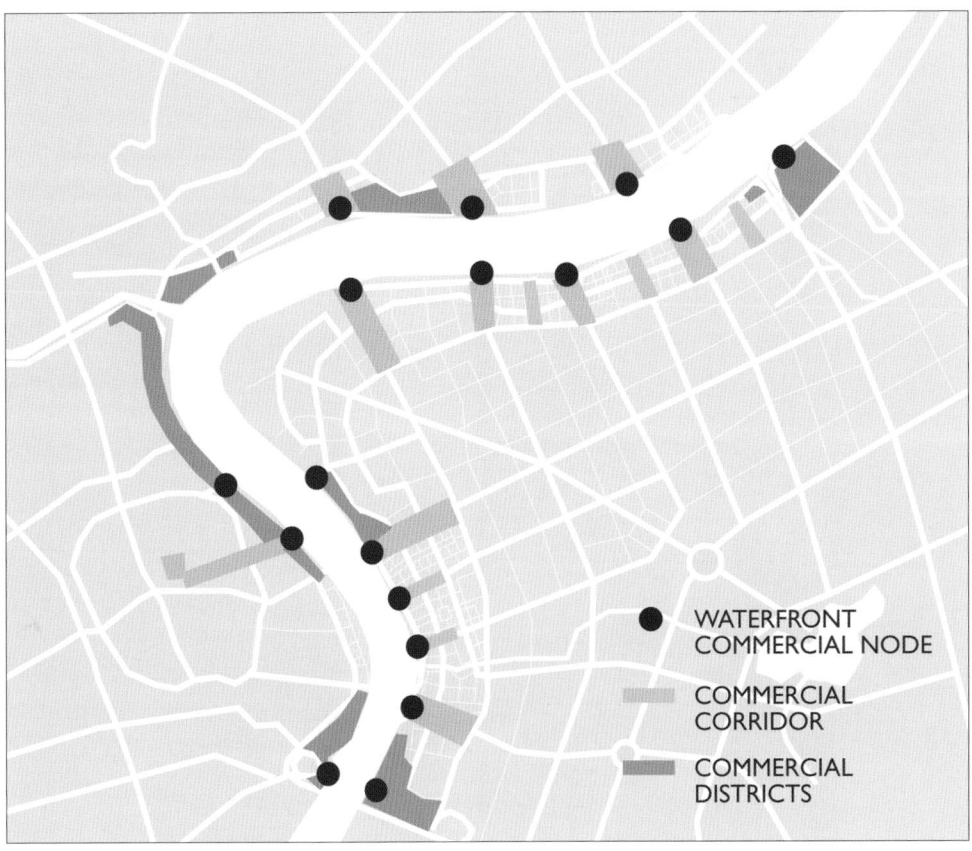

WATERFRONT
COMMERCIAL NODE

COMMERCIAL
CORRIDOR

COMMERCIAL
DISTRICTS

Above: The development plan
Opposite: Views along both banks of the Huangpu

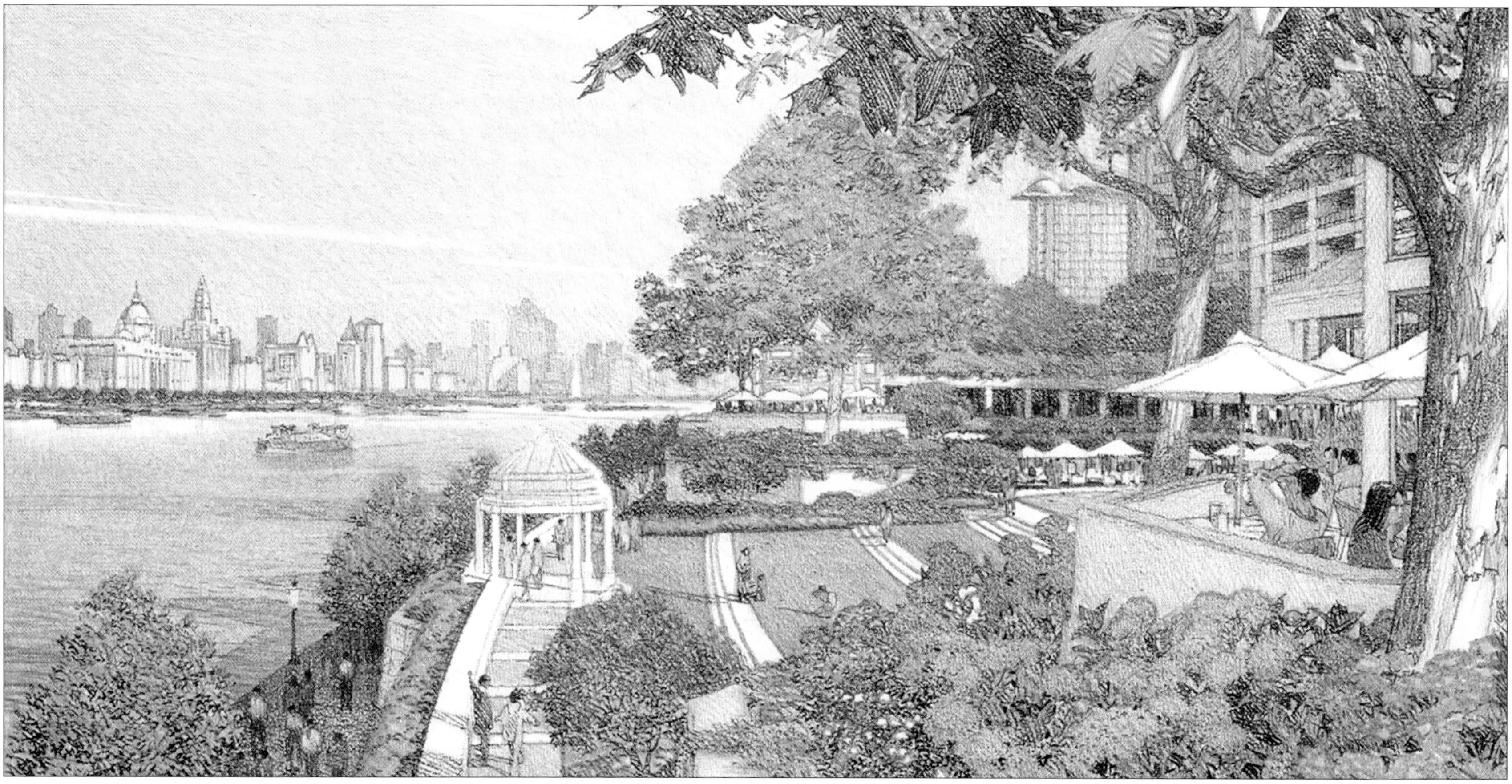

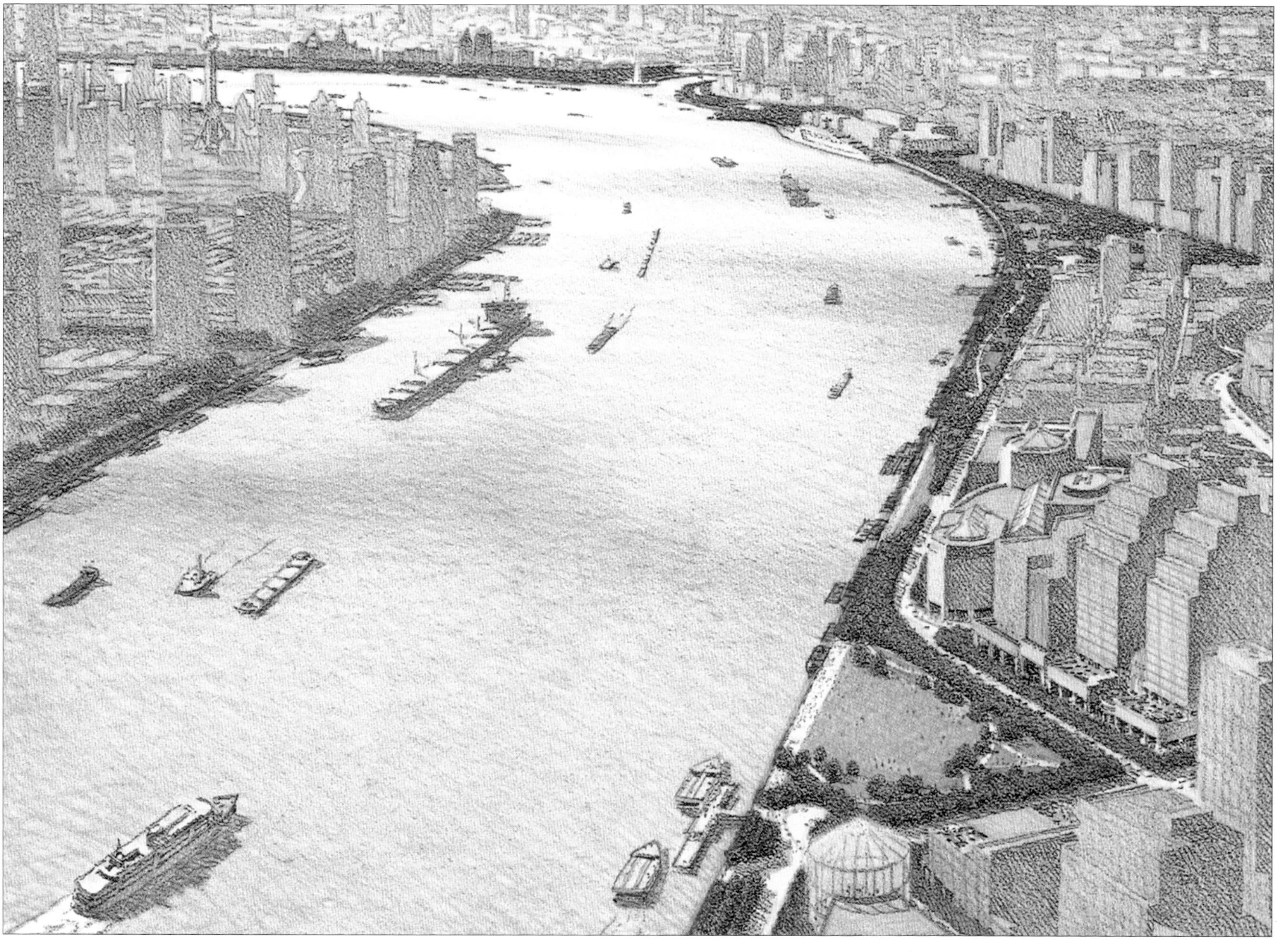

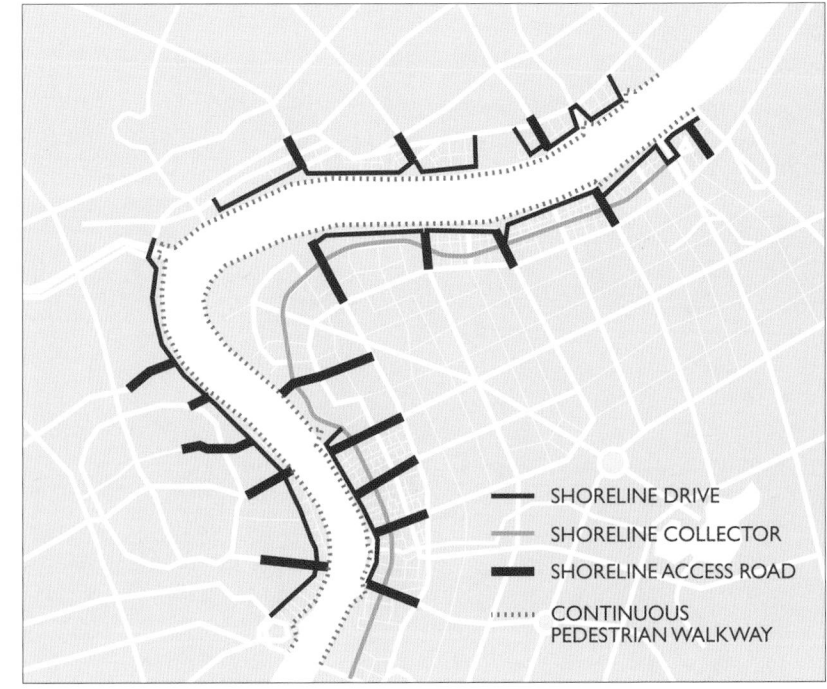

Above: Views up and down the river
Below, left to right: Circulation plan; landscape master plan; significant views

SHORELINE DRIVE
SHORELINE COLLECTOR
SHORELINE ACCESS ROAD
CONTINUOUS
PEDESTRIAN WALKWAY

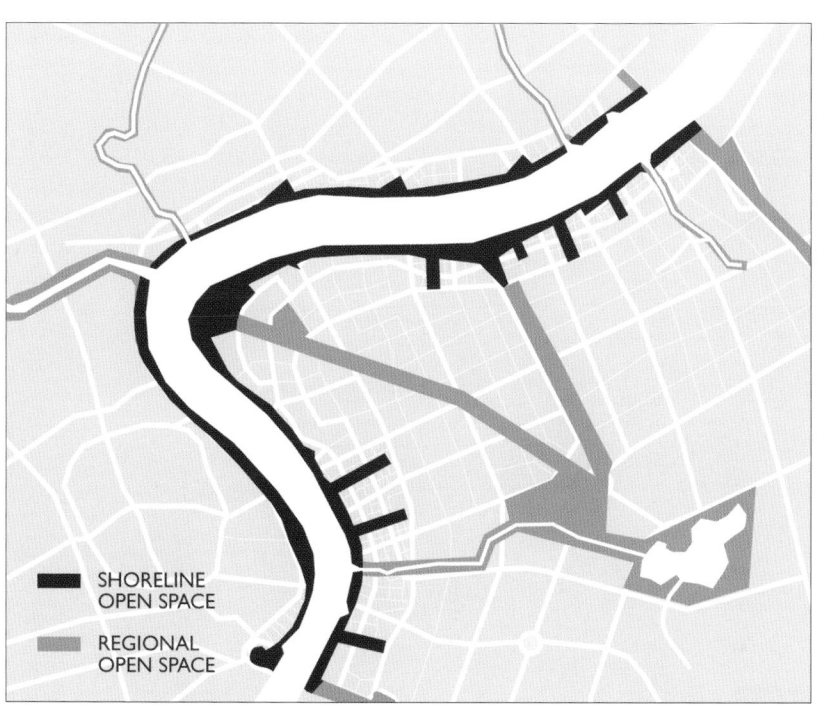

SHORELINE
OPEN SPACE

REGIONAL
OPEN SPACE

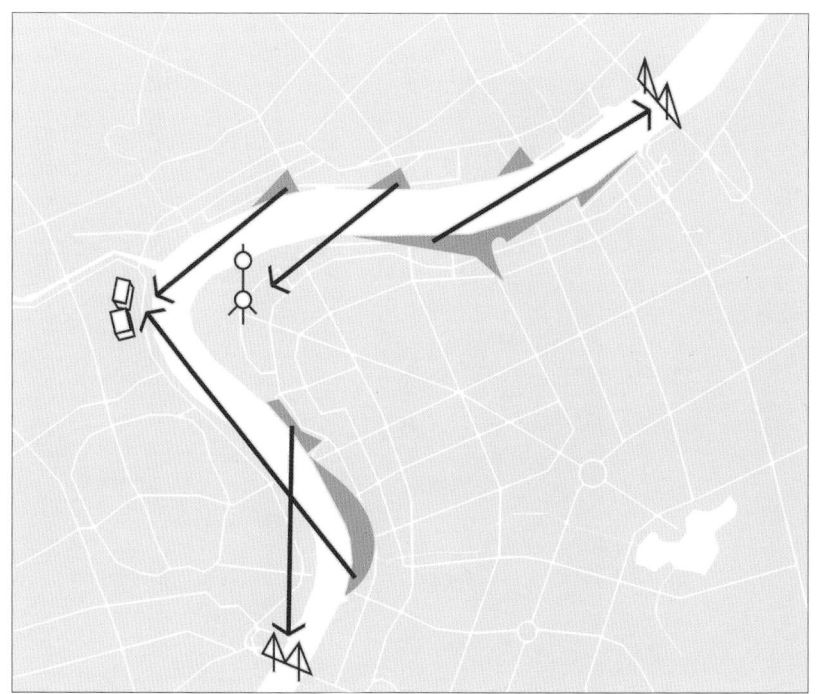

MICHAEL GRAVES & ASSOCIATES
SHANGHAI BUND ARTS CENTRE

All three orientation devices, the two atria and the grand stairway, project past the roof to become lanterns at the top of the building. From the Bund, glimpses of these are visible, and their presence is especially significant from the Pudong, the Financial District, across the Huangpu River. These skylights are akin to the small structures on top of every other building along the Bund, and blend with their surroundings. The steeply pitched skylight over the east atrium is a minimal intrusion above the roof in terms of size and area (especially as seen end-on from east or west) and is clearly not to be confused in any way with the original building. Modest though these lanterns are, they are important elements of the project, symbolising the complete, catalytic reconfiguration of the building.

The east atrium extends toward the sky in a dramatic fashion through the tilting of its walls, which could be described as 'forcing the perspective'. It is therefore essential that they

reach above the roof in such a way that communicates the connection of the internal light with the night sky for the benefit of those enjoying the roof terrace in the evening. The peak of the atrium, as it emerges through the roof, allows the visitor to identify the light emanating both from and to the building, at a large enough scale to seem like a room of light in itself.

The architecture of the Arts Centre is not approached in an outrageous or iconoclastic way. It emphasises the attributes of the present Bund in an inventive way. The new building embodies not architecture for its own sake, but architecture that is understood through one's relationship to it. Every aspect of the new Shanghai Bund Arts Centre, with its convivial, dynamic spaces and quiet, tranquil places, attempts to reflect the character of the people who visit it and of the city of Shanghai which it honours.

Below: Longitudinal section looking north

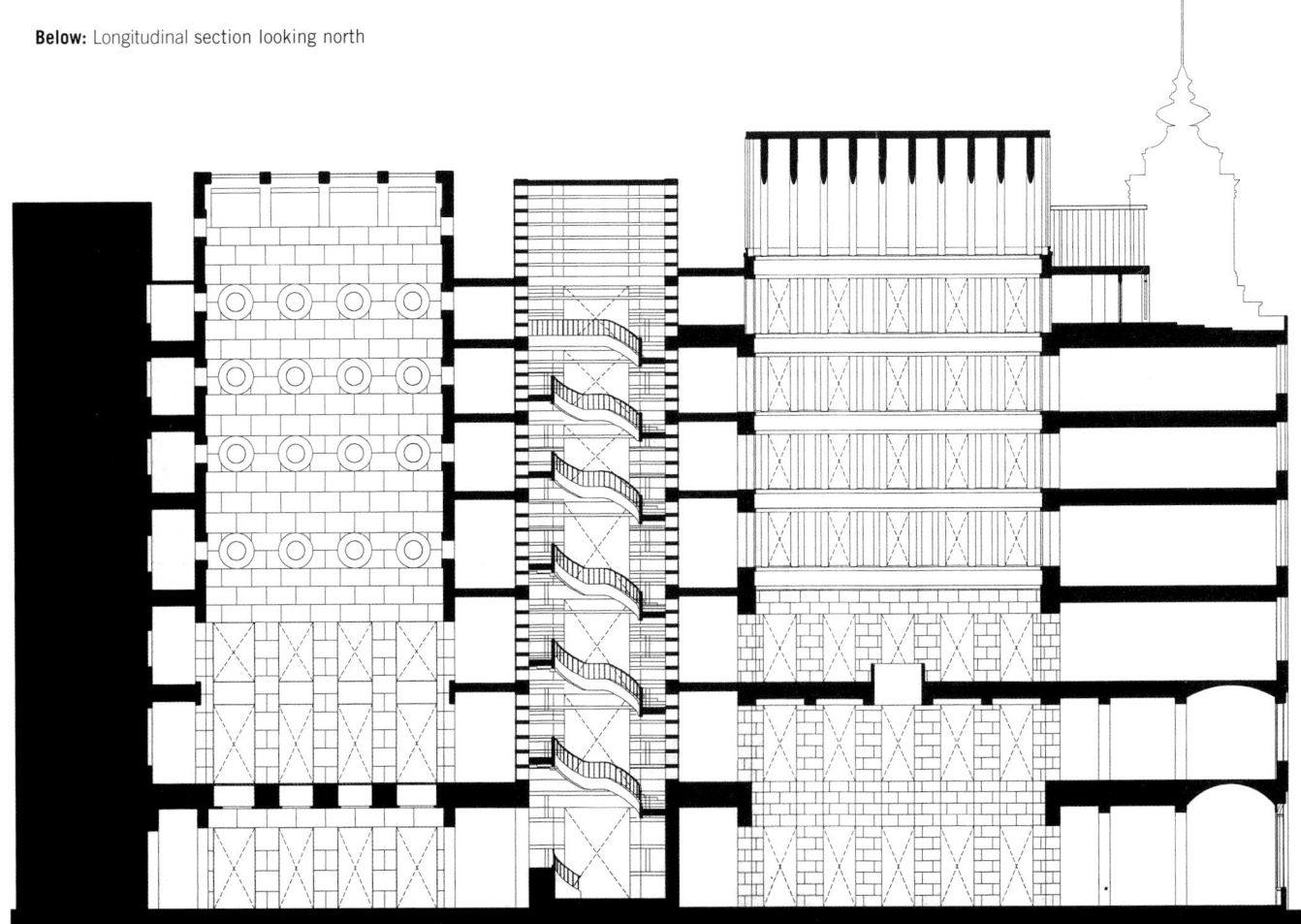

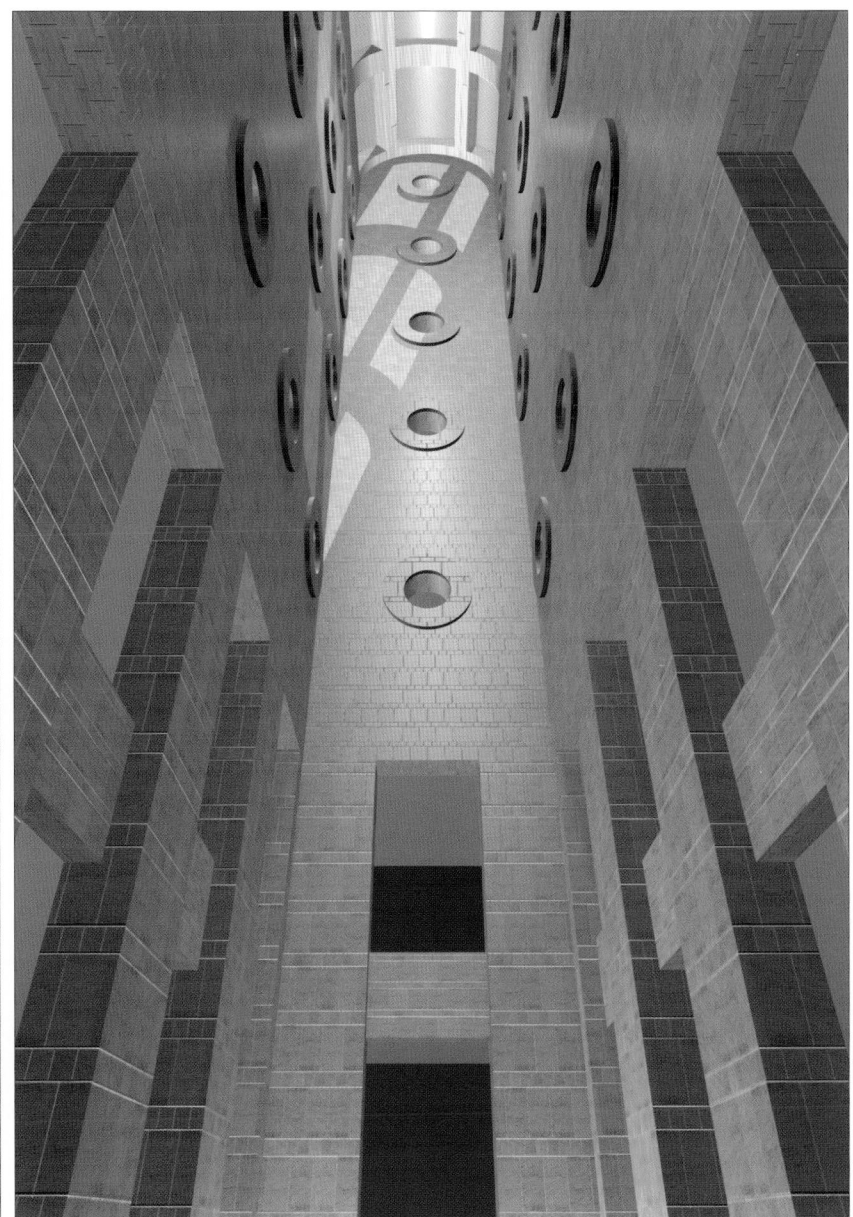

Left: East atrium
Right: West atrium
Below: Ground floor plan

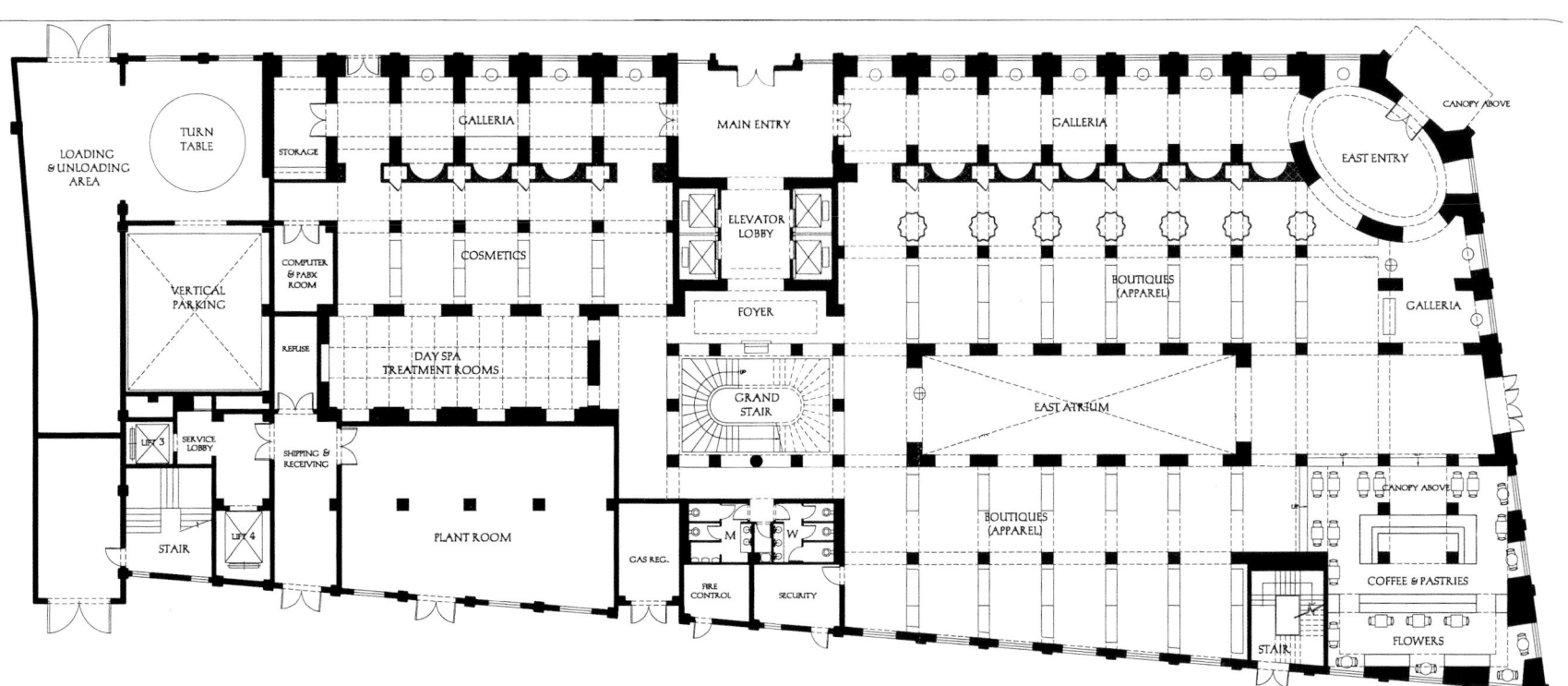

SHANGHAI ZHONGFANG ARCHITECTURAL DESIGN INSTITUTE
MEDICAL SCHOOL

The Multi-Usage Building (24,955 square metres) accommodates several functions such as teaching, research and sports facilities. Sited on the Medical School campus, its style reflects its context. The spatial order is strictly organised and attempts to stimulate all the senses, as well as representing the content and milieu of a medical school.

To the north of the site is an artificial lake some 200 metres wide. On the other side is the old medical school. To the south are the playground and students' dormitory, while an animal laboratory is located in the east. All the surrounding buildings are five to six floors high, and designed to harmonise with the lake. The block is divided into small parts and is linked organically with the environment. The building design is rich in details and includes some curved faces.

The classroom and teaching areas occupy the first four floors, reached via a staircase, while the research area occupies the fifth to seventh floors, accessed by elevator. The facade reflects the different functions of the two parts.

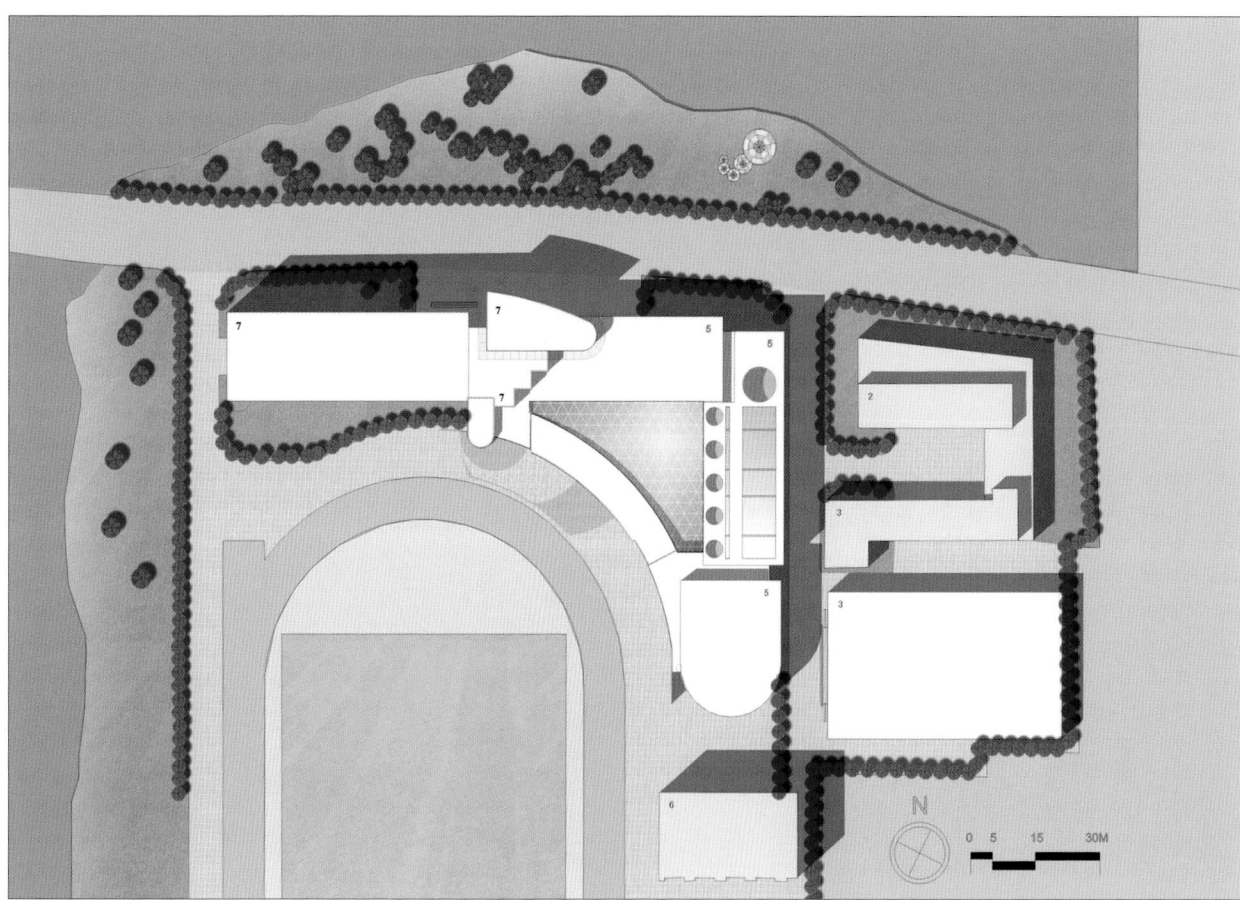

Above: Plan
Opposite above: Perspectives
Opposite below: Elevations

南立面

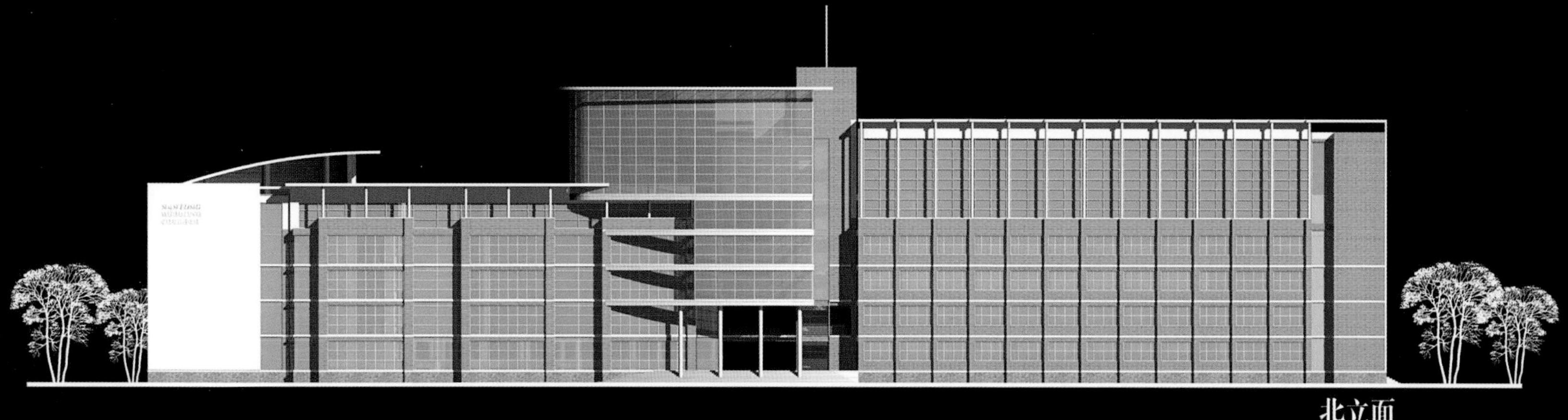

北立面

ASHEN + ALLEN

SHANGHAI WAYTOFUND INTERNATIONAL FINANCE CENTRE

Winner of an international design competition, this 123,000 square-metre, mixed-use complex combines 20-storey and 25-storey live–work towers with retail to create a transition between Shanghai's historic Bund and emerging Pudong business districts. The site occupies a pivotal position in the city near the intersection of Sozhou and Huangpu rivers and marks a transition from the historical Sichuan Bei retail district to a newly emerging business district in downtown Shanghai.

Intended to reinforce historical waterfront development patterns while establishing a precedent for sensitive future growth, the Shanghai WayToFund International Building enhances and celebrates its riverfront location by incorporating the bridge and rivers edge as sources of vitality, tranquillity, recreation, leisure and civic life.

Placement of the two towers to the north creates a public promenade running the length of the site along the river. Pedestrian-oriented public plazas to the south and west draw life into the heart of the complex, creating a physical connection and encouraging movement between the towers and the surrounding district.

The building's vocabulary of bridge, gateway and pagoda elements physically reflect the sense of place and culture of a Chinese waterfront city. The gently curving south facade traces the course of the Sozhou River. An open public lobby links the towers and the site to the Sozhou river and retail district. The central atrium is the heart of the development and contains two distinct parts. The Great Hall, on the first five storeys, provides the primary entrance and links the building, vehicle plaza, and waterfront promenade. The glass-clad Floating Pagoda Hall above it, derived from traditional Chinese architecture, offers a spectacular vertical space for the public as they rise through and cross between the towers. The floating pagoda connects the great hall to the roof terrace.

Shared amenities, including an exhibition hall, conference centre, interactive children's discovery museum, executive club, and health club can be accessed from bridges crossing the open space where the differing floor-to-floor heights of the office and live/work towers align on every fifth storey. Restaurant and banquet spaces occupy the penthouse floors.

Right: Perspective
Opposite above: Model
Opposite, below left: Plans from top to bottom: tower plan at opening levels; tower plan at bridge levels; tower plan at typical levels
Opposite, below right: Section

1
3
2
2
1
3
3
2
1
3
2
2

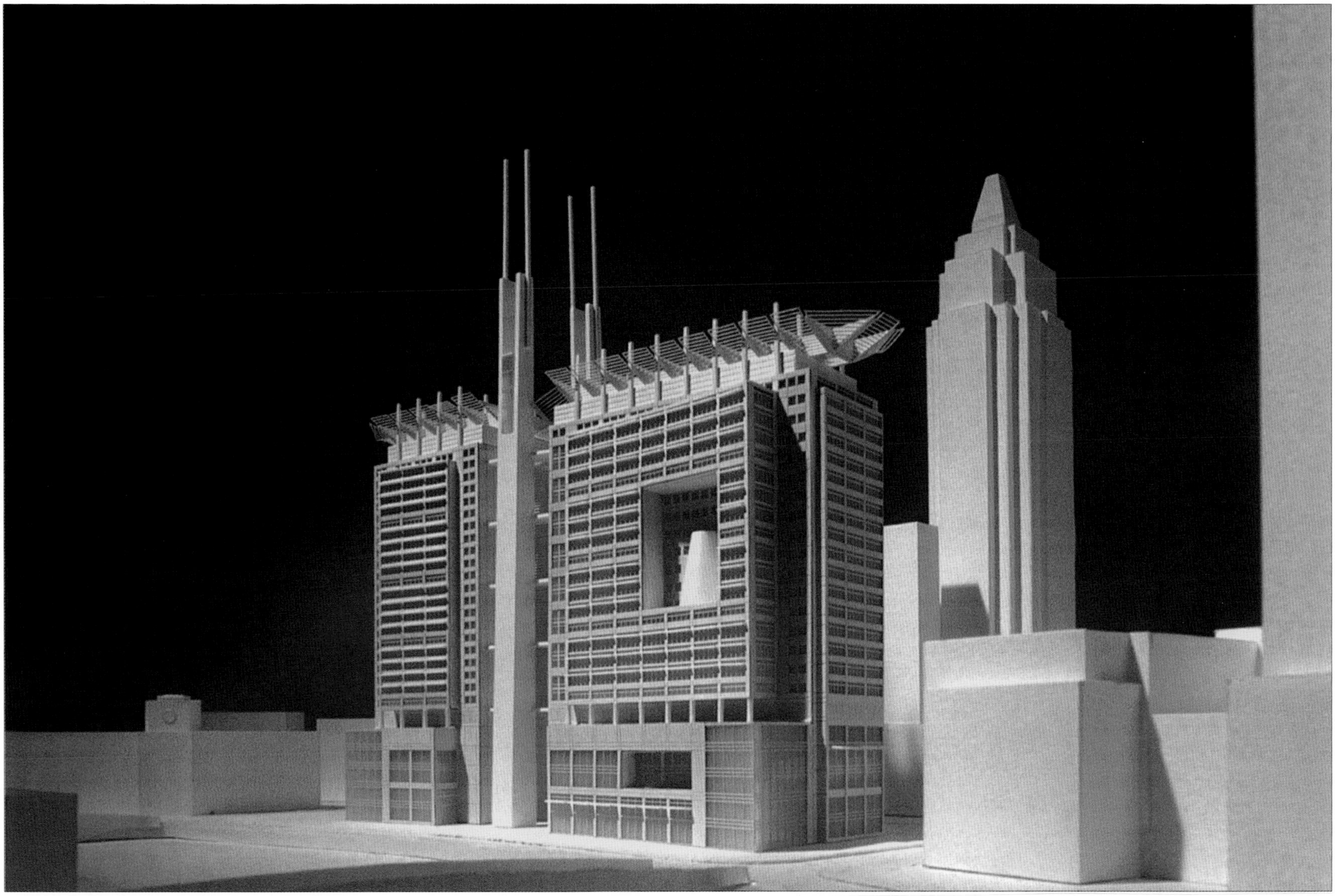

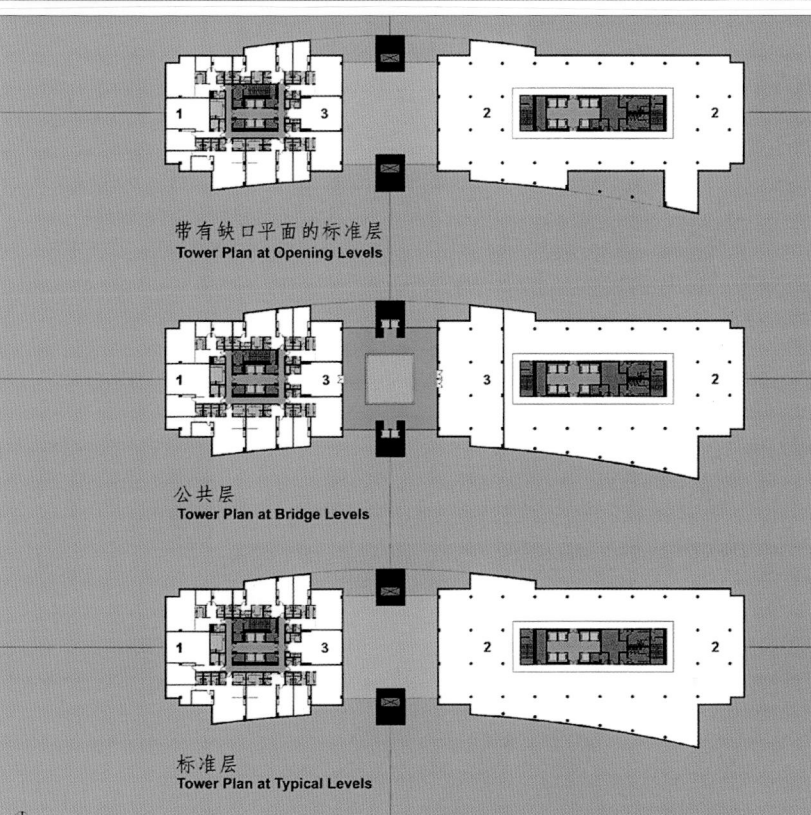

带有缺口平面的标准层
Tower Plan at Opening Levels

公共层
Tower Plan at Bridge Levels

标准层
Tower Plan at Typical Levels

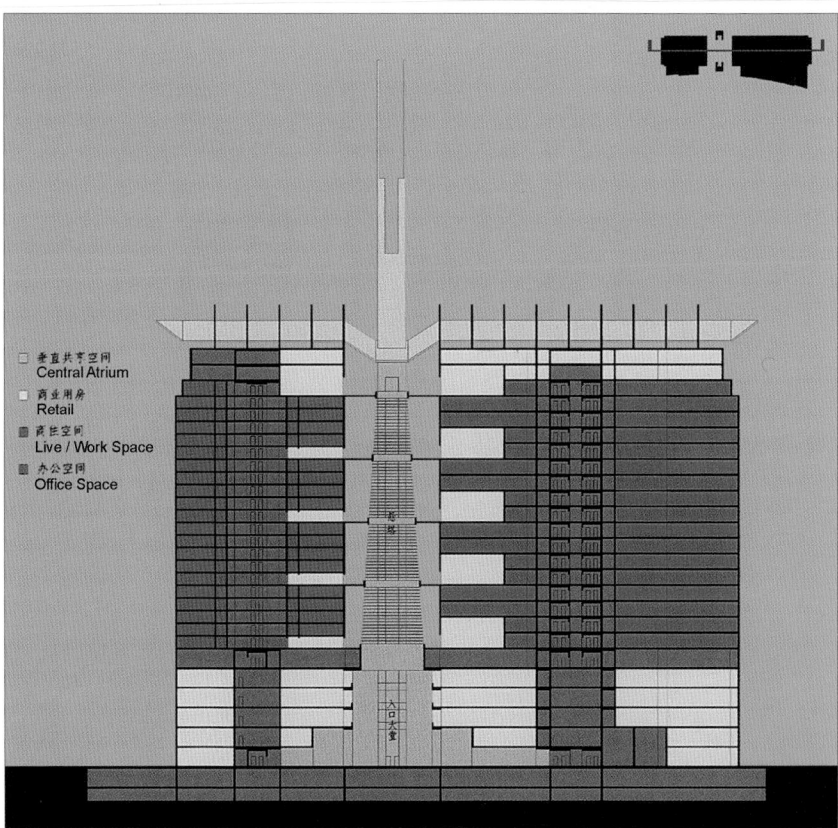

垂直共享空间
Central Atrium
商业用房
Retail
商住空间
Live / Work Space
办公空间
Office Space

MICHAEL GRAVES & ASSOCIATES
FUJIAN XINGYE BANKING TOWER

The extraordinary number of building projects in Shanghai reinforces the significance of the city both as a financial and architectural Asian centre. As impressive as the current developments are in both number and size, it is the 19th and early 20th century buildings of the Bund which remain as the built image of Shanghai. The towers, domes and classical elements of the buildings form both the context of a traditional city and the unforgettable image of cosmopolitan Shanghai.

Given the historical importance of the Bund, and its place in Shanghai's social and architectural history, the task of building in this area is daunting, particularly given the programmatic requirements of modern office buildings. Here the strategy employed was that of stacking elements, in this case base building and tower, as a means of simultaneously addressing the concerns of both the traditional city and the skyline, complementing the wonderfully crenellated and stacked 19th century architectural compilations which line the Bund.

The selected scheme has a tower that is parallel to the Bund. In order to reduce the impact of the parallel alignment, the rectangular plan and subsequent vertical massing is configured so that the main block of the high-rise office building can be read as a series of three small towers intersected by fields of horizontal bands. The small towers are crowned by glass cylinders, modern abstractions of the caps of the 19th-century buildings, which will define the Xingli Bank's place in the Shanghai skyline. The residual area between the ochre towers is composed of horizontal blue bands of glass and tile, their neutral appearance reducing the mass of the building.

The base building which carries the high-rise tower has two large rotundas that are the entry lobbies for the Bank. The periphery of the base continues the existing street line and is filled with retail shops. As the base building steps up, the mass of the building is reduced on the upper floors with open pergolas which line Hanko and Sichuan Road.

Left: Site plan
Right: Front elevation of Scheme One
Opposite: Exterior elevation of Scheme One

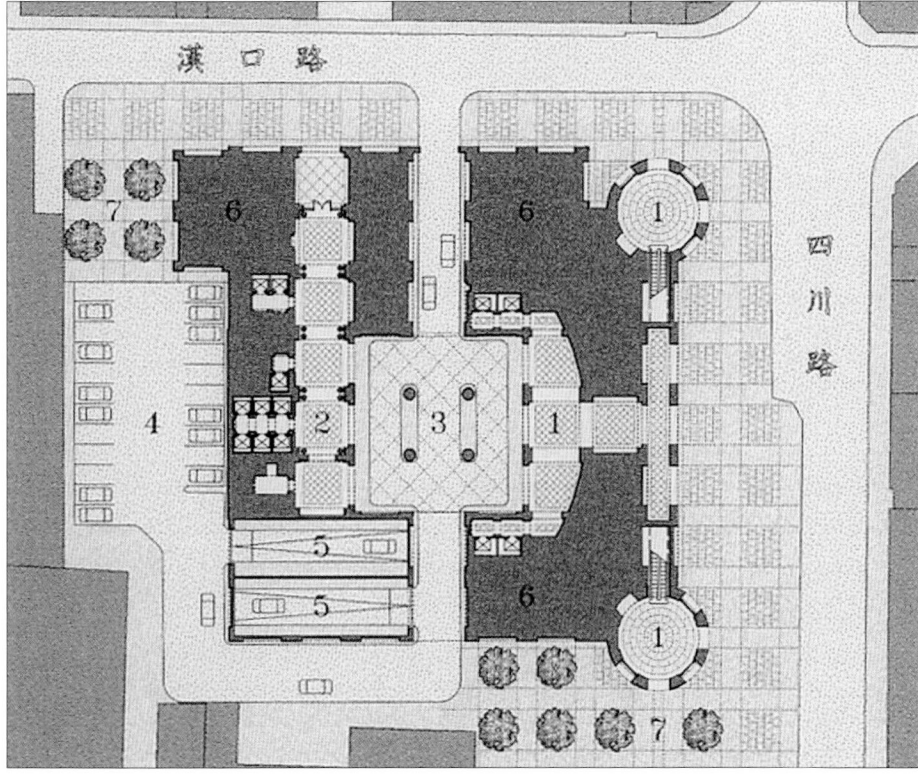

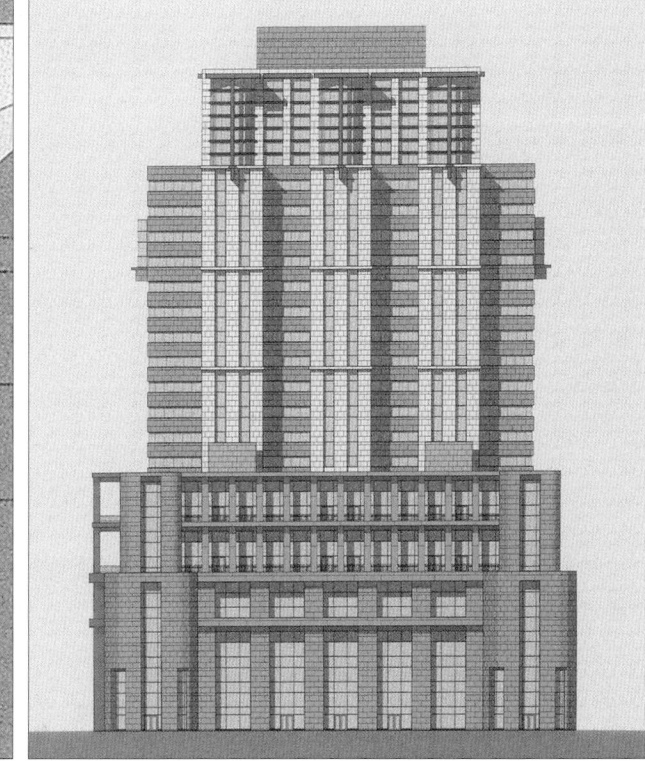

THE JERDE PARTNERSHIP INTERNATIONAL
JOINBUY CITY PLAZA

JoinBuy City Plaza is located at the western end of Nanjing Lu, metaphorically a 'river of people', which twists and turns across the city centre from the Bund on the Huangpu River to the Jing'an district.

The design (completion date 2002), focuses on providing this famous thoroughfare with a new architectural symbol that will unify the surrounding neighbourhood, which includes the 1,700-year-old Jing'an Temple, Jing'an Park and underground station. It will attract pedestrian visitors from all parts of the city, providing a communal destination that combines cafés, offices, retail, restaurants and a cinema.

The form of the building is fluid and playful, echoing the curved roofs of the temple next door and the region's natural river gorges. It bends along Nanjing Lu, offering different views from park, street, terrace and the inside.

The terrace on Nanjing Lu, which floats gently above the overcrowded street, acts as a meeting place, traditional exercise plaza and performance and event space. The Jing'an park is continued across the street like a blanket wrapping over the plaza and down the new pedestrian street. A bold, diagonal internal street acts as a physical connector between Nanjing Lu, the underground station, Yu Yuan Road and the residential quarter to the north; its corner entrance links the street with the wedge-shaped interior.

The eight-level project is rendered distinctive by a steel-framed skylight and its concrete roof deck. Materials incorporated include stone panels, plaster/tile exterior walls, metal column covers, stainless steel window boxes, glass storefronts and skylights.

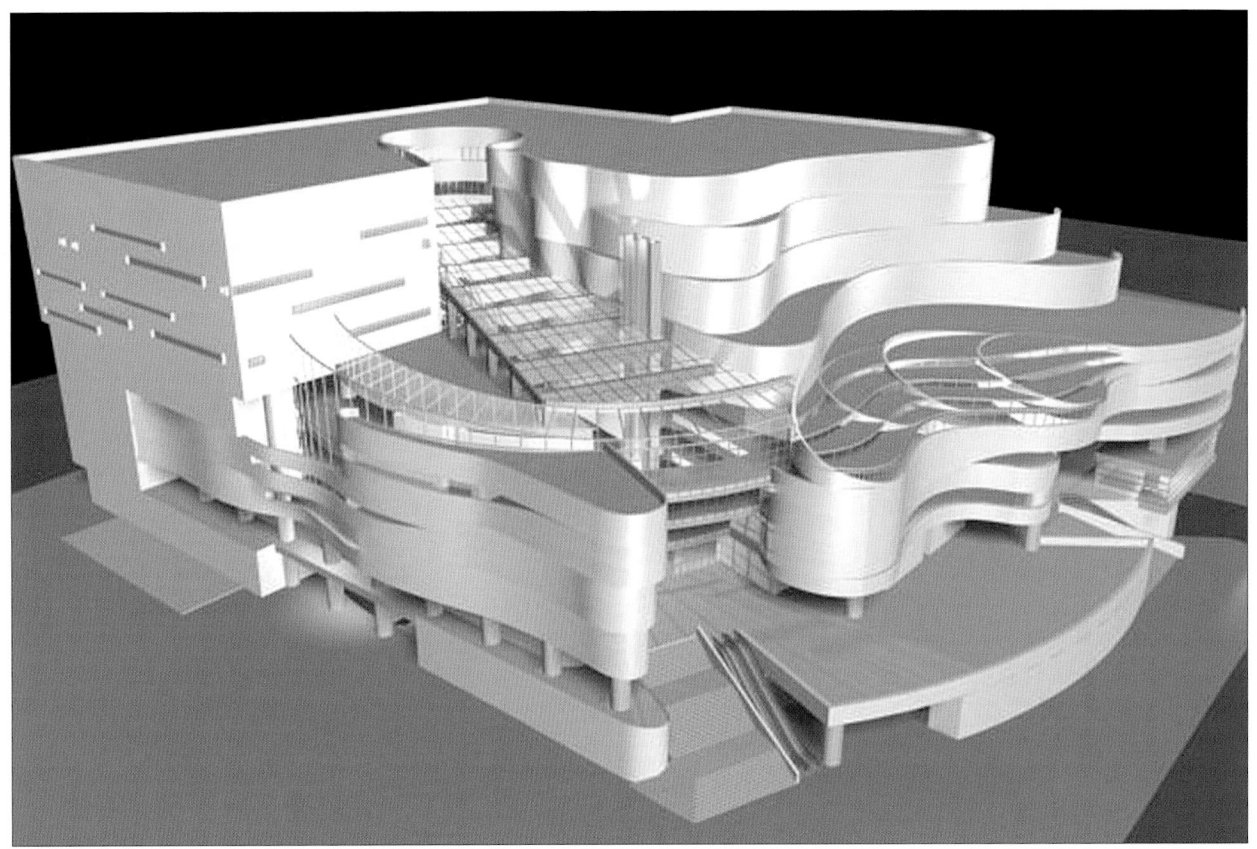

THE JERDE PARTNERSHIP INTERNATIONAL
SUPER BRAND MALL

Across the river from the Bund and centrally located in Pudong's new Lujiazui financial and trade district, Super Brand Mall has been designed as a gateway and entry icon for this dynamic, evolving area. Surrounded by the new Convention Centre, the iconic television tower, Shangri-La Hotel, World Financial Tower, Shanghai Securities Exchange Building and Shanghai World Financial Centre, the 13-storey complex will be experienced by residents, nationals and tourists alike. With a floor space of over 241,000 square metres, ten floors above ground and three below, the $335-million complex will be the largest shopping and entertainment destination in China to date, with 1,000 domestic and international name brands, a supermarket, the largest Internet centre in Shanghai, floor space for trade exhibitions, an auditorium and 13-theatre cineplex.

The planning and design for Super Brand Mall will provide a node of intensity within the larger urban fabric. Outside, where the project connects to the transportation system, is a strong and active exterior. Inside, the levels become complex, experiential spaces within a continuous crescent that surrounds an open, skylit gathering place.

The site of the 31,000 square-metre project places it strategically as a node of transportation and as the centre of key tourist and business activities. Super Brand Mall's symbolic front door and primary orientation is the Huangpu River. The vehicular route from Pudong is Lujiazui Road. A pedestrian tunnel provides access from the northwest.

Super Brand Mall has five exterior 'faces' encompassing the four elevations and the roof. The Bund face is Super Brand Mall's high-profile view. A golden drum anchors this end of the project; its colour, symbolic of fortune, suggests that it can be read also as a stack of gold coins. Movement through the multi-level block starts here at the drum's base and proceeds ultimately to its top. The restaurant massing to the right becomes a glazed box, creating possible views to and from the Bund. The large colonnade in front of the drum is articulated and animated, so that it will be seen from the Bund.

The Lujiazui facade is the main Pudong elevation. The four-level, department-store-like massing is expressed through large granite columns with articulated lanterns. The overall massing, nearly ten storeys high, is clad with a basket weave of red and beige Indian sandstone, providing a richly patterned and coloured exterior base. This face is designed to accommodate large-scale graphics or advertising panels.

A large portal at the sixth level reveals the project's life within and gives visitors inside a glimpse of the contextual environment. A large, yellow, ceramic-tiled and bevelled cornice marks the top edge; a wave-like blue form, which contains the cinemas and multi-purpose hall, expresses a distinctive form complementary to the project's base.

The city face provides the greatest access from Pudong. Its corner is chamfered to address the key intersection of Lujiazui. Glazed its entire height, it extends the street into the project's core. The tower on the southeast corner focuses attention from Pudong's central business district. A burgundy colour provides a backdrop for graphics and project signage. The red and beige sandstone basket-weave pattern is also applied here, and on the side that faces the Shangri-La Hotel. Shingled blue-green slate tracks along the base of this elevation, emphasising the park ramp's diagonal movement up into its core and the undulating dragon wall within. Large portals at both levels five and seven provide glimpses into and out of the project, integrating the context once again. A low-setback requirement through level four results in the lessening of scale at this point. Glazing wraps around this facade to express the restaurants on this side, which is anchored by the burgundy tower to the southeast.

The roof becomes a sculpted, fifth elevation, as viewed from above, composed of the gold drum, the blue wave, and the east court and park ramp skylights, forms that express the project's exuberant spirit by day.

Horizontally, the interior planning moves from the river to the city. Visitors arrive on the second level directly from the river front and park directly in and up into the project by way of a gentle park ramp. Optimal street circulation from Lujiazui is made possible by a corner-to-corner move along the road.

Vertically, the park ramp takes visitors to the top with a switchback from river to city and back to river, up into the project. The project is ten levels high, excluding a private club at the top of the drum, and simplifies into subclusters of levels to ease comprehension and districting. The bottom basement level is the Superstore. Levels one to four comprise the street zone featuring mainstream retailing and food. The park ramp zone, levels three to five, offers lifestyle, fashion and beauty. Levels six and seven concentrate on domestic retail, speciality products and services. Levels eight and nine are for entertainment, including the cineplex and multi-purpose hall. The retail mix includes value, high- and domestic-brand food and entertainment.

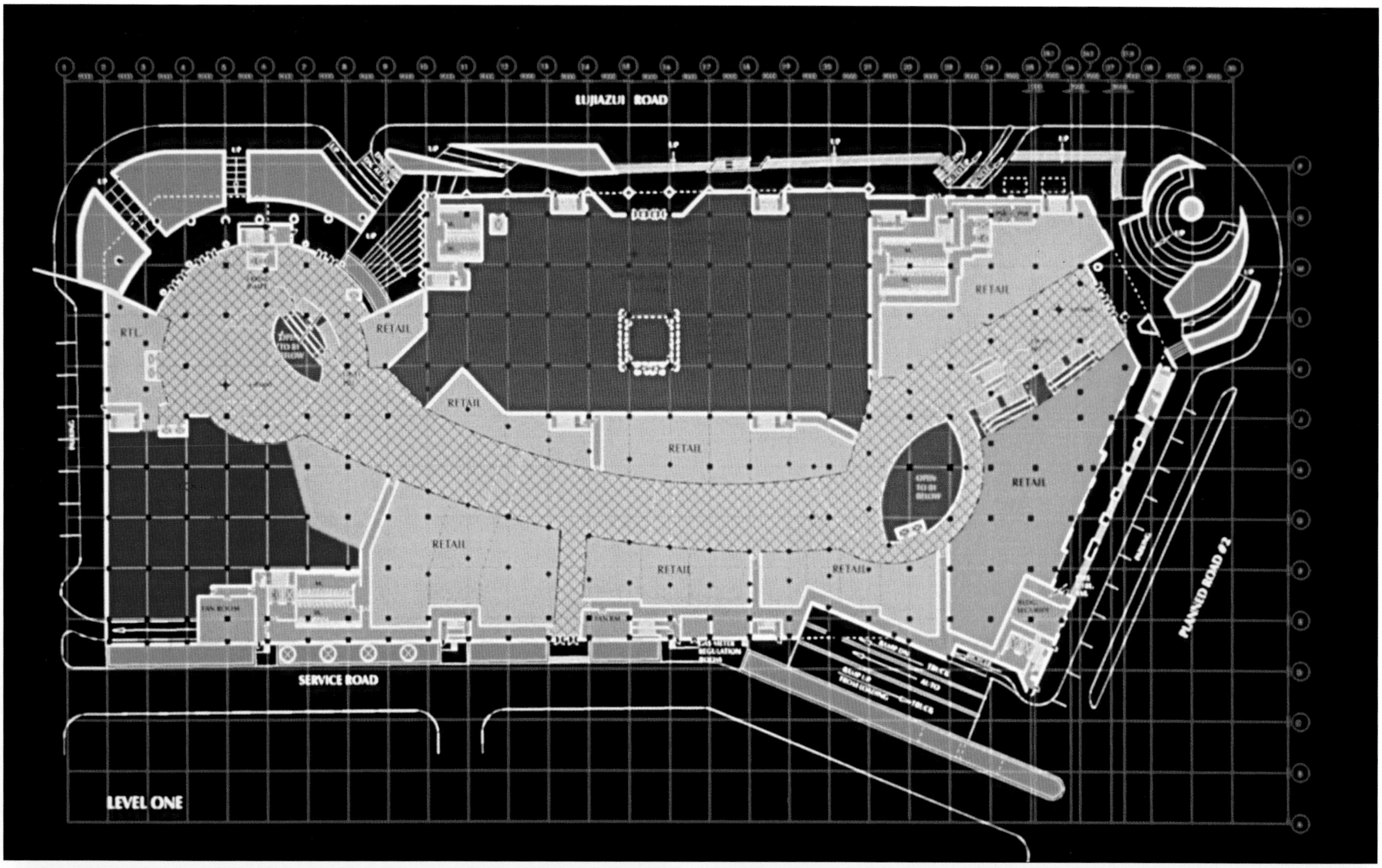

Above: Plan
Below: Model views

Above: Aerial perspective showing the view to the Bund
Opposite above: Perspective
Opposite below: View of the inner arcade

KAPLAN McLAUGHLIN DIAZ

SHANGHAI INTERNATIONAL BUSINESS CENTRE

The project aims to provide a landmark international business centre in the upscale Xi Hui District of Shanghai, intermingling references to Western culture with Chinese tradition. The client wished to set new standards in the built environment while 'stressing the concept of business' and of a 'centre in formation'. Requirements also included quality, comfort, rationality, tranquillity and colour.

The complex includes a 304,800 square metre office building, 304,800 square metres of retail, restaurant and related support services, a 152,400 square metre, four-star, 450-room hotel, a 152,400 square metre office/apartment complex, and 243,840 square metres of parking for 1,500 cars. The office building stands 60-storeys high, and provides the landmark focus of the cluster. A central Civic Plaza anchors the built environment and provides a visual and physical connection to the beautiful park situated across the north end of the site. The 10-acre site will be connected by the proposed new subway linking the districts of Shanghai.

Above: Perspective

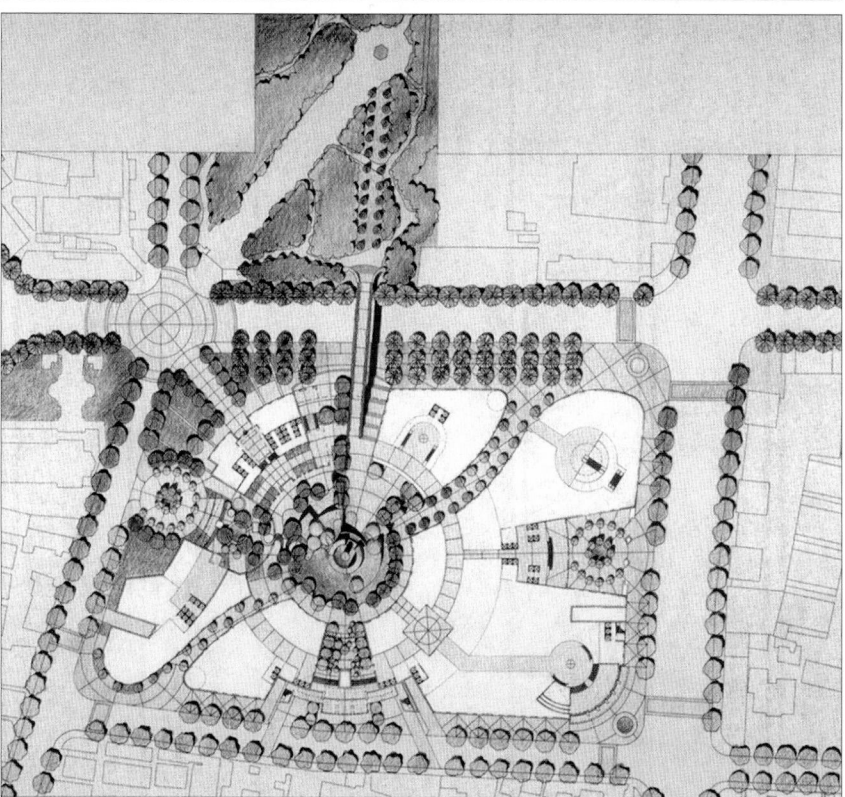

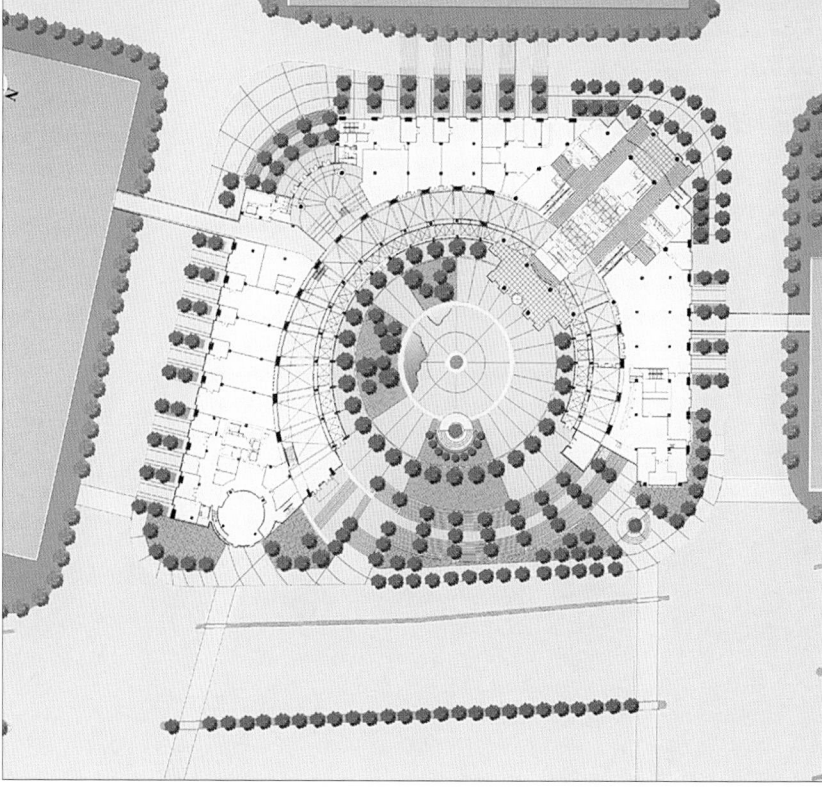

Above: Models
Below left: Site plan
Below right: Plan

Below: Perspectives
Opposite: Elevation

KAPLAN McLAUGHLIN DIAZ
SHANGHAI INTERNATIONAL PLAZA

This project consists of 1.5 million square feet of office, retail and entertainment facilities organised around a central urban plaza. Each level within the project provides an area of intensity focused on various uses. The outer ring features a pedestrian street to encourage street fairs and fruit markets, a landscape buffer, and shaded arcades for local merchants to display their wares. The middle ring is the district/national ring and includes a speciality retail shopping atrium and galleria. Finally, the central core is the community plaza blending private seating, an amphitheatre and a festival stage.

KMD's design solution to the historic Bund district bridges the Bund and Chinese culture with international traditions through a contemporary yet appropriate architecture. By placing the new landmark tower on a northwest axis, the design recognises the divergent elements of Shanghai. The tower faces directly towards the traditional area of Shanghai (the Yu Yuan Gardens, historic Shanghai, and the central business district). The opposite facade rises from the community plaza to offer excellent views of the new Nan Pu Bridge, which is designed to symbolise Shanghai's modern strength and technology. The long curving brow emphasises the view of the Bund and the development of Pudong, while addressing the important feature of the Huangpu River.

Below left: Plan
Below right: Perspective
Opposite, above left: East elevation
Opposite, above right: South elevation
Opposite below: Models

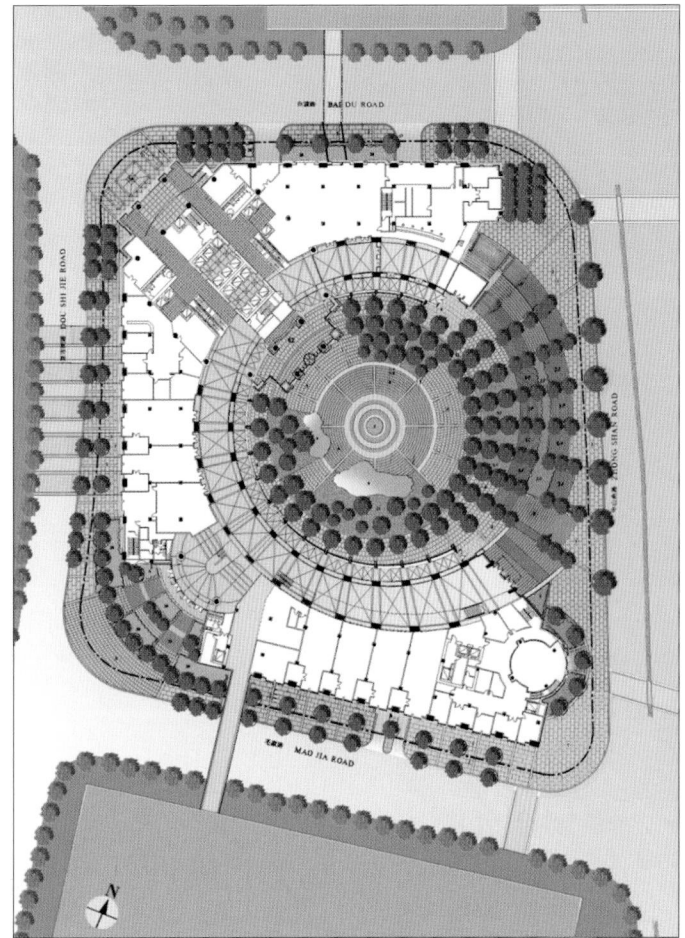

KOHN PEDERSEN FOX ASSOCIATES
SHANGHAI WORLD FINANCIAL CENTRE

When it is completed in the beginning of the 21st century, the Shanghai World Financial Centre will stand 460 metres high, the tallest building in the world.

In association with Mori Building Co Limited, it is being constructed for Forest overseas Co Limited on a key site in the Lujiazhui Financial and Trade District in Pudong. The Chinese government has designated this area as an Asian centre for international banking and trading. The design of the building synthesises characteristics that are meaningful to traditional Chinese architecture but with a view to the future. Two primary geometric forms, a square prism and a cylinder, intersect the building's physical form resulting in a transition from a square base to a line at its top. A 50 metre cylindrical void, or 'moon gate' is carved through the top of the tower to relieve wind pressure. This void, equal in diameter to the sphere of the adjacent Oriental Pearl Television Tower, provides a link for the two structures across the urban landscape.

The programme of this 94-storey project is contained within its two distinctly formal elements: a sculptured tower and a podium. Retail space is contained within the podium. Ground level parking is connected to a series of retail walkways and terraces which overlook a garden planned for the adjacent site. Wall, wing and conical forms penetrate the massive stone base of the tower. The varied geometries of these smaller elements lend human scale and organise the complexities of pedestrian movement at the point of entry, complementing the elemental form of the tower.

Internally, the building transforms its shape to accommodate the space requirements of the entry lobbies and retail functions of its lower levels with office space being located on its intermediate floors. A 300-room luxury hotel will occupy the upper levels of the tower, grandly capped by an observation deck.

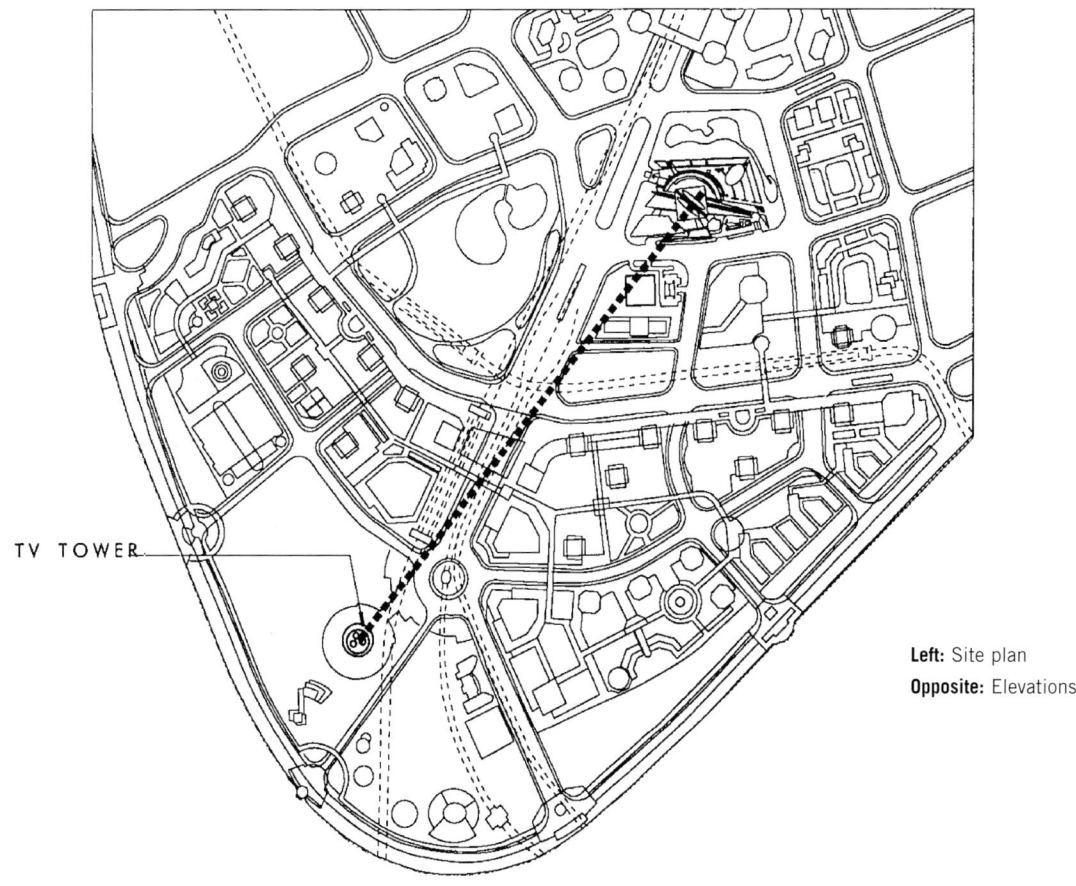

TV TOWER

Left: Site plan
Opposite: Elevations

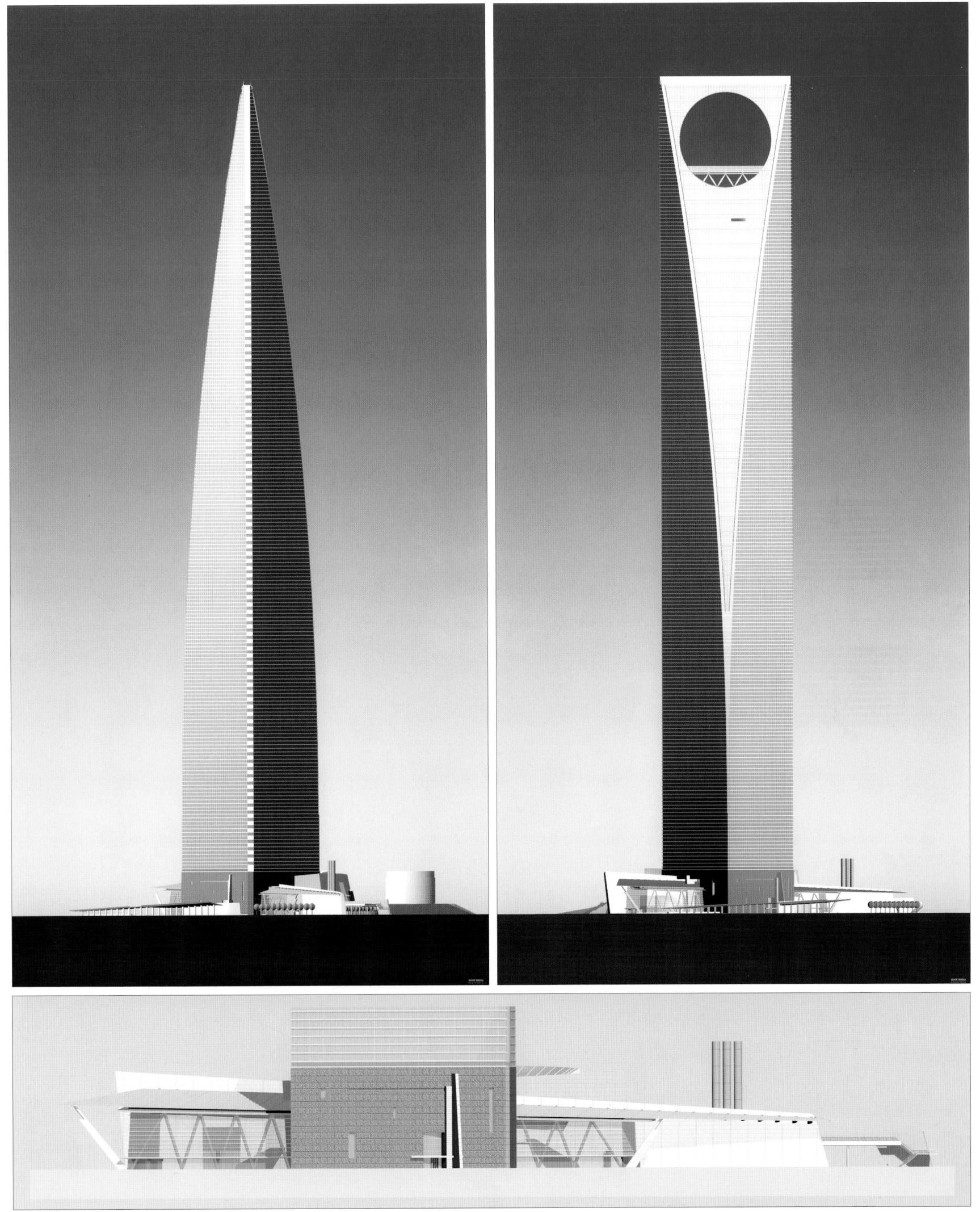

12
20
94

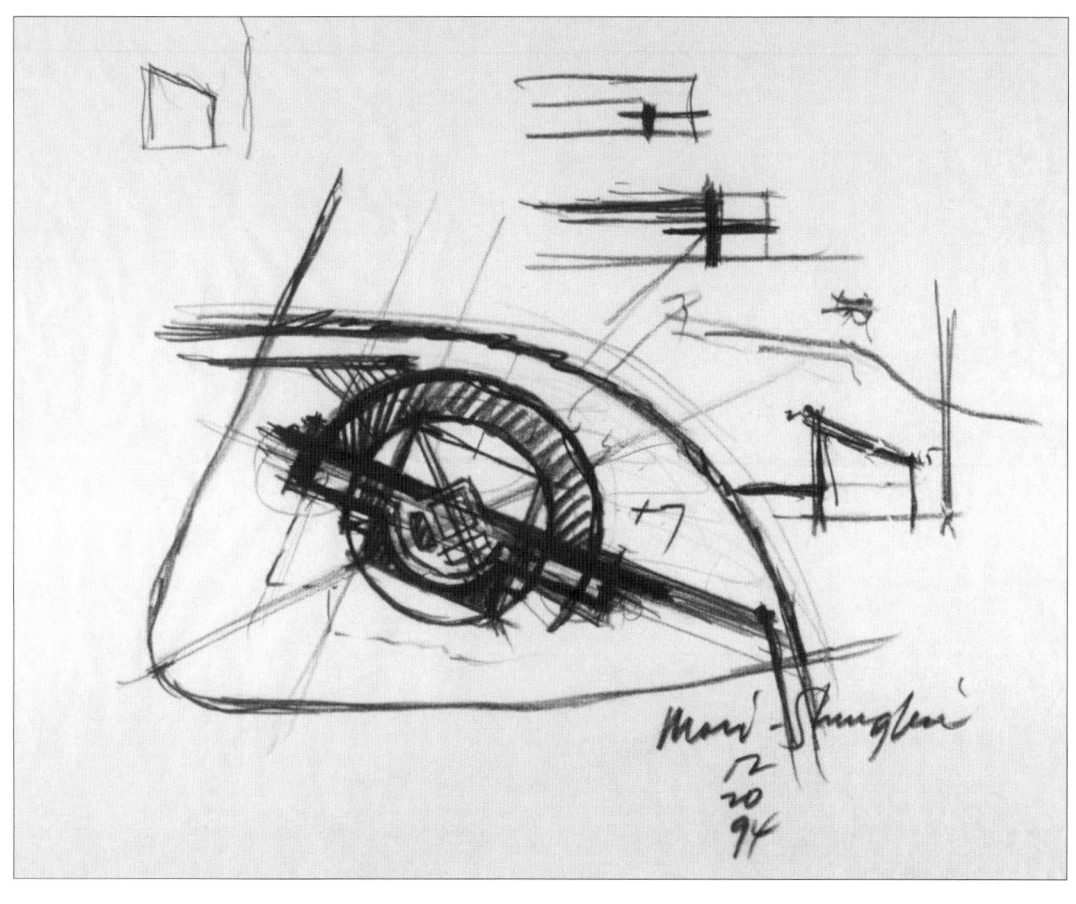

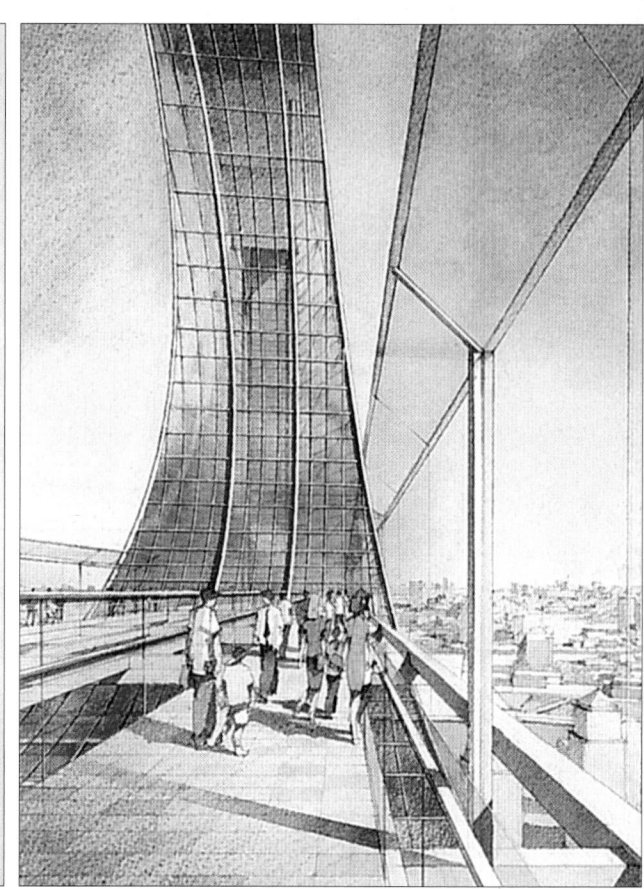

Above, left to right: Early sketch; observation bridge
Below: First floor plan

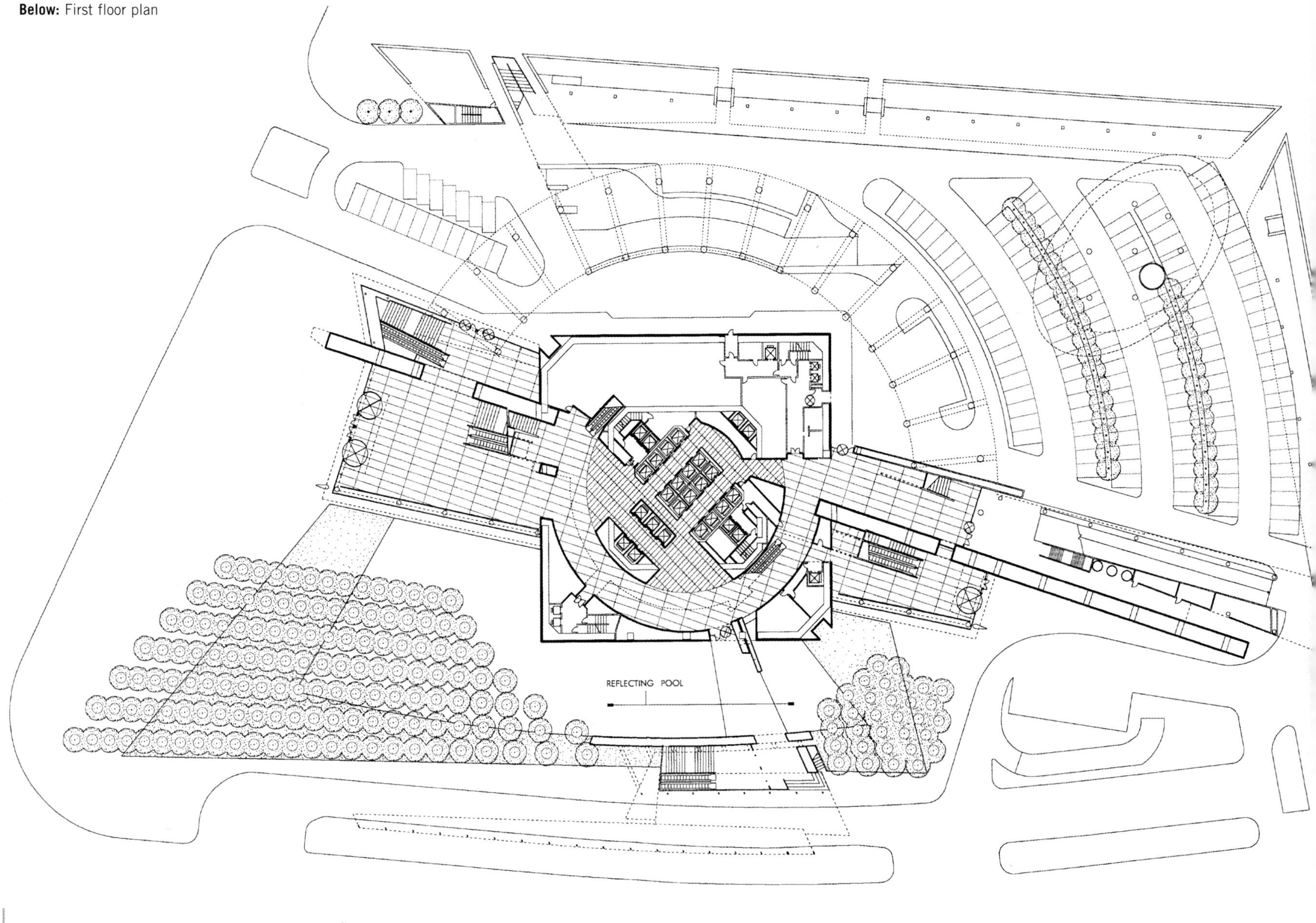

REFLECTING POOL

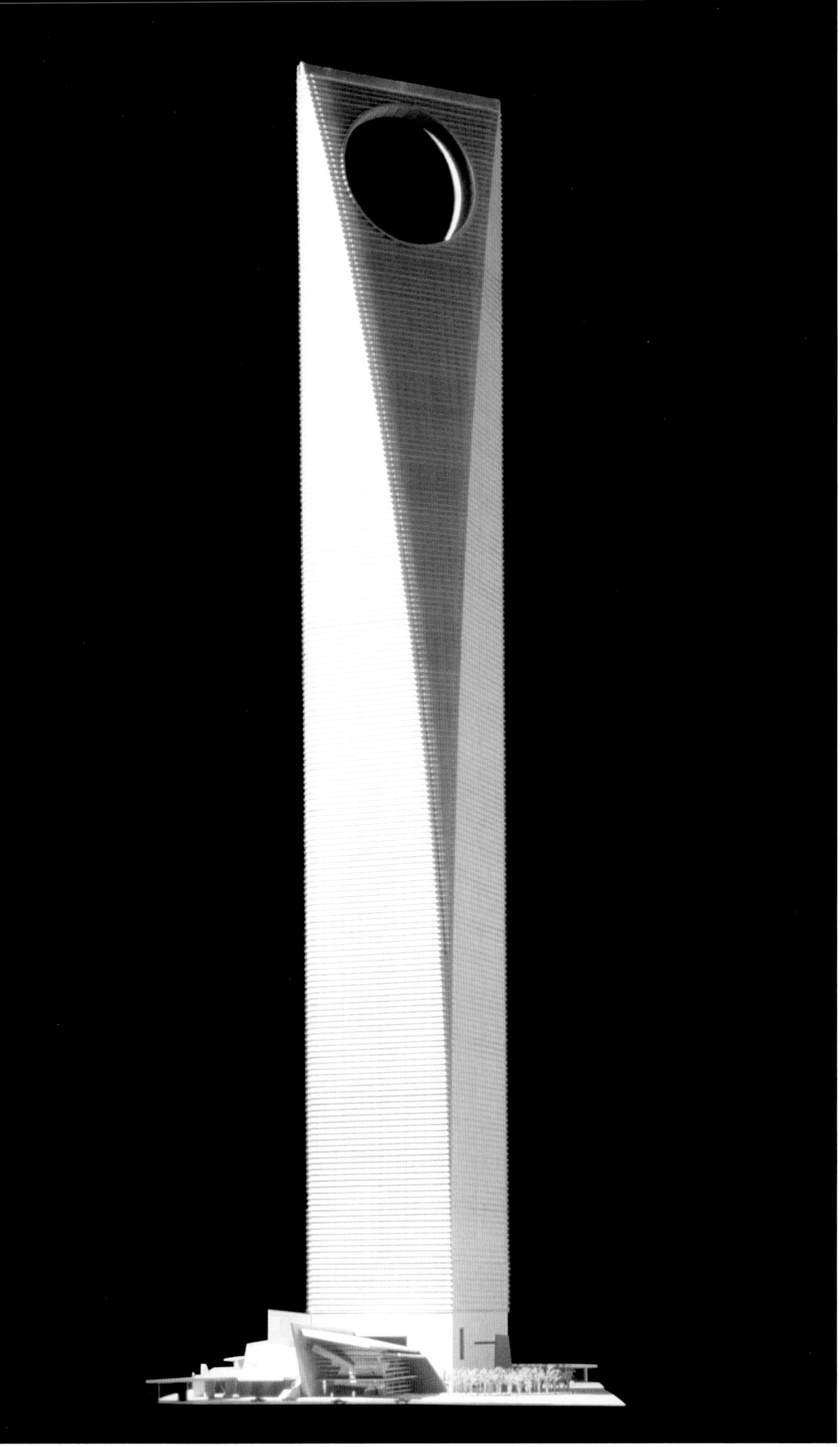

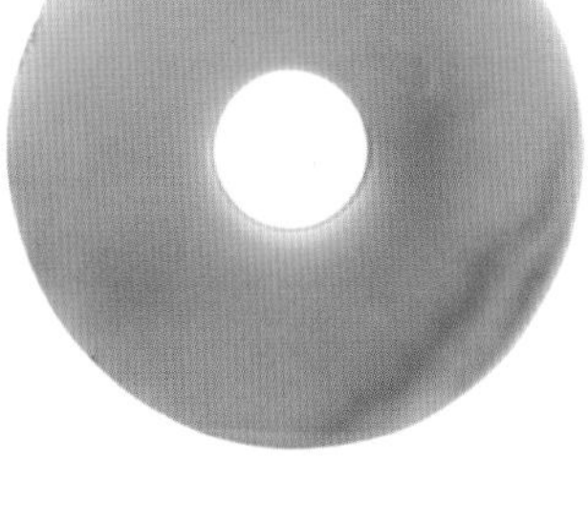

Left: Model

Above: Jade disc (*bi*) and jade prismatic tube (*cong*). These two ancient elements of Chinese art, earliest surviving examples of which are over 5,000 years old, have inspired the fundamental form of the tower

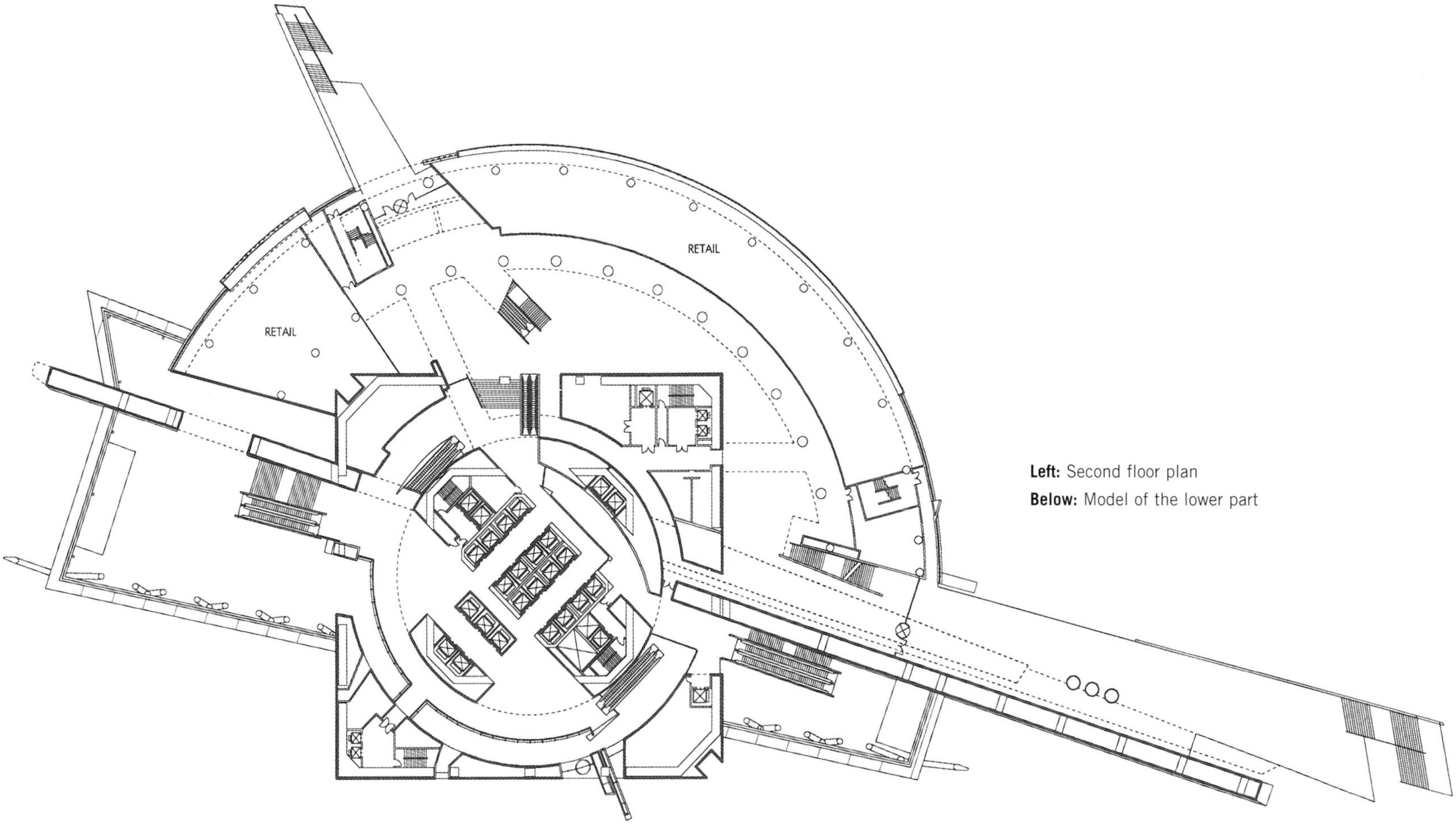

RETAIL

RETAIL

Left: Second floor plan
Below: Model of the lower part

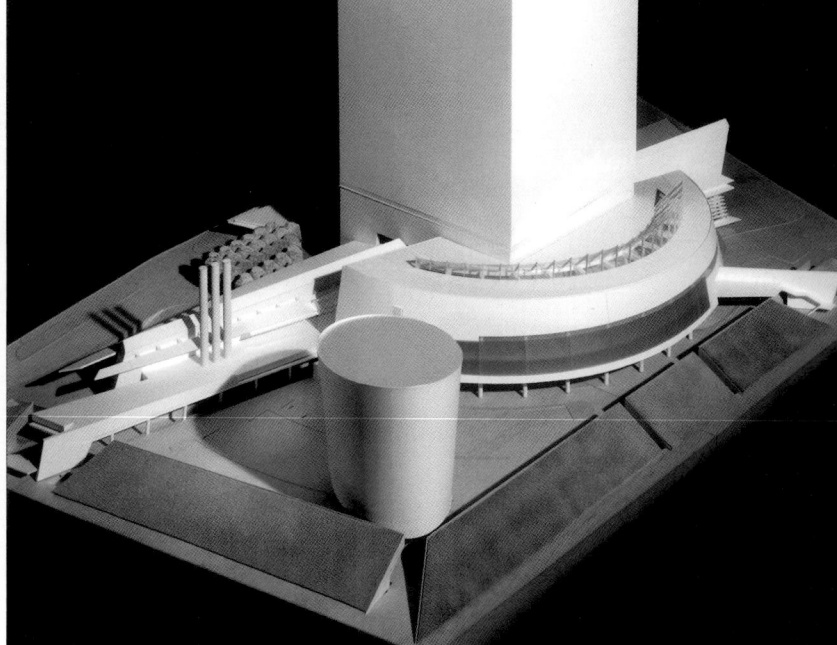

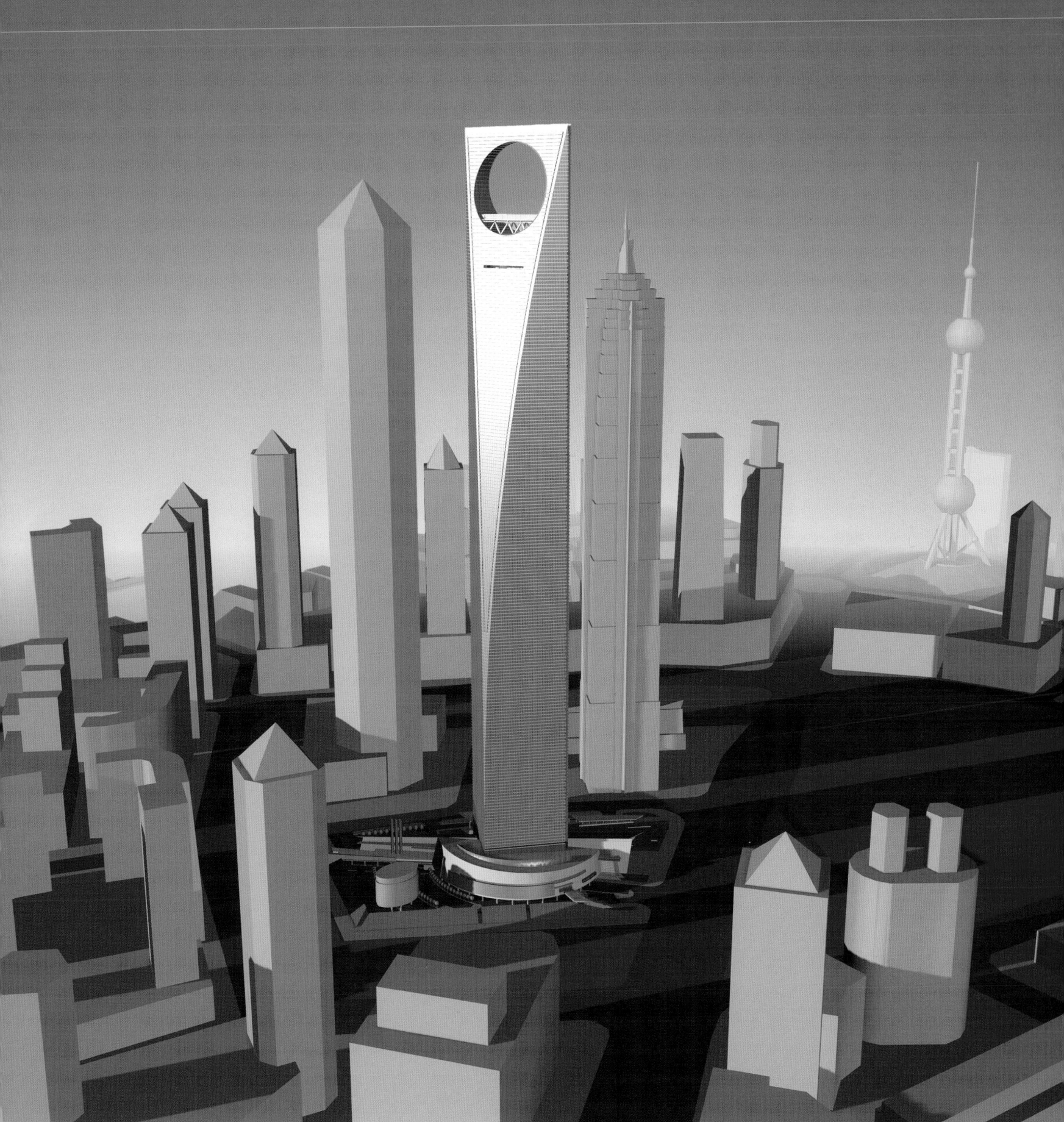

View of the tower in context with other buildings of Pudong

MURPHY / JAHN
21st CENTURY TOWER

This proposal is influenced by an interest in minimalist, geometric form. The building is complex in its integration of structure, materials and technology, shown as a simple and clear diagram.

At Pudong context does not set the limits of scale and materials. No adjustment is necessary. The 'new' can be dramatically presented and can become a symbol for China Everbright and the city.

The design rethinks the high-rise office building in terms of urban planning, function and technology. The resulting formal and aesthetic image is a point tower with a regular plan geometry that is expressed as a singular object or icon. Stacked skygardens complete the formal composition, oriented towards the central space of Pudong, the Jin Mao Tower and the Orient Pearl TV Tower.

Architecturally, the tower is a study in transparency, colour and structural expression. Each of these elements supports and reinforces the other elements so that the structure and architecture are integrated into a single entity. The structural principle employed is that of a braced tube with the expression of this structure being achieved through the detail of the facade. Through its vertical rigour, the structure orders both the use of colour and the skygardens. The structural system allows for the design to eliminate the column at the northwest corner, which faces Central Avenue. The structural gesture marks the ceremonial entrance and identifies the skygarden locations. The application of colour takes its cue from the structural expression. The primary building members are painted red. Neutral Low-E coated glass further reinforces the structural pattern. The skygardens are glazed in clear glass. Through the transparency of the skygardens, the building's edge becomes highly articulated. The podium building at the southwest corner of the site is glazed in clear glass with its metal elements painted a neutral grey. This building is treated as a pavilion that is separated programmatically from the tower. The neutral treatment of the pavilion and plaza become the backdrop to the tower.

The shape and form of the four nine-storey skygardens are determined by the structural frame. These gardens are spaces to be used by the building's tenants for informal meetings, tea, or simply relaxation. The structure, which is independent of the tower, simply supports the glass facade, which in turn provides protection from the exterior environment. A system of horizontal steel plates, vertical cables and horizontal steel spars supports the glass. The environmental systems are designed to supply small quantities of conditioned air at the occupied zone. This results in temperature and humidity control so that the environment is suitable for use in normal work attire. Return air and solar heat gain are recovered at the skygardens' highest point for either heating or cooling. The landscape concept for each space is a simple cast fibreglass tree set against neutral granite paving. Simple metal chairs and tables can be set at the perimeter for small gatherings.

Left to right: Tower lobby; floor 41 – zone 4; floor 48 – meeting rooms

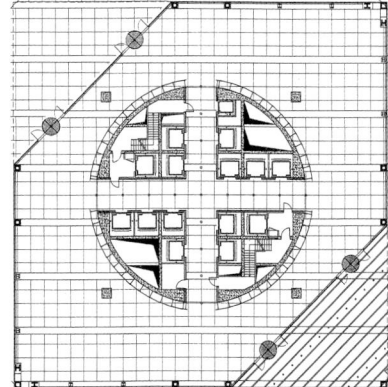
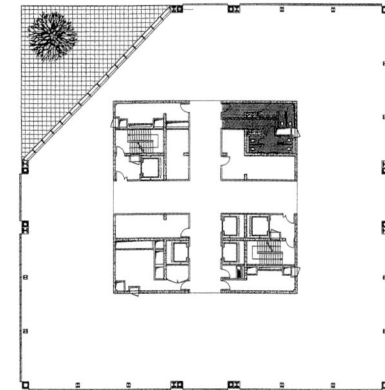
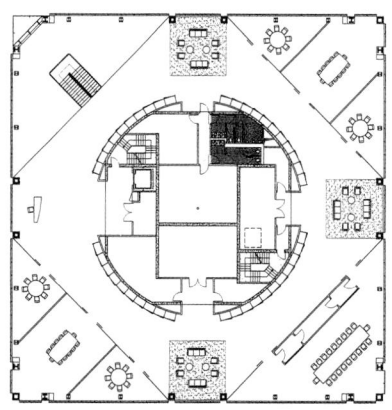

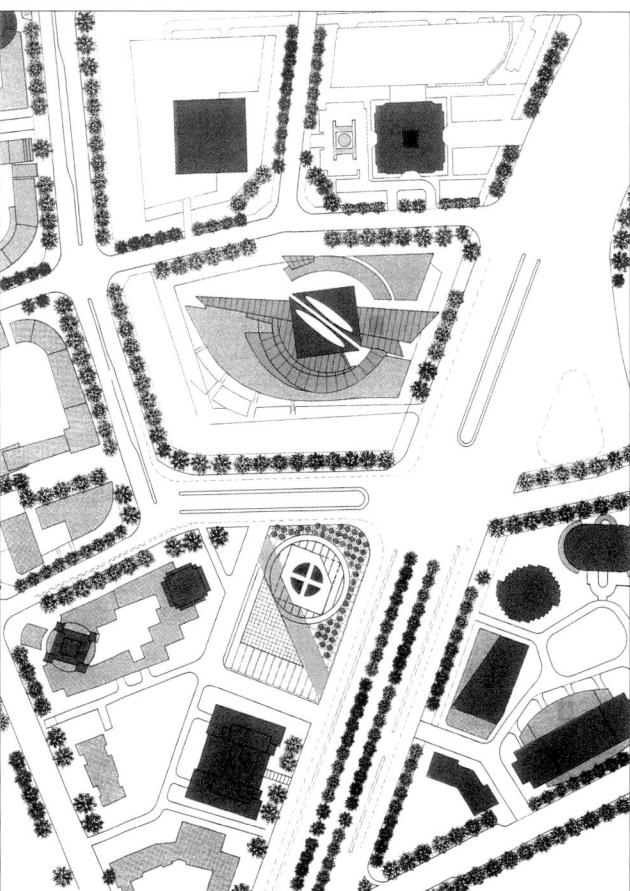

Left: Model
Above: Skygarden
Below: Location

NBBJ
FUXING MANSION

Standing at the important intersection of Zhongshan and Fuxing roads, which links the developing south Bund district with Old Shanghai and the Yu Yuan Gardens, this mixed-use complex serves as a defining architectural nexus between the old and new centres of town.

Both towers collaborate in a single curving composition addressing the main corner of the site. The eastern tower presents to the Huangpu River a formalised frontal posture suitably honouring the architectural traditions of the adjacent historic Central Bund.

A podium moving from five to eight levels acts as a unifying element for the 102,000 square metre office and retail complex, and anchors it at street level to the neighbourhood, while the towers rise to pedestrian bridges linking open public spaces and crossing Zhongshan Road to the Huangpu River.

Building mass in both towers is distributed to the edges to form strong street walls and create a figural centre space open to the sky, 5 metres above the street. This plaza, providing retail-lined upper-level entrance to the office towers, connects the complex's corner to the sequence of public spaces above.

Below and opposite: Model views

JOHN PORTMAN & ASSOCIATES
NEW CI HOU PLAZA

The 134,000 square metre Ci Hou Plaza is comprised of three interrelated buildings on a landscaped pedestrian plaza: a seven-storey office building, a 42-storey residential/retail complex and a five-storey retail podium located beneath a five-storey club and office building. The residential/retail tower is the focal point of the complex. The slender tower appears to be suspended above the retail podium. Its curving north facade on Nanjing Road contrasts with the dramatic recessed south facade. The sleek glass and metal north facade is richly lit so that the building radiates as a unique flowing backdrop for the sophisticated urban lifestyle of Nanjing Road. The

semi-circular form of the office building echoes the curving form of the tower.

Geometric, sculptural form shapes the complex. At the edge of Nanjing Road, a large granite portal marks the entrance to the retail mall and echoes the geometry of the tower glowing behind it. The retail podium adjoins the residential tower, unified beneath the skylight of a spectacular semi-circular atrium. Above the landscaped rooftop plaza of the retail podium, the office and club appear to be majestically suspended. The curved facade of the building is penetrated above the main entrance to reveal the unique glow of the tower beyond.

Left: Section
Right: Elevation

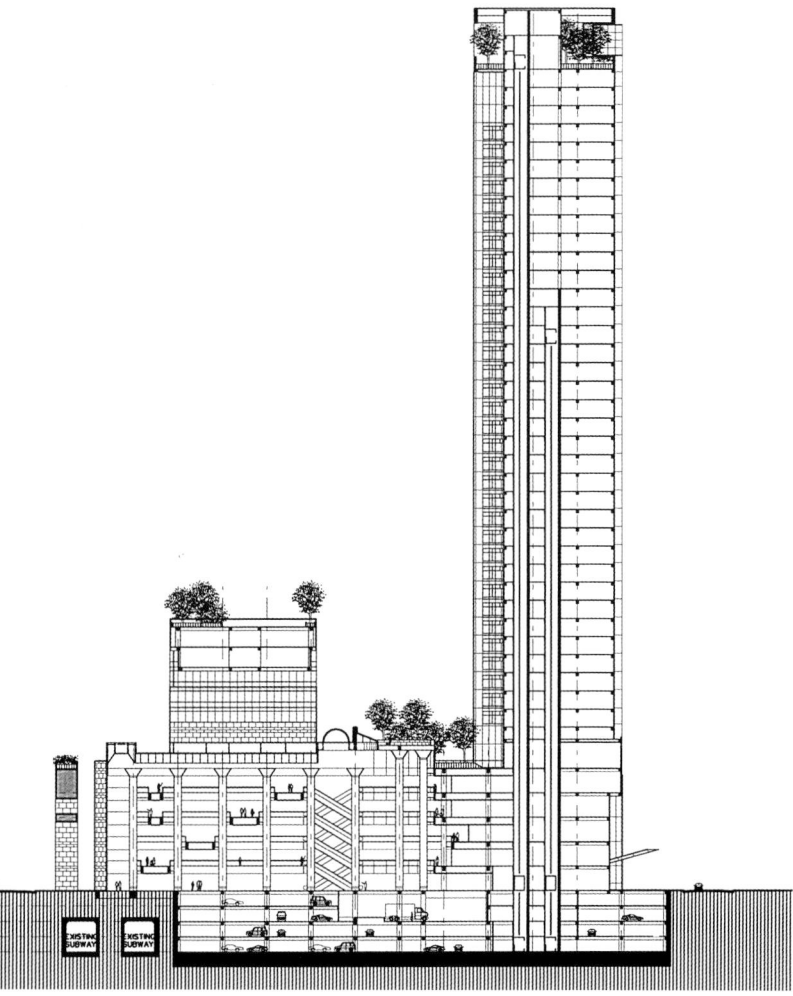

The great atrium

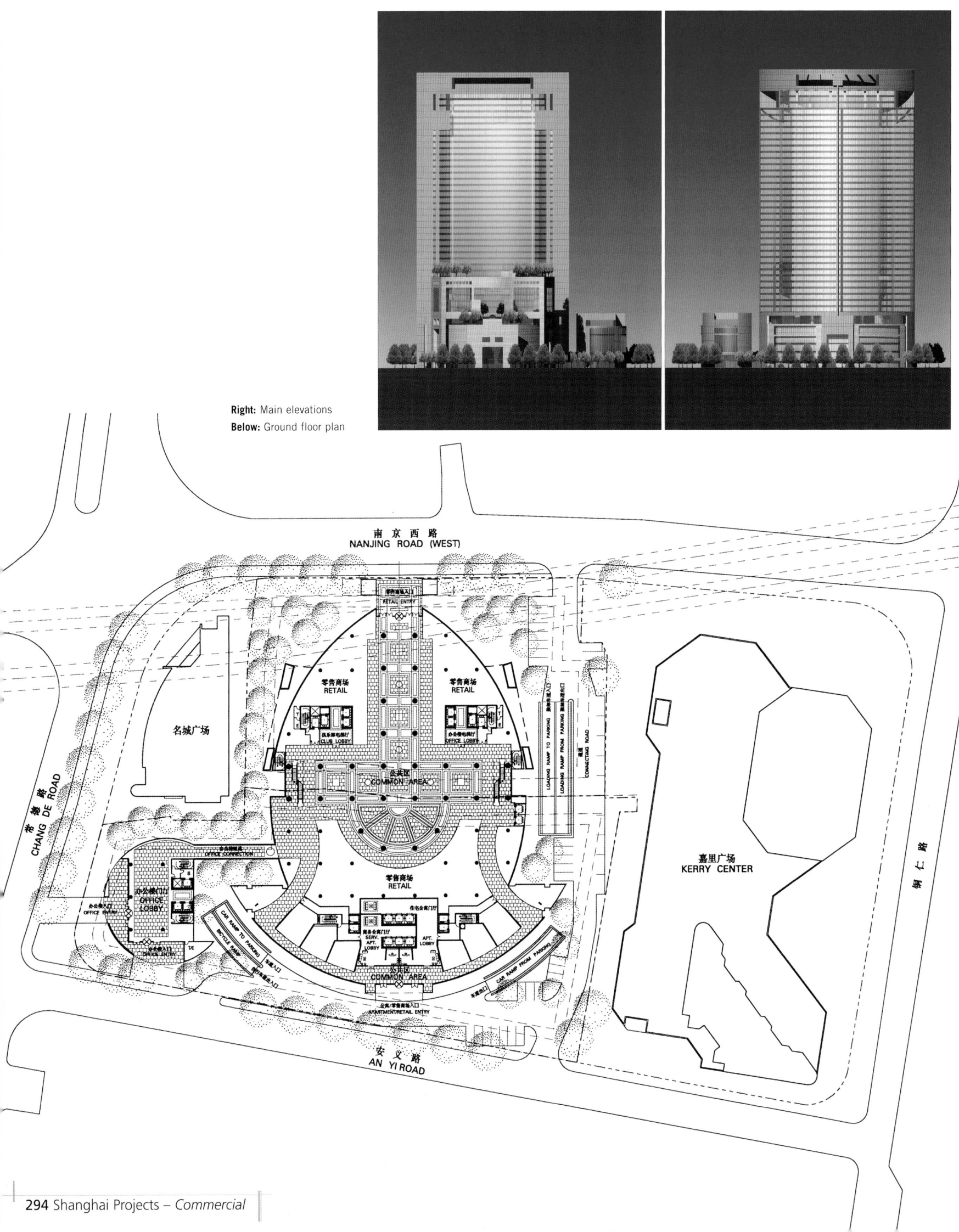

Right: Main elevations
Below: Ground floor plan

南 京 西 路
NANJING ROAD (WEST)

零售商场入口
RETAIL ENTRY

名城广场

常 德 路
CHANG DE ROAD

零售商场
RETAIL

零售商场
RETAIL

办公楼电梯厅
CLUB LOBBY

办公楼电梯厅
OFFICE LOBBY

公共区
COMMON AREA

公共楼通道
OFFICE CONNECTION

办公楼门厅
OFFICE LOBBY

零售商场
RETAIL

住宅公寓门厅
APT. LOBBY

商务公寓门厅

办公楼入口

CAR RAMP TO PARKING

BICYCLE RAMP

SERV.
APT.
LOBBY

APT.
LOBBY

公共区
COMMON AREA

CAR RAMP FROM PARKING

公寓/零售商场入口
APARTMENT/RETAIL ENTRY

安 义 路
AN YI ROAD

LOADING RAMP TO PARKING
LOADING RAMP FROM PARKING

连接
CONNECTING ROAD

嘉里广场
KERRY CENTER

铜 仁 路

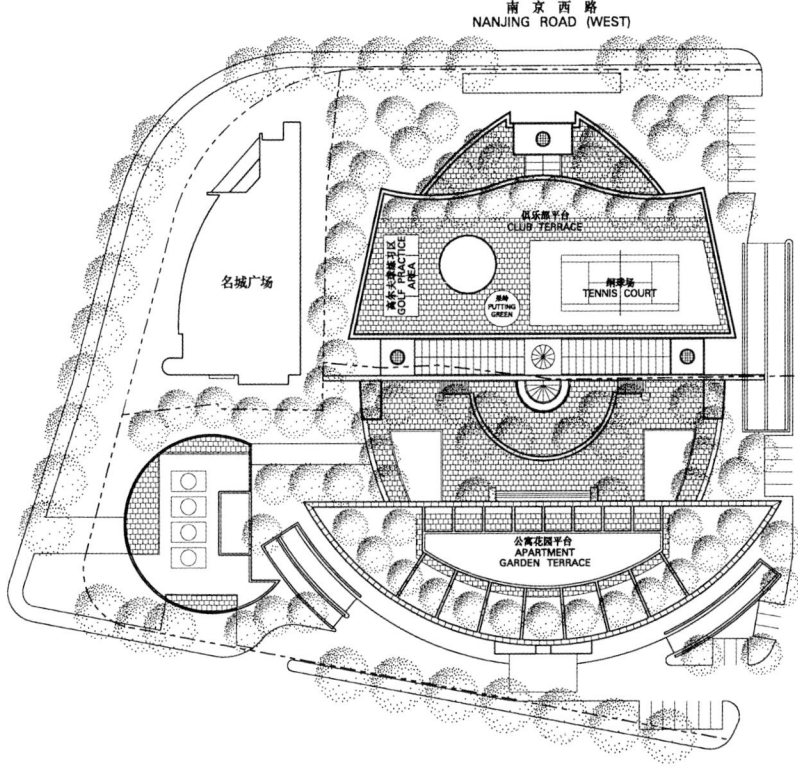

Left: Roof plan
Below left and right: Computer generated night views

The 41-storey Bading Development Finance Mansion is designed as a world-class financial centre. Positioned on the Huangpu River at the heart of Shanghai's Pudong New Area riverfront Bund, the building faces the Puxi Bund and stands as a symbol for the strength and security of the new focal point that is the Lujiazui Financial Centre.

The granite base of the tower is a strong, solid-looking form that gives the building a firm foundation. It rises 24 metres to the height of the podium and relates to the podium building's roofline. The podium itself has horizontal bands that combine a granite course of stone with ribbons of glass. The result is an exciting building, with trees in the high open public spaces and a feeling of transparency appropriate to a complementary construction such as this.

The building has a total proposed gross area of approximately 112,680 square metres, with 89,000 square metres above grade and 25,000 square metres below grade. It consists of three basement levels and 41 occupied levels above grade, including a five-storey podium. In addition, there are three mechanical levels at the top of the building including an area for a communication satellite. The total height of the building is 180 metres. The top occupied floor is at an elevation of 164 metres.

A bank tenant will occupy the southern half of the tower lobby and be accessible both from the tower lobby and from the south plaza podium entrance. The bank facility is located on five levels above grade and extends three levels below grade. The bank is located both within the base of the tower and in the podium. This allows separate and secure access for bank employees located within the tower and the public banking facility located at the ground level.

The retail podium atrium is situated to the east of the office tower and provides amenities for office tenants as well as the public. The upper levels of the podium include a bar overlooking the lobby, a multipurpose room for large gatherings, rest area, coffee bar, business centre and fitness centre. The upper four occupied levels of the office tower contain VIP office space and a club.

The plan of the tower is an octagon, creating a building that stands elegantly when viewed from any vantage point around the city. The facade features ribs that extend up the central portion of each face, giving the building a strong vertical expression as it rises skyward. Each face recesses slightly and rotates, spiralling toward the glass crown, which provides the upper floors with unequalled views of the Puxi Bund from this unique observation point. The podium, whose main entrance opens into a large lobby with 22 metre high ceilings, steps up gradually as the two eight-sided elements intersect harmoniously with the tower and fit into the site perfectly. The glass and granite skin of the podium create a horizontal feeling to contrast with the tower and relate to its base. The public area contains a large array of services for the building's occupants, including restaurants and bars, multipurpose rooms, a business centre, conference rooms, a fitness centre, and an assortment of retail shops. The interior floors of the podium cascade up from one another, and are connected by escalators, creating lines of sight from one level to the next.

Opposite left: Podium
Opposite right: Computer generated view

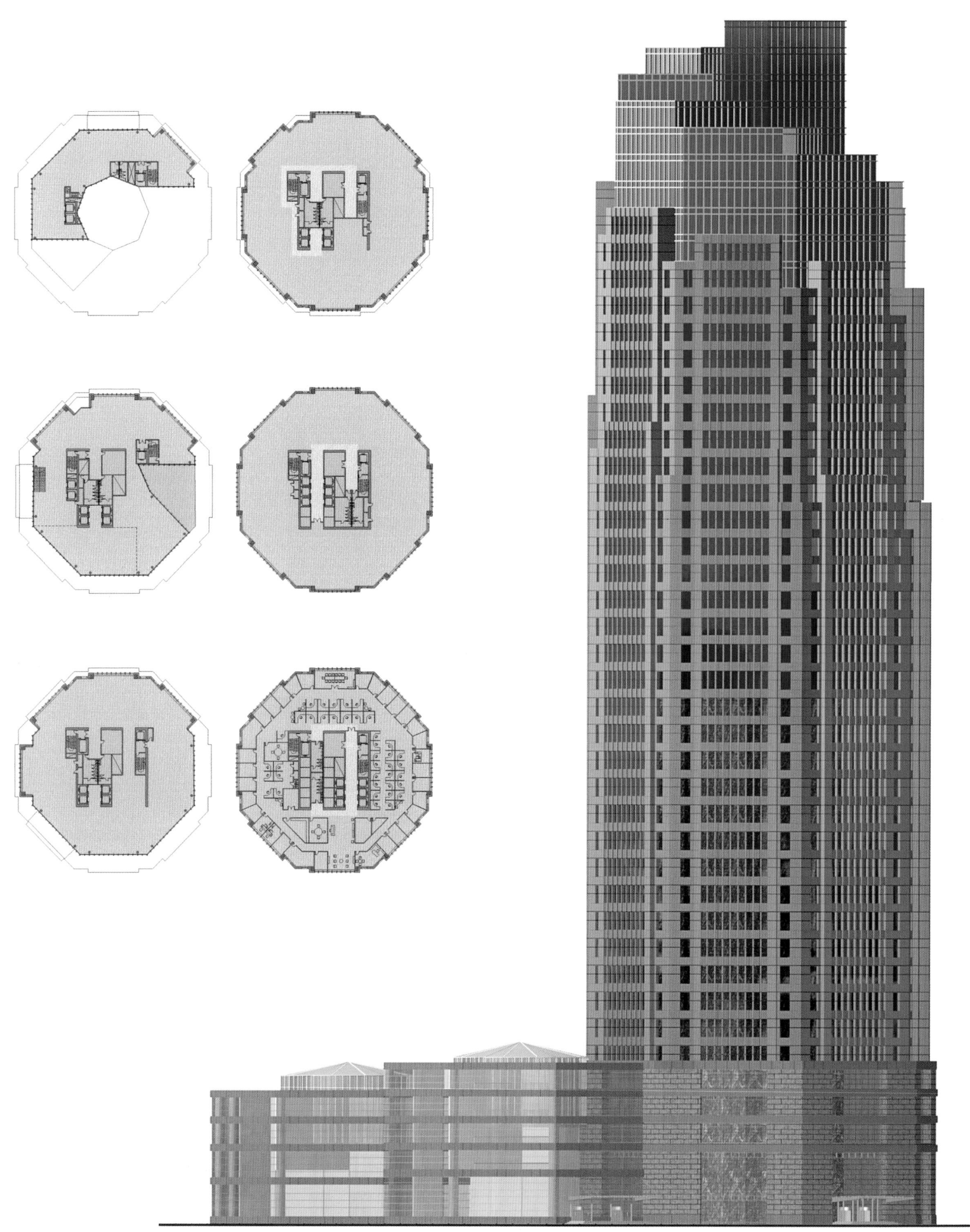

Opposite left: Tower plans
Opposite right: Elevation
Above: Computer generated views
Below: Site plan

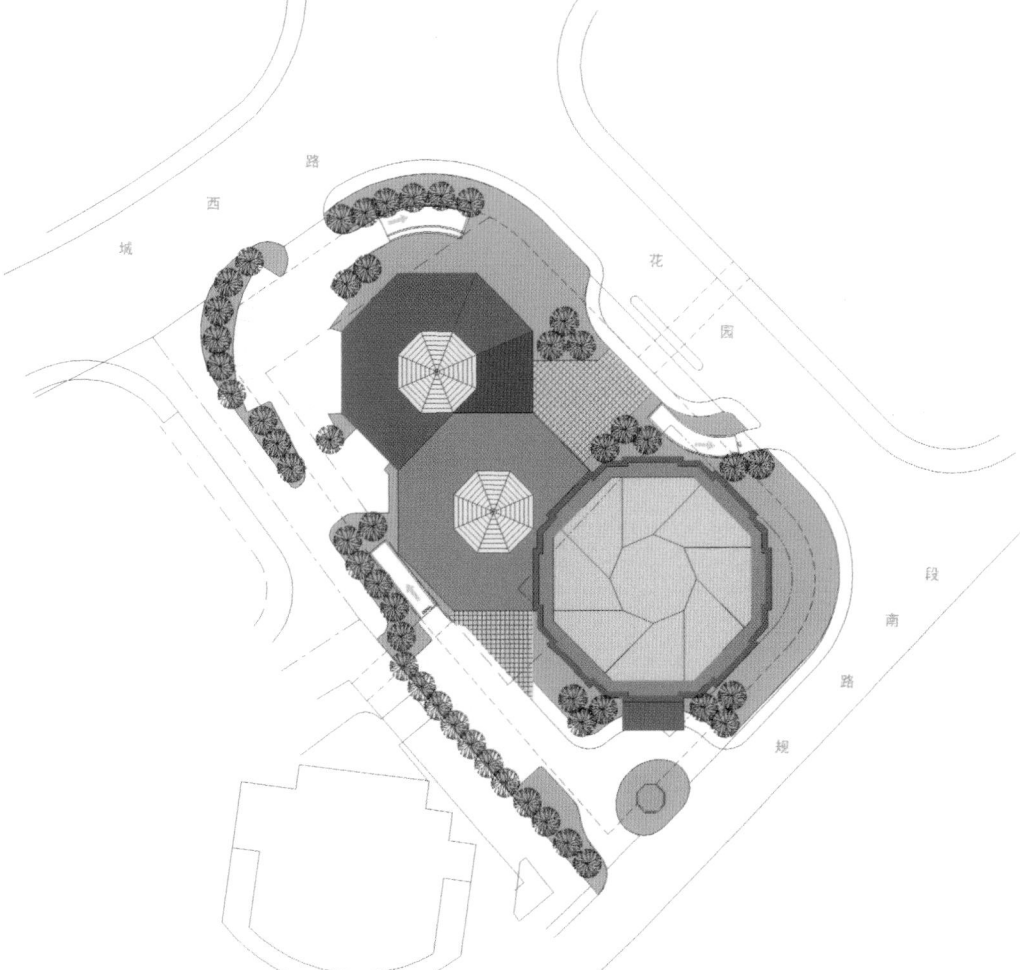

SYDNESS ARCHITECTS
LUJIAZUI ITOCHU DEVELOPMENT BUILDING

Sydness Architects was awarded this commission after winning an international design competition that included contributing architects from Japan, Germany, Great Britain and the United States.

The owners are the Lujiazui Development Company of Shanghai, and Itochu, a Japanese multinational organisation. They will both occupy the building as a headquarters that is located at the heart of the Lujiazui Finance and Trade Zone in the Pudong area of Shanghai.

The building's form is a response to the configuration of the site and to its location on a prominent corner. The plan consists of two semi-circles that are shifted along the diameter to fit snugly within the property lines. The building is then modified in deference to standard office modules and building products, and has a serrated edge on a shifting 1.2-metre module.

The undulating perimeter curtain wall of flamed and polished granite is accented by granite vertical ribs that rise up the tower to a stepped top that echoes the plan against the sky.

The lower floors are clad with horizontal stone mullions and grey vision glass and spandrel glass A large piazza facing southwest leads to a recessed circular glazed entry.

Plan

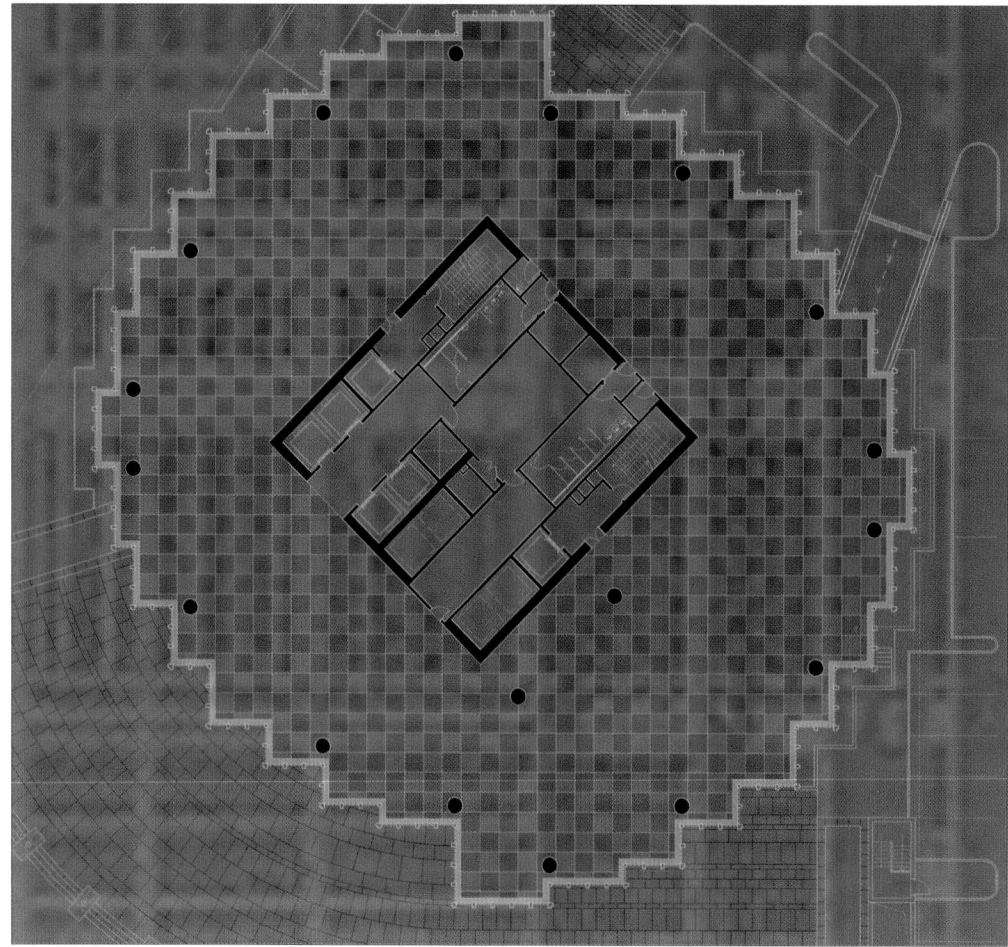

Above: Computer generated views
Below: Elevations

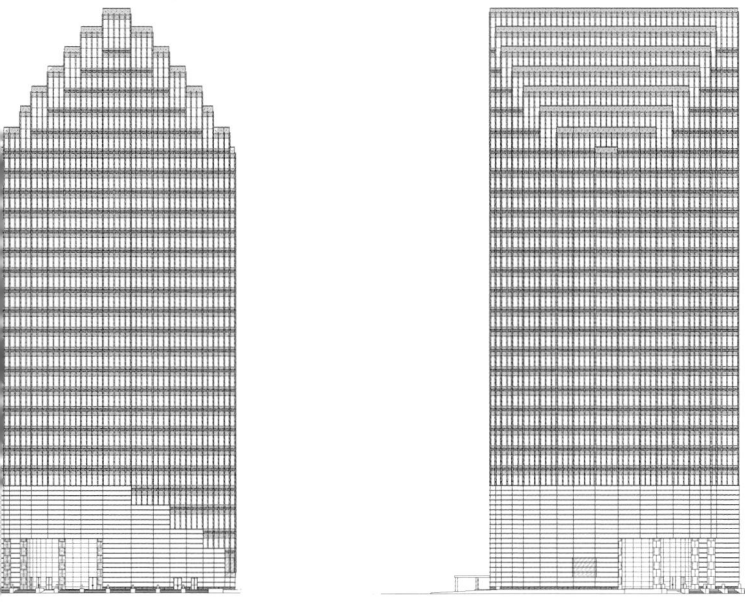
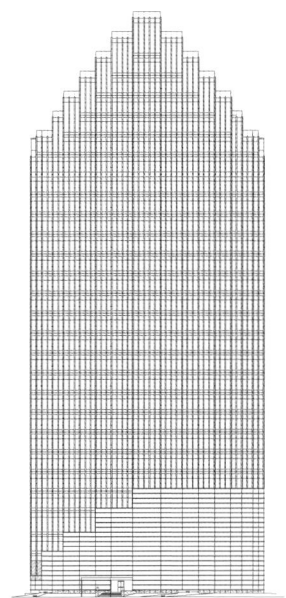
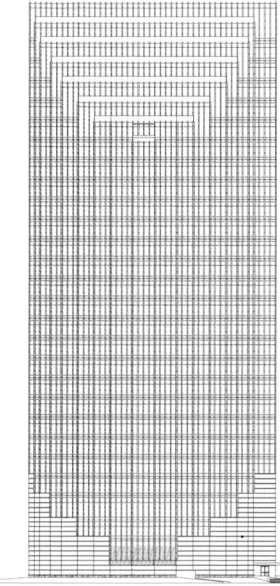

NBBJ
YANLORD LIAN YANG GARDENS

This project for the Shanghai Yanlord Property Co Limited is sited in the new Lian Yang development area in Pudong. The overall development is anchored around the recently completed Central Park. This park, with its dense plantings of trees and vegetation, elaborate water features, winding and strolling pathways and amenity attractions, is a natural oasis and a refreshing contrast to the density of urban life indigenous to Shanghai. Adjacent to Central Park is the civic development of a new Government Centre, a Science and Technology Building, and the Central Public Library. The Lian Yang development area is linked to the major commercial area of Pudong via the grand Century Boulevard and the No 2 subway line, therefore making the area a unique suburban destination within close proximity to all the energy and activity of the new city.

The Yanlord Lian Yang Gardens development is located in the northeast corner of the overall development, with excellent orientation to the south and to Century Park to the southwest. In addition, its northern and eastern boundaries are defined by Yanggao Road and Luoshan Road. These site attributes give the property great visual exposure and ease of access from the major roadways.

Direct access to the site for vehicles and pedestrians is from Jinxiu Road to the south and the A Planning Road, a branch road moving along the site's western edge. This creates an entry sequence that is highly visible, while exclusive and private. Although the site is relatively flat, a significant feature is an existing waterway, which is currently located in the site's northern section. This water element is a major focal point and identity source for the development.

The overarching objective is to create an environment that allows people and nature to coexist in harmony so that they can live in modern comfort while having access to a natural landscape, inspiring a healthy and active lifestyle unique in Shanghai. This is accomplished through the integration of green space, orientation, water features, centres of focus, and organic architecture.

Green space is generally centred within the site and consists of a sequence of landforms, water features (ponds, rivers, canals and streams), natural vegetation, amenity spaces and pathways. It becomes the organising element of the site, which drives the planning and location of the residential buildings. This dialogue between the building and the landscape creates a unique 'outdoor space'. The formation of this outdoor space is critical in that it separates the various tower blocks and additionally creates a visual focal point that is appreciated by all the apartments. The site has been carefully planned to maximise the number of apartment buildings with southern exposure and views to either Century Park to the south and west, the golf course to the south and east, or to the internal green space.

A number of centres of focus give the site a strong presence and sense of orientation. These are typically anchored by amenity functions such as a clubhouse, commercial shops, and a spiritual centre and include a major point tower development that can be seen from afar and becomes part of the development's image. The individual building forms are designed to integrate gracefully into the natural landscape. The masses derived from gently curving forms and sloping rooflines create an undulating wall when in composition with the entire site. It is as if they have been formed by the natural forces of the wind and water running through the site.

All apartments provide equal access to the natural setting, personalised views to the immediate site amenities and to the Lian Yang amenities beyond (Century Park, the commercial area, Pudong commercial core, etc), and individual privacy. A high level of performance is expected from each and every apartment and all of the unit layouts maximise the experience of the inhabitant.

Each building is designed as a series of gently curved layers whose specific articulation is relative to the form and function within, and which work outward from the core at the centre towards screen-like elements at the perimeter. The outermost skin responds to functions adjacent to the exterior, balconies and large openings for special spaces like living areas and master bedrooms, and smaller punched windows where studies, secondary bedrooms and service spaces exist. These outer layers for the most part surround the more transparent core element, which rises above and becomes the special penthouse units. The end conditions of the core element are also transparent and create internal spaces with 180-degree panoramic views. Each apartment building includes floor through units with a minimum of two exposures. There is typically a lift core and an exit stair serving two units per floor.

蜿蜒绿荫带
WEAVING SHADE TREE
SCREEN LAYER

坡状草坪
BERMED LAWN

蜿蜒步道
WEAVING PATHS

地下停车场采光天窗
SKYLIGHT TO PARKING
ACCESS BELOW

零节前庭栽种墙
SEASONAL FOREGROUND
PLANTING

ENLARGED PLAN OF
TYPICAL ENTRY COUNT
典型住宅单体入口
庭院放大平面

网球场
TENNIS COURTS

开花树木
FLOWERING
SHADE TREES

自然化生态河道
NATURALIZED
STREAM CORRIDOR

休闲坐椅平台
SEATING TERRACES

编织印度树丛
WEAVING SHADE
TREE GROVES

河道走廊
RIVER CORRIDOR

步行道通
ACCESS RAMP

机动车桥
VEHICULAR BRIDGE

步行桥
PEDESTRIAN
BRIDGE

人行道
PROMENADE

防洪墙
FLOOD CONTROL
WALLS

休息平台步道
WALK OF SEATING
TERRACES

红砂石步道
RED SANDSTONE
WALKS

ENLARGED PLAN OF
RIVER WALK
滨河步行系统
放大平面

SECTION
步行拉索桥剖面

PEDESTRIAN BRIDGE PLAN
步行拉索桥平面

紫饰球荫树木
ORNAMENTAL SHADE TREE

室外开始空间·雕塑和人工地形
OPEN SPACE
-SCULPTURAL LANDFORMS

蜿蜒步道
WEAVING PATHS

下沉式庭院·停车站通风垂直交通
POCKET GARDEN
-PARKING VENTILATION
VERTICAL CONNECTION

绿荫树丛
WEAVING SHADE TREE GROVE

景观墙
LANDSCAPE WALLS

ENLARGED PLAN OF OPEN
SPACE & POCKET GARDEN
室外开放空间及下沉式
庭院放大平面

NEW WALLS

RESIDENTIAL
GARDENS
住宅花园

PEDESTRIAN WALKS
& LANDSCAPING
人行步道
景观

EXISTING RIVER LOCATION
WITH NEW WALLS AND
PEDESTRIAN WALKS, WIDTH VARIES
现有河道

PEDESTRIAN WALKS
& LANDSCAPING
人行步道
景观

RESIDENTIAL
GARDENS
住宅花园

Previous page: Presentation panels showing the many landscapes of the environmental design
Right: Site plan
Below and opposite: Views north and south within the complex

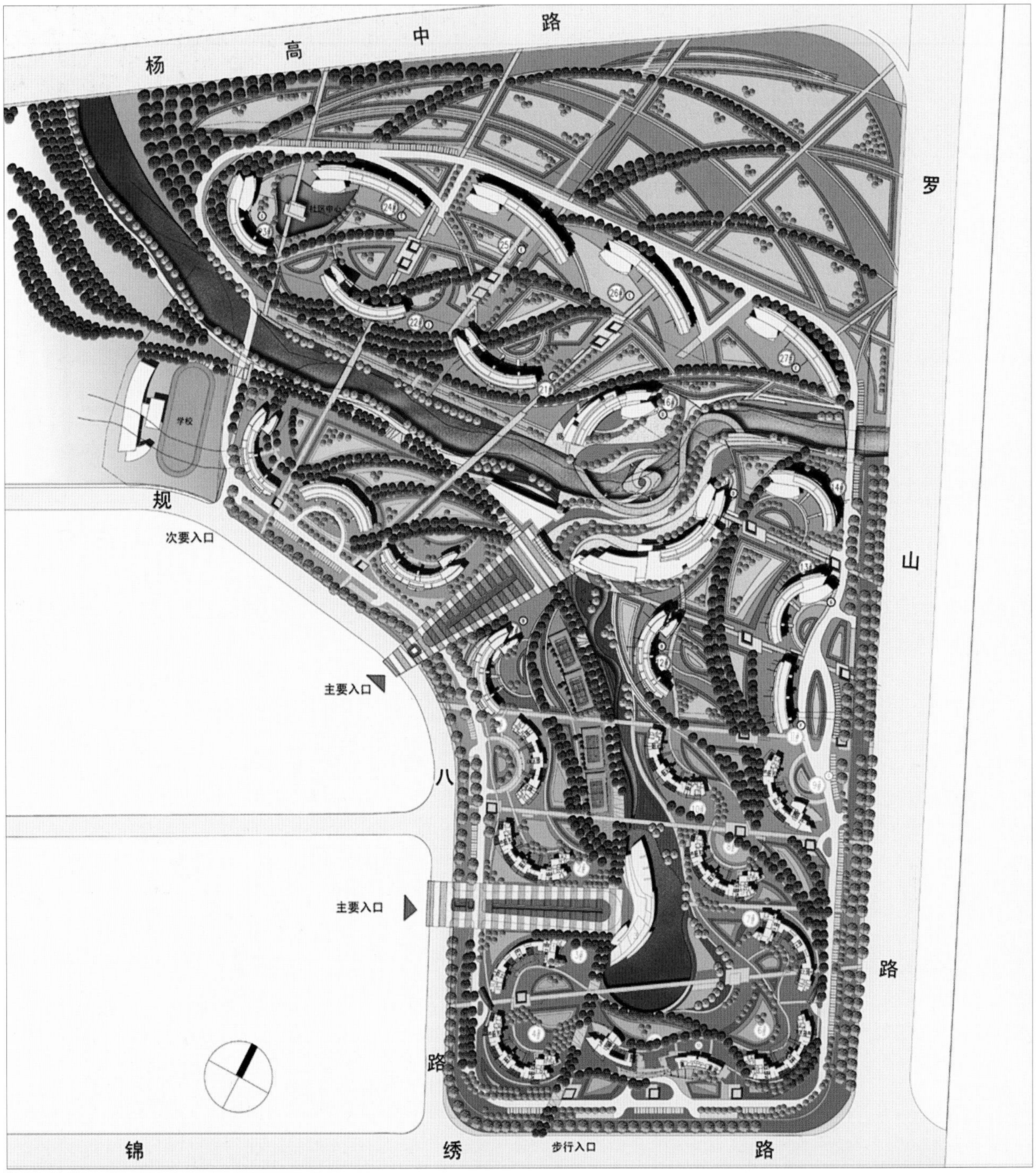

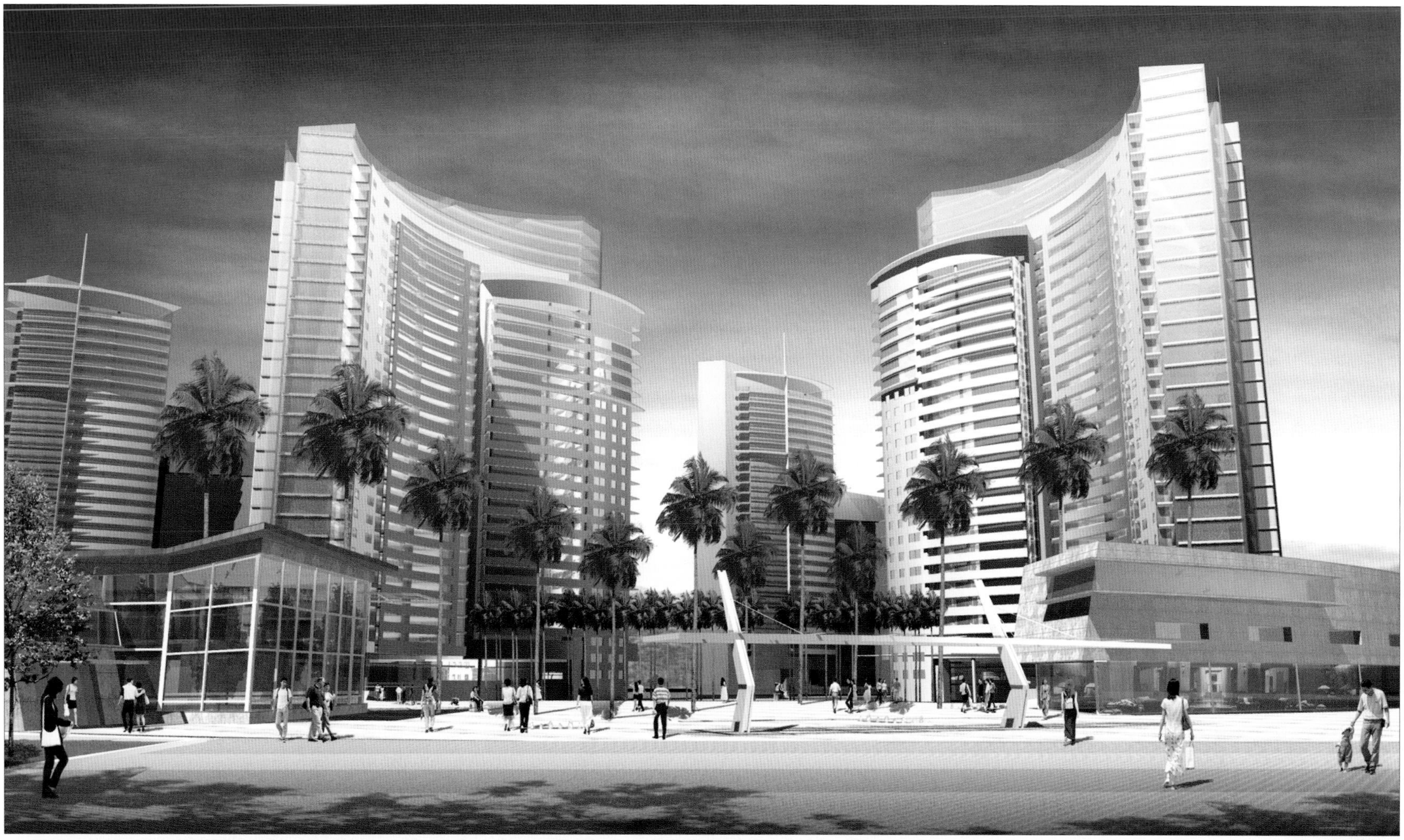

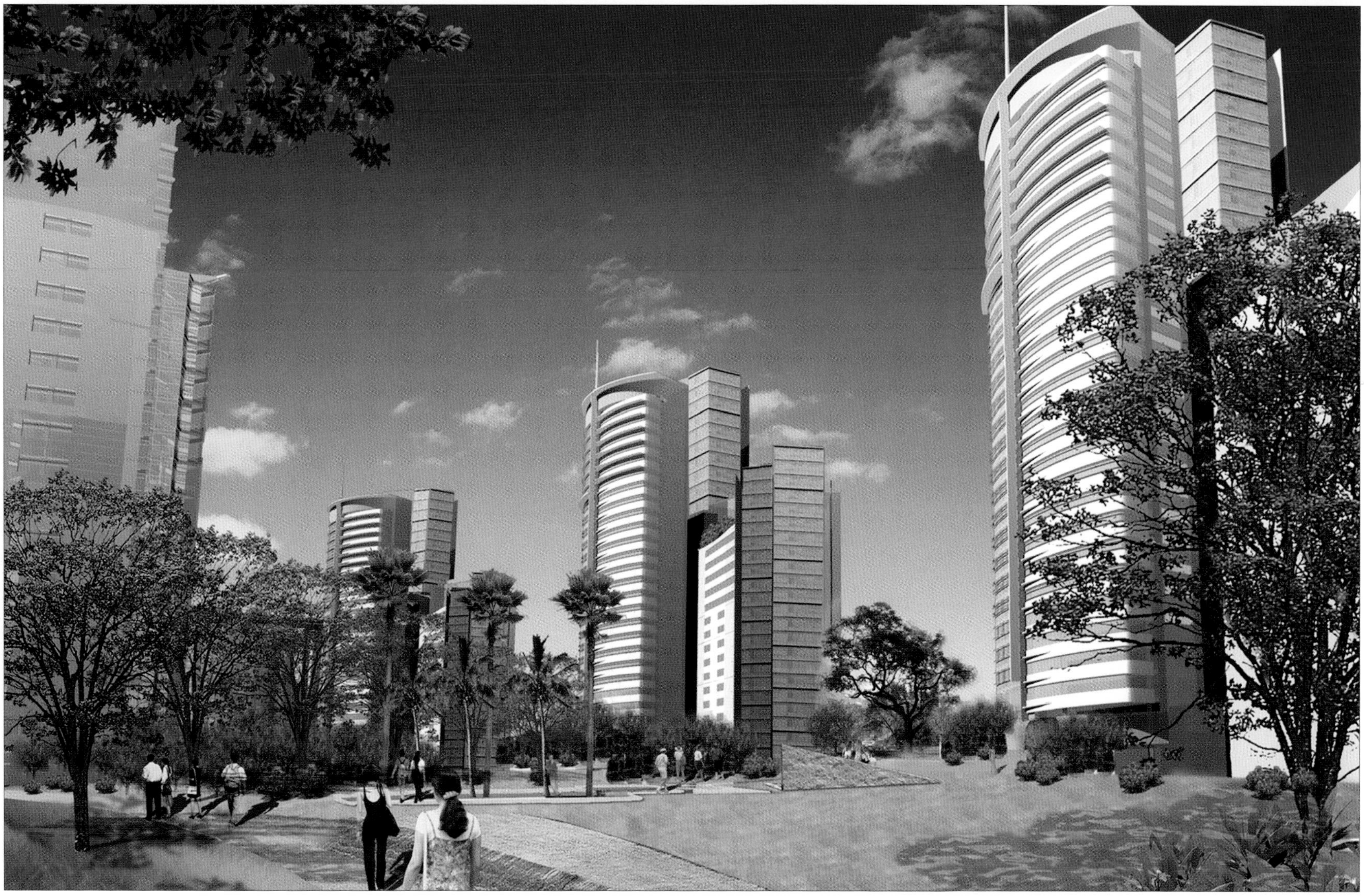

SHANGHAI ZHONGFANG ARCHITECTURAL DESIGN INSTITUTE
YONG-YE APARTMENT BUILDING

This project comprises a 34-floor, high-rise apartment and six 12-floor semi-high-rise apartment buildings, on a general building square of 78,000 square metres. The overall site area is 300,000 square metres, with 40 per cent green space, creating a harmonious environment balancing nature and humanity. With its rich facade and skyline, it has been designed to be both modern and simple in style.

The design is guided by principles of land and energy saving, and a healthy ecology. Areas of high activity are separated from quiet spaces. Natural lighting and south to north ventilation are supplied. The layout of each apartment condenses functions such as a lobby, working terrace, walk-in storage closet, study room, viewing terrace and work room. They vary widely in size from 96 to 200 square metres. Top floor units have two levels and adopt a recognisable facade characterised as 'City-roof window'.

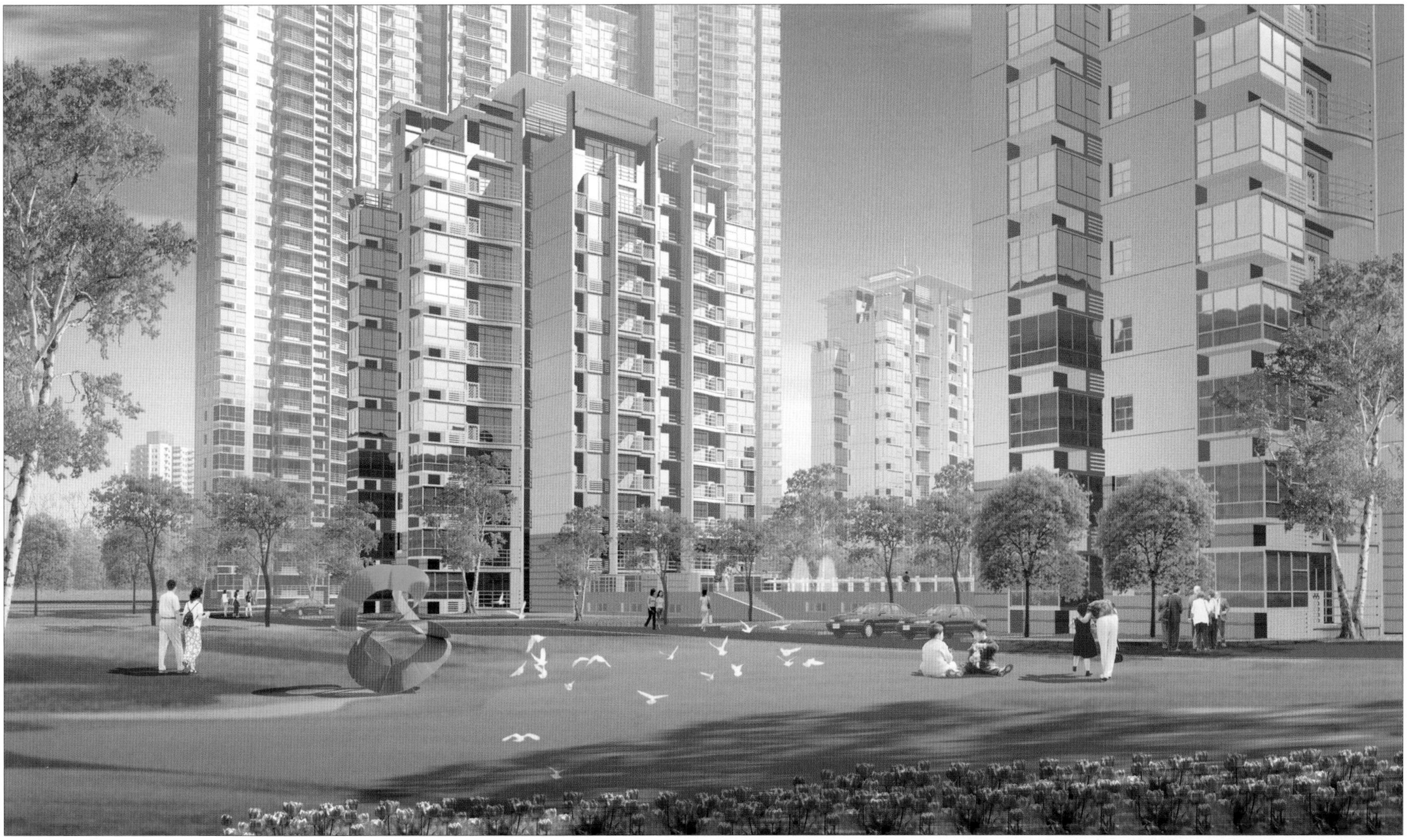

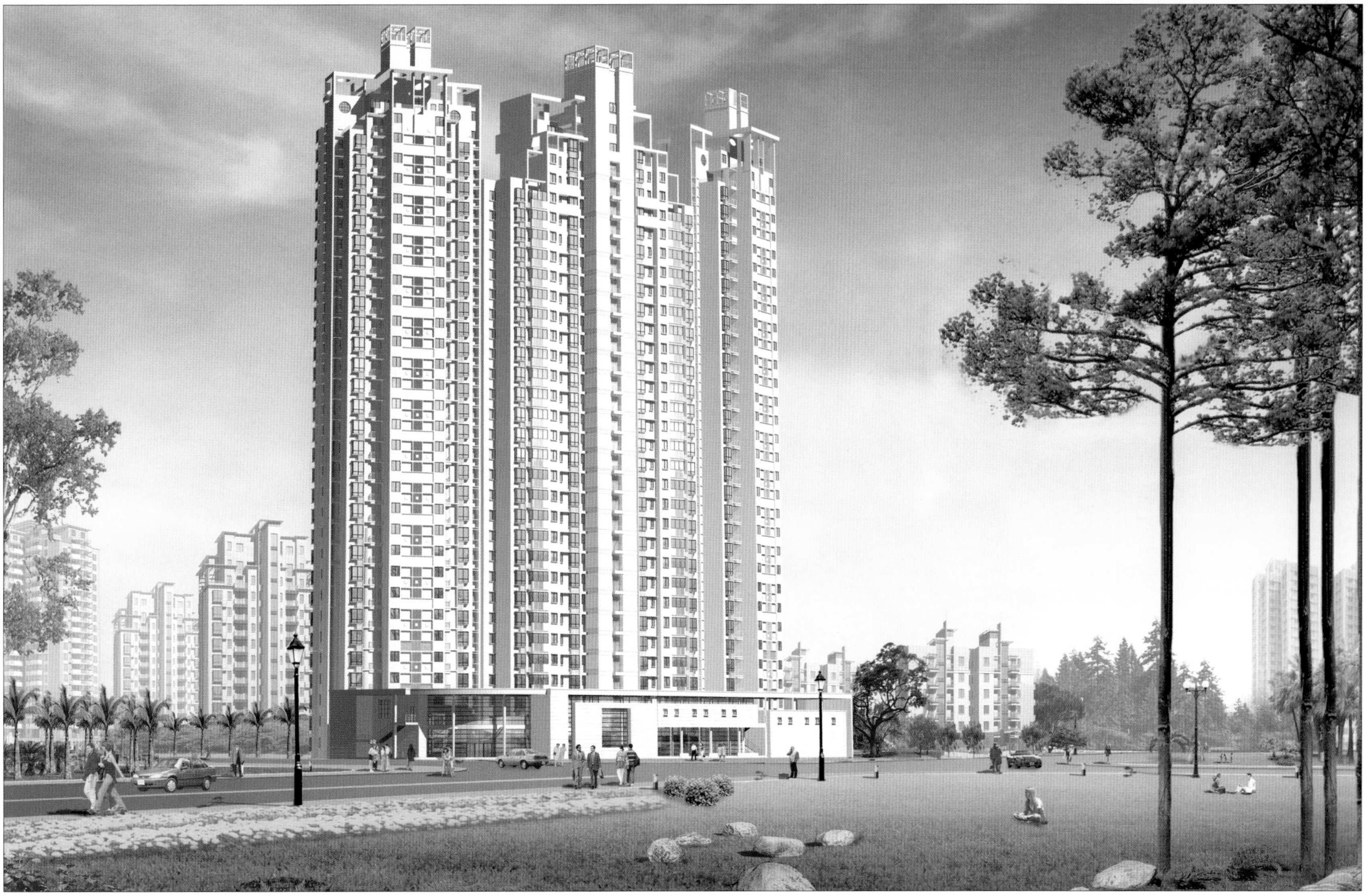

TAOHO DESIGN ARCHITECTS
BAI HUI GARDENS

This middle-class housing development is, perhaps, the first housing project along the massive riverfront renewal programme of the Huangpu River in southern Shanghai. The site was originally an airplane factory with many mature trees. Every effort is made to preserve these trees as an integral part of the master plan. The scale of Bai Hui Gardens is such that it will form a self-contained garden city. A sequence of low rise housing terraces, six storeys in height, runs transverse across the site, each band enclosing a gar-

den, creating its own community and each terminating in a 16-storey tower, marking and adding grandeur to the great promenade along the water's edge.

Since heating is not normally provided in such housing, every unit is designed to have southern exposure to gain maximum solar heat in the winter. There are many different unit types, offering more choice for the purchasers. Specially designed units are located along the eastern end of the site to take full advantage of the Huangpu River.

DREAMS

PAUL ANDREU
ORIENTAL ART CENTRE

Sited at the end of Century Avenue, opposite the Town Hall, the Oriental Art Centre is a place for music and performances. During the day its appearance is enigmatic, the shiny, curving pearl grey material unique in the city. No sign indicates its function, which is not immediately apparent. Like an enormous sculpture set amidst the trees in the middle of a group of roads, it is highlighted by reflections and shadows, its shape changing as one moves around it. It soars up from the ground and opens out to the sky. From the entrance, with its large flight of steps, the building front becomes transparent and one can see another flight of steps inside along with colourful high walls.

At night, the building becomes bright and transparent. There is a sense of gaiety and brightness in the movement of the people, the colours and the lights. The three interior volumes that rise out of the base in which they are rooted, becoming lighter in colour as they reach the ceiling, house and protect three auditoriums. The common space around them, composed as a variation on the twin theme of transparency and curves, comprises an entrance lobby, lounges, a circulation space and exhibition areas. Functionally and visually, this space links the auditoriums to the city. A performance space is the site of an encounter, meticulously prepared yet new and unique each time, a place where artists, public and artworks meet. Everything in the building is designed to facilitate a pleasant experience. In the base, the

rehearsal and dressing rooms are located along the periphery, most of them with discreet windows providing a view onto the outside. The lounge area and technical support facilities are in the centre.

The husk of the auditorium walls houses a functional, limited and modest space, which is transformed, during the time of the show, into a limitless space. Each of the three auditoriums is informed by the same will to discreetly serve the works and the performers in their encounter with the public. In the grand auditorium, the performers are surrounded by the public in a lyrical space in which the seats are spread out over an undulating ground and curves run through the clear sky above. Here, a wide diversity of music, from the most ancient to the most contemporary, can be created, recreated and enjoyed. The theatre auditorium, with its more conventional appearance, will lend itself to a frontal encounter between the orchestra and the public, and also to Chinese or Western opera performances. The 'small' auditorium, which retains its intimacy even when filled to its maximum capacity of 400, will be the site for new music. These three contrasting auditoriums form a single composition around a common circulation and exhibition space. Their exterior colours create a painting that appears at nightfall, like the sound of music emerging from silence, visible amongst the trees, the roads and buildings of Pudong.

Above: Computer generated perspective
Opposite left: Plan of concert hall
Opposite right: Plan of theatre

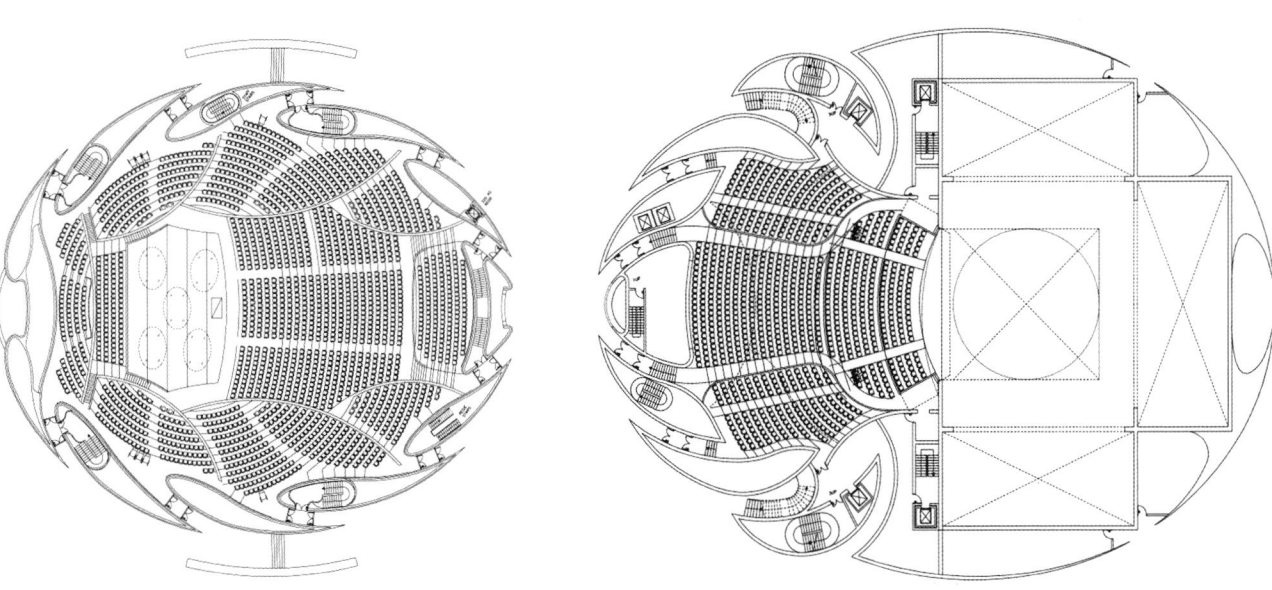

ARTE CHARPENTIER ET ASSOCIES
EXHIBITION CENTRE

This design was the winner of an international competition aimed at supplying the Pudong area with an exhibition centre. A 55,000-square-metre block of five halls is connected together in the shape of a fan, representing the five continents.

A master plan for organising the future fair and exhibition area of Pudong on 94 hectares is in progress.

The Oriental Arts Centre is a new cultural symbol for the Pudong district of Shanghai. The design creates a seven-storey, light-filled and enjoyable building for the performance of music. The building is sited parallel to Ding Xiang Road. The main entrance is oriented towards the central axis with separate and distinct entries for the Symphony Hall, Chamber Hall and the small theatre/public spaces. A separate entrance from Ding Xiang Road provides access to the Art Exchange, as well as entries for the performers and the delivery of materials. Surface parking and below-grade parking are also accessible from this entry. A landscaped garden is located to the east, including a small area for outdoor performances.

The basis for the planning is to allow for simultaneous events in each of the three halls. Therefore, each hall is designed as an acoustically isolated structure. In addition, each is designed to function publicly as an independent building. Some back-of-house facilities and support services will be shared.

The 800-seat Chamber Hall is located in the east third of the complex. This hall is designed with one balcony and two levels of side boxes. A stage house is provided to allow for the performance of opera and theatrical production. The stage control room and simultaneous translation booths are located within this hall.

The 2,000-seat Symphony Hall is located in the middle third of the building. The main seating level is in the first basement. Four balconies with side boxes are accessed from multiple lobbies. Glass elevators and stairs interconnect the different lobby levels. Seating for the choir is located at the second level behind the stage. Reverberation chambers are employed in order to modulate the sound as required by any individual piece of music. Provisions for a pipe organ will also be made.

A small theatre for 200 as well as the restaurant and administrative offices are located in the west third and accessed from the south. The Green Room/VIP Lounge is adjacent to this theatre. A connection is also provided to the Art Exchange, which is accessed from the north end of the complex. Covered terraces at Level 4 provide outdoor dining or simply a break during intermission. Glass elevators and stairs also connect the various levels.

Common spaces such as the rehearsal hall, rehearsal rooms, performers' amenities and the mechanical systems are located to the north and below grade. The two major halls have separate fan systems.

This design represents an architecture that not only relies on form and aesthetic, controlling its environment through design, but also on added technical systems. Form, space, function, materials, construction and technology all enforce and support each other in a totally integrated design.

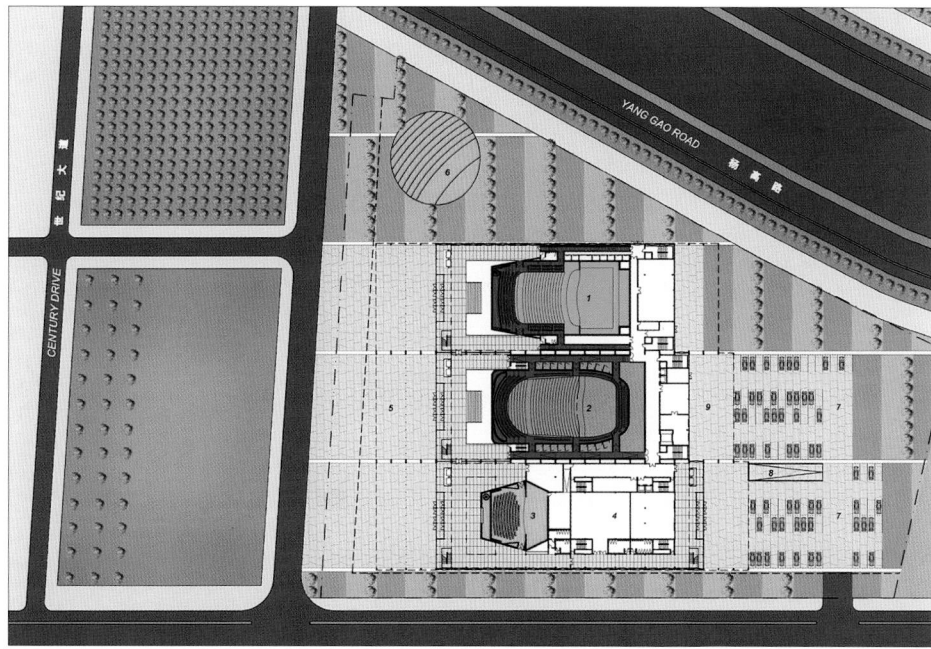

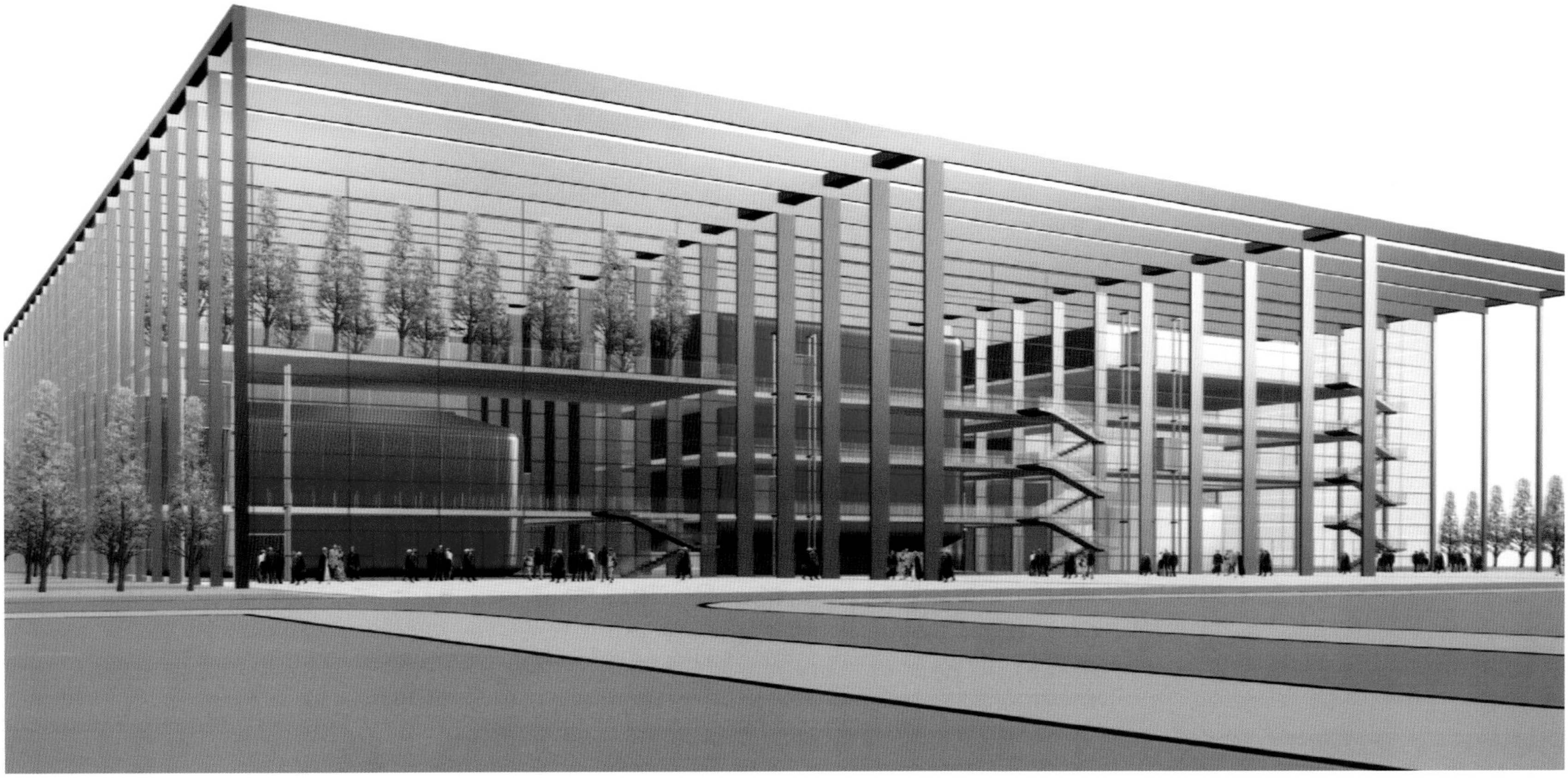

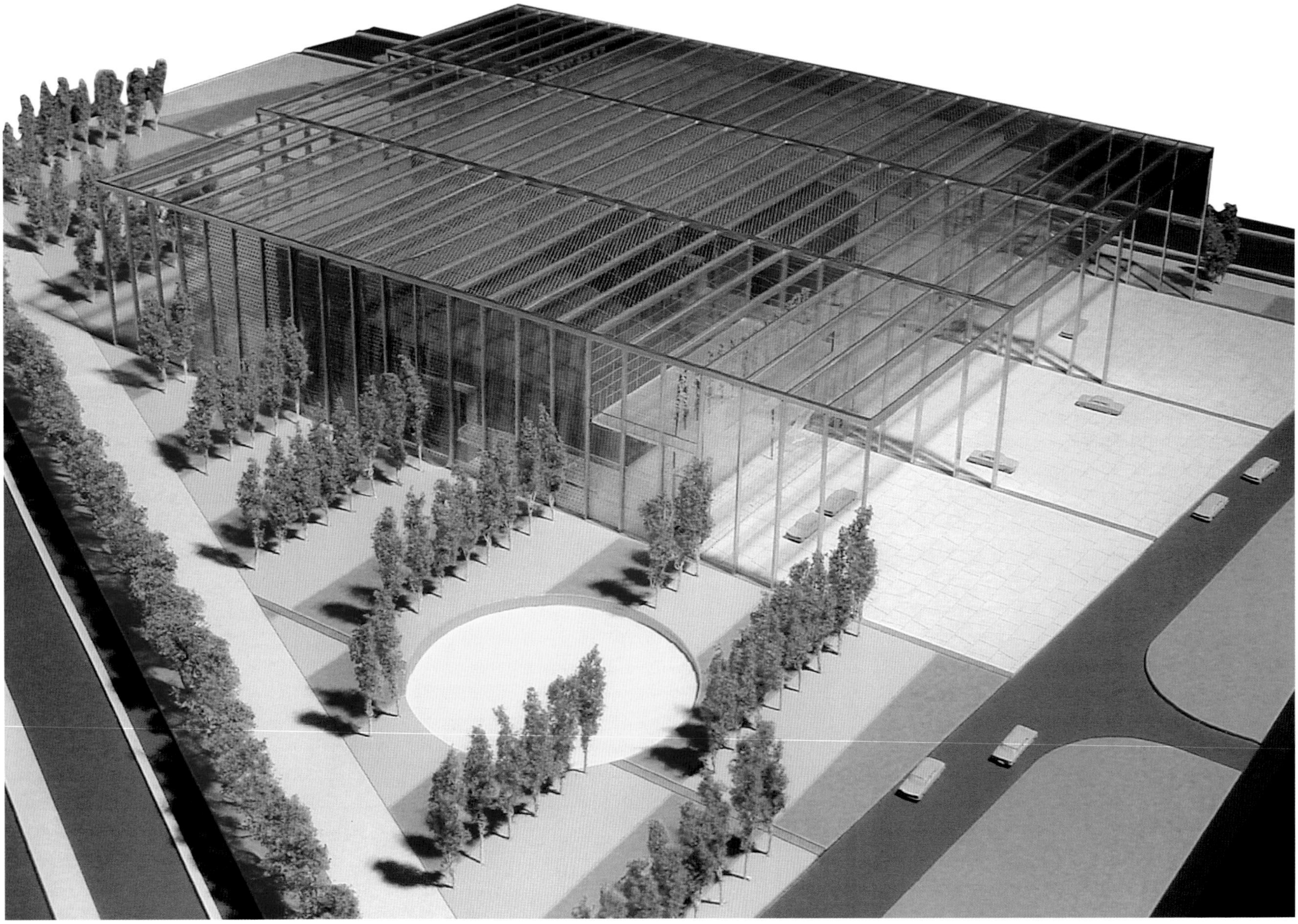

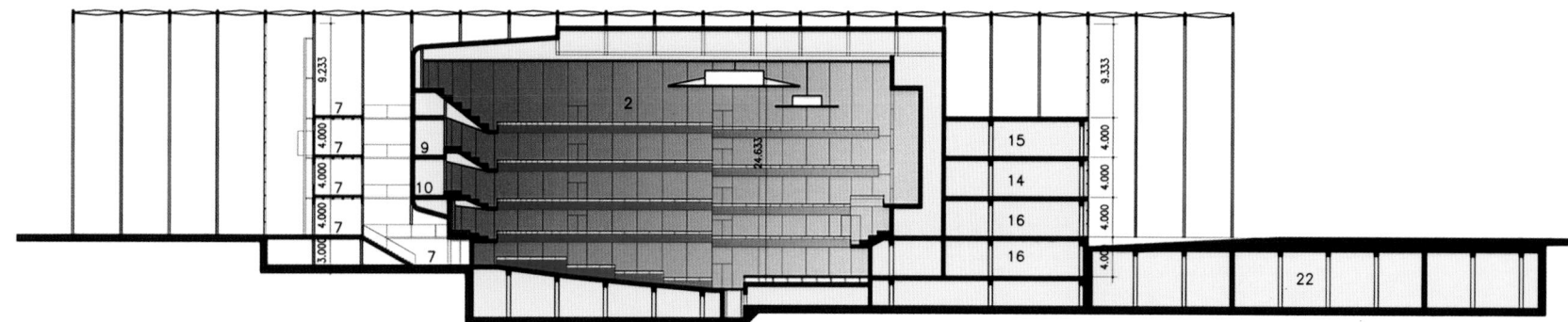

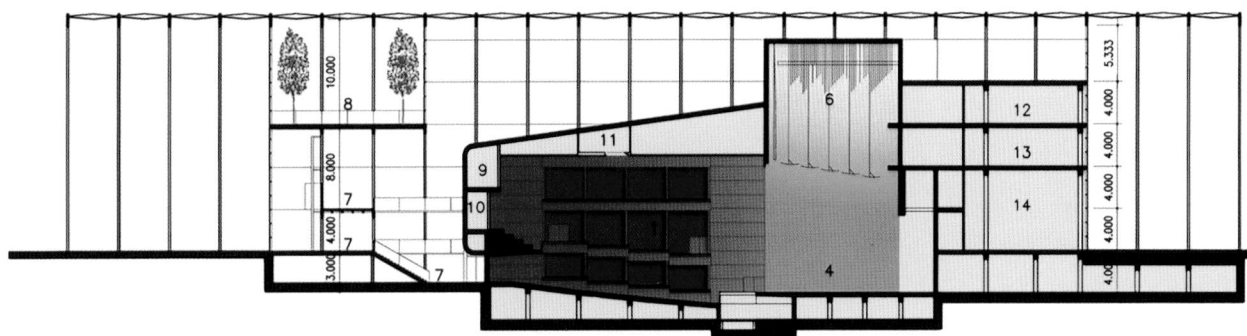

Opposite: Perspective views
From Above:
Section through Symphony Hall
Section through Chamber Music Hall
South elevation
West elevation

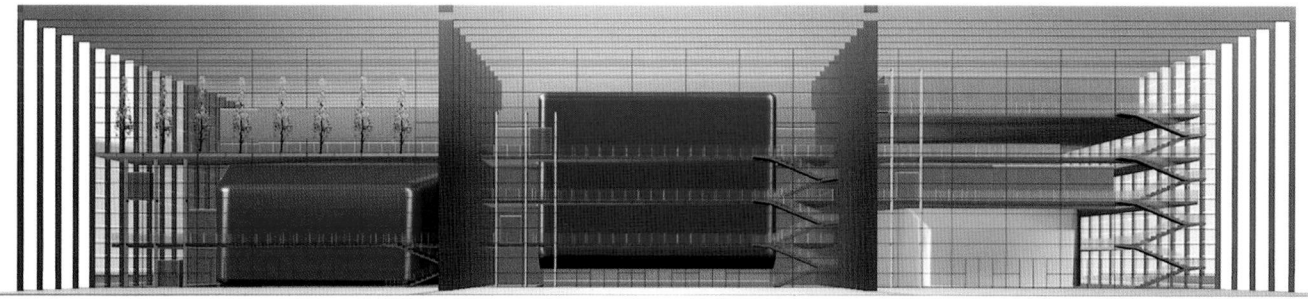

ARCHITECTURAL RESOURCES CAMBRIDGE
SHANGHAI CITY CLUB HOTEL

In 1994, Architectural Resources Cambridge, Inc. (ARC) was commissioned to develop plans for a $30 million, 60,000 square-metre, multi-use high-rise in Shanghai. The building site, overlooking the old French territory park, is in a prime location of mixed commercial use, sometimes referred to as Shanghai's 'Fifth Avenue'. The building will house a 350-room hotel, commercial office space, a business centre, restaurants, convention facilities, a health spa, beauty salon and coffee shop. Underground space will include parking and a six-lane bowling alley.

The original designs explored architectural concepts generated from French and British Colonial influence in the China territories. Traditional building materials and colonial details were incorporated in the early schemes. After a series of meetings, however, both the client and the architect opted for a building design that adopted a more forward-looking spirit. The later schemes became more international and contemporary in style, while incorporating Shanghai's Old World culture and Chinese heritage through symbolic imagery.

The final design, which was completed in 1996, maintains the highly recognisable Chinese cultural presence through the stylised image of a river junk. The strong vertical element of the building, (encompassing the elevator shaft), is the mast, while the layering of the curtain wall portrays the sail. The curtain wall is also gently curved to suggest a billowing sail, just beginning to fill as it catches the harbour breeze.

Indigenous and locally produced materials have been used wherever possible, not only to support the regional economy and reduce costs, but also to create a natural and comfortable environment within its urban setting. This has been carried through to the interior – immediately evident in the design of the lobby, which depicts a 'miniature China', using blue, green and earth-tone Chinese marbles to represent the landscape of rivers, rice paddies and small towns.

The tower's fate remains unclear as it moves through a hesitant planning and review process.

Model

MIXED USE COMMERCIAL COMPLEX

Presentation drawings

ARQUITECTONICA
LZM TOWER

This 80,000 square-metre tower consists of a 350-room hotel, an office building and a sunken courtyard under an elevated six-storey shopping mall.

ARTE CHARPENTIER ET ASSOCIES
MAGNOLIA PLAZA

Two 26-floor towers housing a total of 253 apartments are designed around a landscaped magnolia. In its centre, a five-star, 600-room hotel is being built in a 180-metre-high tower.

FOX & FOWLE ARCHITECTS
WAYTOFUND FINANCIAL CENTRE

This mixed-use, 125,000 square metre complex is located in downtown Shanghai, overlooking Suzhou Creek on the south, and bounded by the landmark post office building on the west. The project is set back from the south property line to form a major new urban park along Suzhou Creek, thus strengthening urban life along Shanghai's waterfront.

The project consists of four office towers rising above a four-storey podium to a height of 23 storeys off the ground. The podium contains flexibly designed retail spaces, and cultural spaces such as exhibition halls and art galleries. At the base of the four towers are located a health club, karaoke club and communal spaces. The two towers at the west and east side of the site are open-office towers, while the two central towers contain apartment/offices. There is below-grade automobile and bicycle parking.

The four towers are designed to permit maximum sunlight penetration as well as to offer optimal views of the magnificent vistas over Suzhou Creek to the Huangpu River and the Shanghai skyline beyond. At the retail base, the clear glass facing south admits welcome sunshine in winter, while abundant greenery inside and out provides shade in summer and a welcome contact with nature.

Above and opposite above: Model views showing relation to Suzhou creek
Opposite below: Site plan

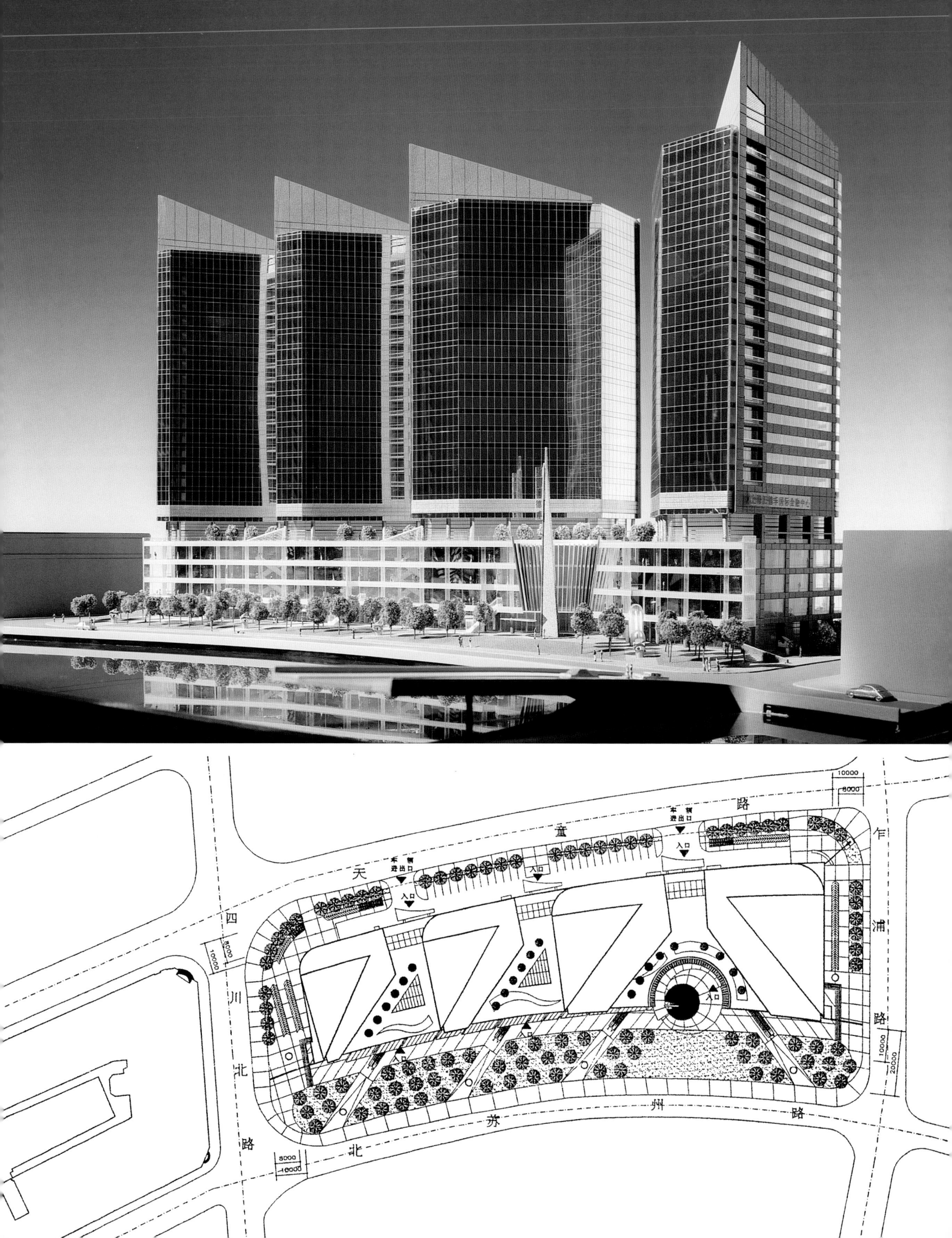

FONG & CHAN ARCHITECTS
BANK OF COMMUNICATIONS TOWER

As the city of Shanghai rapidly positions itself as an international financial centre for the 21st century, the design objective of the Bank of Communications Tower enthusiastically responds to the optimism of Shanghai with a first-class international financial tower. Through the process of creating a project of historical and farsighted significance, the design must balance the rich history of the institution with the needs of an intelligent, international multi-purpose financial office complex geared for the new century. The Bank of Communications Tower must not only meet the functional requirements of safety, organisational clarity and rental profitability, but must also respond on an aesthetic level as a beautiful object sensitively placed in Shanghai's developing financial centre. The tower must definitively balance the universal ideals of the Chinese culture with the specific history of the Bank of Communications by creating a building that both signifies the strength of the bank itself and offers a recognisable landmark for the city of Shanghai.

In an age of a cacophony of trendy architectural styles, the design seeks instead to provide an elegant financial institution by way of universal, timeless qualities and culturally specific forms. The unique characteristics of the site provided the impetus for the idea. Fronting the monumental East Pearl TV Tower, the prominent Huangpu River and the historical Bund of Shanghai, coupled with the developing Pudong Central Park to the back, the form of the tower responds by growing as it rises, creating a maximum of premium floor areas, visually accessible to these views.

In the early part of the 20th century the Bank of Communications was principally founded with the aim of consolidating the banking-related businesses for shipping, roadway, telecommunications and postal industries as its cornerstones. Responding to this established history, the design takes its inspiration from the symbol of a ship steadily sailing the seas, encountering new lands, expanding its horizons. The form of the building evokes the body of the ship on the ground levels and the sail of the ship in the tower, not only creating a beautiful profile, but also metaphorically suggesting the ever-growing prosperity of the Bank of Communications in its ascending form.

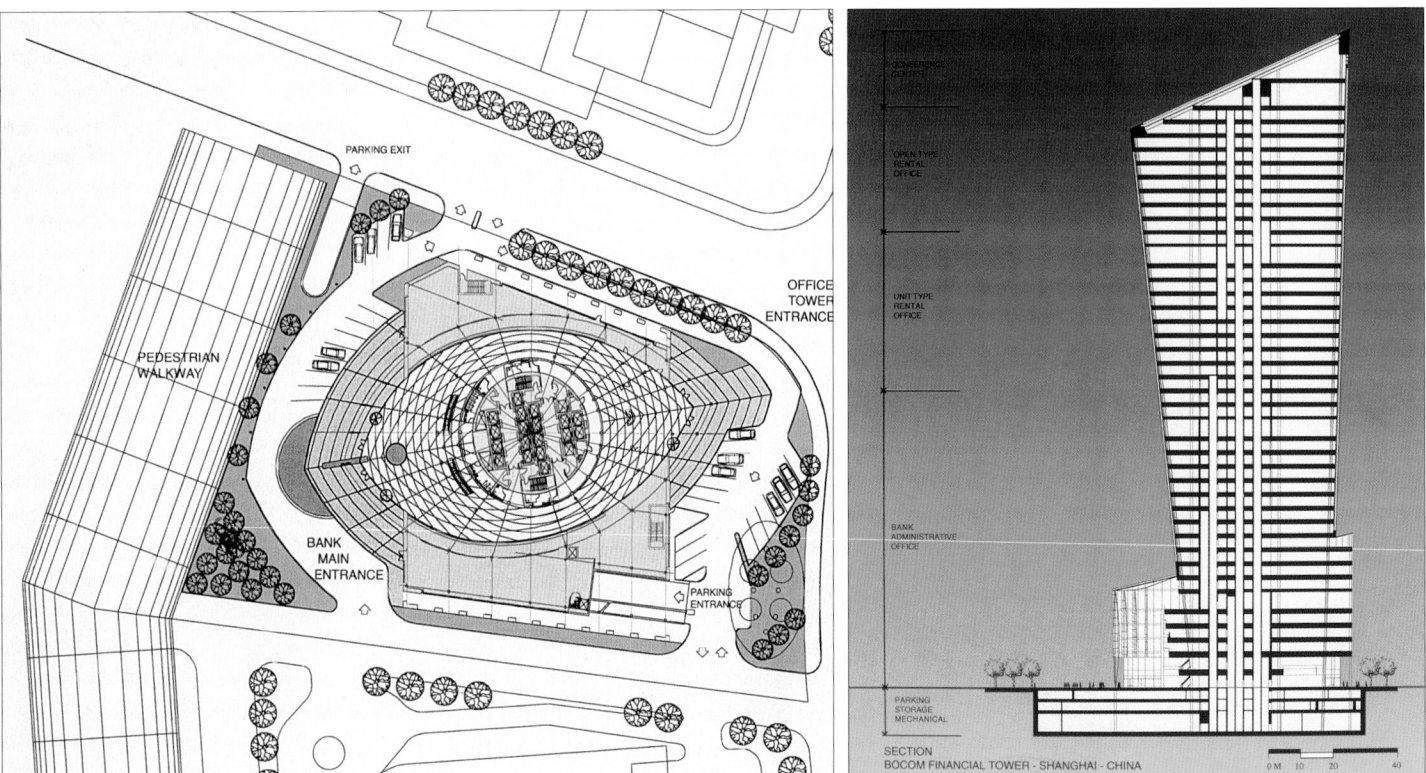

Opposite left: Site plan
Opposite right: Section
Left and above right: Model
Above: Concept sketch

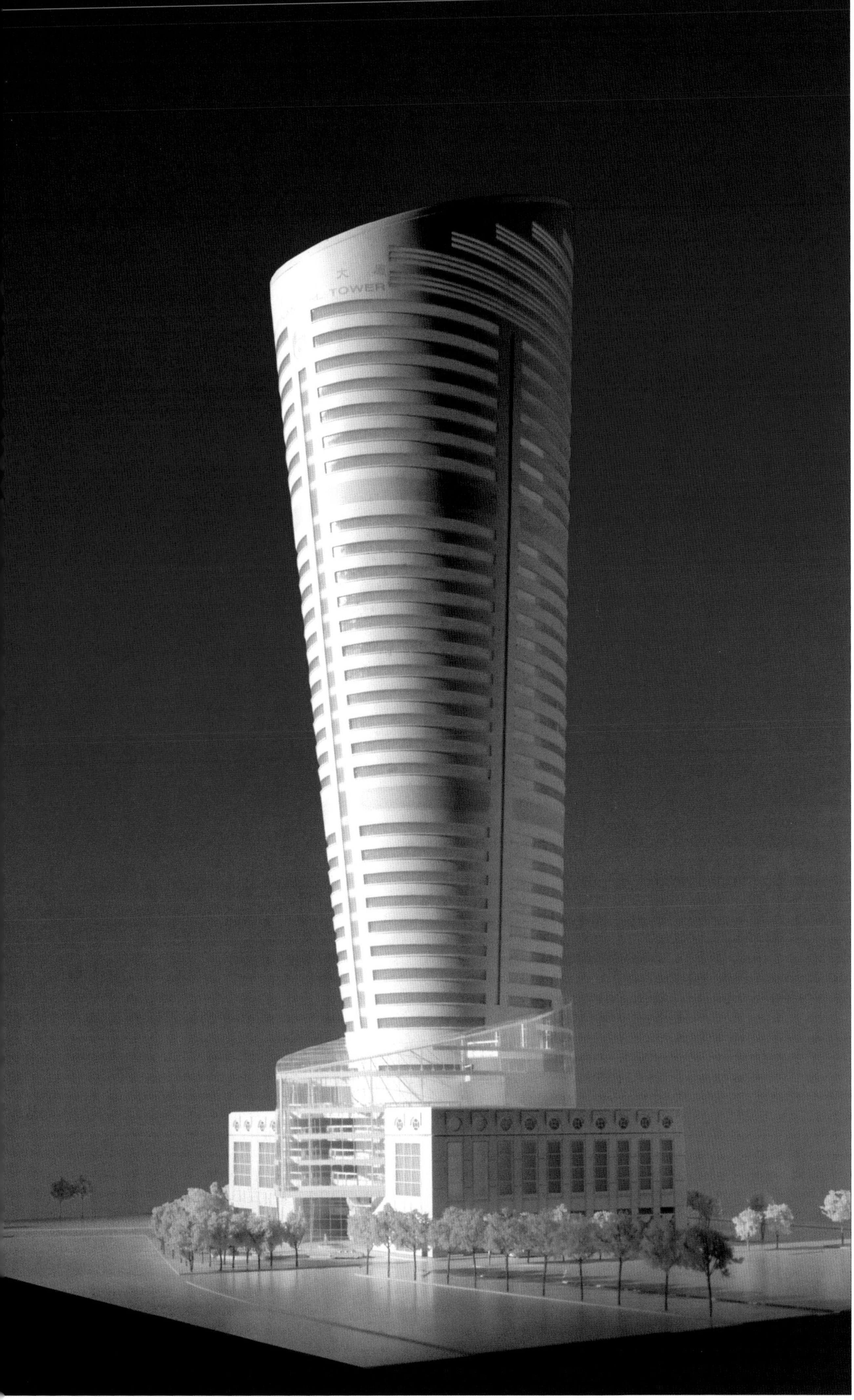

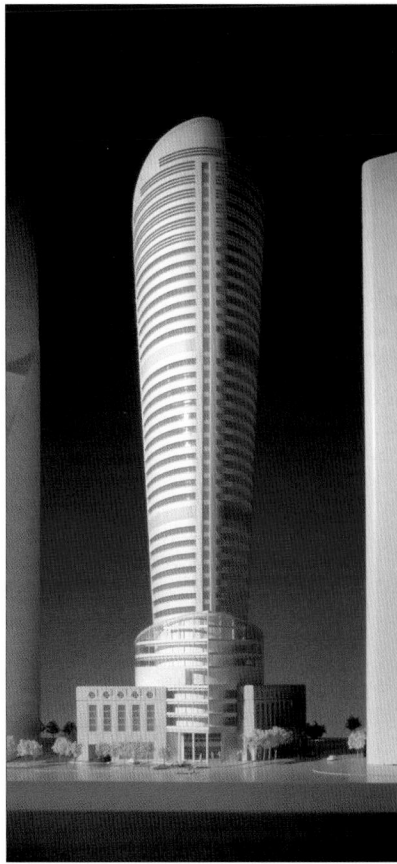

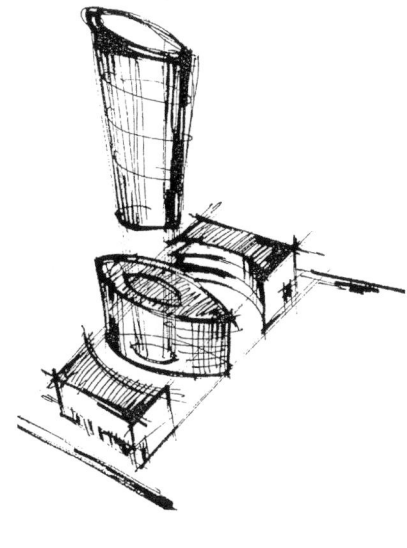

The siting of the building was influenced by a desire to provide two primary grand entrances for the bank and the office tower. To create a relationship between these two entrances and to respond to the unique characteristics of the site the building establishes a primary diagonal axis. This axis is created by orienting the building with the East Pearl TV Tower, reinforcing the strong site references and bringing order to the project. In the process of creating this strong diagonal relationship, the buildings' entrances are placed on an axis reinforcing this order.

By placing the mass of the tower in the centre of the site, routing the driveway on the northwest side and using the planned pedestrian arcade as a backdrop, a court is created for the bank, allowing the user to experience the monumental Bank of Communications on a grand scale. Contributing to this grandeur is the provision for landscaped greenbelts, water elements and a radiating paved plaza floor, allowing the pedestrian to linger comfortably in this charming plaza before entering the building.

Extending the exterior plaza into the building, the plan of the plaza and entry floor draws inspiration from the fish, a distinguished Chinese symbol of wealth and good fortune. The floor pattern and forms of the building's base abstract this symbol, adding further levels of complexity and cultural significance to the design.

Conceived as a combination of three simple geometric forms, the building is artfully composed to create two primary elements. The podium takes the two forms of the curving ship and the rectilinear base and reconciles them into one unified base element. Through sensitive attention to proportion and materials, these two forms interact to create a dynamic balance, bringing harmony and life to the building. The granite rectilinear forms of the base embrace the curve, anchoring it to the site. The curving ship form is meticulously articulated in a transparent high-tech glazing system. This has the added responsibility of acting as the transitional form from the rectilinear base to the elliptical tower.

The compound ellipse of the tower grows from the base as it ascends to the sky, providing an organic composition with the podium element. As it reaches to the sky the tower's top is articulated with a sloped, glass skylight providing a significant profile in the Shanghai skyline. At night the skylight is illuminated, presented as a jewel for the city.

The exterior form of the building achieves a rich complexity in providing an economic, bold design for the 21st century while maintaining the strong, majestic quality the Bank of Communications has proudly earned.

View of the model of the podium

In the past decade Pudong has experienced an unprecedented building boom resulting in the construction of numerous tall buildings, the most notable being the Jin Mao Tower. These buildings emulate the postmodern styles of the 1990s, a catalogue of shapes and forms that visually compete with each other.

What makes the Shanghai Bading Project interesting is that it creates the opportunity to design a building that is spatial and more open and responsive to its context and surroundings; a building that pushes the art and science of design to a new level.

The round plan is in response to the unique site on the Huangpu River and purposely takes advantage of the riverside views and views of the Bund. The lobby and executive bank floors are treated in a spatial and open manner further reinforcing the image of the tower and the Pudong skyline. The transparent glass facade bends to form the roof of the Executive Business Centre at the top of the building. The podium contains commercial and retail spaces providing necessary urban connections to the surrounding development.

The quality of the envelope of a building not only has a great deal of influence on its visual appearance, but also on the building's performance. This building uses high-performance glass to create a unique appearance and optimal performance, especially of the skin. The coating, the shades and their control, together with artificial lighting and the conditioning system, ensure that optimal conditions exist in the building's interior spaces in response to the exterior conditions.

Shanghai Bading is bold and strong in the best modernist tradition. It is contextual, responsive and functional, effective and flexible, technically innovative, ecologically responsive and pleasant and comfortable for its occupants.

The tower has a gross area of 79,465 square metres on 47 floors. Typical floors have a gross area of 1,810 square metres and are serviced by four elevator zones with three elevators each. The 11.5 metre lease space is column-free from the facade to the core. The executive bank floors on the top seven storeys are accessible by two shuttle elevators from the 4th floor and offer panoramic views to the Huangpu River. These are special places that can be developed according to a specific tenant's needs. The 46th and 47th floor Business Club serves as an amenity to the building with

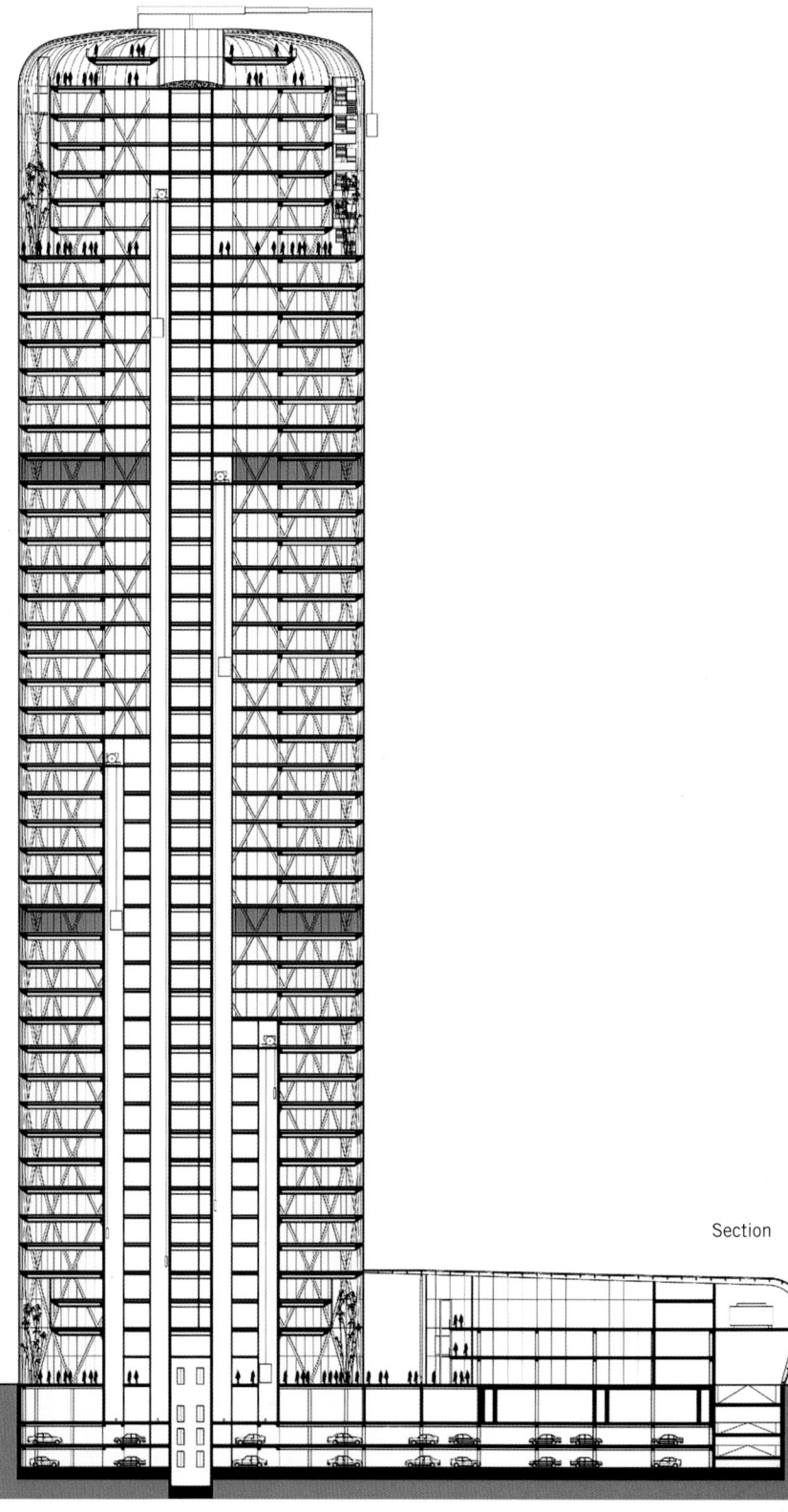

Section

meeting rooms and dining facilities. A three-storey podium of 6,423 square metres houses those public functions such as the Commercial Bank, restaurant, meeting facilities and a fitness centre. The roof of the podium is conceived as a stainless-steel shell punctuated with skylights as needed. The roof extends to form the entrance canopy and to shield the parking ramp and cooling towers. Parking for 430 cars is provided on three below-grade levels.

The facade is fully glazed with high performance, insulated glazing units, giving it a planar, tight quality, which in turn informs the building's shape. From the inside, 10 centimetre perforated blinds give an interesting modulation to the views. The detail of the slab edge is minimised. This innovation allows for more daylight in the offices as well as increased views to the outside. Clear glazing is used on the lobby and bank executive floors, reinforcing those open spaces by increasing their transparency. The support system for these facades consists of lightweight steel cables and rods.

The tower is served by 12 elevators split between four elevator zones. The Bank Executive floors and Business Club,

on floors 40 to 47, will be served by two panoramic glass elevators from the 40th floor. Two dedicated elevators serve the parking levels. Two freight elevators connect all floors. The podium building is served by two panoramic elevators and supported by two service elevators.

The structure is a steel frame with a concrete core. A unique system of interlocking diagonal columns spaced at 9 metres along the perimeter supports the floor slab, which in turn spans to the core. Stiffening, wind resistance and seismic measurements are taken by the exterior support system.

A separate study will be undertaken to determine whether it is economical for condenser water for the refrigeration machines and supplemental tenant cooling to be derived from the Huangpu River. Intake, filters and primary pumping are located in the lower levels.

The HVAC system is a displacement system supplied from a raised floor. Radiant panels are located in the ceiling in a perimeter zone at the facade. A single outdoor air supply serves individual fan rooms at every floor in order to maximise flexibility. The central plant is located in the lower levels.

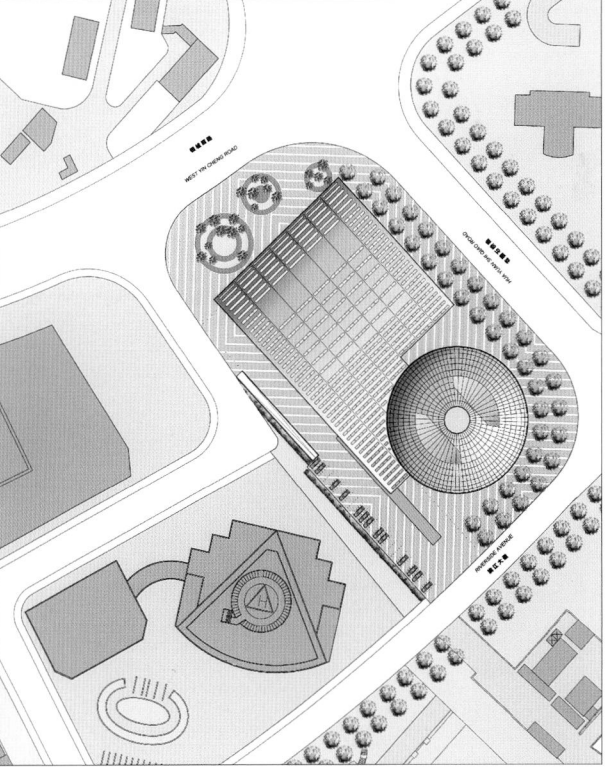

Opposite and above: The Bading office tower with the Jin Mao in the background
Above right: Site plan

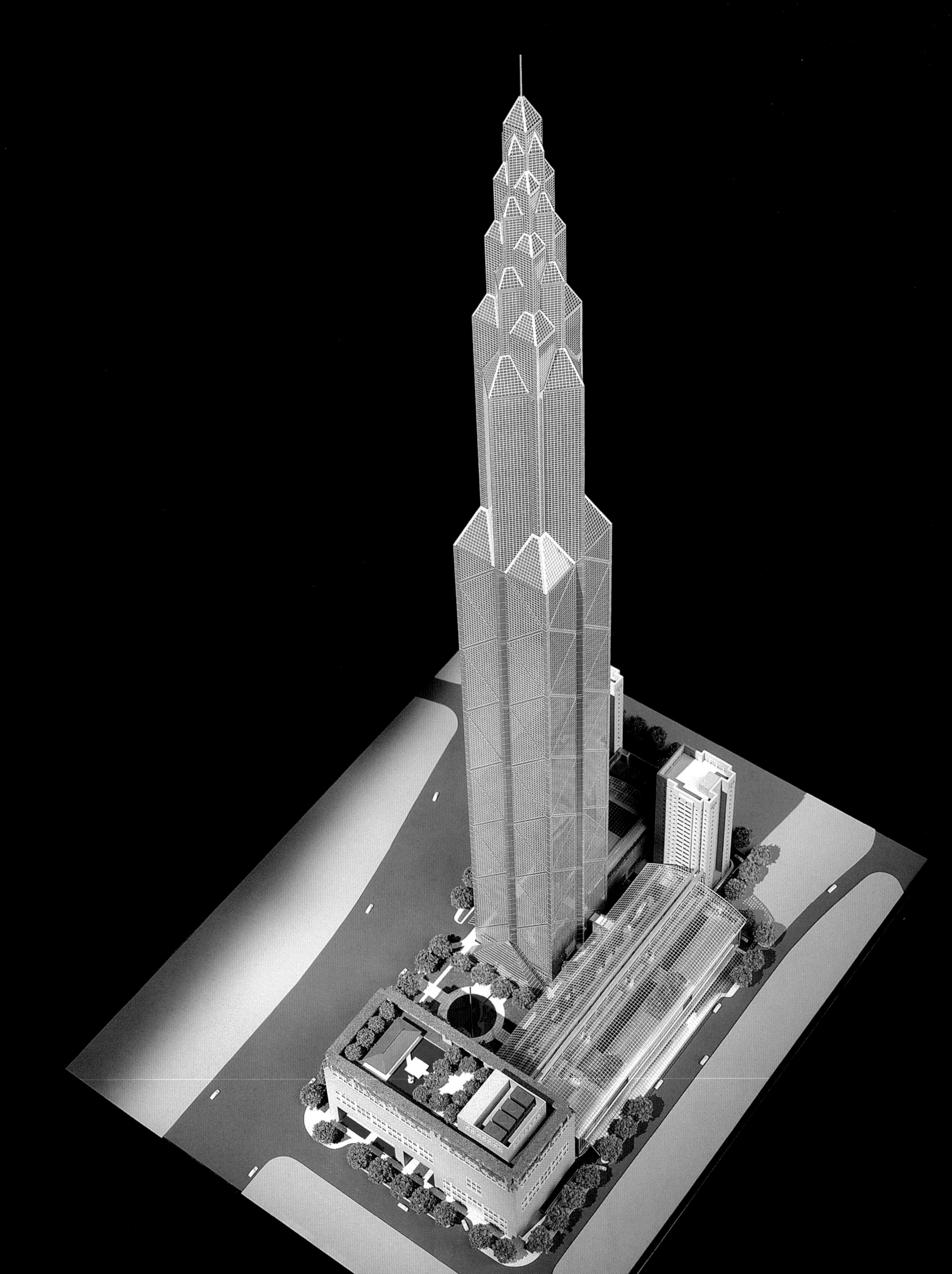

A competition heralding Daewoo's proposed presence in Shanghai resulted in this distinctive 92-storey landmark tower that was designed to symbolise the historic moment in 1992 when China opened its doors to neighbouring South Korea.

The 275,500 square metre business centre is comprised of five components: an office/hotel tower, department store, retail galleria, apartment tower and pedestrian plaza. The 420 metre tower provides offices on the first 61 levels, with a public observation level on the 62nd. The hotel is above. The metal and glass facades rise upward in a straightforward progression that marks the functions within. The dramatic tower is square shaped until it reaches the observation level, where the plan is reduced in size and rotated 45 degrees; the corners slope inward to form large glass triangles. The rotation repeats again at the 92nd level where the tower steps in to form the pinnacle in which planes of fritted glass form four large diamond shapes that encircle a 41 metre spire.

The base of the nine-storey department store embodies large showcase windows that encircle the building at street level, engaging pedestrians and animating the street scene, as does the view through the glass-clad walls of the seven-level retail galleria. The 36-storey apartment tower makes the transition in height from the soaring tower to the surrounding buildings. Its cylindrical form complements the square and triangular shapes that dominate the office/hotel tower and department store and echoes the curvilinear form of the galleria roof.

Opposite and above: Views of the model

ROBERT MATTHEW JOHNSON MARSHALL
EMPEROR STAR CITY

Emperor Star City is an ambitious multi-use complex, a joint venture proposed by Emperor Investment and many of Hong Kong's most famous entertainment personalities. The concept is similar to Planet Hollywood: entertainment endorses and adds glamour to other functions. The complex will offer multiplex cinemas, state-of-the-art electronic games centres, simulator rides, night club and karaoke lounges, ice skating, bowling and other entertainments, together with a retail mall, a variety of dining spaces, including a revolving restaurant with panoramic views and a 12-storey office tower.

RMJM was selected by invited competition, for a design combining modern international principles, exuberant contemporary Chinese style and deeper Chinese cultural references, requested by the planning authorities.

The entertainment drum at the heart of the project is topped by a shallow dome circumnavigating a large-scale media screen. The drum is surrounded by a circular shopping galleria and contained by an outer ring of buildings. The serpentine roof of the outer buildings and the domed drum evoke the metaphor of the dragon and the pearl. More importantly, the design creates a satisfying variety of spaces, both internally and externally. The massing, giving a varied and entertaining appearance from different viewpoints, positively invites one to explore.

An important consideration was the proximity of the famous and historic Yu Yuan Gardens. Terraces spiral up to the 5th level, overlooking the gardens. Emperor Star City renews Shanghai's reputation for providing all of life's pleasures.

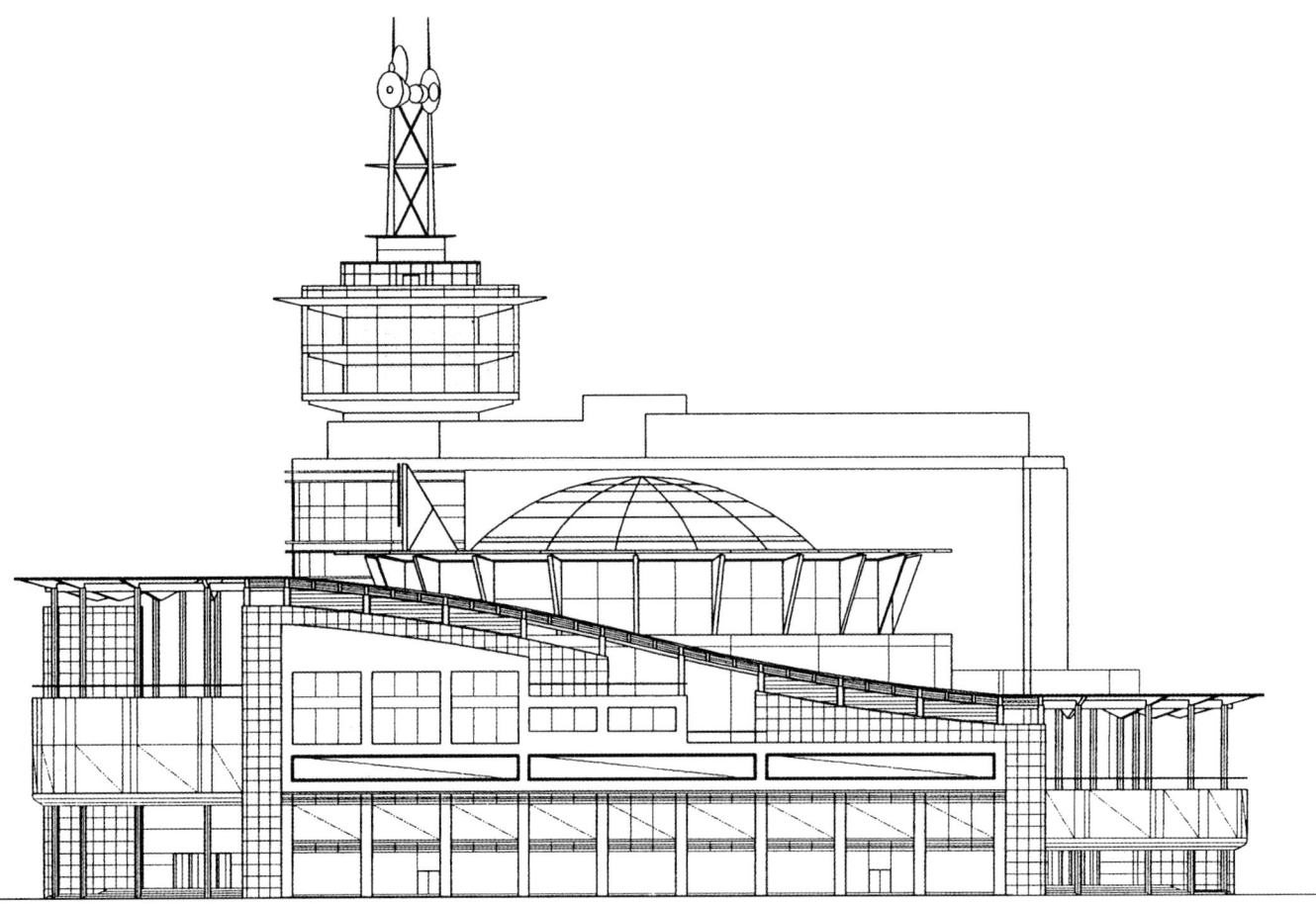

Opposite: Elevation
Above: Computer generated views

SYDNESS ARCHITECTS
SHANGHAI UNITED BANK TOWER

The Shanghai United Bank Tower stands out among the towers in the Pudong New Area. The concept for the design is based on a square plan that shifts slightly as it rises, to generate a unique and dynamic image. The underlying design concept is based on the geometric principles of a square rotating within a square.

The podium is set behind the tower, so that the tower faces the large open space at the centre of the Lujiazui Financial Area. The podium is clad in stone and glass, while the framework of the tower is made of granite to emphasise the strength of the building and the bank it represents. The panels within the frames are warm grey glass, which make up the primary facade of the building.

The main entry brings one into a large open square within the podium. This space is a grand hall that can be used as an exhibition space and display area, and is nearly 24 metres high, with a large overhead skylight. There are shops and service areas located along the two sides of this large space, which also leads into the lobby of the tower, controlled for security. The 50-storey tower becomes more slender as it rises, and as the floor areas decrease. This is an elegant design response to the programme of varied uses the bank has established.

Sydness Architects was invited to design the building as part of a design competition that included a select group of architects from around the world.

Artist's impressions of the project

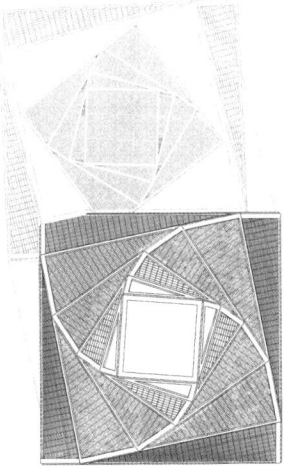

Left: The tower in context with the Shanghai World Financial Centre and the Jin Mao on the right

Above: The footprint

MURPHY / JAHN

SHANGHAI PUDONG INTERNATIONAL AIRPORT

The Shanghai Pudong International Airport is the gateway to Shanghai and one of the major gateway airports to China. As an important hub for international air traffic in the Asia Pacific Region, it must process and accommodate the efficient and economic movement of passengers, aircraft, baggage, cargo and vehicles.

The terminal building is oriented along the north-south axis of the site, the axis of passenger movement. Two separate roadway systems are provided, one for domestic and one for international traffic. The terminal operates as two buildings in one. The domestic side has its own curb-front, ticketing, baggage reclaim and baggage sort. From the standpoint of the 70 million passengers, this is completely separate from the international side, which has its own unique functions. Yet to transfer from domestic to international or vice versa one has merely to cross over to the other side of the building. This scheme has all the functional advantages of separate buildings such as better passenger orientation, more distinct and direct circulation, whilst having the operation advantages of a single build-ing: shared mechanical systems, support functions, staffing, and so on.

The ticketing and baggage reclaim areas will expand to the north as additional concourses are added to the south. The first phase is compact and efficient, with international gates located at the concourse adjacent to the terminal and domestic gates located at the first remote concourse. The concourse is connected to the terminal by a passenger pedestrian tunnel, a tunnel for a future people mover, and a baggage/utility tunnel.

This master plan is the most efficient and most appropriate for the Shanghai Pudong International Airport. Most European airports, and most other Asian airports, have predominantly international traffic. Hong Kong and Macau, for example, are international, while Bangkok and Seoul do not have nearly as much domestic traffic as Shanghai Pudong. Airports in the United States have predominantly domestic traffic. The Shanghai Pudong Airport has a more balanced distribution. This plan best reflects its dual role as both domestic and international hub.

Below: The central terminal
Bottom: Concourses
Opposite above: Junction between terminal and concourse
Opposite below: Overview of the terminal with concourse at the top

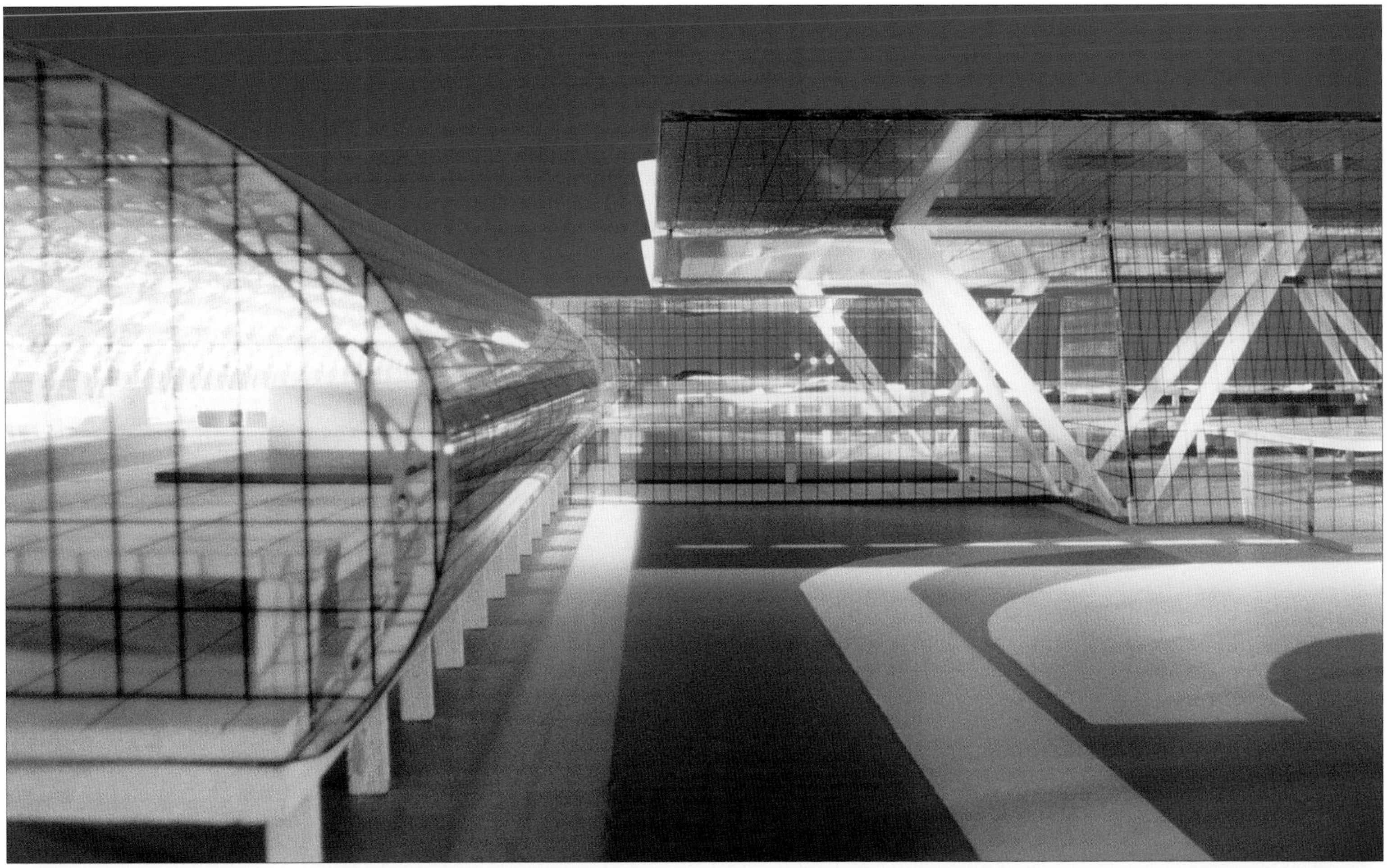

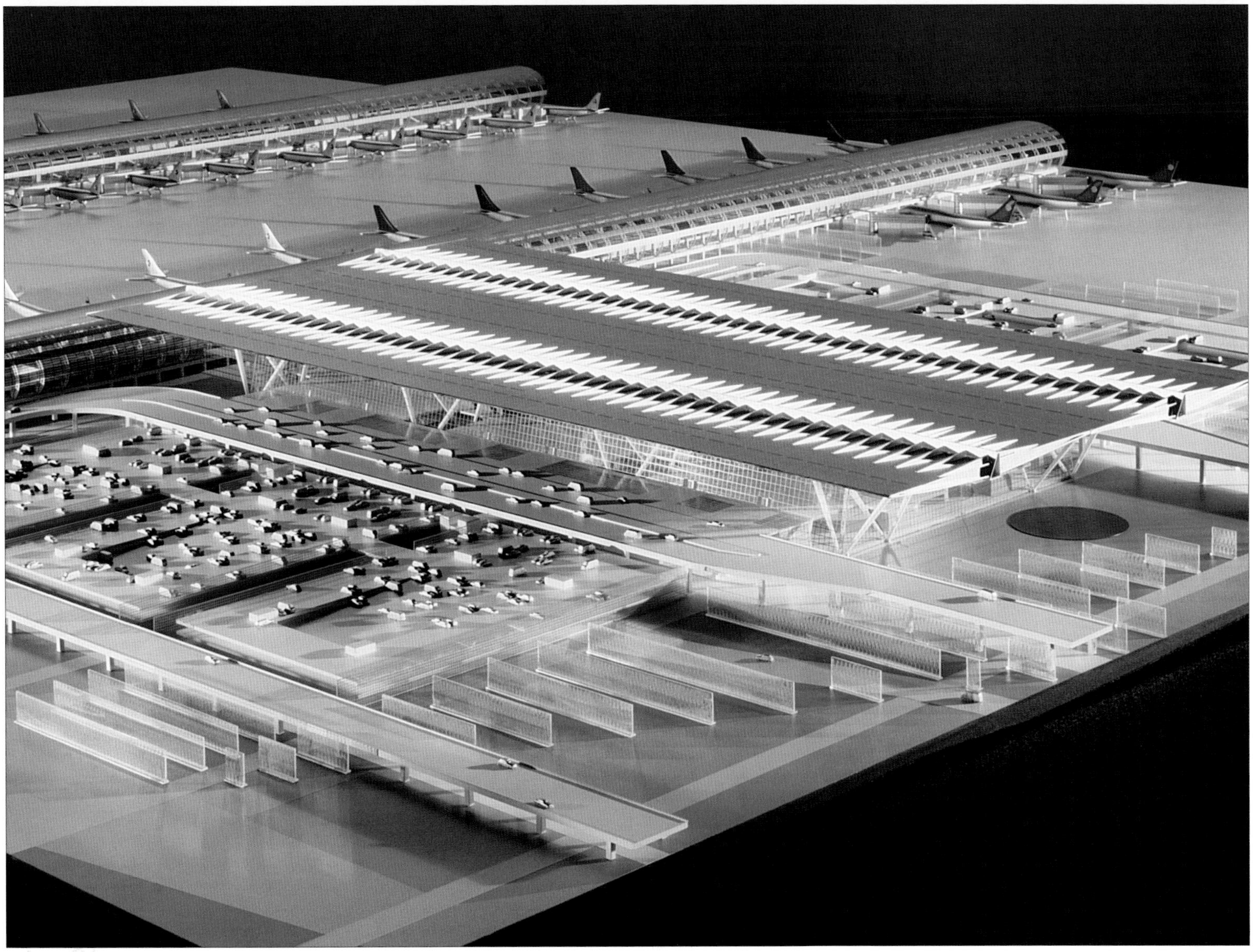

Above: Inside the concourse
Below: The terminal
Opposite: Terminal

PUDONG

Competition entries for the master plan
of the redevelopment of Pudong

Right: Lord Richard Rogers
Below: Massimiliano Fuksas
Opposite top: Dominique Perrault
Opposite bottom: Toyo Ito

SHANGHAI OPERA HOUSE

Selected entries from the competition for the design of Shanghai Opera House

Above left: ECADI
Above right: Zeidler
Below left: Wong Gregersen Architects
Below right: Charles Moore
Opposite above: Nikken Sekkei
Opposite below: Harry Goleman and Mario Bolullo

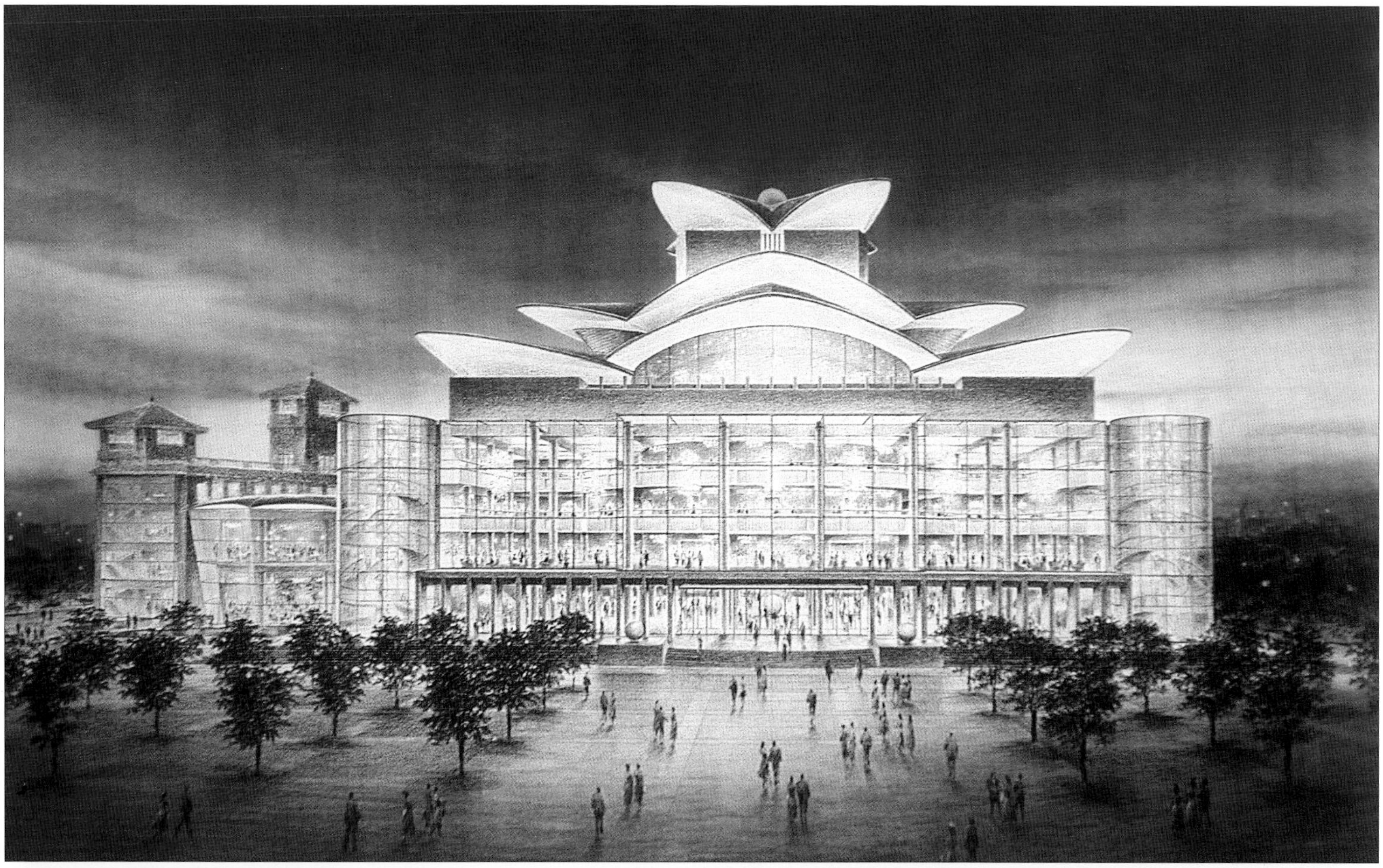

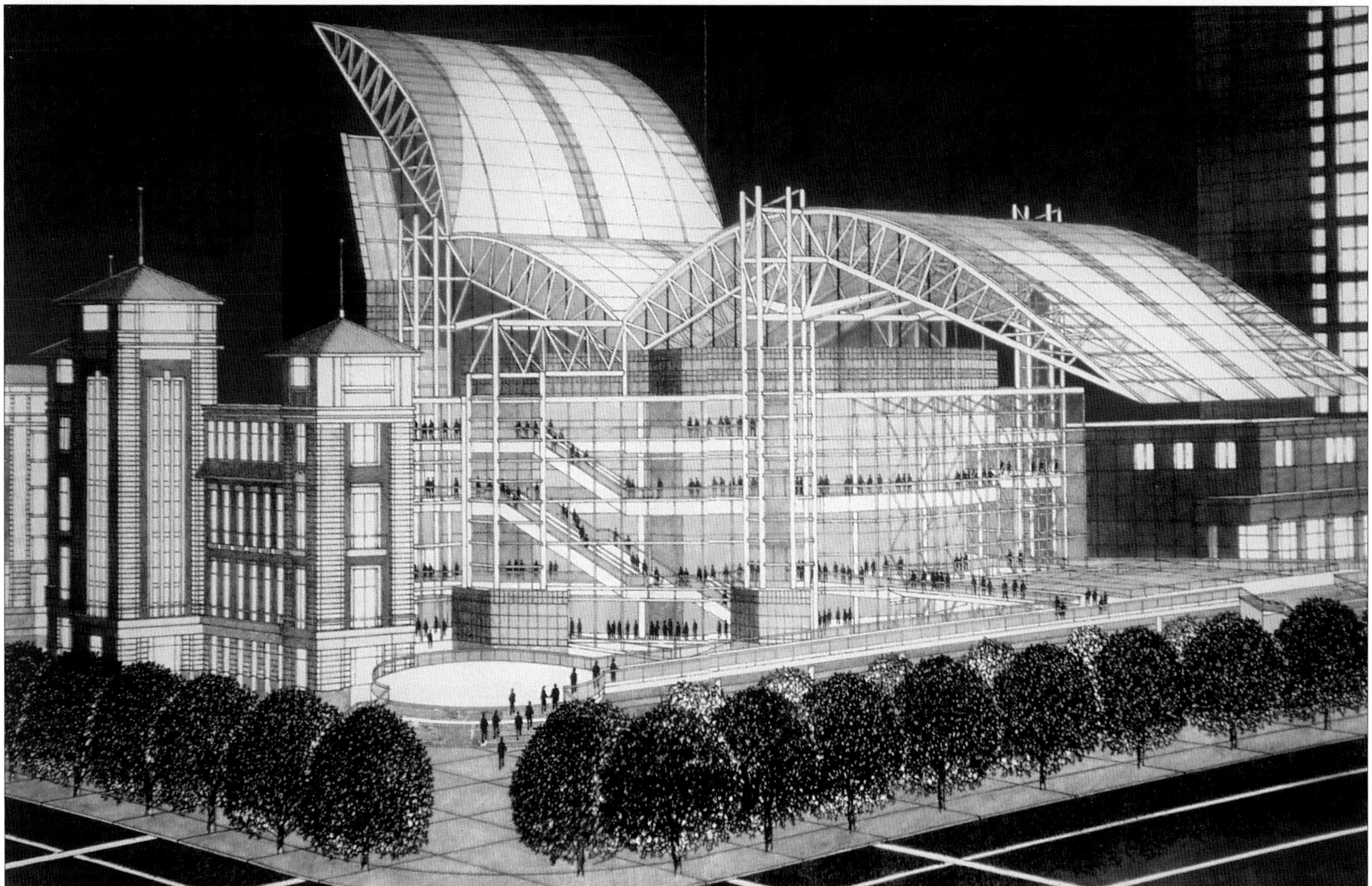

Opposite above: Nihon Sekkei
Opposite below: Bochsler
Above left: Ekon Enterprises
Above right: Annau Associates Architects
Below left: Great March
Below right: Shanghai Architectural Design and Research Institute

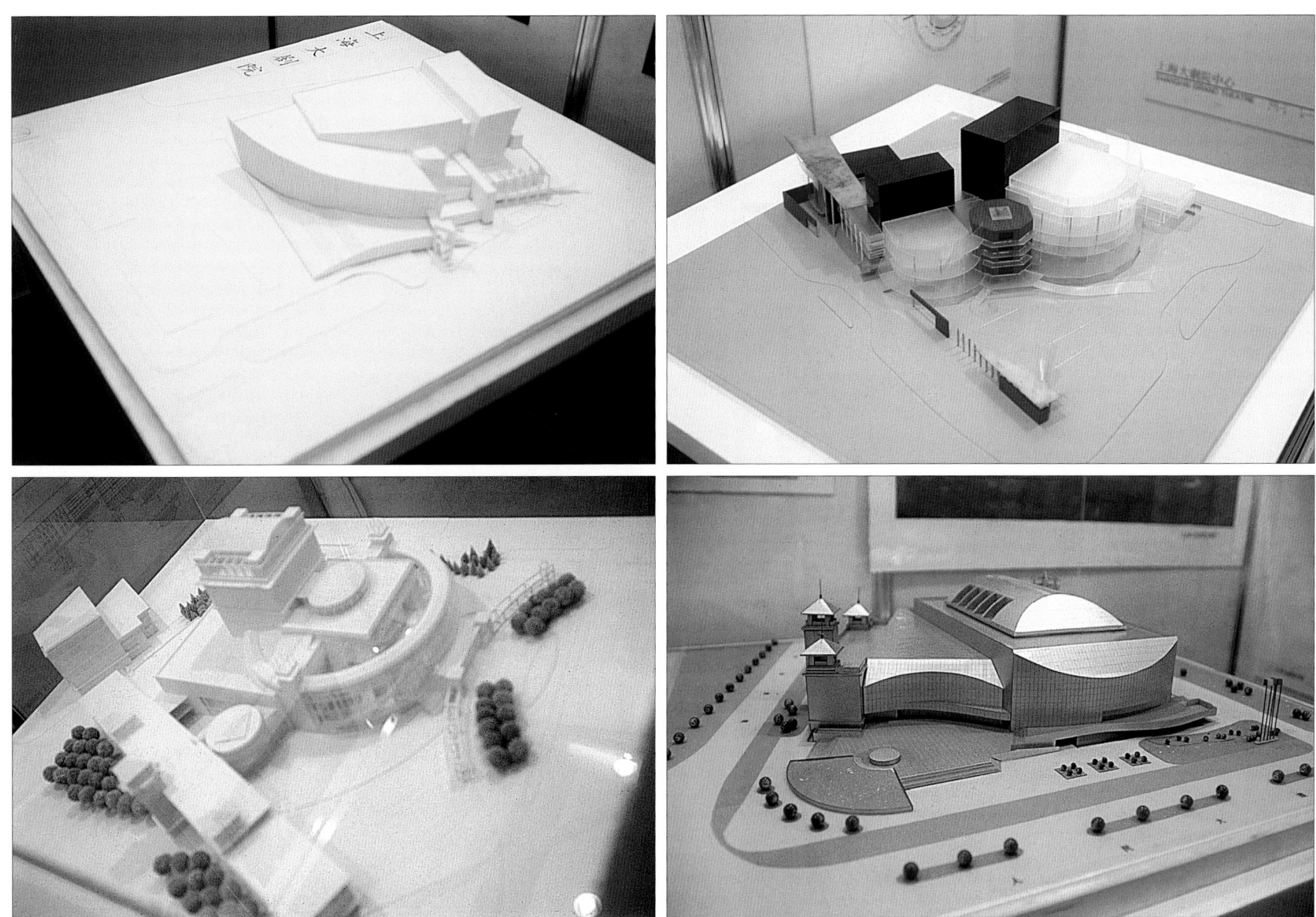

剧
院

GREEN FIELD AND LANE – EXPERIMENTAL HOUSING

Selected entries for the competition to develop new forms of housing to replace the *li long*

Right: Zhu Wenyi
Below: Obermeyer

Selected competition entries for Scienceland, Shanghai's Museum of Science and Technology

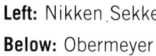
Left: Nikken Sekkei
Below: Obermeyer

Above: Shanghai Architectural Design and Research Institute
Below: East China Architectural Design Institute

SHANGHAI INTERNATIONAL PASSENGER TERMINAL

Selected competition entries

Right: Nikken Sekkei; interior
Below: Nikken Sekkei; general view
Opposite: Carlos Ott and Associates

SOUTH RAILWAY STATION
Selected competition entries

Right: Third Survey and Design Institute
Below: Hangzhou Architectural Design Institute
Opposite above: GMP
Opposite below: East China Architectural Design Institute

PLANNING

1 **Arte Charpentier et Associes** Century Avenue
2 **Arte Charpentier et Associes** Nanjing Road
3 **Arte Charpentier et Associes** Wanli
4 **Hellmuth, Obata + Kassabaum** Huangpu District Development
5 **Lu Jiwei, with Gu Ruzhen, Sun Guanglin, Zhang Bing** Jing-an Temple Plaza
6 **Anshen + Allen** Aetna School of Management
7 **Arte Charpentier et Associes** Shanghai Opera House
8 **NBBJ** Ing Chang-Ki Goe School
9 **NBBJ** Shanghai American School
10 **Pei Cobb Freed & Partners** China-Europe International Business School
11 **RTKL** Shanghai Scienceland
12 **Shanghai Architectural Design and Research Institute,**
   Zhang Jie-zheng, Tang Yu-en Shanghai Library
13 **Shanghai Modern Architectural Design Group (Ling Benli, Tang Lin,**
   Zhang Chi) Shanghai Urban Planning Exhibition Hall
14 **Xing Tonghe and the Shanghai Architectural Design Institute**
   Shanghai Museum

INSTITUTIONAL

15 **Anshen + Allen** Shanghai Far-East International Building
16 **Arquitectonica** Shanghai Information Tower
17 **Foster & Partners** Jiushi Corporation Headquarters
18 **Fox & Fowle Architects** Industrial and Commercial Bank of China
   Headquarters
19 **Kohn Pedersen Fox Associates** Plaza 66
20 **Murphy / Jahn** Shanghai International Expo Centre
21 **Pei Cobb Freed & Partners** Pos Plaza
22 **John Portman & Associates** Bank of Communications
23 **John Portman & Associates** Shanghai Centre
24 **John Portman & Associates** Tomorrow Square
25 **Nikken Sekkei** Pudong International Finance Building
26 **Simon Kwan & Associates** China Merchant's Tower
27 **Simon Kwan & Associates** Shanghai Plaza
28 **Skidmore, Owings & Merrill** Jin Mao Tower
29 **Taoho Design Architects** King Tower
30 **Wong & Ouyang** Kerry Everbright City
31 **Wong & Ouyang** Everbright City
32 **Wong & Ouyang** San Feng Centre
33 **Wong & Ouyang** Shanghai Times Square

COMMERCIAL

34 **Shanghai ZhongFang Architectural Design Institute**
   Housing Project for Ping-Yang Village
35 **Taoho Design Architects** Colourful (Wanzhao) Homestead
36 **Taoho Design Architects** Vanke Waltz Gardens

TRANSPORT

37 **Paul Andreu** Shanghai Pudong International Airport

 Built up area		Other roads
③ Site locations		Water
Elevated roads		·········· Ferry Crossings
Main roads		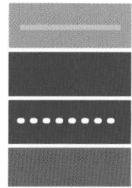 Parks

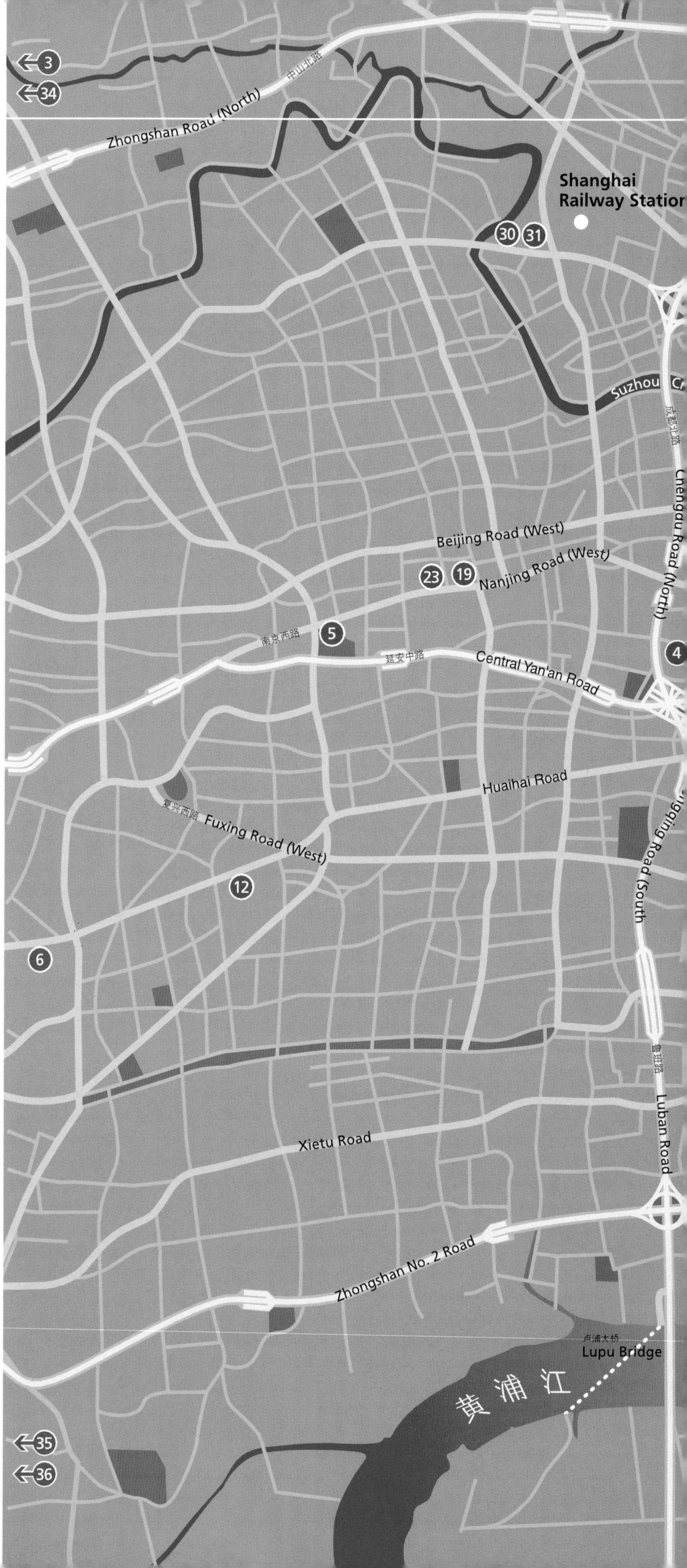

SHANGHAI BUILDS

Beijing Road (East)　北京东路

㉔

Nanjing Road (East)　南京东路

⑧ ②

人民公园
People's Park

⑬

People's Square

⑭ 人民广场

㉝

豫园
Yu Yuan Gardens

OLD CITY

Central Fuxing Road

Fuxing Road (East)

㉒

⑰

③②

● Oriental Pearl
TV tower

㉕

PUDONG

㉘

㉖

①

⑱

㉙

⑩

Lujiazui Financial and Trade Zone

世纪大道

Century Avenue

㉗

⑨

⑮

㉑

⑯

⑪

Pudong Road (South)　浦东南路

世纪公园

Century Park

Zhongshan No. 1 Road

Huangpu River

Longyang Road

龙阳路

⑳

㊲

Ningguo Road

PLANNING

1   **Skidmore, Owings & Merrill** Shanghai Waterfront Redevelopment Master Plan

INSTITUTIONAL

2   **Michael Graves & Associates** Shanghai Bund Arts Centre
3   **Shanghai ZhongFang Architectural Design Institute** Medical School

COMMERCIAL

4   **Ashen + Allen** Shanghai WayToFund International Finance Centre
5   **Michael Graves & Associates** Fujian Xingye Banking Tower
6   **The Jerde Partnership International** JoinBuy City Plaza
7   **The Jerde Partnership international** Super Brand Mall
8   **Kaplan McLaughlin Diaz** Shanghai International Business Centre
9   **Kaplan McLaughlin Diaz** Shanghai International Plaza
10 **Kohn Pedersen Fox Associates** Shanghai World Financial Centre
11 **Murphy / Jahn** 21st Century Tower
12 **NBBJ** Fuxing Mansion
13 **John Portman & Associates** New Ci Hou Plaza
14 **Sydness Architects** Bading Development Finance Mansion
15 **Sydness Architects** Lujiazui Itochu Development Building

RESIDENTIAL

16 **NBBJ** Yanlord Lian Yang Gardens
17 **Shanghai ZhongFang Architectural Design Institute**
    Yong-Ye Apartment Building
18 **Taoho Design Architects** Bai Hui Gardens

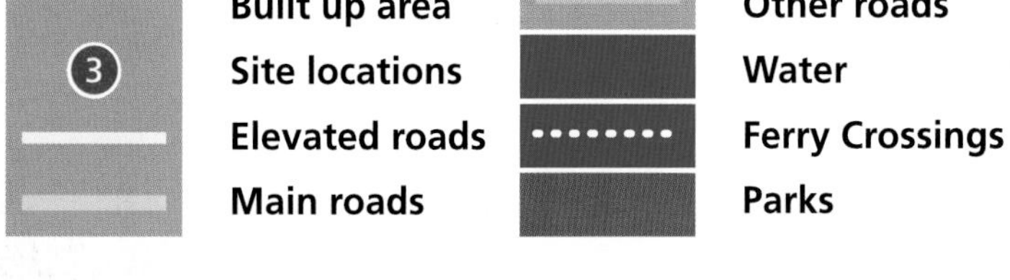

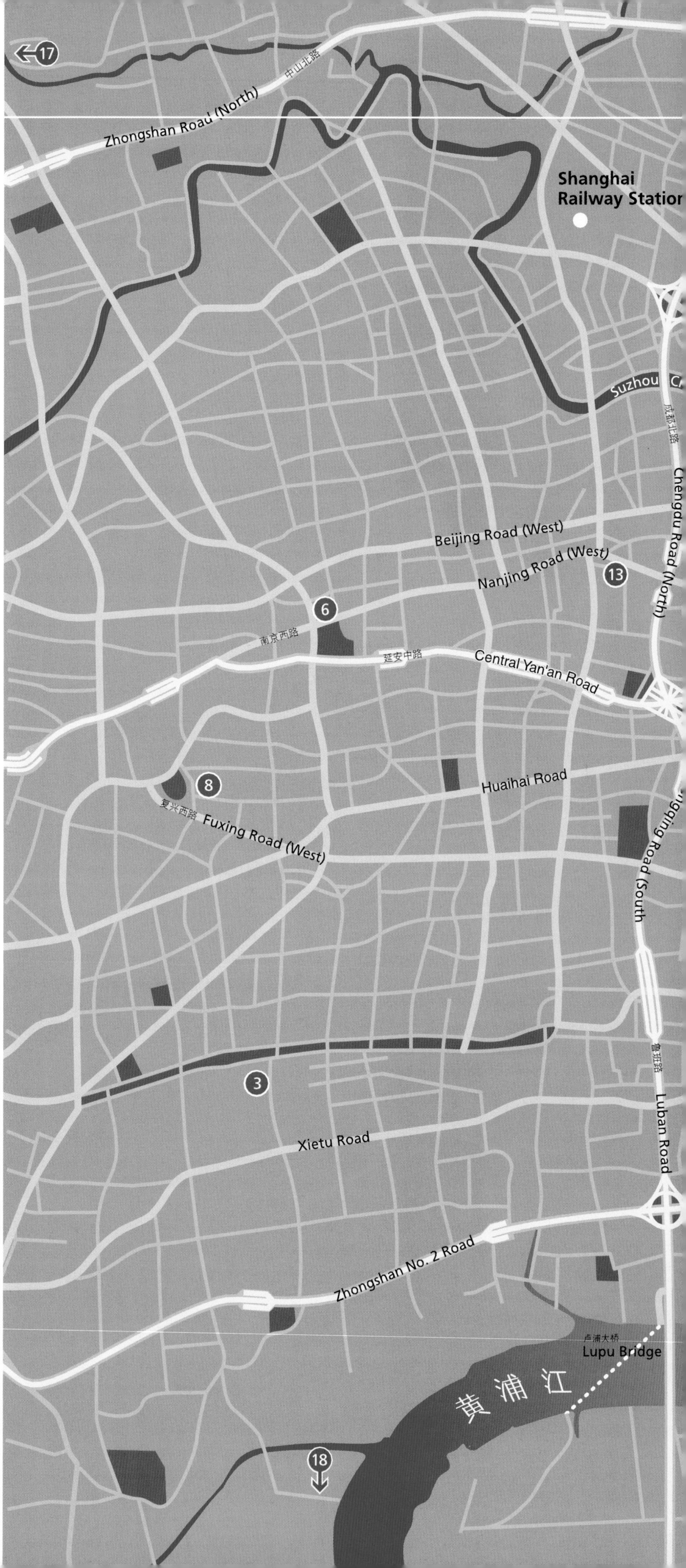

	Built up area		Other roads
	Site locations		Water
	Elevated roads	·········	Ferry Crossings
	Main roads		Parks

Zhongshan Road (North)

中山北路

Shanghai
Railway Station

Suzhou C

Chengdu Road (North)

Beijing Road (West)

Nanjing Road (West)

6

13

南京西路

延安中路

Central Yan'an Road

8

夏兴西路 Fuxing Road (West)

Huaihai Road

Qinqing Road (South

3

Xietu Road

Luban Road

Zhongshan No. 2 Road

卢浦大桥
Lupu Bridge

黄浦江

18

Beijing Road (East) 北京东路

Nanjing Road (East) 南京东路

人民公园
People's Park

People's Square
人民广场

豫园
Yu Yuan Gardens

OLD CITY

Central Fuxing Road   Fuxing Road (East)

○ Oriental Pearl
TV tower

PUDONG

Lujiazui Financial and Trade Zone

世纪大道

Century Avenue

Pudong Road (South) 浦东南路

世纪公园

Century Park

Huangpu River

Longyang Road 龙阳路

Ningguo Road

View toward Nanjing Road and the new pavilions marking the entrance to the Jing'an Temple
seen through the wall of advertising that encloses its western edge.

EPILOGUE

ALAN BALFOUR

COMMUNISM AND CONSUMERISM

Chinese society has no real equivalent in Western civic life. It is a society rooted in and structured by the family. Yet every morning, many thousands gather on the Bund, and in People's Square, dancing and exercising in good-natured groups that have come together naturally, by age and interest, not by neighbourhood, clan or class. They begin at 6.00 am, their participants often travelling some distance to be there. This is a relatively new phenomenon, emerging only in the late 1980s, but it is a distinctly Shanghainese experience. In every other respect, the city's gain in affluence has been matched with a loss of character.

The fabric of physical reality is akin to language – in texture, order and structure, and in the ability to convey meaning and emotion. The physical reality of China previously remained unchanged for centuries, sustaining the strengths and weaknesses of a highly conservative imperial society. Everything had its place and every place had its precise limitations. However, Shanghai has always been a commercial culture, and even the earliest surviving photographs from well over 100 years ago are dominated by advertising. The major distortion in returning the city to a commercial reality after 40 years of socialist austerity has been the overwhelming power of the propaganda of international consumerism. For half a century European Shanghai had cultivated a taste for international consumer goods and Shanghai had come to claim a place in the world as a major centre of production. But in the return to a consumer society, the mixed realities of Shanghai – a faded Westernism and earnest but mean structures of socialism – were no match for the overwhelming force of world commercial reality. The physical realities of a society driven by consumerism and the illusion that sustains it vulgarises all values. The cynical could see in this a continuing pattern over the last 200 years: the manipulation of the mass population's desires, first through the stimulus of opium, then through modernism, then Marxism, and into the present. Assuaging the emotional limitations of an ideological reality, the dictatorship of the state decides to coat the revolution in the multiple veneers of American consumerism. Even at its most authoritarian, Marxist society never had propaganda tools as extensive and precisely constructed as those developed by Coca-Cola and McDonald's et al. Conversely, the global lifestyle producers have never had a more compliant audience and enthusiastic government on which to work. (In a culture celebrated for the subtlety of its food, there is something demeaning in the success of the fast-food chains. In the same week that businessmen and women were invited to join the CCP, McDonald's won the nation's attention by offering 10-cent ice-cream cones, creating queues around the block in city after city.) Watching the relationship develop over the last decade from one of wary scepticism on both sides to the present wholehearted co-operation, one could imagine a time in the not-too-distant future when the lifestyle producers might begin secretly to encourage the administration in Washington to see the benefits of state control – not of industry but of the people – it makes consuming and wealth creation so much easier.

Nowhere in Shanghai is there evidence among the planners, architects and engineers of a conception of a reality unique to Shanghai; a reality able to enlarge and ennoble the distinct character of the culture. Charting the way in which the city transforms and renews itself is at its most complex in Shanghai, distorted by both European mercantilism and Marxist ideology. What context can the imagination now find to establish the form of its future? At present the culture producers seem only to be able to imagine the future in terms of international symbols of power and the trappings of American-driven world consumerism.

It is difficult to explain how a culture that is fiercely proud of its history and of its uniqueness can destroy almost every vestige of historical Shanghai, while listing as significant monuments to be preserved more than 390 faded buildings from the international settlement; a situation that is as absurd as it is disturbing. The systematic destruction in the last five years of the streets and shop houses of the old city that sat within the walls could be justified as necessary renewal, but the housing and office buildings that are being rushed out on the cleared land are unrelated to any idea of city or community. While the poor are being removed to the edges of the city, the wealthy are restructuring the centre. The most extravagant example, an apartment complex at the very heart of the old city, is marked by a great neon sign atop a grand classical colonnade, proclaiming in English, 'Sun Wonderland'. From the grandiose gateways and fountains to the rows of Roman-inspired figures that surround the base, nothing about this building would be out of place in Las Vegas. It sits within yards of the bustling, socially mixed streets of the old town, yet it will serve only the very rich, physically constructing class divisions, which were never so reinforced in the Chinese city's past. The city's culture cannot help but reflect the utter confusion of realities that politicians and the market have spawned in the last decade. This has created a consuming desire for simplistic dreams, for prestige and identity, established by the most crass products of American consumerism. It is a withdrawal from a sensual view of existence, trivialising culture and family, and eroding cultural identity.

This new reality seems driven solely by the images cultivated by consumerism. There is an overwhelming influence of simplistic bourgeois values and manners. Along the highways that snake through the city, all the apartment buildings from the 1970s and 1980s are being given red-tiled pitched roofs, and a variety of little ornamental dormer windows. This is only applied to the buildings that can be seen from the highway – the intention is to sweeten the public view.

The great Buddhist Temple, Jing'an on Bubbling Well Road, founded in 1008 and rebuilt over many years in a consistently modest style, has become very wealthy in the last decade, a direct product of the prosperous Shanghai. A visit in the summer of 2001 found the temple half destroyed in the middle of a complex process of rebuilding. This will be in a form wholly unrelated to its roots. Instead, the temple leaders have chosen to create a powerful public monument using devices from the imperial religious structures of northern China; a choice intended to impress rather than to sustain the historical richness of place.

The most peculiar and extravagant example of this madness is in Ming Hang, described by Edgar Snow as one of the 14 political districts that make up Shanghai and one of five created by the socialist administration as self-contained industrial communities. It remains a remote suburb far to the west of the city. The central area is still basic, except for a large floral clock as the main road enters the town centre. Just beyond the 1970s housing, the hotel and the community shops, are the new district law courts. Each political subdivision has the authority to build as it wishes and the judiciary of Ming Hang has chosen to be housed in a two-thirds scale replica of the US Capitol. Apart from the French-style dormers, it is all colonnades and wings and *folie de grandeur* beneath its dome. Unless one commits a crime it is impossible to enter, so who knows what is on the inside? What was in their minds? 'Create the illusion of a great symbol of democracy and somehow democracy will follow'? 'Build something sufficiently strange that will put this little town on the map'? Or is it just another easy image of consumable power and prestige and, like so much of the renewed city, a simulacrum of reality?

Shanghai is a city out of balance. That most ancient pursuit of the Chinese – continually adjusting forces to find a sympathetic relationship between the *yin* and the *yang* – is so far unresolved as the country transforms. One might claim that the male element is far too prevalent, because of the testosterone of American consumerism, and some profound adjustment in the culture is urgently needed to resurrect the feminine in the fabric of the city.

Such spectacular growth and cultural transformation cannot avoid instability and corruption. In the summer of 2001 the drug Ecstasy flooded into the dance clubs. The drug was popular among the wealthier elements of Shanghai youth, but its consumption was largely driven by young Australians and some Americans. The authoritarian power of the city was quickly in evidence, as the police moved to arrest those suspected of being high; the inability to stop dancing was the measure. Within a week, all the dance clubs had become bars and the young Shanghainese stayed at home.

There is as yet no ideological resolution of the relationship between the ideals of socialism and the manipulations of a consumer-driven society. My visit to Ming Hang was on a day in July 2001 when, for the first time, business people were allowed to become members of the Communist Party. Since the Revolution, the evil for Communism was

capitalism, and the agents of capitalism were the businessmen who manipulated the economy to exploit and subject the population to profit-centred ambition. Yet there are many who believe that the economic arrangements that have driven the spectacular development of Shanghai have all the characteristics of a financial bubble – banks lend to projects that produce no revenue, projects sit empty, banks continue to lend because politicians want visible results, and no one can afford to admit failure. It is a bubble that will burst.

When, over time, Shanghai is able to evolve and define its own reality, its own instruments, its own structures, and apply them with a management equal to its resurrection in the last decade of the 20th century, the Great Model will become nothing more than a historical curiosity, a reflection of the dangers of being seduced again by the Western illusion of progress. And even if the city is unable to escape the seduction of the West, unable to fulfil such unreasonable dreams, the result will not be failure. Throughout its history, this has been a city of wily pragmatism. Apart from the wall built against pirates in the 16th century, the Great Model represents the first attempt to constrain its natural evolution by large-scale planning. So if the economy fails to create the wealth promised, if few can afford the cars, villas, and the corruption needed to construct the modelled reality, 20 million people still need to eat, sleep and make love, to find work. And the mass population of this expedient and disciplined city will create new forms of manufacturing, new kinds of businesses, new communities in their own terms and appropriate them to their own dreams.

Colleagues in Shanghai argue that recent consumerism is a minor part of a revolution that has restored the value of human life, and respect for and readoption of metaphysical forces in Chinese culture. As the ideo-logy of extreme conservatism, which so constrained political and social life over the last 250 years, Confucianism must share some of the blame for the collapse of the empire and the chaos that followed. However, scholars argue that the legalism and authoritarianism of Han Feizi bore greater responsibility, particularly after the end of the Qing Dynasty. They argue the need for a new Hundred Schools of Thought and the emergence of another Spring and Autumn Period (772–481 BC), a time in which a unified and confident China was able to create new ideas and new philosophies that would influence the world over the next 2,000 years.

In an absolute sense, planning for the future of Shanghai demands nothing more than that which has determined its character for almost 1,000 years; the future is laid out as a pragmatic rationally ordered field dedicated above all else to trade, industry and commerce. Over the last 150 years the people of Shanghai have demonstrated exceptional resilience. They have adjusted to continually changing political and physical environments without losing any of their energy or ambition. The reality of the future Shanghai lies much more in the character of its people than in the visions of planners and architects.

One must not judge this process too soon. It will take several generations to find a match between the output of mass production and the deep poetic desires of the vast, brilliant, selfish population. And when this happens it will be the product not of Chinese labour but of Chinese desire, and it will compel the world.

TABLE OF CHINESE DYNASTIES

c. 2000–1500 BC	Xia	夏	534–549	Eastern Wei	東魏
1700–1027 BC	Shang	商	535–557	Western Wei	西魏
1027–771 BC	Western Zhou	西周	550–577	Northern Qi	北齊
770–221 BC	Eastern Zhou	東周	557–588	Northern Zhou	北周
770–476 BC	Spring and Autumn period	春秋時代	581–617	Sui	隋
475–221 BC	Warring States period	戰國時代	618–907	Tang	唐
221–207 BC	Qin	秦	907–960	Five Dynasties	五代
206 BC–AD 9	Western Han	西漢	907–923	Later Liang	後梁
AD 9–24	Xin (Wang Mang interregnum)	新	923–936	Later Tang	後唐
25–220	Eastern Han	東漢	936–946	Later Jin	後晉
220–280	Three Kingdoms	三國	947–950	Later Han	後漢
220–265	Wei	魏	951–960	Later Zhou	後周
221–263	Shu	蜀	907–979	Ten Kingdoms	十國
229–280	Wu	吳	960–1279	Sung	宋
265–316	Western Jin	西晉	960–1127	Northern Sung	北宋
317–420	Eastern Jin	東晉	1127–1279	Southern Sung	南宋
420–588	Southern and Northern Dynasties	南北朝	916–1125	Liao	遼
420–588	Southern Dynasties	南朝	1038–1227	Western Xia	西夏
420–478	Song	宋	1115–1234	Jin	金
479–501	Qi	齊	1279–1368	Yuan	元
502–556	Liang	梁	1368–1644	Ming	明
557–588	Chen	陳	1644–1911	Qing	清
386–588	Northern Dynasties	北朝	1911–1949	Republic of China	中華民國
386–533	Northern Wei	北魏	1949	People's Republic of China	中華人民共和國

BIBLIOGRAPHY

Andrews, Julie F, Kiuyi Shen, *A Century in Crisis: Modernity and Tradition in the Arts of 20th Century China*, Guggenheim Museum, Harry N Abrams (New York), 1998.

Auden, WH,/Isherwood, Christopher, *Journey to a War*, Random House (New York), 1939, p 246.

Bauer, Wolfgang, *China and the Search for Happiness*, The Seabury Press (New York), 1976.

Baum, Vicki, *Shanghai '37*, Oxford University Press (Hong Kong), 1986 (first published in 1939 as *Hotel Shanghai* in the US and *Nanjing Road* in the UK).

Birch, Cyril, *Scenes for Mandarins: The Elite Theater of the Ming*, Columbia University Press (New York), 1995.

Bird, Isabella, *The Yangtze Valley and Beyond*, John Murray (Edinburgh), 1899.

Chan, Evelyn, *Architecture Showcase, Selected Articles from Space Magazine, Pace Publishing Ltd.*, Jiangxi Science and Technology Press (Nanchang), 2001.

Chen, Cong Zhou, *On Chinese Gardens*, Tongji University Press, Shanghai, 1995.

Cheng, Nein, *Life and Death in Shanghai*, Grove Press (New York), 1986.

Denong, Zhou, *A History of Modern Chinese Architecture*, Tianjin Science & Technology Press (Tianjin), 2001.

Dong, Stella, *Shanghai 1842–1942: The Rise and Fall of a Decadent City*, William Murrow, HarperCollins (New York), 2000, p 89.

Dongdong, Jia, *The Selected Works of the Collaborated Design by Chinese and Foreign Architects*, China Architecture and Building Press (Beijing), 1998.

Erming, Liu,/Feng, Yi, *International Architects in China, Selected Works Since 1980*, China Planning Press and Encyclopedia of China Publishing House (Beijing), 1999.Guoxing, Huang, et al, *New and Trans-Century Architecture in Shanghai*, vol. III, Tongji University Press (Shanghai), 2000.

Fitzgerald, CP, *The Horizon History of China*, American Heritage Publishing Co Inc (New York), 1969.

Fu, Polshek, *Passivity, Resistance, and Collaboration*, Stanford University Press (Stanford, California), 1993.

Guobo, *The Fast Vanishing Shanghai Lanes*, Shanghai Pictorial Publishing House, Shanghai, 1996.
Hessler, Peter, *River Town: Two Years on the Yangtze*, HarperCollins (New York), 2001.

Hook, Brian, (ed), *Shanghai and the Yangtze Delta: A City Reborn*, Oxford University Press (Hong Kong), 1998.

Howe, Christopher, (ed), *Shanghai: Revolution and Development in an Asian Metropolis*, Cambridge University Press (Cambridge), 1981.

Jizuo, Yin, *A Report of Economic Development in Shanghai 2000*, Shanghai Academy of Social Science Press (Shanghai), 2000.

Johnson, Linda Cooke, (ed), *Cities of Jiangnan in Late Imperial China*, State University of New York Press (New York), 1993.

Johnson, Linda Cooke, *Shanghai from Market Town to Treaty Port 1074–1858*, Stanford University Press (Stanford, California), 1995.

Johnson, Tess, *Welcome to Shanghai*, Old China Hand Press (Hong Kong), 1997.

Lampugnani, Vittorio Magnago, *The Architectures of the Contemporary City*, Tadahiro Yoshida Press (Tokyo), 1999.

Lee Ou-Fan, Leo, *Shanghai Modern, the Flowering of a New Urban Culture in China, 1930–1945*, Harvard University Press (Cambridge, Mass), 1999.

Lee, Sherman, *China 5000 Years: Innovation and Transformation in the Arts*, Guggenheim Museum/Harry N Abrams (New York), 1998.

Lethbridge, HJ, *All About Shanghai*, The University Press (Shanghai), 1934–5 (reprinted by Oxford University Press, Hong Kong, 1983).

Lewis, John Wilson, (ed), *The City in Communist China*, Stanford University Press (Stanford, California), 1971.

Li, Dun J, *The Civilization of China: Translations and Introductions*, Charles Scribner & Son (New York), 1975.

Ling, Pan, *In Search of Old Shanghai*, Joint Publishing Co (Hong Kong), 1982.

Lu, Hanchao, *Beyond the Neon Lights: Everyday Shanghai in the Early Twentieth Century*, University of California Press (Berkeley and Los Angeles, California), 1999.

Luo Xiao Wei, *A Guide to Shanghai Architecture*, Shanghai People's Fine Arts Press (Shanghai),1996.

Luo, Xiao Wei, Wu Jiang, *Shanghai Longtang*, Shanghai People's Fine Arts Press (Shanghai).

Morris, AEJ, *History of Urban Form*, John Wiley & Sons (New York), 1979.

Perkins, Dorothy, *Concise Encyclopedia of China*, Checkmark Books (New York), 1999.

Rogers, Richard, *Cities for a Small Planet*, Faber and Faber (London), 1997.

Sergeant, Harriet, *Shanghai Collision Point of Cultures 1918–1939*, John Murray (Edinburgh), 1999.

Snow, Edgar, *Red China Today*, Vintage Books (New York), 1971.

Spence, Jonathan D, *The Chan's Great Continent: China in Western Minds*, WW Norton & Co (New York), 1999.

Temperley, J, *Japanese Terror in China*, Modern Age Books Inc (New York), 1938.

Tun, Mao, *Midnight*, Foreign Language Press (Peking), 1979.

Tun, Mao, *Spring Silkworms*, English Language Publishing (Hong Kong), 1965.
Wakeman Jr, Frederick/Wen-hsin Yeh, *Shanghai Sojourners*, University of California Press (Berkeley), 1992.

Wei, Betty Peh-Ti, *Shanghai: Crucible of Modern China*, Oxford University Press (Hong Kong), 1987.

Wheatley, Paul, *The Pivot of the Four Quarters: A Preliminary Enquiry into the Origins and Character of the Ancient Chinese City*, Aldine Publishing Company (Chicago), 1971.

Wood, Frances, *Blue Guide: CHINA*, A & C Black (London), 1992.

Wu, Jiang, *A Guide to Shanghai Architecture*, Shanghai Art Publishing (Shanghai), 1996.

Wu, Jiang, *The History of Shanghai Architecture: 1840–1949*, Tongji University (Shanghai), 1997.

Yan, Kang, *Reading Shanghai, 1990–2000*, Shanghai People's Press (Shanghai), 2001.

Yatsko, Pamela, *New Shanghai: The Rocky Rebirth of China's Legendary City*, John Wiley & Sons (Asia) Ltd (Singapore), 2001.

Yeung, YM,/Yun-wing, Sung *Shanghai, Transformation and Modernization under China's Open Policy*, The Chinese University Press (Hong Kong), 1996.

Yongsheng, Yang,/Mengchao, Gu, *Chinese Architecture of the Twentieth Century*, Tianjin Science and Technology Press, (Tianjin), 1999.

Yule, Colonel Henry, (ed and trans), *The Book of Sen. Marco Polo, the Venetian, Concerning the Kingdom and Marvels of the East*, third edition, John Murray (Edinburgh), 1903.

Yusuf, Shahid,/ Wu, Weiping, *The Dynamics of Urban Growth in Three Chinese Cities*, World Bank/Oxford University Press (Hong Kong), 1997.

Zaknic, Ivan,/Smith, Matthew,/Rice, Dolores, (Council on Tall Buildings and Urban Habitat), *100 of the World's Tallest Buildings*, Images Publishing (Victoria), 1998.

Zhou, Junyan, *Vernacular Housing: Wood Carving in the Ming and Qing Dynasties*, Shanghai Classics Publishing House (Shanghai), 1998.

Zukowsky, John,/Thorne, Martha, *Skyscrapers, The New Millennium*, Prestel (Munich), 2000.

Air Harbour of the 21st Century, Special Edition of Architectural Interior Landscape Design & Decoration of Shanghai Pudong International Airport, Interior Design Construction Press (Jiangsu), 1999.

British Museum History of Chinese Art, Thames & Hudson (London), 1996.

Selected Architectural Works of East China Architectural Design Institute, Selected Works of Chinese Famous Architectural Design Institutes in Series, no 3, Heilongjiang Science and Technology Press (Haerbin), 1998.

New Shanghai Looking Back 50 Years, China Statistical Press (Beijing), 1999.

Selected Architectural Works of Tongji University, Selected Works of Chinese Famous Architectural Design Institutes in Series, no 4, Heilongjiang Science and Technology Press (Haerbin), 1998.

Shanghai Municipal Statistics Bureau, *Statistical Yearbook of Shanghai*, China Statistics Press (Beijing), 2000.

The Evolution of Shanghai Architecture in Modern Times, Shanghai Educational Publishers (Shanghai), 1999.

The Planning of Shanghai, Shanghai Planning Ministry (Shanghai), 1994.

INDEX

Figures in italics indicate illustrations.

Shanghai Huangpu Riverfront 121
Shanghai Information Centre 123, *124*
Shanghai Information Tower, Phase 1 (Lower Tower) 192, *192-3*, 356
Shanghai International Business Centre 276, *276-9*, 358
Shanghai International Conference Centre 113, 130, *131*, 136
Shanghai International Expo Centre 208, *208-11*, 356
Shanghai International Finance Centre 123, *124*
Shanghai International Passenger Terminal 352-3
Shanghai International Plaza 280, *280-81*, 358
Shanghai International Trade Centre *122*, 123
Shanghai Jiao Tong University 164, *164*, *165*
Shanghai Library *128*, 130, 147, 184, *184-5*, 356
Shanghai Mansions *93*
Shanghai Mercury 56
Shanghai Modern Architectural Design Group: Shanghai Urban Planning Exhibition Hall 186, *186*, 356
Shanghai Municipal Administration 112
Shanghai Municipal Bureau *91*
Shanghai Municipal Council 68, 71, 72, 100, 101
Shanghai Municipal Council Building *91*, 92, 101
Shanghai Municipal Government 110, 125-6, 134, 135, 147
Shanghai Museum 110, *127*, 129, 187, *187-9*
Shanghai Nextage Shopping Centre 123, *124*
Shanghai Opera House 110, 121, *121*, 128, 147, 166, *166-9*, 186, 344, *344-7*, 356
Shanghai Oriental Art Centre 121
Shanghai Plaza 231, *231*, 356
Shanghai Post Office Building *91*, 92, 95
Shanghai Power Company 92, *93*
Shanghai Pudong International Airport (SPIA) 121, 126, *252-5*, 253, 338, *338-41*
Shanghai Railway Station 241
Shanghai Scienceland 121, *121*, 178, *179-83*, *349-51*, 356
Shanghai Securities Exchange Building 123, *124*, 272
Shanghai South Railway Station 121
Shanghai Special Municipal Government Building 92
Shanghai Stadium *129*, 130, 147
Shanghai State Guest House *127*, 129
Shanghai Subway 86
Shanghai Times Square 243, *243*, 356
Shanghai TV Station Building *128*, 130
Shanghai United Bank Tower 336, *336-7*
Shanghai Urban Planning Administration 109
Shanghai Urban Planning & Design Institute *94*
Shanghai Urban Planning Exhibition Hall *149*, 186, *186*, 356
Shanghai Waterfront Redevelopment Master Plan 258, *258-61*, 358
Shanghai Waytyfund International Finance Centre 266, *266-7*, 358
Shanghai Yanlord Property Co Limited 302
Shanghai World Financial Centre 121, 272, 282, *282-7*, *337*, 358
Shanghai Yu Garden Shopping City *128*, 130, *140*, 147
Shanghai Zhongfang Architectural Design Institute
    Housing Project for Ping-Yang Village 244, *244-5*, 356
    Medical School 264, *264-5*, 358
    Yong-Ye Apartment Building 306, *306-7*, 358
Shanghai Zoo 110
Shanghighlanders 79, 103
Shangri-La Hotel 272
Shao Xin 119
Shaoxing 51
Sheen, Vincent 72-3
Shen-tsung, Emperor 16
Sheng Xuanhui residence *91*, 92
Shengzhen 114
Shimizu 121
Shimizu Corporation 123, *124*
Shintoism 35
shipping 32, 35, 51, 60, 148
    coastal 58
    routes 36
Shiwan township 253
shopping centres 123, *124*, *128*, 130, *140*, 147, 162, 322
shrines

Buddhist 35, 38
    Confucian 67
    Shinto 35
Shunji Temple (Tian Hou Temple) 30
Shuyuan Academies 30
Sichuan Bei retail district 266
Sichuan Road 147
Siena 24
    Palazzo Publico 24
Sikhs 55
silk 14, 15, 16, 25, 31, 32, 37, 40, 71, 79, 105, 108, *140*
Silk Road 14, 17
silver 58
Silver Crown Tower *see* POS Plaza
Simon Kwan & Associates
    China Merchant's Tower 230, *230*, 356
    Shanghai Plaza 231, *231*, 356
Sincere Company 95, 134
Singapore 51, 60, 121
Sino-French War (1884-5) 69
Sino-Japanese War (1894-5) 69
Sino-Soviet Friendship Mansions 119, *119*, *202*, 220
Skidmore, Owing and Merrill International LLP (SOM) 112, 121, *127*, 129-30, 135, 136, *137*
    Jin Mao Tower 112-13, *127*, 129-30, 232, *232-7*, 356
    Shanghai Waterfront Redevelopment Master Plan 258, *258-61*, 358
skygardens 288, *289*
slavery 53
Small Sword Society 54, 55, 58
Snow, Edgar 105, 107-8, 362
Social Realistic style 119
socialism 361, 362
Society of Righteousness and Harmony 69
SOM *see* Skidmore, Owings & Merrill LLP
Song army 24-5
Song Danjing (City God) Temple 30
Song Jingan Shrine *30*
Song (Sung) Dynasty (960-1279 AD) 9, 16, 17, 24, 30, 89, 129
Songjiang City 134-5
Songjiang region 30, 36, 129
Soria, Arturo 135
South Korea 333
South Railway Station 99, 100, *354-5*
Southern Seas 32
Southern Song Dynasty 25, 29
Soviet Communist Party 75
Soviet Union 107, 119
    see also Russia
Sozhou River 266
Spain 69
Spanish vernacular 67, 92
Speer, Albert 77, 121
Spence, Robinson & Partners 97
SPIA *see* Shanghai Pudong International Airport
Spielberg, Steven 109
Spring and *Autumn Annals* 12
Spring and Autumn Period Dynasty (772-481 BC) 12, 29, 362
Spring Dew Garden 33
Square Pagoda *see* Xing-Sheng-Jiao Temple Pagoda
Square Pagoda Garden *125*, 129
Sri Lanka 14
stadia 95, *129*, 130
Stalinist Classicism 107
State Council of China 95, 126, 134
state shops 16
Sternberg, Joseph von: *Fun in a Chinese Laundry* 80
Stewardson & Spence *91*
street committees 16
streets
    width of 38
    names 40, 52
    Western settlement 67
strikes 71, 74
subway system 86, 109, 112, 152, 162, 186, 276
sugar 36, 37
Sui Dynasty (581-618 AD) 11-12, *12*, 14-15, 29
Sumatra 51
Sun Company 134
Sun Company Department Store 95
Sun Guanglin *see* Lu Jiwei
Sun Wonderland Residential Quarter 130, *131*, 361
Sun Yat-sen, Dr 69, 71, 72

former residence in Shanghai 95
    memorial 75, 76
Sun-Sun Company 134
Sunqiao Modern Agriculture District 147
Super Brand Mall 272, *273-5*, 358
Susongpang Circuit 50
Suzhou 15, 25, 29, 32, 34, 35, 37, 38, 51, 54, 56, 68
Suzhou Creek 29, 30, 31, 51, 57, 99, 100, 126, 135, 324, *324*
Suzhou River 147
Sweden 69
Switzerland 69
Sydness Architects
    Bading Development Finance Mansion 297, *298-9*, 358
    Lujiazui Itochu Development Building 300, *300-301*, 358
    Shanghai United Bank Tower 336, *336-7*
symbolism 77, 128-9, 166, 230, 280, 328
Szechwan 36

Taipei Palace Museum 187
Taiping army 54
Taiping Rebellion 53-6, 63
Taiping Tiangu 53
Taiwan 66, 69, 69, 104, 121
Taizu, Emperor 16
Tan Hou Miau 63
Tang Dynasty (618-907 AD) 15-16, 29, 89
Tang Lin 186, 356
Tang Yu-en *128*, 184, 356
Tange, Kenzo 121
Tao Xingzhi Memorial Hall *127*, 129
Taoho Design Architects
    Bai Hui Gardens 308, *308-9*, 358
    Colourful (Wanzhao) Homestead 246, *246-8*, 356
    King Tower *127*, 130, 238, *238-9*, 356
    Vanke Waltz Gardens 249, *249-51*, 356
Taotai 61
tariffs 32, 49, 50, 57
Tartars 15
taxation
    grain 15, 16, 32
    and Tongeng Tang 68
tea 36, 40, 49
    drinking 16
    tea rooms *28*, *37*
    teahouses 38, 60, 129
technology 65, 66, 111, 112, 126, 280, 288
    construction 95
telegraph 60
telephones 90
television 112, 115
Temple of the City God 89
temple of the God of War 60-61
temple halls 67
Temple Square 35
temples 33, 37, 38, 40, 41, 67
    Buddhist 67
    Confucian 53
    cult 40, 41
    Ming 33
    Yuan *30*
    see also individual temple names
tenants 13
textiles 16
Thames Embankment, London 66
Thames River 58
theatre 33, 312, *314*
Third Survey and Design Institute *354*
Three Dragons King temple 33
Three Kingdoms era 14
Three Officials temple 33
Tian Hou Temple *see* Shunji Temple
Tianjin 53, 56, 69, 99
Tianjin Road 170
tobacco 36, 37
Tokyo 89, 113
Tomorrow Square 135, *137*, *222-5*, 223, 356
Tongji University *111*
Tongli 34, *44*
Tongren Tang 38, 68
Tower Restaurant 98
Town Hall 77, 312
Townsend, Frederick Ward 54
trade unions 71, 74
trade guilds 38
trade routes 14, 16, 36, 49
traffic 126, 146, 147, 148, 156, 244
    see also transport
trams 90
transport 104, 109, 115, 148, 152

see also traffic
Treaty Ports 50, 53, 65, 66, 90
tribal groups 40
Tsien Dynasty 14
Tu Yueh-sen 74
21st Century Tower 288, *288-9*, 358

Uighurs 16
'Unequal Treaties' 72
United States of America 102, 121
    republicanism 9
    consumerism 9, 361, 362
    and Treaty Ports 53
    bombing of Hiroshima and Nagasaki 57
    a 'favoured nation' in Shanghai 69
    Congress 76
    design influences 78
    cinema 80, 98
    culture 90
    bombs Shanghai 104
United States Court for China 69
US Army 104

Vanke Waltz Gardens 249, *249-51*, 356
Vietnam 69, 100
Viguier, Jean-Paul 121
villas *94*, 95, 101, 111, 147, 362
Volkswagen 115

Waigaoqiao tax-free district 147
wall paintings 109
walls: Shanghai's city walls 32-4, 40, *40*, 41, 52, 57, 58, 63, 64, 65, 69, 71, 111, 112
Wang Boqun, Residence of 92, *93*
Wang Dingzhen *120*
Wang Jingwei 101
Wang Xiaoan *128*
Wanko City Garden Residential Quarter 130, *130*
Wanli Residential Area 130, 159, *159*, 356
warehouses 40, 90
warlords
    'warlord period' (1916-28) 71
    campaign against 72-5
    and Japanese military activity in Manchuria 98
Warsaw 107
Washington DC 9, 77
    plan for 75, *75*, 76
    Capitol Hill 130, 362
water supply 68, 90, 107
waterways 9, 15-16, 29, 30, 31, 33, 41, *44*, 58, 68
Waytyfund Financial Centre 324, *324-5*
weaving 36, 40
Webb Zerafa Menkès Housden Partnership Architects 121, 123, *124*
Wei Dunshan *120*, 129
Wei Dynasty (AD 220-300) 14
Wei Zhida *127*
Wen-Yuan Building, Tongji University 119
Wendi, Emperor 14-15
Wengchang Temple *30*
wenren (urban literati) 16
West Gate 40
Western art, history of 17
Western Association of Schools and Colleges 171
Western culture 55, 90, 128, 276
Western Empire 14
Western mercantilism 65
Whangpoo River 100, 105
Whitney, Eli 31
Wine Distribution Warehouse (Yuan Dynasty) 30, *30*
Wing On Company 134
Wong & Ouyang
    Everbright City 241, *241*, 356
    Kerry Everbright City 240, *240*, 356
    San Feng Centre 242, *242*, 356
    Shanghai Times Square 243, *243*, 356
Wong & Tung International Ltd *120*, 121
Wong Gregersen Architects *344*
Wood, DV, Residence of 92, *94*
'Workers' New Village' 146
World Exposition (2010) 135
World Financial Tower 272
Worship of God Society 53
Wu people 15, 29
Wu Yae 29
Wu-jing Chemical Industry Zone 119
Wuchang uprising (1911) 69, 71
Wuden 29
Wuhan, Hubei Province 72

Wujia Chiang 77
Wujiang Road Pedestrian Area 134
Wukou pirates 32, 35, 49
Wusong 57
Wusong Creek 52
Wusong River 29, 32, 51
Wusong Shanghai Railway Company 65

Xi Hui District 276
Xi Yuan (the West Gardens) 89
    see also Yu Yuan Gardens
'Xia' Dynasty 13
Xia Liqing 109
Xi'an (previously Chang'an) 9, 13, 14, 17, 36, 69, 99
Xian College (Yuan Dynasty) 30, *30*, 38, 40
Xin-Jing-Gang green belt 244
Xing-Sheng-Jiao Temple Pagoda (the Pagoda of the Rising Sacred Buddhist Temple; Square Pagoda) 89, *89*, 129
Xing Tonghe 110, *127*, 128
    Lu Xun Memorial Hall (2000) *128*
    Shanghai Museum 110, *127*, 187, *187-9*, 356
Xu Guong (Paul Xu) 35
Xu-Jia-Hui 123, *124*, 126
Xuantong (later Henry Pu-yi, the Last Emperor) 69, 71
Xungzaisuo 25

Ya'an, Shanxi Province 99
Yamen of the Circuit Intendant 37
Yamens 33, 61
Yan'an Road doubling tunnel 147
Yang 54
Yang Chien, Duke of Sui *see* Wendi, Emperor
Yang Ti, Emperor 15
Yang Zhou 15
Yangpu Bridge 147
Yangpu Bridge High Tech Centre 258
Yangtze Creek 51
Yangtze Delta 15, 135
Yangtze River 11, 14, 15, 25, 29, 32, 49, 51, 53, 58, 60, 75, 253
Yangtze Valley 14, 15, 135
Yangzhou (previously Jiangdu) 15
Yanlord Lian Yang Gardens 302, *303-5*, 358
Yellow Emperor temple 33
'Yellow Peril' 60
Yellow River 17
Yellow Turban rebellion (184 AD) 14
YMCA Building 92
Yokohama Specie Bank of Shanghai 61, 97, *97*
Yong-Ye Apartment Building 306, *306-7*, 358
Yongle, Emperor 32
'Young Shoots Law' 16
Yu Yuan Gardens 33, 34, *37*, 38, 39, 40, *42*, *43*, 49, 52, 54, 63, 67, 79, 89-90, 110-13, 280, 290, 334
    see also Xi Yuan
Yuan Dynasty (1279-1368) 29-31, 30, 89
Yuan emperors 25
Yuan Shikai 71
Yuanggialu 112

Zeidler *344*
Zeidler, Eberhard 121
Zhang Bing *see* Lu Jiwei
Zhang Chi 186, 356
Zhang Jie-zheng *128*, 184, 356
Zhang Nanyung 33, 90
Zhang Zeduan: 'Life along the River on the Eve of the Qing Ming Festival' 17, *18*
Zhang Zhimo *120*
Zhang Zhongmin.31
Zhangjiang High-tech Park 147
Zhejiang 36
Zhen Shiling *127*, 129
Zhou Dynasty 12, 15
Zhou Enlai 67, 99, 109, 110
Zhou Li 13, *13*
Zhou Zhuang 34, *44*
Zhu De 99
Zhu Jia Jiao 41
    City Temple 35
Zhu Qizhan Art Museum *127*, 129
Zhu Wenyi *348*
Zhu-Jia-Jiao Town 135
Zhuangzi 12
Zhuqiao township 253
Zig-Zag Bridge 360
Zoroastrianism 16